QuickBooks® 2004
The Official Guide

KATHY IVENS

McGraw-Hill/Osborne
New York   Chicago   San Francisco
Lisbon   London   Madrid   Mexico City   Milan
New Delhi   San Juan   Seoul   Singapore   Sydney   Toronto

The McGraw·Hill Companies

McGraw-Hill/Osborne
2100 Powell Street, 10th Floor
Emeryville, California 94608
U.S.A.

To arrange bulk purchase discounts for sales promotions, premiums, or fund-raisers, please contact **McGraw-Hill**/Osborne at the above address.

QuickBooks® 2004 The Official Guide

34567890 CUS CUS 01987654

ISBN 0-07-223139-4

Publisher
Brandon A. Nordin

Vice President & Associate Publisher
Scott Rogers

Acquisitions Editor
Megg Morin

Project Editor
Jenn Tust

Acquisitions Coordinator
Athena Honore

Technical Editor
Thomas E. Barich

Copy Editor
Sally Engelfried

Proofreaders
Paul Medoff, Linda Medoff

Indexer
Valerie Perry

Composition
Tabitha M. Cagan, George Toma Charbak, John Patrus

Illustrators
Kathleen Fay Edwards, Melinda Moore Lytle, Lyssa Wald

Cover Design
Pattie Lee

Series Design
Peter F. Hancik

This book was composed with Corel VENTURA™ Publisher.

Contents at a Glance

Part III

Tracking Time and Mileage

Part IV

Managing QuickBooks

Part V

Appendixes

Contents

Part II
Bookkeeping

Part IV
Managing QuickBooks

Acknowledgments

This book wouldn't exist without the support and expert input of a whole bunch of talented people, and there are few I need to thank, in person (well, at least virtually in person), right here.

Acquisitions editor Megg Morin is always a pleasure to work with because she stays on top of every stage of this book's process and offers plenty of expertise and common sense. Project editor Jenn Tust was a miracle worker as she juggled all sorts of details, tracking every step of the road this book took to get to the bookstores. Acquisitions coordinator Athena Honore showed her usual efficiency as she made sure everything fell into place and kept little (but extremely important) details from falling through the cracks.

I owe tons of thanks and gratitude to one of the world's great technical editors, Thomas E. Barich, who provided expert insights about QuickBooks functions and features in addition to making sure that the facts and instructions in this book are correct.

Kudos and thanks to a genius of a copy editor, Sally Engelfried, who found every mistake I made, asked all the right questions, and made all the appropriate corrections to hide my sloppiness and my lack of expertise about spelling and punctuation from you.

For Intuit, here's a grateful nod of appreciation for all that support, with special thanks to Rupesh Shah for his unfailing assistance, and extra special thanks to one of my favorite Intuit geniuses, Roger Kimble, for his expertise and cheerful cooperation.

Introduction

How to Use This Book

I tried to organize this book with a certain amount of logic connected to the way you'll probably use your QuickBooks software. You can consult the table of contents, where you'll notice that the topics start with the tasks you perform immediately after installing the software, move on to the tasks you perform often, and then cover the tasks you perform less frequently.

The index guides you to specific tasks and features, so when you absolutely must know immediately how to do something, it's easy to find the instructions.

However, there are some sections of this book you should read first, just because accounting software is much more complex than most other types of software. You should read Appendix A to learn what information to have at hand in order to set up your accounting system properly. Then, you should read the first two chapters so you can configure your system properly. After that, read the chapter or section you need to in order to perform the tasks that have to be accomplished immediately.

What's Provided in This Book to Help You

There are some special elements in this book that you'll find extremely useful:

- **Tips** Give you some additional insight about a subject or a task. Sometimes they're shortcuts, and sometimes they're tricks I've learned from working with clients.
- **Notes** Provide extra information about a topic or a task. Sometimes they provide information about what happens behind the scenes when you perform a task, and sometimes they have additional information I think you might be curious about.
- **Cautions** Are presented to help you avoid the traps you can fall into if a task has a danger zone.

- **FYI boxes**   Are filled with facts you don't necessarily need to perform a task, but the information may be helpful. Some FYI boxes help you understand the way QuickBooks "thinks" (all software applications have a predictable thinking pattern); others are designed to point out the way certain procedures help you run your business.

You and Your Accountant

One of the advantages of double-entry bookkeeping software like QuickBooks is that a great many simple bookkeeping tasks are performed automatically. If you've been keeping manual books or using a check-writing program such as Quicken, your accountant will probably have less work to do now that you're using QuickBooks.

Many accountants visit clients regularly or ask that copies of checkbook registers be sent to the accountants' offices. Then, using the data from the transactions, a general ledger is created, along with a trial balance and other reports based on the general ledger (Profit & Loss statements and Balance Sheets).

If you've had such a relationship with your accountant, it ends with QuickBooks. Your accountant will only have to provide tax advice and business planning advice. All those bookkeeping chores are performed by QuickBooks, which keeps a general ledger and provides reports based on the data in the general ledger.

Throughout this book, I've provided information about general ledger postings as you create transactions in QuickBooks, and you'll also find references from me when I think specific information is going to be important to your accountant. Accountants tend to ask questions about how software handles certain issues (especially payroll, inventory, accounts receivable, and accounts payable), and I've had many years of experience working with accountants who asked me "why?" and "what's this?" as I set up bookkeeping software. As a result, you'll see comments from me such as "your accountant will probably ask how QuickBooks handles this," followed by an explanation that you can give your accountant. There are also a number of places in this book where I advise you to call your accountant before making a decision about how to handle a certain transaction.

Don't worry, your accountant won't complain about losing the bookkeeping tasks. Most accountants prefer to handle more professional chores, and they rarely protest when you tell them they no longer have to be bookkeepers. Their parents didn't spend all that money on their advanced, difficult educations for that.

Part One

Getting Started

ongratulations on deciding to use QuickBooks to track your business finances. This is a big decision, and one that will change your business life for the better. However, installing QuickBooks isn't the same as installing most other software programs. For example, with a word processor you can open the program and dive right in, sending letters to your family or memos to your staff.

Accounting software such as QuickBooks, however, has to be set up, configured, and carefully tweaked before you can begin using it. If you don't do the preliminary work, the software won't work properly. In fact, the first time you use QuickBooks, you'll be asked to take part in an interview that's designed to help you configure your QuickBooks system properly.

In Part One of this book, you'll learn how to get through the interview that QuickBooks presents to help you set up your company file. I'll explain what's really important, what can wait until later, and what you can do all by yourself instead of through the interview process. I'll even explain when it's okay to lie and how to lie in a way that makes your QuickBooks company file accurate. Part One also includes a chapter containing instructions and hints about putting all those boring details into your accounting system, like customers, vendors, and general ledger information. (Sorry, but these tasks are necessary; you cannot keep accurate books without them.)

Before you read the chapters in Part One, be sure you've looked at Appendix A, which I've titled "Do This First!" Take that title seriously; it'll make getting through all this setup stuff easier.

Using QuickBooks for the First Time

I n this chapter:

- Open QuickBooks

- Go through the setup interview

- Decide whether to continue the interview

- Perform a manual setup

- Navigate the QuickBooks window

Chapter 1

The first time you launch QuickBooks, you have to introduce yourself and your
company to the software by means of a rather substantial setup process. This process
has a lot of tasks to wade through, but it's a one-time-only job.

Launching the Software

The QuickBooks installation program may have offered to put a shortcut to the
software on your desktop. If you opted for a desktop shortcut, the easiest way to
open QuickBooks is to double-click that shortcut. If you chose not to put a shortcut
on your desktop, you can use the Start menu, where you'll find QuickBooks in the
Programs menu. Place your pointer on the QuickBooks listing in the Programs
menu and choose QuickBooks from the submenu.

 TIP: For even faster access to QuickBooks, copy or move the desktop shortcut
to your Quick Launch toolbar, which requires only a single click to open software.
Right-drag the shortcut icon onto the Quick Launch toolbar, and then choose Move
Here (or Copy Here, if you want a shortcut in both places).

When QuickBooks opens for the first time, you see the Welcome to QuickBooks
window, displaying your options for using QuickBooks for the first time:

Here's the scoop on what those options offer:

Create A New Company   Select this option to begin the process of creating a
company file. All of the steps involved in this task are covered in this chapter.

Open An Existing Company   Select this option if you're upgrading from a previous
version of QuickBooks. The Open A Company dialog box appears so you can select
your company file. QuickBooks offers to upgrade the file to your new version, and
after you type **Yes** and click OK to accept the offer, QuickBooks insists on making
a backup of your file first. When the backup is complete, the file is converted to
QuickBooks 2003, and you can go back to work.

> **C A U T I O N :** If you're working in a multi-user environment, upgrade QuickBooks on the computer that holds the company datafile first. Then upgrade QuickBooks on the other computers. Users on the other computers won't be able to open the file until their copies of QuickBooks are upgraded.

Convert From Quicken   Select this option if you are moving to QuickBooks from Quicken. There are a number of preliminary steps to take before selecting this option to make sure the conversion process works properly. It's beyond the scope of this book to discuss converting Quicken files to QuickBooks companies, but if you need additional help, look for articles at http://www.cpa911.com. Select the QuickBooks Tips link, and then select the article Converting From Quicken To QuickBooks.

Open A Sample File   Click this option to display a list of two sample companies you can explore and play with in order to get familiar with QuickBooks. One company is designed for product-based businesses, the other for service-based businesses.

If you're not ready to start using QuickBooks, you can exit the software by clicking the X in the top-right corner of the QuickBooks window, or by choosing File | Exit from the menu bar. The next time you open QuickBooks, all the processes described here will start again.

For now, choose Create A New Company because that's what this chapter is all about.

Starting the Setup Interview

The EasyStep Interview window, shown in Figure 1-1, opens to begin the company creation process. Click Next to begin the interview.

The Welcome Interview

The first section of the interview is the Welcome section, and you click Next to move through the windows. The opening window offers a link to a QuickBooks website where you can find a QuickBooks expert if you feel you need to hire one to help you set up your file. The following window has a button you can click if you're creating your company file by converting a Quicken file, as well as a Next button to move on with the EasyStep Interview. I'm not covering Quicken conversions in this book, so I'm assuming you clicked Next.

The next window offers you the opportunity to skip the interview altogether. If you do want to skip it, you can always return later. On the other hand, you can enter the information QuickBooks needs by using the functions available on the QuickBooks menu bar, instead of using the interview. Chapter 2 has a great deal of information that will help you do this. Incidentally, even if you opt to skip the

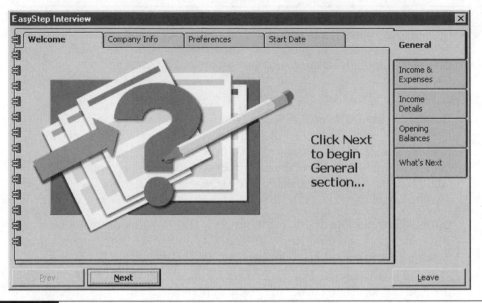

FIGURE 1-1 The EasyStep Interview takes you on a walk through the processes involved in setting up your company file.

interview, you still have to answer several questions by filling out a dialog box with basic information about your company, which is covered in the section "Performing a Manual Setup," later in this chapter.

For now, however, move on with the interview by clicking Next, so you can learn more about the process before deciding whether to set up a company without the interview.

The Company Info Interview

After you read all the information on the ensuing pages of the Welcome section (clicking Next to move through all this stuff), the Company Info portion of the interview begins. Remember to click Next to keep chugging along throughout the entire interview process.

The first item of information QuickBooks needs is your company name, for which two entry fields are available. The first field is for the real company name, the one you do business as. The second entry is optional and is used only if the legal name of your company differs from the company name you use for doing business. For instance, if your company does business as WeAreWidgets, but the legal or corporate name is WAW, Inc., you should fill out both name fields.

Continue to the following windows and fill out the company address and then the basic tax information—your federal tax ID number and the starting month of your fiscal and tax year. The federal ID number is a nine-digit number in the format *XX-YYYYYYY*.

You already have a federal tax ID number if you have employees, and you may have one if you have a business bank account (many banks require this, although some banks merely ask for a copy of a fictitious name registration certificate and will accept your social security number instead of a federal ID).

TIP: If you are a sole proprietor and haven't bothered applying for a federal ID number but instead are using your social security number for tax reporting, think again. You should separate your business and personal taxes/finances. The best way to do this is to have an EIN (employer identification number) and a separate bank account in your business name. Additionally, because you should be thinking in terms of business growth, you're going to need a federal ID number eventually to pay subcontractors, consultants, or employees. Get it now and avoid the rush.

QuickBooks also asks which tax form you use for your business. The common forms for small businesses are

- 1120 for C Corporations
- 1120S for S Corporations
- 1065 for Partnerships
- 1040 for Proprietorships

Note that these are the tax forms on which income (or loss) is reported, but there are lots of other tax forms you'll use in addition to these.

In the next window, tell QuickBooks the type of business you have (see Figure 1-2). If you don't see an exact match for your business type, choose one that comes close. QuickBooks uses this information to create the chart of accounts, and that's better than entering your entire chart of accounts manually.

Move through the next windows (which provide information and don't require user input) to get to the point at which QuickBooks creates the company file you'll use when you work in the software. A Filename For New Company dialog box opens, asking for a filename. QuickBooks suggests a name based on the company name you've entered, so just click Save to use that filename. Or, if you prefer, you can change the name of the file (especially if your company name is long or complicated). It takes a few seconds for QuickBooks to save the company and set up all the files for the company.

TIP: It's a good idea to use a filename that hints at your company name, instead of choosing a name such as Myfiles. Then, if you start another business, you can choose another specific filename for your new venture. Of course, you may end up using QuickBooks for your personal financial records, in which case you'll want a specific filename for that, too.

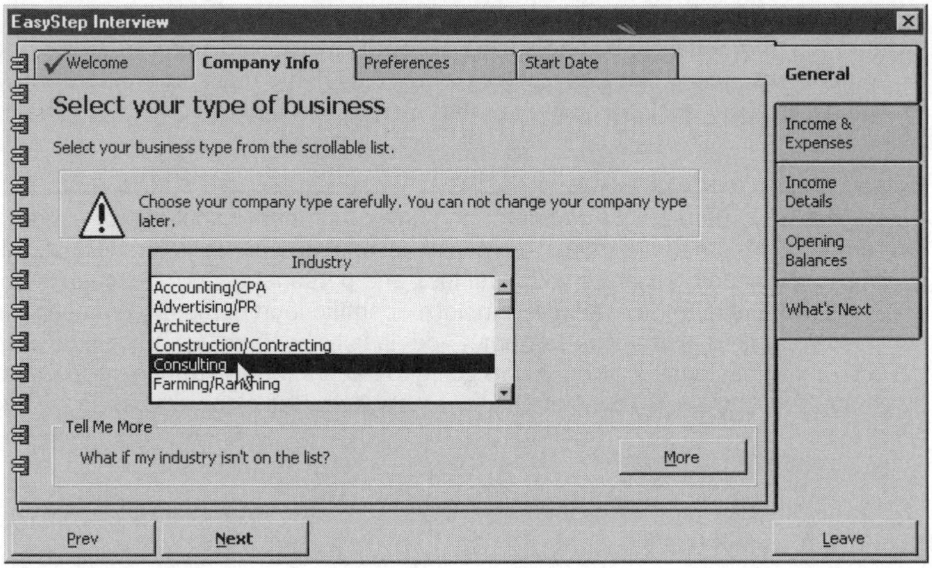

FIGURE 1-2 Scroll through the list to find the type of business that matches your company.

QuickBooks displays the Income and Expense accounts it has established for your company, based on the response you made to the interview question regarding your type of business. You can accept the chart of accounts QuickBooks shows you, or select the option to create your own chart of accounts (covered in Chapter 2). It doesn't really matter which option you select, because you and your accountant will be adding, changing, and removing accounts as you fine-tune your QuickBooks files.

NOTE: If you have a QuickBooks expert available (perhaps your accountant), you can develop your chart of accounts outside of QuickBooks, and then import it. It's beyond the scope of this book to discuss the techniques of building a delimited file with all the right headings that QuickBooks requires, but most QuickBooks experts know how to do this. It's my own preferred method of building a chart of accounts for QuickBooks: I keep a spreadsheet that I can adapt for any client's business, which I modify for each client, and then export to a delimited file that can be imported to QuickBooks.

Click Next to move to the next wizard window. You're asked how many people will have access to your QuickBooks file (which really means the computer on which it resides). This is not connected to running QuickBooks on a network; it refers only to this QuickBooks software on this computer. Many small businesses permit multiple users access to the computer and accounting software, and if you plan to do so, you should tell QuickBooks about it. Then, you'll be able to determine who sees which part of your accounting records. This is a good way to keep payroll records away from everyone except the person who enters payroll data, or to keep employees out of the general ledger (where the totals and profit/loss reports are).

The question about additional users is worded to mean "in addition to yourself," so if nobody but you uses your computer, zero is an appropriate answer. Incidentally, you can always add users later, so it's fine to enter zero and postpone the decision about letting others into your bookkeeping. The next window asks you for an administrator password. Don't enter a password if you're not planning to set up users and passwords. In fact, even if you're going to use passwords, you can wait until after you've finished the EasyStep Interview and implement the feature later, when you're concentrating on the task and taking notes on the passwords you enter. If you forget the administrator password, you cannot open QuickBooks, and you'll have to pay Intuit a lot of money to fix the problem.

NOTE: Restrictions on users are implemented with the use of passwords that are attached to user names. Those features are covered in Chapter 21.

Deciding Whether to Continue the Interview

At this point, having completed the basic steps for creating your company file, you can continue the interview process or leave it. Everything else you do in the EasyStep Interview can be accomplished manually. To help you make the decision, this section presents some things to consider.

In the setup interview, you will be asked about the features you need (such as inventory tracking or collecting sales tax from customers). You can turn on these features manually via the menu system or take care of setting them up now. It's six of one and a half dozen of the other; there's no particular advantage to either approach.

The setup interview will ask for a starting date, which means you need to decide on the date your use of QuickBooks begins. Any activity that occurred in your system before that date is entered as a series of totals. For example, QuickBooks asks you about the amount of money owed to you by customers as of that date, and you must fill out the customer information (and the balance as of the starting date) for each of those customers. The same process occurs for vendors and, in fact, for all the totals of your accounts (banks, liabilities, and so on) as of the starting date. QuickBooks adds up all the customer balances and uses the total as the starting accounts receivable balance.

You can enter customer invoices yourself manually, pretty much in your spare time. That's because QuickBooks is date-sensitive. If you tell QuickBooks your starting date is 3/30, you can enter customer invoices that predate that starting date (invoices that aren't yet paid) instead of entering totals in the interview. This creates the same accounts receivable balance, but you have details about the invoices.

If it's early in the year, you can tell QuickBooks that your starting date is the first day of the year and enter all the transactions for the year. You don't have to enter them before you can begin using QuickBooks for current transactions; you can make your entries in your spare time. If it's November or December, you might want to wait until January to start using QuickBooks.

A major problem with doing all of this within the EasyStep Interview is that you're forced to set up accounts in your chart of accounts during the procedure, and you may want to use a different naming system from the one QuickBooks presents. Specifically, I'm talking about using numbers for your chart of accounts instead of names. Numbered accounts also have names, but the accounts are sorted by numbers. You assign the first digit to reflect the type of account; for example, assets always start with 1, liabilities with 2, and so on. After you finish the interview process and begin to use QuickBooks, you can configure the software to use numbers. However, that choice isn't offered during the interview process, so you're stuck with names instead of numbers (even though you can switch later). Check with your accountant—I think you'll find that he or she is an enthusiastic advocate of numbered accounts.

Chapter 2 explains how to enter all the information QuickBooks needs manually, from customers to the chart of accounts.

In the meantime, this section describes the interview process, so you can follow along if you've decided to complete the interview, read this section in order to make your final decision, or read this section to get an idea of the type of information you'll need if you set up your company file manually.

The Preferences Interview

The QuickBooks features you plan to use, and assorted other preferences, are determined in the Preferences section of the EasyStep Interview. Nothing you enter is etched in stone. You'll probably change your mind about some of the responses you give here, because as you work in QuickBooks and get to know it better, you'll think of a better way to customize it for yourself.

Inventory Feature

The first thing you're asked is whether or not you want to use inventory. Actually, you are first asked whether you maintain inventory in your business, and *then* you're asked whether you want to turn on the inventory features.

If you use inventory, answer Yes to the first question. Regarding the second question about turning on the inventory feature, I can give you a good argument for either choice. If you do turn it on, you are walked through the process of entering all of your inventory items at the end of the interview.

Personally, I think this is really onerous and I wouldn't do it. You can enter your inventory items later, perhaps one morning when your telephones aren't ringing off the hook and you've had plenty of sleep and several cups of coffee (and you haven't just gone through this long interview process). Inventory is one of those things that has to be entered accurately and precisely if the feature is going to work properly. If you stock only a few inventory items, you might want to complete this now; otherwise, wait a while, and when you're ready, start by reading Chapters 2 and 10, which cover entering inventory items.

Sales Tax Feature

If you collect sales tax from your customers, you have to tell QuickBooks about it so it can be added to your invoices. First, answer Yes to the question about whether or not you are responsible for collecting (and remitting) sales tax. Then, specify whether or not you collect a single tax or multiple taxes. If you collect a single tax, fill in the information. If you collect multiple taxes, you cannot set them up during the interview; you must do that later. Multiple taxes can be defined in several ways:

- You do business in more than one state and collect sales tax and remit it to the appropriate states.
- You do business in only one state, but different tax rates apply depending on the city in which you or your customer resides.
- You have both of the preceding situations.

If you do business in a state that has a different sales tax for one city than it does for other cities (for example, New York City has a higher tax rate than the rest of New York state, and Philadelphia has a higher tax rate than the rest of Pennsylvania), then be sure to read the tax law carefully. Some tax rates are determined by the address of the vendor (which is you), not the address of the customer.

Invoice Form Preference

Choose the invoice form you prefer from the formats available in QuickBooks (see Figure 1-3). All forms can be modified, so pick the one that comes closest to your own taste, and then read Chapter 3 (see the section called "Customizing Forms") to learn how to tweak it to a state of perfection. When you're actually creating invoices, all the forms are available, and you can use any of them for any specific invoice, so the decision you make here isn't irrevocable.

Payroll Feature

If you have employees and you plan to do your own payroll processing in QuickBooks, select Yes to the question about using QuickBooks payroll. If you have employees and use an outside payroll service, select No.

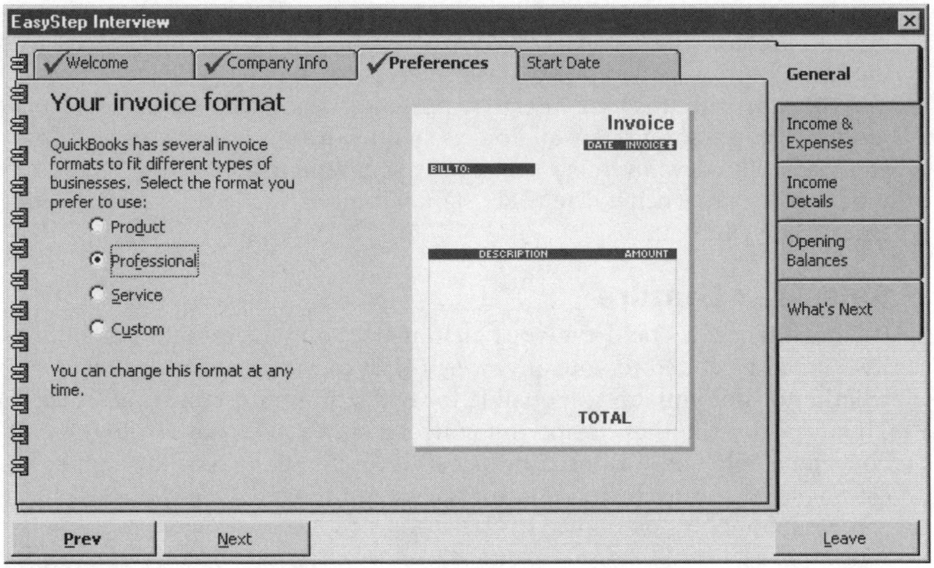

FIGURE 1-3 Choose an invoice form that comes close to your needs to make it the default form.

An employee is someone you pay for whom you withhold taxes and issue a W-2 form at the end of the year. This includes you, if that's how you pay yourself (instead of writing a check that's a draw against the business income). Subcontractors for whom you report payments on Form 1099 are not employees.

See Chapters 8 and 9 to learn everything about doing your own payroll.

Estimating Preferences

If you provide estimates and then bill your customers according to a formula that tracks the progress of a job, QuickBooks has some features you may want to use. If you answer Yes to this question, the next question inquires whether you submit more than one invoice against the estimate (which usually means at certain intervals, based on the percentage of the job that's completed).

Time Tracking Preferences

If you bill for time and want to track the amount of time you or your employees spend on each job, an interview question is provided for that, also. You can use time tracking to calculate payroll for hourly workers, or to track time for internal analysis of your payroll expense. See Chapters 18 through 20 for information about using this feature.

Classes Preferences

You also are given an opportunity to turn on the classes feature, which is a way to combine categories and accounts to create reports that are more detailed than the standard reports. The feature can be useful for tracking types of customers, types of jobs, or even profit and loss at branch offices. More information about setting up and using classes is in Chapter 21. If you turn on the classes feature here, you must establish the classes at some point after the interview (or you can answer No now and turn on the feature when you're ready to set up the classes).

TIP: I usually advise people who are just getting started with QuickBooks to wait before turning on the classes feature. After you've been using QuickBooks for a while, you may find that some QuickBooks reports don't provide exactly the information you want. At that point, you can turn on the classes feature and configure it for exactly the type of information you're currently lacking.

Accounts Payable Preferences

The next section in the interview process is the determination of the method for handling your bills from vendors. In any accounting system (even manual bookkeeping), you have two choices, and both offer advantages and disadvantages:

- Enter the checks when you're ready to pay your bills (this is called direct disbursement).
- Enter the bills and then pay those bills.

If you opt to enter your checks directly, it means that as bills arrive in your office, you put them somewhere (an envelope, a folder, or a shoebox) until you're ready to pay them. Then, you just have to enter the checks in the QuickBooks check register, place the checks in the envelopes, and attach a stamp. The advantage of this method is that it takes less time and less data entry. The disadvantage is that the only way to know how much money you owe at a given moment is to take the bills out of the container and total them manually. Also, unless you specially mark and store those bills that offer a discount for timely payment, you might inadvertently miss a deadline and lose the discount.

If you decide to enter the bills first and then go through the process of paying them in QuickBooks, you can let the software remind you about due dates and simultaneously get a total for your current accounts payable.

If you opt to enter your bills into the software, your accountant might have to make an adjustment when it's time to figure your taxes. Tracking accounts payable (and accounts receivable, for that matter) is called *accrual accounting*. If you file your taxes on a cash basis instead of an accrual basis, the accrued amount owed is not considered an expense and has to be subtracted from your total expenses. This isn't terribly unusual or difficult, but you should be aware of it. Most small businesses that don't have inventory considerations file taxes on a cash basis.

Reminders Preferences

QuickBooks has a feature that tracks the things you need to do and shows you a To Do list when you start the software. Included in the list are any due dates that exist (as a result of your data entry) in addition to any notes you wrote yourself and opted to be reminded about.

You can continue to let QuickBooks show you the reminder list when you open the software, or opt to display it manually through the menu. Make your decision based on the way you're most comfortable working. (You can always change it later.)

Cash or Accrual Reporting

QuickBooks has a specific interview question about the way you want to print or display reports, offering cash or accrual options. Before you make the decision, check with your accountant. The smart way to do that is to ask your accountant to give a full explanation (don't just say, "Which way?" and accept a one-word answer).

> **NOTE:** One important fact that both you and your accountant should be aware of is that when you use QuickBooks, the decision of accrual versus cash isn't as important as it is with some other accounting software programs. QuickBooks is capable of producing reports either way (there's a button you can click on every report), regardless of the decision you make in the interview.

Here's a quick overview of what's really involved in this decision. (For details that apply specifically to your business, you should have a fuller discussion with your accountant.)

In cash-based accounting, an expense doesn't exist until you write the check. Even if you enter the bill into the software and post it to an expense account in the general ledger, it isn't really an expense until the check is written. The same is true for revenue, meaning income isn't considered to be real until payment is received from your customer. Even though you enter an invoice and post it to a revenue account in the general ledger, it isn't revenue until it's paid.

In accrual-based accounting, as soon as you incur an expense (receive a bill from a vendor) or earn income (send an invoice to a customer), it counts on your reports.

Because most accounting software is accrual-based, most businesses, especially small businesses, keep accrual books and report to the IRS on a cash basis. Most accounting software is accrual-based because business owners want to know those accrued totals: "How much did I earn (invoice customers for)?" and "How much do I owe?"

My own advice is you should choose accrual-based reports in the QuickBooks interview so you can obtain information about your earning and spending in greater detail.

Start Date Interview

If today is the first day of your fiscal year (usually January 1), your accountant has just completed all the accounting stuff for last year, and your numbers are pristine and perfect, you can keep going now. It's almost impossible to believe that this scenario exists. If any other situation exists, you should stop and read the section in Appendix A on selecting a start date. (You might also want to call your accountant.)

The start date you select has an enormous impact on the amount of detail your QuickBooks reports will have. In fact, it has an enormous impact on the accuracy of the numbers QuickBooks reports.

Without repeating all the information in Appendix A, the following is a quick overview of the choices you have:

- Choose the start date that represents the first day of your fiscal year and enter every transaction.
- Choose a start date that represents some accounting period, such as the end of a specific month or a specific quarter, enter totals as of that date, and then enter all the transactions since that date.
- Choose today (or some other non-meaningful date) and enter totals.

If the start date is not the first day of your fiscal year, you will have to enter the totals for each account in your chart of accounts as of the start date. This is called an *opening trial balance*.

NOTE: Even if today is the first day of your fiscal year, you'll need an opening trial balance, but it's a much smaller one (a balance sheet) and doesn't involve income and expenses incurred so far.

If you enter year-to-date totals, you won't have the details about how those totals were accrued in your QuickBooks file. That's not necessarily awful; it simply means that if you want to know how you reached a total income of a gazillion dollars by June 30, you'll have to go back to your manual records (or your old software) to get the information. If a customer calls and wants details about the account, the individual invoices won't be in your QuickBooks system and you'll have to walk to the filing cabinet and pull the paperwork.

If you're starting your QuickBooks software (and reading this book) in the first half of your fiscal year, I recommend using the first day of your fiscal year as your start date, and then entering each historical transaction. You don't have to enter all of them today, or even tomorrow; you can take your time.

> **TIP:** If other people in your office will be using QuickBooks, having them enter the historical transactions is a terrific way for them to learn how to use the software. Make sure everyone participates.

Ready? Okay, enter the date. As Figure 1-4 shows, QuickBooks provides a graphical calendar you can use to move through the months and select a date (click the calendar's icon to open it). Or you can enter a date directly.

The Accounts Configuration Interview

Next on your interview agenda is the configuration of your income and expense accounts. Remember that QuickBooks entered a partial chart of accounts earlier in the interview process, when you indicated the type of business you have (unless you selected the business type "Other" or chose to create your own chart of accounts).

Income Accounts Configuration

At this point, the income accounts are displayed, and you're asked whether you want to add any income accounts. By default, the Yes option is selected. I suggest you switch the option to No, even if you do need more income account types; you can add those accounts later. Chapter 2 covers this process in detail.

If you didn't choose a business type, and therefore have no income accounts, you must enter one now. Create an account and name it appropriately (e.g., income, revenue, fees, etc.). You can fine-tune your income accounts later.

Expense Accounts Configuration

There are a large number of interview screens connected to configuring expense accounts, because QuickBooks walks you through an explanation of accounts and subaccounts. You can skip the explanations by choosing No when you're asked if you want detailed information about expense accounts.

The expense accounts already entered into your chart of accounts are displayed, and you're offered the opportunity to add additional accounts. There's no particular

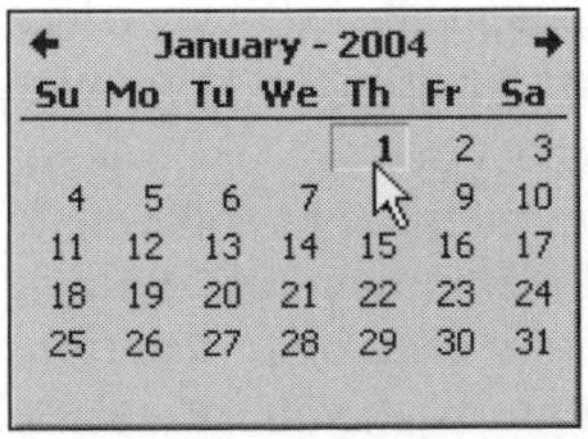

FIGURE 1-4 Any time you need to enter a date in any transaction window, QuickBooks offers a graphical calendar.

reason to add accounts now. When you're ready to add accounts, refer to Chapter 2 for directions.

If you didn't accept the preconfigured chart of accounts, you'll still see Payroll Expenses as an existing expense account. QuickBooks adds this account automatically, even if you didn't pick a business type and therefore don't have a chart of accounts.

In fact, this Payroll Expenses account appears even if you answered No to the question of whether or not you are using QuickBooks for payroll. You can never delete this account, even if you never use it. QuickBooks does this by design, on purpose, for some unfathomable reason, so I can't call it a bug (but I can call it an annoyance). You can make this account inactive if you don't want it to appear on the list of accounts during transaction entry (see Chapter 2 to learn how to make accounts inactive).

The Income Details Interview

Here's where you set up the income and accounts receivable features you'll use in QuickBooks. Move through the questions and respond according to the way you do business. For example, you're asked about the manner in which customer payments are made and whether you use statement charges (charges that are added to the statements you mail to customers).

After you respond to all those questions, you're asked whether you want to set up the items for which you invoice customers. The Items portion of the Income Details Interview displays different types of items, starting with services you provide and noninventory parts and moving through other charges (shipping fees, postage, and other expenses you might want to charge to your customers). From there, the wizard asks if you want to enter inventory items. I advise you to respond No to each invitation to enter an item. When you decide to put these items into your system (which you can do any time before you send your first invoice to a customer), Chapter 2 will walk you through the process.

If you want to accomplish these tasks now (make that decision only if you have a small number of items you'll be using for customer invoices), answer Yes and fill out the dialog boxes with the appropriate information. Chapter 2 provides assistance.

The Opening Balances Interview

The next series of interview windows asks about balances—all sorts of balances.

Customer and Vendor Balances

QuickBooks wants to know about the balances owed by your customers as of the opening date. If you fill out the interview questions, be prepared to fill out the customer information as well as the balance due (and the revenue account you posted the balance to, which you had to enter in the interview section about the chart of accounts).

The balances you owe your vendors are also requested, requiring you to fill out vendor cards and the expense accounts used for your purchases.

If you don't want to fill in these amounts now, just lie. Tell QuickBooks that none of your customers owe you money as of your start date. (I'm assuming that's a lie, unless you have a retail business, because it's normal to have customers with balances due.) Or, answer that you don't owe any money to vendors (wouldn't that be nice!).

You can enter the balances later, or enter each transaction to let QuickBooks keep track of the totals (and have a record of each customer and vendor transaction).

Balance Sheet Accounts

This part of the interview is designed to establish the balances for your balance sheet accounts: assets, liabilities, and equity.

The interview starts by asking whether you want to set up credit card accounts. That means QuickBooks wants to track the money you spend via plastic for business expenses. It tracks the credit card as a liability, an outstanding loan. The theory is that when you use your credit card, you automatically incur an obligation, even before the bill arrives from the credit card company. A message on the window warns you that you must set up a credit card account for each credit card you use to make purchases for your business. It's perfectly okay to ignore that message, because you don't have to set up credit cards in this manner.

If you pay off your credit card balances each month, there is no reason to incur the extra work involved in handling credit cards as a liability. If you make partial payments on your credit cards and frequently have a running balance, you can choose to track the credit card as a regular accounts payable item for which you make partial payments instead of as a liability. Even if you decide to use a liability account, you don't have to set it up during the interview; you can establish it later.

Personally, I don't understand why QuickBooks makes the assumption that the only way to handle credit cards with running balances is as a liability. It means that you open the credit card account to record your purchases as you make them, and then reconcile the account (filling in the finance charges and interest charges) when the bill arrives.

I hate that—I'm far too lazy for that process. I like to treat my credit card as just another vendor. I apply the appropriate amounts to the appropriate expense accounts when I enter the bill (or write a check if I don't want to enter the bill). If I don't want to pay off the whole balance, I make a partial payment. I enter any finance charges as just another expense when I enter the vendor invoice.

> **($) TIP:** Credit card interest or finance charges you incur for a business are deductible. They are not deductible if the credit card is used for personal purchases.

This option has no right and wrong answer. I just want to point out that QuickBooks takes the liability account connection for granted, and you don't have to do it that way if you don't want to. You might want to discuss this with your accountant before making the decision.

This is also the place to set up loans (including lines of credit) and bank accounts.

The interview process next walks through all the different types of asset accounts you might have on your balance sheet, asking for the name of the account, the type of asset, and the balance as of your start date. You can, if you wish, set up at least one bank account in the bank account section of the interview, in addition to other important asset accounts in other interview windows. Or, you can wait and set up your bank accounts manually. Either way, you don't have to enter opening balances as you set up accounts.

Following asset accounts is an interview section for equity accounts. These are the accounts that represent the worth of your business. Generally, your current equity is the difference between your income and your expenses (your profit or loss), along with the original capital you put into the business. If you take a draw instead of being on the payroll, the amount you draw is subtracted from that number.

QuickBooks automatically provides two equity accounts:

- Opening Bal Equity, which is the worth of your business as of your opening date
- Retained Earnings, which is the difference between income and expenses for the current fiscal year

Other equity accounts may exist, depending on the type of business organization you indicated earlier in the interview.

The What's Next Interview

The last section of the interview process is called What's Next, and it begins with a list of recommended actions, as shown in Figure 1-5. The list contains items that are specific to your company setup, and the contents of the list reflect the information you decided to omit during the interview process, along with reminders about QuickBooks goods and services you can purchase.

As you continue to click Next, each window displays instructions about how to accomplish the task QuickBooks is recommending. You don't perform the task in the interview; these windows just contain recommendations and reminders.

Finishing Up

Guess what? You're finished. This is the last window in the EasyStep Interview. If you failed to make entries in any section of the interview, no check mark appears on the tab to the right.

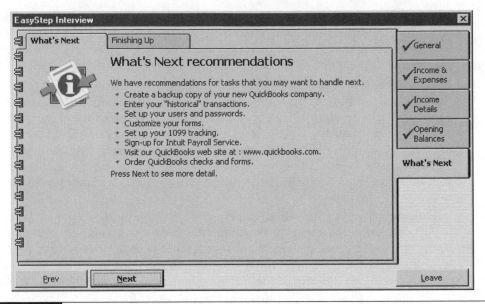

FIGURE 1-5 Here's a list of things to do.

You can click any tab on the right side of the window to return to an interview section. If you can't face that now (and I can't blame you), you can always return to the EasyStep Interview by choosing File | EasyStep Interview from the menu bar.

Choose Leave to close the EasyStep Interview and start working in the QuickBooks window. QuickBooks displays a page full of information, including links for more information about QuickBooks features and services. You can close this window by clicking the X in its top-right corner (not the top-right corner of the QuickBooks software window). See the section "The QuickBooks Software Window" later in this chapter to continue learning about using the QuickBooks window.

Performing a Manual Setup

You can configure your QuickBooks company file manually either by choosing Skip Interview on the third interview window, or by clicking the Leave button at the point in the interview where QuickBooks saves your company file (or at any other point after that).

Manual Company Setup

If you click Skip Interview on the third interview window, the Creating New Company dialog box opens, and you can enter the basic information quickly (see Figure 1-6).

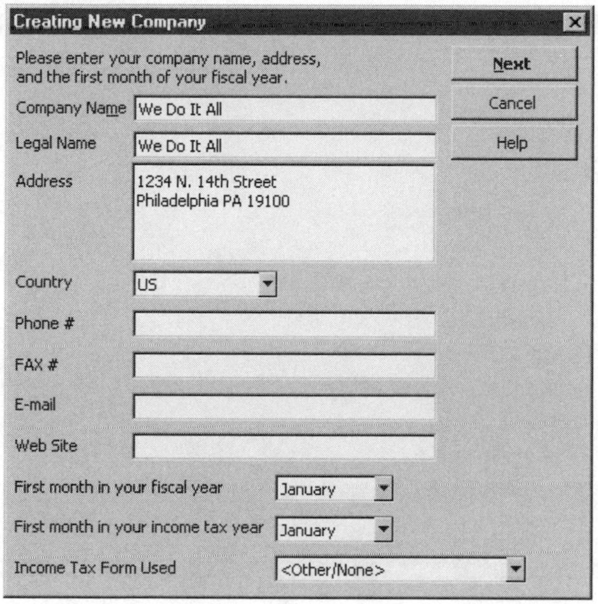

FIGURE 1-6   You can enter company information directly in the Creating New Company dialog box.

Click Next to select a type of business so QuickBooks can install the appropriate chart of accounts, or choose (No Type) to enter or import your own chart of accounts. Then click Next to save the company file.

Now you can use the QuickBooks menu system to turn on preferences (the features you want to use), and also to enter data.

Manual Preferences Setup

Choose Edit | Preferences from the menu bar to select the QuickBooks features you want to use. The Preferences dialog box appears with the General category selected, as shown in Figure 1-7.

Each category has two tabs: My Preferences and Company Preferences. The My Preferences tab offers options that are universally applied in QuickBooks, no matter which company you're working in. If you have multiple users set up, QuickBooks remembers the settings on a user-by-user basis and applies those settings when each user logs in to QuickBooks.

The Company Preferences tab offers options for the currently opened company (QuickBooks remembers the preferences you set for each company). The majority of categories have no options available in the My Preferences tabs; you can only set company preferences.

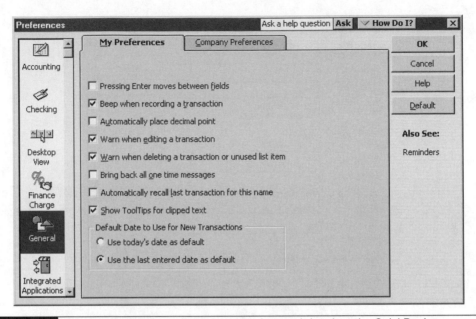

FIGURE 1-7 Use the Preferences dialog box to select and deselect the QuickBooks features you want to use.

For this discussion, I'm covering only the company preferences, and you can read Chapter 21 to learn how to set the My Preferences features. In fact, I'm not going to cover all of the company preferences here, I'm going to concentrate on those that are connected to basic bookkeeping tasks. The other preferences are discussed throughout this book, as each feature is discussed.

Following are some guidelines for establishing the features you want to use in QuickBooks using the Company Preferences tab. To see each category, select its icon from the left pane (and make sure you click the Company Preferences tab, so we're all talking about the same thing).

Accounting Preferences   Specify whether or not you want to use account numbers (numbers are always a better idea). Also, you can indicate whether you want to use class tracking (see Chapter 21 for more information) and whether you want to keep an audit trail. An *audit trail* is a list of changes made to transactions, and if you turn this feature on, you may notice a small slowdown in the software. Despite this inconvenience, it's sometimes handy to track changes, particularly if you need to be reminded why some numbers have changed in your reports. Detailed information on using audit trails is in Chapter 21.

Checking Preferences   You can choose what you want to print on check vouchers (stubs) and decide the way you want to date checks (when you fill in the data or when you actually print the check). You can also choose the default bank accounts to use for payroll and payroll liabilities. Learn about printing checks in Chapter 7, about payroll in Chapter 8, and about paying payroll liabilities in Chapter 9.

Finance Charge Preferences   Use this dialog box to turn on finance charges for late-paying customers. You can set a default rate and the circumstances under which finance charges are assessed. Learn about assessing finance charges in Chapter 5.

Integrated Applications Preferences   Use this dialog box to allow or disallow access to the company file from other applications. See Appendix B for more information on integrating other software with QuickBooks.

Jobs & Estimates Preferences   This is the place to configure estimating and progress billing (billing a percentage of the price of a job as you reach a percentage of completion), if you need it. You can also configure the terminology you want to use for describing the status of jobs. Learn about estimates in Chapter 3.

Payroll & Employees Preferences   If you're doing your own payroll processing in QuickBooks, set the preferences for creating employees and printing paychecks. Chapter 8 takes you through the steps for performing these tasks.

Purchases & Vendors Preferences   Use this dialog to configure the way you handle bills and bill paying. You can also turn on inventory and purchase orders (you have to enable both features; you can't pick only one of them, but you don't actually have to use purchase orders). Entering bills and working with purchase orders are covered in Chapter 6. Paying bills is covered in Chapter 7.

Sales & Customers Preferences   Here's where you establish your shipping preferences and the default markup on inventory products. In addition, you can configure the way you want to handle reimbursed expenses.

One of the important preference options on this dialog box is whether or not you want to apply customer payments automatically or manually. This really means that if the feature is turned on, customer payments are applied starting with the oldest invoice first. I find that this frequently doesn't work well, because customers skip invoices that they want to contend (the product didn't arrive, or it arrived damaged, or they think the price is wrong). If you apply the payments against the invoices manually, you have a more accurate record of payments. Most customers are applying the payment to one of your specific invoices when they cut the check, so if you follow their lead, you and your customer will have identical payment records. The features listed in this dialog are discussed in a variety of places throughout this book.

TIP: If you don't apply payments by invoice and use balance-forward billing, it's okay to leave the automatic application feature turned on.

Sales Tax Preferences   This is the place to turn sales tax on or off. You must also specify when you have to remit the sales tax to the taxing authority, as well as whether the tax is due when it's charged or collected (check the state law). Information about charging and remitting sales tax appears in several places in this book.

Tax 1099 Preferences   If you pay subcontractors and need to send Form 1099s at the end of the year, this is the dialog box to use for configuration. After you configure your 1099 forms, you must remember to specify the 1099 check box in each applicable vendor card. See Chapter 2 for information on setting up vendors.

As you go through the Preferences dialog boxes, each time you make a change and move to the next category, you're asked whether you want to save the changes in the category you just completed. Answer Yes. When you're finished with all the categories, choose OK to close the Preferences dialog box.

These are the important system categories, and if you've completed them, you're ready to finish your manual setup. Chapter 2 introduces you to all the lists you need to enter.

The QuickBooks Software Window

When the EasyStep Interview window closes, QuickBooks displays several windows providing information: automatic updates, a Getting Started window (read any article you wish by clicking its link), and the Company Navigator.

You can close any window by clicking the X in the top-right corner. Don't click the X in the QuickBooks window, or you'll close the software.

> **TIP:** To close the window in the foreground (the window currently in use), you can press CTRL-F4. To close QuickBooks, you can press ALT-F4.

Navigators

QuickBooks has a number of Navigator windows, which are dedicated to a particular subject, containing links to tasks, transaction windows, and information about features. By default, QuickBooks displays the Company Navigator shown in Figure 1-8 every time you open the company file.

Basic QuickBooks Window Elements

Some people find it easier to access transaction windows and other components of the company file from the QuickBooks toolbars and menus instead of the Company Navigator. If you close the Company Navigator by clicking the X in the top-right corner of the navigator window, you see the basic QuickBooks window, which is shown in Figure 1-9.

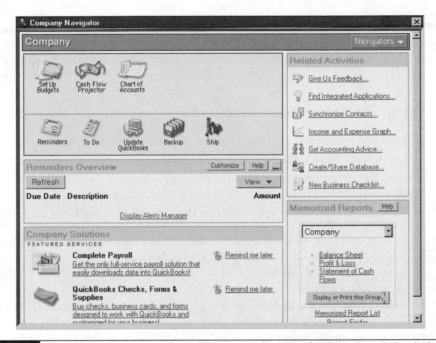

FIGURE 1-8 The Company Navigator lets you access features for the currently loaded company file.

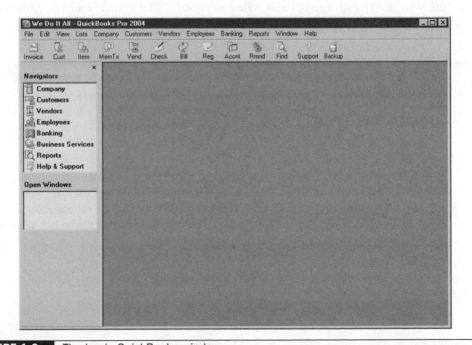

FIGURE 1-9 The basic QuickBooks window

($) **TIP:** To eliminate the appearance of the Company Navigator permanently, choose Edit | Preferences and click the Desktop View icon. On the My Preferences tab, deselect the option Show Company Navigator When Opening A Company File.

By default, the QuickBooks basic window has the following elements:

- Title bar, which displays the name of your company file
- Menu bar, which contains all the commands for working in QuickBooks
- Icon Bar, which contains buttons for quick access to oft-used functions (see Chapter 21 to learn how to customize the Icon Bar)
- Navigators List, which also contains the Open Windows List

Clicking any item on the Navigators List opens the associated Navigator window. For example, click the Customers listing on the Navigators List to open the Customers Navigator, which contains icons and links for accessing functions and information related to customers.

The Open Windows List lets you move between multiple open QuickBooks windows easily—click a window's name to put that window in the foreground of your QuickBooks window.

You can close the Navigators List by clicking the X at the top-right corner of its panel (QuickBooks asks you to confirm the fact that you want to close the window). To bring it back, choose View | Open Windows List from the menu bar.

($) **NOTE:** Even though the top of the panel says Navigators, that's not the name of this QuickBooks toolbar—the name is really Open Windows List. This seems confusing to me—the name in the View menu should match the title on the panel.

QuickBooks also offers another left-side panel for easy access to functions; it's called the Shortcut List, and you can choose it from the View menu. Like the icon bar, it provides quick access to commonly used functions, but it organizes those icons by category (see Figure 1-10). The Shortcut List is customizable, and you can learn how to optimize it by reading Chapter 21.

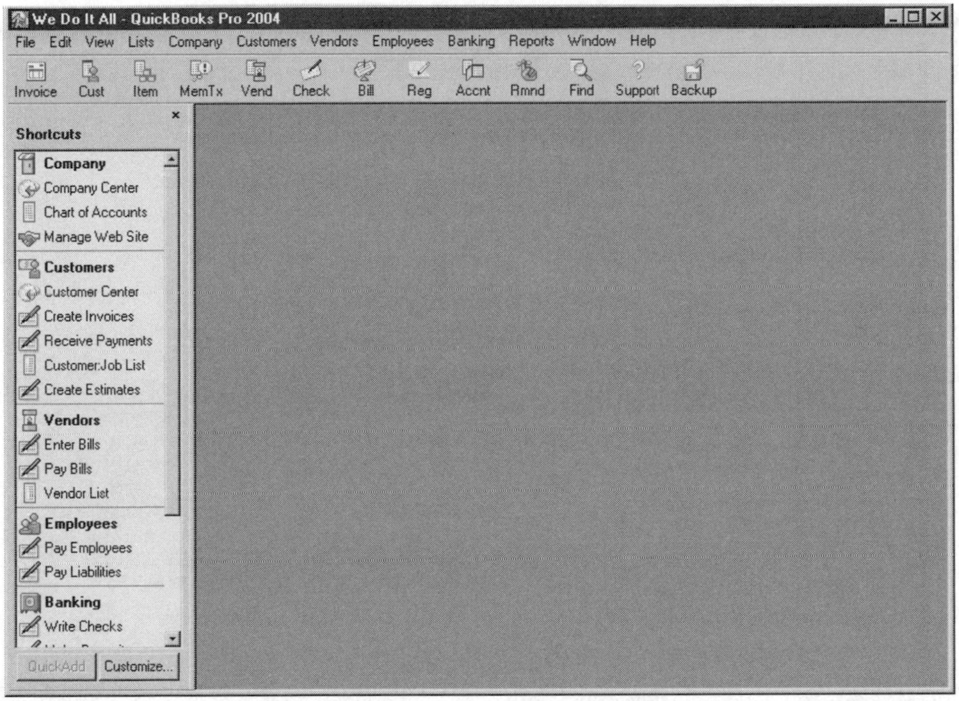

FIGURE 1-10 You can use the Shortcut List instead of (or in addition to) the Open Windows List.

QuickBooks Centers

QuickBooks centers are windows in which information is displayed about specific areas of your company. You can see current data, analyze that data, and perform tasks. The following centers are available:

- Company Center
- Customer Center
- Customer Detail Center
- Vendor Detail Center

You can open any center from the menu bar; for example, the Company center is listed on the Company menu, the Vendor detail center is on the Vendors menu, and so on. Figure 1-11 shows the Customer center window.

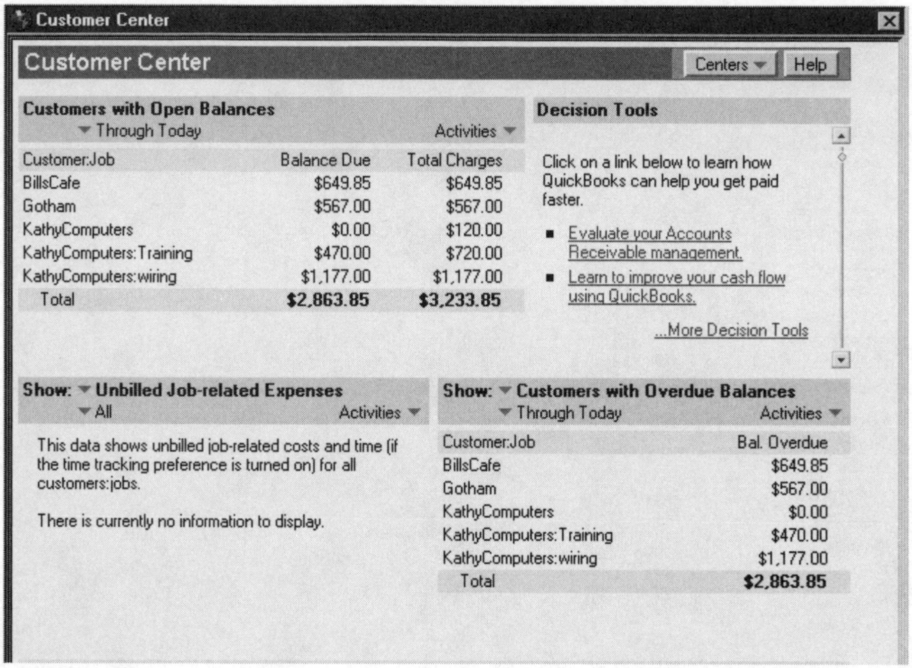

FIGURE 1-11 You can see a quick summary of current conditions in a center's window.

Closing QuickBooks

To exit QuickBooks, click the X in the top-right corner of the QuickBooks window or choose File | Exit from the menu bar. The company file that's open at the time you exit the software is the file that opens the next time you launch QuickBooks.

If you have any report or transaction windows open when you close QuickBooks, they're opened again the next time you use the software. You can change that behavior by configuring the Desktop View in the Preferences dialog box—see Chapter 21 for instructions.

Setting Up Your Lists

n this chapter:

- Create a full chart of accounts
- Enter all your lists
- Invent your own fields to make your lists more useful

In this chapter, I'm going to cover a lot of basic chores. They aren't terribly exciting or creative, but if you don't do them now, you'll regret it later. That's because every time you enter a transaction or fill out a form, you'll have to enter some basic data at the same time. Talk about annoying! So take the time now to get the basic data into the system. This is the preparation stuff, the work that makes future work faster and more efficient.

QuickBooks has a spell checker, and some of the List windows contain a Spelling button. Click it to check the text you entered. Then you won't have to worry about spelling errors in transactions (for instance, invoices) because you've prechecked the elements.

Each of the lists you create in QuickBooks has its own List window, which you can open by selecting the list from the Lists menu. When you view the items in a list, you can sort the list by any column in the window. Just click the column heading to sort the list by the category of that column.

Creating a Full Chart of Accounts

The first priority is your chart of accounts. QuickBooks created some accounts for you during the initial setup of your company, but most people need lots of additional accounts in order to keep books accurately. You do the chart of accounts first because many of the other lists you create require you to link the items in the list to accounts. For example, service and inventory items are linked to income accounts.

Using Numbers for Accounts

As you go through the entry of accounts, remember that I'm using numbers as the primary element in my chart of accounts. There's a title attached to the number, but the primary method of sorting my account list is by number (see the sidebar "How QuickBooks Sorts Accounts"). Even though the QuickBooks default is to use names, it's a simple matter to change the default and use numbers. Your accountant will be grateful, and you'll find you have far fewer mistakes in posting to the general ledger. If you prefer to stick to names, see the next section for some hints about creating account names.

To switch to a number format for your accounts, you just need to spend a couple of seconds changing the QuickBooks preferences:

1. Choose Edit | Preferences from the menu bar to open the Preferences dialog.
2. Select the Accounting icon from the scroll bar in the left pane.
3. Click the Company Preferences tab.
4. Select the Use Account Numbers check box (see Figure 2-1).

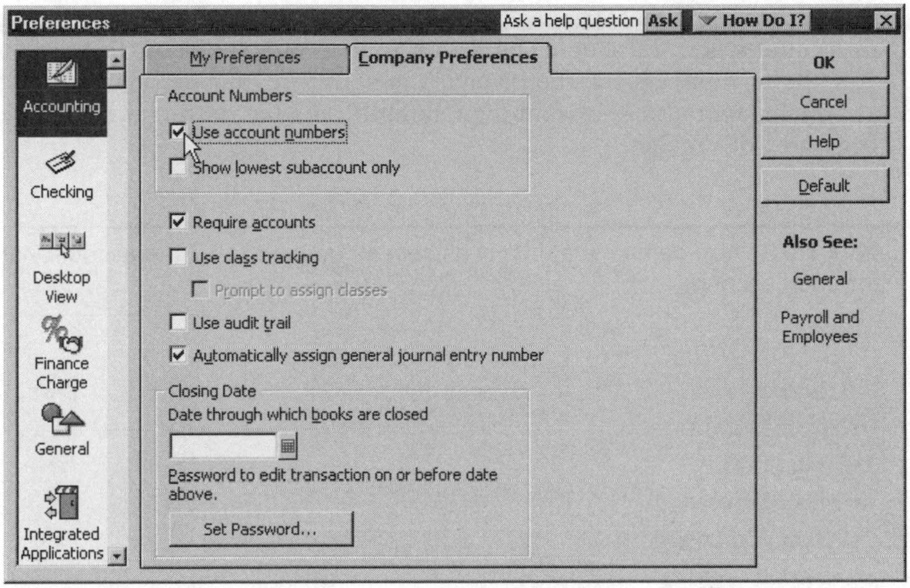

Preferences | Ask a help question | Ask | ▼ How Do I? | ✕

| My Preferences | **Company Preferences** | | OK |

Accounting

Account Numbers
- ☑ Use account numbers
- ☐ Show lowest subaccount only

- ☑ Require accounts
- ☐ Use class tracking
  - ☐ Prompt to assign classes
- ☐ Use audit trail
- ☑ Automatically assign general journal entry number

Closing Date
Date through which books are closed

Password to edit transaction on or before date above.

Set Password...

OK
Cancel
Help
Default

Also See:

General

Payroll and Employees

Icons on left: Accounting, Checking, Desktop View, Finance Charge, General, Integrated Applications

FIGURE 2-1   Change the accounting options to add numbers to your accounts.

If you chose a prebuilt chart of accounts during the EasyStep Interview, those accounts are switched to numbered accounts automatically. You may want to change some of the numbers, and you can do so by editing the accounts (see "Editing Accounts" later in this chapter). Some accounts (those you added yourself during or after the interview) have to be edited manually to turn them into numbered accounts.

When you select the option to use account numbers, the option Show Lowest Subaccount Only becomes accessible (it's grayed out if you haven't opted for account numbers). This option tells QuickBooks to display only the subaccount on transaction windows instead of both the parent account and the subaccount, making it easier to see precisely which account is receiving the posting. (Subaccounts are discussed later in the section "Using Subaccounts.")

If all your accounts aren't numbered and you select Show Lowest Subaccount Only, when you click OK, QuickBooks displays an error message that you cannot enable this option until all your accounts have numbers assigned. After you've edited existing accounts that need numbers (any accounts that QuickBooks didn't automatically number for you), you can return to this preferences window and enable the subaccount option.

After you've set up numbered accounts, you have a more efficient chart of accounts; now you, your bookkeeper, and your accountant will have an easier time. Numbers give you a quick clue about the type of account you're working with. As you enter the accounts, you must use the numbers intelligently, assigning ranges of numbers to account types. You should check with your accountant before finalizing the way you use the numbers, but the example I present here (and use in my own books) is a common approach. I use four-digit numbers, and the starting digit represents the beginning of a range:

NOTE: You can have as many as seven numbers (plus the account name) for each account.

- 1*xxx* Assets
- 2*xxx* Liabilities
- 3*xxx* Equity
- 4*xxx* Income
- 5*xxx* Expenses
- 6*xxx* Expenses
- 7*xxx* Expenses
- 8*xxx* Expenses
- 9*xxx* Other Income and Expenses

Notice the amount of room for further breakdowns, especially in the expenses. (Most companies need more expense categories than income categories.)

You can, if you wish, have a variety of expense types and reserve the starting number for specific types. Many companies, for example, use 5*xxx* for sales expenses (they even separate the payroll postings between the sales people and the rest of the employees), then use 6000 through 7999 for general operating expenses, and 8*xxx* for other specific expenses that should appear together in reports (perhaps taxes and late fees).

Some companies use one range of expense accounts, such as 7000 through 7999 for expenses that fall into the "overhead" category. This is useful if you bid on work and need to know the total overhead expenses so you can apportion them to appropriate categories in your bid.

If you have inventory and you track cost of sales, you can reserve a section of the chart of accounts for those account types. Some companies use 4300 through 4999 for cost of sales; other companies use the numbers in the 5000 range.

Also, think about the breakdown of assets. You might use 1000 through 1099 for cash accounts and 1100 through 1199 for receivables and other current assets, then use 1200 through 1299 for tracking fixed assets such as equipment, furniture, and so on. Follow the same pattern for liabilities, starting with current liabilities and moving to long term. It's also a good idea to keep all the payroll withholding liabilities together.

Usually, you should add accounts by increasing the previous account number by ten, so that if your first bank account is 1000, the next bank account is 1010, and so on. For expenses (where you'll have many accounts), you might want to enter the accounts in intervals of five. This gives you room to squeeze in additional accounts that belong in the same general area of your chart of accounts when they need to be added later.

➡ FYI

How QuickBooks Sorts Accounts

You have to create a numbering scheme that conforms to the QuickBooks account types because QuickBooks sorts your chart of accounts by account type. If you have contiguous numbers that vary by account type, you won't be able to view your chart of accounts in numerical order. QuickBooks uses the following sort order for the chart of accounts:

- Assets
  - Bank
  - Accounts Receivable
  - Other Current Asset
  - Fixed Asset
  - Other Asset
- Liabilities
  - Accounts Payable
  - Credit Card
  - Other Current Liability
  - Long-Term Liability
- Equity
- Income
- Cost Of Goods Sold
- Expense
- Other Income
- Other Expense
- Non-Posting Accounts

(Non-posting accounts are created automatically by QuickBooks when you enable features that use those account types, such as Estimates and Purchase Orders).

Using Names for Accounts

Okay, I didn't convince you, or your accountant is just as happy with names for accounts. Or you've imported your accounts from another software application and you cannot bear the thought of changing all that data. Here's an important rule: memorize it, print it out in big letters, and post it all over the office:

Follow the company protocol for naming and using accounts

The company protocol is a system you invent for naming accounts. Your protocol must be clear so that when everyone follows the rules, the account naming convention is consistent.

Why is this important? Because when I visit clients who haven't invented and enforced protocols, I find accounts with names such as the following:

- Telephone Exp
- Exps-Telephone
- Tele Expense
- Telephone
- Tele

You get the idea, and I'll bet you're not shocked to hear that every one of those accounts had amounts posted to them. That's because users "guess" at account names and point and click on whatever they see that seems remotely related. If they don't find the account the way they would have entered the name, they invent a new account (using a name that seems logical to them). Avoid all of those errors by establishing protocols about creating account names, and then make sure everyone searches the account list before applying a transaction.

Here are a few suggested protocols—you can amend them to fit your own situation, or invent different protocols that you're more comfortable with. The important thing is consistency, absolute consistency.

- Avoid apostrophes
- Set the number of characters for abbreviations. For example, if you permit four characters, telephone is abbreviated "tele"; a three-character rule produces "tel".
- Decide whether to use the ampersand (&) or a hyphen. For example, is it "repairs & maintenance" or "repairs-maintenance"?
- Make a rule about whether spaces are allowed. For example, would you have "repairs & maintenance" or "repairs&maintenance"?

Using Subaccounts

Subaccounts provide a way to post transactions more precisely using subcategories for main account categories. For example, if you create an expense account for insurance expenses, you may want to have subaccounts for vehicle insurance, liability insurance, equipment insurance, and so on. Post transactions only to the subaccounts, never to the parent account. When you create reports, QuickBooks displays the individual totals for the subaccounts, along with the grand total for the parent account. To create a subaccount, you must first create the parent account, as described in the section, "Creating Subaccounts," later in this chapter.

If you're using numbered accounts, when you set up your main (parent) accounts, be sure to leave enough open numbers to be able to fit in all the subaccounts you'll need. If necessary, use more than four digits to make sure you have a logical hierarchy for your account structure. For example, suppose you have the following parent accounts:

- 6010 Insurance
- 6020 Utilities
- 6030 Travel

You can create the following subaccounts:

- 6011 Insurance:Vehicles
- 6012 Insurance:Liability
- 6013 Insurance:Equipment
- 6021 Utilities:Heat
- 6022 Utilities:Electric
- 6031 Travel:Sales
- 6032 Travel:Seminars and Meetings

The colon in the account names listed here is added by QuickBooks—you only have to create the subaccount name and number.

Adding Accounts

After you've done your homework, made your decisions, invented your protocols, and checked with your accountant, adding accounts is a piece of cake:

1. Press CTRL-A to open the Chart of Accounts window.

NOTE: QuickBooks provides various ways to get to the Chart of Accounts list. You can click the Accnt icon on the icon bar; select Company in the Navigators list, and then click the Chart of Accounts icon in the Company Navigator window; or choose Lists I Chart of Accounts from the menu bar.

2. Press CTRL-N to enter a new account. The New Account dialog box opens so you can begin entering information.

3. Click the down arrow to the right of the Type box and select an account type from the drop-down list.

The dialog box for entering a new account changes its appearance depending on the account type, because different types of accounts require different information. In addition, if you've opted to use numbers for your accounts, there's a field for the account number. Figure 2-2 shows a blank New Account dialog box for an Expense account.

The Description field is optional, and I've found that unless there's a compelling reason to explain the account, descriptions only make your account lists busier and harder to read. The Note field, which only appears on some account types, is also optional, and I've never come up with a good reason to use it.

TIP: Remember that every character you enter adds bytes to the size of your file. The larger a file is, the slower your work with it proceeds.

If you're not currently using an account, or you don't want anyone to post transactions to the account at the moment, you can select the Account Is Inactive option, which means the account won't be available for posting amounts while you're entering transactions. Entering a new account and marking it inactive

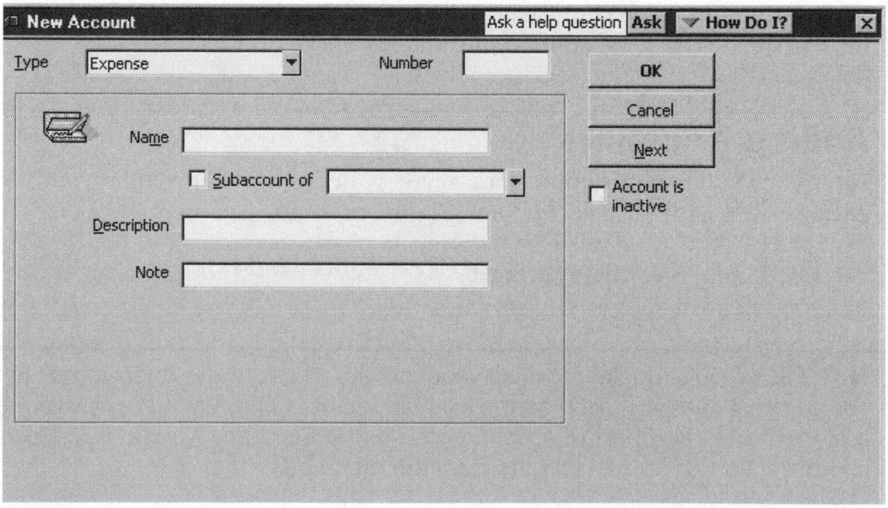

FIGURE 2-2 The only required entries for an account are the number (if you're using numbers) and the name.

immediately means you're really good at planning ahead. (Okay, I really wanted to say, "you're compulsive.")

Some account types (for example, accounts connected to banks) have a field for an opening balance. Don't worry about it during this initial entry of new accounts. The priority is to get all of your accounts into the system; you don't have to worry about balances now. In fact, the fastest and easiest way to put the account balances into the system is to enter an opening trial balance as a journal entry (see Appendix A).

As you finish entering each account, click Next to move to another blank New Account dialog box. When you're finished entering accounts, click OK and then close the Chart of Accounts list by clicking the X in the top-right corner.

Editing Accounts

If you need to make changes to any account information, select the account's listing in the Chart of Accounts list, and press CTRL-E. The Edit Account dialog box appears, which looks just like the account card you just filled out. Make your changes and click OK to save them.

To add a number to an account that wasn't automatically numbered when you changed your preferences to indicate numbered accounts, follow these steps:

1. Open the Chart of Accounts list.
2. Select an account that lacks a number.
3. Press CTRL-E to open the Edit Account dialog box.
4. Enter the account number.
5. Click OK.

Creating Subaccounts

To create a subaccount, you must have already created the parent account. Then take these steps:

1. Open the Chart of Accounts list.
2. Press CTRL-N to create a new account.
3. Select the appropriate account type.
4. Click the Subaccount check box to place a check mark in it.
5. In the drop-down box next to the check box, select the parent account. (This gives you access to the parent account number if you're using numbered accounts, which makes it easier to create the appropriate number for this subaccount.)
6. If you're using numbered accounts, enter the appropriate number.
7. Enter the account name.
8. Click OK.

You can have multiple levels of subaccounts. For example, you may want to track income in the following manner:

Income

   Income:Consulting

      Income:Consulting:Engineering

      Income:Consulting:Training

   Income:Products

      Income:Products:Technical

      Income:Products:Accessories

Creating the sub-subaccounts is as easy as creating the first level; just make sure you've already created the first-level subaccounts (which are the parents of the sub-subaccounts). When you fill in the New Account dialog box, after you check the Subaccount check box, select the appropriate subaccount to act as the parent account.

When you view the Chart of Accounts List, subaccounts appear under their parent accounts, and they're indented. When you view a subaccount in a transaction window, it appears in the format: *ParentAccount:Subaccount* or *ParentAccount: Subaccount:Subaccount*.

For example, if you create a parent account named Income with a subaccount Consulting, the Account field in transaction windows shows Income:Consulting. If you've used numbers, the Account field shows 4000-Income:4001-Consulting. Because many of the fields in transaction windows are small, you may not be able to see the subaccount names without scrolling through each account. This can be annoying, and it's much easier to work if only the subaccount name is displayed. That's the point of enabling the preference Show Lowest Subaccount Only, discussed earlier in this section. When you enable that option, you see only the subaccounts when you're working in a transaction window, which makes it much easier to find the accounts you need.

Merging Accounts

Sometimes you have two accounts that should be one. For instance, you may have accidentally created two accounts for the same purpose. As I discussed earlier in this chapter, I've been to client sites that had accounts named Telephone and Tele, with transactions posted to both accounts. Those accounts badly need merging. Accounts must meet the following criteria in order to be merged:

- The accounts must be of the same type.
- The accounts must be at the same level (parent or subaccount).

If the accounts aren't at the same level, move one of the accounts to the same level as the other account. After you merge the accounts, you can move the newly merged account to a different level.

Take the following steps to merge two accounts:

1. Open the Chart of Accounts List window.
2. Select (highlight) the account that has the name you *do not* want to use.
3. Press CTRL-E to open the Edit Account dialog box.
4. Change the account name and number to match the account you want to keep.
5. Click OK.
6. QuickBooks displays a dialog box telling you that the account number you've entered already exists for another account and asks if you want to merge the accounts. Click Yes to confirm that you want to merge the two accounts.

Customers and Jobs

In QuickBooks, customers and jobs are handled together. In fact, QuickBooks doesn't call the list a Customer List, it calls it a Customer:Job List. You can create a customer and consider anything and everything you invoice to that customer a single job, or you can have multiple jobs for the same customer.

NOTE: If you're using QuickBooks Basic Edition, you don't have the job tracking feature.

Many small businesses don't worry about jobs; it's just the customer that's tracked. But if you're a building contractor or subcontractor, an interior decorator, or some other kind of service provider who usually bills by the job instead of at an hourly rate for an ongoing service, you should track jobs. For example, I find it useful and informative to track income by jobs (books) instead of just tracking my customers (publishers).

Jobs don't stand alone as an entity in QuickBooks; they are attached to customers, and you can attach as many jobs to a single customer as you need to. If you are going to track jobs, it's a good idea to enter all the customers first (now), and then attach the jobs second (later).

If you enter your existing customers now, when you're first starting to use QuickBooks, all the other work connected to the customer is much easier. It's bothersome to have to stop in the middle of every invoice you enter to create a new customer record.

Entering a New Customer

Putting all your existing customers into the system takes very little effort:

1. Press CTRL-J to open the Customer:Job List window. (Alternatively, you can click the Cust icon on the icon bar, or click the Customers listing in the Navigator list and then click the Customers icon in the Customers Navigator window.)
2. Press CTRL-N to open a blank customer card and fill in the information for the customer (see Figure 2-3).

Consider the Customer Name field a code rather than just the billing name. It doesn't appear on your invoices. (The invoices print the company name, the primary contact name, and the address.)

You must invent a protocol for this Customer Name field so that you'll enter every customer in the same manner. Notice the Customer Name field in Figure 2-3. This customer code entry has no apostrophe or space, even though the customer name contains both. Avoiding punctuation and spaces in codes is a good protocol for filling in code fields.

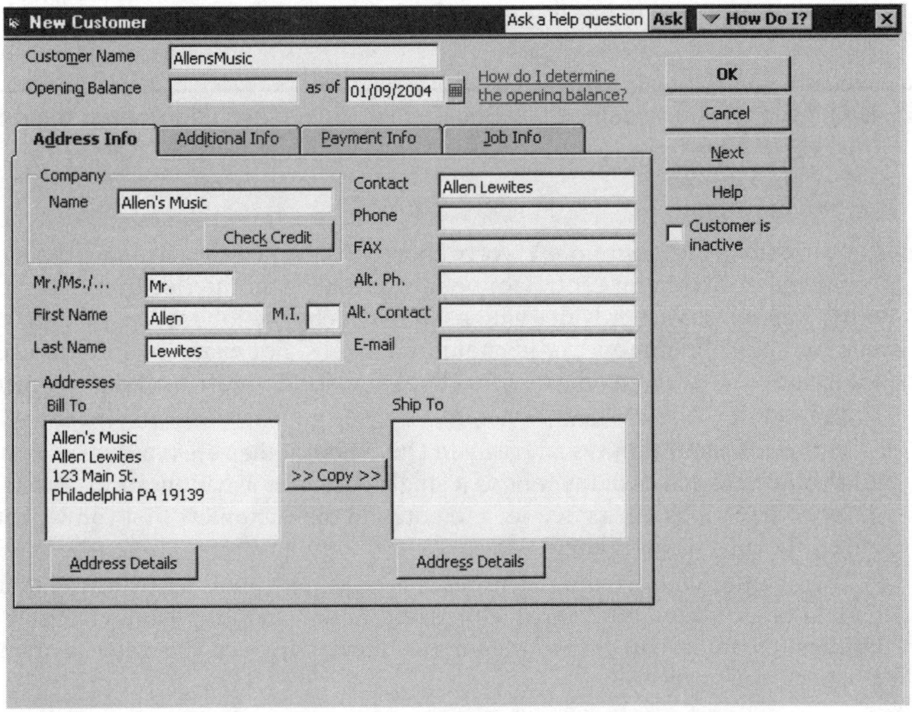

FIGURE 2-3   The customer card has plenty of fields for storing information.

Your lists and reports use this field to sort your customer list, so if you want it alphabetized, you must make sure you use the last name if there's no company name. Each customer must have a unique entry in this field, so if you have a lot of customers named Jack Johnson, you may want to enter them as JohnsonJack001, JohnsonJack002, and so on.

QuickBooks makes an Opening Balance field available, along with the date for which this balance applies (by default, the current date is inserted). You may want to use this if you're just setting up your company files, but don't use it if you're adding a customer after you've begun using QuickBooks. The amount you enter in this field is the total amount owed by this customer as of the date you specify. If you enter that amount, you'll have no detailed records on how the customer arrived at this balance, which makes it difficult to accept payments against specific invoices. It's better to skip this field and then enter an invoice, or multiple invoices, to post this customer's balance to your books. However, if the customer has a large quantity of outstanding invoices, you could consider using this field to avoid the need to enter each invoice separately. Then you can accept payments against the balance as they come in.

Address Info Tab

In the Name and Addresses sections of the window, enter the company name, optionally enter a contact, and enter the billing address. When you enter the company name and the contact name, that information is automatically transferred to the address field, so all you have to do is add the street address.

Enter a shipping address if it's different from the billing address. If the shipping address isn't different (or if you have a service business and don't ship products), you can click Copy to duplicate the billing address, or ignore the shipping address field.

TIP: If you've been storing customer names and addresses in another software program (such as a word processor), you can copy and paste the information between that program and the Address field in the customer dialog box. Starting with QuickBooks 2004, you can paste the entire address—in previous versions of QuickBooks you could only copy or paste a single line at a time, which was incredibly annoying.

If you've subscribed to the QuickBooks Credit Check Services, you can check the customer's Dun & Bradstreet credit rating by clicking the Check Credit button.

Click Address Details to enter or view the address as a series of fields, including fields for additional information.

Edit Address Information

Address	Allen's Music / Allen Lewites / 123 Main St.
City	Philadelphia
State / Province	PA
Zip / Postal Code	19139
Country / Region	
Note	

OK / Cancel

☑ Show this window again when address is incomplete or unclear

Use the check box to tell QuickBooks to display this window whenever you enter an incorrectly formatted address in a transaction window. For example, if you enter an incomplete address, after you click OK on the transaction window (such as an invoice), this address window opens. On the transaction window, your cursor flashes in the field where you made the mistake.

Additional Info Tab

The information you enter in the Additional Info tab of a customer card (see Figure 2-4) ranges from essential to convenient. Prepopulating the fields with information makes your work go faster when you're filling out transaction windows, and it makes it easier to create in-depth reports. It's worth spending the time to design some rules for the way data is entered. (Remember, making rules ensures consistency, without which you'll have difficulty getting the reports you want.)

NOTE: The fields you see on the Additional Info tab may not be the same as the fields shown in Figure 2-4. The preferences you configure (for example, whether you track sales tax) determine the available fields.

Let's spend a minute going over the fields in this tab. Most of the fields are also QuickBooks lists, and if you haven't already entered items in those lists, you can do so as you fill out the fields in the customer card. Each field that is also a list has an entry named <Add New>, and selecting that entry opens the appropriate new blank entry window.

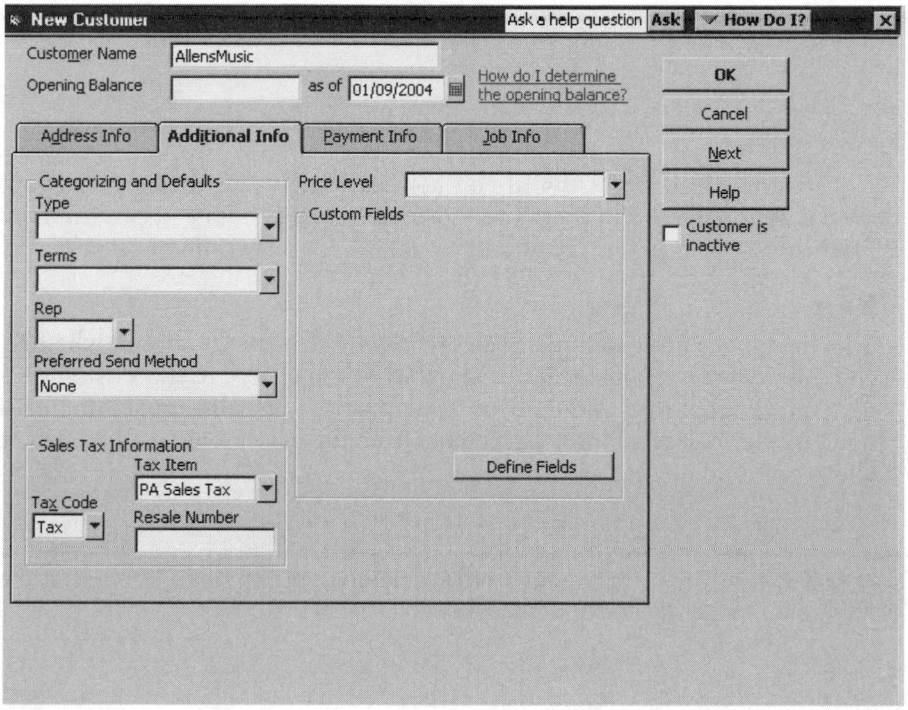

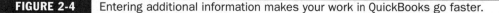

FIGURE 2-4   Entering additional information makes your work in QuickBooks go faster.

N O T E : The Preferred Send Method does not have an <Add New> entry.

Type

Use the Type field to sort your customers by a type you find important (or convenient) when you create reports. QuickBooks maintains a Type list (see the section "Customer Type List" later in this chapter). For example, you may want to consider wholesale and retail customers as your customer types. To use the field, click the arrow to select a type that you already entered, or create a new type.

Terms

Terms, of course, refers to payment terms. Click the arrow to the right of the text box to see the terms that are already defined, or choose <Add New> to define a new one. QuickBooks automatically adds the following terms to the Terms list:

- 1% 10 Net 30
- 2% 10 Net 30

- Due on Receipt
- Net 15
- Net 30
- Net 60

The terms in the Terms list are for both customers and vendors, and you may need additional terms to meet your customers' and vendors' needs. See the section "Terms List" later in this chapter to learn how to create different types of terms.

Rep

This field is the place to track a sales representative, and it's useful whether you pay commissions, or you just want to know who is in charge of this customer. Sales reps can be employees, vendors, or "other names" (usually applied to owners who don't receive commissions). Select a rep from the list of reps or add a new rep by choosing <Add New>.

 N O T E : If you're upgrading from QuickBooks 99 or earlier, note that the Rep field is no longer limited to employees.

Preferred Send Method

This field stores the default value for the way you want to send invoices, statements, or estimates to this customer. The choices are None (you don't send the documents), Mail, and E-mail. Regardless of the method you choose as your default, you can use any send method when you're creating a transaction.

Sales Tax Information

If you've configured QuickBooks to collect sales tax, the sales tax information uses several fields. If the customer is liable for sales tax, select the appropriate sales tax item for this customer, or create a new sales tax item. If the customer does not pay sales tax, select Non and enter the Resale Number provided by the customer (this is handy to have when the state tax investigators pop in for a surprise audit).

Price Level

Price levels are a pricing scheme, usually involving special discounts that you want to use for this customer's purchases. Select an existing price level or create a new one. See the section, "Price Level List" to learn about creating and assigning price levels.

Custom Fields

Custom fields provide an opportunity to invent fields for sorting and arranging your QuickBooks lists. See the section "Using Custom Fields" later in this chapter.

Payment Info Tab

This tab (see Figure 2-5) puts all the important information about customer finances in one place.

Account No.

This is an optional field you can use if you assign account numbers to your customers.

Credit Limit

A credit limit is a way to set a threshold for the amount of money you'll extend to a customer's credit. If a customer places an order, and the new order combined with any unpaid invoices exceeds the threshold, QuickBooks displays a warning. QuickBooks won't prevent you from continuing to sell to and invoice the customer, but you should consider rejecting the order (or shipping it COD).

 T I P : If you aren't going to enforce the credit limit, don't bother to use the field.

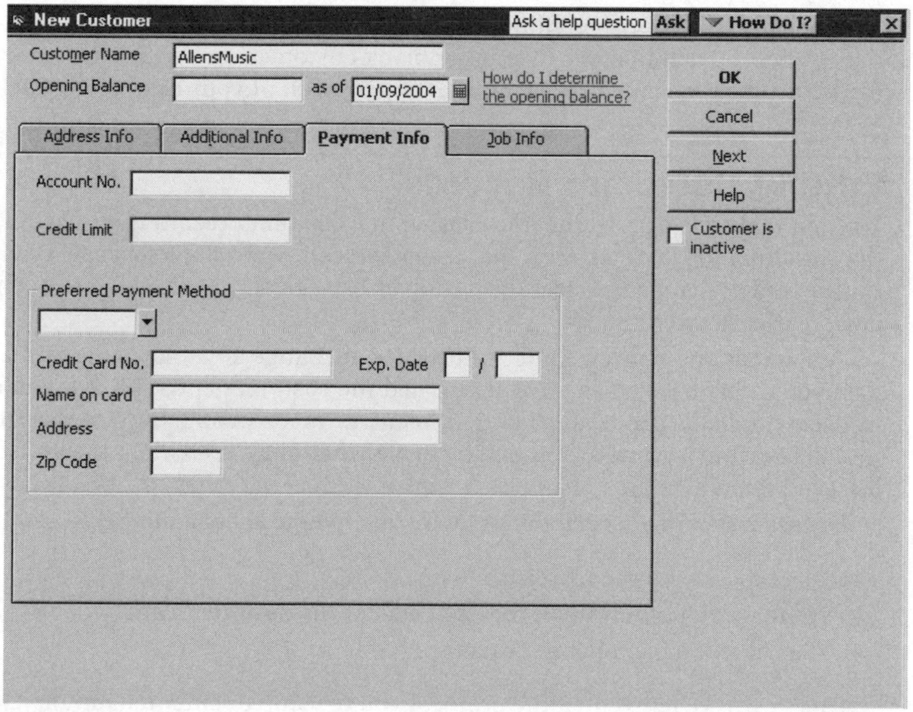

FIGURE 2-5 Use the Payment Info tab to track details for entering customer transactions.

Preferred Payment Method

This means the customer's preferred method for payments, and a list of payment methods is offered in drop-down list. You can select the appropriate item from the list or add a new one by selecting <Add New>. See the section "Payment Method List" later in this chapter for more information.

> **TIP:** The payment method you select automatically appears on the Receive Payments window when you are using this customer in the transaction. You can change the payment method at that time, if necessary.

Credit Card No.

This field is intended to contain this customer's credit card number, if that's the customer's preferred payment method. Don't fill it in unless your computer and your QuickBooks file are protected with all sorts of security. In fact, the laws (both government and merchant card providers) about keeping credit card numbers on file are changing, and it's probably illegal for you to keep anything more than the last four or five digits of the card number on file.

When you have finished filling out the fields (I'm skipping the Job Info tab for now), choose Next to move to another blank customer card so you can enter the next customer. When you have finished entering all of your customers, click OK.

Editing Customer Records

You can make changes to the information in a customer record quite easily. Open the Customer:Job List and select the customer record you want to change. Double-click the customer's listing or select the customer listing and press CTRL-E to open the customer card in Edit mode.

When you open the customer card, you can change any information or fill in data you didn't have when you first created the customer entry. In fact, you can fill in data you *did* have but didn't bother to enter. (Some people find it's faster to enter just the customer name and company name when they're creating their customer lists, and then fill in the rest at their leisure or the first time they invoice the customer.)

However, there are several things I want you to note about editing the customer card:

- Don't mess with the Customer Name field.
- There's a Notes button on the right side of the customer card.
- You can't enter an opening balance.

Unless you've reinvented the protocol you're using to enter data in the Customer Name field, don't change this data. Many high-end (translate that as "expensive and

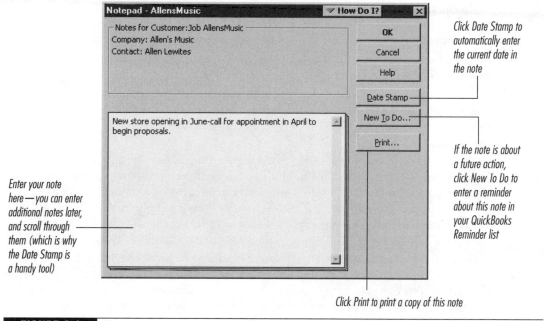

Click Date Stamp to automatically enter the current date in the note

Enter your note here — you can enter additional notes later, and scroll through them (which is why the Date Stamp is a handy tool)

If the note is about a future action, click New To Do to enter a reminder about this note in your QuickBooks Reminder list

Click Print to print a copy of this note

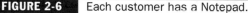

FIGURE 2-6   Each customer has a Notepad.

incredibly powerful") accounting software applications lock this field and never permit changes. QuickBooks lets you change it, so you have to impose controls on yourself.

Click the Notes icon to open a Notepad window that's dedicated to this customer, as shown in Figure 2-6. This is a useful feature, and I bet you'll use it frequently.

The Notepad is a great marketing tool because you can use it to follow up on a promised order, track a customer's special preferences, and notify the customer when something special is available. When you view the Customer:Job List, an icon appears in the Notes column for each customer that has a note in its record. You can open the note by double-clicking the note icon; you don't have to open the customer record to get to the note.

Vendors

The vendors you purchase goods and services from have to be entered into your QuickBooks system, and it's far easier to do it now. Otherwise, you'll have to go through the process of establishing the vendor and entering all the important information when you want to enter a vendor bill or write a check.

To open the Vendor List, click the Vend icon on the icon bar. (You can also select Vendors from the Navigators list, and then click the Vendors icon on the Vendors Navigator window, or choose Lists | Vendor List from the menu bar.)

When the Vendor List window opens, press CTRL-N to open a New Vendor card and fill out the fields (see Figure 2-7).

If you wish, you can enter the opening balance for this vendor, along with the date on which that balance exists. However, it's better to skip this field and enter an invoice (or multiple invoices) to represent that balance, so you have details about the transaction(s).

As with customers, you should have a set of rules about entering the information in the Vendor Name field. This field doesn't appear on checks or purchase orders; it's used to sort and select vendors when you need a list or a report. Think of it as a code. Notice that in Figure 2-7, the vendor code is a telephone number, but the vendor is the telephone company. This is how I create separate checks for each telephone bill I receive.

The Address field is important if you're planning to print checks and the vendor doesn't enclose a return envelope, making it necessary for you to put the address on the check. You can purchase window envelopes, and when you insert the check in the envelope, the vendor name and address block is in the right spot.

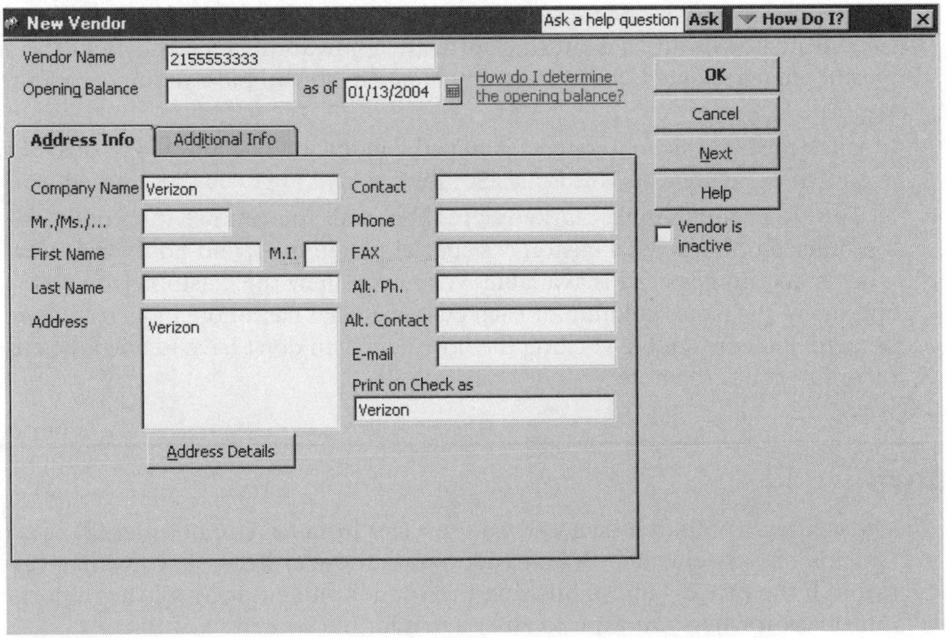

FIGURE 2-7 Vendor records are less complicated than customer records.

The Additional Info tab (see Figure 2-8) for vendors has several important categories:

- **Account No.** Enter your account number with this vendor (to the vendor, it's your customer number), and the number will appear in the memo field of printed checks.
- **Type** Select a type or create one. This optional field is handy if you want to sort vendors by type, which makes reports more efficient. For example, you can create vendor types for inventory suppliers, tax authorities, and so on.
- **Terms** Enter the terms for payment this vendor has assigned to you.
- **Credit Limit** Enter the credit limit this vendor has given you.
- **Tax ID** Use this field to enter the social security number or EIN if this vendor receives a Form 1099.
- **1099 status** If appropriate, select the check box for Vendor Eligible For 1099.
- **Custom Fields** As with customers, you can create custom fields for vendors (see the section "Using Custom Fields" later in this chapter).

After you fill in the information, choose Next to move to the next blank card and enter the next vendor. When you're finished, click OK.

| FIGURE 2-8 | Add information to the vendor record to make it easier to print checks and produce detailed reports. |

When you view or edit a vendor card by selecting the vendor's listing and pressing CTRL-E, you'll find a Notes button just like the one in the customer card. You can use it in the same way.

Payroll Lists

If you plan to use QuickBooks for payroll, you must enter all of your employees, including their pertinent tax information. To do that, you have to define the tax information, which requires you to define the items that make up the payroll check. This means you have two lists to create—the payroll items and the employees. I'm assuming all the vendors who receive checks from the payroll system have been entered into your Vendor List (the IRS, the state and local tax authorities, the medical insurance companies, pension providers, and so on). Of course, your chart of accounts should have all the accounts you need in order to post payroll items.

Entering Payroll Items

The number of individual elements that go into a paycheck may be more than you thought. Consider this list, which is typical of many businesses:

- Salaries
- Wages (hourly)
- Overtime
- Double-time
- Federal tax withholdings (including FIT, FICA, and Medicare)
- State tax withholdings
- State unemployment and disability withholdings
- Local tax withholdings
- Pension plan deductions
- Medical insurance deductions
- Life insurance deductions
- Garnishes
- Union dues
- Reimbursement for auto expenses
- Bonuses
- Commissions
- Vacation pay
- Sick pay
- Advanced Earned Income Credit

Whew! And don't forget that you also have to track company-paid payroll items, such as matching FICA and Medicare, employer contributions to unemployment (both state and federal), state disability funds, pension and medical benefit plans, and more!

Each payroll item has to be defined and linked to the chart of accounts. The vendors who receive payments (for example, the government and insurance companies) have to be entered and linked to the payroll item.

To create or add to your list of payroll items (you may have some items listed as a result of your EasyStep Interview or because you enabled payroll in the Preferences dialog box), choose Lists | Payroll Item List from the menu bar. QuickBooks displays a message asking if you want help setting up payroll. If you click Yes, QuickBooks opens the Payroll Setup Interview Wizard, which walks you through the necessary steps. I discuss this method in Chapter 8. If you click No, you're taken to the Payroll Item list (see Figure 2-9) where you can edit existing items and add new items.

If anything is missing (for example, wages, sick/vacation pay, state and local taxes, medical benefits deductions, and other payroll items are probably not listed), add a new item by pressing CTRL-N to open the Add New Payroll Item Wizard shown in Figure 2-10.

The Custom Setup method provides a wizard that walks you through the creation of the payroll item. The Easy Setup method displays payroll items from which you can select the items you need, so you won't accidentally leave an item out. When you're running payroll checks, it's a real pain to have to stop the task and create payroll items.

Easy Setup Method

If you select Easy Setup, the wizard closes and the Payroll Setup window opens (see Figure 2-11). Select the items you need and click Create. Then click Continue at the bottom of the window, and follow the prompts on the screen to fill in the details for the items you're creating.

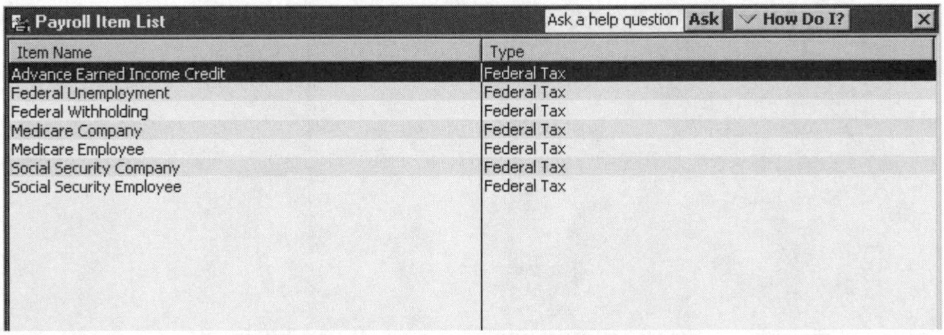

Item Name	Type
Advance Earned Income Credit	Federal Tax
Federal Unemployment	Federal Tax
Federal Withholding	Federal Tax
Medicare Company	Federal Tax
Medicare Employee	Federal Tax
Social Security Company	Federal Tax
Social Security Employee	Federal Tax

Payroll Item List   Ask a help question [Ask] ∨ How Do I? [X]

FIGURE 2-9 The payroll items automatically added by QuickBooks may not include everything you need.

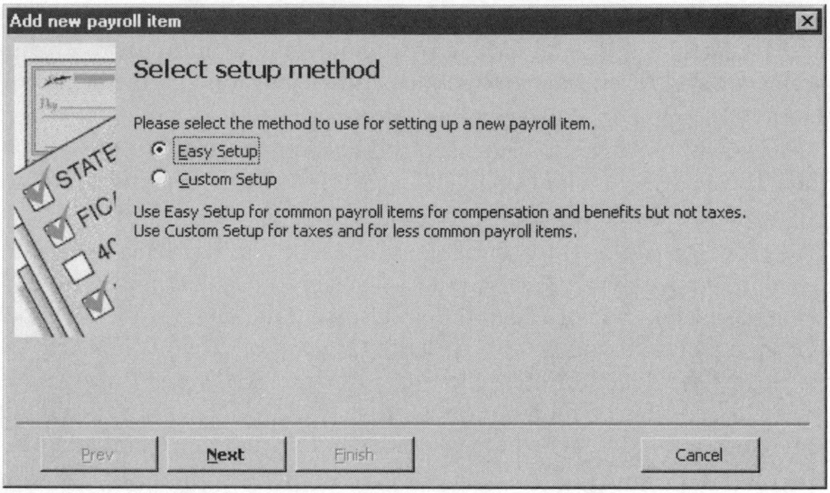

Add new payroll item ☒

Select setup method

Please select the method to use for setting up a new payroll item.

● Easy Setup
○ Custom Setup

Use Easy Setup for common payroll items for compensation and benefits but not taxes.
Use Custom Setup for taxes and for less common payroll items.

Prev | **Next** | Finish | Cancel

FIGURE 2-10 The method you select for creating a payroll item depends on the type of item.

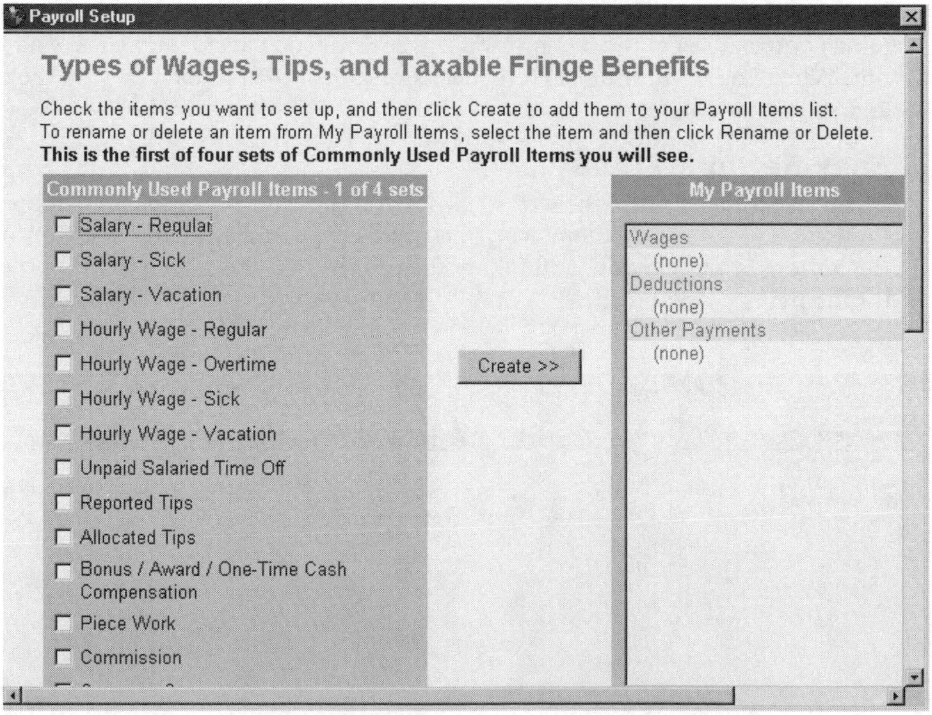

Payroll Setup ☒

Types of Wages, Tips, and Taxable Fringe Benefits

Check the items you want to set up, and then click Create to add them to your Payroll Items list.
To rename or delete an item from My Payroll Items, select the item and then click Rename or Delete.
This is the first of four sets of Commonly Used Payroll Items you will see.

Commonly Used Payroll Items - 1 of 4 sets | **My Payroll Items**

☐ Salary - Regular
☐ Salary - Sick
☐ Salary - Vacation
☐ Hourly Wage - Regular
☐ Hourly Wage - Overtime
☐ Hourly Wage - Sick
☐ Hourly Wage - Vacation
☐ Unpaid Salaried Time Off
☐ Reported Tips
☐ Allocated Tips
☐ Bonus / Award / One-Time Cash Compensation
☐ Piece Work
☐ Commission

Create >>

Wages
  (none)
Deductions
  (none)
Other Payments
  (none)

FIGURE 2-11 The Payroll Setup window lets you select an item and enter all the attendant required information.

Custom Setup Method

For Custom Setup items, step through the wizard by clicking Next, answering all the questions and filling in all the information.

> **NOTE:** More information about setting up payroll (including information about using the Payroll Setup window) is in Chapter 8.

Here are some tricks and tips you should be aware of as you enter payroll items:

- Check everything with your accountant.
- QuickBooks already has information on many state taxes, so check for your state before you add the information manually.
- You'll probably have to enter your local (city or township) taxes manually, because QuickBooks only has built-in information on a few cities.
- For deductions, the wizard will ask about the vendor who receives this money. (It's called an *agency*, but it's a vendor.)
- If you want the employer contributions to pension, health insurance, life insurance, and so on to appear on the payroll check stubs, you must enter those items as payroll items.
- When you enter a pension deduction, you must make sure to specify the taxes that are *not* calculated (I said *calculated,* not *deducted*) before you deduct the new payroll item. If you forget one, the paychecks and deductions may be incorrect. Some plans permit employees to choose between pre- and post-tax deductions. Some states have pre-tax deduction allowances.

When you have entered all your payroll items, you're ready to move on to the next step in entering your payroll information: employees.

Create an Employee Template

There is a great deal of information to fill out for each employee, and some of it is probably the same for all or most of your employees. For example, you may have many employees who share the same hourly wage or the same deductions for medical insurance.

To avoid entering the same information over and over, you can create a template and then apply the information to all the employees who match that data. You'll save yourself lots of time, even if some employees require one or two entries that differ from the template.

To get to the template, you have to start with the Employee List, which you open by choosing Lists | Employee List from the menu bar. The first time you access the

Employee List, a message appears asking if you want help setting up payroll. If you click Yes, the Payroll Setup window opens. If you click No, the Employee List opens. To create a template, click No to go right to the Employee List window.

In the Employee List window, click the Employee button at the bottom of the window and choose Employee Defaults from the menu that appears. This opens the Employee Defaults window, where you can enter the data that applies to most or all of your employees.

The information you put into the template is used on the Payroll Info tab for each employee (discussed in the next section, "Entering Employees").

- Click in the Item Name column of the Earnings box, then click the arrow to see a list of earnings types that you've defined in your Payroll Items. Select the one that is suitable for a template.

- In the Hourly/Annual Rate column, enter a wage or salary figure if there's one that applies to most of your employees. If there's not, just skip it and enter each employee's rate on the individual employee card later.

- Use the arrow to the right of the Pay Period field to see a list of choices and select your payroll frequency. The available choices are Daily, Weekly, Biweekly, Semimonthly, Monthly, Quarterly, and Yearly. That should suffice, but if you're planning to pay your employees with some unusual scheme (alternate Tuesdays if it rains??), you can't create a new choice for this field.

- Use the Class field if you've created classes for tracking your QuickBooks data. (See Chapter 21 for information on using classes.)

- If you're using QuickBooks' time-tracking features to pay employees, you also see a check box labeled Use Time Data To Create Paychecks. Put a check mark in the check box to enable the feature. (See Chapter 19 to learn how to transfer time tracking into your payroll records.)

- If all or most of your employees have the same additional adjustments (such as insurance deductions, 401(k) deductions, or reimbursement for car expenses), click in the Item Name column in the Additions, Deductions, And Company Contributions box, then click the arrow to select the appropriate adjustments.
- Click the Taxes button to see a list of taxes and select those that are common and therefore suited for the template (usually all or most of them).
- Click the Sick/Vacation button to set the terms for accruing sick time and vacation time if your policy is similar enough among employees to include it in the template.

When you are finished filling out the template, click OK to save it.

Entering Employees

Finally, you're ready to tell QuickBooks about your list of employees. In the Employee List window, press CTRL-N to bring up a New Employee form (see Figure 2-12).

The New Employee window displays three tabs: Personal, Address And Contact, and Additional Info. Additional tabs exist, and you need to use the drop-down list

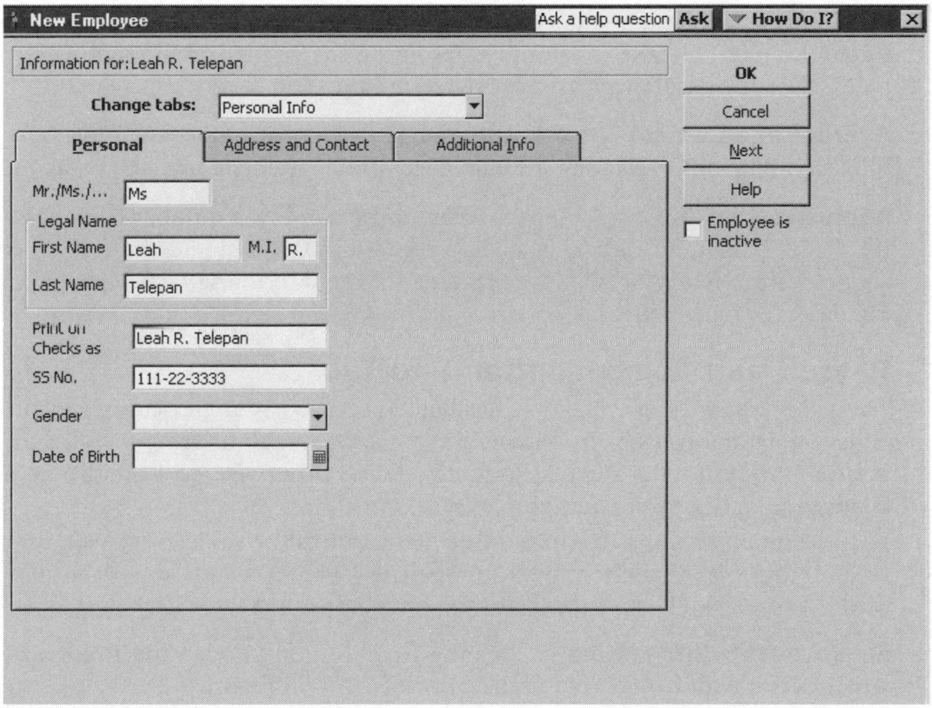

FIGURE 2-12   Enter employee information carefully because payroll has a zero tolerance for errors.

in the Change Tabs field at the top of the window to access them. The following tab categories are available in the drop-down list:

- **Personal Info**   A three-tab dialog where you enter personal information about the employee (the three tabs in Figure 2-12)
- **Payroll And Compensation Info**   Where you enter information about earnings, taxes, deductions, and other financial data.
- **Employment Info**   Where you enter information about the employee's hiring date and other employment history.

I'll discuss all of these tabs in this section.

Personal Info Tab

The Personal Info tab is the place to record personal information about this employee. It's really three tabs, because the information is divided into three categories.

Personal Tab   Enter the employee's name, social security number, and the way the name should be printed on paychecks. QuickBooks automatically inserts the data from the name fields, which is usually the way paychecks are written, but you may want to make a change (for instance, omitting the middle initial).

Enter the Gender and/or Date Of Birth if you have a company policy of recording this information, or if any tax or benefits agency requires it. For example, your state unemployment form may require you to note the gender of all employees; your medical or life insurance carrier may require the date of birth.

Address and Contact Tab   Use this tab to record the employee's address, as well as information about contacting the employee (phone number, e-mail, fax, and so on).

Additional Info Tab   Use this tab to enter the employee number (if your company uses employee numbers). This tab also contains a Define Fields button, so you can create custom fields for employee records (covered in the section "Using Custom Fields" later in this chapter).

Payroll and Compensation Info Tab

This tab contains the information QuickBooks needs to pay employees (see Figure 2-13). Where the employee's payroll items and amounts match information already filled in on the default template, just select the items. Otherwise, make additions and changes as necessary for this employee.

If the amount of the earnings or the deduction is the same every week, enter an amount. If it differs from week to week, don't enter an amount on the employee card. Instead, you'll enter that information when you create the payroll check.

Employee Tax Information   Click the Taxes button to open the Taxes dialog box, which starts with Federal tax information, as seen in Figure 2-14.

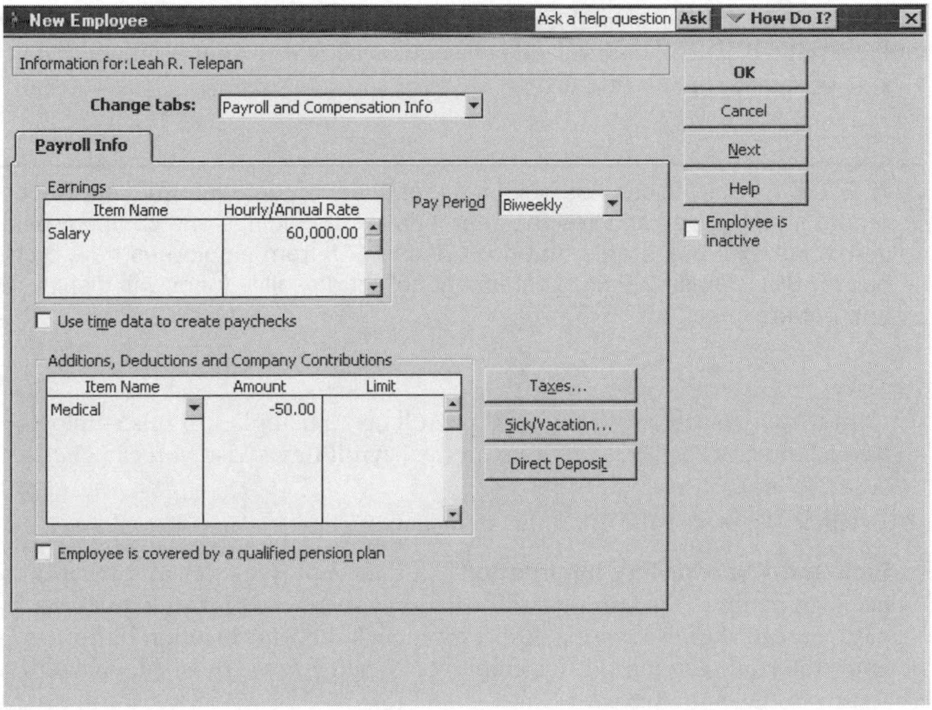

FIGURE 2-13 Enter the information about this employee's compensation and deductions—but not taxes.

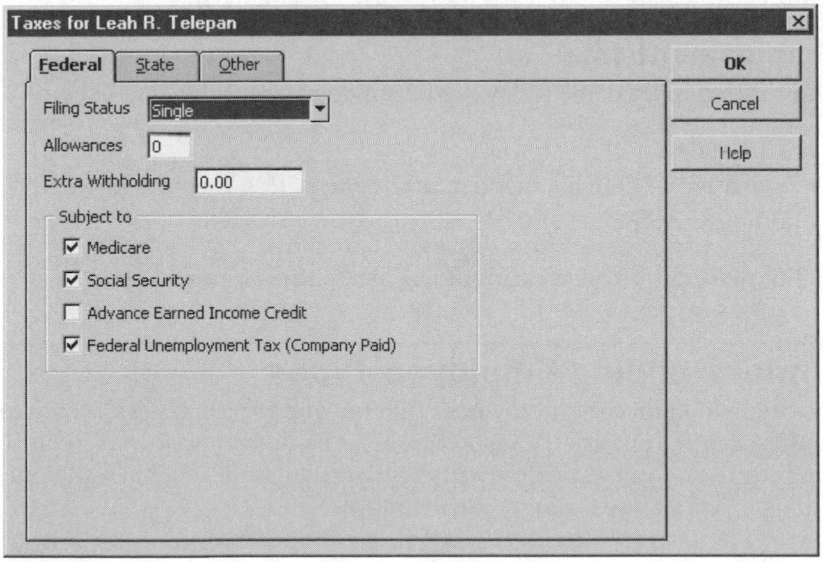

FIGURE 2-14 Set up the employee's tax rate.

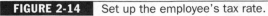

Move to the State tab and configure the employee's status for the state. This varies from state to state, of course, and you should check with your accountant if you aren't sure of something you find there.

> **NOTE:** QuickBooks has built in a great deal of state information. Depending on the state, you should see the appropriate withholdings and company-paid items. For example, states that don't deduct SUI from employees have a check box for SUI (Company Paid); states that collect disability funds will display the appropriate check box.

In the Other tab, apply any local payroll tax that applies to this employee. If you haven't already configured that tax in the Payroll Items List, you can click <Add New> to enter it now.

Click OK to save the tax status information.

Sick and Vacation Pay Information   If this employee's sick and vacation pay package matches the template information you entered for sick and vacation pay, you can skip this section. Otherwise, click the Sick/Vacation button and enter the configuration for this employee. When you are finished, click OK to return to the employee card.

Direct Deposit   The employee card has a Direct Deposit button, which you can use to establish direct deposit of the employee's paycheck to his or her bank account. The button won't work until you've set up direct deposit as an online feature. See Chapter 8 to learn how to use direct deposit.

Employment Info Tab

Use this tab to track the following information about the employee:

- Hiring date
- Release date (fill this in when an employee leaves your company)
- Employee type

For more information on employee types, see the next section.

Understanding Employee Types

The Type field on the Employment Info tab offers four choices, which are explained in this section. The selection you make has an impact on the way your tax returns are prepared. You must check with your accountant if you have any question about the type you should assign to any employee.

Regular Employee

A Regular employee is exactly what it seems to be: a person you hired, for whom you deduct withholdings, issue a W-2, and so on. It's important to have every employee fill out a W-4 form every year (don't accept "I did that last year, nothing has changed").

TIP: If you need extra W-4 forms, you can download them from the IRS at /www.irs.ustreas.gov. Go to the forms section, select W-4, and print or download the form. Then make as many copies as you need.

Officer Employee

An Officer is someone who is an officer of a corporation. If your business isn't incorporated, you have no officers. Corporate tax returns require you to report payroll for officers of the corporation separately from the regular payroll amounts. Selecting Officer as the type has no impact on running your payroll (calculations, check printing, etc); it only affects reports.

Statutory Employee

A Statutory employee is someone who works for you that the IRS has decided qualifies as an employee instead of as an independent contractor. The list of the job types that the rules cover isn't very long, and the definition of *independent contractor* is the subject of much debate (especially in IRS audit hearings). The IRS has a list of criteria that must be met in order to qualify as an independent contractor (which means you don't have to put that person on your payroll, you don't have to withhold taxes, and you don't have to pay employer taxes). The rules that govern this change frequently, so it's important to check the rules in Circular E or with your accountant.

The IRS has issued a list of activities and circumstances that defines independent contractors, which is not at all comprehensive because under the right conditions many independent contractors could be considered employees. However, if any independent contractors are performing any of the following types of duties for you, you must put them on your payroll and configure them as Statutory Employee Types:

- An agent (or commission) driver who delivers food, beverages (other than milk), laundry, or dry cleaning for someone else.
- A full-time life insurance salesperson.
- A traveling or city salesperson (other than an agent driver or commission driver) who works full time (except for sideline sales activities) for one firm or person getting orders from customers. The orders must be for items for resale or use as supplies in the customer's business. The customers must be retailers, wholesalers, contractors, or operators of hotels, restaurants, or other businesses dealing with food or lodging.

- A home worker who works by guidelines of the person for whom the work is done, with materials furnished by and returned to that person or to someone that person designates.

While I'm amused by the exception of milk delivery agents (which probably means the milk delivery folks hired a good lobbyist to go to Washington D.C. to plead their case), the important item is the last one. Someone who works for you at home (usually in a home office) as a freelance professional could be deemed an employee, which increases your expenses. For example, if you hire a consultant, make sure that person doesn't use your materials, doesn't follow your orders about the days and hours for working, and generally works totally independently. Many computer consultants who work long term for a single company get caught in this bind.

Owner Employee

Owner and Employee are mutually exclusive terms to the IRS. If you own a company, that means the company is a proprietorship; it's not a corporation (a corporation doesn't have owners, it has officers and directors). The same thing is true of a partnership, which has multiple owners. You cannot put yourself on the payroll; you must draw regular checks and post the amounts against a Draw account in the Equity section of your accounts.

QuickBooks puts this type in the list in case it's too late and you have already listed yourself or a partner in the Employee List. The QuickBooks payroll program won't perform payroll tasks for any employee of this type. If you did add your name to the Employee List, delete it rather than assign this type.

Entering Items

If you are a service business, this is going to be a snap. If you sell a few items, it'll still be pretty easy. But if you have a large inventory, get a cup of coffee or a soda or take a bathroom break, because this is going to take some time.

Understanding Items

Items are the things that appear on your invoices when you send an invoice to a customer. If you think about it, that's a bit more complicated than it might appear. Do you charge sales tax? If you do, that's an item. Do you subtotal sections of your invoices? That subtotal is an item. Do you show prepayments or discounts? They're items, too.

While you can issue an invoice that says "Net amount due for services rendered" or "Net amount due for items delivered" and enter one total in the invoice, your customers aren't going to be very happy with the lack of detail. More important, when you try to analyze your business to see where you're making lots of money and where you're making less money, you won't have enough information to determine the facts.

This is another setup chore that requires some planning. Each of your items must have a code, a unique identification (QuickBooks calls that the Item Name/Number). Try to create a system that has some logic to it so your codes are recognizable when you see them listed.

Understanding Item Types

It isn't always clear how and when some of the item types are used (or why you must define them). Here are some guidelines you can use as you plan to enter your items:

Service   A service you provide to a customer. You can create services that are charged by the job or by the hour.

Inventory Part   A product you buy for the purpose of reselling. This item type isn't available if you haven't enabled inventory during the EasyStep Interview or activated inventory in the Purchases & Vendors section of the Preferences dialog box.

Non-Inventory Part   A product you don't stock in inventory or don't track even though it's in your inventory warehouse. Most of the time, you use this item type for products that you don't resell, such as office supplies. You generally only need to enter non-inventory parts if you use purchase orders when you order these items, and if you only use purchase orders for real inventory items, you don't have to create any items of this type.

T I P : You should use purchase orders only for inventory items, which are those things you buy in order to resell. It's an unnecessary complication to use purchase orders for your own purchases, such as office supplies.

Other Charge   You'll need this item type for things like shipping charges, or other line items that appear on your invoices. In fact, some people create one for each method of shipping.

Subtotal   This item type adds up everything that comes before it. It gives a subtotal before you add shipping charges or subtract any discounts or prepayments.

Group   This item type is a clever device. You can use it to enter a group of items (all of which must exist in your Item list) all at once. For example, if you frequently have a shipping charge and sales tax on the same invoice, you can create a group item that includes those two items.

Discount   You can't give a customer a discount as a line item if the item type doesn't exist. You may have more than one item that falls within this item type—for example, a discount for wholesale customers and a discount for a volume purchase. When you enter the item, you can indicate a percentage as the rate.

> **TIP:** I have an income item in my chart of accounts called "customer discounts," and items are posted there as discounts (reverse income) instead of as expenses. (This system gives me a better picture of my revenue.) Check with your accountant about the best method for posting discounts; you can use income or expense accounts.

Payment   If you receive a prepayment (either a total payment or a partial payment as a deposit), you must indicate it as a line item. You can use this item type to do that (or you can create a discount item to cover prepayments if you prefer).

Sales Tax Item   Create one of these item types for each sales tax authority for which you collect.

Sales Tax Group   This is for multiple sales taxes that appear on the same invoice.

> **TIP:** I've described all of the item types in terms of their use on your invoices, but many of them are used on your purchase orders, too.

Entering the Data for Items

To put your items into the system, click the Item icon on the icon bar, or choose Lists | Item List from the menu bar. When the Item List window opens, any items that were created during your EasyStep Interview are listed.

To create a new item, press CTRL-N. The New Item window opens, displaying a list of item types, as described in the previous paragraphs. Select an item type to display the appropriate fields in the blank New Item window.

Figure 2-15 shows a blank New Item window for an Inventory Part. Other item types (such as Service items) have fewer fields.

The Item Name/Number field is the place to insert a unique identifying code for the item. When you are filling out invoices (or purchase orders), this is the listing you see in the drop-down list.

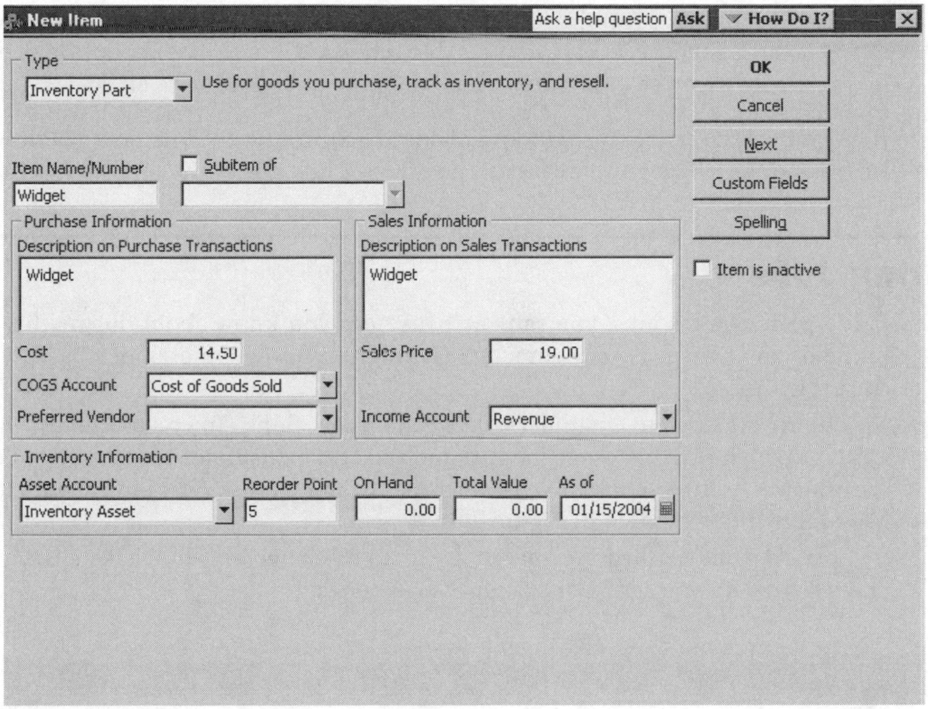

FIGURE 2-15 The fields in the New Item dialog box hold the information you need to use this item in transactions and to produce reports about the item.

NOTE: After you've created an item, you can create subitems. For example, if you sell shoes as an item, you can create subitems for dress shoes, sneakers, boots, and so on. Or use subitems for a parent item that comes in a variety of colors. Not all item types provide subitems.

Many of the rest of the fields in the New Item window change depending on the item type you select. Most of them are self-explanatory, but some are important enough to merit discussion:

- If you're entering an inventory item, fill in the cost of the item and enter the account to which you post the cost of goods (COG). Optionally, fill in the name of the vendor from whom you purchased the item.
- In the Sales Price field, you can enter a rate for those items that you've priced; leave the rate at zero for the items you want to price when you are preparing the invoice. Don't worry—nothing is etched in stone. You can change any rate that appears automatically when you're filling out an invoice. Link the price

to an income account in your chart of accounts and indicate whether the item is taxable (choose Tax) or not taxable (choose Non). (The tax option is only available if you've configured your company to collect sales tax.)

When you complete the window, choose Next to move to the next blank New Item window. When you finish entering items, click OK.

Entering Jobs

If you plan to track jobs, you can enter the ones you know about during this setup phase or enter them as they come up. (If you're running QuickBooks Basic, you can't track jobs).

Jobs are attached to customers; they can't stand alone. To create a job, press CTRL-J to open the Customer:Job List and select the customer for whom you're creating a job. Right-click the customer listing and choose Add Job to open the New Job window, shown in Figure 2-16.

Create a name for the job (you can use up to 41 characters) and make it descriptive enough for both you and your customer to understand.

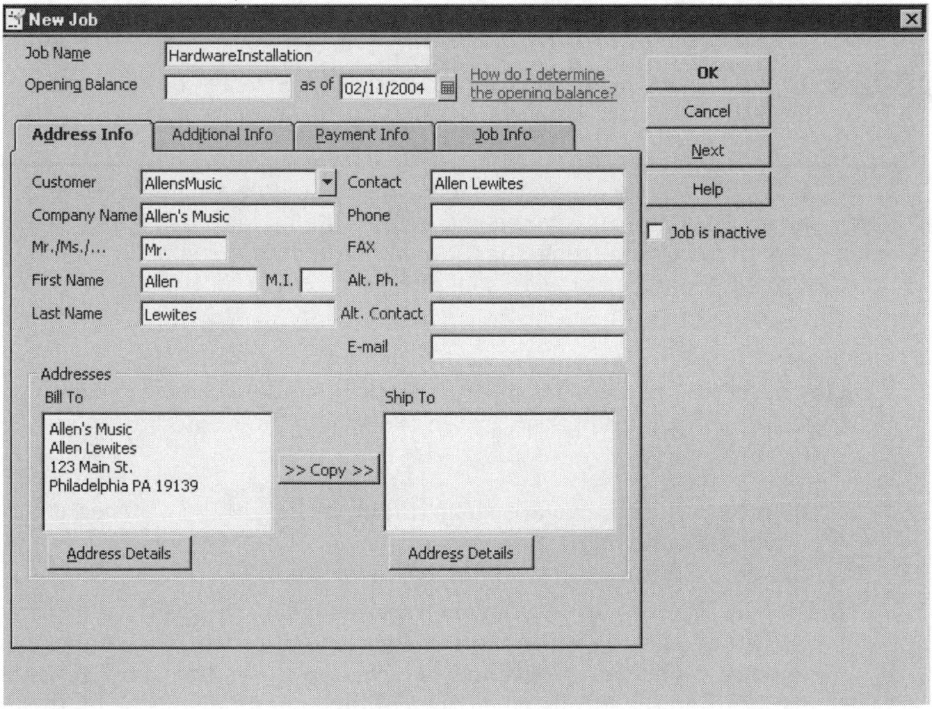

FIGURE 2-16 To create a new job, just enter the job name—all the basic information is already filled in from the customer record.

If this job requires you to bill the customer at an address that's different from the address you entered for this customer, or to ship goods to a different shipping address than the one that's entered, make the appropriate changes. QuickBooks maintains this information only for this job and won't change the original shipping address in the customer record.

The Additional Info tab and the Payment Info tab are related to the customer rather than the job, so you can skip them.

Move to the Job Info tab (see Figure 2-17) to begin configuring this job. All of the information on the Job Info tab is optional; the job exists for invoicing purposes without entering these details. For example, I track book royalties as jobs and never have to use the Job Info tab at all.

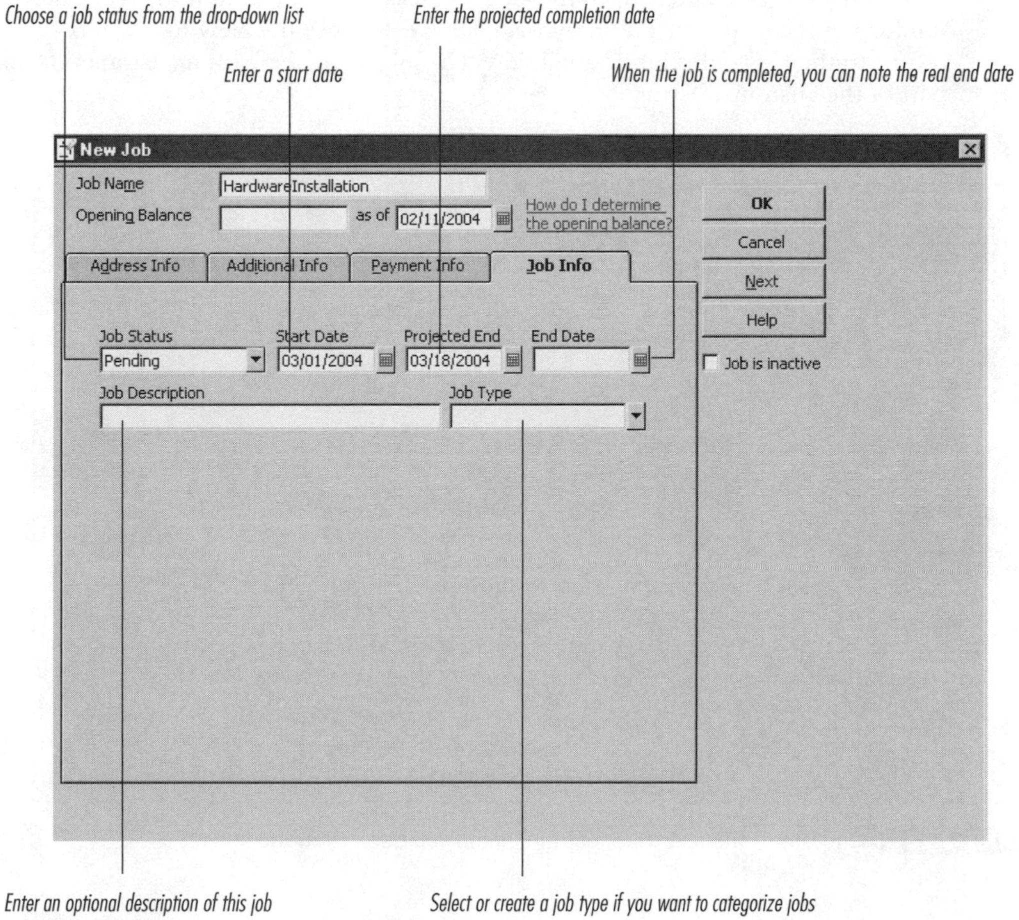
Choose a job status from the drop-down list
Enter the projected completion date
Enter a start date
When the job is completed, you can note the real end date
New Job
Job Name
HardwareInstallation
Opening Balance
as of 02/11/2004
How do I determine the opening balance?
OK
Cancel
Next
Help
Address Info
Additional Info
Payment Info
Job Info
Job Status
Pending
Start Date
03/01/2004
Projected End
03/18/2004
End Date
Job is inactive
Job Description
Job Type
Enter an optional description of this job
Select or create a job type if you want to categorize jobs

FIGURE 2-17 Track job details on the Job Info tab.

The Job Status drop-down list offers choices that you can change as the progress of the job moves along. You can change the text that describes each progress level to suit your own business. To accomplish this, follow these steps:

1. Choose Edit | Preferences to open the Preferences dialog.
2. Click the Jobs & Estimates icon in the left pane.
3. Click the Company Preferences tab in the right pane to see the current descriptive text for each status level (see Figure 2-18).
4. Change the text of any status levels if you have a descriptive phrase you like better. For example, you may prefer "Working" to "In Progress".
5. Click OK.

The new text is used on every job in your system.

When you finish entering all the data, choose Next if you want to create another job for the same customer. Otherwise, click OK to close the New Job window and return to the Customer:Job List window. The jobs you create for a customer become part of the customer listing.

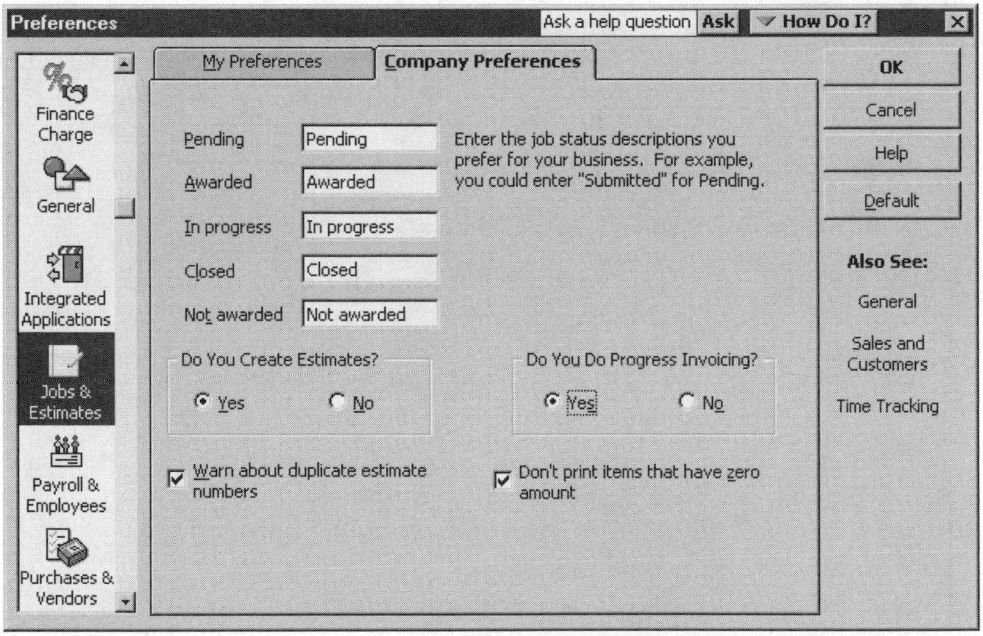

FIGURE 2-18   Customize the text to reflect the jargon you use in your business.

Entering Other Lists

There are a few items in the Lists menu that I haven't covered in detail. They don't require extensive amounts of data, and you may or may not choose to use them. If you do plan to use them, here's an overview of the things you need to know.

Some of these items are in the Lists menu and some of them are in a submenu of the Lists menu called Customer & Vendor Profile Lists. I'll cover all of them, and you can find the items in one place or another.

 N O T E : One item in the Lists menu, Templates, isn't covered here. These are the lists of invoice, purchase order, sales receipt, and other forms you use in transactions. Working with and customizing those templates is discussed throughout this book in the appropriate chapters.

Fixed Asset Item List

New in QuickBooks 2004, you can use this list to store information about fixed assets. This list is meant to track data about the assets you depreciate. As you can see in Figure 2-19, each asset's record includes detailed information and even has fields to track the sale of a depreciated asset.

If you're using QuickBooks Pro (the new list isn't available in QuickBooks Basic), this is merely a list, and it doesn't provide any method for calculating depreciation, nor does it link to any depreciation feature in the software. It's designed to let you use QuickBooks to track your asset list instead of whatever list you're keeping outside of QuickBooks.

You can generate a report on this list, customizing its contents to match the information your accountant needs to calculate your depreciation, and give it to your accountant. See Chapter 15 to learn how to generate and customize reports.

QuickBooks 2004 Premier: Accountant Edition has a nifty tool, Fixed Asset Manager, that uses the information in the Fixed Asset Item list to generate depreciation amounts and automatically perform depreciation transactions, applying depreciation amounts to the appropriate fixed asset accounts. If tracking depreciation is an important financial task, consider upgrading to Accountant Edition. At the very least, make sure your accountant is using Accountant Edition, because the depreciation processes can take place more quickly (which will probably reduce your accounting fees expense). To learn more about Fixed Asset Manager, and the other advanced tools in QuickBooks 2004 Premier Editions, look for *Running QuickBooks 2004 Premier Editions* from CPA911 Publishing (www.cpa911.com).

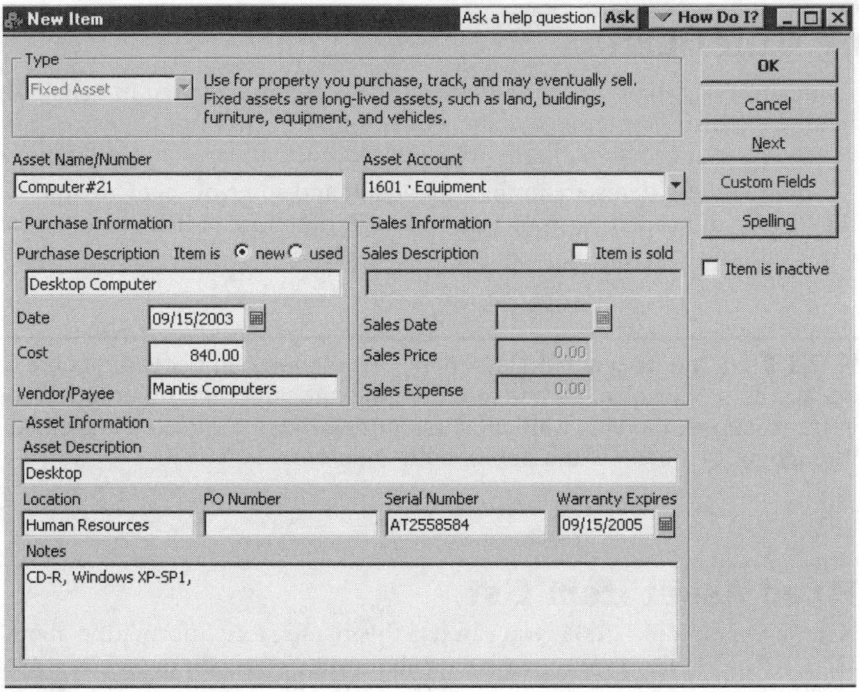

FIGURE 2-19 Keep detailed information about depreciable assets in the Fixed Asset Item List.

N O T E : QuickBooks Pro 2004 has a new tool named Depreciate Your Assets, and you can use it to determine depreciation rates in QuickBooks, but it doesn't open the Fixed Asset Item list—instead you have to enter asset information to use the tool. Depreciate Your Assets is a planning tool, and it does not perform depreciation tasks. You have to depreciate your assets in regular QuickBooks transaction windows.

Price Level List

This list is only available if you've enabled Price Levels in the Sales & Customers section of your Preferences (choose Edit | Preferences). The Price Level list is a nifty, easy way to connect special pricing to customers and jobs. Each price level has two components: a name and a formula. The name can be anything you wish, and the formula is based on the already-entered price of items (the formula increases or reduces that price by a percentage).

For example, you may want to give your favorite customers an excellent discount. Name the price level something like "Special" or "StarCustomer." Then enter a healthy percentage by which to reduce the price of items purchased by this customer. Or you may want to create a discount price level for customers that are nonprofit organizations.

On the other hand, you may want to keep your regular prices steady (assuming they're competitive) and increase them for certain customers (perhaps customers who don't pay in a timely fashion). It's probably politically incorrect to name the price level "Deadbeat," so choose something innocuous such as "DB." You could also use numbers for the price-level names, perhaps making the highest numbers the highest prices.

To apply price levels to customers, open the Customer:Job List and select a customer. Press CTRL-E to edit the customer card and select a price level on the Additional Info tab.

TIP : QuickBooks Premier Editions have a price level feature that's more robust—you can apply price levels to items in addition to customers, which makes it easier to provide discounts (or increases) while you're creating invoices. These per-item price levels let you set custom prices (using either a specific amount or a percentage) for items. If you've purchased a Premier Edition of QuickBooks, or are considering upgrading to Premier Edition, you can learn how to use price levels (and other Premier-only features) in *Running QuickBooks 2004 Premier Editions* (CPA911 Publishing). More information is available at www.cpa911.com.

Sales Tax Code List

This list is available if you configured your business to collect sales tax. If you only collect tax for one taxing authority, you don't have to add another tax code item. If you collect tax for multiple authorities, enter a code for that tax, using a three-letter abbreviation. This is not where you set up the tax rate for a code; you perform that task when you add this tax code to the Items List.

Unfortunately, QuickBooks continues to limit the size of the tax code item field to three characters, even though many states are enacting tax rules that assign multiple taxes that use four- and five-character codes for identification of those taxes. I've asked QuickBooks to change the number of characters permitted in the software's tax code field and have received information that this request is on the list of considerations for QuickBooks 2005.

In the meanwhile, if you conduct business in a state with multiple tax codes, the only workaround is to use three-character codes in QuickBooks to represent the state's tax codes. For example, you can create tax codes named 001, 002, and so on. In the description, enter the appropriate state code. However, to make sure tax codes are entered properly, you should create a list of your QuickBooks tax codes and their meaning (the state tax codes) and distribute that list to all users who enter invoices and estimates.

Class List

The Class List command appears in the Lists menu only if you've enabled the classes feature. Classes provide a method of organizing your activities (income and disbursement activities) to produce reports that you need. Many times, a well-designed chart of accounts will eliminate the need for classes, but if you do want to use them, you can create them ahead of time through the Lists menu.

It's a better idea to work with QuickBooks for a while and then, if you feel you need a report that can only be produced with the use of classes, create the class at that point. Chapter 21 covers the use of classes.

Other Names List

QuickBooks provides a list called Other Names, which is the list of people whose names come up in transactions, but whose activity you don't want to track. This list will appear when you write checks, but the names are unavailable for invoices, purchase orders, and any other QuickBooks transaction type.

If your business is a proprietorship, put yourself on the list to make sure your name is listed when you write your draw check. If there are several partners in your business, use this list for the checks you write to the partners' draws.

When you open a New Name window, there are fields for the address (handy for printing checks), telephone numbers, and other contact information.

> **TIP:** Many people overuse this category and end up having to move these names to the Vendor List because they do need to track the activity. Unless you're a proprietor or partner, it's totally possible to use QuickBooks efficiently for years without using this list.

Memorized Transaction List

This list (which isn't really a list, but rather a collection of transactions) should be built as you go, instead of created as a list. QuickBooks has a clever feature that memorizes a transaction you want to use again and again. Paying your rent is a good example. You can tell QuickBooks to memorize the transaction at the time you create it, which adds the transaction to this list. You can learn how to memorize specific types of transactions throughout this book in the chapters devoted to creating transactions.

Customer Type List

(This list appears in the submenu of Customer & Vendor Profile Lists.) When you create your customer list, you may decide to use the Customer Type field as a way to categorize the customer. This gives you the opportunity to sort and select customers in reports, perhaps to view the total income from specific types of customers.

You can predetermine the customer types you want to track by opening this list item and creating the types you need during setup. (Oops, it's too late if you've followed this chapter in order.) Or you can create them as you enter customers.

Vendor Type List

(This list appears in the submenu of Customer & Vendor Profile Lists.) See the two preceding paragraphs and substitute the word "vendor" for the word "customer."

Job Type List

(This list appears in the submenu of Customer & Vendor Profile Lists.) If you're using QuickBooks Pro, you can set up categories for jobs by creating job types. For example, if you're a plumber, you may want to separate new construction from repairs.

Terms List

(This list appears in the submenu of Customer & Vendor Profile Lists.) QuickBooks keeps both customer and vendor payment terms in one list, so the terms you need are all available whether you're creating an invoice, entering a vendor bill, or creating a purchase order. To create a terms listing, open the Terms List window and press CTRL-N to open the New Terms window, shown in Figure 2-20.

Use the Standard section to create terms that are due at some elapsed time after the invoice date:

- Net Due is the number of days you allow for payment after the invoice date.
- To give customers a discount for early payment, enter the discount percentage and the number of days after the invoice date that the discount is in effect. For example, if you allow 30 days for payment but want to encourage customers to pay early, enter a discount percentage that is in effect for 10 days after the invoice date.

Use the Date Driven section to describe terms that are due on a particular date, regardless of the invoice date:

- Enter the day of the month the invoice payment is due.
- Enter the number of days before the due date that invoices are considered payable on the following month (but it's not fair to insist that invoices be paid on the 10th of the month if you mail them to customers on the 8th of the month).
- To give customers a discount for early payment, enter the discount percentage and the day of the month at which the discount period ends. For example, if the standard due date is the 15th of the month, you may want to extend a discount to any customer who pays by the 8th of the month.

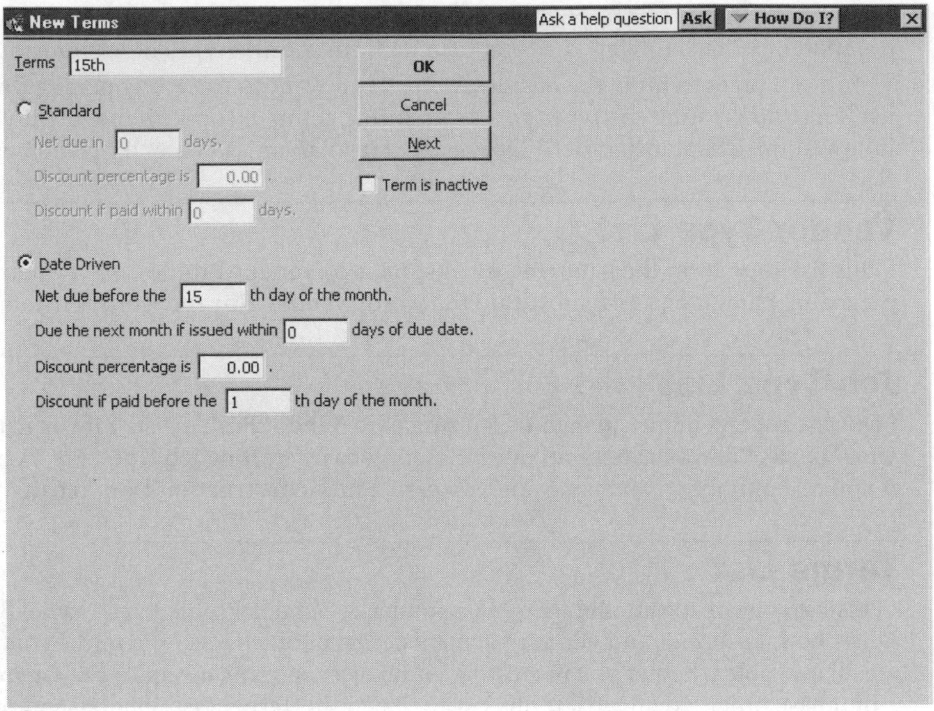

FIGURE 2-20 Give the new terms item a name and configure it so QuickBooks can calculate it.

TIP: Date-driven terms are commonly used by companies that send invoices monthly, usually on the last day of the month. If you send invoices constantly, as soon as a sale is completed, it's very difficult to track and enforce date-driven terms.

Customer Message List

(This list appears in the submenu of Customer & Vendor Profile Lists.) If you like to write messages to your customers when you're creating an invoice, you can enter a bunch of appropriate messages ahead of time and then just select the one you want to use. For example, you may want to insert the message "Thanks for doing business with us," or "Pay on time or else."

Press CTRL-N to enter a new message to add to the list. You just have to write the sentence (which can't be longer than 101 characters, counting spaces)—this is one of the easier lists to create.

Payment Method List

(This list appears in the submenu of Customer & Vendor Profile Lists.) You can track the way payments arrive from customers. This not only provides some detail (in case you're having a conversation with a customer about invoices and payments), but also allows you to print reports on payments that are subtotaled by the method of payment, such as credit card, check, cash, and so on. (Your bank may use the same subtotaling method, which makes it easier to reconcile the bank account.)

QuickBooks prepopulates the payment methods with cash, check, and a variety of credit cards. If you have a payment method that isn't listed, you can add that method to the list. To do so, press CTRL-N to open the New Payment Method window. Name the payment method, and select a payment type.

Ship Via List

(This list appears in the submenu of Customer & Vendor Profile Lists.) You can describe the way you ship goods on your invoices (in the field named Via), which many customers appreciate. QuickBooks prepopulates the list with a variety of shipment methods, but you may need to add a shipping method. To do so, press CTRL-N to add a new Ship Via entry to the list. All you need to do is enter the name, for example Our Truck, or Sam's Delivery Service.

If you use one shipping method more than any other, you can select a default Ship Via entry, which appears automatically on your invoices (you can change it when the shipping method is different). In addition, if you charge clients for shipping, you can specify a default markup for shipping costs. To perform these tasks, follow these steps:

1. Choose Edit | Preferences.
2. Select the Sales & Customers icon.
3. Select the Company Preferences tab.
4. In the Usual Shipping Method field, click the drop-down list and select the Ship Via entry you want to make the default. (Select <Add New> if you want to enter a new shipping method.)
5. Enter a default markup percentage.
6. Enter the FOB site you want to appear on invoices, if you wish to display this information.

FOB (Free On Board) is the site from which an order is shipped and is also the point at which transportation costs are the buyer's responsibility. (There are no accounting implications for FOB—it's merely informational.)

Sales Rep List

(This list appears in the submenu of Customer & Vendor Profile Lists.) By common definition, a sales rep is a person who is connected to a customer, usually because he or she receives a commission on sales to that customer. However, it's frequently advantageous to track sales reps for other reasons: to know which noncommissioned person is attached to a customer (some people call this a service rep), or to track the source of referrals.

To enter a new sales rep, press CTRL-N to open a New Sales Rep form, and select the person's name from the drop-down list. If that name doesn't already exist as an employee, vendor, or other name, QuickBooks asks you to add the name to one of those lists.

Vehicle List

(This list appears in the submenu of Customer & Vendor Profile Lists.) New in QuickBooks 2004 is the ability to track mileage for vehicles used in your business. You can use the mileage information for tax deductions for your vehicles and to bill customers for mileage expenses. The transaction windows for these new features use the business vehicles list. However, even if you don't bill customers for mileage, or your accountant uses a formula for tax deductions, the Vehicle list is a handy way to track information about the vehicles (yours or your employees) used for business purposes.

To add a vehicle to your list, choose Lists | Customer & Vendor Profile Lists | Vehicle List. In the Vehicle List window, press CTRL-N to open a New Vehicle dialog box. The box has two fields:

- Vehicle, in which you enter a name or code for a specific vehicle. For example, you could enter BlueTruck, MikesToyota, FordExplorer, or any other recognizable name.
- Description, in which you enter descriptive information about the vehicle.

While the Description field is handy for standard description terms (such as black, or blue/white truck), take advantage of the field by entering information you really need. For example, the VIN, the license plate number, the expiration date for the plate, the insurance policy number, or other "official" information are good candidates for inclusion. You can enter up to 256 characters in the field. You can learn how to track mileage and bill customers for mileage in Chapter 6.

Using Custom Fields

You can add your own fields to the customer, vendor, employee, and item records. Custom fields are useful if there's information you just have to track, but QuickBooks doesn't provide a field for it. For example, if it's imperative for you to know what color eyes your employees have, add an Eye Color field. Or perhaps you have two offices and you want to attach your customers to the office that services them. Add an Office field to the customer card. If you maintain multiple warehouses, you can create a field for items to indicate which warehouse stocks any particular item (you can do the same thing for bins).

Adding a Custom Field for Names

To add one or more custom fields to names, open one of the names lists (Customer:Job, Vendor, or Employee) and then follow these steps:

1. Select any name on the list.
2. Press CTRL-E to edit the name.
3. Move to the Additional Info tab.
4. Click the Define Fields button.
5. When the Define Fields dialog box opens, name the field and indicate the list for which you want to use the new field (see Figure 2-21).

That's all there is to it, except you must click OK to save the information. When you do, QuickBooks flashes a message reminding you that if you customize your templates (forms for transactions, such as invoices), you can add these fields

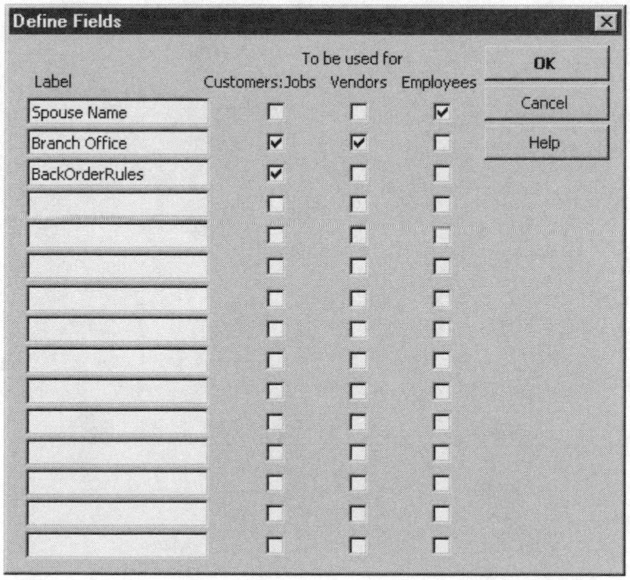

FIGURE 2-21 You can track all sorts of information by creating custom fields.

(instructions are found throughout this book in chapters covering invoices, estimates, purchase orders, and so on). Click OK to make the message disappear (and select the option to stop showing you the message, if you wish). The Additional Info tab on the card for each name on the list to which you attached the fields now shows those fields (see Figure 2-22).

To add data to the custom fields for each name, select the name and press CTRL-E to edit the name. Then add the appropriate data to the field.

Adding a Custom Field for Items

You can add custom fields to your items (except subtotal items and sales tax items) in much the same manner as you do for names, using the following steps:

1. Click the Item icon on the toolbar to open the Item List.
2. Select any item.
3. Press CTRL-E to edit the item.
4. Click the Custom Fields button.

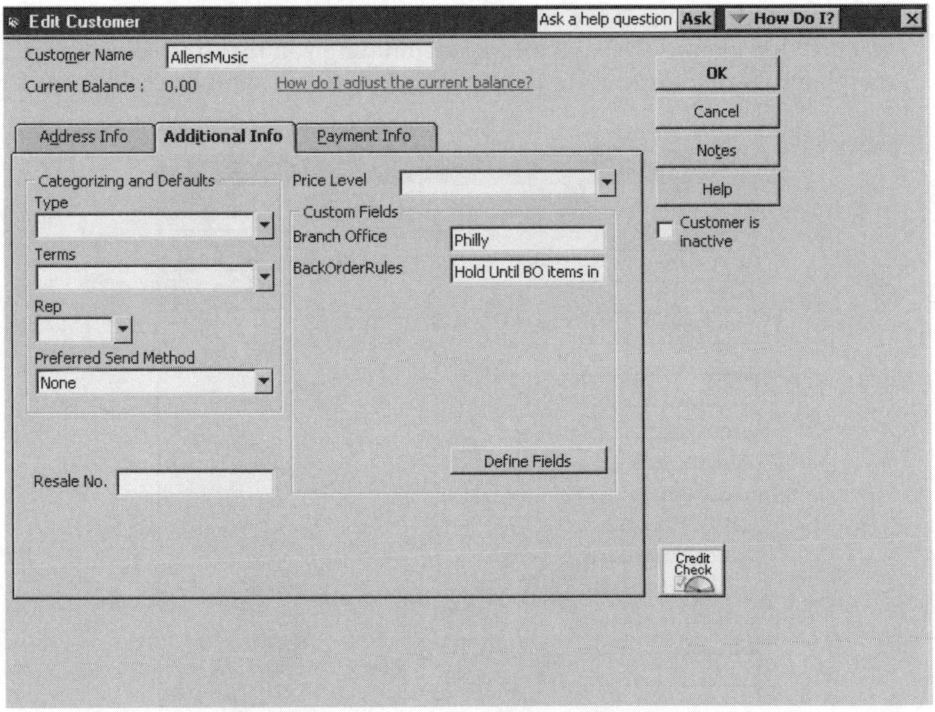

FIGURE 2-22 Custom fields appear on the name records you indicated (in this case, Customers), so you can add appropriate data.

5. When a message appears telling you that there are no custom fields yet defined, click OK.
6. When the Custom Fields dialog box appears, it has no fields on it (yet). Choose Define Fields.
7. When the Define Custom Fields For Items dialog box opens, enter a name for each field you want to add. You can add fields that fit services, inventory items, and so on, and use the appropriate field for the item type to enter data.

8. Click the Use box to use the field. (You can deselect the box later if you don't want to use the field any more.)
9. Click OK.

The first time you enter a custom field on an item, a dialog box appears to tell you that you can use these fields on templates (forms such as Invoices, Purchase Orders, or Packing Slips). Click OK and select the option to stop displaying this message in the future.

When you click Custom Fields on the Edit Item dialog box for any item, your existing custom fields appear. If you want to add more custom fields, click the Define Fields button to open the Define Custom Fields For Items dialog box and add the additional custom field. You can create up to five custom fields for items.

To enter data for the custom fields in an item, open the item from the Items list and click the Custom Fields button on the Edit Item window.

Merging Entries in Lists

After you've been working in QuickBooks for a while, you may find that some lists have entries that should be combined. For example, a vendor was entered twice (with different spellings) or you realize that several items in your chart of accounts are covering similar expenses and should be merged. One common scenario is an Item list that's far too large and complicated. For example, I've seen Inventory Items such as the following:

- Cable-cut to 2ft long
- Cable-cut to 3ft long
- Cable-cut to 4ft long

This makes the item list too long and invites careless errors as users click the wrong item (because they all look alike at first glance). It would be easier and smarter to have one item, named Cable, and enter the length in the Description field of the invoice or purchase order.

If you find a list entry you don't need and you've never used it, you can delete it. But if the entry has been used in a transaction, you can't delete it because you'd lose the data you need to generate reports. To save that data, QuickBooks won't let you delete an item that has been used in a transaction.

You can only merge entries from the following lists:

- Chart of Accounts
- Item
- Customer:Job
- Vendor
- Other Name

Performing a Merge Operation

The solution is to merge entries, which is a rather simple process, using the following steps:

1. Select the list entry you want to get rid of, and press CTRL-E to open the entry in Edit mode.
2. Change the entry's name to match the name of the entry you want to keep.
3. Click OK.
4. QuickBooks opens a message box to tell you the name is already in use and asks if you want to merge them. Click Yes.

All the information, including transaction data, is merged into the entry you're keeping.

Guidelines and Restrictions for Merging List Entries

Bear the following information in mind when you decide to merge entries:

- You cannot "unmerge"—the process is not reversible.
- For accounts and items, you cannot merge entries that have subentries. Change the subentries to parent entries by removing the Subaccount Of or Subitem Of check mark. Merge the parent entries, and then reapply the Subaccount Of or Subitem Of check mark (all of which will now be subentries of the new, single, merged, parent entry).
- You can merge subentries of the same parent (which is in fact the most common type of merge).
- You can merge jobs that are subentries of the same customer.

Now that all your lists exist and they're fine-tuned, you can work quickly and easily in QuickBooks transaction windows. The following chapters walk you through those tasks.

Bookkeeping

Part Two contains chapters about the day-to-day bookkeeping chores you'll be performing in QuickBooks. The chapters are filled with instructions, tips, and explanations. There's even a lot of information that you can pass along to your accountant, who will want to know how QuickBooks and you are performing tasks.

The chapters in Part Two take you through everything you need to know about sending invoices to your customers and collecting the money they send back as a result. You'll learn how to track and pay the bills you receive from vendors. There's plenty of information about dealing with inventory—buying it, selling it, and counting it—and keeping QuickBooks up to date on those figures. Payroll is discussed, both in-house payroll systems and outside services.

All the reports you can generate to analyze the state of your business are covered in Part Two. So are the reports you run for your accountant—and for the government (tax time is less of a nightmare with QuickBooks).

Finally, you'll learn about budgets, general ledger adjustments, and all the other once-in-a-while tasks you need to know how to accomplish to keep your accounting records finely tuned.

Invoicing

In this chapter:

- Create and edit invoices
- Create and edit credit memos
- Print invoices and credit memos
- Use invoices for sales orders
- Create pick lists and packing slips
- Work with estimates
- Customize invoice forms

For many businesses, the only way to get money is to send an invoice to a customer (the exception is retail, of course). Creating an invoice in QuickBooks is easy once you understand what all the parts of the invoice do and why they're there. In addition to invoices, you often have to create credits, packing slips, estimates, and other business financial documents.

In this chapter, I'll go over all those documents, and after I've explained how to create them, I'll move on to describe the choices you have for getting those documents to your customers.

Creating Standard Invoices

To create an invoice, click the Invoice icon on the toolbar, or press CTRL-I. Either action opens the Create Invoices window, which is a blank invoice form (see Figure 3-1).

There are several invoice templates built into QuickBooks, and you can use any of them (as well as create your own, which is covered later in this chapter in the section "Customizing Templates"). The first thing to do is decide whether or not the displayed template suits you, and you should probably look at the other templates

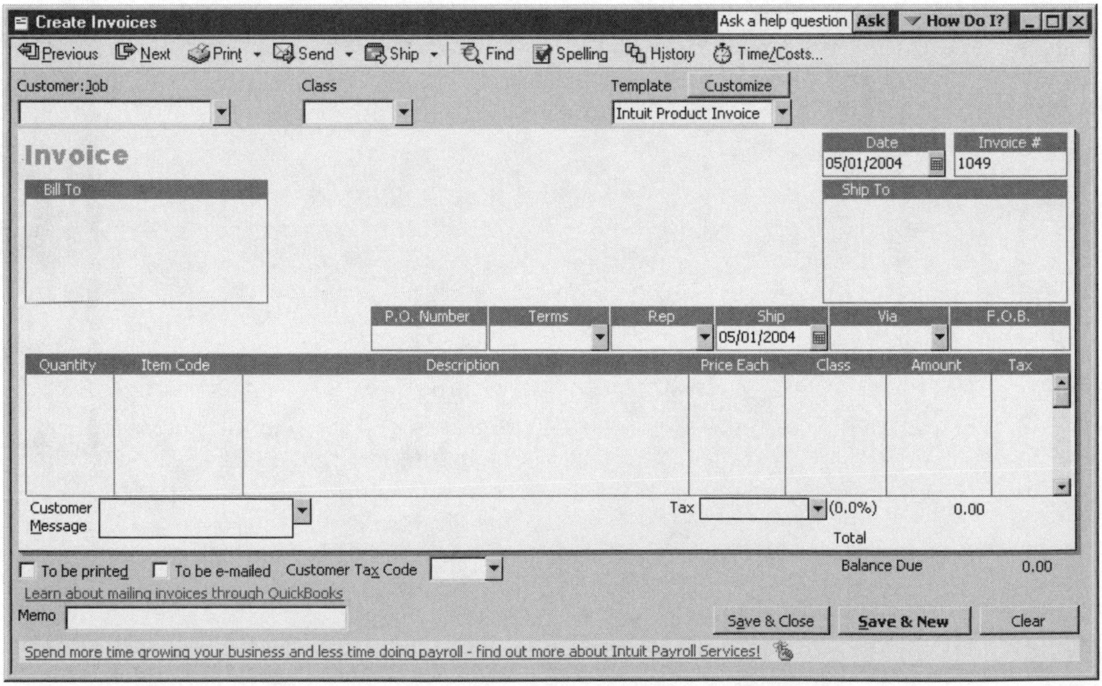

FIGURE 3-1   The Invoice template you chose during the EasyStep Interview loads the first time you create an invoice.

before settling on the one you want to use. To do that, click the arrow next to the Template field and select another invoice template from the drop-down list:

- The Professional and Service templates are almost identical. There's a difference in the order of the columns, and the Service template has a field for a purchase order number.
- The Product template has more fields and columns because it contains information about the items in your inventory.
- The Progress template, which is covered later in this chapter in the "Creating Progress Billing Invoices" section, is designed specifically for progress billing against a job estimate. It doesn't appear in the Template list unless you have specified Progress Invoicing in the Company Preferences tab of the Jobs & Estimates category of the Preferences dialog box. (Estimates are not available in QuickBooks Basic).
- The Packing Slip template, new to QuickBooks 2004, is discussed in the section "Printing Packing Slips," later in this chapter.

 N O T E : The template drop-down list also includes the item Download Templates. This choice takes you to the QuickBooks Web page that has templates you can use to design your own templates.

For this discussion, I'll use the Product template, because it's the most complicated. If you're using any other template, you'll still be able to follow along, even though your invoice form lacks some of the fields related to products.

The top portion of the invoice is for the basic information and is called the *invoice heading*. The middle section is where the billing items (called *line items*) are placed. The bottom contains the totals (called *totals*). Each section of the invoice has fields into which you must enter data.

Entering Heading Information

Start with the customer or the job. Click the arrow to the right of the Customer: Job field to see a list of all your customers. If you've attached jobs to any customers, those jobs are listed under the customer name. Select the customer or job for this invoice. If the customer isn't in the system, choose <Add New> to open a new customer window and enter all the data required for setting up a customer. Read Chapter 2 for information on adding new customers.

 N O T E : After you select the customer, a Credit Check icon appears in the window. If you sign up for the QuickBooks credit check service, you can learn about the customer's financial status.

If you've charged reimbursable expenses or time charges to this customer, QuickBooks displays a message reminding you to add those charges to this invoice. You can learn how to do that in Chapter 6.

In the Date field, the current date is showing, which usually suffices. If you want to change the date, you can either type in a new date, or click the calendar icon at the right side of the field to select a date.

TIP: For service businesses, it's a common practice to send invoices on the last day of the week or month. If you have such a regular invoicing date, you can start preparing your invoices ahead of time and set the invoice date for the scheduled date. That way, the actual billing day isn't a zoo as you scramble to put together your information and enter the invoices.

The first time you enter an invoice, fill in the invoice number you want to use as a starting point. Hereafter, QuickBooks will increment that number for each ensuing invoice.

The Bill To address is taken from the customer record, as is the Ship To address that's available on the Product Invoice template. You can change either address for this invoice.

If you have a purchase order from this customer, enter it into the P.O. Number field.

The Terms field is filled in automatically with the terms you entered for this customer when you created the customer. You can change the terms for this invoice if you wish. If terms don't automatically appear, it means you didn't enter that information in the customer record. If you enter it now, when you finish the invoice, QuickBooks offers to make the entry the new default for this customer by adding it to the customer record.

In fact, if you enter or change any information about the customer while you're creating an invoice, QuickBooks offers to add the information to the customer record. If the change is permanent, click the Yes button in the dialog box that displays the offer. This saves you the trouble of going back to the customer record to make the changes. If the change is only for this invoice, click the No button.

The Rep field is for the salesperson attached to this customer. If you didn't indicate a salesperson when you filled out the customer record, you can click the arrow next to the field and choose a name from the drop-down list.

The Ship field is for the ship date (which also defaults to the current date).

The Via field is for the method of shipping. Click the arrow next to the field to see the available shipping choices. (See Chapter 2 for information about adding to this list.)

The FOB field is used by some companies to indicate the point at which the shipping costs are transferred to the buyer and the assumption of a completed

sale takes place. (That means, if it breaks or gets lost, the customer owns it.)
If you use FOB terms, you can enter the applicable data in the field; it has no impact
on your QuickBooks financial records and is there for your convenience only.

Entering Line Items

Now you can begin to enter the items for which you are billing this customer. Click
in the first column of the line item section.

If you're using the Product invoice template, that column is Quantity. (If you're
using the Professional or Service invoice template, the first column is Item). Enter
the quantity of the first item you're billing for.

In the Item Code column, an arrow appears on the right edge of the column—
click it to see a list of the items in your inventory. (See Chapter 2 to learn how
to enter items.) Select the item you need. The description and price are filled in
automatically, using the information you provided when you created the item. If
you didn't include the information when you created the inventory item, you can
enter it manually now.

QuickBooks does the math, and the Amount column displays the total of
the quantity times the price. If the item and the customer are both liable for
tax, the Tax column displays "Tax."

Repeat this process to add all the items that should be on this invoice. You
can add as many rows of items as you need; if you run out of room, QuickBooks
automatically adds additional pages to your invoice.

Applying Price Levels

If you've created items for your Price Levels List (explained in Chapter 2), you can
change the amount of any line item by applying the price level. Most of the time,
your price levels are a percentage by which to lower (discount) the price, but you
may also have created price levels that increase the price.

When your cursor is in the Price column, an arrow appears to the right of the
price that's entered for the item on this line. Click the arrow to see a list of price
level items, and select the one you want to apply to this item. As you can see in
Figure 3-2, QuickBooks has already performed the math, so you not only see the
name of your price level, you also see the resulting item price for each price level.

After you select a price level, QuickBooks changes the amount you're charging
the customer for the item and adjusts the amount of the total for this item (if the
quantity is more than 1).

The customer sees only the price on the invoice; there's no indication that you've
adjusted the price. This is different from applying a discount to a price (covered in
the next section), where a discrete line item exists to announce the discount.

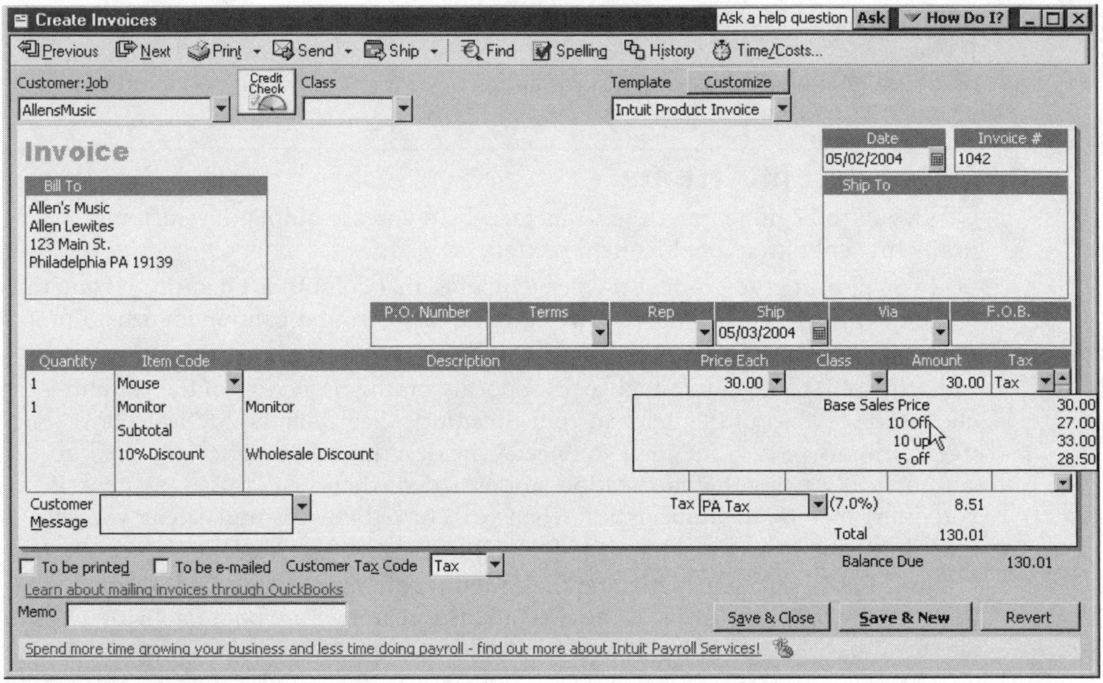

FIGURE 3-2   Assign a predefined price level to the price of an item.

NOTE: You can apply price levels as you enter a line item, or finish all the line items, and then return to the Price column for the items you want to change with a price level. QuickBooks adjusts line totals and the final total, as you apply the price levels.

Entering Discounts

You can also adjust the invoice by applying discounts. Discounts are entered as line items, so the discount has to exist as an item in your Items List.

When you enter a discount, its amount (usually a percentage) is applied based on the line item immediately above it. For example, let's suppose you have already entered line items as follows:

- Qty of 1 for Some Item with a price of $100.00 for a total line item price of $100.00
- Qty of 2 for Some Other Item with a price of $40.00 for a total line item price of $80.00.

Now you want to give the customer a 10 percent discount (you created a 10 percent discount item in your Items List). If you enter that item on the next line, QuickBooks will calculate its value as 10 percent of the last line you entered—an $8.00 discount.

If you want to apply the discount against all the line items, you must first enter a line item that subtotals those lines. To do this, use a subtotal item type that you've created in your Items List. Then enter the discount item as the next line item, and when the discount is applied to the previous amount, that previous amount is the amount of the subtotal. The discount is based on the subtotal.

You can use the same approach to discount some line items, but not others. Simply follow these steps:

1. Enter all the items you're planning to discount.
2. Enter a subtotal item.
3. Enter a discount item.
4. Enter the remaining items (the items you're not discounting).

This method makes your discounts, and your discount policies, very clear to the customer.

Checking the Invoice

When you're finished entering all the line items, you'll see that QuickBooks has kept a running total, including taxes (see Figure 3-3).

Check Spelling

Click the Spelling icon on the toolbar of the Create Invoices window to run the QuickBooks spell checker. If the spell checker finds any word in your invoice form that isn't in the QuickBooks dictionary, that word is displayed. You can change the spelling, add the word to the QuickBooks dictionary (if it's spelled correctly), or tell the spell checker to ignore the word. Information on customizing and using the spell checker is in Chapter 21.

T I P : If you check the spelling each time you create a customer or an item, you eliminate the need to worry about spelling on an invoice—everything is pre-checked before you insert the items in the invoice form.

N O T E : The spell checker is turned on by default, which I find annoying. If you want to control the spell checker, remove its automatic behavior in the Spelling section of the Preferences dialog.

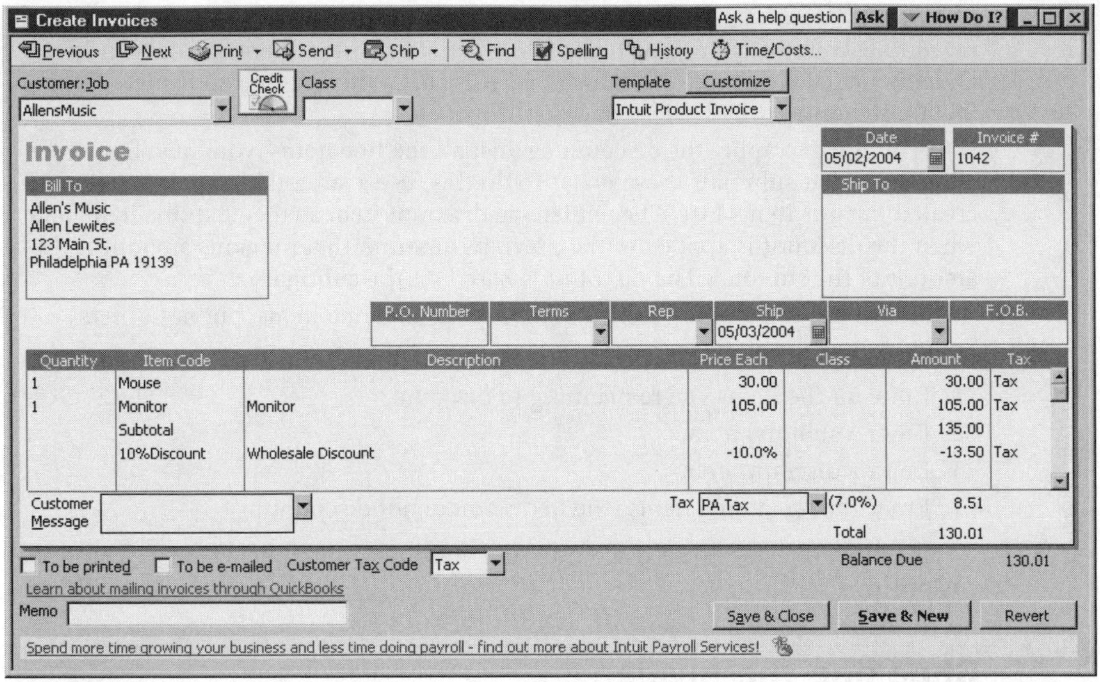

FIGURE 3-3 The invoice is complete, and there are no math errors because computers never make mistakes in math.

Add a Message

If you want to add a message, click the arrow in the Customer Message field to see all the available messages (that you created in the Customer Message List, as described in Chapter 2). You can create a new message if you don't want to use any of the existing notes. To do so, choose <Add New> from the message drop-down list, and enter your text in the New Customer Message window. Click OK to enter the message in the invoice and automatically save the message in the Message list so you can use it again.

Add a Memo

You can add text to the Memo field at the bottom of the invoice. This text doesn't print on the invoice—it appears only on the screen (you'll see it if you re-open this invoice to view or edit it). The memo text also appears on sales reports.

However, the memo text *does* appear on statements, next to the listing for this invoice. Therefore, be careful about the text you use—don't enter anything you wouldn't want the customer to see.

➡ **FYI**

The QuickBooks Invoice Save Options– Annoying and Dangerous

QuickBooks' inability to save an invoice and keep it in the Create Invoices window is a paradigm I find annoying. However, the ability to print an invoice without saving it is more than annoying, it's dangerous.

The removal of an invoice from the Create Invoices window when you save the invoice is annoying because you can't easily save and keep working. You have to select Save & New, and then click the Prev icon to return to the invoice. When I train users in other accounting software applications, I always teach them to save the invoice as they work. If they're entering a long list of line items, and the computer freezes or the network goes down after they've entered the fifteenth item, they have to start all over (talk about annoying!).

As to danger, all accounting software should force you to save an invoice before you can print it (or before you can print a packing slip or a pick slip). Every time I've worked with a client to investigate suspected embezzlements or stolen inventory, we've uncovered schemes involving fake invoices with payments directed to the miscreant, or fake customers (friends of the employee-thief) who are shipped products. With any accounting software except QuickBooks, these schemes are difficult to hide, and almost always come to light rather quickly.

With QuickBooks, however, the lack of the rule that forces users to save invoices before printing, along with the ability to delete transactions, combines to make this software an embezzler's best friend. You can protect yourself from the side effects of transactions that were deleted for nefarious reasons by turning on the Audit Trail feature (discussed in Chapter 21). You have no protection against fake invoices that are never saved but are printed and sent with payments directed to someone other than you.

Choose the Method for Sending the Invoice

At the bottom of the invoice template are two options for sending the invoice: To Be Printed and To Be E-mailed. Select the appropriate method if you're going to print or e-mail all your invoices after you finish entering them. (If you select the e-mail option, you have to provide more information, all of which is covered in the section "Sending Invoices and Credit Memos," later in this chapter.)

You can also print or e-mail each invoice as you complete it. All of the options for printing sending invoices are explained later in this chapter, in the section "Sending Invoices and Credit Memos."

Save the Invoice

Choose Save & New to save this invoice and move on to the next blank invoice form. If this is the last invoice you're creating, click Save & Close to save this invoice and close the Create Invoices window.

You're ready to send the invoices to your customers, which is discussed later, in the section "Sending Invoices and Credit Memos."

Creating Progress Billing Invoices

If you work with estimates, you can use the Progress invoice template to invoice your customers as each invoicing plateau arrives. See the section "Using Estimates" later in this chapter to learn how to create the estimates.

 N O T E : Estimates and Progress Billing are not available in QuickBooks Basic.

Choosing the Estimated Job

Progress invoices are just regular invoices that are connected to estimates. Open the Create Invoices window, select Progress Invoice from the Template drop-down list, and choose the customer or job for which you're creating the Progress invoice. Because you've enabled estimates in your QuickBooks preferences, the system always checks the customer record to see if you've recorded any estimates for this job, and if so, presents them.

Available Estimates				
Customer:Job Greene:Wiring ▾				OK
Select an estimate to invoice				Cancel
Date	Num	Customer:Job	Amount	Help
02/15/2004	2	Greene:Wiring	889.00	

Select the estimate you're invoicing against and click OK. QuickBooks then asks you to specify what to include on the invoice:

Fill out the dialog box, using the following guidelines:

- You can bill for the whole job, 100 percent of the estimate. When the line items appear, you can edit any individual items. In fact, you can bill for a higher amount than the original estimate (you should have an agreement with your customer regarding overruns).

- You can create an invoice for a specific percentage of the estimate. The percentage usually depends upon the agreement you have with your customer. For example, you could have an agreement that you'll invoice the job in a certain number of equal installments, or you could invoice a percentage that's equal to the percentage of the work that's been finished.

TIP: You can use a percentage figure larger than 100 to cover overruns (make sure your customer has agreed to permit that option).

- You can create an invoice that covers only certain items on the estimate, or you can create an invoice that has a different percentage for each item on the estimate. This is the approach to use if you're billing for completed work on a job that has a number of distinct tasks. Some of the work listed on the estimate may be finished, other work not started, and the various items listed on the estimate may be at different points of completion.

After you've created the first Progress billing invoice for an estimate, a new option is available for subsequent invoices. That option is to bill for all remaining amounts in the estimate. This is generally reserved for your last invoice, and it saves you the trouble of figuring out which percentages of which items have been invoiced previously.

As far as QuickBooks is concerned, the items and prices in the estimate are not etched in cement; you can change any amounts or quantities you wish while you're creating the invoice. Your customer, however, may not be quite so lenient, and your ability to invoice for amounts that differ from the estimate depends on your agreement with the customer.

Entering Line Items

After you choose your progress billing method and click OK, QuickBooks automatically fills in the line item section of the invoice based on the approach you selected. For example, in Figure 3-4, I opted to create a progress bill for 50 percent of the estimate (because half the work was done).

Changing Line Items

Because I chose 50 percent of the estimate's total as the basis for this invoice, the amount of every line item on the estimate was halved, which doesn't work terribly well for those lines that have products (it's hard to sell a percentage of a physical product). I can leave the invoice as is, because the customer will certainly understand that this is a progress invoice. Or, I can make changes to the invoice.

In addition to strange or inaccurate line items for products, the line items for services rendered may not be totally accurate. For example, some of the line items may contain service categories that aren't at the same percentage of completion as others.

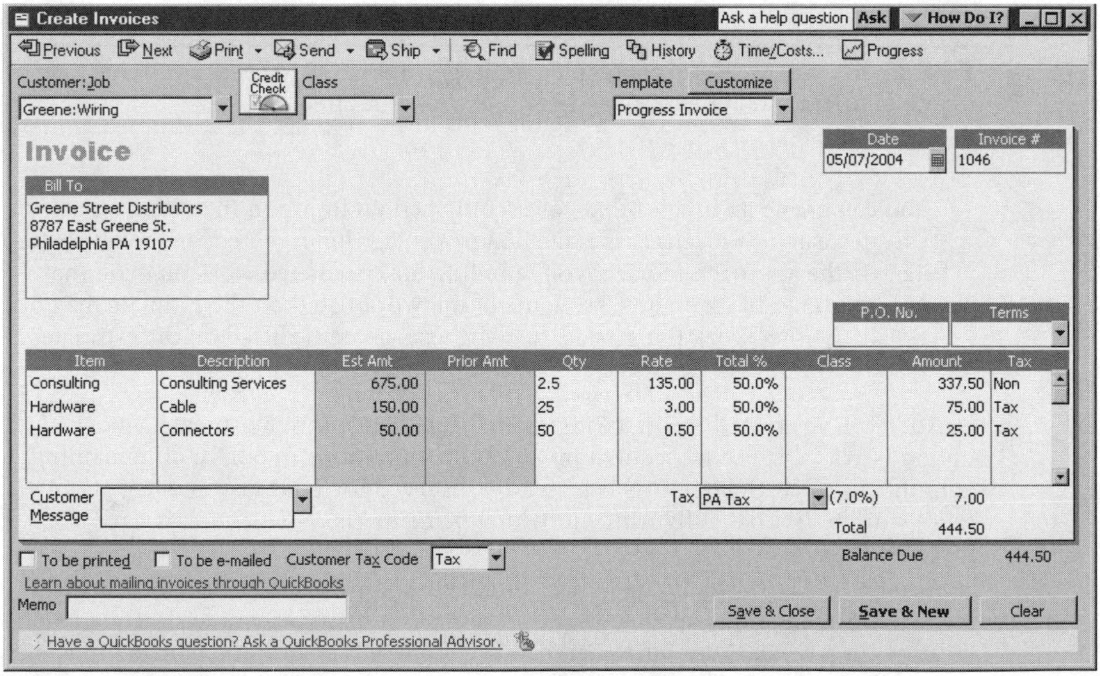

FIGURE 3-4   Progress invoices are filled in automatically, using the information in the estimate.

To change the invoice and keep a history of the changes against the estimate, click the Progress icon on the toolbar of the Create Invoices window. This opens a dialog box (see Figure 3-5) that allows reconfiguration of the line items.

You can change the quantity, rate, or percentage of completion for any individual line item. Here's how to make changes:

1. Select Show Quantity And Rate. The columns in the dialog box change to display the columns from the estimate, and you can make changes to any of them.

2. Click the Qty column for any line item to highlight the default number that's been used to calculate the invoice.

3. Replace the number with the amount you want to use for the invoice. You can also change the rate, but generally that's not cricket unless there are some circumstances that warrant it (which you and the customer have agreed upon).

4. Select Show Percentage to display the column that has the percentage of completion for this and previous billings. The percentages compare the dollar amounts for invoices against the estimated total.

5. Click the Curr% column to change the percentage for any line item.

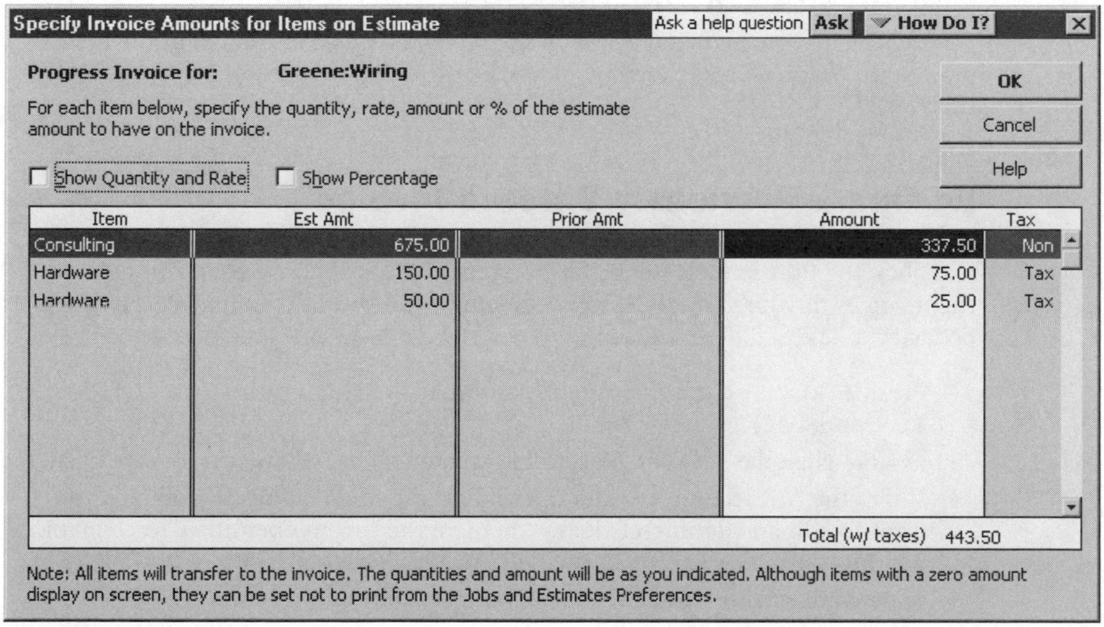

Item	Est Amt	Prior Amt	Amount	Tax
Consulting	675.00		337.50	Non
Hardware	150.00		75.00	Tax
Hardware	50.00		25.00	Tax

Specify Invoice Amounts for Items on Estimate

Progress Invoice for: **Greene:Wiring**

For each item below, specify the quantity, rate, amount or % of the estimate amount to have on the invoice.

☐ Show Quantity and Rate ☐ Show Percentage

OK Cancel Help

Total (w/ taxes) 443.50

Note: All items will transfer to the invoice. The quantities and amount will be as you indicated. Although items with a zero amount display on screen, they can be set not to print from the Jobs and Estimates Preferences.

FIGURE 3-5 You can make changes to the line items that QuickBooks automatically inserted.

6. Select both options if you need to make changes to one type of progress on one line item, and another type of progress on another line item. All the columns (and all the history from previous billings, if any exists) appear in the window.

Click OK when you have finished making your adjustments. You return to the invoice form where the amounts on the line items have changed to match the adjustments you made. Click Save & New to save this invoice and move on to the next invoice, or click Save & Close to save this invoice and close the Create Invoices window.

Using this method to change a line item keeps the history of your estimate and invoices intact (as opposed to making changes in the amounts directly on the invoice form, which does not create a good history).

Editing Invoices

If you want to correct an invoice (perhaps you charged the wrong amount or forgot you'd promised a different amount to a particular customer), you can do so quite easily.

Editing the Current Invoice

Editing the invoice that's currently on the screen is quite easy. Click in the field or column that requires changing and make the changes (you probably figured this out).

Editing a Previously Entered Invoice

You can open the Create Invoices window (or perhaps you're still working there) and click the Prev (which stands for Previous) button to move back through all the invoices in your system. However, if you have a great many invoices, it might be faster to take a different road:

1. Press CTRL-A or click Accnt on the toolbar to bring up the Chart Of Accounts list.
2. Double-click the Accounts Receivable account (that's where invoices are posted).
3. When the A/R account register opens, find the row that has the invoice you want to edit and double-click anywhere on the row to open the Create Invoices window with the selected invoice displayed.
4. Make your changes and click OK. Then close the A/R register.

If you've printed the invoice, when you finish editing be sure to check the To Be Printed box so you can reprint it with the correct information.

TIP : Click the Go To icon on the register window to open a search box that makes it easy to find a transaction.

Voiding and Deleting Invoices

There's an enormous difference between voiding and deleting an invoice. Voiding an invoice makes the invoice nonexistent to your accounting and customer balances. However, the invoice number continues to exist (it's marked "VOID") so you can account for it—missing invoice numbers are just as frustrating as missing check numbers.

Deleting an invoice removes all traces of it—it never existed, you never did it, the number is gone, and a couple of months later you probably won't remember why the number is gone. You have no audit trail, no way to tell yourself (or your accountant) why the number is missing. *Never delete an invoice.*

CAUTION : If you choose to ignore my advice and delete invoices (perhaps you believe you have the memory of an elephant, and when someone questions the missing number you'll be able to explain it no matter how much time has passed), here's another warning–do not ever delete an invoice to which a customer payment has been attached. Straightening out that mess is a nightmare.

Voiding an invoice isn't difficult, just use these steps:

1. Press CTRL-A or click the Accnt button on the toolbar to bring up the Chart Of Accounts list.
2. Select the Accounts Receivable account and double-click.
3. When the A/R account register opens, find the row that has the invoice you want to void and click anywhere on the row to select it.
4. Right-click and choose Void Invoice from the shortcut menu. The word "VOID" appears in the memo field. (If you've entered a memo, the word "VOID" is placed in front of your text.)
5. Click Record to save your action.
6. Close the register by clicking the X in the top-right corner.

NOTE : When you void an invoice, QuickBooks also enters the status Paid in the last column of the Accounts Receivable register. This means nothing more than the fact that the invoice isn't "open," but QuickBooks should have thought of a different word (like, maybe "void"?). It's a bit startling to see that notation.

If you want to delete an invoice, follow the preceding Steps 1 through 3, then press CTRL-D. You'll have to confirm the deletion.

Understanding the Postings for Invoices

It's important to understand what QuickBooks is doing behind the scenes, because everything you do has an impact on your financial reports. Let's look at the postings for an imaginary invoice that has these line items:

- $500.00 for services rendered
- $30.00 for sales tax

Because QuickBooks is a full, double-entry bookkeeping program, there is a balanced posting made to the general ledger. For this invoice, the following postings are made to the general ledger:

ACCOUNT	DEBIT	CREDIT
Accounts Receivable	530.00	
Sales Tax		30.00
Income—Services		500.00

If the invoice includes inventory items, the postings are a bit more complicated. Let's post an invoice that sold ten widgets to a customer. The widgets cost you $50.00 each and you sold them for $100.00 each. This customer was shipped ten widgets, and was also charged tax and shipping.

ACCOUNT	DEBIT	CREDIT
Accounts Receivable	1077.00	
Income—Sales of Items		1000.00
Sales Tax		70.00
Shipping		7.00
Cost of Sales	500.00	
Inventory		500.00

There are some things to think about as you look at these postings. To keep accurate books, you should fill out the cost of your inventory items when you create the items. As you purchase replacement items, QuickBooks updates the cost (from the vendor bill). This is the only way to get a correct posting to the cost of sales and the balancing decrement in the value of your inventory.

You don't have to separate your income accounts (one for services, one for inventory items, and so on) to have accurate books. Income is income. However, you may decide to create accounts for each type of income so you can analyze where your revenue is coming from.

There are two theories on posting shipping:

- Separate your own shipping costs (an expense) from the shipping you collect from your customers (revenue)
- Post everything to the shipping expense

To use the first method, create an income account for shipping and link that account to the shipping item you created to use in invoices.

If you use the latter method, don't be surprised at the end of the year if you find your shipping expense is reported as a negative number, meaning that you collected more than you spent for shipping. You won't have a shipping expense to deduct from your revenue at tax time, but who cares—you made money.

Issuing Credits and Refunds

Sometimes you have to give money to a customer. You can do this in the form of a credit against current or future balances, or you can write a check and refund money you received from the customer. Neither is a lot of fun, but it's a fact of business life.

Creating Credit Memos

A credit memo reduces a customer balance. This is necessary if a customer returns goods, has been billed for goods that were lost or damaged in shipment, or wins an argument about the price of a service you provided.

The credit memo itself is usually sent to the customer to let the customer know the details about the credit that's being applied. The totals are posted to your accounting records just as the invoice totals are posted, except there's an inherent minus sign next to the number.

Creating a credit memo is similar to creating an invoice:

1. Choose Customers | Create Credit Memos/Refunds from the menu bar to open a blank form (see Figure 3-6).

2. Select a customer or job, and then fill out the rest of the heading.

3. Move to the line item section and enter the quantity and rate of the items for which you're issuing this credit memo. Don't use a minus sign—QuickBooks knows what a credit is.

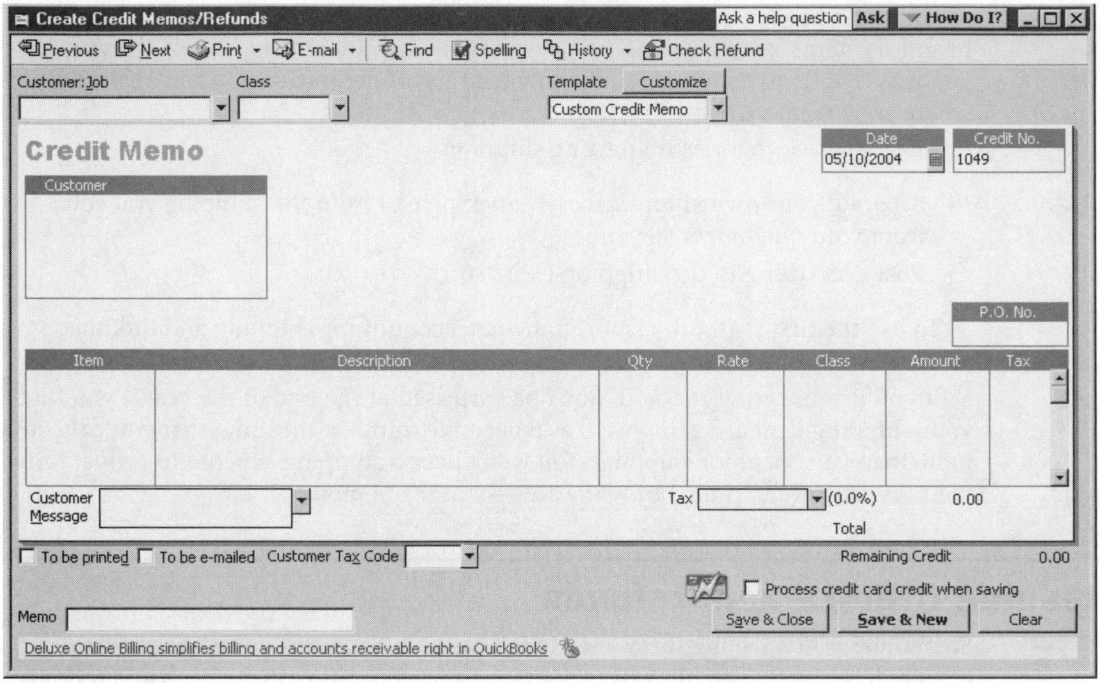

FIGURE 3-6 The credit memo template has all the fields needed to provide information to the customer about the credit.

TIP: By default, the credit memo number is the next available invoice number. If you change the number because you want a different numbering system for credit memos, you'll have to keep track of numbers manually. QuickBooks will use the next number (the one after this credit memo) for your next invoice. Therefore, it's easier to use the default procedure of having one set of continuous numbers for invoices and credit memos.

4. Remember to insert all the special items you need to give credit for, such as taxes, shipping, and so on.
5. You can use the Customer Message field to add any short explanation that's necessary.
6. Click Save & Close to save the credit memo (unless you have more credit memos to create—in which case, click Save & Next).

See the section "Sending Invoices and Credit Memos" later in this chapter to learn about delivering your credit memos.

Issuing Refund Checks

Sometimes a customer is current (is all paid up) and then is entitled to a credit against a paid invoice. This usually occurs because after paying your invoice, the customer returns products or has a serious complaint about your billings for services. When that happens, the customer may ask for a refund instead of a credit memo against the next purchase.

Refunds start as credit memos, then they keep going, requiring a few extra steps to write the check and post the totals to your general ledger properly.

To create a refund check, first create a credit memo, using Steps 1 through 5 from the previous section. Then click the Check Refund button at the top of the Credit Memo window. This opens the Write Checks window, as shown in Figure 3-7.

Make sure that everything on the check is the way it should be. (The only items you may want to change are the date and the bank account you're using for this check; everything else should be accurate.) Then either print the check or click Save & Close to save it. If you're not printing the check now, make sure the To Be Printed check box is checked so you can print it later. Information about check printing is in Chapter 7.

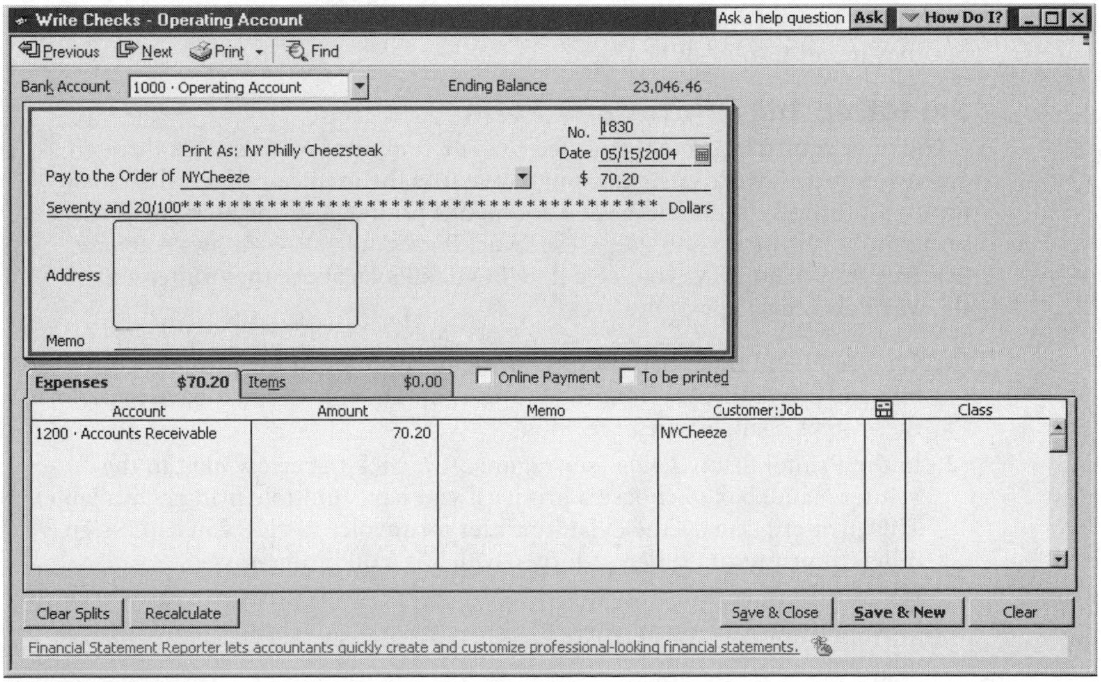

FIGURE 3-7 A refund check gets its data from the credit memo, so there's nothing to fill in.

You're returned to the Credit Memo window, and you can print or e-mail the Credit Memo if you wish. Click Save & Close to close the window.

QuickBooks automatically links the check to the credit memo, which washes the amount. The credit memo is no longer decrementing the customer's balance.

Sending Invoices and Credit Memos

You have several choices about the method you use to send invoices and credit memos. You can print and mail them, or send them via e-mail--and within those options are other options, which I discuss in this section.

For those of you who print invoices, insert them in envelopes, and put them in the mail, I'll start with instructions for printing. Then I'll explain how to e-mail invoices.

Printing Invoices and Credit Memos

You can print on blank paper, preprinted forms on a single sheet of paper, preprinted multipart forms, or your company letterhead. You have to set up your printer for invoices and credit memos, but once you complete this task you don't have to do it again. There are several steps involved in setting up a printer, but they're not terribly difficult.

Selecting the Printer and Form

If you have multiple printers attached to your computer or accessible through a network, you have to designate one of them as the invoice printer. If you use multipart forms, you should have a dot matrix printer. Your printers are already set up in Windows (or should be), so QuickBooks, like all Windows software, has access to them. Now you have to tell QuickBooks about the printer and the way you want to print invoices:

1. Choose File | Printer Setup from the menu bar to open the Printer Setup dialog box and select Invoice from the Forms drop-down list (you'll have to perform these steps again for credit memos).
2. In the Printer Setup dialog (see Figure 3-8), click the arrow next to the Printer Name box to choose a printer if you have multiple printers available. This printer becomes the default printer for Invoice forms (you can assign different printers to different forms, which is a nifty time-saver).

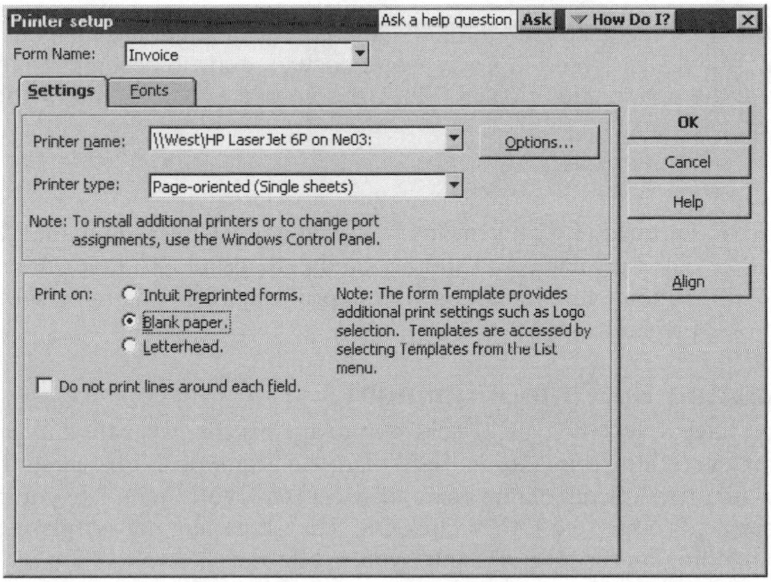

FIGURE 3-8   This printer is on another computer on a network–if your printer is attached to your computer you won't see a network path in the Printer Name field.

3. In the bottom of the dialog, select the type of form you're planning to use for invoices from the following options:

- **Intuit Preprinted Forms**   Templates with all your company information, field names, and row and column dividers already printed. These forms need to be aligned to match the way your invoice prints. You can also purchase the forms from a company that knows about QuickBooks' invoice printing formats, and everything should match just fine. Selecting this option tells QuickBooks that only the data needs to be sent to the printer because the fields are already printed.

- **Blank Paper**   This is easiest, but it may not look as pretty as a printed form. Some of us don't care about pretty—we just want to ship invoices and collect the payments. But if you care about image this may not be a great choice. On the other hand, if you don't need multipart printing (which requires a dot matrix printer), you can use the fonts and graphic capabilities of your laser or inkjet printer to design a professional-looking invoice that prints to blank paper. Selecting this option tells QuickBooks that everything, including field names, must be sent to the printer.

> **TIP:** It's a good idea to print lines around each field to make sure the information is printed in a way that's easy to read. To accomplish that, make sure the option titled Do Not Print Lines Around Each Field does not have a check mark.

- **Letterhead** This means you print your invoices on paper that has your company name and address (and perhaps a logo) preprinted. Selecting this option tells QuickBooks not to print the company information when it prints the invoice.

Setting Up Form Alignment

You have to test the QuickBooks output against the paper in your printer to make sure everything prints in the right place. To accomplish this, click the Align button in the Printer Setup dialog box and select the invoice template you're using (e.g., Service, Product, etc.), then click OK. The Alignment dialog box you see differs depending on the type of printer you've selected.

Aligning Dot Matrix Printers If you're using a continuous feed printer (dot matrix using paper with sprocket holes), you'll see a dialog box that lets you perform both coarse and fine adjustments. This is necessary because you must set the placement of the top of the page, which you cannot do with a page printer (laser, deskjet):

Start by clicking the Coarse button. A dialog box appears telling you that a sample form is about to be printed and warning you not to make any physical adjustments to your printer after the sample has printed. QuickBooks provides another dialog box where you can make any necessary adjustments. Make sure the appropriate preprinted form, letterhead, or blank paper is loaded in the printer. Click OK.

The sample form prints to your dot matrix printer and QuickBooks displays a dialog box asking you to enter pointer line position. You can see the pointer line at the top of the printed sample. Enter the line it's on in the dialog box and click OK (the printout numbers the lines). Continue to follow the instructions as

QuickBooks takes you through any adjustments that might be needed. (I can't give specific instructions because I can't see what your sample output looks like.)

If you want to tweak the alignment a bit further, choose Fine. (See the information on using the Fine Alignment dialog box in the section "Aligning Laser and Inkjet Printers" that follows this section.) Otherwise, choose OK.

When the form is printing correctly, QuickBooks displays a message telling you to note the position of the form now that it's printing correctly. That means you should note exactly where the top of the page is in relation to the print head and the bar that leans against the paper.

TIP: Here's the best way to note the position of the forms in your dot matrix printer: get a marker and draw an arrow with the word "invoice" or the letter "I" at the spot on the printer where the top of the form should be. I have mine marked on the piece of plastic that sits above the roller.

Aligning Laser and Inkjet Printers If you're using a page printer, you'll see only this Fine Alignment dialog box:

Click Print Sample to send output to your printer. Then, with the printed page in your hand, make adjustments to the alignment in the dialog box. Use the arrows next to the Vertical and Horizontal boxes to move the positions at which printing occurs.

Click OK, and then click OK in the Printer Setup dialog box. Your settings are saved, and you don't have to go through this again for printing invoices.

Repeat all these steps to create settings for Credit Memos.

Batch Printing

If you didn't print each invoice or credit memo as you created it, and you made sure that the To Be Printed check box was selected on each invoice you created, you're ready to start a print run.

Place the correct paper in your printer and, if it's continuous paper in a dot matrix printer, position it properly. Then use the following steps to print your invoices:

1. Choose File | Print Forms | Invoices.
2. In the Select Invoices To Print window, all your unprinted invoices are selected with a check mark.
3. If there are any invoices you don't want to print at this time, click the check marks to remove them.
4. If you need to print mailing labels for these invoices, you must print them first (see the next section).
5. Click OK to print your invoices

The Print Invoices dialog appears, where you can change or select printing options. Click Print to begin printing.

Repeat the steps to print credit memos.

Printing Mailing Labels

If you need mailing labels, QuickBooks will print them for you. You must print the mailing labels before you print the invoices.

In the Select Invoices To Print window, click the Print Labels button to bring up the Select Labels To Print dialog box.

The options have been selected to match a label run for selected customers—the definition of "selected customers" is "customers receiving invoices." You may need to tweak the options, if you know you have customer types or other particular situations that require making changes. If you created a discrete invoice for each customer job, and you need a label for each (perhaps the billing names or addresses

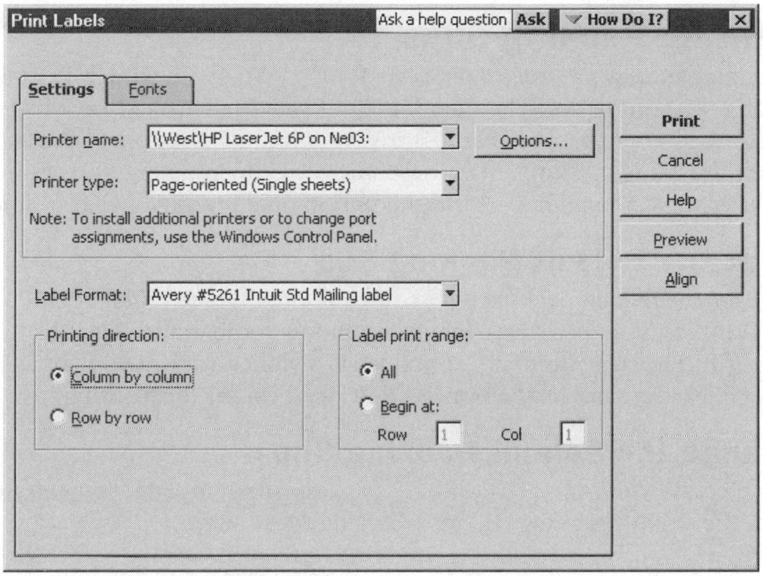

FIGURE 3-9 Configure the label printing options you need.

differ among a customer's jobs) select the option Print Labels For Jobs. When you're finished, click OK.

The Print Labels dialog box appears (see Figure 3-9), and it assumes you've loaded Avery labels into your printer. Select the appropriate printer, specify the label format you use (if you purchased pre-printed labels from QuickBooks, they're in the drop-down list), and click Print.

After the labels are printed, you're returned to the Select Invoices To Print dialog box. Choose OK to open the Print Invoices dialog and begin printing your invoices.

After you've finished printing invoices, check the print job to make sure nothing went wrong (the printer jammed, you had the wrong paper in the printer, whatever). If anything went amiss, you can reprint the forms you need when the following dialog box appears. (Use the invoice number as the form number.)

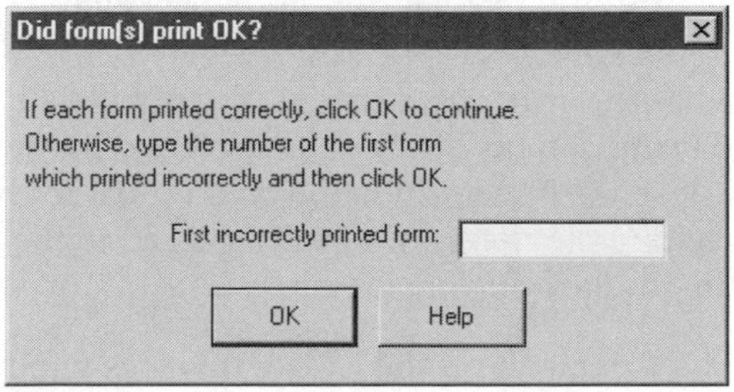

If everything is hunky-dory, click OK.

Printing Packing Slips

QuickBooks now provides a template for a packing slip, which is basically an invoice without prices. The theory behind packing slips is that for the warehouse personnel who unpack and store arriving products, the cost of those products falls under the category "none of your business". Unfortunately, you cannot batch print packing slips, you must perform this action on a one-invoice-at-a-time basis.

Print the Default Packing Slip

To print the default packing slip, complete the invoice. Then click the arrow next to the Print icon on the Create Invoices window toolbar and select Print Packing Slip. The Print Packing Slip dialog box opens so you can select your printing options (which are the same as the options described earlier for printing invoices).

Change the Default Packing Slip

If you create your own, customized, packing slip template, you can make that new form the default packing slip by following these steps:

1. Choose Edit | Preferences to open the Preferences dialog box.
2. Go to the Sales & Customers section and click the Company Preferences tab.
3. In the Choose Template For Packing Slip field, select your new packing slip form from the drop-down list.
4. Click OK.

Choose a Different Packing Slip for a Specific Invoice

If you've created one or more customized packing slips, you can choose any packing slip for printing. With the completed invoice in the Create Invoices window, change the form by selecting a packing slip template from the drop-down list in the Template field. The Create Invoices window changes to display the packing slip, as shown in Figure 3-10.

I know I just told you that a packing slip doesn't display any amounts, and there they are! Well, no they're not. Confused? Don't be--the packing slip in Figure 3-10 is the Intuit Packing Slip, which has one set of configuration options for the screen, and another set of configuration options for the printed version. This is true for many templates, and it's a handy feature, as you'll learn when you read the section on customizing templates later in this chapter.

To see what the printed version of the packing slip looks like, click the arrow next to the Print icon on the Create Invoices window toolbar, and choose Preview. Satisfied? Close the Preview window and return to the Create Invoices window. To print the packing slip that's currently displayed in the window, instead of the default packing slip, do the following:

1. Click the Print icon on the Create Invoices window toolbar to print the packing slip.

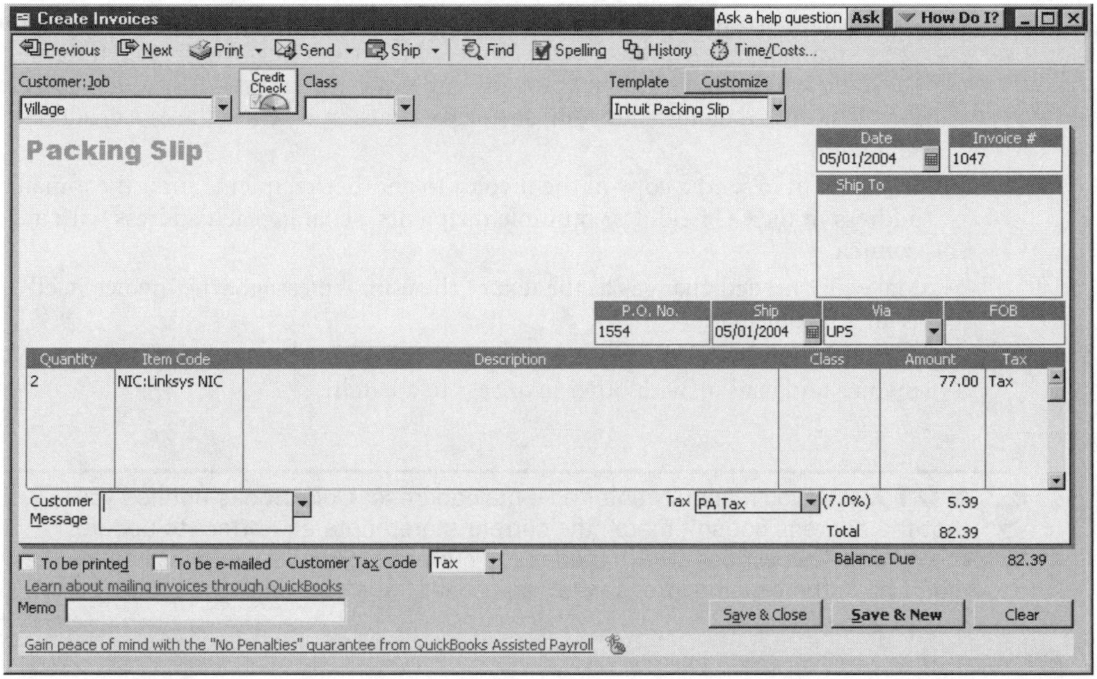

FIGURE 3-10 View a packing slip before you print it.

2. From the drop-down list in the Template field, select the original template you used to create the invoice.
3. Save the invoice.

E-mailing Invoices and Credit Memos

QuickBooks provides a way to e-mail invoices and credit memos to customers. (From here on I'll refer to invoices in the discussion, but all the same instructions apply to credit memos and other billing forms.)

To e-mail an invoice, make sure the completed invoice is in the Create Invoices window. (If you saved the invoice previously, open the Create Invoices window and use the Prev button to move backwards through saved invoices.) Then follow these steps:

1. Click the arrow to the right of the Send icon on the Create Invoices window toolbar, and select E-mail.

2. In the Send Invoice dialog box (see Figure 3-11), select E-mail, and make sure the e-mail addresses in the To and From fields are correct (they're taken from the data you entered for your company and your customers). If you didn't enter e-mail address data for your company or your customer, enter the e-mail address manually.

3. If you want to send a copy of the invoice to another recipient, enter the e-mail address in the CC field. For multiple recipients, separate each address with a comma.

4. Make any needed changes to the text of the e-mail message (the invoice itself is an attachment).

5. Click Send to e-mail the invoice immediately, or click Send Later to save the invoice and mail it (with other invoices) in a batch.

 NOTE: If you manually enter an e-mail address, QuickBooks notifies you that the address doesn't match the current stored data and offers to update the record. This almost always means the current stored data is missing (you didn't fill in the e-mail address field), so accept the offer.

Send Invoice	✕

Send by ⦿ E-mail
        ○ Mail through QuickBooks

To   ak@allensmusic.net

Cc

From   acctspayable@wedoitall.com

Subject Invoice from We Do It All

QuickBooks BILLING SOLUTIONS

Get paid faster!
    Sign up to let customers
     pay you online

    Sign up to send payment
    reminders, track e-mail, and more

E-mail Text

Dear Mr. Lewites :

Your invoice is attached. Please remit payment at your earliest convenience.

Thank you for your business - we appreciate it very much.

Sincerely,

We Do It All

Edit Default Text

Check Spelling

[Your Invoice will be attached to the message as a PDF file]

Send Now	Send Later	Cancel	Help

FIGURE 3-11   Make sure the e-mail addresses and the message text are correct before you send the invoice.

E-mail the Invoice Immediately

If you clicked Send to e-mail this invoice immediately, QuickBooks opens a browser window and takes you to the Business Services section. Your regular e-mail software doesn't open, this is all done by QuickBooks, through the Internet. Follow the prompts to complete the process. When your e-mail is sent, QuickBooks issues a success message:

E-mail Invoices in a Batch

If you clicked Send Later, QuickBooks saves the message, along with any others you save, until you're ready to send all of them.

When you want to e-mail all the invoices, choose File | Send Forms to open the Select Forms To Send dialog box shown in Figure 3-12.

Here are some guidelines for working with the Select Forms To Send dialog box:

• By default, all e-mails are selected. Deselect an e-mail by clicking the check mark in the leftmost column of its listing. Click again to put the check mark back.

• You can delete any item by selecting it and clicking Remove. You're not deleting the invoice, you're deleting the e-mail. You can return to the invoice and send it anytime.

• To edit the message text of any e-mail, select its listing and click Edit E-mail. Make your changes and click OK.

• Click Send Now to e-mail all the selected items.

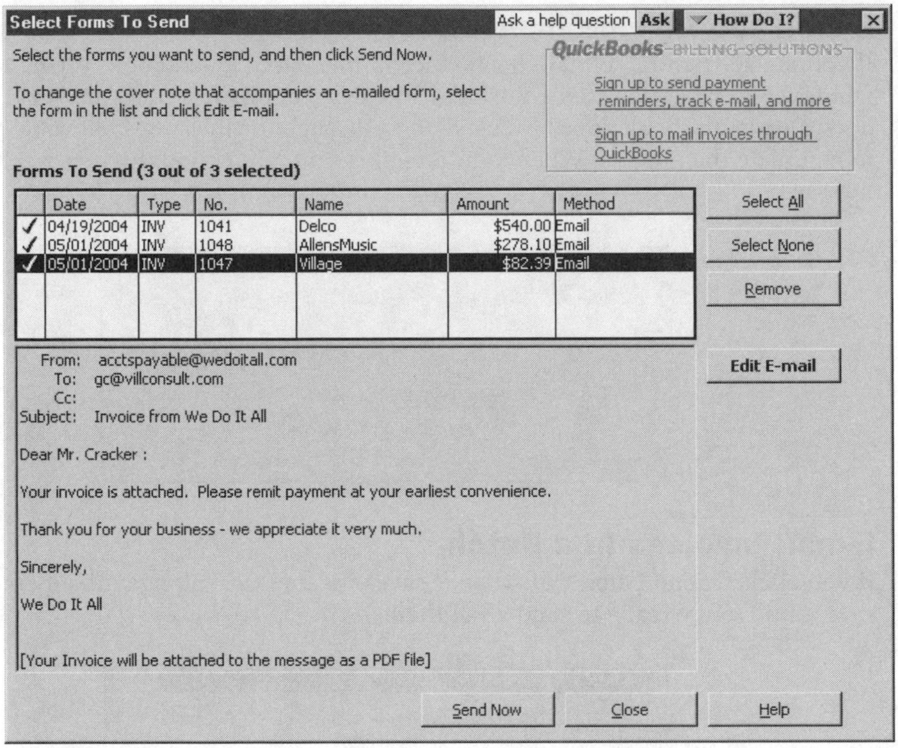

FIGURE 3-12 E-mail all the invoices and credit memos at once.

Change the Default Message

If you want to change the default message that appears in the e-mail message, choose Edit | Preferences and move to the Send Forms section of the Preferences dialog box. In the Company Preferences tab (see Figure 3-13), make changes to any part of the message header or text.

You can use this dialog box to change the e-mail for all QuickBooks forms that can be sent by e-mail (look at the list, it's amazingly complete). Select the appropriate form from the drop-down list in the Change Default For field.

You can change the way the salutations are inserted in the message, change the text of the Subject field, and change the text in the message.

The Customer-Side of E-mailed Invoices

When the customer receives your e-mail invoice, the invoice is a PDF attachment. In addition to the message text you sent, below your signature, the e-mail message body contains information about the attached invoice file.

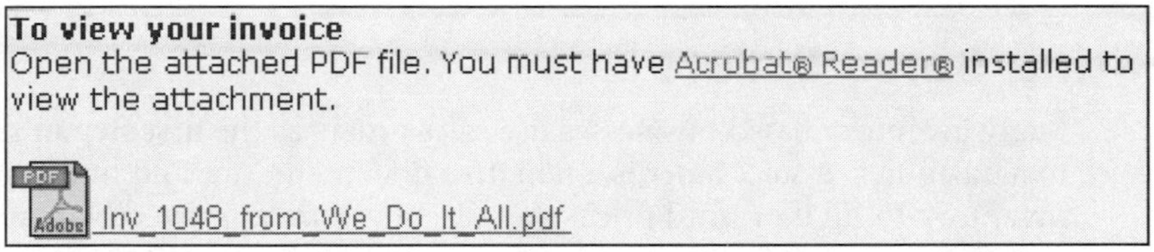

To view your invoice
Open the attached PDF file. You must have Acrobat® Reader® installed to view the attachment.

PDF Adobe Inv_1048_from_We_Do_It_All.pdf

If your customer doesn't have Acrobat Reader installed, clicking the link (the words "Acrobat Reader" are a link) sends your customer to the Adobe website, where the software is available for downloading (and it's free).

Additional Send Features for Forms

The Send drop-down list on the invoice form (and other forms) includes a choice named Mail Invoice. This refers to a feature you can sign up for (for a fee) to let QuickBooks print and mail your invoices. The printed form has a tear-off remittance slip, a return envelope, and other features.

You can add power to your e-mail delivery options by adding a "pay online" feature for customers, available (for a fee) from QuickBooks. See Appendix B to learn how to sign up for additional invoicing features.

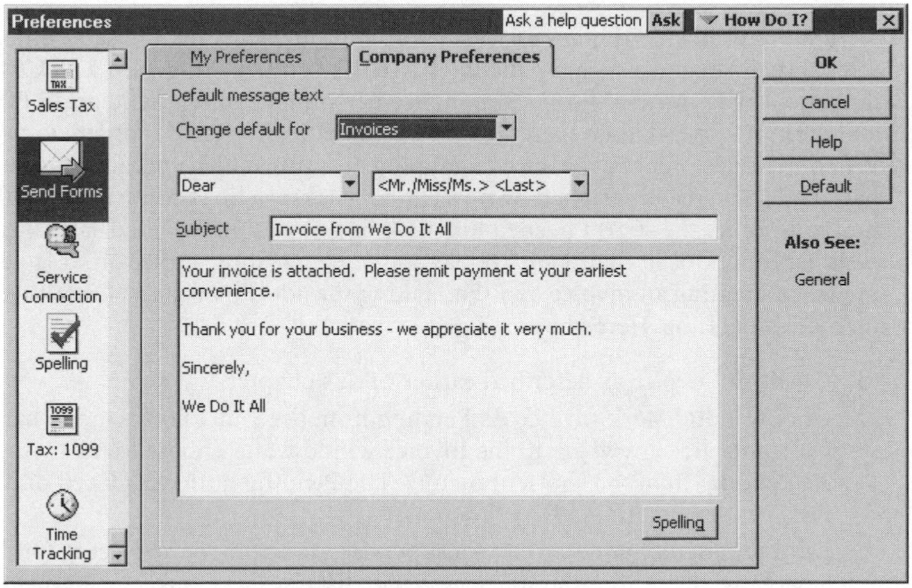

FIGURE 3-13 Customize the e-mail forms you use.

Creating Sales Orders

Many inventory-based businesses use sales orders as the first step in selling products to a customer. A *sales order* is a tentative document, on hold until there is sufficient inventory to fill it or until prices and discounts are approved by management. Some companies don't want to consider a sale as a final step until the items are packed, weighed, and on the truck. Other companies don't want an invoice processed until a sales manager approves the prices (especially if the sales person has the right to give discounts to favorite customers). Nothing on a sales order is posted to the general ledger.

QuickBooks Pro and QuickBooks Basic do not offer a sales order form. However, you can imitate this protocol if you need it. I discovered I could set up sales order processing in those editions of QuickBooks by using a little imagination and a couple of keystrokes.

NOTE: QuickBooks Premier Editions provide sales orders. To learn how to use them, read *Running QuickBooks 2004 Premier Editions* from CPA911 Publishing (www.cpa911.com).

In more robust (and more expensive) accounting software, the sales order is a separate form and a separate menu choice. It's printed along with a *pick list* (a document that's printed for the warehouse personnel, listing the items in bin order, and omitting prices); then there's a menu item that converts sales orders to invoices. When the sales order is converted, shipping costs are added (because the shipment has been packed and weighed by now) and a packing slip is printed. I found it easy to duplicate all the steps I needed for small businesses that wanted sales order and pick list functions in their QuickBooks software. Creating a sales order is just a matter of creating an invoice and then taking the additional step of marking the invoice as pending. Here's how:

1. Create an invoice as described earlier in this chapter.
2. Choose Edit | Mark Invoice As Pending from the QuickBooks menu bar (or right-click anywhere in the Invoice window and choose Mark Invoice As Pending from the shortcut menu). The Pending notice is placed on the invoice (see Figure 3-14).
3. Print the invoice and send it to a supervisor to approve the pricing (and send a packing slip to the warehouse as a pick list).
4. When the order is through the system, bring the invoice back to the window and add the shipping costs.

5. Choose Edit | Mark Invoice As Final. Now you have a regular invoice and you can proceed accordingly.

> **TIP:** Some of my clients purchase multipart invoice forms that have areas of black on the last form, covering the columns that hold the pricing information. They use this copy as the pick list and the packing slip. Other clients have created pick lists and packing slips by customizing the invoice template. See information on customizing later in this chapter.

If you have a service business, the sales order protocol can be handy for tracking specific jobs or tasks that customers request. It's a good first step, even before the estimating process (if you use estimates).

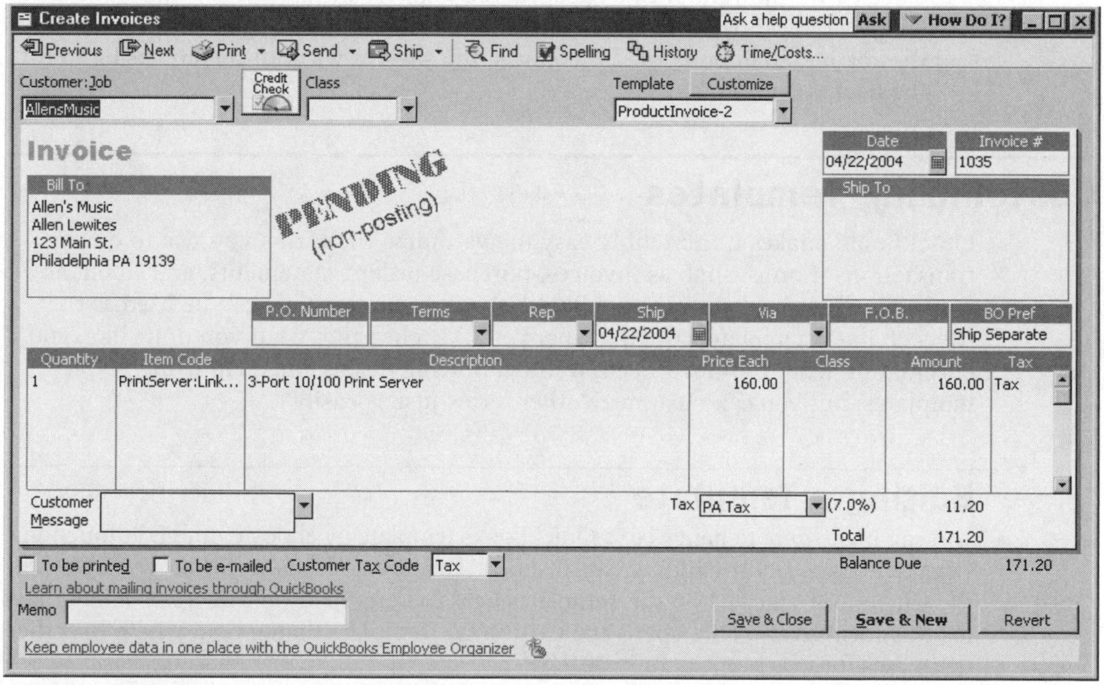

FIGURE 3-14 There's no mistaking the fact that this invoice isn't ready to send to the customer.

Creating Backorders

If you're selling inventory, there's nothing more frustrating than getting a big order when you're out of some or all of the products being ordered. You can ship the items you do have in stock and consider the rest of the items a backorder. The problem is that there's no backorder button on a QuickBooks invoice, nor is there a backorder form.

Instead of a backorder form, use the Pending Invoice feature described in the previous section. Here are some guidelines for making that feature work for backorders:

- As the items arrive in your warehouse from the vendor, remove them from the pending invoice (and save the invoice again) and place them on a regular invoice form.
- Use the Notes feature on customer records to indicate whether this customer accepts backorders, automatically cancels the portion of the order that must be backordered, or wants you to hold the shipment until the entire order can be sent.
- Check with the vendor of a backordered item regarding delivery date, and then create a QuickBooks reminder. The reminder tells you to grab the products as they arrive, so nobody puts them onto the shelves without remembering to fill the backorder.

Customizing Templates

QuickBooks makes it incredibly easy to customize the forms you use to create transactions. Forms, such as invoices, purchase orders, statements, and so on, are actually called *templates* in QuickBooks. An existing template can be used as the basis of a new template, copying what you like, changing what you don't like, and eliminating what you don't need. In the following discussions, I'm using invoice templates, but you can customize other forms just as easily.

Editing a Template

You can make minor changes to a QuickBooks template by choosing the Edit function. Open the transaction window (for instance, the Create Invoices window), and click the Customize button atop the Templates field (where the drop-down list of templates for this form lives). This opens the Customize Template dialog box, which lists the templates for this transaction window.

Customize Template

Select a template:

Intuit Packing Slip
Intuit Product Invoice
Intuit Professional Invoice
Intuit Service Invoice
Progress Invoice

Select an action:

Edit — Edit the selected template.

New — Create a new template based on the selected template.

Go to List — Go to the template list for advanced options.

Cancel   Help

Select the template you want to tweak, and click Edit. After a message appears telling you that this Edit process has limited features (remember, I said it was for minor adjustments), the Customize Invoice dialog box appears with the Edit mode options. For this example, I'm using an invoice, but the same options are available for other templates.

The Format tab (see Figure 3-15) lets you change the font for the various parts of your invoice form.

Select the part of the invoice you want to change and click the Change button. (If your printer setup is configured for blank paper, the options to change the font you use to print the company name and address are available). You can change the font, the font style (bold, italic, etc.), the size, the color, and the special effects (such as underline).

You can also disable the printing of any status stamps, such as the Pending notification, that may appear on the invoice. The status stamp continues to appear on the screen when you display the invoice.

On the Company tab, you can change some of the elements on your invoice. If you're switching from blank paper to preprinted forms, deselect the check boxes that enable printing of company information. Don't forget to go through a new printer setup, including alignment, when you use this edited template.

If you want to add a logo to your printed form, select the Use Logo option. In the Select Image dialog box that appears, click File. Locate your logo file, select it, and click Open. Click OK to confirm the use of this file.

The logo is positioned in the upper-left corner of your invoice form. You cannot change the positioning of the logo when you're working in Edit mode. See the section "Designing the Layout" to learn how to change the location of your logo on your invoices.

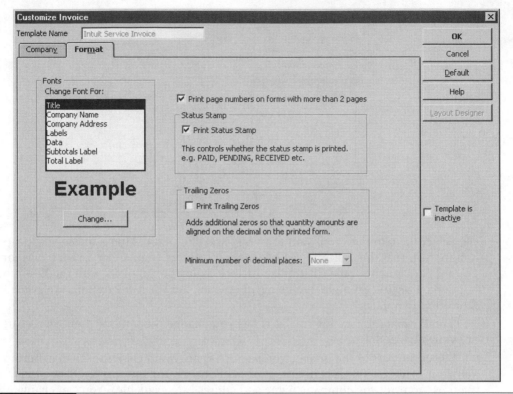

FIGURE 3-15 Alter the look of your invoices by changing fonts.

If you want to change the file you're using for your logo, return to this Customize Invoice dialog box and click Specify to tell QuickBooks where to locate the new file.

TIP: By default, QuickBooks assumes your logo file is in the same folder in which you've installed QuickBooks. If it's not, QuickBooks asks if it's okay to copy the file to the folder in which you installed QuickBooks.

Designing a New Template

If you want to add, remove, or reposition elements in your invoice, you have to design a new template. This is also the way to put any custom fields you may have created for any of your lists (customers, items, and so on) onto the appropriate transaction form.

To begin, click the Customize button above the Template drop-down list. Select the template you want to use as the basis of this new template, and choose New in the Customize Template dialog box. The Customize Invoice dialog box opens with a whole raft of choices (see Figure 3-16).

Notice that unlike the dialog box you see when you merely edit a template, QuickBooks doesn't enter the name of the template you're using as a model in the Template Name box. That's because the changes you make here are more sweeping than a minor edit, and you must give the template a name to create a new form. Enter a name for the form—something that reminds you of the format (such as "FootersAdded" or "CustomFields") or just call it "ProductInvoice2."

Move through the tabs to make changes, as follows:

- Add a field to the printed copy of the form if you want the customer to see the new field and its information.
- Add a field to the screen display of the form if the information is only important to the person who is entering the data.

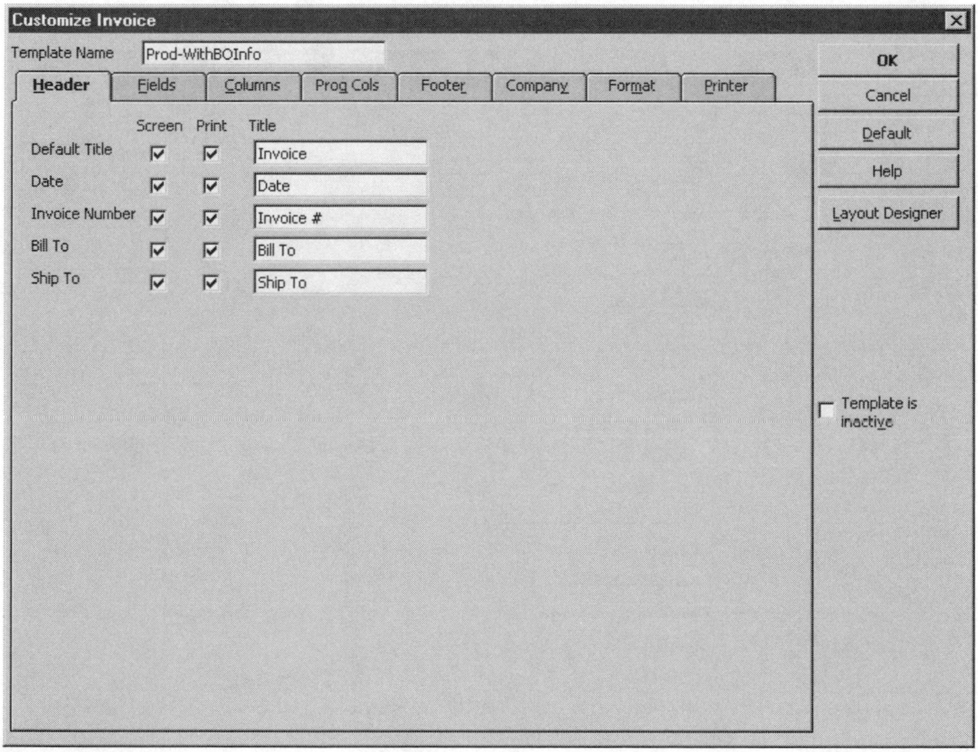

FIGURE 3-16 Each tab has specific customization options.

- Add a field to both the printed form and the screen display if it's appropriate for everybody to see the data.
- Remove fields from the printed copy of the form, the screen display, or both, if it's appropriate to skip that data.

Any custom fields you created (as discussed in Chapter 2) are available for you to add to the printed form, the onscreen display, or both.

> **NOTE:** Some fields can only be removed from the printed version of the form, not the onscreen display.

For example, as you can see in Figure 3-17, the custom field that was created for customer records to track backorder preferences has been added to the onscreen version of the invoice (the custom field is named Backorder, the invoice form will have the label BO Pref). This data needs to be tracked for internal purposes, to let

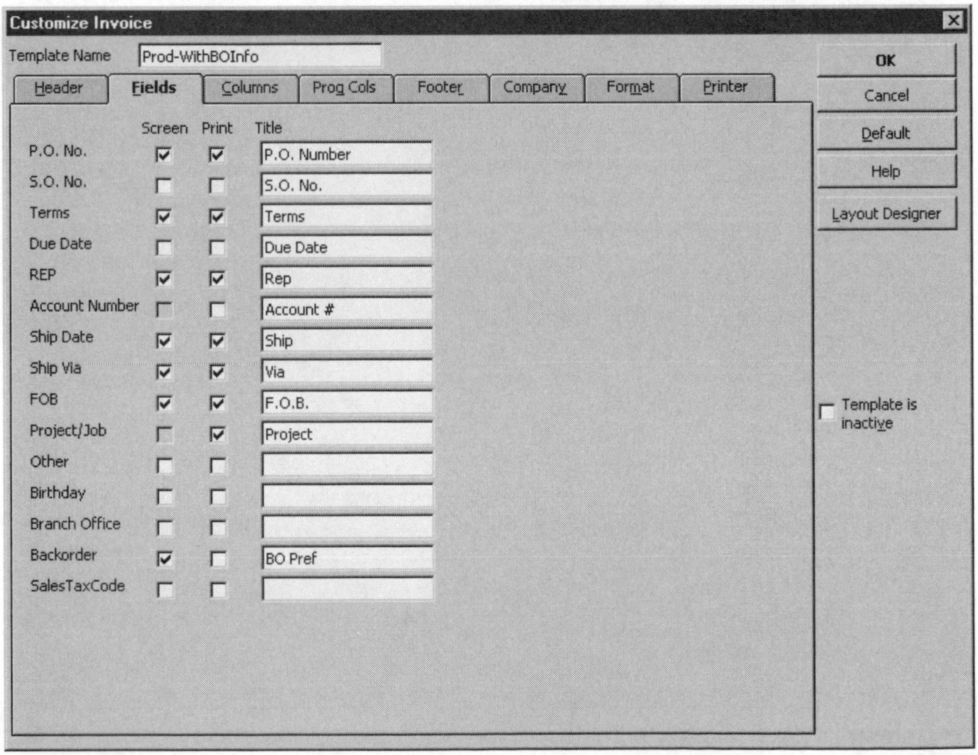

FIGURE 3-17 This customized data entry form is more efficient.

the user who is creating the invoice know whether to create a backorder if goods
are not in the warehouse. The field is of no interest to the customer who receives
the printed invoice.

Go through all the tabs on the dialog, making changes as needed. Notice that
you can add the current balance due for each customer in the Footer of the invoice
template. This is information that is usually reserved for statements, and unless you
have some cogent reason to avoid sending statements, I wouldn't add this information
to each invoice. It can be confusing to customers, most of who are used to the paradigm
of invoices for services and products, followed by statements to summarize invoices,
payments, and credits.

Designing the Layout

If you're comfortable with designing forms (or if you like to live on the edge), click
the Layout Designer button on the Customize window. The Layout Designer window
opens (see Figure 3-18) and you can plunge right in, moving elements around,
changing margins, and building your own layout.

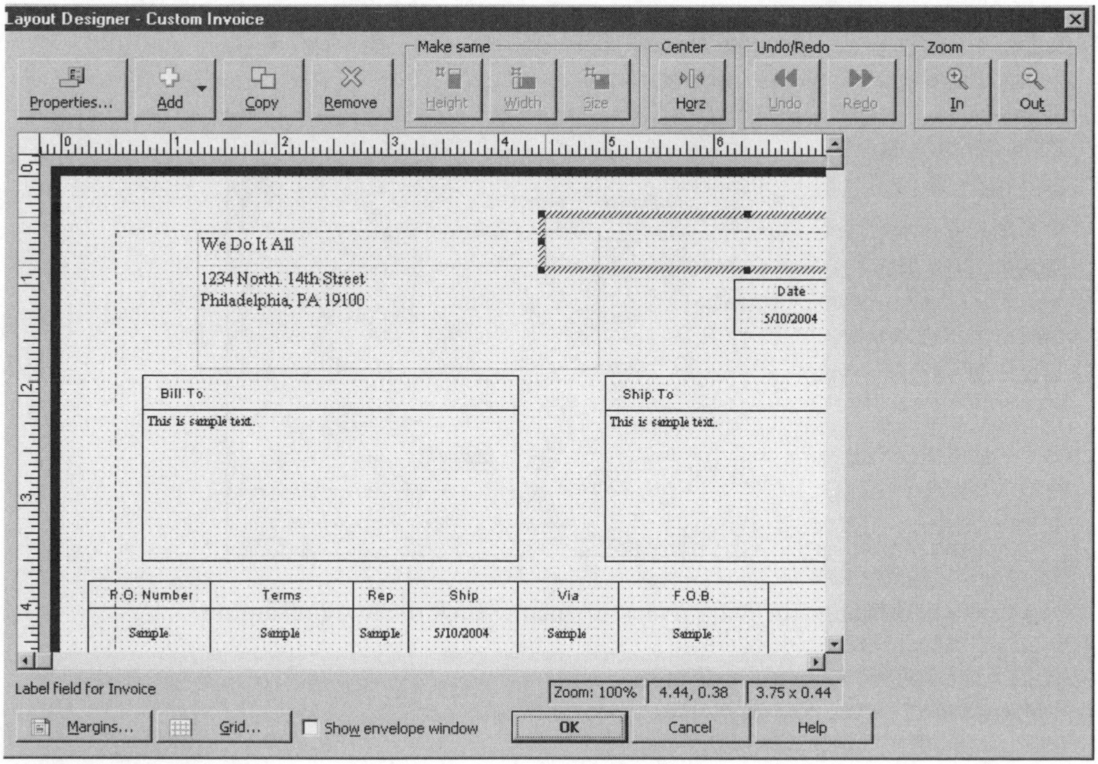

FIGURE 3-18 Move components around to create your own design.

NOTE: If you've added custom fields to the template, the Layout Designer warns you that these fields may overlap existing fields. You can choose to skip automatic redesigning (and manually move any fields that overlap), or tell the system to re-layout the design

Before you start, select the Show Envelope Window option if you use window envelopes to mail your invoices. This helps you avoid moving any fields into that area. Then select any element to put a frame around it. Now you can perform an action on the frame, as follows:

- To change the size of the element, position your pointer on one of the sizing handles on the frame, then drag the handle to resize the element.
- To move an element, position your pointer inside the frame and, when your pointer turns into a four-headed arrow, drag the frame to a different location on the form.
- Double-click an element's frame to see a dialog box that permits all sorts of option changes for the selected element.

- To change the margin measurements, click the Margins button.

- Click the Grid button to eliminate the dotted line grid from the screen, to change the spacing between grid lines, or to turn off the Snap To Grid option (automatically aligns objects to the nearest point on the grid).

- Use the toolbar buttons to align, resize, and zoom into the selected elements. There's also an Undo/Redo choice, thank goodness. When you finish with the Layout Designer, click OK to move back to the Customize Invoice window.

Once everything is just the way you want it, save your new template by clicking OK. This new template name appears on the drop-down list when you create invoices.

TIP: You can also use this new template as the basis for other customizations.

Using the Template List

You can also select a template for customization from the Template List, which you open by choosing Lists | Templates to see a list of all the templates that can be customized. Right-click the listing for the form you want to work with, and choose Edit or New to begin customizing the template as described in the previous paragraphs.

Duplicating a Template

You can duplicate existing templates, which is a good idea. You're not messing around with the original (always a safe way to approach making changes), and after you make changes to a duplicate template you have a new starting place for additional changes (creating duplicates of duplicates). This is a good way to experiment with template configuration, because you can always return to the last version if the latest set of changes proves to be inefficient when you're entering transactions.

To duplicate a template, open the Templates list by choosing Lists | Templates from the QuickBooks menu bar. Right-click the listing for the template you want to clone, and choose Duplicate from the shortcut menu to open the Select Template Type dialog box.

Select a template type for the duplicate you're creating, which doesn't have to be the same as the original template type. The duplicate template is saved in the Template list, with the name DUP:<*original template name*>, along with a notation of its type. This means you can have a template name that doesn't match the template type, or two templates with similar names.

To eliminate any confusion, you should change the name of a duplicated template, as follows:

1. Double-click the listing of the duplicate template to open the Customize Invoice dialog box, with the template name selected (highlighted).

TIP: The name of the dialog box changes to match the type of template you're editing.

2. Enter a new name for this template.
3. Click OK.

Notice that when you select Edit for a duplicate template, you don't see the same Edit dialog you see when you edit a built-in template. Instead, you see the same dialog you'd see if you selected New as your edit mode. That's because it's okay to make sweeping changes to duplicate templates; it's not as dangerous as making changes to the basic, built-in templates.

Using Memorized Invoices

If you have a recurring invoice (most common if you have a retainer agreement with a customer), you can automate the process of creating it. Recurring invoices are those that are sent out at regular intervals, usually for the same amount.

Create the first invoice, filling out all the fields. If there are any fields that will change each time you send the invoice, leave those fields blank and fill them out each time you send the invoice. Then press CTRL-M to open the Memorize Transaction dialog.

Fill in the fields using the following guidelines:

- Change the title in the Name box to reflect what you've done. It's easiest to add a word or phrase to the default title (the customer name or job), such as "Retainer."
- Choose Remind Me and specify how and when you want to be reminded in the How Often and Next Date fields. The reminder will appear in the automatic QuickBooks Reminder window.
- Choose Don't Remind Me if you have a great memory, or only use this memorized invoice for special occasions.
- Choose Automatically Enter if you want QuickBooks to issue this invoice automatically. If you opt for automatic issuing of this invoice, you must fill in the fields so that QuickBooks performs the task accurately, as follows:
  - The How Often field is where you specify the interval for this invoice, such as monthly, weekly, or so on. Click the arrow to see the drop-down list and choose the option you need.
  - The Next Date field is the place to note the next instance of this invoice.
  - The Number Remaining field is a place to start a countdown for a specified number of invoices. This is useful if you're billing a customer for a finite number of months because you only have a one-year contract.
  - The Days In Advance To Enter field is for specifying the number of days in advance of the next date you want QuickBooks to create the invoice.

Click OK when you have finished filling out the dialog box. Then click Save & Close in the Invoice window to save the transaction. Later, if you want to view, edit, or remove the transaction, you can select it from the Memorized Transaction List by pressing CTRL-T, or by clicking the MemTx icon on the QuickBooks toolbar.

Using Estimates

For certain customers, or certain types of jobs, it may be advantageous to create estimates. An estimate isn't an invoice, but it can be the basis of an invoice (you can create multiple invoices to reflect the progression of the job).

 N O T E : Estimates aren't available in QuickBooks Basic Edition.

Creating an Estimate

The first (and most important) thing to understand is that creating an estimate doesn't impact your financial records. When you indicate that you use estimates in your QuickBooks preferences, a nonposting account named Estimates is added to your Chart Of Accounts. The amount of the estimate is posted to this account (invoices, on the other hand, are posted to the Accounts Receivable account).

To create an estimate, choose Customers | Create Estimates from the menu bar, which opens an Estimate form. As you can see in Figure 3-19, the form is very much like an invoice form. Fill out the fields in the same manner you use for invoices.

Estimates permit you to invoice customers with a markup over cost. This is often the approach used for time and materials on bids. Just enter the cost and indicate the markup in dollars or percentage. Incidentally, if you decide to change the total of the item, QuickBooks will change the markup so your math is correct.

Creating Multiple Estimates for a Job

You can create multiple estimates for a customer or a job, which is an extremely handy feature. You can create an estimate for each phase of the job, or create multiple estimates with different prices. Of course, that means each estimate has different contents; you never want to let customers know you could do exactly the same job for less money.

When you create multiple estimates for the same job, each estimate is marked Active. If a customer rejects any estimates, you can either delete them or change the status to Closed in order to have a permanent record.

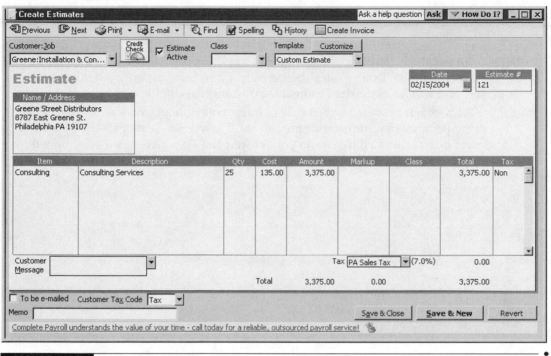

FIGURE 3-19 Estimates provide a way to track and invoice a job.

Duplicating Estimates

You can also duplicate an estimate, which provides a quick way to create multiple estimates with slightly different contents. Choose Edit | Duplicate Estimate while the estimate is displayed in your QuickBooks window. The Estimate Number field changes to the next number, while everything else remains the same. Make your changes, and then click Save & Close.

Memorizing Estimates

If you frequently present the same estimated items to multiple customers, you can use the Memorize Estimates feature to create boilerplate estimates for future use. Memorized estimates do not contain the customer name (QuickBooks removes the name when memorizing the document).

1. Create an estimate, filling in the items that belong on this type of estimate. Don't fill in amounts (quantities, prices, or both) that usually change.
2. Press CTRL-M to memorize the estimate.
3. Give the estimate a name that reminds you of its contents.

4. Select the option Don't Remind Me.

5. Click OK.

To use the boilerplate estimate, press CTRL-T, or choose Lists | Memorized Transaction List. Double-click the estimate, fill in the Customer:Job information, and save it. The memorized estimate isn't changed, only the new estimate is saved.

This chapter covered a great deal of information about invoices, and that reflects the importance of your invoicing procedures. The more accurate your invoices are, the fewer questions you'll have from your customers. This increases the likelihood that your customers will send checks right away.

Receiving Payments

*I*n this chapter:

- Apply customer payments

- Handle cash sales

- Deposit payments and cash sales into your bank account

- Apply credits and discounts to invoices

The best part of Accounts Receivable chores is receiving the payments. However, you need to make sure you apply customer payments correctly, so that you and your customers have the same information in your records.

Receiving Invoice Payments

As you create invoices and send them to your customers, there's an expectation that money will eventually arrive to pay off those invoices. And, in fact, it almost always works that way. In accounting, there are two ways to think about the cash receipts that pay off invoices:

Balance forward   This is a system in which you consider the total of all the outstanding invoices as the amount due from the customer, and you apply payments against that total. It doesn't matter which particular invoice is being paid, because it's a running total of payments against a running total of invoices.

Open item   This is a system in which payments you receive are applied to specific invoices. Most of the time, the customer either sends a copy of the invoice along with the check, or notes the invoice number that is being paid on the check stub, to make sure your records agree with the customer's records.

QuickBooks assumes you're using a balance forward system, but you can override that default easily. In fact, applying payments directly to specific invoices is just a matter of a mouse click or two.

N O T E : QuickBooks refers to the process of handling invoice payments from customers as "Receive Payments." The common bookkeeping jargon for this process is "cash receipts." You'll find I use that term frequently throughout this chapter (it's just habit).

Recording the Payment

When a check arrives from a customer, follow these steps to apply the payment:

1. Choose Customers | Receive Payments from the menu bar to bring up a blank Receive Payments window, as shown in Figure 4-1.
2. Click the arrow to the right of the Received From field to display a list of customers and select the customer or job as follows:
   - If the payment is from a customer for whom you're not tracking jobs (or for an invoice that wasn't related to a job), select the customer. The current balance for this customer automatically appears in the Customer Balance Field.
   - If the payment is for a job, select the job. The current balance for this job automatically appears in the Customer Balance field.

- If the payment covers multiple jobs, select the customer to see all invoices for all jobs. The current balance for this customer automatically appears in the Customer Balance field.

3. In the Amount field, enter the amount of this payment.
4. Click the arrow to the right of the Pmt. Method field and select the payment method:
   - If the payment method is a credit card, complete the Card No. and Exp. Date fields. If you have a merchant account with the QuickBooks Merchant Account Service, click the option Process Credit Card Payment When Saving, which automatically puts the credit card payment into your bank account. (See Appendix B for information about using the QuickBooks Merchant Account Service.)
   - If the payment method is a check, enter the check number in the Ref./Check No. field.

The Memo field is optional, and I've never come across a reason to use it, but if there's some important memorandum you feel you must attach to this payment record, feel free.

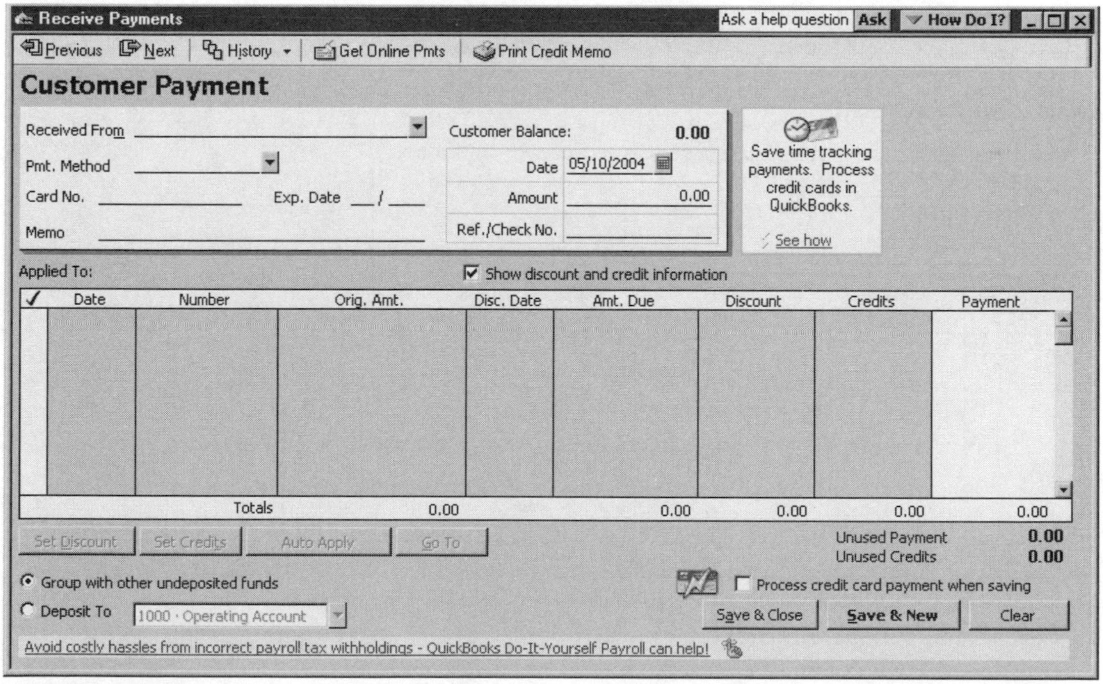

FIGURE 4-1   Fill in all the data to make sure you apply payments accurately.

N O T E : You can add all the payment methods you need in the Payment Method list, as described in Chapter 2.

Applying Payments to Invoices

Now you have to apply the payment against the customer invoices. As you can see in Figure 4-2, QuickBooks automatically applies the payment to the oldest invoice. However, if the payment exactly matches the amount of another invoice, QuickBooks applies it correctly.

T I P : You can force QuickBooks to let you apply payments to specific invoices instead of automatically heading for the oldest invoice by changing the options in the Preferences dialog. Choose Edit | Preferences and click the Sales & Customers icon in the left pane. On the Company Preferences tab, deselect the option Automatically Apply Payments.

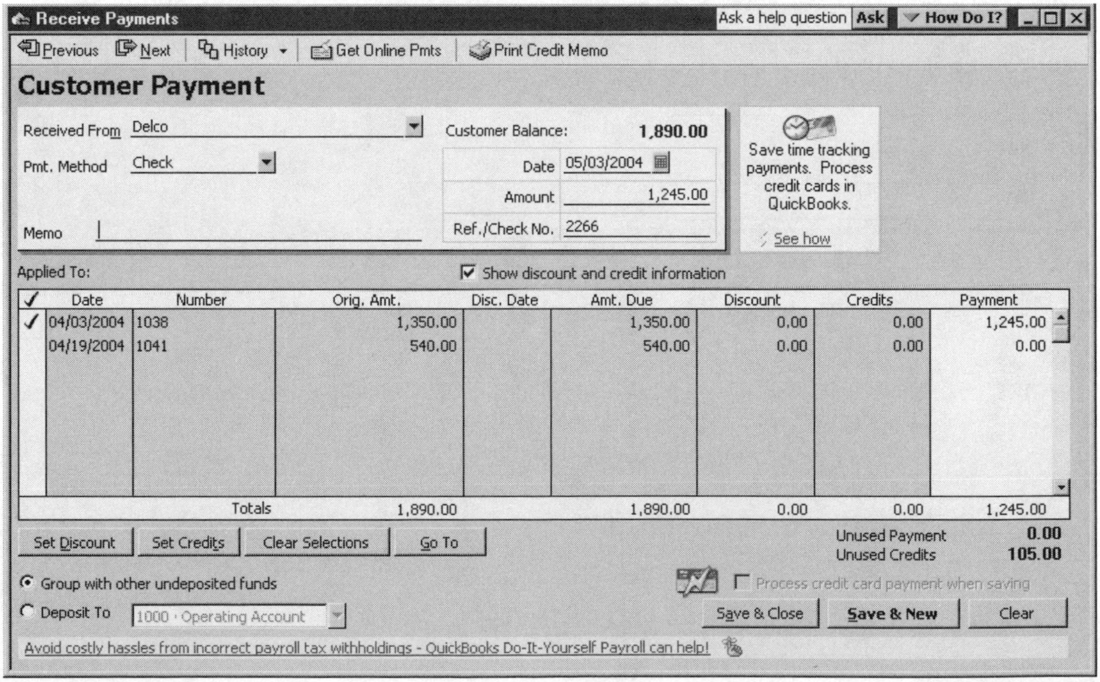

FIGURE 4-2 QuickBooks automatically applies payments logically.

You could face several scenarios when receiving customer payments:

- The customer has one unpaid invoice, and the payment is for the same amount as that invoice.
- The customer has several unpaid invoices, and the payment is for the amount of one of those invoices.
- The customer has one or more unpaid invoices, and the payment is for an amount lower than any single invoice.
- The customer has several unpaid invoices, and the payment is for an amount greater than any one invoice but not large enough to cover two invoices.
- The customer has one or more unpaid invoices, and the payment is for a lesser amount than the current balance. However, the customer has a credit equal to the difference between the payment and the customer balance.

You have a variety of choices for handling any of these scenarios, but for situations in which the customer's intention isn't clear, the smart thing to do is call the customer and ask how the payment should be applied. You can manually enter the amount you're applying against an invoice in the Payment column. You must, of course, apply the entire amount of the payment.

If you are not tracking invoices and are instead using a balance forward system, just let QuickBooks continue to apply payments against the oldest invoices.

If the customer sent a copy of the invoice with the payment or indicated the invoice number on the check or stub, always apply the payment to that invoice, even if it means an older invoice remains unpaid. Customers do this deliberately, usually because there's a problem with the older invoice. The rule of thumb is "apply payments according to the customers' wishes." Otherwise, when you and the customer have a conversation about the current open balance, your bookkeeping records won't match.

If the customer payment doesn't match the amount of any invoice (it's a partial payment), check to see whether the customer indicated a specific invoice number for the payment. If so, apply the payment against that invoice; if not, let the automatic selection of the oldest invoice stand.

If the check is for the same amount as a later invoice, QuickBooks should automatically select that invoice. If that doesn't happen, click the check mark next to the one that QuickBooks automatically selected incorrectly to remove the check mark. Then click the check mark column next to the invoice that's being paid with this payment.

Applying Credits to Invoices

You can apply any existing credit to an invoice in addition to this payment. If credits exist, QuickBooks displays the amount of credit due on the Receive Payments window (refer to the item Unused Credits shown in Figure 4-2). Usually, customers let you know how they want credits applied, and it's not unusual to find a note written on the copy of the invoice that the customer sent along with the check.

Click the Set Credits button to apply existing credits via the Discount And Credits dialog box.

Depending on the circumstances, here's how QuickBooks handles the credits:

The Credit Total Is Equal to or Less than the Unpaid Amount of the Oldest Invoice   This reduces the balance due on that invoice. If the customer sent a payment that reflects a deduction for the amount of his credits (a common scenario), so that the credit total is equal to the unpaid amount, the invoice has no remaining balance.

If applying the existing credit along with the payment doesn't pay off the invoice, the balance due on the invoice is reduced by the total of the payment and the credit.

The amount of the credit is added to the postings for the invoice. Don't worry—this change only affects the invoice balance and the Accounts Receivable posting; it doesn't change the amount of the payment that's posted to your bank account.

The Credit Total Is Larger than the Amount Required to Pay Off an Invoice
If the customer payment is smaller than the amount of the invoice, but the amount of credit is larger than the amount needed to pay off the invoice, the balance of the credit is available for posting to another invoice.

To apply the unapplied credit balance to another invoice, click Done and select the next invoice in the Receive Payments window. Then click Set Credits and apply the credit balance (or as much of it as you need) against the invoice. Any unused credits remain for the future.

You should send a statement to the customer to reflect the current, new invoice balances as a result of applying the payments and the credits (even though the customer's accounting software probably reflects the facts accurately).

> **TIP:** Be sure the option Show Discount And Credit Information is selected on the Receive Payments window, or you won't know about existing credits that have been applied.

Applying Credits to a Different Job

You may have a situation in which a customer has already paid the invoices for a job when the credit is created, or has paid for part of the job, exceeding the amount of the credit. If the customer tells you to apply the credit balance to another job, or to float the credit and apply it against the next job, you have a problem.

Sigh! QuickBooks does not permit you to apply a credit from one job to another job. You have the same problem if you created a credit for a customer that has one or more jobs, but you applied the credit directly to the customer instead of a job. You can't use the credit amount against an invoice payment for one of that customer's jobs.

However, as a workaround, you can unapply and reapply credits, and you have a couple of methods to choose from, as described here.

Wash (zero out) the original credit with an invoice against the same job (or the same customer if you mistakenly applied a credit to the customer name instead of the job name). If the credit is a partial credit (you applied some of it against its job), make the invoice amount equal to the credit balance. In the Description column, enter **Offset to CM *xxx***, where *xxx* is the original credit memo number, so you can mail the invoice to the customer to explain what you're doing. Then create a new credit for an equal amount and apply it to the other job.

There are some minor problems (well, *irritations…*) with this approach, due to the fact that QuickBooks does not have an element called a debit memo (traditionally used to offset and correct credit memos). Therefore, when your customer gets a statement at the end of the month, an invoice is listed that makes no sense to the customer. I solved this for my clients by instructing them to use the letters "DM" in front of the invoice number in the Invoice # field. Then they customized their Statement template to add a footer that explained the DM invoices. (See Chapter 5 to learn how to customize Statement forms.) Of course, if you use this approach, you have to remember to remove the DM from the Invoice # field when you next open the Create Invoices window.

Another technique is to wash the credit with a debit via a journal entry. To do this, you need to have a "wash" account. For my clients, I create an account named "Exchanges" with an account type of Other Expense. Then I take the following steps:

1. Choose Banking | Make Journal Entry to open the General Journal Entry window.
2. In the Account column, select the Accounts Receivable account and press TAB.

3. In the Debit column, enter the amount of the credit.

4. Optionally, enter a note to yourself in the Memo column (e.g., **Moving CM # *xxx***) and press TAB.

5. In the Name column, select the Customer:Job listing from which you are *removing* the credit and press TAB to move to the next line.

6. In the Account column, select the "wash" account.

7. QuickBooks automatically puts the correct amount in the Credit column.

8. Click Save & New to open a new, blank General Journal Entry window.

9. In the Account column, select the Accounts Receivable account and press TAB twice to move to the Credit column.

10. In the Credit column, enter the amount of the credit and press TAB.

11. Optionally, write a note to yourself in the Memo column (e.g., **Moving CM # *xxx***) and press TAB.

12. In the Name column, select the Customer:Job listing to which you are *applying* the credit and press TAB.

13. In the Account column, enter the "wash" account.

14. QuickBooks automatically puts the correct amount in the Debit column.

15. Click Save & Close.

Now, before you send me an e-mail to ask (sarcastically) why I didn't put all four lines on the same journal entry, I'll explain. QuickBooks, unlike other accounting software programs, does not permit you to use the A/R or A/P account multiple times in the same journal entry. There are lots of situations that arise during the course of business bookkeeping activities that would be much easier if you could have multiple entries to A/R or A/P, but QuickBooks has had this restriction forever. Also annoying is the fact that QuickBooks doesn't permit you to put both an A/R and A/P entry on the same journal entry (making entering opening trial balances a real pain). Further, you can't post anything to A/R or A/P in a journal entry without charging the amount to a customer or a vendor, which is frequently a bother. I can't explain their reasons for imposing these restrictions, I can only explain the ramifications.

Both of these solutions create an audit trail that you can understand in the future, and that your accountant will approve of. However, even though I continuously rail against the practice of deleting transactions, I know that many of you will have figured out that merely deleting the credit memo and creating a new one for the right job will be easy (and that's what you'll do). The math works, but you're not following good accounting/bookkeeping practices. The ability to delete a transaction is another feature QuickBooks offers that most, if not all, other accounting software companies shun. As a result, if I ever decide to stop writing books and become a professional embezzler, I'll only work at companies that use QuickBooks because otherwise I won't be able to hide (delete) my devious transactions.

Applying Discounts for Timely Payments

If you offer your customers terms that include a discount if they pay their bills promptly (for instance, 2% 10 net 30), you must apply the discount to the payment if it's applicable. You must also make sure the option Show Discount And Credit Information is selected on the Receive Payments window.

Figure 4-3 shows the Receive Payments window for a customer who has been offered a discount for timely payment and has taken it by reducing the amount of the payment. The only clue you have to explain the difference between the payment amount and the invoice amount is the fact that the Disc Date column shows the date by which the invoice must be paid to receive the discount. For customers or invoices without discount terms, that column is blank in the Receive Payments window.

QuickBooks doesn't apply the discount automatically, for instance by offering a column with the discount amount and selecting that amount as part of the payment. Instead, you must select the invoice (unless QuickBooks

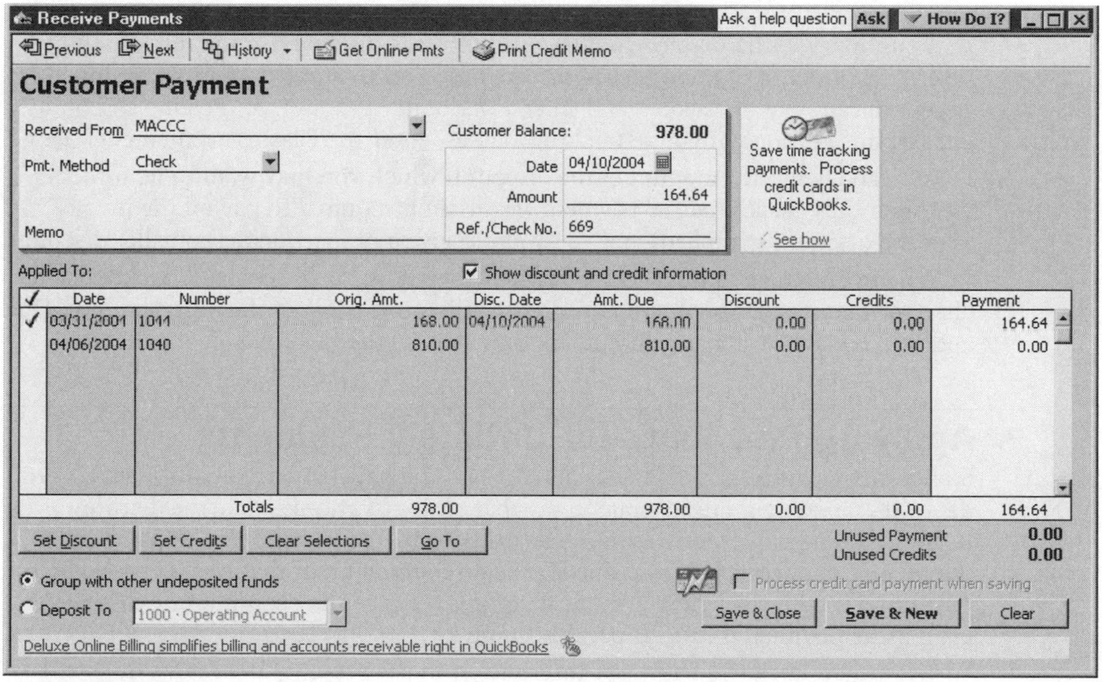

FIGURE 4-3   A discount date appears for invoices that have terms with discounts.

automatically selected it in order to apply the payment) and click the Set Discount button to see the Discount And Credits dialog box connected to this invoice.

A summary of the invoice and discount terms is displayed, and QuickBooks inserts the amount of the discount to use, based on the information in the invoice. Accept the amount of discount and enter a Discount Account (see "Posting Discounts" later in this section). If you're tracking classes, enter the Class, and then click Done.

You can change the amount of the discount, which you may want to do if the customer only made a partial payment (less than is required to pay off the invoice after the discount is applied) and you want to give a proportionately smaller discount.

When you return to the Receive Payments window, you'll see that QuickBooks has changed the Amt. Due column to reflect the discount. Most of the time, the Amt. Due and the customer payment amount are the same, so the invoice is now paid off.

Applying Discounts for Untimely Payments

Sometimes customers take the discount even if the payment arrives after the discount date. (It's probably more accurate to say that customers *always* take the discount even if the payment arrives later than the terms permit.) You can apply the payment to the invoice and leave a balance due for the discount amount that was deducted by the customer, if you wish. However, most companies give the customer the discount even if the payment is late, as part of "good will."

When you click the Discount Info button in that case, QuickBooks does not automatically fill in the discount amount—it's too late, and QuickBooks is not forgiving, generous, or aware of the need to humor customers to preserve good will. Simply enter the amount manually and then click Done to apply the discount to the invoice.

Posting Discounts

To track the amount of money you've given away with discounts, you should create a specific account in your chart of accounts. You could post discounts to your standard income account(s), which will be reduced every time you apply a discount. The math is right, but the absence of an audit trail bothers me (and bothers many accountants). It's better to create an Income account (I call mine "Discounts Given").

CAUTION: If there's an account named "Discounts" in the part of your chart of accounts that's devoted to expenses, don't use that account for your customer discounts, because it's there to track the discounts you take with your vendors.

Turning Payments into Bank Deposits

QuickBooks offers two options for depositing your payment on the Receive Payments window: Group With Other Undeposited Funds, and Deposit To (which you use to name a specific bank account). By default, the first option is selected. This section explains the choices so you can decide how to handle deposits.

Group with Other Undeposited Funds

Each payment you receive is entered into an account named Undeposited Funds (QuickBooks establishes this account automatically). It's an account type of Other Current Asset. When you finish applying customer payments in QuickBooks and are ready to make your bank deposit, you move the money from the Undeposited Funds account into the bank account by choosing Banking | Make Deposits from the menu bar. (See the section "Depositing Income" later in this chapter for the rest of the details.) While the Undeposited Funds account shows each individual payment you received, the bank account shows only the total amount of each bank deposit. This matches the bank statement that shows up each month, making it easier to reconcile the account.

Deposit to Bank Account

Depositing each payment directly to the bank means you don't have to take the extra step involved in using the Make Deposits window. However, each payment you receive appears as a separate entry when you reconcile your bank account. If you received six payments totaling $10,450.25 and took the checks to the bank that day, your bank statement shows that amount as the deposit. When you reconcile the bank statement, you'll have to select each payment individually to mark them as cleared, which requires some calculations at the time you perform the reconciliation. (See Chapter 12 for detailed instructions on reconciling bank accounts.)

Understanding Customer Payment Postings

When you receive money in payment for customer invoices, QuickBooks automatically posts all the amounts to your general ledger. Following are the postings if you select the option Group With Other Deposits.

ACCOUNT	DEBIT	CREDIT
Undeposited Funds	Total of cash receipts	
Accounts Receivable		Total of cash receipts

When you make the actual deposit, using the Make Deposit window, QuickBooks automatically posts the following transaction:

ACCOUNT	DEBIT	CREDIT
Bank	Total of deposit	
Undeposited Funds		Total of deposit

Here are the postings for a sale to a customer who has terms that permit a 1% discount. Let's assume the sale was for $100.00. The original invoice posted the following amounts:

ACCOUNT	DEBIT	CREDIT
Accounts Receivable	$100.00	
Income		$100.00

Notice that the postings are unconcerned with the discount amount. You don't have to account for the discount until it occurs.

When the customer's payment arrived, the 1% discount was deducted from the invoice total. When you enter the customer payment, which is in the amount of $99.00, the following postings occur:

ACCOUNT	DEBIT	CREDIT
Undeposited Funds	$99.00	
Accounts Receivable		$100.00
Discounts Given	$1.00	

Handling Cash Sales

A cash sale is a sale for which you haven't created an invoice, because the exchange of product and payment occurred simultaneously. Cash sales are the same as invoiced sales insofar as an exchange of money for goods or services occurs. The difference is that there's no period of time during which you have money "on the street." You can have a cash sale for either a service or a product, although it's far more common to sell products for cash. Most service companies use invoices.

NOTE: QuickBooks uses the term Sales Receipt instead of Cash Sale. However, the term Cash Sale is the common jargon (a sales receipt is a piece of paper).

I'm assuming that a cash sale is not your normal method of doing business (you're not running a candy store). If you *are* running a retail store, the cash sale feature in QuickBooks isn't an efficient way to handle your cash flow. You should either have specialized retail software (that even takes care of opening the cash register drawer automatically and also tracks inventory) or use QuickBooks only to record your daily totals of bank deposits as a journal entry. You might want to look at the QuickBooks Point of Sale product, which is designed for retailers. More information is available on the QuickBooks website, www.quickbooks.com.

NOTE: Don't take the word "cash" literally, because a cash sale can involve a check or a credit card.

There are two methods for handling cash sales in QuickBooks:

- Record each cash sale as a discrete record. This is useful for tracking sales of products or services to customers. It provides a way to maintain records about those customers in addition to tracking income and inventory.
- Record sales in batches (usually one batch for each business day). This method tracks income and inventory when you have no desire to maintain information about each customer that pays cash.

To record a cash sale, choose Customers | Enter Sales Receipts from the menu bar to open the Enter Sales Receipts window, shown in Figure 4-4.

Entering Cash Sale Data

If you want to track customer information, enter a name in the Customer:Job field or select the name from the drop-down list. If the customer doesn't exist, you can add a new customer by choosing <Add New>.

If you're not tracking customers, invent a customer for cash sales (I named the customer "Cash Sale," which seemed appropriate, if not creative).

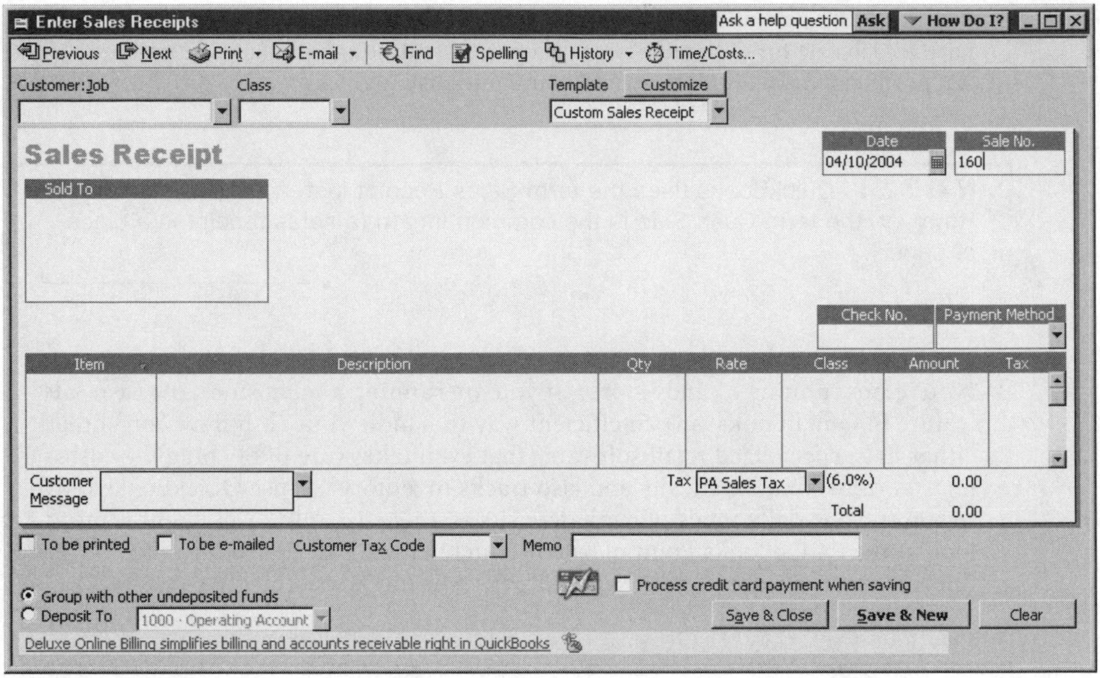

FIGURE 4-4   The Sales Receipts window is an invoice, a payment form, and a receipt.

TIP: If you track customers who always pay at the time of the sale, you might want to consider creating a customer type for this group ("Cash" seems an appropriate name for the type). You can separate this group for reports or for marketing and advertising campaigns.

Every field in the Enter Sales Receipts window works exactly the way it works for invoices and payments—just fill in the information. To save the record, click Save & New to bring up a new blank record, or click Save & Close to stop using the Enter Sales Receipts window.

Printing a Receipt for a Cash Sale

Most cash customers want a receipt. Click the Print button in the Enter Sales Receipts window to open the Print One Sales Receipt window, shown in Figure 4-5. (You may see a promotional message from QuickBooks about printing shipping labels, which you can turn off.) If you're not printing to a dot-matrix printer with multipart paper and you want a copy of the receipt for your files, be sure you change the specification in the Number Of Copies check box.

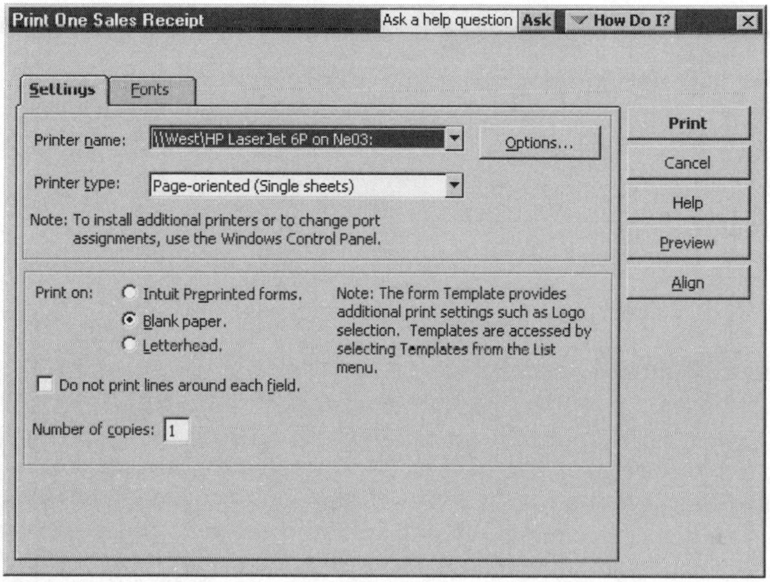

FIGURE 4-5 Choose the appropriate option for the type of paper you use to print receipts.

Customizing the Cash Receipts Template

I think a lot is missing from the QuickBooks cash receipts template. For example, there's no place for a sales rep, which is needed if you're paying commissions on cash sales, or you just want to track the person who made the sale. There's no Ship To address if the customer pays cash and wants delivery, nor is there a Ship Via field.

The solution is to customize the Custom Sales Receipts form. Here's how to do that:

1. Click the Customize button on top of the Template box in the upper-right corner of the form to open the Customize Template dialog box. There aren't multiple forms to use as a basis for the new form, so Custom Sales Receipts is selected.
2. Click New to open the Customize Sales Receipt window, shown in Figure 4-6.
3. Give the form a name in the Template Name box.

Following are some suggestions and guidelines for customizing this template.

Change Options in the Header Tab

Depending on your needs, you should consider one or more of the following suggestions for making changes in the Header tab:

- If you wish, change the Default Title. You might prefer the term Cash Receipt, or just Receipt.
- If you ever ship products to cash customers, select the Ship To field for both the Screen and the Print forms.

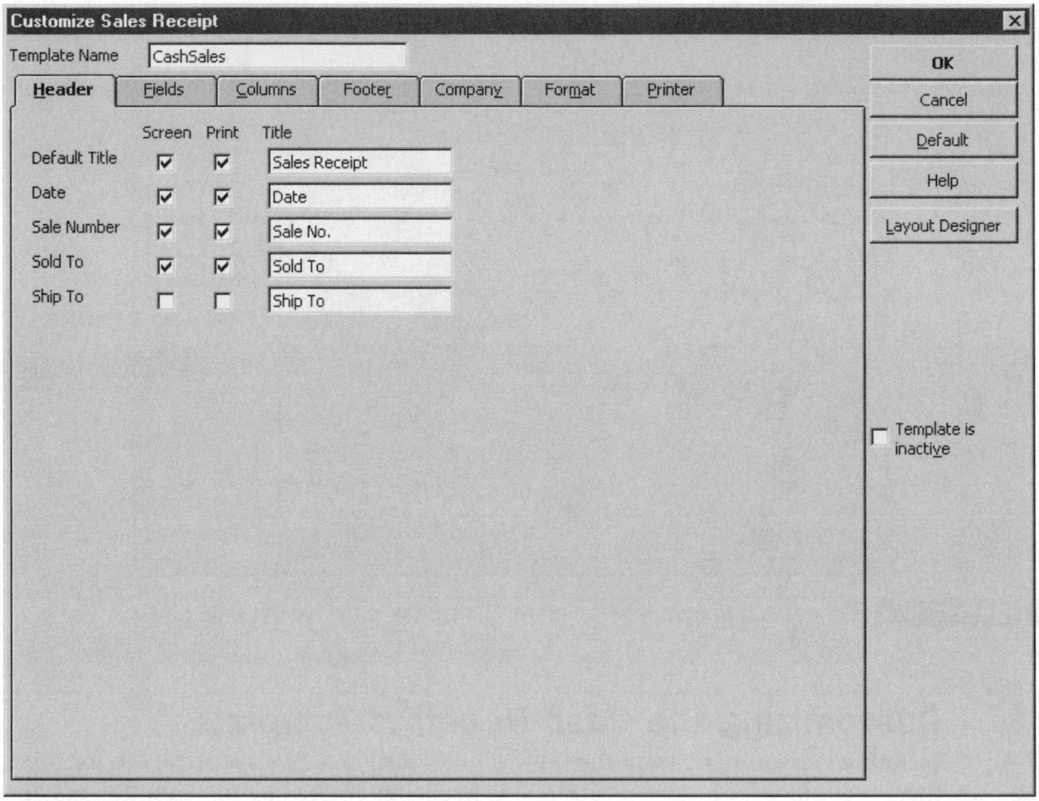

FIGURE 4-6 Build your own, more useful, form for cash sales.

Change Options in the Fields Tab

In the Fields tab, you can add any fields you need. If you're tracking sales persons (either for commission or just to know who made the sale), add the Rep field. You can add the field to the screen version and omit it from the print version.

If you ship products to cash customers, add the Ship Date, and Ship Via fields to the template.

Change Options in the Columns Tab

Use the Columns tab to add or remove columns in the line item section of the form. You can also change the order in which the columns appear. (For instance, perhaps you'd rather have Qty in the first column instead of the Item number.)

After you finish making the changes you need, click OK. You're returned to the Enter Sales Receipts window, and your new form is ready to use (see Figure 4-7).

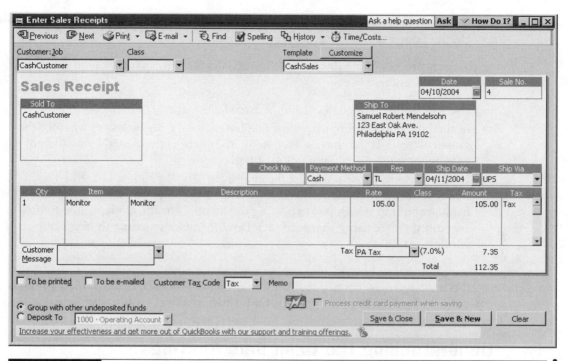

FIGURE 4-7 This customized template works better for me.

TIP: Even if you don't track individual cash customers, you can put the customer's name and address in the Ship To box. After you print and save the transaction, QuickBooks asks if you want to change the Ship To information in the customer record of your generic cash customer. Click No. In the future, when you view this transaction, the name and address remain in the box.

Handling Batches of Cash Sales

If you sell products or services and receive instant payment on a more frequent basis, you might want to consider batching the transactions. This works only if you don't care about maintaining information about the customers, and no customer expects a receipt. This technique also works if you have a business in which sales and service personnel return to the office each day with customer payments in hand.

Create a customized form, using the steps described in the previous section, with the following guidelines:

- Name the form appropriately (for example, "Batch Sales" or "Sales Batch").
- On the Header tab, keep only the Date and Sale Number fields in the heading.

- On the Fields tab, deselect all the optional fields.
- On the Footer tab, remove the Message field.

To batch-process cash sales, use the Enter Sales Receipts window with the following procedures:

- Use a customer named "Cash" or "CashSale."
- In the line item section, use a new line for each sale, regardless of whether the same customer is purchasing each item, each item is purchased by a different customer, or there's a combination of both events.
- Use the Save & Close button at the end of the day. If you need to close the window during the day (perhaps you'd like to get some work done), open the bank account to which you're posting the income (or the Undeposited Funds account if you're using that account). Double-click the listing to re-open the window.

If you use this technique, you cannot track the method of payment, and all receipts are treated as "money in." You can create a money-in item in the Customer Payment Method list (see Chapter 2 for information about creating list items).

Understanding the Cash Sale Postings

QuickBooks treats cash sales in the simplest, most logical manner. If you've sold a service instead of an inventory item for cash (perhaps a service call for a one-time customer you don't want to invoice), the postings are very straightforward:

ACCOUNT	DEBIT	CREDIT
Undeposited Funds	Total cash sales	
Revenue		Total cash sales

If the cash sale involved inventory items, here are the postings:

ACCOUNT	DEBIT	CREDIT
Undeposited Funds	Total cash sales	
Income		Total cash sales
Cost of Sales	Total cost of items sold	
Inventory		Total cost of items sold

Now I'm going to suggest you make it a bit more complicated, but don't panic, because it's not difficult. In the long run, these suggestions will make your bookkeeping chores easier. There's also a chance you'll make your accountant happier.

The Enter Sales Receipts window provides two choices for depositing the cash you receive:

- Group With Other Undeposited Funds
- Deposit To (you're expected to enter the bank account into which you place your cash receipts)

If you use the Deposit To option, your sales won't appear in the Payments To Deposit window when you tell QuickBooks you're taking your cash receipts to the bank. (See the section "Depositing Income" later in this chapter.) In fact, your bank account will be incremented by the amount of cash you post to it from cash sales, even though the money isn't really there until you make the trip to the bank.

There are two other ways to track receipts from cash sales separate from customer payments; pick the one that appeals to you:

- Opt to post the receipts to the Undeposited Funds account, but make those deposits separately when you work in the QuickBooks Payments To Deposit window.
- Opt to post the receipts to a new account called "Undeposited Till" (or something similar) and move the money into your bank account with a journal entry.

If you want to have an account to represent the cash till, to which you post cash in the Enter Sales Receipts window, create an Other Current Asset account for this purpose.

If you deal in real cash and have a cash register, you need to fill the till to make change. Write a check from your operating account (the payee should be Cash) and post the amount to the new account (which I call "Undeposited Till"). This produces the following posting (assuming $100.00 is allocated for change).

ACCOUNT	DEBIT	CREDIT
Checking		$100.00
Undeposited Till	$100.00	

When it's time to go to the bank, leave the original startup money (in this example, $100.00) in the till, count the rest of the money, and deposit that money into your checking account. When you return from the bank, make the following journal entry:

ACCOUNT	DEBIT	CREDIT
Checking	Amt of deposit	
Undeposited Till		Amt of deposit

In a perfect world, after you make the deposit and the journal entry, you can open the register for the Undeposited Till account and see a balance equal to your original startup cash. The world isn't perfect, however, and sometimes the actual amount you were able to deposit doesn't equal the amount collected in the Enter Sales Receipts transaction window. To resolve this, see the section "Handling the Over and Short Problem" later in this chapter.

Incidentally, if you want to raise or lower the amount you leave in the till for change, you don't have to do anything special. Just deposit less or more money, and the remainder (in the register for the Undeposited Till account and also in the physical till) just becomes the new base.

Depositing Income

With all of those checks you've received for invoice payments and the cash hanging around from the cash sales, it's time to go to the bank. Wait, don't grab those car keys yet! You have to tell QuickBooks about your bank deposit. Otherwise, when it's time to reconcile your checkbook, you'll have a nervous breakdown.

Choosing the Payments to Deposit

As you've been filling out the payment and cash sales forms, QuickBooks has been keeping a list it calls Undeposited Funds. That list remains designated as Undeposited Funds until you clear it by depositing them. (If you've been depositing every payment and cash receipt to a specific bank account, this section doesn't apply.)

To tell QuickBooks to make a deposit, choose Banking | Make Deposits from the QuickBooks menu bar, which brings up the Payments To Deposit window, shown in Figure 4-8.

 N O T E : You may have other deposits to make, perhaps refunds, loan proceeds, capital infusion, or some other type of deposit. Don't worry—you can tell QuickBooks about them in the next transaction window. This window is only displaying the cash receipts you've entered into QuickBooks through the Payments And Sales Receipts transaction windows.

Notice the following about the Payments To Deposit window:

- The Type column displays information about the payment type for each transaction—PMT for payment of an invoice and RCPT for a cash sale.
- The Payment Method column displays the specific payment method for each transaction, such as cash, check, a specific credit card, and so on.

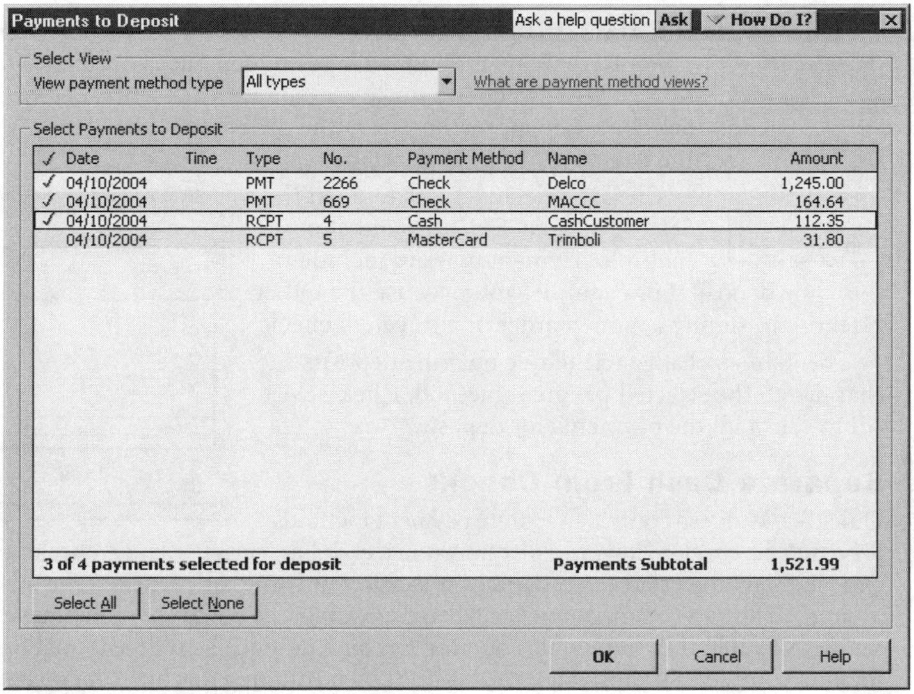
Payments to Deposit
Ask a help question Ask
How Do I?
Select View
View payment method type
All types
What are payment method views?
Select Payments to Deposit
✓ Date Time Type No. Payment Method Name Amount
✓ 04/10/2004 PMT 2266 Check Delco 1,245.00
✓ 04/10/2004 PMT 669 Check MACCC 164.64
✓ 04/10/2004 RCPT 4 Cash CashCustomer 112.35
04/10/2004 RCPT 5 MasterCard Trimboli 31.80
3 of 4 payments selected for deposit
Payments Subtotal 1,521.99
Select All
Select None
OK
Cancel
Help

FIGURE 4-8 All the money you've collected since the last bank deposit is waiting to be deposited.

This information is important because you should match it to the way your bank records deposits; otherwise, bank reconciliation becomes much more complicated. For example, your bank probably lists credit card deposits separately from a deposit total for cash and checks, even if all the money was deposited the same day. That's because your credit card deposits are probably made directly to your bank account by your merchant account bank. Even if you take deposit slips for credit card transactions to the bank and hand them to the teller along with your regular (cash/checks) deposit slip, the credit card deposits are probably listed separately on your bank statement.

Select Deposit Items

If you only have a few transactions to deposit, select those you just deposited into the bank by clicking their listings to place a check mark in the left column. Notice that in Figure 4-8, my cash and checks are selected because they went into today's deposit. I'll deposit the credit card income when I know my merchant bank has transferred the funds to my account.

Separate Deposit Items by Payment Method

If you have many individual deposits, separate your deposits by Payment Method to make it easier to work with this window. Select a payment method from the drop-down list at the top of the Payments To Deposit window.

Choose Selected Types to open the Select Payment Types list and choose multiple payment types to include in the same deposit. For example, you may use the Other category to signify a money order or a traveler's check.

The listings change to include only the deposits that match the selected payment method. Click Select All to select all the payments for deposit.

Separate Cash From Checks

QuickBooks doesn't provide separate payment methods for cash and checks. However, if you turn in a cash bag, select only the checks and deposit them; then start the process over to select only the cash (or do it the other way around). This is a common practice when depositing cash, because sometimes the bank notifies you that their automatic counting machine produced a different total from the total on your deposit slip (you probably don't own counting machines for coins and paper money). If that happens, you can edit the cash sales deposit item in your bank register, and the cause of the edit will be obvious. (I'm a stickler for good audit trails.)

Separate Deposits by Bank Account

If you're depositing money into multiple bank accounts, select only the transactions that go into the first account. After you complete the deposit, start this process again and deposit the remaining transactions into the appropriate account.

Credit Card Deposits

You can't deposit credit card payments until your merchant bank notifies you that the funds have been placed in your account.

- If you have QuickBooks online banking, the deposit shows up in the QuickReport (see Chapter 16 to learn about managing online banking transactions).
- If you have online access to your merchant card account, the transfer will appear on the activities report.
- If you don't have any form of online access, you'll have to wait for the monthly statement to arrive (or, contact the bank periodically to see if anything showed up in your account).

If your merchant bank deducts fees before transferring funds, learn how to deposit the net amount in the section "Calculating Merchant Card Fees," later in this chapter.

Deselect Items to Delay Their Deposit

If you want to hold back the deposit of any item, deselect it by clicking its listing (the check mark is a toggle). Only the items that have a check mark will be cleared from the undeposited payments list. There are several reasons to deselect deposit items:

- You received a payment in advance from a customer and don't want to deposit it until you're sure you can fill the order.
- You've accepted a post-dated check and it cannot yet be deposited.

After you make your selections, click OK.

Filling Out the Deposit Slip

Clicking OK in the Payments To Deposit window brings up the Make Deposits window, shown in Figure 4-9.

Select the bank account you're using for this deposit. Then make sure the date matches the day you're physically depositing the money. (If you're doing this at night or during the weekend, use the next business date so your records match the bank statement.)

Adding Items to the Deposit

If you want to add deposit items that weren't in the Payments To Deposit window, click anywhere in the Received From column to make it accessible, and select an existing name by clicking the arrow, or click <Add New> to enter a name that isn't

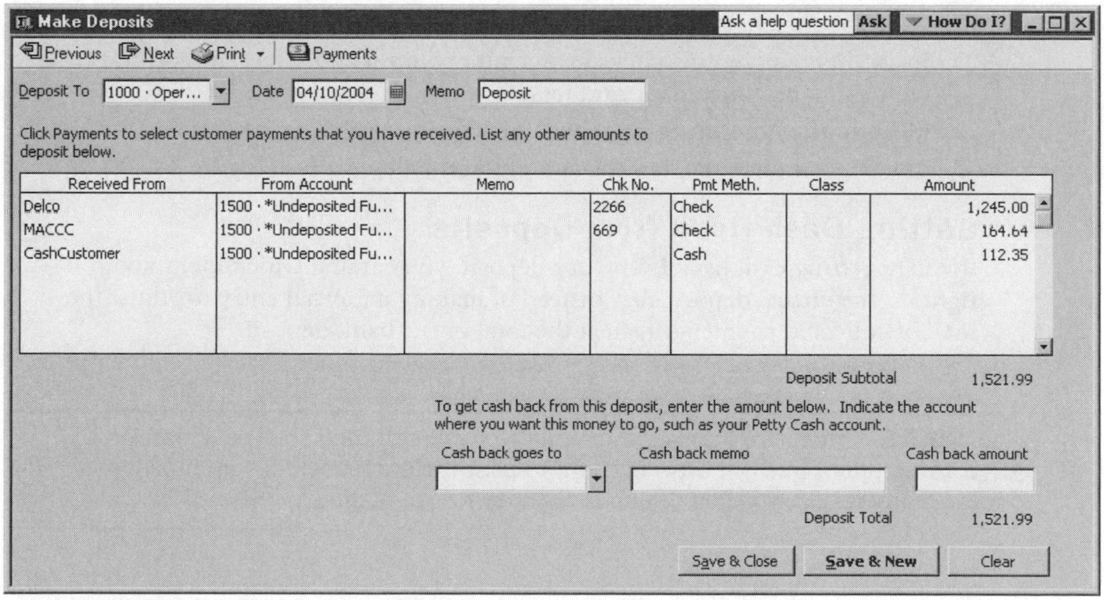

FIGURE 4-9 The Make Deposits window is a virtual bank deposit slip.

in your system. If the source of the check is a bank, or yourself, or any other entity that isn't a customer or vendor, use the Other Name classification for the type of name.

Press TAB to move to the From Account column and enter the account to which you're posting this transaction. For example, if the check you're depositing represents a bank loan, use the liability account for that bank loan (you can create it here by choosing <Add New> if you didn't think to set up the account earlier). If the check you're depositing represents an infusion of capital from you, use the owner's capital account in the Equity section of your chart of accounts. If the check is a refund for an expense (perhaps you overpaid someone, and they're returning money to you), post the deposit to that expense. Use the TAB key to move through the rest of the columns, which are self-explanatory.

Calculating Merchant Card Fees

If your merchant card bank deposits the gross amount of each transaction and charges your bank account for the total fees due at the end of the month, you don't have to do anything special to deposit credit card payments. You can deal with the fees when you reconcile your bank account.

If your merchant card bank deducts fees from transactions and deposits the net proceeds to your account, use the following steps to track credit card transactions and deposit the correct amount:

1. Select the credit card transactions in the Payments To Deposit window. These are gross amounts.
2. Click OK to move the deposits to the Make Deposits window.
3. In the first empty line, click the Account column and select the account to which you post merchant card fees.
4. Move to the Amount column and enter the fee as a negative number.
5. The deposit total matches the amount of the deposit (see Figure 4-10).

Getting Cash Back from Deposits

If you're getting cash back from your deposit, you can tell QuickBooks about it right on the virtual deposit slip, instead of making a journal entry to adjust the total of collected payments against the total of the bank deposit.

 N O T E : If you're keeping the money for yourself, and your business isn't a corporation, use the Draw account to post the cash back. If your business is a corporation, you can't keep the money for yourself.

Enter the account to which you're posting the cash (usually a petty-cash account); optionally, enter a memo as a note to yourself, and enter the amount

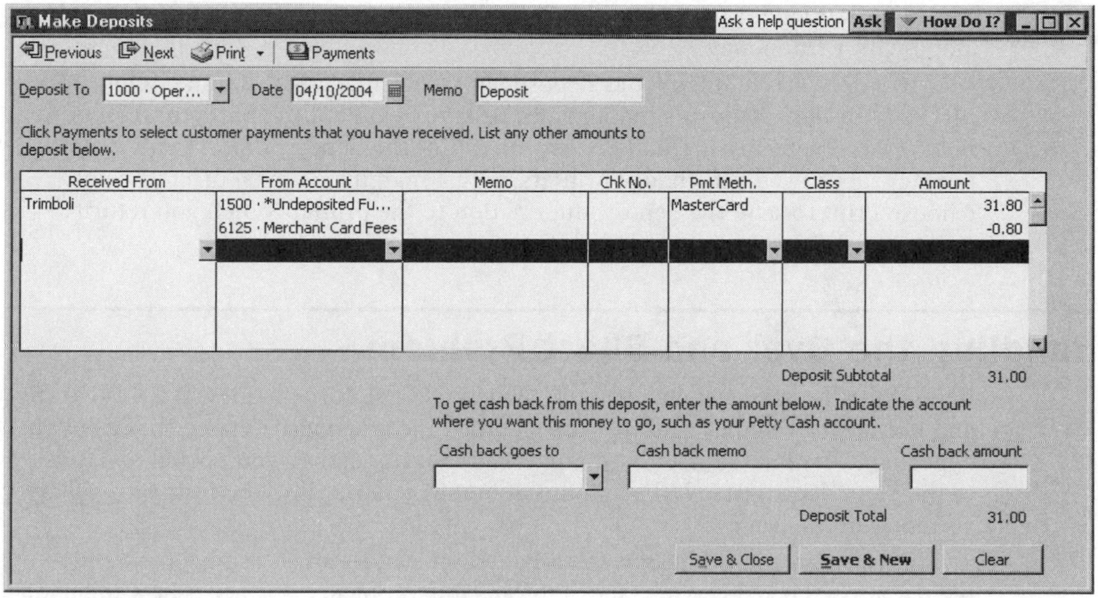

FIGURE 4-10 Deposit the correct amount and post your expenses for merchant card fees in one fell swoop.

of cash you want back from this deposit. Even though you can put the cash in your pocket, you must account for it, because these are business funds. As you spend the cash for business expenses, post the expense against a petty-cash account with a journal entry.

C A U T I O N : Many banks will not cash checks made out to a company, so your ability to get cash back may be limited to checks made out to you, personally.

Printing Deposit Slips

If you want to print a deposit slip or a deposit summary, click the Print button in the Make Deposits window. QuickBooks asks whether you want to print a deposit slip and summary, or just a deposit summary.

If you want to print a deposit slip that your bank will accept, you must order printable deposit slips from QuickBooks. Visit their website, which is at www.quickbooks.com/services/supplies/.

The QuickBooks deposit slips are guaranteed to be acceptable to your bank. You must have a laser printer or inkjet printer to use them. When you print the deposit slip, there's a tear-off section at the bottom of the page that has a deposit summary.

Keep that section for your own records and take the rest of the page to the bank along with your money.

If you don't have QuickBooks deposit slips, select Deposit Summary Only and fill out your bank deposit slip manually. Be sure to fill out the payment method field (cash or check), or QuickBooks won't print the deposit slip. A Print dialog box appears so you can change printers, adjust margins, or even print in color. Choose Print to send the deposit information to the printer. When you return to the Make Deposits window, click OK to save the deposit.

Handling the Over and Short Problem

If you literally take cash for cash sales, when you count the money in the till at the end of the day, you may find that the recorded income doesn't match the cash you expected to find in the till. Or you may find that the money you posted to deposit to the bank doesn't match the amount of money you put into the little brown bag you took to the bank.

This is a common problem with cash, and, in fact, it's an occasional problem in regular accrual bookkeeping. One of the ensuing problems you face is how to handle this in your bookkeeping system. QuickBooks is a double-entry bookkeeping system, which means the left side of the ledger has to be equal to the right side of the ledger. If you post $100.00 in cash sales, but only have $99.50 to take to the bank, how do you handle the missing 50 cents? You can't just post $100.00 to your bank account (well, you could, but your bank reconciliation won't work and, more importantly, you're not practicing good bookkeeping).

The solution to the Over/Short dilemma is to acknowledge it in your bookkeeping procedures. Track it. You'll be amazed by how much it balances itself out—short one day, over another. (Of course, if you're short every day, and the shortages are growing, you have an entirely different problem, and the first place to look is at the person who stands in front of the cash register.) To track Over/Short, you need to have some place to post the discrepancies, which means you have to create some new accounts in your chart of accounts.

Create two new accounts as follows:

1. Click the Accnt button on the icon bar to open the Chart of Accounts list.
2. Press CTRL-N to create a new account.
3. In the New Account window, select an account type of Income.
4. If you're using numbered accounts, choose a number that's on the next level from your regular Income accounts; for example, choose 4290 if your regular Income accounts are 4000, 4010, and so on.
5. Name the account "Over."
6. Click Next and repeat the processes, using the next number and naming the account "Short."

If you want to see a net number for Over/Short (a good idea), create three accounts: Name the first account (the parent account) "Over-Short," and then make the Over and Short accounts subaccounts of Over-Short.

In addition, you need items to use for your overages and shortages (remember, you need items for everything that's connected with entering invoices and cash sales). Create these new items as follows:

1. Click the Item button on the icon bar to open the Item List.
2. Press CTRL-N to create a new item.
3. Create a noninventory part item named "Overage."
4. Don't assign a price.
5. Make it nontaxable.
6. Link it to the account (or subaccount) named Over that you just created.
7. Click Next to create another new, noninventory part item.
8. Name this item "Short" and link it to the account (or subaccount) named Short.
9. Click OK to close the Items List window.

Now that you have the necessary accounts and items, use the Over and Short items right in the Sales Receipts window to adjust the difference between the amount of money you've accumulated in the cash-sale transactions and the amount of money you're actually depositing to the bank. It's your last transaction of the day. Remember to use a minus sign before the figure if you're using the Short item.

Tracking Accounts Receivable

n this chapter:

- Set up finance charges
- Send customer payment reminders
- Print customer statements
- Run A/R aging reports
- Use the Customer Centers

Collecting your money is one of the largest headaches in running a business. You have to track what's owed and who owes it, and then expend time and effort to collect it. All of the effort you spend on the money your customers owe you is called *tracking Accounts Receivable (A/R)*.

You can use finance charges as an incentive to pay on time, and you can track overdue invoices and then remind your customers to pay in gentle, or not-so-gentle, ways. In this chapter I go over the tools and features QuickBooks provides to help you track and collect the money your customers owe you.

Using Finance Charges

One way to speed up collections is to impose finance charges for late payments. Incidentally, this isn't "found money"; it probably doesn't cover its own cost. The amount of time spent tracking, analyzing, and chasing receivables is substantial, and in all businesses "time is money".

Configuring Finance Charges

To use finance charges, you have to establish the rate and circumstances under which they're assessed. Your company's finance charges are configured as part of your company preferences. Choose Edit | Preferences to open the Preferences window. Then click the Finance Charge icon in the left pane and select the Company Preferences tab (see Figure 5-1).

Here are some guidelines for filling out this window:

- Notice that the interest rate is annual. If you want to charge 1.5 percent a month, enter **18%** in the Annual Interest Rate field.
- You can assess a minimum finance charge for overdue balances. QuickBooks will calculate the finance charge, and if it's less than the minimum, the amount will be rolled up to the minimum charge you specify here.
- Use the Grace Period field to enter the number of days of lateness you permit before finance charges are assessed.
- During setup, QuickBooks probably created an account for finance charges. If so, it's displayed in this window. If not, enter (or create) the account you want to use to post finance charges (this is an income account).
- The issue of assessing finance charges on overdue finance charges is a sticky one. The practice is illegal in many states. Selecting this option means that a customer who owed $100.00 last month and had a finance charge assessed of $2.00 now owes $102.00. As a result, the next finance charge is assessed on a balance of $102.00 (instead of on the original overdue balance of $100.00). Regardless of state law, the fact is that very few businesses opt to use this calculation method.

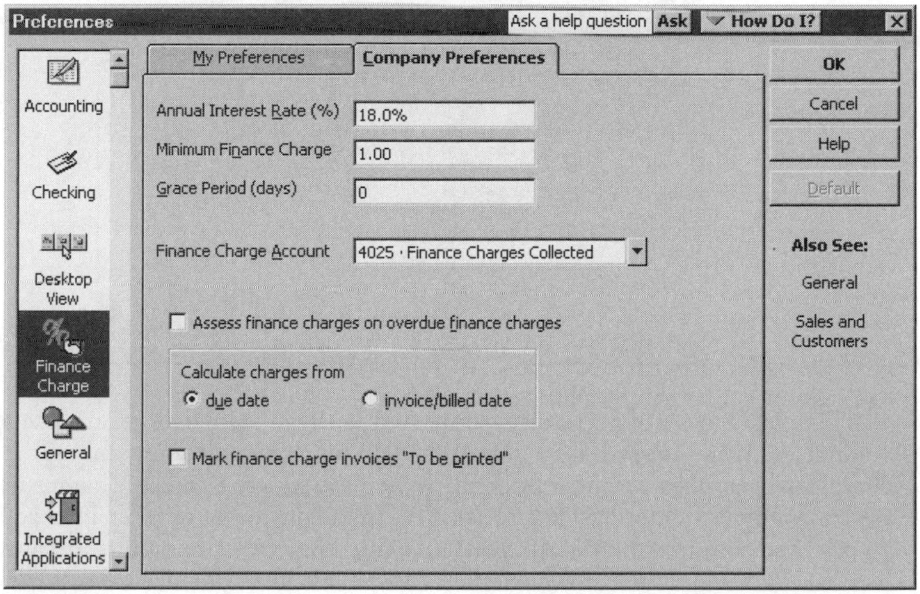

FIGURE 5-1 Configure the way in which you'll impose finance charges on overdue invoices.

- Specify whether to calculate the finance charge from the due date or the invoice date.
- QuickBooks creates an invoice when finance charges are assessed in order to have a permanent record of the transaction. By default, these invoices aren't printed; they're just accumulated along with the overdue invoices so they'll print out on a monthly statement. You can opt to have the finance charge invoices printed, which you should do only if you're planning to mail them to nudge your customers for payment.

Click OK to save your settings after you've filled out the window.

Assessing Finance Charges

You should assess finance charges just before you calculate and print customer statements. Choose Customers | Assess Finance Charges from the menu bar. The Assess Finance Charges window opens (see Figure 5-2), with a list of all the customers with overdue balances.

Before you see the window, if you have any customers that have made payments that you haven't yet applied to an invoice, or if any customers have credits that you haven't yet applied to an invoice, QuickBooks displays a message to that effect.

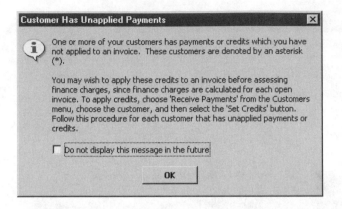

This message is not necessarily connected to the customers who are due to have finance charges assessed; it's a general statement that somewhere in your system there's an unapplied payment or credit. When the Assess Finance Charges window opens, if any customer has an asterisk next to the customer or job name, you have to pay attention to the message about unapplied payments or credits, because the asterisk indicates an affected customer. Close the Assess Finance Charges window and correct the situation, then return to this window.

Assess	Last FC	Customer	Overdue Bal.	Finance Charge
✓		AllensMusic	2,137.35	3.50
✓		Charity	675.00	8.99
✓		Delco	1,890.00	20.91
✓	03/31/2004	Kates	4,860.00	71.91
✓		SoftwareInstallation	945.00	13.51
✓		MACCC	810.00	9.59
✓	03/31/2004	NYCheeze	540.00	7.99
✓	03/31/2004	Trimboli	1,774.03	26.25
✓	03/31/2004	Village	726.80	10.76

Assess Finance Charges

Click the assess column for each customer for whom you wish to create a finance charge invoice.

Assessment Date: 04/30/2004
Template: Finance Charge   [Customize]

[Mark All] [Unmark All]   ☐ Mark Invoices "To be printed"

Customers with *s have payments or credit memos which have not been applied to any invoice. The overdue balance does not include these credits.

[Settings...] [Collection History]   [Assess Charges] [Cancel]

FIGURE 5-2   QuickBooks automatically assesses the finance charge as of the assessment date you enter.

Choosing the Assessment Date

Change the Assessment Date field to the date on which you want the finance charge to appear on customer statements. It's common to assess finance charges on the last day of the month. When you press TAB to move out of the date field, the finance charges are recalculated to reflect the new date.

Selecting the Customers

You can eliminate a customer from the process by clicking in the Assess column to remove the check mark. QuickBooks, unlike many other accounting software packages, does not have a finance charge assessment option on each customer record. Therefore, all customers with overdue balances are included when you assess finance charges. It can be time consuming to deselect each customer, so if you have only a few customers for whom you reserve this process, choose Unmark All, then reselect the customers you want to include.

Changing the Amounts

You can change the calculated total if you wish (a good idea if there are credit memos floating around that you're not ready to apply against any invoices). Just click the amount displayed in the Finance Charge column to activate that column for that customer. Then enter a new finance charge amount. If you need to calculate the new figure (perhaps you're giving credit for a floating credit memo), press the equal sign (=) on your keyboard to use the built-in QuickMath calculator.

Checking the History

To make sure you don't assess a charge that isn't really due, you can double-check by viewing a customer's history from the Assess Finance Charges window. Select a customer and click the Collection History button to see a Collections Report for the selected customer (see Figure 5-3). Your mouse pointer turns into a magnifying glass with the letter "z" (for "zoom") in it when you position it over a line item. Double-click any line item to display the original transaction window if you need to examine the details.

Saving the Finance Charge Invoices

Click Assess Charges in the Assess Finance Charges window when all the figures are correct. If you've opted to skip printing, there's nothing more to do. (If you chose to print the finance charges, see the next paragraph). When you create your customer statements, the finance charges will appear.

Selecting Printing Options

If you want to print the finance charge invoices (they really are invoices because they add charges to the customer balance), be sure to select the Mark Invoices To Be Printed check box on the Assess Finance Charges window. You can send the printed copies to your customers as a nagging reminder. If you just want the customer to see the finance charge on the monthly statement, deselect the printing option.

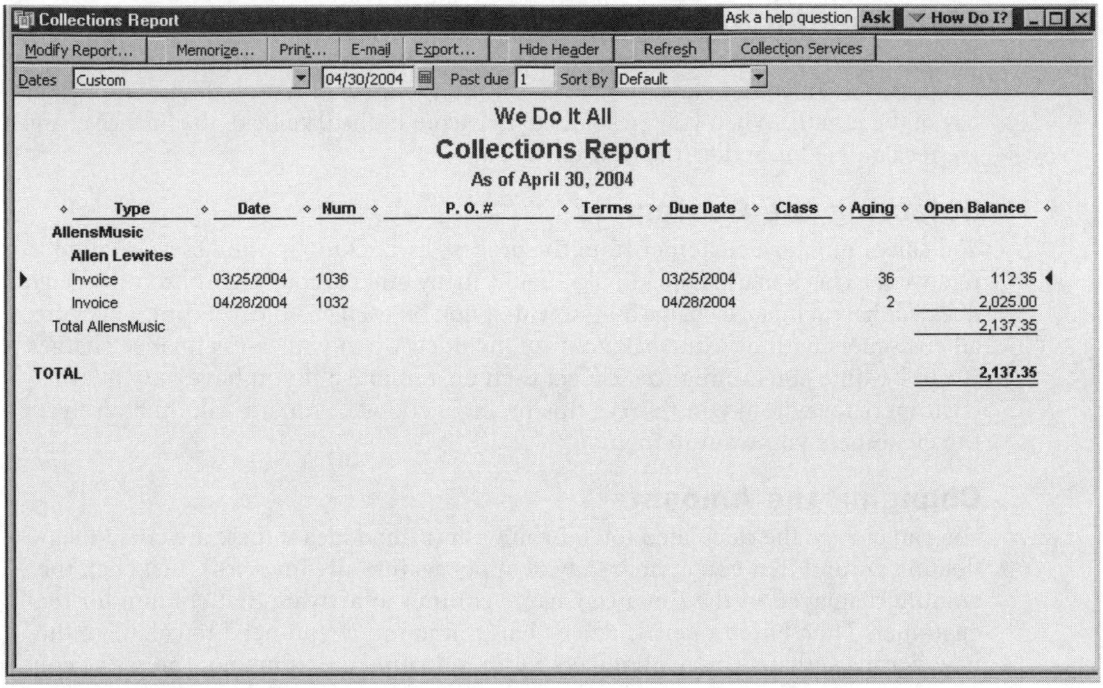

FIGURE 5-3   You can double-check transactions to make sure the finance charges are legitimate.

To print the finance charge invoices, choose File | Print Forms | Invoices. The list of unprinted invoices appears, and unless you have regular invoices you didn't print yet, the list includes only the finance charge invoices. If the list is correct, click OK to continue on to the printing process. Chapter 3 has detailed information about printing invoices.

Sending Statements

On a periodic basis, you should send statements to your customers. (Most businesses send statements monthly.) They serve a couple of purposes: they remind customers of outstanding balances, and they ensure that your records and your customers' records reflect the same information.

If you're coming to QuickBooks from a manual system, statements will seem like a miraculous tool, because creating statements from manual customer cards is a nightmare. As a result, companies without accounting software generally don't even bother to try.

Entering Statement Charges

A *statement charge* is a charge you want to pass to a customer for which you don't create an invoice. You can use statement charges for special charges for certain customers, such as a general overhead charge, or a charge you apply instead of using reimbursements for expenses incurred on behalf of the customer. You can also use statement charges for discounts for certain customers, such as reducing the total due by a specific amount instead of creating and applying discount rates or price levels. Some companies use statement charges instead of invoices for invoicing regular retainer payments.

You must add statement charges before you create the statements (or else the charges won't show up on the statements). Statement charges use items from your Item List, but you cannot use any of the following types of items:

- Items that are taxable
- Items that have percentage discounts
- Items that represent a payment transaction

Statement charges are recorded directly in a customer's register, or in the register for a specific job. You can reach the register to enter a statement charge in either of two ways:

- Choose Customers | Enter Statement Charges and then select the customer or job in the Customer:Job field at the top of the register that opens. (By default, QuickBooks opens the register for the first customer in your Customer:Job List.)
- Press CTRL-J to open the Customer:Job List, right-click the appropriate listing and choose Enter Statement Charges from the shortcut menu.

The Customer:Job register opens, as shown in Figure 5-4.

Use the TAB key to move through the register line as you perform the following steps:

1. Select the statement charge item from the Item drop-down list (or use <Add New> to create a new item).
2. Enter a quantity in the Qty field if the item is invoiced by quantity.
3. Enter a rate (or accept the default rate if one exists) if you're using the Qty field.
4. Enter the amount charged if the Qty and Rate fields aren't used (if they are, the total amount is entered automatically).
5. Optionally, edit the item description.
6. Enter the billed date, which does not have to match the transaction date in the first column of the register. Post-dating or predating this field determines which statement it appears on.

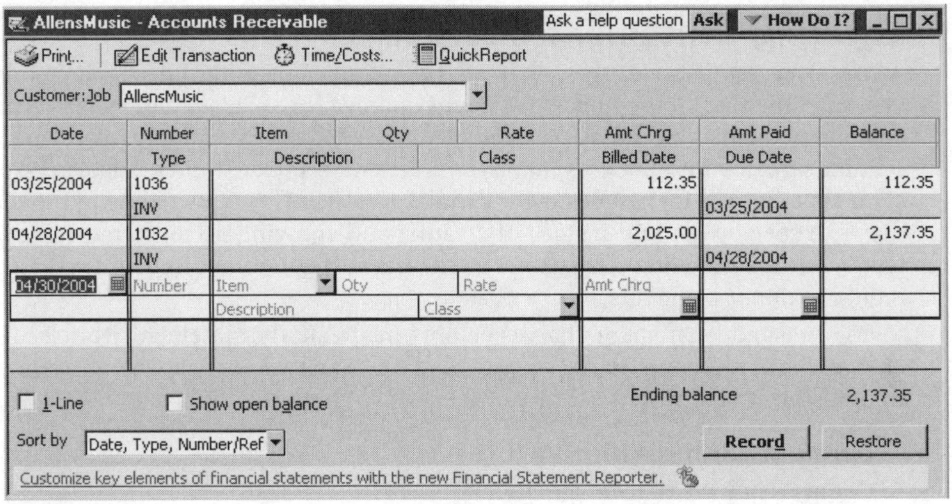

FIGURE 5-4 Statement charges are entered directly in a customer or job register.

7. Enter the due date, which affects your aging reports and your finance charge calculations.

8. Click Record to save the transaction.

If your statement charges are recurring charges, you can memorize them to have QuickBooks automatically create them. After you create each charge, right-click its listing in the register and select Memorize Stmt Charge from the shortcut menu. This works exactly like memorized invoices (covered in Chapter 3).

Creating Statements

Before you start creating your statements, be sure that all the transactions that should be included on the statements have been entered into the system. Did you forget anything? Credit memos? Payments? Finance charges? Statement charges?

Choose Customers | Create Statements from the menu bar to open the Create Statements window, shown in Figure 5-5.

Selecting the Date Range

The statement date range determines which transactions appear on the statement. The printed statement displays the previous balance (the total due before the starting date) and includes all transactions that were created within the date range. Your opening date should be the day after the last date of your last statement run. If you do monthly statements, choose the first and last days of the current month; if you send statements quarterly, enter the first and last dates of the current quarter—and so on.

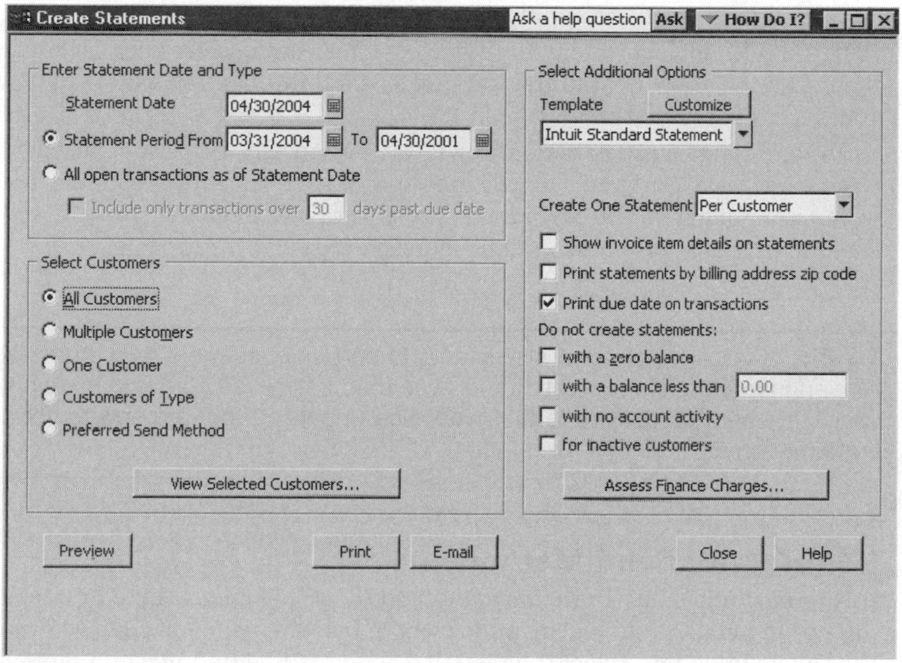

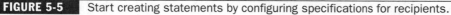

FIGURE 5-5   Start creating statements by configuring specifications for recipients.

If you choose All Open Transactions As Of Statement Date, the printed statement just shows unpaid invoices and charges and unapplied credits. You can narrow the criteria by selecting the option to include only transactions overdue by a certain number of days (which you specify). This makes the printed statement more of a list than a standard statement.

Selecting the Customers

It's normal procedure to send statements to all customers, but if that's not the plan, you can change the default selection.

If you want to send statements to a group of customers, click the Multiple Customers option to activate the Choose button that's next to it. Then click the Choose button to bring up a list of customers and select each customer you want to include. You can manually select each customer, or select Automatic and then enter text to tell QuickBooks to match that text against all customer names and select the matching customers.

TIP : Automatic selection is handy if you have a customer naming protocol that lets you group customers by type. For instance, if you decided to name all your retail customers with an R at the beginning of the name, you could filter by selecting all customers with names that start with R.

Click OK when all the appropriate customers are selected.

If you're sending a statement to one customer only, select One Customer, and then click the arrow next to the text box to scroll through the list of your customers and select the one you want.

To send statements to customers who are designated with a specific customer type, select the Customers Of Type option, and then select the customer type you want to include from the drop-down list. This works, of course, only if you created customer types as part of your QuickBooks setup.

 TIP: If you want to send statements to certain customers only, that's a good reason in itself to create a customer type (name the type "stmnts"). Then link your statement customers to that type. See Chapter 2 to learn how to set up customer types.

Filtering for Send Methods

If your customers vary in the way you send them statements (mail or e-mail), you can opt to handle your statement delivery in batches, using one delivery method per batch. To do this, select the Preferred Send Method option, and then select the send method for this batch. Note that there isn't any send method named Mail; that's what the None option is for.

NOTE: If you want to send statements by e-mail, you'll find instructions in Chapter 3.

Specifying the Printing Options

You can specify the way you want the statements to print, using the following criteria and options:

- You can print one statement for each customer, which lists all transactions for all that customer's jobs, or you can print a separate statement for each job.
- You can opt to show invoice item details instead of just listing the invoice on the statement. If your invoices have a lot of line items, this could make your statements very long (possibly too many pages to get away with a single postage stamp). I don't see any particular reason to select this option, because most customers have copies of the original invoices—if they don't, they'll call you with questions and you can look up the invoice number and provide details.

Printing statements in order by ZIP code is handy if you're printing labels that are sorted by ZIP code. This option is also important if you have a bulk mail permit, because the post office requires bulk mail to be sorted by ZIP code.

By default, the original due date for each transaction listed on the statement is displayed. If you have some reason to hide this information from your customers (I can't think of a good reason), you can deselect the option.

Specifying the Statements to Skip

You may want to skip statement printing for customers who meet the criteria you set in this part of the dialog. If you use statements only to collect money, selecting any of these options makes sense.

If, however, you use statements to make sure you and your customers have matching accounting records, you should create statements for all customers except inactive customers.

Last Call for Finance Charges

If you haven't assessed finance charges, and you want them to appear on the statements, click the Assess Finance Charges button. The Assess Finance Charges window opens, showing customers who have been selected for finance charges.

If you've already assessed finance charges, QuickBooks will warn you that finance charges have already been assessed as of the selected date. Unfortunately, if you ignore the message, QuickBooks is perfectly willing to add another round of finance charges (and you'll have a lot of angry and distrustful customers). Therefore, this window is useful only if you don't assess finance charges as described earlier in this chapter.

Previewing the Statements

Before you commit the statements to paper, you can click the Preview button to get an advance look (see Figure 5-6). This is not just to see what the printed output will look like; it's also a way to look at the customer records and to make sure that all the customers you selected are included.

Use the Zoom In button to see the statement and its contents close up. Click the Next Page button to move through all the statements. Click Close to return to the Create Statements window.

 T I P : If you see a statement that seems "funny," open a customer report to check the transactions.

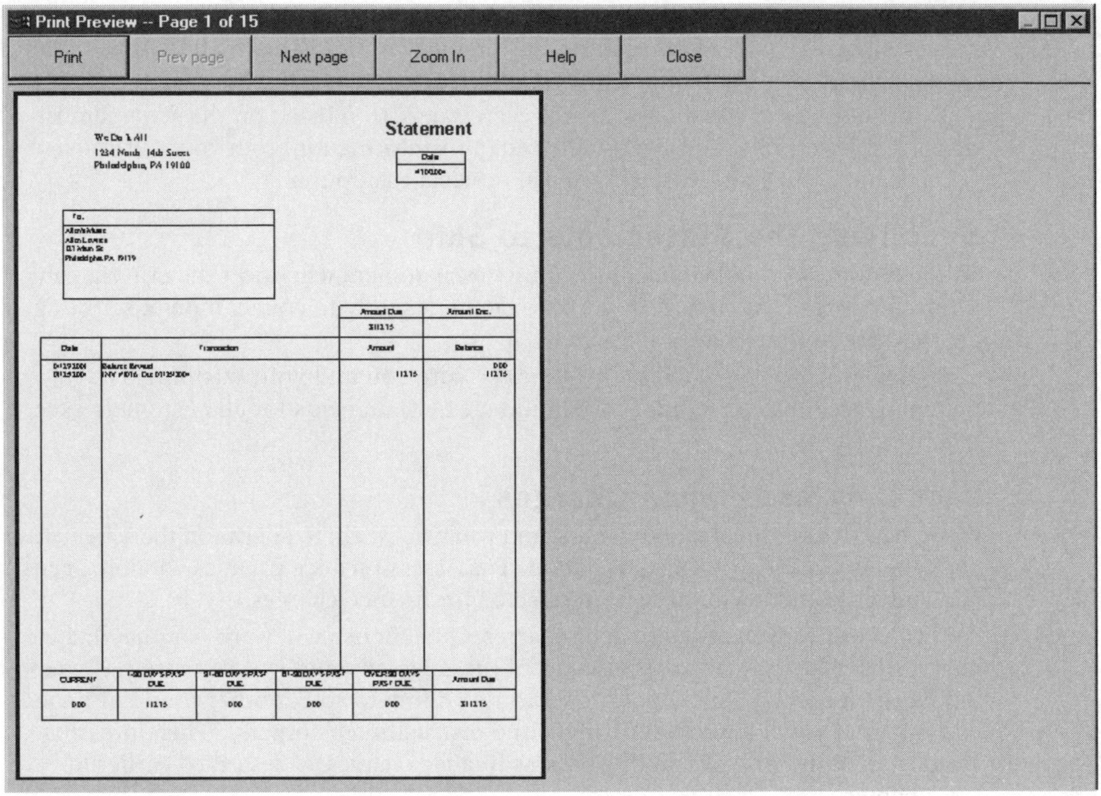

FIGURE 5-6   The Preview window provides a quick check before you send statements.

Printing the Statements

When everything is just the way it should be, print the statements by clicking the Print button in either the Print Preview window or the Create Statements window. If you click Close in the Preview window, you return to the Create Statements window—click Print to open the Print Statement(s) window. You change the printing options as needed.

Customizing Statements

You don't have to use the standard statement form—you can design your own. To accomplish this, in the original Create Statements window, click the Customize button to open the Customize Template window. Choose New in that window to open the Customize Statement window shown in Figure 5-7.

On the Fields tab, you might want to think about changing the following fields:

Terms   It's a good idea to select the Terms column title. It doesn't seem fair to tell a customer of amounts past due without reminding the customer of the terms.

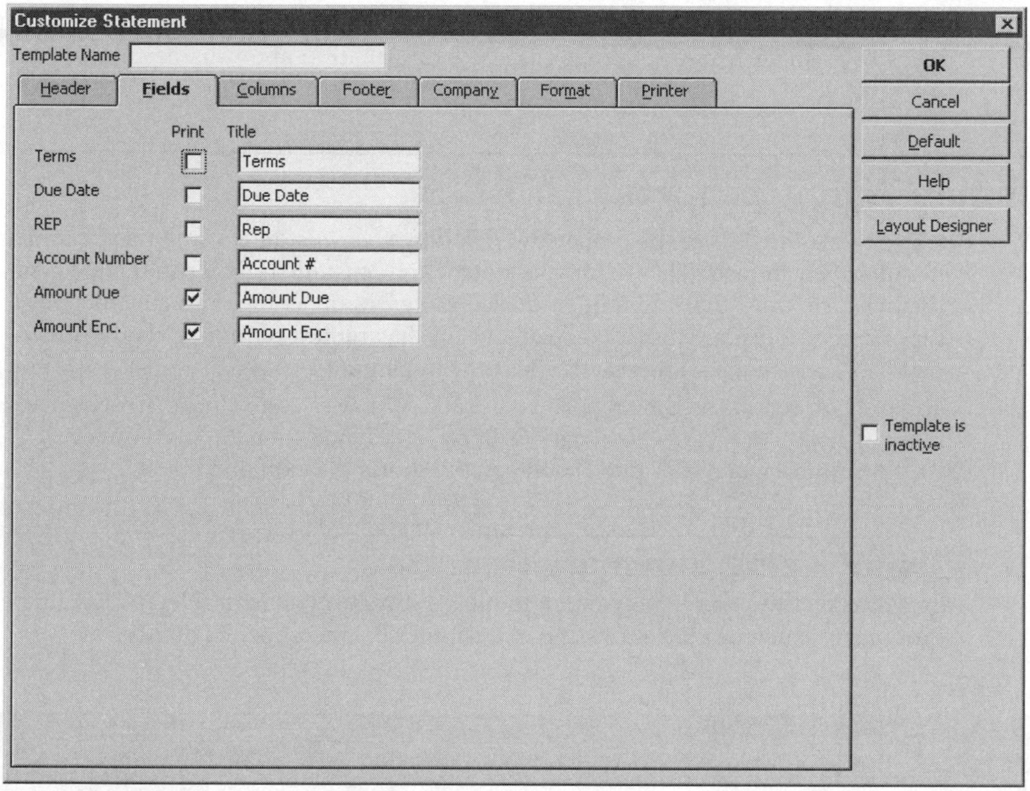

FIGURE 5-7 I move right to the Fields tab, because that's the common place to make changes.

Amount Due   This field isn't really necessary, because the same field and its data are positioned at the bottom of the statement page.

Amount Enc   If you use statements as bills, or expect payment for the amount of the statement, this field is supposed to contain an amount filled in by the customer. (The amount is supposed to match the amount of the check that's returned with the statement.) If you mail invoices and use statements as reminders (and your customers never send checks attached to the statements), deselect this field.

On the Footer tab, you can add text if you think there's anything to explain about the items on the statement. For example, if you create and list debit memos (see Chapter 4), you may want to explain what they are.

You must also supply a new name for this new template, because you cannot save the new design with the existing name. Click OK when you're finished.

When you add fields to a template, QuickBooks may issue a warning that the fields overlap existing fields. If you choose Relayout, QuickBooks will attempt to fit all the fields onto the top of the statement columns. If you choose Skip, the fields will overlap; you should then choose the Layout Designer in the Customize Statement window to make everything neat and tidy. Information about using the Layout Designer is in Chapter 3.

Running Aging Reports

Aging reports are lists of the money owed you by your customers, and they're available in quite a few formats. They're for you, not for your customers. You run them whenever you need to know the extent of your receivables. Many companies run an aging report every morning, just to keep an eye on the amount of money on the street.

A couple of aging reports are available in QuickBooks, and you can also customize any built-in reports so they report data exactly the way you want it. To see an aging report, choose Reports | Customers & Receivables, and then choose either A/R Aging Summary or A/R Aging Detail (these reports are explained next).

Using Aging Summary Reports

The quickest way to see how much money is owed to you is to select A/R Aging Summary, which produces a listing of customer balances (see Figure 5-8).

	Current	1 - 30	31 - 60	61 - 90	> 90	TOTAL
AllensMusic	20.00	0.00	2,025.00	112.35	0.00	2,157.35
BigTime						
Equipment&Install	0.00	0.00	0.00	0.00	-100.00	-100.00
Total BigTime	0.00	0.00	0.00	0.00	-100.00	-100.00
Charity	0.00	104.00	675.00	0.00	0.00	779.00
Crows	0.00	5,216.47	0.00	0.00	0.00	5,216.47
Delco	0.00	0.00	1,890.00	0.00	0.00	1,890.00
Kates						
SoftwareInstallation	0.00	0.00	945.00	0.00	0.00	945.00
Kates - Other	0.00	0.00	0.00	511.56	4,860.00	5,371.56
Total Kates	0.00	0.00	945.00	511.56	4,860.00	6,316.56
MACCC	0.00	0.00	810.00	0.00	0.00	810.00
NYCheeze	0.00	0.00	0.00	102.53	540.00	642.53
Trimboli	0.00	0.00	0.00	318.46	1,774.03	2,092.49
Village	0.00	0.00	0.00	96.57	726.80	823.37
TOTAL	**20.00**	**5,320.47**	**6,345.00**	**1,141.47**	**7,800.83**	**20,627.77**

FIGURE 5-8 A/R totals for each customer appear in the Aging Summary report.

Let's pause a moment and talk about the importance of the number for that A/R asset. After all, banks give lines of credit and loans using the A/R balance as collateral.

When your accountant visits, you can bet one of the things he or she will ask to see is this report. When your accountant asks for an aging report, another safe bet is that you'll receive a request to see the amount posted to A/R in your general ledger. The general ledger A/R balance and the total on the aging report must be the same (for the same date)—not close, not almost, but *exactly* the same. If the figures are not identical, your general ledger isn't "proved" (jargon for, "I'm sorry, we can't trust your general ledger figures because they don't audit properly").

Using Aging Detail Reports

If you choose Aging Detail from the Accounts Receivable reports menu, you see a much more comprehensive report, such as the one seen in Figure 5-9. The report is sorted by aging interval, showing individual transactions, including finance charges, for each aging period.

Type	Date	Num	P. O. #	Name	Terms	Due Date	Class	Aging
1 - 30								
Invoice	05/03/2004	1037		Charity		05/03/2004		28
Invoice	04/30/2004	1033		Crows	Net30	05/30/2004		1
Total 1 - 30								
31 - 60								
Invoice	04/01/2004	1034		Kates:SoftwareIns...		04/01/2004		60
Invoice	04/03/2004	1038		Delco		04/03/2004		58
Invoice	04/03/2004	1039		Charity		04/03/2004		58
Invoice	04/06/2004	1040		MACCC		04/06/2004		55
Invoice	04/19/2004	1041		Delco		04/19/2004		42
Invoice	04/28/2004	1032		AllensMusic		04/28/2004		33
Total 31 - 60								
61 - 90								
Invoice	03/25/2004	1036		AllensMusic		03/25/2004		67
Invoice	03/31/2004	FC 1		Kates		03/31/2004		61
Invoice	03/31/2004	FC 2		NYCheeze		03/31/2004		61
Invoice	03/31/2004	FC 3		Trimboli		03/31/2004		61

FIGURE 5-9 Scroll through the report to see detailed information about the money owed to you.

Customizing Aging Reports

If you don't use (or care about) all of the columns in the aging detail report, or you'd prefer to see the information displayed in a different manner, you can customize the report. Start by clicking the Modify Report button on the report to see the Modify Report window shown in Figure 5-10.

Customizing the Columns

The most common customization is to get rid of any column you don't care about. For example, if you use the classes feature, but don't care about that information in your aging report, get rid of the column. Or you might want to get rid of the Terms column since it doesn't impact the totals. To remove a column, scroll through the list of columns and click to remove the check mark. The column disappears from the report.

While you're looking at the list of column names, you may find a column heading that's not currently selected but that contains information you'd like to include in your report. If so, click that column listing to place a check mark next to it. The column appears on the report and the data linked to it is displayed.

Filtering Information

If you want to produce an aging report for a special purpose, you can easily filter the information that appears so that it meets criteria important to you. To filter your aging report, click the Filters tab (see Figure 5-11).

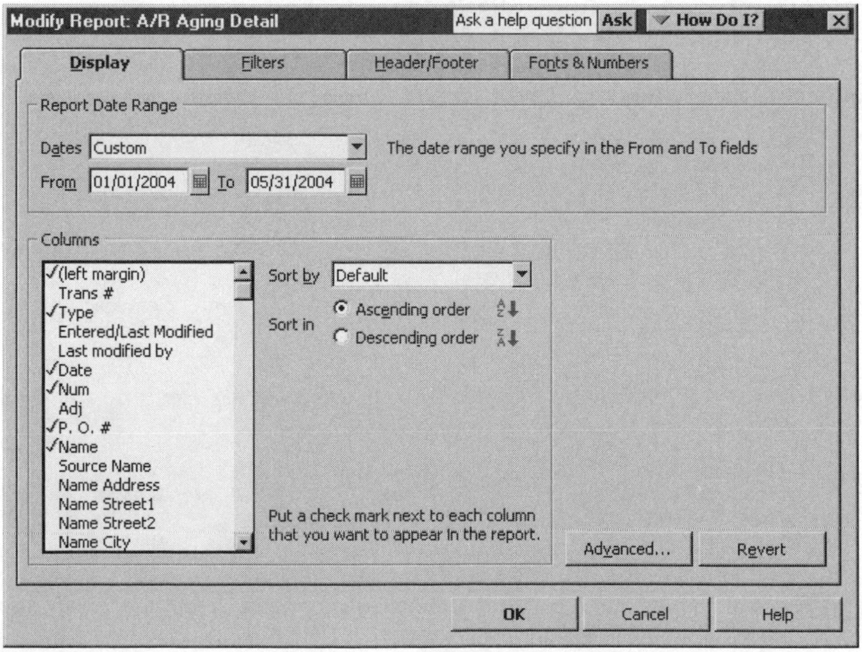

FIGURE 5-10   Customize aging reports to get exactly the information you need.

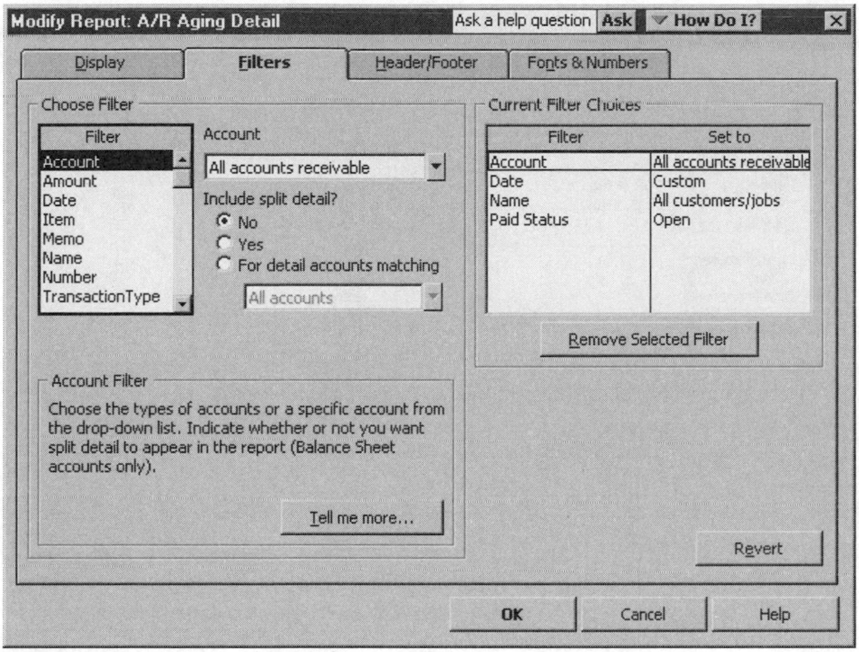

FIGURE 5-11 Filters let you specify the criteria for displaying data.

Select a filter and then set the limits for it. (Each filter has its own specific type of criteria.) For example, you can use this feature if you want to see only those customers with receivables higher than a certain figure, or older than a certain aging period

Configuring Header/Footer Data

You can customize the text that appears in the header and footer of the report by making changes in the Header/Footer tab shown in Figure 5-12.

You'll probably find that your decisions about the contents of the header and footer depend on whether you're viewing the report or printing it. And, if you're printing it, some stuff is more important if an outsider (a banker or your accountant) will be the recipient of the report, rather than your credit manager.

For example, the date and time of preparation is more important for outsiders than for you. That reminds me, on the Header/Footer tab, the Date Prepared field has a meaningless date—don't panic, your computer hasn't lost track of the date. That date is a format, not today's date. Click the arrow to the right of the field to see the other formats for inserting the date. The Page Number field also has a variety of formats to choose from.

You can remove fields by removing the check mark from the check box. For fields you want to print, you can change the text. You can also change the layout by choosing a different Alignment option from the drop-down list.

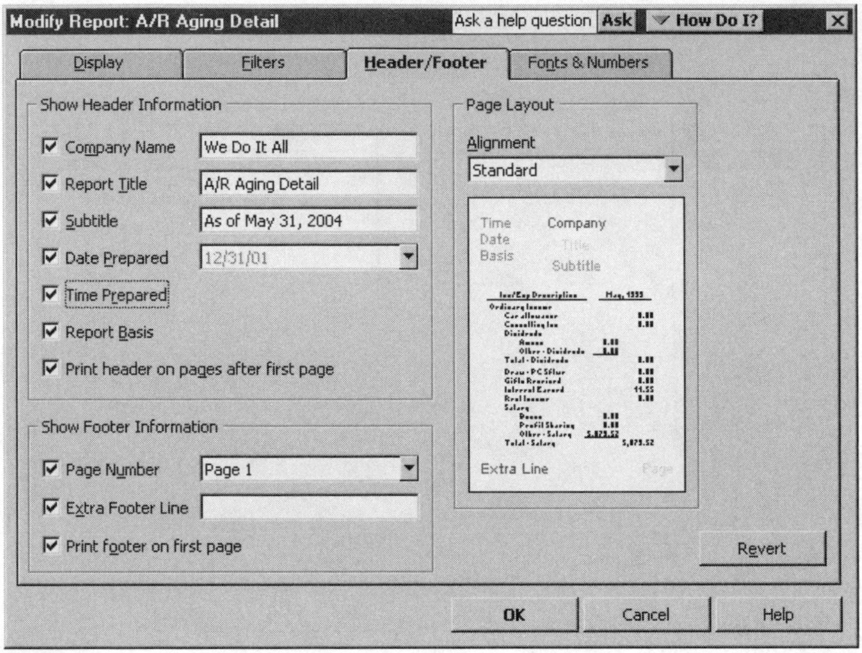

FIGURE 5-12 Decide on the text you want to see at the top and bottom of the report.

Customizing the Appearance

Click the Fonts & Numbers tab (which looks like Figure 5-13) to change the format of the report.

You can change the way negative numbers are displayed, and you can change the fonts for any or all the individual elements in the report.

When you close the report window, QuickBooks asks if you want to memorize the report with the changes you made. Click Yes so you don't have to go through all the modifications again (see the next section on memorizing reports).

Memorizing Aging Reports

If you've customized a report and have the columns, data, and formatting you need, there's no reason to reinvent the wheel the next time you need the same information. Instead of going through the customization process again next month, memorize the report as you designed it. Then you can fetch it whenever you need it.

Click the Memorize button in the report window. When the Memorize Report window appears, enter a new name for the report, optionally save it within a report group, and click OK.

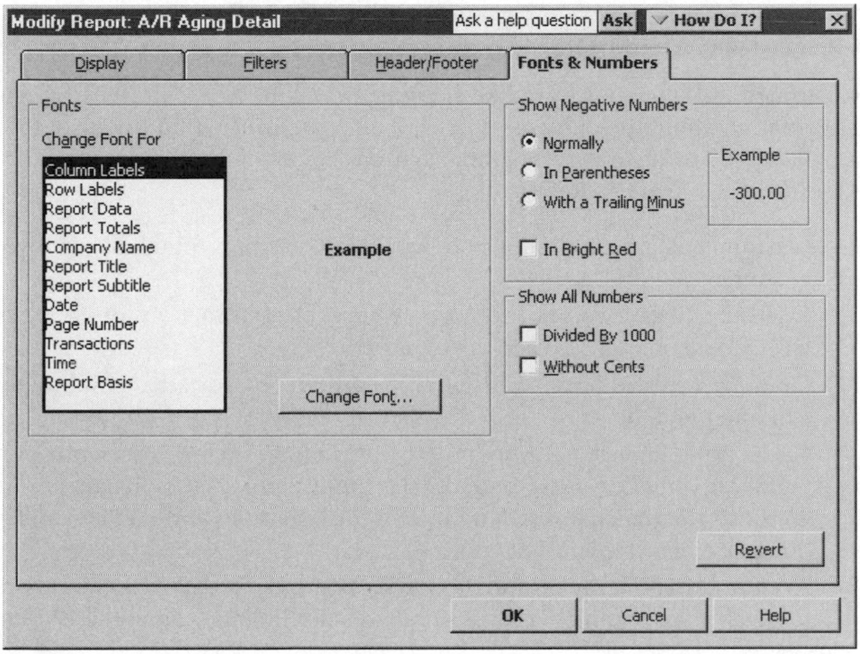

FIGURE 5-13   Change the look of the report by modifying the options in the Fonts & Numbers tab.

From now on, this report name will be on the list of memorized reports you can select from when you choose Reports | Memorized Reports from the menu bar.

N O T E : When you use a memorized report, only the criteria and formatting is memorized. The data is generated from the QuickBooks transaction records, so you get current, accurate information.

Printing Reports

Whether you're using the standard format or one you've customized, you'll probably want to print the report. When you're in a report window, click the Print button at the top of the window to bring up the Print Reports window. If the report is wide, use the Margins tab to set new margins, and use the options on the Settings tab to customize other printing options.

Running Customer and Job Reports

Customer and job reports are like aging reports, but they're designed to give you information about the customers instead of concentrating on financial totals. There are plenty of customer reports available from the menu that appear when you choose Reports | Customers & Receivables:

- **Customer Balance Summary Report**   Lists current total balance owed for each customer.
- **Customer Balance Detail Report**   Lists every transaction for each customer, with a net subtotal for each customer.
- **Open Invoices Report**   Lists all unpaid invoices, sorted and subtotaled by customer and job.
- **Collections Report**   A nifty report for nagging. Includes the contact name and telephone number, along with details about invoices with balances due. You're all set to call the customer and have a conversation, and you can answer any questions about invoice details.
- **Accounts Receivable Graph**   Shows a graphic representation of the accounts receivable. For a quick impression, there's nothing like a graph (see Figure 5-14).

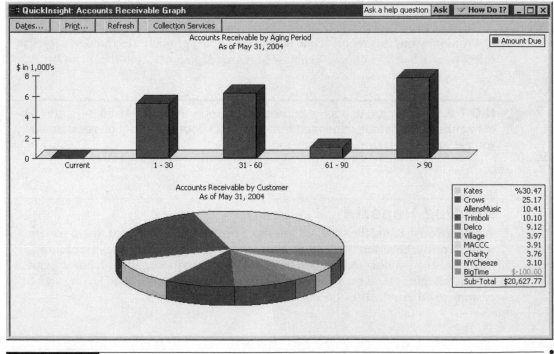

FIGURE 5-14   Get a bird's eye view of your receivables with a graph.

- **Unbilled Costs By Job** Tracks job expenses you haven't invoiced.
- **Transaction List By Customer** Displays individual transactions of all types for each customer.
- **Customer Phone List** Displays an alphabetical list of customers along with the telephone number for each (if you entered the telephone number in the customer record).
- **Customer Contact List** Displays an alphabetical list of customers along with the telephone number, billing address, and current open balance for each. Give this list to the person in charge of collections.
- **Item Price List** Lists all your items with their prices and preferred vendors.

Viewing Data in Customer Centers

QuickBooks provides windows, called Customer Centers, that display data about your customers, their balances, and other important information. You can examine the data for your customers as a group in the Customer Center and information about each individual customer is available in the Customer Detail Center.

Customer Center

To see a summary overview of the current state of your customers, choose Customers | Customer Center to open the Customer Center window seen in Figure 5-15.

The upper-right quadrant (Decision Tools) of the Customer Center window has links to information and tools. The other sections of the Customer Center display financial information about your customers, and include the following tools:

- A date range field with an arrow next to the label. Click the arrow to select a different date range for the displayed data.
- An Activities field with an arrow next to the label. Click the arrow to accomplish a task or view a report related to the data in that quadrant.

The bottom quadrants have a Show field that offers a menu of information categories (see the section "Changing the Categories").

Viewing Open Balances

The section labeled Customers With Open Balances displays accounts receivable information for each customer, as of the current date. A high number is not necessarily a reason to be concerned about late payments, because this figure includes the current period. Double-click any listing to see the details behind the number.

Viewing Information About Specific Categories

The Show sections in the lower part of the Customer Center window display specific information about your customers. By default, the lower-left quadrant displays current

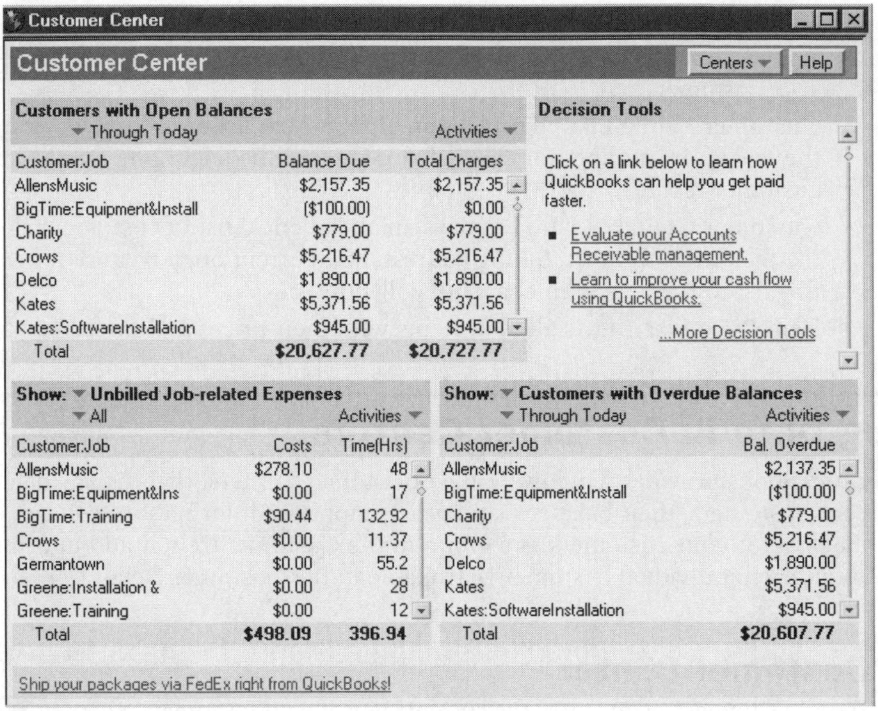

FIGURE 5-15 The Customer Center displays customer balances and other financial data.

unbilled job-related expenses (if you've enabled that feature, which is discussed in Chapter 6). Double-click any listing to see the details behind the number.

The lower-right quadrant displays overdue balances as of the current date, and you can change the date range to examine the numbers from a different date perspective. Double-click any listing to see the details behind the number.

Changing the Categories

You can change the data category for either of the lower sections by clicking the arrow next to the Show label.

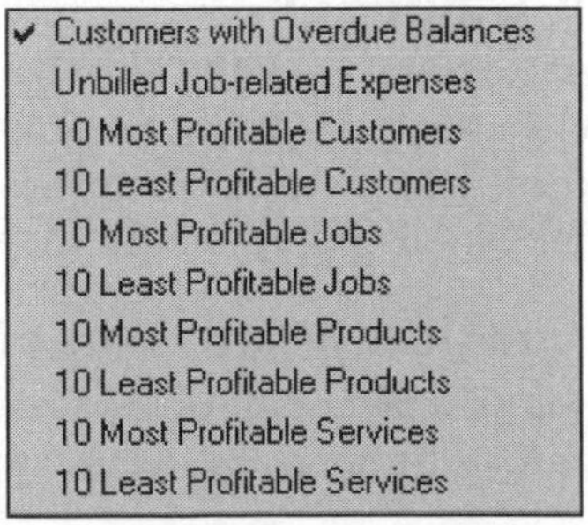

> ✓ Customers with Overdue Balances
> Unbilled Job-related Expenses
> 10 Most Profitable Customers
> 10 Least Profitable Customers
> 10 Most Profitable Jobs
> 10 Least Profitable Jobs
> 10 Most Profitable Products
> 10 Least Profitable Products
> 10 Most Profitable Services
> 10 Least Profitable Services

The choices are the same in both Show sections of the window, so you can view two categories at once. For example, it might be interesting to view your most profitable customers next to your most profitable services or products, and then view the details to see if there's a connection. You may find that some of the most profitable customers aren't necessarily purchasing the most profitable products, but are instead profitable because your costs were decreased by invoicing those customers for expenses. This might warrant a discussion with those customers with whom you don't have an agreement for reimbursing expenses—and certainly this information should influence the way you approach agreements with new customers.

Compare Information by Date Range

If you compare customer figures between separate date ranges, choose the same category in both of the bottom quadrants and change the date range in one quadrant. This is a good way to see if you have a "busy season," which is useful information when you're planning for part-time hires, using subcontractors, or buying products in larger amounts to take advantage of volume discounts. On the other hand, discovering a pattern of a "slow" season lets you plan your own vacation without worrying that your absence will cause problems (most of us who are small business owners believe the business will collapse if we're not in the office).

Customer Detail Center

The Customer Detail Center puts everything QuickBooks knows about a given customer into one place. Choose Customers | Customer Detail Center to open this window, and choose a customer from the drop-down list at the top of the window. Basic data about the customer is displayed, as seen in Figure 5-16.

The customer's contact information appears at the top of the center, and you can view, add, or change information by clicking Edit/More Info.

The two sections at the bottom of the window display current open balances and recently received payments and credits. As in the Customer Center, clicking the arrow next to the Show label displays a list of the available categories of information. However, the only additional item is Outstanding Items On Order, and that category is only available if you've enabled inventory tracking.

> **TIP:** If you have a lot of money on the street, you can speed up collections by sending letters targeted to customers according to their degree of lateness. QuickBooks automates this process, which requires Microsoft Word. You can learn about collection letters in Appendix B.

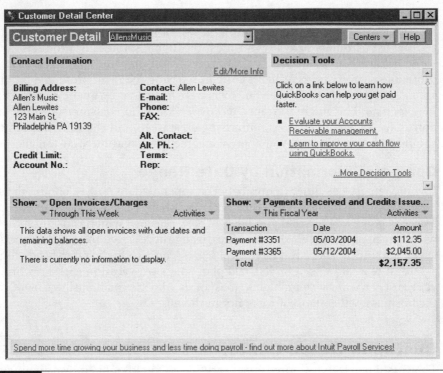

FIGURE 5-16 Take a close-up look at customer data in the Customer Detail Center.

Entering Accounts Payable Bills

In *this chapter:*

- Enter vendor bills

- Track reimbursable expenses

- Enter inventory item purchases

- Use purchase orders

- Enter vendor credit memos

- Enter recurring bills

Entering your bills and then paying them through QuickBooks is *accrual accounting*. That means an expense is posted to your Profit & Loss statement when you enter the bill, not when you actually pay the bill. The total of unpaid bills is the amount posted to the Accounts Payable account. However, if your taxes are filed on a cash basis (an expense isn't posted until you pay the bill), be assured (and assure your accountant) that QuickBooks understands how to report your financial figures on a cash basis. (See Chapter 15 for information on financial reports.)

Recording Vendor Bills

When the mail arrives, after you open all the envelopes that contain checks from customers (I always do that first), you should tell QuickBooks about the bills that arrived. Don't worry—QuickBooks doesn't automatically pay them. You decide when to do that.

To enter your bills, click the Bill icon on the Icon Bar, or choose Vendors | Enter Bills from the menu bar.

When the Enter Bills window opens (see Figure 6-1), you can fill out the information from the bill you received. The window has two sections: the heading section, which contains information about the vendor and the bill, and the details section, which records the data related to your general ledger accounts. The details section has two tabs: Expenses and Items. In this section, I'll cover bills that

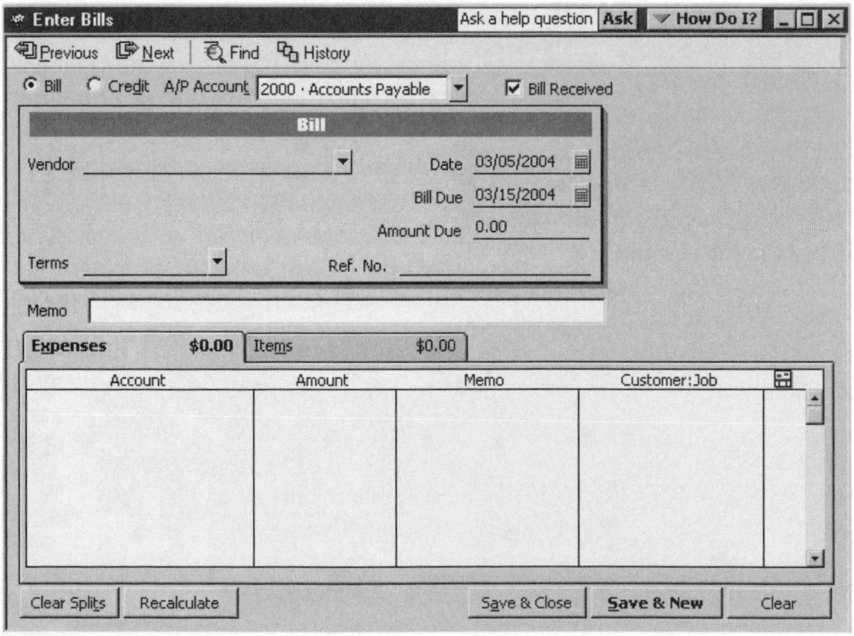

FIGURE 6-1 The Enter Bills window has a heading section and a details section.

are posted to Expenses; the Items are covered later in this chapter when I cover purchasing inventory items.

> $ **N O T E :** The Accounts Payable Account field appears in the heading section only if you have multiple Accounts Payable accounts.

Depending on the bill, you may be able to assign the entire bill to one expense account, or you may have to split the bill among multiple expense accounts. For example, your utility bills are usually posted to the appropriate utility account (electric, heat, and so on). However, credit card bills may be split among numerous expenses.

Easy One-Account Posting

In the Vendor field, click the arrow to choose this vendor from the list that appears. If the vendor isn't on the list, choose <Add New> to add this vendor to your QuickBooks vendor list. Then fill out the rest of the bill as follows:

1. Enter the bill date. The bill due date fills in automatically, depending on the terms you have with this vendor. You can change this date if you wish. (If you didn't set up terms for this vendor, the due date is automatically filled out using the default number of days for paying bills. QuickBooks sets this at 10 days, but you can change it by choosing Edit | Preferences and going to the Purchases & Vendors section.)

2. Enter the amount due.

3. Enter the vendor's invoice number in the Ref. No. field.

4. In the Terms field, click the arrow to display a list of terms, and select the one you need. If the terms you have with this vendor aren't available, choose <Add New to create a new Terms entry. The due date changes to reflect the terms.

5. When you click in the Account column, an arrow appears. Click the arrow to display your chart of accounts. Select the account to which this bill is assigned. QuickBooks automatically assigns the amount you entered in the Amount Due field

6. If you wish, enter a note in the Memo column.

7. In the Customer:Job column, enter a customer or job if you're paying a bill that you want to track for job costing, or if this bill is a reimbursable expense. See the discussions on tracking and charging customers for expenses later in this chapter

8. If you're tracking classes, a Class column appears; enter the appropriate class.

9. When you're finished, click Save & New to save this bill and bring up another blank Enter Bills window. When you've entered all your bills, click Save & Close.

Splitting Expenses Among Multiple Accounts

Some bills aren't neatly assigned to one account in your general ledger; instead, they're split among multiple accounts. The most common example is a credit card bill.

Here's how to split a bill among multiple general ledger accounts:

1. Follow the first four steps in the instructions for entering bills in the previous section.
2. Click in the Account column to display the arrow you use to see your chart of accounts.
3. Select the first account to which you want to assign some portion of this bill.
4. If you've entered an amount in the Amount Due field on the bill heading, QuickBooks automatically applies the entire amount of the bill in the Amount column. Replace that data with the amount you want to assign to the account you selected.
5. Click in the Account column to select the next account and enter the appropriate amount in the Amount column.

As you add each additional account to the column, QuickBooks assumes that the unallocated amount is assigned to that account (see Figure 6-2). Repeat the process of changing the amount and adding another account until the split transaction is completely entered.

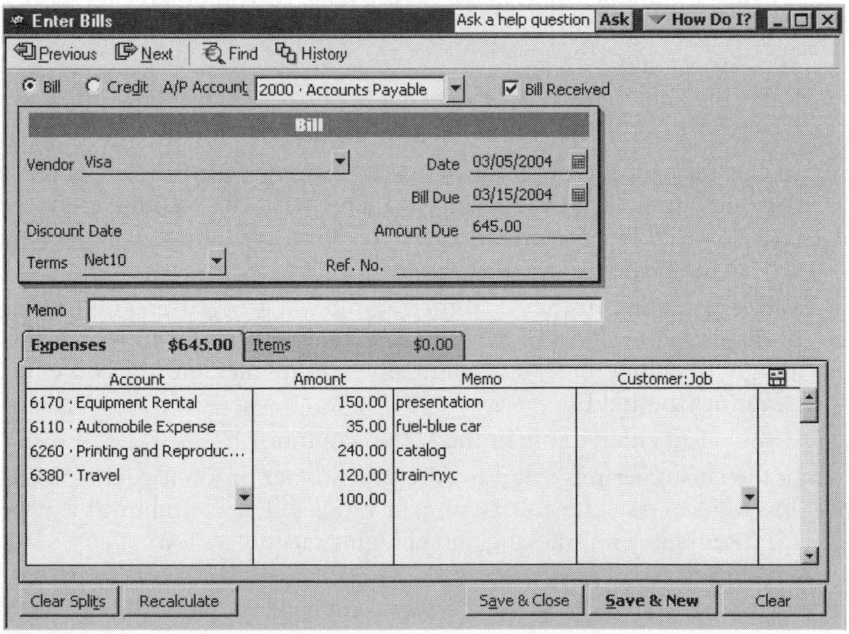

FIGURE 6-2 QuickBooks keeps recalculating, so the last account posting entry you make automatically has the correct amount.

Reimbursable Expenses

A reimbursable expense is one that you incurred on behalf of a customer. Even though you pay the vendor bill, there's an agreement with your customer that you'll send an invoice to recover your costs. There are two common types of reimbursable expenses:

- General expenses, such as long-distance telephone charges, parking and tolls, and other incidental expenses, are incurred on behalf of a client. Those portions of the vendor bill that apply to customer agreements for reimbursement are split out when you enter the bill.
- Specific goods or services are purchased on behalf of the customer.

Options for Managing Reimbursable Expenses

You have two ways to manage reimbursable expenses:

- Pay the bill, post it to an expense, and then let QuickBooks automatically post the customer's reimbursement to the same expense account. This cancels the original expense and reduces the expense total in your Profit & Loss statements.
- Pay the bill and then let QuickBooks automatically post the customer's reimbursement to an income account that's created for posting reimbursements. This lets you track totals for both the expense and the reimbursement (so you can see if they're equal).

You may want to discuss these choices with your accountant, but many businesses prefer the second option—tracking the expenses and reimbursements separately—just because it's more accurate. I'll therefore go over the steps you have to take to configure reimbursement tracking, and you can ignore them if you don't mind reducing your expense totals.

Configuring Reimbursement Tracking

To track reimbursed costs from customers, you need to enable reimbursement tracking in QuickBooks and create income accounts that are used for collecting reimbursements.

Enable Reimbursement Tracking

To tell QuickBooks that you want to track reimbursable costs, you must enable the feature in the Preferences dialog box, using the following steps:

1. Choose Edit | Preferences to open the Preferences dialog.
2. Select the Sales & Customers icon in the left pane.
3. Click the Company Preferences tab.
4. Click the check box next to the option labeled Track Reimbursed Expenses As Income to put a check mark in the box.
5. Click OK.

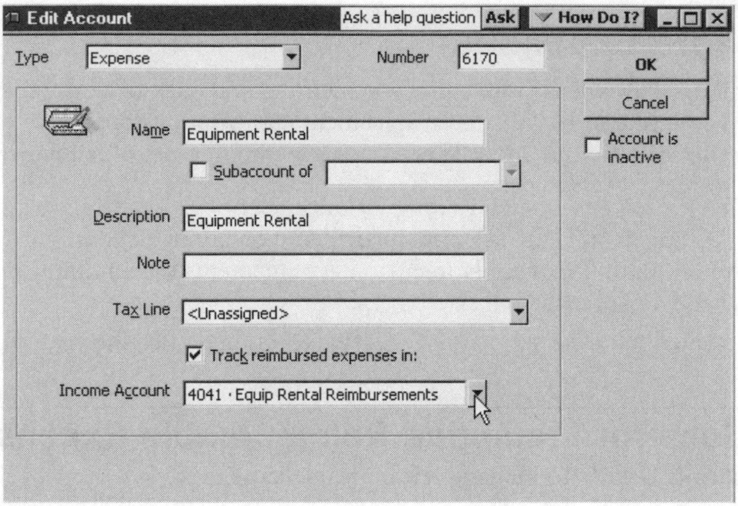

FIGURE 6-3 QuickBooks automatically posts reimbursements for this expense account to an income account.

As a result of enabling this option, QuickBooks adds a new field to the dialog box you use to create or edit expense accounts. As you can see in Figure 6-3, you can configure an expense account to post reimbursements to an income account. Whenever you post a vendor expense to this account and also indicate that the expense is reimbursable, the amount you charge to the customer when you create an invoice for that customer is automatically posted to the income account that's linked to this expense account.

Set Up Income Accounts for Reimbursement

You may have numerous expense accounts that you want to use for reimbursable expenses; in fact, that's the common scenario. Portions of telephone bills, travel expenses, subcontractor expenses, and so on are frequently passed on to customers for reimbursement.

The easiest way to manage all of this is to enable those expense accounts to track reimbursements, and post the income from customers to one account. After all, it's only important to know how much of your total income was a result of reimbursements (separating that income from the income you generate as the result of sales).

Alas, QuickBooks doesn't approach this with the logic inherent in this paradigm. Instead, the software insists on a one-to-one relationship between a reimbursable expense and the reimbursement income from that expense. As a result, if you have multiple expense accounts for which you may receive reimbursement (a highly likely scenario), you must also create multiple income accounts for accepting reimbursed expenses.

This is a one-time chore, however, so when you've finished setting up the accounts, you can just enter transactions, knowing QuickBooks will automatically post reimbursed expenses to your new income accounts.

Because you probably only care about totals for income received as reimbursement, the best way to set up the income accounts you'll need is to use subaccounts. That way, your reports will show the total amount of income due to reimbursed expenses, and you can ignore the individual account totals unless you have some reason to audit a number.

Depending on the company type you selected during the EasyStep Interview, QuickBooks may have already created a Reimbursed Expenses account in the Income section of your chart of accounts. If so, you already have a parent account, and you can skip this section on setting up the account and move directly to the instructions for creating subaccounts.

Here's the most efficient way to set up your income accounts to track reimbursements:

1. Open the chart of accounts by clicking the Accnt icon on the toolbar, or by pressing CTRL-A.
2. Press CTRL-N to open a New Account window.
3. Select Income as the account type.
4. Enter an account number (if you use numbers) and name the account Reimbursed Expenses (or something similar).
5. Click OK.

You've created the parent account—now create the subaccounts as follows:

1. Press CTRL-N to open the New Account window.
2. Select Income as the account type.
3. If you're using numbered accounts, use the next sequential number after the number you used for the parent account. Also enter a name for the account, such as "Telephone Reimbursements."
4. Select the Subaccount check box and link it to the parent account you created.
5. Click Next to create the next account.

Repeat this process as many times as necessary (click OK instead of Next when you're finished). For example, my chart of accounts has the following accounts for this purpose:

    4040 Reimbursed Expenses

        4041 Equip Rental Reimbursements

        4042 Telephone Reimbursements

        4043 Travel Reimbursements

        4044 Subcontractor Reimbursements

My reports show the individual account postings as well as a subtotal for all postings for the parent account (which is the only number I really look at).

Don't forget to edit your expense accounts by selecting the check box to track reimbursed expenses and entering the appropriate income account.

Recording Reimbursable Expenses

If you want to be reimbursed by customers for expenses you incurred on their behalf, you must enter the appropriate data while you're filling out the vendor's bill. After you enter the account and the amount, click the arrow in the Customer:Job column and select the appropriate customer or job from the drop-down list. Entering data in the Customer:Job column automatically places an icon in the column, with the strange-looking icon that appears to the right of the Customer:Job column. The icon represents an invoice, and its appearance means you're tracking this expense in order to invoice the customer for reimbursement.

You can click the icon to put an X atop it if you don't want to bill the customer for the expense but you do want to track what you're spending for the customer. This disables the reimbursement feature, but the expense is still associated with the customer in your records (which is how you perform job costing).

Sometimes, a vendor's bill is for an amount that's not entirely chargeable to a customer. Some of the amount may be your own responsibility, and it may also be that multiple customers owe you reimbursement for the amount. (This is often the case with telephone expenses when your customers reimburse you for long distance charges.) Here's how to enter the transaction:

1. Select the expense account, and then enter the portion of the bill that is your own responsibility.
2. In the next line, select the same account, and then enter the portion of the bill you are charging back to a customer.
3. Enter an explanation of the charge in the Memo column. (When you create the invoice, the text in the Memo column is the only description the customer sees.)
4. In the Customer:Job column, choose the appropriate customer or job.
5. If you're only tracking expenses, and don't want to include the amount in your invoice to this customer, click the invoice icon to place an X on it.
6. Repeat steps 2 through 5 to include any additional customers for this expense account.

When you're finished, the total amount entered should match the amount on the vendor's bill (see Figure 6-4).

Invoicing Customers for Reimbursable Expenses

When you save the vendor bill, the amounts you linked to a customer are saved in the customer file. If you placed an Invoice icon in the column next to the Customer:Job column on the vendor bill, you can collect the money by adding those amounts to the next invoice you create. In fact, you're free to create an invoice specifically for the purpose of collecting reimbursable expenses.

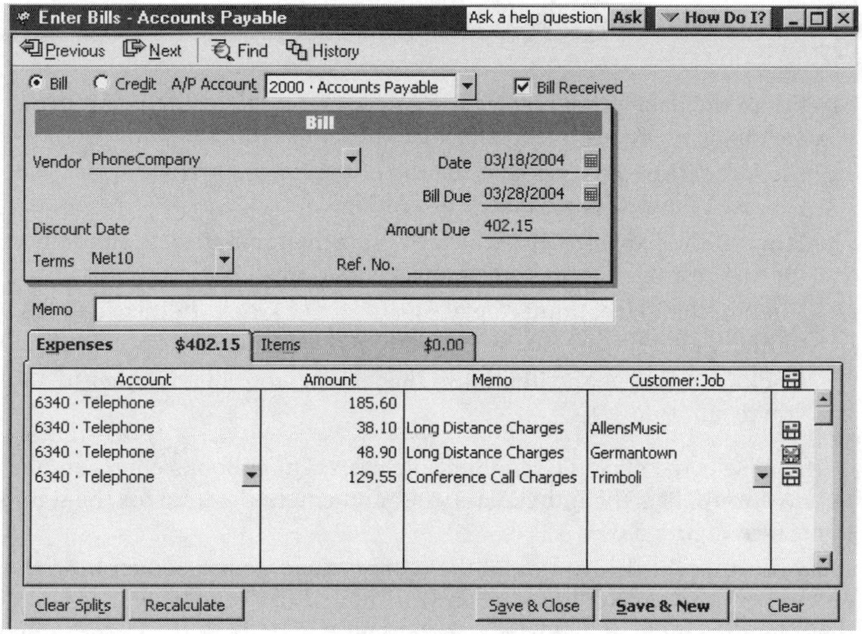

FIGURE 6-4 Charge portions of an expense to one or more customers by splitting the entry when you create the vendor bill.

Chapter 3 has complete information about creating invoices for customers, but in this section I'll discuss the particular steps you take when you want to create an invoice that includes costs for which you're seeking reimbursement.

As soon as you select a customer in the Invoice window, QuickBooks checks to see if that customer has any outstanding billable time or costs. If so, you're notified of that fact.

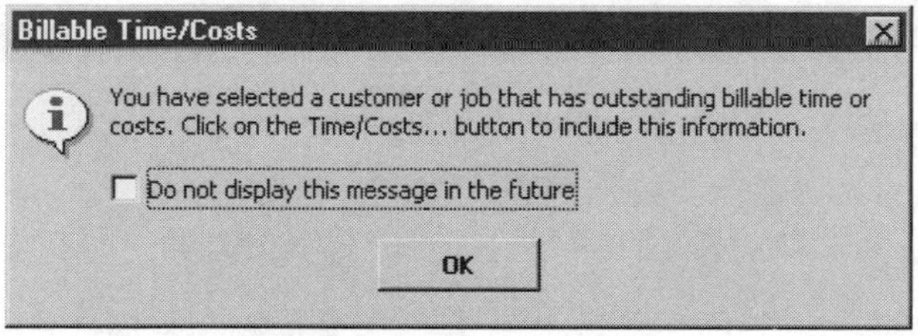

NOTE: The automatic alert about existing time and expense charges is new to QuickBooks 2004. The message contains an option to stop showing this reminder when you're creating invoices, but I can't think of any reason to stop this handy reminder from appearing. Tracking time for customer billing is covered in Chapter 18.

Use the following steps to collect reimbursement for costs the customer has agreed to pay:

1. Fill in the data in the invoice heading (and line items if you're invoicing this customer for goods or services in addition to reimbursable costs).
2. Click the Time/Costs icon at the top of the Create Invoices window to open the Choose Billable Time And Costs window.
3. Move to the Expenses tab, which displays the reimbursable amounts you posted for this customer when you entered vendor bills.
4. Click in the Use column to place a check mark next to the expenses you want to include on the invoice you're currently creating (see Figure 6-5).
5. Click OK to move the item(s) to the invoice, to join any other invoice items you're entering.

If you selected multiple reimbursable costs, QuickBooks enters an item called Reimb Group, lists the individual items, and enters the total for the reimbursable items (see Figure 6-6).

Notice that the description of the reimbursable items is taken from the text you entered in the Memo column when you entered the vendor's bill. If you don't use that Memo column, you'll have to enter text manually in the Description column of the invoice (which is a real test of your memory). Otherwise, the customer sees only an amount and no explanation of what it's for.

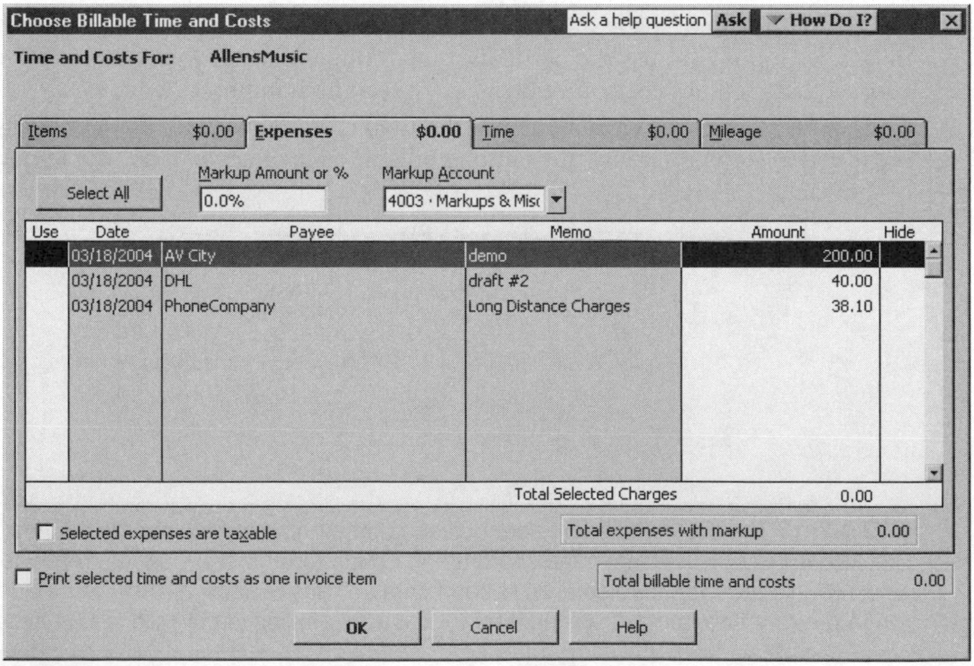

FIGURE 6-5   Select the expenses you want to add to the invoice you're preparing.

QuickBooks creates a group item for reimbursable charges and displays the total on the invoice.

Adding Taxes to Reimbursable Expenses

If an item is taxable, and the customer is not tax exempt, choose the option Selected Expenses Are Taxable. When the items are passed to the invoice, the appropriate taxes are applied. If you select the taxable option, and the customer is tax exempt, QuickBooks won't add the sales tax to the invoice.

If some items are taxable and others aren't, you have to separate the process of moving items to the invoice. First, deselect each nontaxable item by clicking its check mark to remove it (it's a toggle). Click OK to put those items on the invoice. Then return to the Choose Billable Time And Costs window, put a check mark next to each nontaxable item, deselect the Selected Expenses Are Taxable option, and click OK.

Omitting the Details on the Invoice

If you have multiple reimbursable items, you can combine all of them into a single line item on the invoice. Choose the option Print Selected Time And Costs As One Invoice Item. When you click OK and view the results in the invoice, you still see each individual item. Don't panic—you're not losing your mind. The screen version of the invoice continues to display the individual items. However, when you print the invoice, you'll see a line item named Total Reimbursable Expenses with the correct total in the Amount column.

> **$ TIP:** You can preview the printed invoice by clicking the arrow next to the Print icon on the invoice window and choosing Preview.

QuickBooks changes the format of the printed invoice to eliminate the details, but doesn't change the screen version. This means you can open the invoice later and see the detailed items, which is handy when the customer calls to ask, "What's this reimbursable expenses item on my bill?"

Excluding a Reimbursable Expense

If you have some reason to exclude one or more expenses from the current invoice, just avoid putting a check mark in the Use column. The item remains in the system and shows up on the Choose Billable Time And Costs window the next time you open it. You can add the item to the customer's invoice in the future.

Removing a Reimbursable Expense from the List

As explained earlier, when you're entering a vendor's bill and assigning expenses to customers and jobs, you can track the expense, but not invoice the customer for it, by putting an X over the invoice icon. Leaving the invoice icon intact automatically moves the expense to the category "reimbursable."

But suppose when it's time to invoice the customer, you decide that you don't want to ask the customer to pay this expense; you've changed your mind. The Choose Billable Time And Costs window has no Delete button and no method of selecting an item and choosing a delete function. You could deselect the check mark in the Use column, but afterwards, every time you open the window, the item is still there—it's like a haunting.

The solution lies in the Hide column. If you place a check mark in the Hide column, the item is effectively deleted from the list of reimbursable expenses, but not from your system. This means you won't accidentally invoice the customer for the item, but the link to this expense for this customer continues to appear in reports about this customer's activity.

Changing the Amount of a Reimbursable Expense

You're free to change the amount of a reimbursable expense. To accomplish this, select (highlight) the amount in the Amount column of the Billable Time And Costs window, and enter the new figure.

If you reduce the amount, QuickBooks does not keep the remaining amount on the Billable Time And Costs window. You won't see it again, because QuickBooks makes the assumption you're not planning to pass the remaining amount to your customer in the future.

You may want to increase the charge for some reason (perhaps to cover overhead), but if you're increasing all the charges, it's easier to apply a markup (covered next) than to change each individual item.

Marking Up Reimbursable Expenses

You can mark up any expenses you're invoicing, which many companies do to cover any additional costs incurred such as handling, time, or general aggravation. To apply a markup, select the items you want to mark up by placing a check mark in the Use column in the Choose Billable Time And Costs window. Then enter a markup in the Markup Amount or % field in either of the following ways:

- Enter an amount.
- Enter a percentage (a number followed by the percent sign).

Specify the account to which you're posting markups. You can create an account specifically for markups (which is what I do because I'm slightly obsessive about analyzing the source of all income), or use an existing income account.

The item amounts and the total of the selected charges don't change when you apply the markup; the change is reflected in the amounts for Total Expenses With Markup, and Total Billable Time And Costs.

When you click OK to transfer the reimbursable expenses to the customer's invoice, you'll see the reimbursable expenses and the markup as separate items (see Figure 6-7).

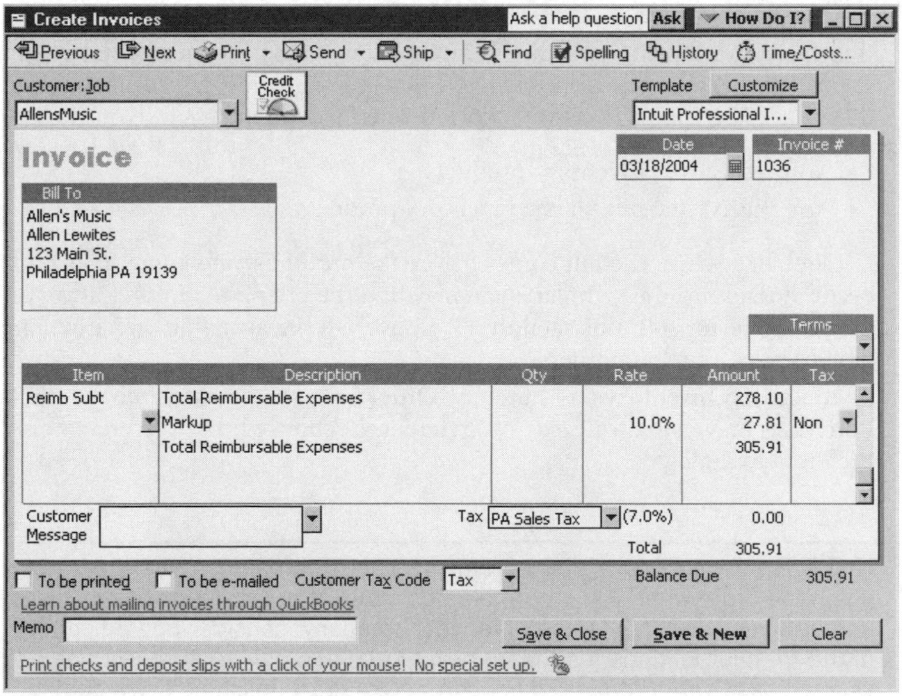

FIGURE 6-7 The markup is clearly indicated—it has its own line item.

Although it would be unusual for you to be marking up items without having discussed this with your customer, if you don't want your customer to see the markup amounts, select the Print Selected Time And Costs As One Invoice Item option. You'll see the breakdown on the screen version of the invoice, but the printed invoice will contain only the grand total.

One big difference between using the markup function and just changing the amount of the reimbursable expense in the Amount column is the way the amounts are posted to your general ledger. If you use the markup function, the difference between the actual expense and the charge to your customer is posted to the markup account. If you change the amount of the expense, the entire amount is posted to the income account you linked to the reimbursable expense account.

NOTE: In addition to the ability to mark up specific reimbursable expenses, QuickBooks provides a way to apply markups across the board. See Chapter 21 for more information.

Managing Inventory Item Purchases

If the vendor bill you're recording is for inventory items, you need to take a different approach, because the accounting issues (the way you post amounts) are different. Two transactions are involved when you buy items for your inventory:

- You receive the inventory products.
- You receive the bill for the inventory products.

Once in a while, the bill comes before the products, and sometimes both events occur at the same time. (In fact, you may find the bill pasted to the carton or included inside the carton.) In this section, I'll go over all the available scenarios, including how to track purchase orders.

To use the Inventory and Purchase Order features, you must enable them in the Purchases & Vendors category of Preferences (choose Edit | Preferences to open the Preferences dialog box).

NOTE: QuickBooks 2004 Premier Editions can automatically create a purchase order when you create a sales order or estimate involving inventory items. If you think this is useful for your company, consider upgrading to one of the Premier Editions, and learn how to use this nifty feature in *Running QuickBooks 2004 Premier Editions* from CPA911 Publishing (www.cpa911.com).

Using Purchase Orders

You can use purchase orders to order inventory items from your suppliers. It's not a great idea to use purchase orders for goods that aren't in your inventory, such as office supplies or consulting services—that's not what purchase orders are intended for.

Creating and saving a purchase order has no effect on your financials. No amounts are posted, because purchase orders exist only to help you track what you've ordered against what you've received.

> **TIP:** When you enable the Inventory and Purchase Order features, QuickBooks creates a non-posting account named Purchase Orders. You can double-click the account's listing to view and manipulate the purchase orders you've entered, but the data in the register has no effect on your finances and doesn't appear in financial reports.

Here's how to create a purchase order:

1. Choose Vendors | Create Purchase Orders to open a blank Create Purchase Orders window.
2. Fill in the purchase order fields, which are easy and self-explanatory (see Figure 6-8).

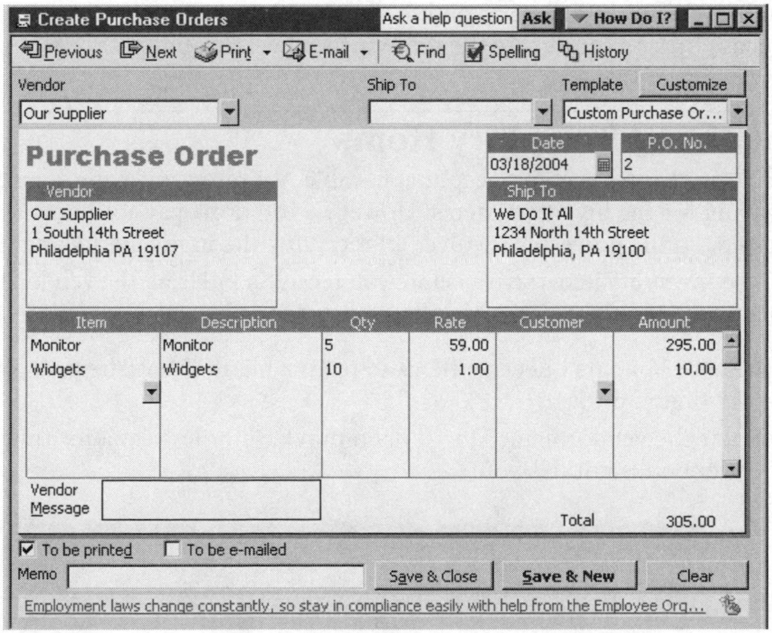

FIGURE 6-8 A purchase order looks like a vendor bill, but you don't incur any accounts payable liability.

3. Click Save & New to save the purchase order and move on to the next blank purchase order form, or click Save & Close if you have created all the purchase orders you need right now.

> **TIP:** As with expenses, you can use the Customer column to treat the purchase as a reimbursable transaction when you enter the vendor's bill for this purchase.

You can print the purchase orders as you create them by clicking the Print button as soon as each purchase order is completed. If you'd prefer, you can print them all in a batch by clicking the arrow to the right of the Print button on the last purchase order window and selecting Print Batch. If you want to print them later, be sure the option To Be Printed is selected on each PO. When you're ready to print, choose File | Print Forms | Purchase Orders from the QuickBooks menu bar.

> **TIP:** Many companies don't print purchase orders; instead, they notify the vendor of the purchase order number when they place the order over the telephone, via e-mail, or by logging into the vendor's Internet-based order system.

When the inventory items and the bill for them are received, you can use the purchase order to automate the receiving and vendor bill entry processes.

Receiving Inventory Items

Since this chapter is about accounts payable, we must cover the steps involved in paying for the inventory items. However, you don't pay for items you haven't received, so the processes involved in receiving the items merits attention.

If the inventory items arrive before you receive a bill from the vendor, you must tell QuickBooks about the new inventory, so the items are available for sales. Here's how:

1. Choose Vendors | Receive Items to open a blank Create Item Receipts window (see Figure 6-9).
2. Enter the vendor name, and if open purchase orders exist for this vendor, QuickBooks notifies you.

Open PO's Exist

⚠ Open purchase orders exist for this vendor. Do you want to receive against one or more of these orders?

[Yes]   [No]

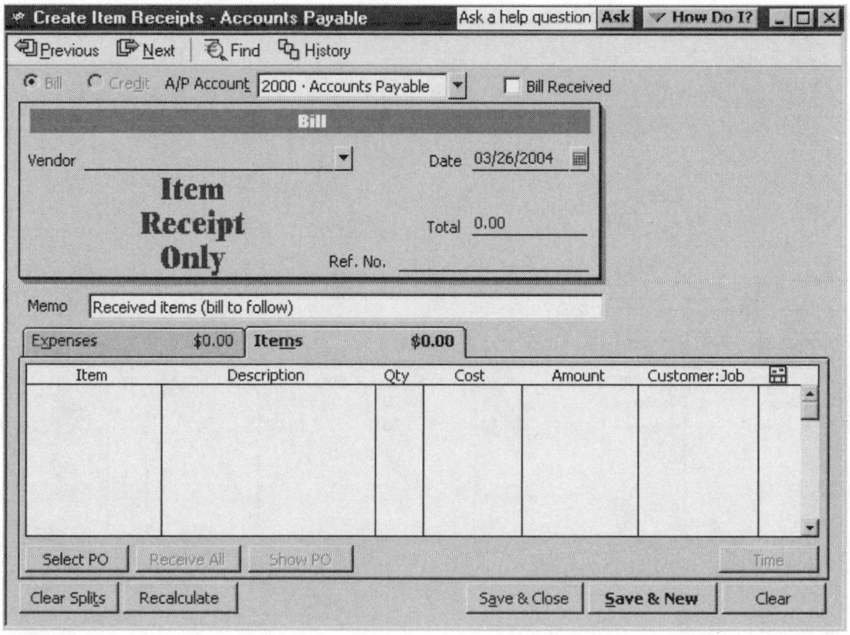

FIGURE 6-9 Receive items into inventory so you can sell them.

3. If you know there isn't a purchase order for this particular shipment, click No, and just fill out the Create Item Receipts window manually.

4. If you know a purchase order exists for this shipment, or if you're not sure, click Yes. QuickBooks displays all the open purchase orders for this vendor so you can put a check mark next to the appropriate PO, or multiple POs if the shipment that arrived covers more than one. If no PO for this shipment is listed on the Open Purchase Orders List for this vendor, click Cancel on the Open Purchase Orders window to return to the receipts window and fill in the data manually.

5. QuickBooks fills out the Create Item Receipts window using the information in the PO (see Figure 6-10). Check the shipment against the PO and change any quantities that don't match.

6. Click Save & New to receive the next shipment into inventory, or click Save & Close if this takes care of all the receipts of goods.

QuickBooks posts the amounts in the purchase order to your Accounts Payable account. This is not the standard, generally accepted accounting procedure (GAAP) method for handling receipt of goods, and if your accountant notices this QuickBooks action, you can stop the screaming by explaining that QuickBooks has a workaround for this (see the section "Understanding the Postings" later in this chapter).

I'll take a moment here to explain why your accountant might start screaming: First, an accounts payable liability should only be connected to a bill. When a bill comes, you owe the money. While it's safe to assume that if the goods showed up,

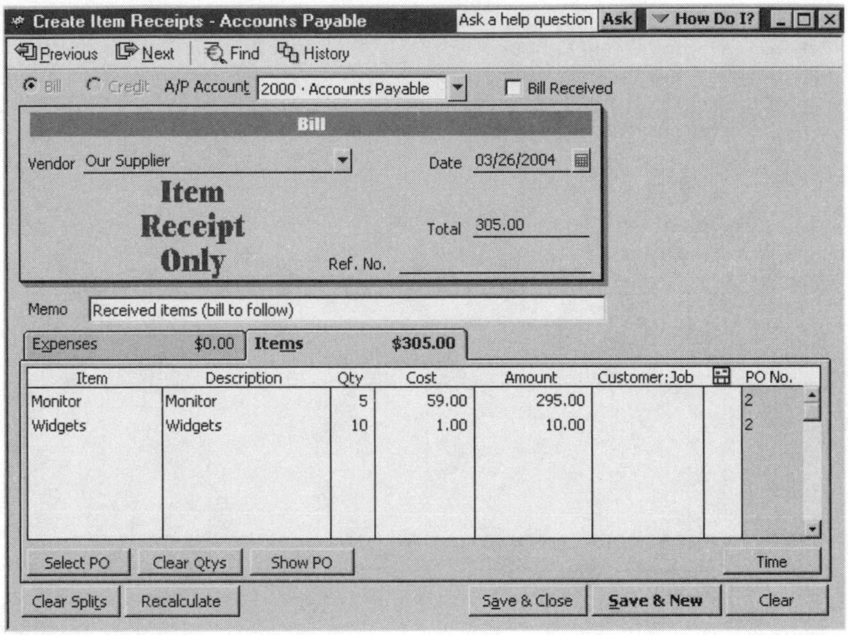

FIGURE 6-10   The line items are auto-filled based on the data in the PO—the Memo field is automatically filled in to remind you that the bill hasn't arrived yet.

the bill will follow, and you'll owe the money in the end, technically you don't incur the A/P liability until you have a bill.

Second, costs on the PO may not be the current costs for the items, and the vendor bill that shows up may have different amounts. The PO amounts you filled in were taken from your inventory records, or by your own manual entry. It's not uncommon for purchasing agents to fill out a PO without calling the vendor and checking the latest cost. The bill that arrives will have the correct costs, and those costs are the amounts that are supposed to be posted to the A/P account. If this situation occurs, QuickBooks changes the posting to A/P to match the bill.

Third, in order to avoid double-posting the A/P liability when the bill does arrive, you must use a special QuickBooks transaction window (discussed next). Because warehouse personnel frequently handle the receipt of goods, and receipt of bills is handled by a bookkeeper, a lack of communication may interfere with using the correct transaction methods. QuickBooks prevents this problem by alerting the data-entry person of a possible error. If the bookkeeper uses the standard Enter Bills transaction window, as soon as the vendor is entered in the window, QuickBooks displays a message stating that a receipt of goods record exists for this vendor and the bill should not be recorded with the standard Enter Bills window.

Recording Bills for Received Items

After you receive the items, eventually the bill comes from the vendor.

To enter the bill, do *not* use the regular Enter Bills icon in the Vendors Navigator window, which would cause another posting to Accounts Payable. Instead, do the following:

1. Choose Vendors | Enter Bill For Received Items to open the Select Item Receipt window. Choose the vendor, and you see the current items receipt information for that vendor.

2. Select the appropriate listing and click OK to open an Enter Bills window. The information from the items receipt is used to fill in the bill information.
3. Change anything that needs to be changed: a different cost per unit, taxes and shipping costs that were added, and so on. If you make any changes, you must click the Recalculate button so QuickBooks can match the total due to the changed data.
4. Click Save & Close.

Whether you've made changes to the amounts or not, QuickBooks displays a message warning you that the transaction is linked to other transactions, and asking if you're sure you want to save the changes. Say Yes. Even if you didn't make changes to the line items, you've changed the transaction from a receipt of goods transaction to a vendor bill transaction, and QuickBooks replaces the original posting to Accounts Payable that was made when you received the items.

Receiving Items and Bills Simultaneously

If the items and the bill arrive at the same time (sometimes the bill is in the shipping carton), you must tell QuickBooks about those events simultaneously. To do this, choose Vendors | Receive Items And Enter Bill. This opens the standard Enter Bills window, and when you enter the vendor's name you see a message telling you an open PO exists.

Click Yes to see the open POs for this vendor and select the appropriate PO. The line items on the bill are filled in automatically, and you can correct any quantity or price difference between your original PO and the actuals. When you save the transaction, QuickBooks receives the items into inventory in addition to posting the bill to A/P.

Understanding the Postings

You need to explain to your accountant (or warn your accountant) about the way QuickBooks posts the receipt of goods and the bills for inventory items. It seems a bit different from standard practices if you're a purist about accounting procedures, but as long as you remember to use the correct commands (as described in the preceding sections), it works fine.

QuickBooks makes the same postings no matter how, or in what order, you receive the items and the bill. Let's look at what happens when you receive $400.00 worth of items and fill out the Receive Items window:

ACCOUNT	DEBIT	CREDIT
Accounts Payable		$400.00
Inventory	$400.00	

Notice that the amount is posted to Accounts Payable, even if the bill hasn't been received. The entry in the Accounts Payable register is noted as a receipt of items with a transaction type ITEM RCPT.

When the vendor bill arrives, as long as you remember to use Vendors | Enter Bill For Received Items, the amount isn't charged to Accounts Payable again; instead, the A/P register entry is changed to reflect the fact that it is now a bill (the item type changes to BILL). If you made changes to any amounts, the new amounts are posted, replacing the original amounts.

It's that "replacing" approach that is bothersome to many accountants, because when you overwrite one transaction (the receipt of goods) with another transaction (the receipt of the vendor bill), you have an incomplete audit trail. This is especially bothersome if amounts are changed during the replacement.

 CAUTION: If you use the standard Enter Bills transaction, QuickBooks will warn you that this vendor has receipts pending bills and instructs you to use the correct command if this bill is for that receipt. If you ignore the listing, and the bill is indeed for items already received into QuickBooks, you'll have double entries for the same amount in your Accounts Payable account.

Just for your information, and for your accountant's information, here's the posting you could expect from the receipt of $400.00 worth of items if you take the purist approach. In fact, most accounting software systems do use this two-step method, which separates the receipt of items from the receipt of the bill from the vendor. This approach requires an account in your chart of accounts that tracks received items. (It's usually placed in the Liabilities section of the Chart of Accounts.)

ACCOUNT	DEBIT	CREDIT
Inventory	$400.00	
Receipts holding account		$400.00

Then, when the vendor bill arrives, a separate posting is made to the general ledger:

ACCOUNT	DEBIT	CREDIT
Receipts holding account	$400.00	
Accounts Payable		$400.00

Because the postings to the receipts holding account are washed between the receipt of goods and the receipt of the bill, the bottom-line effect to your general ledger is the same when QuickBooks does it. However, the QuickBooks approach denies you the ability to look at the amount currently posted to the receipts holding account to see where you stand in terms of items in but bills not received (or vice versa). Some accountants and company bookkeepers want to track that figure. Additionally, some purchasing agents want to track the differences in prices between POs and vendor bills. If you need these functions, you'll have to track those amounts outside of QuickBooks.

In terms of bottom-line financials, however, as long as you use the correct commands on the Vendor menu to enter these transactions, you won't have a problem.

Recording Vendor Credits

If you receive a credit from a vendor, you must record it in QuickBooks. Then, you can apply it against an open vendor bill or let it float until your next order from the vendor. (See Chapter 7 for information about paying bills, which includes applying vendor credits to bills.)

QuickBooks doesn't provide a discrete credit form for accounts payable; instead, you can change a vendor bill form to a credit form with a click of the mouse, as follows:

1. Click the Bill icon on the QuickBooks toolbar (or choose Vendors | Enter Bills from the menu bar) to open the Enter Bills window.
2. Select Credit, which automatically deselects Bill and changes the available fields in the form (see Figure 6-11).
3. Choose the vendor from the drop-down list that appears when you click the arrow in the Vendor field.
4. Enter the date of the credit memo.
5. Enter the amount of the credit memo.
6. In the Ref. No. field, enter the vendor's credit memo number.

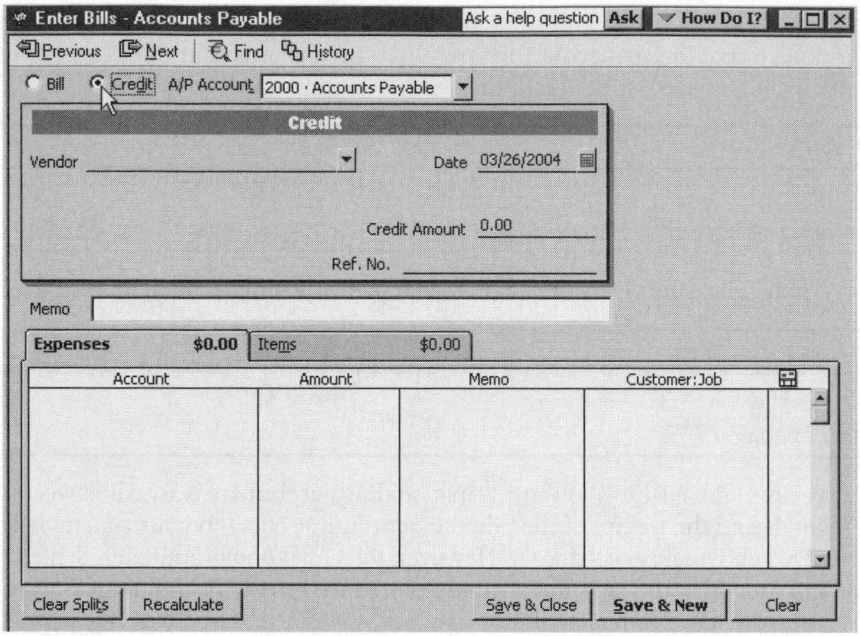

FIGURE 6-11 When you click the Credit option, the Enter Bills transaction window changes—the fields for terms and due date disappear.

7. If the credit is not for inventory items, use the Expenses tab to assign an account and amount to this credit.

8. If the credit is for inventory items, use the Items tab to enter the items, along with the quantity and cost, for which you are receiving this credit.

NOTE: If you've agreed that the vendor pays the shipping costs to return items, don't forget to enter that amount in the Expenses tab.

9. Click Save & Close to save the credit (unless you have more credits to enter—in which case, click Save & New).

Here are the postings to your general ledger when you save a vendor credit:

ACCOUNT	DEBIT	CREDIT
Inventory Asset		Amount of returned items
Applicable expense accounts		Amounts of expenses in the credit
Accounts Payable	Total credit amount	

> **TIP:** Don't use an RA (Return Authorization) number from your vendor as the basis for your credit. Wait for the credit memo to arrive so your records and the vendor's records match. This makes it much easier to settle disputed amounts.

Entering Recurring Bills

You probably have quite a few bills that you must pay every month. Commonly, the list includes your rent or mortgage payment, payments for assets you purchased with a loan (such as vehicles or equipment), or a retainer fee (for an attorney, accountant, or subcontractor). You might even need to order inventory items on a regular basis.

You can make it easy to pay those bills every month without reentering the bill each time. QuickBooks provides a feature called *memorized transactions,* and you can put it to work to make sure your recurring bills are covered.

Creating a Memorized Bill

To create a memorized transaction for a recurring bill, first open the Enter Bills window and fill out the information, as shown in Figure 6-12.

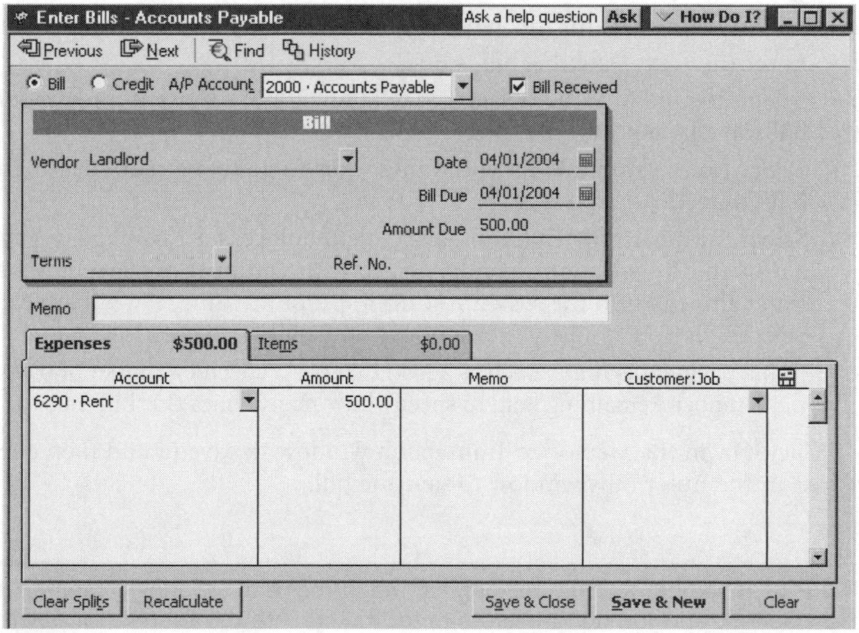

FIGURE 6-12 Enter the bill in the normal fashion, then memorize it to use it again and again.

> **TIP :** If the recurring bill isn't always exactly the same—perhaps the amount is different each month (your utility bills, for instance)—it's okay to leave the Amount Due field blank. You can fill in the amount when you use the memorized bill.

Before you save the transaction, memorize it. To accomplish this, press CTRL-M (or choose Edit | Memorize Bill from the menu bar). The Memorize Transaction window opens.

Use these guidelines to complete the Memorize Transaction window:

- Use the Name field to enter a name for the transaction. QuickBooks automatically enters the vendor name, but you can change it. Use a name that describes the transaction so you don't have to rely on your memory.
- Select the interval for this bill from the drop-down list in the How Often field.
- Enter the Next Date this bill is due.
- Select Remind Me (the default) to tell QuickBooks to issue a reminder that this bill must be put into the system to be paid.
- Select Don't Remind Me if you want to forego getting a reminder and enter the bill yourself.
- Select Automatically Enter to have QuickBooks enter this bill as a payable automatically, without reminders. Specify the number of Days In Advance To Enter this bill into the system. At the appropriate time, the bill appears in the Select Bills To Pay List you use to pay your bills (covered in Chapter 7).
- If this payment is finite, such as a loan that has a specific number of payments, use the Number Remaining field to specify how many times this bill must be paid.

Click OK in the Memorize Transaction window to save it, and then click Save & Close in the Enter Bills window to save the bill.

> **TIP :** If you created the bill only for the purpose of creating a memorized transaction, and you don't want to enter the bill into the system for payment at this time, after you save the memorized transaction, close the Enter Bills window and respond No when QuickBooks asks if you want to save the transaction.

CAUTION: When you select the reminder options for the memorized bill, the reminders only appear if you're using reminders in QuickBooks. Choose Edit | Preferences and click the Reminders category icon to view or change reminders options.

Using a Memorized Bill

If you've opted to enter the memorized bill yourself (either by asking QuickBooks to remind you to do this, or by trusting your memory), you must bring it up to make it a current payable.

To use a memorized bill, press CTRL-T (or click the MemTx icon on the Icon Bar, or choose Lists | Memorized Transaction List from the menu bar). This opens the Memorized Transaction List window.

Double-click the appropriate listing to open the bill in the usual Enter Bills window, with the next due date showing.

If the amount is blank, fill it in. Click Save & Close to save this bill, so it becomes a current payable and is listed as a bill that must be paid when you write checks to pay your bills. (See Chapter 7 for information about paying bills.)

Creating Memorized Bill Groups

If you have a whole bunch of memorized transactions to cover all the bills that are due the first of the month (rent, mortgage, utilities, car payments, whatever), you don't have to select and convert them to payables one at a time. You can create a group and then invoke actions on the group (automatically invoking the action on every bill in the group).

The steps to accomplish this are easy:

1. Press CTRL-T to display the Memorized Transaction List.
2. Right-click any blank spot in the Memorized Transaction window and choose New Group from the shortcut menu. In the New Memorized Transaction Group window, give this group a name.
3. Fill out the fields to specify the way you want the bills in this group to be handled.
4. Click OK to save this group.

Now that you've created the group, you can add memorized transactions to it as follows:

1. In the Memorized Transaction List window, select the first memorized transaction you want to add to the group.
2. Right-click and choose Edit from the shortcut menu.
3. When the Schedule Memorized Transaction window opens with this transaction displayed, select the option named With Transactions In Group.

Then select the group from the list that appears when you click the arrow next to the Group Name field.

4. Click OK and repeat this process for each bill in the list.

As you create future memorized bills, just select the same With Transactions In Group option.

If you have other recurring bills with different criteria (perhaps they're due on a different day of the month, or they're due annually), create groups for them and add the individual transactions to the group.

Now that all of your vendor bills are in the system, you have to pay them. Chapter 7 covers everything you need to know about accomplishing that task.

Track Loan Payments with Loan Manager

All QuickBooks 2004 editions except QuickBooks Basic have a new Loan Manager program you can use to track and pay loans. Loan Manager can post principal and interest to the appropriate accounts automatically (saving you the work of a split transaction, a journal entry after the fact, and a lookup of an amortization schedule). In addition, you can perform "what if" tests to see the financial ramifications of interest rates, payback periods, and increased payments against principal.

Loan Manager only works with amortized loans (loans where each payment is distributed differently between principal and interest). You cannot use Loan Manager for standard loans that have a fixed payment distribution and a defined length, or for one-payment loans, or interest-only loans with balloons.

Setting Up a Loan in Loan Manager

You can't create a loan in Loan Manager, you can only track a loan that already exists in QuickBooks. If your loan is brand new, you still must go through the steps within QuickBooks to set up the loan, posting the amounts to the appropriate accounts, before you can use Loan Manager.

I'm not going to give you instructions about entering your loan in QuickBooks, because the account postings vary according to the type of loan and the reason for the loan. Of course, the loan is always a liability. However, the offsetting debit posting differs. For example, if you borrow money to meet expenses, the offset debit may be to your bank account. If you borrow money for a vehicle or real estate, the offset debit is a fixed asset. Consult with your accountant about the postings for a loan.

Assuming you already have a liability account with the loan balance (Loan Manager doesn't care about the debit side of the posting), and you also have an expense account to which you post the interest you pay on the loan, you're ready to track the loan in Loan Manager.

Choose Banking | Loan Manager to load the Loan Manager program in your QuickBooks software window.

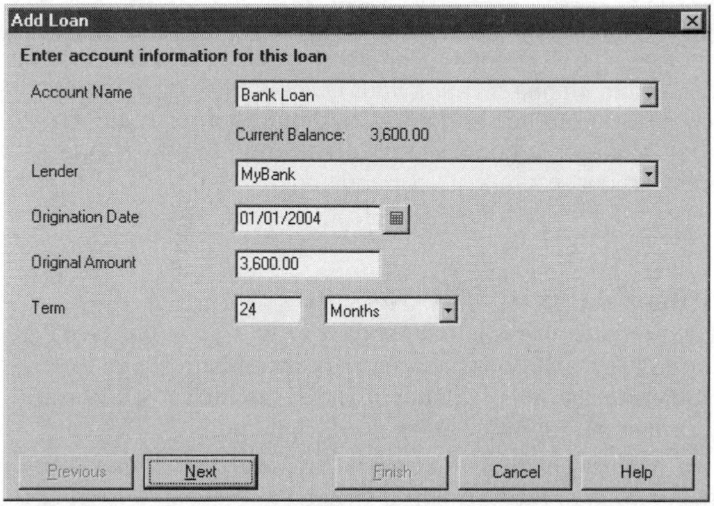

FIGURE 6-13 The first step is to enter basic data about your loan.

Entering Loan Information in Loan Manager

Select Add Loan to begin creating your loan in Loan Manager (see Figure 6-13).

Select the Account Name from the drop-down list, which contains all the Current Liability accounts in your chart of accounts. Only the account names are listed, because Loan Manager does not read account numbers. Loan Manager displays the current balance of the liability account beneath this field and assumes this is the current balance of the loan. If you've been posting payments to this account as split transactions, the current balance is probably accurate. If, however, you've been posting the full payment to the account, and then using a journal entry to move the interest portion of the payment to an interest expense account, your journal entries must be up to date. The balance in Loan Manager should be the current balance of the loan. If you have to adjust for interest, click Cancel, close Loan Manager, make the journal entry, and start again.

Select the Lender name from the drop-down list, which displays all your vendors. Your lender must already be configured as a vendor in QuickBooks. If your lender is not a vendor, click Cancel, close Loan Manager, enter the lender as a vendor, and start Loan Manager again.

Enter the Origination Date of the loan (which you can find on the paperwork you received when your loan was approved). Loan Manager uses this date to calculate interest and remaining balances.

Enter the Original Amount of the loan. Unless this is a new loan, that amount is higher than the current balance displayed under the Account Name field.

Enter the Term, by entering a number in the text box on the left, and selecting Weeks, Months, or Years from the drop-down list in the text box on the right.

> **N O T E :** You must always exit Loan Manager and then restart it if you have to create entries in QuickBooks (such as an account or a vendor) in order to create your loan. Loan Manager reads your QuickBooks data once and keeps it in memory. If you open the Vendor list, or the Account list, and create a new entry while Loan Manager is open, when you return to that field in Loan Manager, the drop-down list doesn't reflect your addition.

Entering Payment Information

Click Next to enter information about your loan payment (see Figure 6-14). Note that if you have QuickBooks configured to automatically place a decimal point when you enter amounts (a handy feature I couldn't live without), Loan Manager doesn't cooperate. You must enter the decimal point.

If your payment includes an escrow payment (usually for insurance and taxes), enter the amount of the payment dedicated to escrow. Also enter the account to which escrow payments are posted (escrow payment accounts are asset accounts).

The bottom of the payment information window has an option for an alert that occurs ten days before each payment is due. This alert is sent from Loan Manager; it is not part of the QuickBooks reminder feature, so you can't change the number of days.

Entering Interest Information

Click Next to enter information about interest rates and the way interest is calculated for this loan (see Figure 6-15).

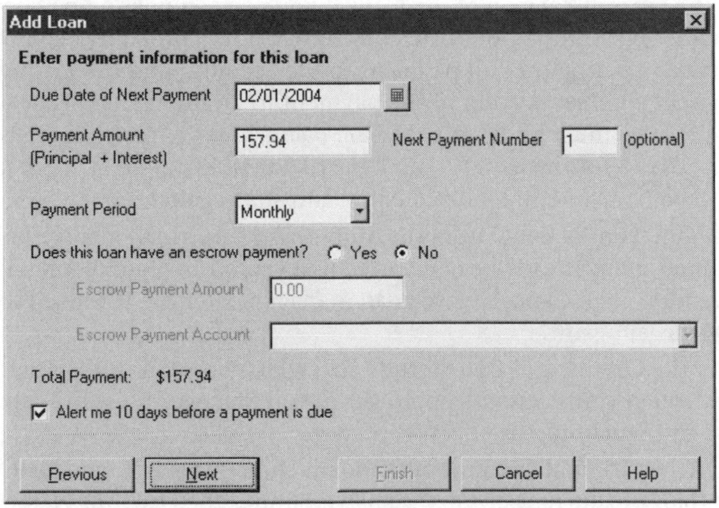

FIGURE 6-14 Enter the information about your loan payments.

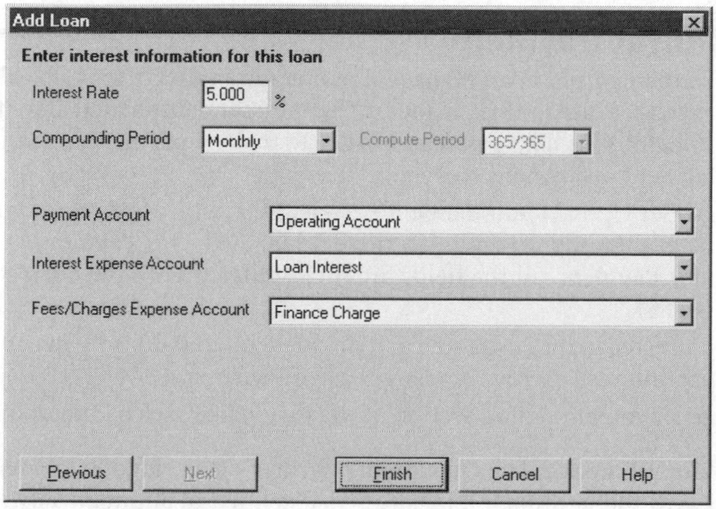

FIGURE 6-15 Provide information about interest and the accounts to which amounts are posted.

Interest on your loan is compounded according to the terms of the loan, and the compounding period affects the amount of interest you pay on the loan. The drop-down list in the Compounding Period field offers two choices:

- Monthly, which means interest is compounded monthly, on a given day of the month.
- Exact Days, which means your loan interest is computed based on a specific number of days in the year. If you select Exact Days, the Compute Period field is activated. Choose a compute period of 365/365 or 365/360. Check your loan origination paperwork to see which compute period your lender uses.

In the remaining fields, enter the appropriate accounts for payments (the bank account from which payments are made), interest, and fees/late charges.

Viewing Information About the Loan

Click Finish to see a summary of the information you entered about the loan. You may notice a balloon payment, even though I said Loan Manager can't handle loans with balloon payments. If the payment amount you entered doesn't exactly pay down the last payment, Loan Manager treats the last payment as a balloon payment. If it bothers you, re-do your math or check your loan origination documents to see if you made a mistake in the number you entered as a payment.

Click the Payment Schedule tab to see the amortized payment schedule. The Contact Info tab has contact information about your lender; the information is drawn from the vendor's QuickBooks record—you cannot enter data in Loan Manager.

Making a Payment

Loan payments from Loan Manager are not automated; this is not like a recurring bill (covered earlier in this chapter). The only semiautomated activity is a reminder, ten days before the next payment is due. To make a payment, open Loan Manager and click Set Up Payment.

In the Set Up Payment dialog box, select the type of payment you want to make from the drop-down list in the field labeled This Payment Is. If you choose A Regular Payment, all the fields are prepopulated with the correct data (see Figure 6-16).

If you select Extra Payment, each field reverts to 0.00, so you can apply principal, interest, escrow, or charges as you wish.

In the payment method section of the dialog box, select one of following actions:

- **Write A Check**   The QuickBooks Write Checks window opens after you click OK. All the information for the check is filled in automatically.
- **Enter A Bill**   The QuickBooks Enter Bills Window opens after you click OK. All the information for the bill is filled in automatically.

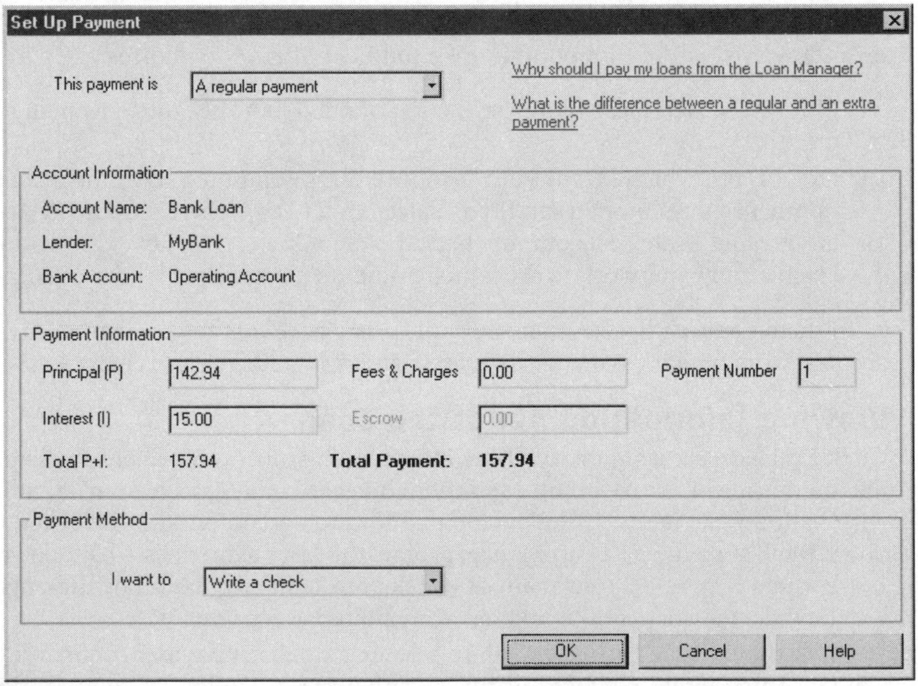

FIGURE 6-16   When you set up a regular payment, Loan Manager fills in all the data.

Editing Loans

You can edit any loans you're tracking in Loan Manager by selecting the loan's listing and clicking the Edit Loan Details button on the opening Loan Manager window. Loan Manager walks you through the same windows you saw when you created the loan, and you can make changes where necessary. For example, it's not unusual for your escrow payment to change (usually it goes up), and if you have a variable rate loan, you'll want to change the interest rate when the lender notifies you of the change.

Playing "What If?" with Loan Manager

You can test different scenarios with your loans, and loan payments, and even evaluate the effects of applying for new loans. Click the button labeled What If Scenarios to open the dialog box seen in Figure 6-17.

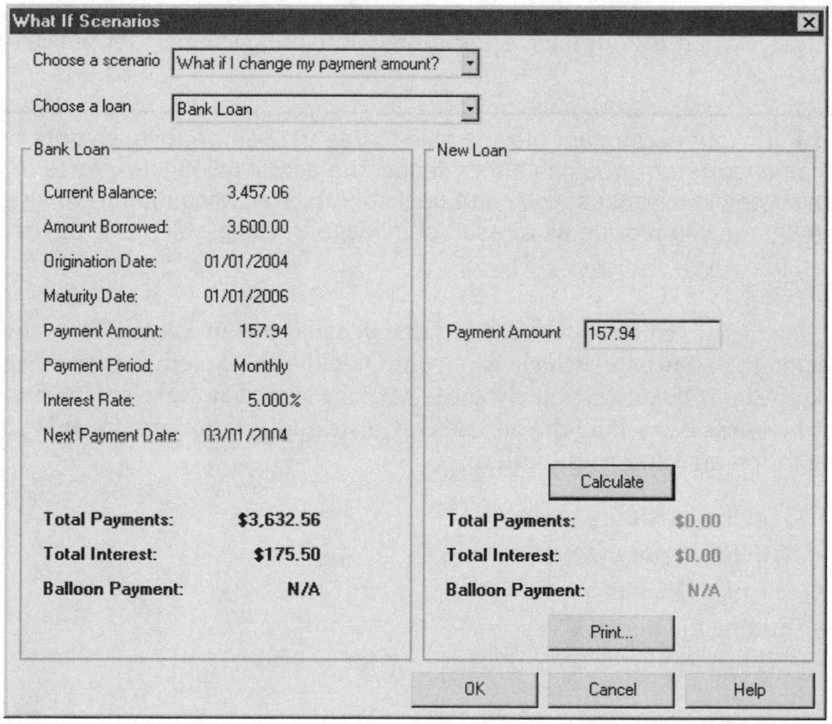

FIGURE 6-17   Check the ramifications before you change the way you manage a loan

Pick your "If" from the drop-down list in the Choose A Scenario field, and fill out the rest of the dialog box appropriately.

```
What if I change my payment amount?        ▼
What if I change my payment amount?
What if I change my interest rate?
How much will I pay with a new loan?
What if I refinance my loan?
Evaluate two new loans
```

Then, armed with information, you can change the payment amount, call your lender to renegotiate, or apply for a new loan.

Tracking Mileage Expense

QuickBooks 2004 introduces a way to track the mileage of your vehicles. You can use the mileage information to track the expenses connected to vehicle use, to use mileage as part of your job costing efforts, or to bill customers for mileage expenses.

TIP: Your accountant may be able to use the vehicle mileage data on your income tax return. You can either deduct the actual mileage expense or your other vehicle expenses; you can't deduct both. Your accountant, working with the figures you provide as a result of mileage tracking, will make the decision.

To track a vehicle, you must add that vehicle to your Vehicle List (covered in Chapter 2). Once the vehicle is in your QuickBooks system, you can begin tracking its mileage. Of course, you also need to make sure that everyone who uses a vehicle for business is tracking the odometer. Create and print a form for this purpose, with the following categories to fill in:

- Trip Start Date
- Trip End Date
- Starting Odometer
- Ending Odometer
- Customer:Job

Entering Mileage Rates

To track the cost of mileage, you must make sure you have accurate mileage rates in your system. These change frequently, so you'll have to keep up with the latest IRS figures. QuickBooks calculates the cost of mileage based on the information you enter.

To get the current rate, check with the IRS (www.irs.gov) or ask your accountant. Then use the following steps to enter the rate:

1. Choose Company | Enter Vehicle Mileage to open the Enter Vehicle Mileage window.
2. Click the Mileage Rates button on the toolbar to open the Mileage Rates window.
3. Select a date from the calendar as the Effective Date.
4. Enter the IRS rate for that date.

5. Click Close.

Notice that you can continue to add dates and rates, and QuickBooks will use the appropriate rate, based on the date of your mileage entry, to calculate costs.

Creating a Mileage Item

If you plan to use mileage expenses for job costing, or to bill customers for mileage, you must create an item (call it mileage, travel, or something similar). The item is a Service type. This is the item you select when you're filling in a mileage window.

Attach an income account to the item (for example, Mileage Invoiced). You could create another reimbursement income account to attach to this item, because you're collecting reimbursements for travel expenses. However, don't create an expense account for mileage and link the reimbursement account to it, because you don't enter accounts payable expenses for mileage—this mileage item is just one part of your existing vehicle expenses (such as vehicle fuel, travel, and so on).

It's important to understand that the mileage rate you entered in the Mileage Rates window (described in the previous section) is not automatically transferred to the item you create for mileage. Therefore, you must independently fill in the rate for the item, and update it when the IRS rate changes. You can use the same rate you used in the Mileage Rates window, or enter a different rate to create a mark up (or a mark down if you wish to take that approach).

Entering Mileage

Use the following steps to enter mileage:

1. Choose Company | Enter Vehicle Mileage to open the Enter Vehicle Mileage window.

2. Select the vehicle from the drop-down list in the Vehicle field.
3. Enter the dates of the trip.
4. Enter the odometer readings—QuickBooks calculates the total miles.
5. If you want to bill the customer for mileage, place a check mark in the Billable check box, and select the Customer:Job, the item you created for mileage, and the Class (if you're tracking classes).
6. If you don't want to bill a customer, but you want to track job costs, select the Customer:Job, the item you created for mileage, and the Class (if you're tracking classes). Do *not* place a check mark in the Billable check box.
7. Optionally, enter a note.
8. Click Save & New to enter another trip, or click Save & Close if you're finished entering mileage.

To add the billable mileage to a customer's invoice, follow the instructions for recovering reimbursable expenses earlier in this chapter.

Creating Mileage Reports

QuickBooks includes four vehicle mileage reports, which you can access by choosing Reports | Jobs, Time & Mileage, and selecting the appropriate mileage report from the submenu. If you're working in the enter Vehicle Mileage dialog box, the reports are available in the drop-down list you see if you click the arrow next to the Mileage Reports button.

Mileage by Vehicle Summary

Use the Mileage By Vehicle Summary report to see the total miles and the mileage expense for each vehicle you're tracking. You can run this report for any date range that you want to check, which is a way to determine whether vehicles need servicing. For example, you may need to change the oil and filter every 6,000 miles, or schedule a 50,000 checkup. If you deduct mileage expenses on your income tax form, use the entire year as the date range.

Mileage by Vehicle Detail

Use the Mileage By Vehicle Detail report to view details about each mileage slip you created. For each vehicle, the report displays the following information:

- Trip end date
- Total miles
- Mileage rate
- Mileage expense

No customer information appears in the report, but you can double-click any listing to open the original mileage slip, which shows you whether the trip is linked to a job, and whether it's marked billable.

Mileage by Job Summary

Use the Mileage By Job Summary report to view the total number of miles linked to customers or jobs. The report displays total miles for all customers or jobs for which you entered an item, and displays billable amounts for any mileage entries you marked billable.

Mileage by Job Detail

Use the Mileage By Job Detail report to see the following information about each trip for each customer or job:

- Trip end date
- Total miles
- Billing status

The report doesn't display any amounts, which I find annoying. To gain more knowledge, you can modify the report by clicking the Modify Report button on the report window to open the Modify Report dialog box. In the Display tab, select additional columns to reflect what you want to see in this report. For example, you may want to add the Mileage Rate or Mileage Expense (or both). You may even want to add the start date for the trip. I've added all three of those columns to my report (see Figure 6-18), and of course I memorized the report so I don't have to repeat the modifications next time.

Vehicle	Trip Start Date	Trip End Date	Total Miles	Billing Status	Mileage Rate	Mileage Expense
AllensMusic						
Ford	04/21/2004	04/21/2004	150.00	Billable	0.36	54.00
Total AllensMusic			150.00			54.00
Charity						
Ford	04/11/2004	04/11/2004	23	Not Billable	0.36	8.28
Total Charity			23			8.28
Germantown						
Ford	04/11/2004	04/11/2004	102	Billed	0.36	36.72
Total Germantown			102			36.72
MACCC						
Toyota	04/16/2004	04/16/2004	108	Billable	0.36	38.88
Total MACCC			108			38.88
TOTAL			**383.00**			**137.88**

FIGURE 6-18   This report is customized to provide more information.

Reimbursing Employees and Subcontractors

You can use the vehicle mileage tracking feature to reimburse employees, subcontractors, and yourself. Enter each person's car in the Vehicle List (use the person's name for the vehicle), and have everyone keep mileage logs.

QuickBooks cannot transfer this money directly to paychecks, the way the system can transfer time, but you can run reports to reimburse everyone, using the following steps:

1. Open the Mileage By Vehicle Detail report.
2. Enter the date range for which you're reimbursing individuals.
3. Click the Modify Report button to open the Modify Report dialog box.
4. In the Filters tab, select the first person's car from the drop-down list in the Vehicle field.
5. Click OK to return to the report window, which now displays information about that person's mileage only.
6. Memorize the report, naming it *person* mileage (substitute the real name for *person*).
7. Repeat the process for each remaining person.

Print each person's report and attach it to the reimbursement check.

Paying Bills

In this chapter:

- Choose bills to pay
- Apply discounts and credits
- Write checks
- Make direct disbursements
- Set up sales tax payments

The expression "writing checks" doesn't have to be taken literally. You can let QuickBooks do the "writing" part by buying computer checks and printing them. Except for signing the check, QuickBooks can do all the work.

Choosing What to Pay

You don't have to pay every bill that's entered, nor do you have to pay the entire amount due for each bill. Your current bank balance and your relationships with your vendors have a large influence on the decisions you make.

There are all sorts of rules that business consultants recite about how to decide what to pay when money is short, and the term "essential vendors" is prominent. I've never figured out how to define "essential," since having electricity can be just as important as buying inventory items. Having worked with hundreds of clients, however, I can give you two rules to follow that are based on those clients' experiences:

- The government (taxes) comes first. Never, never, never use payroll withholding money to pay bills.
- It's better to send lots of vendors small checks than to send gobs of money to a couple of vendors who have been applying pressure. Vendors hate being ignored much more than they dislike small payments on account.

Incidentally, I'm not covering the payment of payroll tax obligations in this chapter, so be sure to read Chapter 9 to stay on top of those accounts payable items.

Viewing Your Unpaid Bills

Start by examining the bills that are due. The best way to see that list is in detailed form, instead of a summary total for each vendor. To accomplish this, choose Reports | Vendors & Payables | Unpaid Bills Detail. In the report window, set the Date field to All to make sure all of your outstanding vendor bills are displayed (see Figure 7-1).

Double-click any entry if you want to see the original bill you entered, including all line items and notes you made in the Memo column.

You can filter the report to display only certain bills. To accomplish this, click Modify Report and go to the Filters tab in the Modify Report dialog box. Use the filters to change the display in any of the following ways:

- Filter for bills that are due today (or previously), eliminating bills due after today.
- Filter for bills that are more or less than a certain amount.
- Filter for bills that are more than a certain number of days overdue.

Print the report, and if you're short on cash, work on a formula that will maintain good relationships with your vendors.

Unpaid Bills Detail			Ask a help question	Ask ▼ How Do I?	_ □ ×

Modify Report... | Memorize... | Print... | E-mail | Export... | Hide Header | Refresh | Cash Advance Services

Dates | All ▼ | | Sort By | Default ▼

We Do It All
Unpaid Bills Detail
All Transactions

◇ Type	◇ Date	◇ Num	◇ Due Date	◇ Aging	◇ Open Balance	◇
AV City						
Bill	03/18/2004		03/28/2004		200.00 ◄	
Total AV City					200.00	
DHL						
Bill	03/18/2004		03/28/2004		40.00	
Total DHL					40.00	
Landlord						
Bill	04/01/2004		04/11/2004		650.00	
Total Landlord					650.00	
Our Supplier						
Credit	05/01/2004				-59.00	
Credit	04/21/2004				-5.00	
Bill	03/26/2004		04/05/2004		305.00	
Total Our Supplier					241.00	
PhoneCompany						
Bill	03/18/2004		03/28/2004		402.15	

FIGURE 7-1 Check the current state of your Accounts Payable balance.

Selecting the Bills to Pay

When you're ready to tell QuickBooks which bills you want to pay, choose Vendors | Pay Bills. The Pay Bills window appears (see Figure 7-2), and you can begin to make your selections using the following guidelines.

Due On Or Before Displays all the bills due within ten days, by default, but you can change the date to display more or fewer bills. If you have discounts for timely payments with any vendors, this selection is more important than it seems. The due date isn't the same as the discount date. Therefore, if you have terms of 2%10Net30, a bill that arrived on April 2 is due on May 2, and won't appear on the list if the due date filter you select is April 30. Unfortunately, the discount date is April 12, but you won't know, because the bill won't appear. If you want to use a due date filter, go out at least 60 days. (See the section "Applying Discounts" later in this chapter.)

Show All Bills Shows all the bills in your system, regardless of when they're due. This is the safest option, because you won't accidentally miss a discount date. On the other hand, if you don't get discounts for timely payment (usually offered only by vendors who sell inventory products), it's probably not the best choice because the list can be rather long.

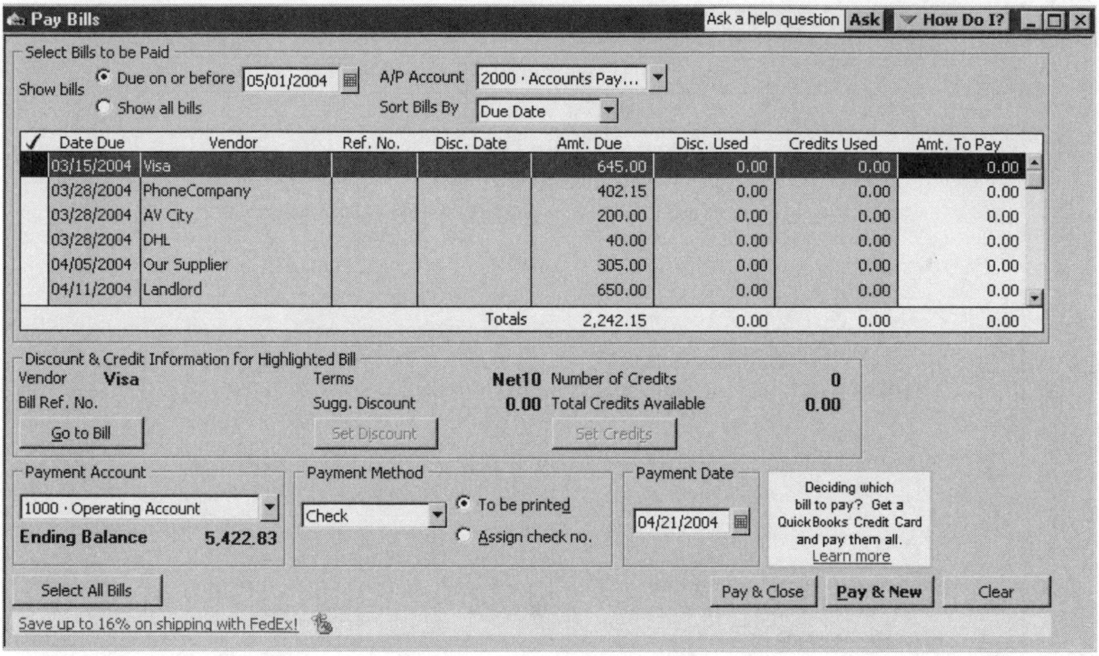

FIGURE 7-2   Paying bills starts in the Pay Bills window.

A/P Account   If you have multiple A/P accounts, select the account to which the bills you want to pay were originally posted. If you don't have multiple A/P accounts, this field doesn't appear in the window.

Sort Bills By   Determines the manner in which your bills are displayed in the Pay Bills window. The choices are

- Due Date (the default)
- Discount Date
- Vendor
- Amount Due

Payment Account   The checking or credit card account you want to use for these payments.

Payment Method   The drop-down list displays the available methods of payment: Check and Credit Card are the default options, but if you've signed up for QuickBooks online bill payment services, you can use that payment method.

If you are paying by check and QuickBooks prints your checks, be sure the To Be Printed option is selected. If you're using manual checks, select Assign Check No., and when you finish configuring bill payments, QuickBooks opens the Assign Check Numbers dialog box so you can specify the starting check number for this bill paying session in the Check No. column.

Payment Date   This is the date that appears on your checks. By default, the current date appears in the field, but if you want to predate or postdate your checks, you can change that date. If you merely select the bills today and wait until tomorrow (or later) to print the checks, the payment date set here still appears on the checks.

> **TIP:** You can tell QuickBooks to date checks by the day of printing by changing the Checking Preferences (see Chapter 21 to learn about preferences).

If you made changes to the selection fields (perhaps you changed the due date filter), your list of bills to be paid may change. If all the bills displayed are to be paid either in full or in part, you're ready to move to the next step. If there are still some bills on the list that you're not going to pay, you can just select the ones you do want to pay. Selecting a bill is simple—just click the leftmost column to place a check mark in it.

Selecting the Payment Amounts

If you want to pay in full all the bills that are listed in the Pay Bills window, and there aren't any credits or discounts to worry about, the easiest thing to do is to click the Select All Bills button. This selects all the bills for payment (and the Select All Bills button changes its name to Clear Payments, so you have a way to reverse your action).

Here's what happens in your general ledger when you pay all bills in full:

ACCOUNT	DEBIT	CREDIT
Accounts Payable	Total bill payments	
Bank		Total bill payments

I've had clients ask why they don't see the expense accounts when they look at the postings for bill paying. The answer is that the expenses were posted when they entered the bills. That's a major difference between entering bills and then paying them, or writing checks without entering the bills into your QuickBooks system (called direct disbursement). If you just write checks, you enter the accounts to which you're assigning those checks. For that system (the cash-based system) of paying bills, the postings debit the expense and credit the bank account. See the section "Using Direct Disbursements" later in this chapter for more information.

Making a Partial Payment

If you don't want to pay a bill in full, you can easily adjust the amount:

1. Click the check mark column on the bill's listing to select the bill for payment.
2. Click in the Amt. To Pay column and replace the amount that's displayed with the amount you want to pay. The total will change to match your payment when you save the window.

When the transaction is posted to the general ledger, the amount of the payment is posted as a debit to the Accounts Payable account (the unpaid balance remains in the Accounts Payable account) and as a credit to your bank account.

Applying Discounts

When you want to take advantage of discounts for timely payment, the amount displayed in the Amt. Due column (or the Amt. To Pay column if you've selected the bill for payment) doesn't reflect the discount. You have to apply it:

1. Select the bill by clicking the check mark column. If a discount is available for this bill, information about the discount appears in the Discount & Credit Information For Highlighted Bill section when you select the bill's listing. If the information about the discount doesn't include the amount of the discount, check the date in the Payment Date field, which must be equal to or earlier than the discount date. (If it's too late, don't worry, you can still take the discount—see the next section "Taking Discounts After the Discount Date.")
2. Click the Set Discount button to open the Discount And Credits window, which displays the amount of the discount based on the terms for this bill. You can accept the amount or change it (useful when you're taking the discount after the discount date, explained in the next section), and then click Done to apply it.

When you return to the Pay Bills window, the discount is applied and the Amt. To Pay column has the correct amount.

Taking Discounts After the Discount Date

Many businesses fill in the discount amount even if the discount period has expired. The resulting payment, with the discount applied, is frequently accepted by the vendor. Businesses that practice this protocol learn which vendors will accept a discounted payment and which won't (most will). Seeing that the discount you took has been added back in the next statement you receive is a pretty good hint that you're not going to get away with it.

To take a discount after the discount date, use the same steps explained in the preceding section for applying a discount. When you click the Set Discount button to open the Discount And Credits window, the amount showing for the discount is zero. Enter the discount you would have been entitled to if you'd paid the bill in a timely fashion, and click Done.

Understanding the Discount Account

Notice that the Discount tab of the Discounts And Credits window has a field for the Discount Account. This account accepts the posting for the amount of the discount. If you don't have an account for discounts taken (not to be confused with the account for discounts given to your customers), you can create one now by clicking the arrow to the right of the field and choosing <Add New>.

The account for the discounts you take (sometimes called *earned discounts*) can be either an income or expense account. There's no right and wrong here, although I've seen accountants get into heated debates defending a point of view on this subject. If you think of the discount as income (money you've brought into your system by paying your bills promptly), make the account an income account. If you think of the discount as a reverse expense (money you've saved by paying your bills promptly), make the account an expense account (it posts as a minus amount, which means it reduces total expenses).

If the only vendors who offer discounts are those from whom you buy inventory items, you should put the discount account in the section of your chart of accounts that holds the Cost of Goods Sold accounts. In fact, the most efficient way to do this is to have a parent account called Cost of Goods Sold, and then create two subaccounts:

- Cost of Goods
- Discounts Taken

You'll be able to see the individual amounts on your financial reports, and the parent account will report the net COGS.

> ($) **TIP:** QuickBooks may have created a Cost of Goods Sold account automatically during your company setup. If not, create one and then create the subaccounts.

Here's what posts to your general ledger when you take a discount. For example, suppose the original amount of the bill was $484.00 and the discount was $9.68; therefore, the check amount was $474.32. (Remember that the original postings when you entered the bill were for the total amount without the discount.)

ACCOUNT	DEBIT	CREDIT
Accounts Payable	$484.00	
Bank		$474.32
Discounts Taken		$9.68

Applying Credits

If the list of bills includes vendors for whom you have credits, you can apply the credits to the bill. Select the bill, and if credits exist for the vendor, information about the credits appears on the Pay Bills window. Click Set Credits to open the Discounts And Credits window. Select the credit, and click Done to change the Amt. To Pay column to reflect the credit.

Saving the Pay Bills Information

There are two ways to save information about paying bills: save as you go or save at the end. You can select a bill, make adjustments (make a partial payment, apply a discount or a credit), and then click Pay & New to save that bill payment. That bill disappears from the list if it's paid in total, and reappears with the balance owing if it's partially paid. Or you can select each bill, making the appropriate adjustments. Then, when you're finished applying all the credits, discounts, and partial payments, click Pay & Close.

Regardless of the approach, when you're finished selecting the bills to pay, QuickBooks transfers all the information to the general ledger and fills out your checkbook account register (or credit card account register) with the payments. If you're paying bills online, QuickBooks retains the information until you go online.

After you've paid the bills in QuickBooks, the bills aren't really paid; your vendors won't consider them paid until they receive the checks. You can write manual checks or you can print checks.

When you click Pay & Close in the Pay Bills window, all the bills you paid are turned into checks (albeit unwritten checks). You can see those checks in the bank account register, as shown in Figure 7-3 (click the Accnt icon on the Icon Bar and double-click the listing for your bank).

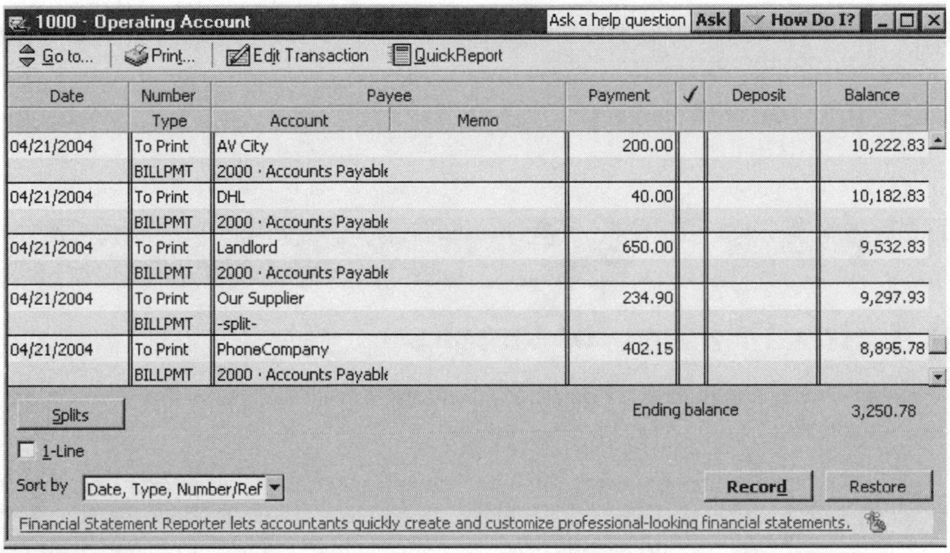
1000 · Operating Account
Ask a help question
Ask
How Do I?
Go to...
Print...
Edit Transaction
QuickReport
Date
Number
Type
Payee
Account
Memo
Payment
✓
Deposit
Balance
04/21/2004
To Print
BILLPMT
AV City
2000 · Accounts Payable
200.00
10,222.83
04/21/2004
To Print
BILLPMT
DHL
2000 · Accounts Payable
40.00
10,182.83
04/21/2004
To Print
BILLPMT
Landlord
2000 · Accounts Payable
650.00
9,532.83
04/21/2004
To Print
BILLPMT
Our Supplier
-split-
234.90
9,297.93
04/21/2004
To Print
BILLPMT
PhoneCompany
2000 · Accounts Payable
402.15
8,895.78
Splits
Ending balance
3,250.78
1-Line
Sort by
Date, Type, Number/Ref
Record
Restore
Financial Statement Reporter lets accountants quickly create and customize professional-looking financial statements.

FIGURE 7-3 The checks that pay your bills have been posted to your bank account.

If you indicated in the Pay Bills window that you would be printing checks (by selecting the To Be Printed option), your bank account register displays To Print as the check number. See the section "Printing Checks" later in this chapter.

If you selected the Assign Check No. option because you manually write checks, your bank account register uses the check number you specified in the Assign Check Numbers dialog box.

Writing Manual Checks

If you're not printing checks, you must make sure the check numbers in the register are correct. In fact, it's a good idea to print the register and have it with you as you write the checks. To accomplish that, with the register open in the QuickBooks window, click the Print icon at the top of the register window. When the Print Register dialog opens, select the date range that encompasses these checks (usually they're all dated the same day), and click OK to open the Print Lists dialog, where you can select print options before clicking Print to print. Then, as you write the checks, use the check numbers on the printout.

Printing Checks

Printing your checks is far easier and faster than using manual checks. Before you can print, however, you have some preliminary tasks to take care of. You have to purchase computer checks and set up your printer.

C A U T I O N : Lock the room that has the printer with the checks in it when you're not there.

➡ **FYI**

Dot Matrix Printers for Checks

I use dot matrix printers for checks. I gain a few advantages with this method, and you might like to think about them:

- I never have to change paper when it's time to print checks. I never accidentally print a report on a check. I never accidentally print a check on plain paper.
- They're cheap. Not just cheap—they're frequently free. Gazillions of companies have upgraded to networks and can now share laser printers. As a result, all of those dot matrix printers that were attached to individual computers are sitting in storage bins in the basement. Ask around.
- They're cheap to run (you replace a ribbon every once in a while), and they last forever. I have clients using old printers (such as an OKI 92) that have been running constantly for about 15 years. And I mean constantly—dot matrix printers are great for warehouse pick slips and packing slips, and some of my clients pick and pack 24 hours a day, 7 days a week.

My dot matrix printer is connected to a second printer port that I installed in the computer I use as a print server on my network (the first printer port is for my laser printer). Printer ports cost less than $10 and are easy to install.

I have two checking accounts and still never have to change paper, because I have one of those dot matrix printers (an OKI 520) that holds two rolls of paper at the same time; one feeds from the back and the other from the bottom. I flip a lever to switch between paper (my personal checking account and the corporate checking account).

I have clients who want the additional security of making copies of printed checks. You can buy multipart checks where the second page is marked "COPY" so nobody tries to use it as a check. Law firms, insurance companies, and other businesses that file a copy of a check appreciate multipart checks, which require a dot matrix printer.

Don't use a dot matrix printer that has a pull tractor for checks, because you'll have to throw away a couple of checks to get the print head positioned. Use a push-tractor printer.

Purchasing Computer Checks

Many vendors sell computer checks, and my own experience has been that there's not a lot of difference in pricing or the range of styles. Computer checks can be purchased for dot matrix printers (the check forms have sprocket holes) or for page printers (laser and inkjet).

- Intuit, the company that makes QuickBooks, sells checks through its Internet marketplace, which you can reach at http://www.intuitmarket.com.
- Business form companies (there are several well-known national companies) sell them.
- Your bank may supply them (some banks have a computer-check purchasing arrangement with suppliers).

If you purchase checks from any supplier except Intuit, you have to tell them you use QuickBooks. All check makers know about QuickBooks and offer a line of checks that are designed to work perfectly with the software.

Computer checks come in several varieties (and in a wide range of colors and designs). For QuickBooks, you can order any of the following check types:

- Plain checks
- Checks with stubs (QuickBooks prints information on the stub)
- Checks with special stubs for payroll information (current check and year-to-date information about wages and withholding)
- Wallet-sized checks

Setting Up the Printer

Before you print checks, you have to go through a setup routine. Take heart: you only have to do it once. After you select your configuration options, QuickBooks remembers them and prints your checks without asking you to reinvent the wheel each time.

Your printer needs to know about the type of check you're using, and you supply the information in the Printer Setup window. To get there, choose File | Printer Setup from the menu bar. Select Check/PayCheck as the form. Choose the Printer name and type that match the printer you're using for checks. Your Printer Setup window should look similar to Figure 7-4.

Choosing a Check Style

You have to select a check style, and it has to match the check style you purchased, of course. Three styles are available for QuickBooks checks, and a sample of each style appears in the window to show you what the style looks like.

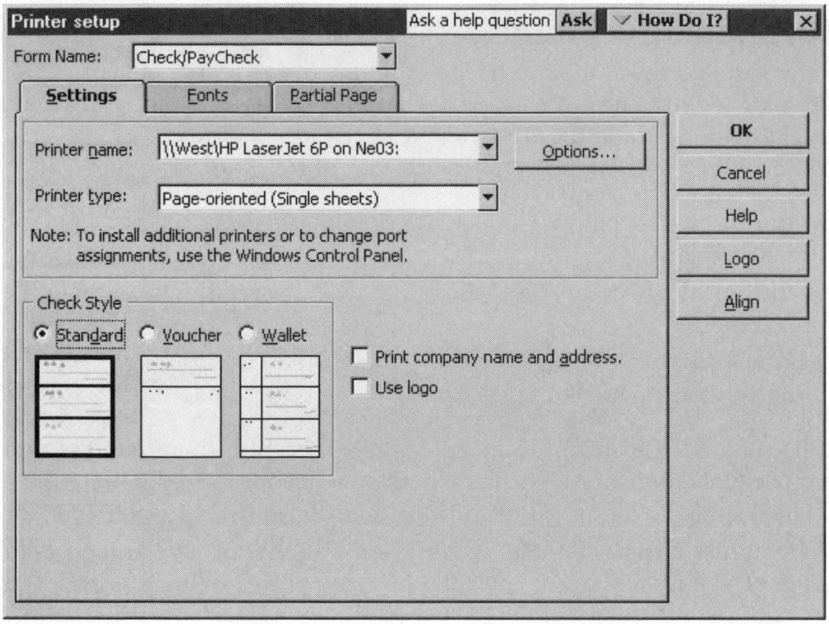

FIGURE 7-4 Set up your printer for check printing.

- **Standard checks**   Are just checks. They're the width of a regular business envelope (usually called a *#10 envelope*). If you have a laser printer, there are three checks to a page. A dot matrix pin-feed printer just keeps rolling, since the checks are printed on a continuous sheet with perforations separating the checks.

- **Voucher checks**   Have additional paper attached to the check form. QuickBooks prints voucher information if you have voucher checks, including the name of the payee, the date, and the individual amounts of the bills being paid by this check. The voucher is attached to the bottom of the check. The check is the same width as the standard check (it's longer, of course, so you have to fold it to put it in the envelope if you're including the voucher).

- **Wallet checks**   Are narrower than the other two check styles (so they fit in your wallet). The paper size is the same as the other checks (otherwise, you'd have a problem with your printer), but there's a perforation on the left edge of the check, so you can tear off the check.

Adding a Logo

If your checks have no preprinted logo and you have a file of your company logo, you can select the Use Logo box and then click the Logo button to open the Logo dialog box. Click the File button to locate the graphics file, which must be a bitmapped graphic (the file extension is .bmp).

There's also a selection box for printing your company name and address, but when you buy checks, you should have that information preprinted.

CAUTION: Dot matrix printers can't handle graphics printing, so don't bother choosing a logo if you're using a dot matrix printer for your checks.

Changing Fonts

Click the Fonts tab in the Printer Setup window to choose different fonts for the check information, such as the amounts, or the payee's address block. Click the appropriate button and then choose a font, a font style, and a size from the dialog box that opens.

CAUTION: Before you change fonts, make a note of the current settings. No Reset or Default button exists in the Fonts tab. If you make changes and they don't work properly, without knowing the original settings you'll have to mess around with fonts for a long time to get back to where you started.

Handling Partial Check Pages on Laser and Inkjet Printers

If you're printing to a laser or inkjet printer, you don't have the advantage that a pin-fed dot matrix printer provides—printing a check and stopping, leaving the next check waiting for the next time you print checks. QuickBooks has a nifty solution for this problem, found on the Partial Page tab (see Figure 7-5). Click the selection that matches your printer's capabilities.

Printing the Checks

After your printer is configured for your checks, click OK in the Printer Setup window to save the configuration data. Now you can print your checks. Choose

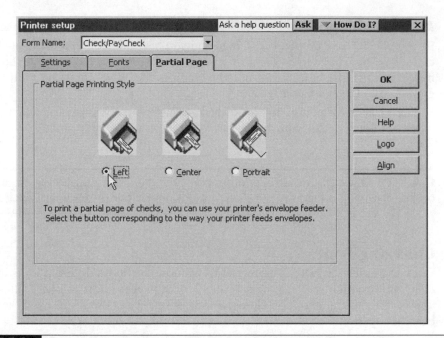

FIGURE 7-5 The partial page solution is based on the way your printer handles envelopes.

File | Print Forms | Checks from the menu bar to bring up the Select Checks To Print window.

By default, all the unprinted checks are selected for printing. The first time you print checks, the first check number is 1; just replace that number with the first check number in the printer. Click OK when everything is correct to open the Print Checks window.

If you're not using a dot matrix printer, QuickBooks asks how many checks are on the first page (in case you have a page with a check or two remaining). Fill in the number and place the page with leftover checks in the manual feed tray (QuickBooks prints those checks first). Then let the printer pull the remaining check pages from your standard letter tray. If you indicate there are three checks on the page, printing starts with the checks in the standard letter tray.

> **NOTE:** Voucher checks for laser and inkjet printers are one to a page, so you don't have to worry about using remaining checks on a page.

Click Print to begin printing your checks.

Reprinting in Case of Problems

Sometimes things go awry when you're printing. The paper jams, you run out of toner, the ribbon has no ink left, the dog chews the paper as it emerges, the paper falls off the back tray and lands in the shredder—all sorts of bad things can occur. QuickBooks knows this and checks the print run before it finalizes the printing process.

```
┌─────────────────────────────────────────────────┐
│ Did check(s) print OK?                      [X]   │
├─────────────────────────────────────────────────┤
│ Remember to sign your checks!                     │
│ If checks 1824 through 1827 printed correctly, click OK │
│ to continue.  Otherwise, type the number of the first check │
│ which printed incorrectly and then click OK.      │
│                                                   │
│         First incorrectly printed check: [        ]│
│                                                   │
│              [   OK   ]    [  Help  ]             │
└─────────────────────────────────────────────────┘
```

If everything is fine, click OK. If anything untoward happened, enter the number of the first check that is messed up. Put more checks into the printer (unless you're using a dot matrix printer, in which case you don't have to do anything). Then click OK and choose File | Print Forms | Checks. Your unprinted checks are listed in the Select Checks To Print dialog box, and the first check number is the next available check number.

After your checks have printed properly, put them in envelopes, stamp them, and mail them. *Now* you can say your bills are paid.

> **TIP:** Just for the curious: open the register for your bank account, and you'll see that the checks are numbered to match the print run.

Using Direct Disbursements

A *direct disbursement* is a disbursement of funds (usually by check) that is performed without matching the check to an existing bill. This is check writing without entering bills.

If you're not entering vendor bills, this is how you'll always pay your vendors. However, even if you are entering vendor bills, you sometimes need to write a quick check without going through the process of entering the vendor bill, selecting it, paying it, and printing the check—for example, when the UPS delivery person is standing in front of you waiting for a C.O.D. check and doesn't have time for you to go through all those steps.

Writing Direct Disbursement Manual Checks

If you use manual checks, you can write your checks and then tell QuickBooks about it later. Or you can bring your checkbook to your computer and enter the checks in QuickBooks as you write them. You have two ways to enter your checks in QuickBooks: in the bank register or in the Write Checks window.

Using the Register

To use the bank register, open the bank account register with either of the following actions:

- Click the Accnt icon on the QuickBooks toolbar, and then double-click the listing for the bank account.
- Click the Reg button on the toolbar and select your bank account.

When the account register opens, you can enter the check on a transaction line, as follows:

1. Enter the date.
2. Press the TAB key to move to the Number field. QuickBooks automatically fills in the next available check number.
3. Press TAB to move through the rest of the fields, filling in the name of the payee, the amount of the payment, and the expense account you're assigning to the transaction.
4. Click the Record button to save the transaction.
5. Repeat the steps for the next check and continue until all the manual checks you've written are entered into the register.

Using the Write Checks Window

If you prefer a graphical approach, you can use the Write Checks window to tell QuickBooks about a check you manually prepared. To get there, click the Check

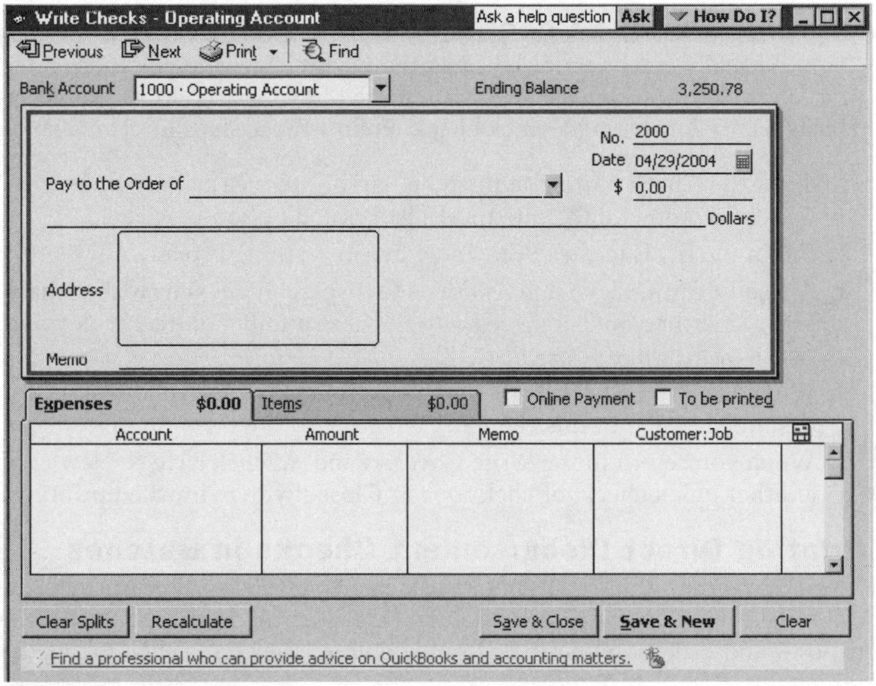

FIGURE 7-6 Fill out the onscreen check the same way you'd fill out a paper check—they look the same.

icon on the Icon Bar, press CTRL-W, or choose Banking | Write Checks from the menu bar. When the Write Checks window opens (see Figure 7-6), select the bank account you're using to write the checks.

The next available check number is already filled in unless the To Be Printed option box is checked (if it is, click it to toggle the check mark off and put the check number in the window). QuickBooks warns you if you enter a check number that's already been used (although the warning doesn't appear until you've filled in all the data and attempt to save the check).

Fill out the check, posting amounts to the appropriate accounts. If the check is for inventory items, use the Items tab to make sure the items are placed into inventory. When you finish, click Save & New to open a new blank check. When you're through writing checks, click Save & Close to close the Write Checks window. All the checks you wrote are recorded in the bank account register.

Printing Direct Disbursement Checks

You can print checks immediately, whether you normally enter bills and print the checks by selecting bills to pay or you normally print checks as direct disbursements.

Printing a Single Check Quickly

If you normally enter vendor bills and then print checks to pay those bills, you can print a check for an expense that isn't entered in your accounts payable system. This is handy for writing a quick check. Follow these steps to print a single check:

1. Click the Check button on the Icon Bar, or press CTRL-W to open the Write Checks window. Make sure the To Be Printed option is selected.
2. Fill in the fields in the check and when everything is ready, click Print.
3. A small Print Check window opens to display the next available check number. Make sure that number agrees with the next number of the check you're loading in the printer, and then click OK.
4. When the Print Checks window opens, follow the instructions for printing described earlier in this chapter.
5. When you return to the Write Checks window, click Save & New to write another quick check, or click Save & Close if you're finished printing checks.

Printing Direct Disbursement Checks in Batches

If you don't enter vendor bills but instead pay your bills as direct disbursements, you can print checks in a batch instead of one at a time. To do so, open the Write Checks window and make sure the To Be Printed option is selected. Then follow these steps:

1. Fill out all the fields for the first check and click Save & New to move to the next blank Write Checks window.
2. Repeat step 1 for every check you need to print.
3. Print the checks using one of the following methods:
   - Click Save & Close when you are finished filling out all the checks, and then choose File | Print Forms | Checks from the menu bar.
   - In the last Write Checks window, click the arrow to the right of the Print button and choose Print Batch.

Postings for Direct Disbursements

The postings for direct disbursements are quite simple:

ACCOUNT	DEBIT	CREDIT
Bank account		Total of all checks written
An expense account	Total of all checks assigned to this account	
Another expense account	Total of all checks assigned to this account	
Another expense account	Total of all checks assigned to this account (as many as needed)	

Sending Sales Tax Checks and Reports

If you collect sales tax from your customers, you have an inherent accounts payable bill because you have to turn that money over to the state taxing authorities. The same thing is true for payroll withholdings; those payments are discussed in Chapter 9.

In order to print reports on sales tax (so you can fill out those complicated government sales tax forms) you have to configure your sales tax collections in QuickBooks (and if you collect multiple sales taxes, this can be more complicated than the government forms).

While I will sometimes use the term "state" in the following sections, your tracking and reporting needs may not be limited to state-based activities. In recent years many states have created multiple sales tax authorities within the state (usually a specific location such as a county, or a group of ZIP codes, each having its own tax rate). Businesses in those states remit the sales tax they collect to both the state and the local sales tax authority (or to multiple local sales tax authorities). As a result, tracking sales tax properly (which means in a manner that makes it possible to fill out all the forms for all the authorities) has become a very complicated process.

I've received hundreds of messages asking for help from readers on this subject, mostly from readers in states that have made sales taxes more complicated. In the following sections I'll present a rather comprehensive discussion in an effort to cover these complicated scenarios. If your sales tax issues aren't at all complicated, you probably don't have to read the rest of this chapter.

Configuring Sales Tax Settings

If you collect and remit sales tax, you need to configure the sales tax features in QuickBooks. You must set up tax codes to link to your customers, so you know whether a customer is liable for sales tax. You must also set up tax items, so you can set a rate (a percentage rate) and link the item to a taxing authority.

Start your sales tax setup by choosing Edit | Preferences from the menu bar. Click the Sales Tax icon in the left pane and select the Company Preferences tab to see the window shown in Figure 7-7.

If you didn't enable the sales tax feature during the EasyStep Interview, do it now by selecting the Yes option in the section labeled Do You Charge Sales Tax? In the following sections I'll go over the other options in this dialog box.

Sales Tax Payment Basis

There are two ways to remit sales tax to the taxing authorities, and they're listed in the Owe Sales Tax section of the Sales Tax Preferences dialog box:

- **Accrual-basis method** Means the tax is due when the customer is charged (the invoice date).
- **Cash-basis method** Means the tax is due when the customer pays.

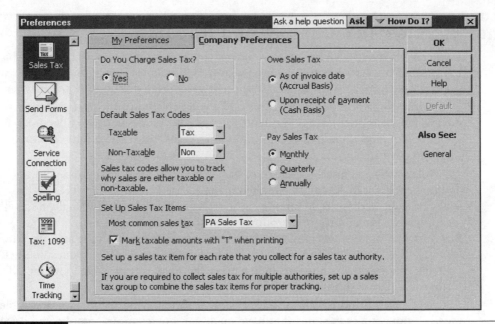

FIGURE 7-7 Be sure the specifications are correct, because QuickBooks goes on autopilot using these choices.

Check with your accountant (and the taxing authority law) to determine the method you need to select.

Sales Tax Payment Dates

You must indicate the frequency of your remittance to the taxing authority in the Pay Sales Tax section of the Preferences dialog box. You don't get to choose—your sales tax license indicates the schedule you must use. Many states base the frequency on the amount of tax you collect, usually looking at your returns for a specific period of time—perhaps one specific quarter, which is usually referred to as the *lookback* period. If your sales tax liability changed dramatically during the lookback period, you may receive notice from the state that your remittance interval has changed. (They'll probably send you new forms.) If that occurs, don't forget to return to the Preferences window to change the interval.

Default Sales Tax Codes

QuickBooks has two discrete entities for configuring sales tax: Tax Codes and Tax Items. Lots of people get them confused, so I'll attempt to clarify their definitions and use. Let's start with definitions:

- A tax code indicates tax liability, which means the entity to which it's linked (a customer or a tax item) is deemed to be taxable or nontaxable, depending on the code. In addition, if you take the trouble to do so, you can have tax codes that explain *why* an entity is taxable or nontaxable. Tax codes contain no information about the tax rate or the taxing authority (the payee for the check you write).
- Tax items contain information about the tax rate and the taxing authority to which you remit taxes and reports. Like all other items, they appear on sales forms, and the tax is calculated when you add the tax item to the taxable line items (products and services) on an invoice or sales receipt.

Linking a sales tax code to customers and items lets you (and the QuickBooks invoicing feature) know whether sales tax should be calculated for that item for this customer. If a customer is liable for sales tax, it doesn't mean that every item you sell the customer is taxable, because some items aren't taxable. I can't give you a list of categories, because each state sets its own rules. For example, in Pennsylvania, food and some other necessities of life aren't taxable, but some types of consulting services are. Other states don't tax services at all, reserving the sales tax for products. Some states seem to tax everything—California comes to mind. If an item is taxable, it's taxable only to customers whose tax code indicates they are liable for sales tax.

When you create items in your company file, you indicate whether the item is taxable under your state tax laws. If the item is taxable, the rate that's applied is connected to the customer, not to the item. Technically, a customer's sales tax liability is like a light switch; it's either on or off (techies call this scenario "boolean," which means the only possible answers or definitions are On/Off, or Yes/No). In the spirit of boolean mathematics, QuickBooks prepopulates the Sales Tax Preferences dialog box with the following two tax codes:

- Tax, which means liable for sales tax
- Non, which means not liable for sales tax

For many of us, that's enough; we don't need any additional tax codes for customers or for items. We can move on to creating tax items so their rates are calculated on sales forms. However, for some companies, those two tax codes aren't enough. State rules governing sales tax reports and state reporting forms require more information.

For nontaxable customers, some states want to know why a nontaxable customer isn't charged sales tax. Is a customer nontaxable because it's out of state and the rules say you don't have to collect taxes for out-of-state sales? Is a customer nontaxable because it's a nonprofit organization? Is a customer nontaxable because it's a government agency? Is a customer nontaxable because it's a wholesale business and collects sales tax from its own customers? (The last definition probably describes your business, and your suppliers have you configured as nontaxable.) If your state requires this information, you must create tax codes to match the reporting needs (covered in the next section "Creating Sales Tax Codes").

For taxable customers, you may want to use tax codes to specify customers as taxable in another state (if you collect taxes from out-of-state customers and remit those taxes to that state's taxing authority).

States that have instituted multiple tax rates depending on a customer's location want to know which location within the state the customer occupies, because that location determines the tax rate. Your reports on sales taxes have to subtotal your collections by location. In fact, in some states, you have to send individual sales tax reports to individual local tax authorities. If your state operates in this manner, you should solve this with tax items, not tax codes, because part of your configuration task is the tax rate (which isn't part of a tax code, it's only part of a tax item).

Creating Sales Tax Codes

If you want to create codes to track customer sales tax status in a manner more detailed than "taxable" and "nontaxable," follow these steps to add a new sales tax code:

1. Choose Lists | Sales Tax Code List.
2. Press CTRL-N to open the New Sales Tax Code window.
3. Enter the name of the new code, using up to three characters.
4. Enter a description to make it easier to interpret the code.
5. Select Taxable if you're entering a code to track taxable sales.
6. Select Non-taxable if you're entering a code to trace nontaxable sales.
7. Click Next to set up another tax code.
8. Click OK when you've finished adding tax codes.

This procedure works nicely for specifying different types of nontaxable customers. For example, you could create the following tax codes for nontaxable categories:

- NPO for nonprofit organizations
- GOV for government agencies
- WSL for wholesale businesses
- OOS for out-of-state customers (if you aren't required to collect taxes from out-of-state customers)

For taxable customers, the permutations and combinations are much broader, of course. If you're required to collect and remit sales tax for some additional states, just create codes for customers in those states, using the postal abbreviations for each state.

The problem is that QuickBooks' tax code setup doesn't work well for categorizing taxable customers if you do business in a state with complicated multiple tax rates. Those states issue codes that match the rules and rates (frequently location-based), and the codes are almost always more than three characters—but three characters is all QuickBooks permits for a sales tax code. The workaround for this is in the ability to assign a sales tax item to a customer, as long as the customer's configuration indicates "taxable" (using the built-in Tax code, or any taxable code you created). Sales tax items are discussed next.

A larger problem is that sales tax codes don't contain any real information (tax rate, taxing authority), so they aren't used in reports that generate your sales tax liabilities. However, you can generate reports about tax codes, and use that information in addition to the sales tax reports, if you have to send incredibly detailed reports to your taxing authorities. Or, you can eschew the notion of creating additional tax codes for taxable and nontaxable categories, and apply sales tax items to customers (see the following sections to understand that recommendation).

Sales Tax Items

A sales tax item is a collection of data about a sales tax, including the rate and the agency to which the sales tax is remitted. QuickBooks uses sales tax items to calculate the Tax field on sales forms and to prepare reports for tax authorities. The Sales Tax Preferences dialog box has a section named Set Up Sales Tax Items, and you can create sales tax items here or in the Items list (see the section "Creating Sales Tax Items").

Most Common Sales Tax

The Sales Tax Preferences dialog box has a field named Most Common Sales Tax, and you must enter a sales tax item in that field. Of course, to do that, you must first create at least one sales tax item (covered next). This item becomes the default sales tax item for any customers you create hereafter, but you can change any customer's default sales tax item.

Creating Sales Tax Items

You can create a sales tax item in either of the following ways:

- In the Sales Tax Preferences dialog box, click the arrow next to the Most Common Sales Tax field, and choose <Add New> from the drop-down list.
- Click the Item icon on the toolbar, or choose Lists | Item List from the menu bar, to open the Items list. Then Press CTRL-N.

Either action opens the New Item dialog box. Follow these steps to create the new sales tax item:

1. Select Sales Tax Item as the item type.
2. Enter a name for the item.
3. Enter a description to describe this sales tax on your transaction forms.
4. Enter the tax rate. QuickBooks knows the rate is a percentage, so it automatically adds the percent sign to the numbers you type (for instance, enter **6.5** if the rate is 6.5 percent).

5. Select the tax agency (which is a vendor) to whom you pay the tax from the drop-down list, or add a new vendor by choosing <Add New>.

6. Click OK.

Use the Name field to enter those complicated, pesky tax rate codes if you're in a state that has codes you couldn't use because of the three-character limitation of the tax code. In fact, if you'd created specific tax codes for multiple state rates, you'd still have to create these tax items in order to calculate rates and track the tax authorities.

Does this make you wonder why QuickBooks doesn't just use tax items and get rid of the tax codes altogether? It certainly makes me wonder. And it seems to me that it would be easy to do this, by adding a "Taxable?" field to the tax item, to put everything in one place. Then you'd only have to assign a tax item to each customer, instead of both a tax code and a tax item. On the other hand, QuickBooks could do it the other way around, making tax codes the container of rate and payee information, but they'd have to make the number of characters allowed greater than the current limit of three.

Assigning Codes and Items to Customers

By default, QuickBooks assigns the Tax (taxable) tax code to all customers, as well as the tax item you specify in the Sales Tax Preferences dialog box. These fields are on the Additional Info tab of the customer's record, and you can edit each customer's record to make changes to either field. Most of the time, it's the default tax item (not the tax code) for a customer that requires changing, especially if you're in a state that bases tax rates (and perhaps taxing authorities) on the delivery location for customers.

If you already created a great many customers, opening each record to make changes can be onerous, and you might want to wait until you use a customer in a sales transaction. Then select a new tax code or tax item (or both) from the drop-down list in the appropriate field, as seen in Figure 7-8

When you save the transaction, QuickBooks cooperates with this approach by offering the option to make permanent any changes you make during sales transaction entries.

The customer record changes, and hereafter the new tax information appears in any transaction window for this customer.

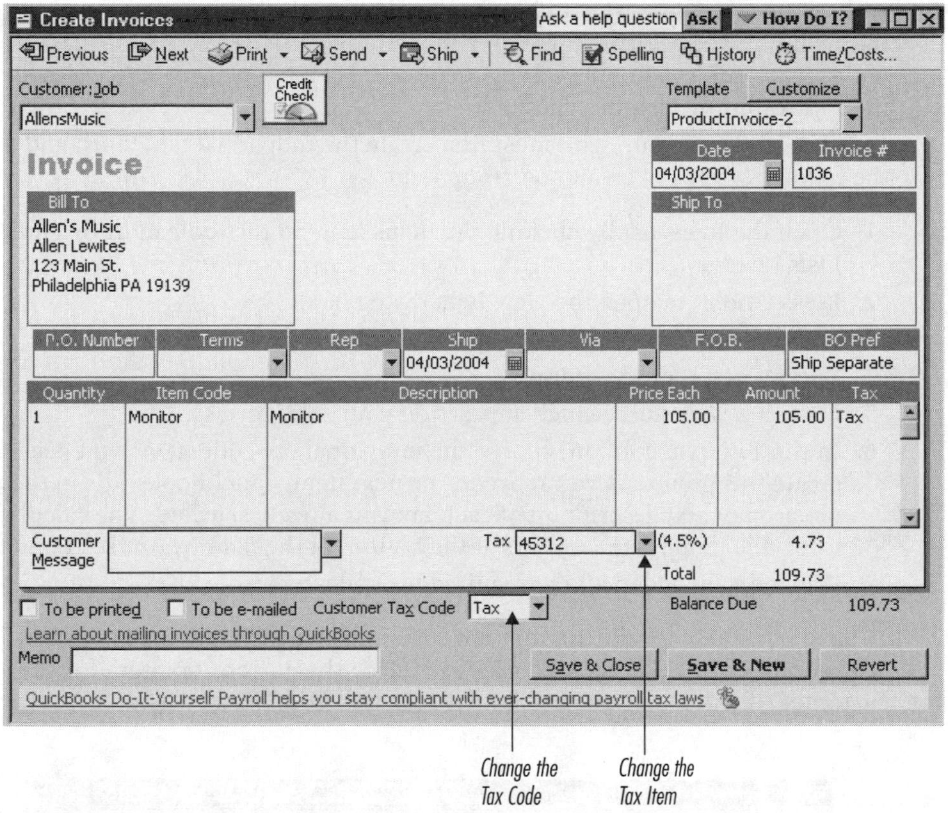

Change the Tax Code   Change the Tax Item

FIGURE 7-8 Changes made on the transaction window can be changed permanently.

Creating Tax Groups

In some states, the tax imposed is really two taxes, and the taxing authority collects a single check from you, but insists on a breakdown in the reports you send. For example, in Pennsylvania, the state sales tax is 6 percent, but businesses in Philadelphia and Pittsburgh must charge an extra 1 percent. The customer pays 7 percent, a check for 7 percent of taxable sales is remitted to the state's revenue department, but the report that accompanies the check must break down the remittance into the individual taxes. In other states, the customer pays a single tax, but the portion of that tax that represents the basic state sales tax is remitted to the state, and the locally added tax is remitted to the local taxing authority.

The challenge is to display and calculate a single tax for the customer and report multiple taxes to the taxing authorities. Tax groups meet this challenge. A tax group is a single entity that appears on a sales transaction, but it is really multiple entities that have been totaled. QuickBooks creates the tax amount by calculating each of the multiple entries and displaying their total (the customer is being charged the "combo" rate). For example, in Pennsylvania, a Philadelphia business would use a tax group (totaling 7 percent) that includes the 6 percent state sales tax and the 1 percent Philadelphia sales tax.

To create a tax group, you must first create the individual tax items, and then use the following steps to create the group item:

1. Open the Items list by clicking the Items icon on the toolbar, or by choosing Lists | Items.
2. Press CTRL-N to open the New Item dialog box.
3. Select Sales Tax Group as the Type.
4. Enter a name for the group.
5. Enter a description (which appears on your sales forms).
6. In the Tax Item column, choose the individual tax code items you need to create this group. As you move to the next item, QuickBooks fills in the rate, tax agency, and description of each tax you already selected. The calculated total (the group rate) appears at the bottom of the dialog box (see Figure 7-9).
7. When you've added all the required tax code items, click OK.

Select this item for the appropriate customers when you're creating sales transactions. QuickBooks will offer to replace the current tax item for the customer (if a different one exists) with the tax group in the customer's record.

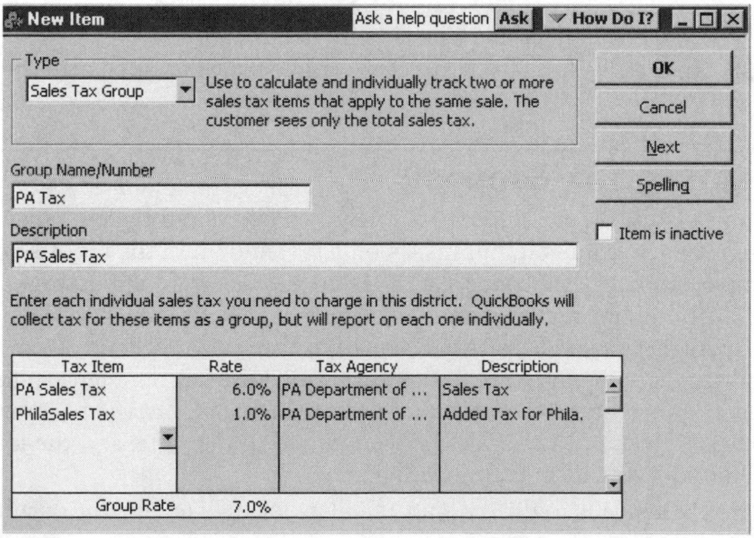

FIGURE 7-9 Create a Sales Tax Group to apply to transactions.

Running Sales Tax Reports

At some interval, determined by your taxing authority, you need to report your total sales, your nontaxable sales, and your taxable sales, along with any other required breakdowns. Oh, yes, you also have to write a check to remit the taxes.

Sales Tax Liability Report

QuickBooks has reports to help you fill out your sales tax forms. Choose Reports | Vendors & Payables | Sales Tax Liability. Use the Dates drop-down list to select an interval that matches the way you report to the taxing authorities. By default, QuickBooks chooses the interval you configured in the Preferences dialog, but that interval may only apply to your primary sales tax. If you collect multiple taxes, due at different intervals, you must create a separate report with the appropriate interval to display those figures.

Figure 7-10 shows a Sales Tax Liability report for a monthly filer. In this case, the report is for Pennsylvania, for which the rules have been explained in this chapter.

Tax Code Reports

If you have to report specific types of taxable or nontaxable sales, you can obtain that information by creating a report on the tax code you created to track that information. Choose Lists | Sales Tax Code List and select (highlight) the tax code for which you need a report. Press CTRL-Q to see a report on the activity of customers with this tax code (see Figure 7-11). Change the date range to

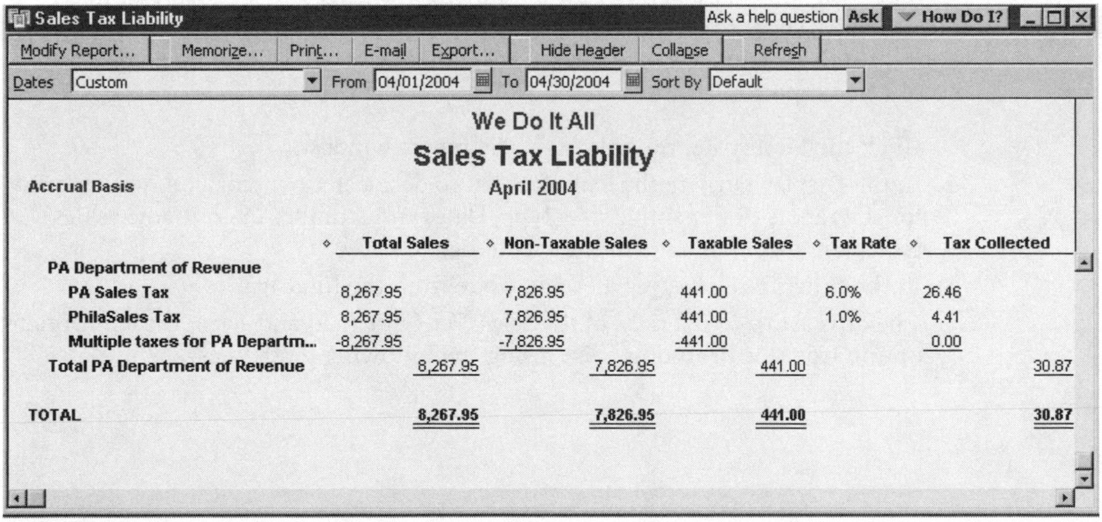

	Total Sales		Non-Taxable Sales		Taxable Sales		Tax Rate	Tax Collected	
PA Department of Revenue									
PA Sales Tax	8,267.95		7,826.95		441.00		6.0%	26.46	
PhilaSales Tax	8,267.95		7,826.95		441.00		1.0%	4.41	
Multiple taxes for PA Departm...	-8,267.95		-7,826.95		-441.00			0.00	
Total PA Department of Revenue		8,267.95		7,826.95		441.00			30.87
TOTAL		**8,267.95**		**7,826.95**		**441.00**			**30.87**

FIGURE 7-10 The Sales Tax Liability report displays taxable and nontaxable sales for each tax code.

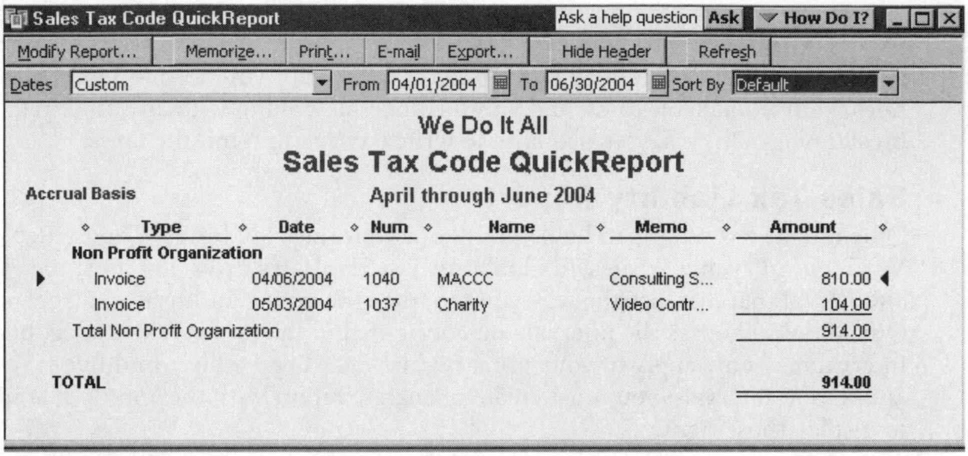

FIGURE 7-11 It's easy to get an activity report on any tax code.

match your reporting interval with the sales tax authority (this isn't a sales tax report, so QuickBooks doesn't automatically match the settings in the Sales Tax Preferences dialog box).

You don't have to create these reports one code at a time; you can modify the report window so it reports all of your tax codes, or just those you need for a specific tax authority's report. In fact, you can modify the report so it reports totals instead of every sales transaction. Use the following steps to modify this report:

1. Click the Modify Report button on the report window.
2. In the Display tab, use the Columns list to deselect any items you don't require for the report (for example, the Type, Date, and Number of an invoice/sales receipt, and the contents of the Memo field).
3. In the Filters tab, choose Sales Tax Code from the filter list.
4. Click the arrow to the right of the Sales Tax Code field and select the appropriate option from the drop-down list, using the following guidelines:

- All Sales Tax Codes, which displays total activity for the period for every code.
- Selected Sales Tax Codes, which opens the Select Sales Tax Code window, listing all codes, so you can select the specific codes you want to report on.
- All Taxable Codes, which displays total activity for the period for each taxable code.
- All Nontaxable Codes, which displays total activity for the period for each nontaxable code.

5. Click OK to return to the report window, where your selections are reflected.
6. Unless you want to take all these steps again when you need this report, click the Memorize button to memorize the report.

Remitting the Sales Tax

After you check the figures (or calculate them, if you have multiple reports with different standards of calculation), it's time to pay the tax:

1. Choose Vendors | Sales Tax | Pay Sales Tax to open the Pay Sales Tax window.

2. Select the bank account to use, if you have more than one.
3. Check the date that's displayed in the field named Show Sales Tax Due Through. It must match the end date of your current reporting period (for instance, monthly or quarterly).

NOTE: QuickBooks doesn't ask for a start date because it uses the period duration defined in your Sales Tax Preferences.

4. Click in the Pay column to insert a check mark next to those you're paying now. If you're lucky enough to have the same reporting interval for all taxing authorities—it never seems to work that way, though—just click the Pay All Tax button.
5. If you're going to print the check, be sure to select the To Be Printed check box at the bottom of the dialog box.
6. Click OK when you've completed filling out the information. The next time you print or write checks, the sales tax check is in the group waiting to be completed.

If, for some reason, you need to adjust the amount of sales tax due, select that item and click the Adjust button to open the Sales Tax Adjustment dialog box. Specify the amount by which to increase or reduce the tax amount, and specify an Adjustment Account to which you want to post the adjustment.

Sales Tax Adjustment ☒

Adjustment Date 04/30/2004 ▦

Entry No. 1

Sales Tax Vendor MyStateRevDept ▼

Adjustment Account 2900 · Adjustments ▼

┌─ Adjustment ──────────────────────────────┐
│ ◉ Increase Sales Tax By   │
│   Amount 1.00   │
│ ○ Reduce Sales Tax By   │
└──┘

Memo Sales Tax Adjustment

[**OK**] [Cancel] [Help]

TIP: If you have customers in a state other than the state in which you do business, you might be able to use another approach to sales tax. Technically, some states call this tax a Sales and Use tax, where the "use" part of the name means that the customer is responsible for remitting the tax. If the state permits it, you can skip the sales tax charge (and therefore skip the need to fill out forms and remit payments) and leave it up to the customer. The customer has to tell his or her state taxing authority that he or she purchased taxable goods from an out-of-state vendor (that's you) and remit the appropriate amount. Businesses that take advantage of this usually print a message on the invoice that says, "Sales taxes for this purchase are not collected by us and are your responsibility," or something to that effect. The truth is, you have no legal obligation to warn the customer if the out-of-state taxing authority is willing to let you skip sales tax collections, but it's nice to do.

Running Payroll

In *this chapter:*

- Set up payroll

- Check tax status, deductions, and other employee information

- Enter historical data

- Write payroll checks

If you plan to do your own payroll rather than employ a payroll company, you'll find all the tools you need in QuickBooks. All the information you need to set up and run payroll is covered in this chapter.

Setting Up Payroll

To set up payroll, you can use the QuickBooks Payroll Setup feature, which walks you through each required step, or you can set up each element of payroll manually. Until all your setup tasks are completed, each time you access any payroll function, QuickBooks offers to help you set up payroll. If you click Yes, QuickBooks loads the Payroll Setup program, which lists all the steps involved in getting started with payroll.

As you can see in Figure 8-1, the program tracks your progress as you complete each task. All the steps enumerated by the setup program are covered in this chapter, although I won't be specifically walking through (or referring to) the Payroll Setup window all the time—some things, such as creating payroll items, or running a Payroll Checkup in order to make sure your setup is correct, are just as easily done directly from the menu system.

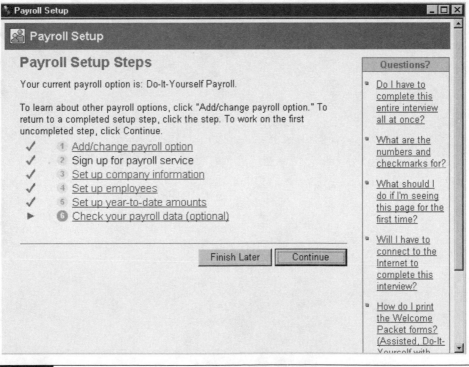

FIGURE 8-1 Each step involved in setting up payroll is available in the Payroll Setup window.

QuickBooks Payroll Services

You cannot do payroll within QuickBooks without signing up for payroll services. Actually, you can perform some payroll chores, such as generating gross payroll data. However, unless you've signed up for QuickBooks payroll services, no calculations occur against the gross amount of the paycheck. No withholding appears, no amounts are posted to employee and employer liability accounts, and there is no net amount.

You can, if you wish, use your own printed tax table (Employer's Circular E from the IRS), calculate the deductions manually, and then issue a paycheck for the net amount to each employee. If you don't want to face that, you must sign up for payroll services.

Do-It-Yourself Payroll

Sign up for this service if you want to run your payroll totally in-house. For an annual fee, QuickBooks keeps your tax table up to date, so calculations are automatic. You can print all federal tax forms from QuickBooks (940, 941, 1099, and W-2).

For an additional fee, Do-It-Yourself Payroll can provide direct deposit services and electronic payment of federal and state payroll taxes.

Assisted Payroll

This option includes all the functions in the Do-It-Yourself Payroll Service and then adds the following features:

- Automatic payment, by electronic transfer, of your federal and state withholdings
- Automatic electronic filing of all the federal and state forms required throughout the year
- Preparation of W-2 forms for each employee
- Preparation of W-3 forms for transmitting W-2 forms

NOTE: QuickBooks also offers Complete Payroll Service, which is a fully outsourced payroll service company. If you don't use a payroll service company, or you are unhappy with your current payroll service company, you might want to check out this QuickBooks company. You can get more information by choosing Employees | Employer Services | Payroll Options and clicking the links that provide information about the Complete Payroll Service.

QuickBooks Direct Deposit Services

With either payroll service, you can purchase direct deposit services for your employees. Employees must sign a form giving permission for direct deposit, and you can print those forms directly from your QuickBooks software (QuickBooks provides a link to display and print the forms during the sign-up process).

Employees can opt to deposit their entire paychecks into one bank account, or split the amount between two bank accounts.

Applying for Payroll Services

To sign up for either payroll service, choose Employees | Payroll Services | Set Up Payroll to open the Payroll Setup Options window. Click Choose a Payroll Option to begin your setup (see Figure 8-2).

Make your choice and click Continue. An ad for the QuickBooks Employee Organizer appears, and I'm going to assume you're not stopping now to learn about,

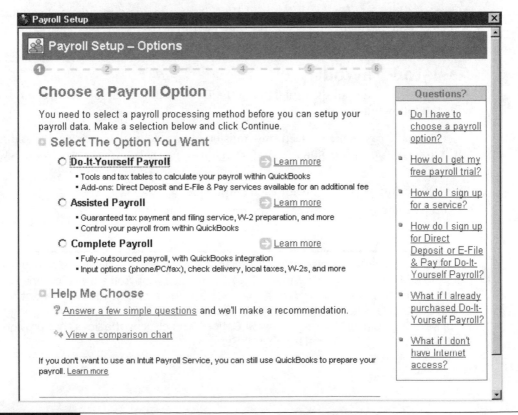

FIGURE 8-2 Payroll setup starts with signing up for a payroll service.

or buy, this program, so click Continue (you can examine the Employee Organizer add-on at any time by selecting its listing from the Payroll menu). The Payroll Setup window opens, displaying all the steps required for setting up payroll. Click Sign Up For Payroll Service, and if you chose Do-It-Yourself, select the manner in which you prefer to update tax tables: online or on a CD. The tax table updates aren't enormous, so even if you connect to the Internet via a telephone modem, online updates are a better choice. QuickBooks charges extra for shipping you a CD every time the tax table changes, and sometimes the changes are only state-tax changes that may not even affect your state.

Click Continue to open the Company Information window (if you chose Assisted Payroll, you jump right to this window). Make sure your company EIN, company name, and company address is correct, and then click Continue.

If you chose Do-It-Yourself Payroll, the next window invites you to complete your application online. Click Sign Up Now. QuickBooks opens your web browser and travels to the QuickBooks payroll sign-up site. Click Continue to move through the windows (most of which contain information about the service). You can sign up for the payroll service and for direct deposit services. If QuickBooks has a problem with the company or credit card information you provide, a message appears asking you to contact Intuit to resolve the issue (a telephone number is included in the message).

If you chose Assisted Payroll, you see a window that explains you must first contact QuickBooks to make arrangements for the service. A telephone number is displayed; when you call, have the following information available:

- Number of employees
- Your EIN
- Your state and local tax ID numbers
- Bank account information (bank, routing number, your account number, etc.)
- Name and address of company principals

When you receive your subscription number, return to the Payroll Setup window and go through the online sign-up process, entering the number when instructed.

When the sign-up process is completed, QuickBooks downloads the files you need to run payroll (unless you chose to receive your files on a CD). The new files are automatically added to your QuickBooks system; you don't have to do anything to install them. In addition to the payroll software, the current tax table is added to your system.

Configuring Payroll

Before you run the first payroll, all your setup tasks must be completed. You can't produce accurate payroll checks unless QuickBooks knows everything there is to know about the payroll taxes you have to withhold, the payroll taxes you have to pay as an employer, and the deductions you need to take for benefits, garnishes, union dues, or any other reason. And, of course, you need to configure each employee for dependents and deductions.

In the following sections, I'll go over all the elements and components involved in setting up payroll. You can perform all the tasks either by moving through the Payroll Setup windows, or by performing each task manually, using the QuickBooks menus and setup dialog boxes.

Payroll Items

A QuickBooks *payroll item* is any element that is part of a payroll check. That means the elements that go into determining the gross amount of the payroll check (salary, wages, bonuses, and commissions), as well as the elements that determine the net amount of the payroll check (withheld taxes, deductions for benefits, and any other deductions). Additionally, if you have expenses that are attached to payroll, such as company-paid benefits that don't deduct amounts from employee paychecks, you should set up those elements as well.

QuickBooks creates many payroll items during your EasyStep Interview when you indicate you'll be using payroll, but you'll probably have to create additional items. Each item you create has to be linked to an account in your chart of accounts. And because all the money you withhold or pay out as a company expense is turned over to somebody else (the government, an insurance company, or a pension administrator), you must have vendors associated with each deduction.

Before you run your first payroll, it's a good idea to check your Payroll Item List to make sure everything you need has been entered and also to double-check the links to accounts and vendors.

Open your list of payroll items by choosing Lists | Payroll Item List from the menu bar. Every item that's used to generate a paycheck must exist in the Payroll Item List. Double-click each item to make sure it's linked properly. Double-clicking puts the item in Edit mode, which brings up a wizard-like series of windows. Click Next to see the links for the item. If any data is missing or incorrect, you must make the necessary entries. You can create any additional vendor or general ledger accounts you need by selecting <Add New> from the appropriate drop-down list. See Chapter 2 for detailed information about creating payroll items.

TIP: Some payroll items have only two wizard windows; others have more because there's additional information needed about the item. If you come across anything you don't understand or don't know how to fill out, it's best to call your accountant.

Employee Information

The information about your employees must be perfectly, pristinely accurate, or you may hear about it in a very unfriendly manner. Your employees won't be happy if the deductions are incorrect; the IRS won't be happy if your payroll records don't accurately reflect employee tax status categories. Chapter 2 covers the procedure for adding employees to your company records; in this section I'll go over some of the details in those records.

 TIP: Make sure you pass around W-4 forms every year and insist that employees fill them out completely. Don't accept blank forms back with a notation that says "same as last year." This is your bible for entering employee data, and it's important to be able to prove that you entered information from the horse's mouth.

To view your employee list, choose Lists | Employee List from the menu bar. When the list appears, double-click each employee's listing to put the record into Edit mode. For each record, select Payroll And Compensation Info from the Change Tabs drop-down list. Check the information against the W-4 form or any other documents that this employee may have provided to have specific deductions taken from paychecks (medical benefits, pension plans, and so forth). Then click the Taxes button to check the federal, state, and local tax status for this employee against the W-4 form.

Click OK to return to the Payroll Info tab. If you've established policies for sick and vacation days, click the Sick/Vacation button to make sure the settings are correct. Click the Direct Deposit button to configure the employee's direct deposit choices, if you've signed up for direct deposit services with QuickBooks.

TIP: If your business is a corporation, you must separate compensation for corporate officers from the other employee compensation when you file your business taxes. To avoid having to perform all sorts of calculations outside of QuickBooks to determine these amounts, create a separate payroll item called "Officer Compensation." Assign it to its own account (e.g. Payroll-Officers). Then open the Employee card for each officer and change the Earnings item to this new payroll item.

Entering Historical Data

If you're not starting your use of QuickBooks at the very beginning of the year, you must enter all the historical information about paychecks. This is the only way to perform all those tasks required at the end of the year. You cannot give your employees two W-2 forms, one from your manual system and another from QuickBooks, nor can you file your annual tax reports on any piecemeal basis.

NOTE: No matter what your fiscal year is, your payroll year is the calendar year. Even though you can start using payroll for the current period before you enter the historical data, remember that the absence of historical data may affect some tax calculations. If there are withholding amounts that cease after a certain maximum (perhaps your state only requires SUI for the first $8,000.00 in gross payroll), you'll have to adjust those current paychecks manually to remove the withholding if the historical payroll data isn't entered.

Entering the History Manually

The truth is, payroll is so easy to do if everything is set up properly that I usually advise clients to enter each historical payroll run individually. It's great training. For the first couple of pay periods, stop to look at the details (the postings to general ledger accounts) and compare them to your manual records. This gives you an opportunity to understand what QuickBooks is doing, in addition to checking accuracy.

If it's late in the year when you first begin using QuickBooks, I usually advise waiting until next year to move to QuickBooks payroll. If it's somewhere around the middle of the year, you may decide that my suggestion is crazy and refuse to go through the process of entering 26 or 30 weeks of payroll runs. I can understand your reluctance (although there's no such thing as being too careful when it comes to payroll), so read on to learn how to enter historical data in batches, using the QuickBooks Payroll Data Wizard.

Using the QuickBooks Payroll Data Wizard

QuickBooks provides assistance for entering prior payroll records in the form of a wizard. Choose Employees | Payroll Services | Set Up Payroll from the QuickBooks menu bar. This opens the same Payroll Setup window you used to sign up for payroll. Complete all the tasks up to Step 5. If you performed any of the steps manually, just select the tasks that are not marked as completed, and click the Continue button until you're returned to this window and the setup steps are marked as completed.

Assuming you've completed all the previous steps, select Step 5: Set Up Year To Date Amounts. The YTD Introductory window opens. Read the information and then click Set Up YTD Amounts to start the Set Up YTD Amounts Wizard. The wizard walks you through all the necessary steps. You'll need all your manual payroll records for the year, or this won't go smoothly.

Set the Dates for Payroll History

The opening screen is informational. Once you've digested it, click Next to proceed. The initial wizard questions (spanning two wizard pages) are about the dates you want QuickBooks to use for postings as you enter historical data. The dates you enter depend on the way you've been managing payroll data in QuickBooks up to this point.

The first wizard window asks about dates for posting liability and expense account data, and net paycheck amounts (see Figure 8-3).

Payroll Liability and Expense Postings   The wizard wants to know the first date that payroll liability and expense accounts are affected by the historical information you'll be entering for each employee. This is the date you want QuickBooks to use to post payroll liability and expense data. If you've had an outside payroll service, or you've been doing payroll manually, enter the first date in the current year that doesn't already have liability and expense postings.

If you've been making journal entries or individual transaction entries (paychecks for which you posted amounts to the liability and expense accounts) in QuickBooks, the first date for posting payroll liability and expense information is the first day you begin using QuickBooks for payroll. When you enter historical data, QuickBooks doesn't have to post this data, because you've been doing it.

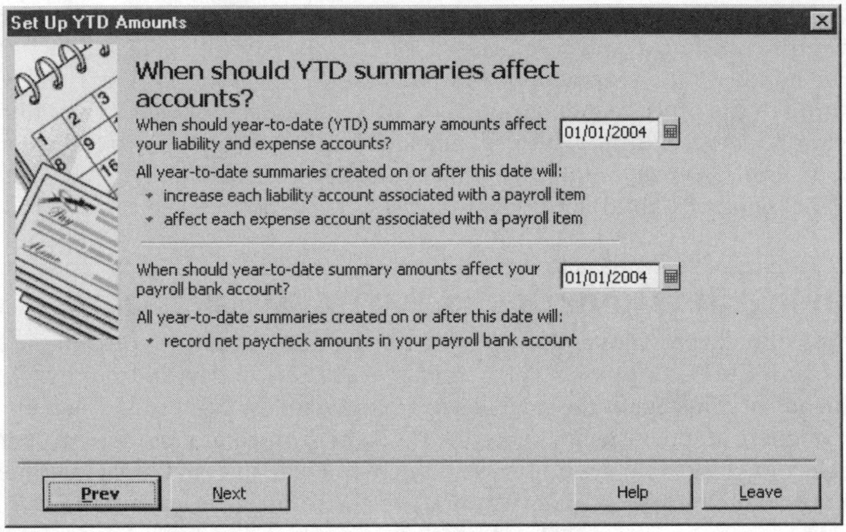

FIGURE 8-3 Tell QuickBooks the date as of which the historical data is posted.

If you haven't been posting your liability and expense payroll data into QuickBooks, the first date to enter payroll liability and expense data is the first day of the calendar year. As you enter historical data for each employee, QuickBooks will post the liability and expense data to your general ledger.

Payroll Bank Account Postings This is the date you want QuickBooks to use to post the net paycheck amounts to your bank account, whether it's a separate payroll account or your regular operating account.

If you've been entering the net payroll checks into your bank account, QuickBooks doesn't have to post the amount when you enter historical data. Therefore, the first date QuickBooks should use is the day you start doing your payroll in QuickBooks. If you've been entering the net amount of paychecks in your checkbook and not entering the liability and expense postings, then the date for posting to the bank account is later than the date you specified for liability and expense postings.

After you enter the two dates, click Next.

Starting Date for Using QuickBooks Payroll The next wizard window asks for the date on which you plan to go "live" with payroll.

Set Up YTD Amounts

Earliest QuickBooks payroll date

Enter the date that you will begin using QuickBooks payroll to create paychecks. For information that will help you determine this date, click Help.

07/01/2004

Prev   Next   Help   Leave

QuickBooks defines historical data as any data that precedes this date. On the live date, you'll be entering payroll checks and distributing them; those checks are not part of the historical data. It's important to understand how the live date affects the task in front of you.

- Payroll records are summarized quarterly, because your 941 reports are due quarterly.
- You can't enter summarized data for the quarter that's current (the quarter that the live date falls in). Instead, for the current quarter, you must enter data for each individual pay period (weekly, biweekly, semimonthly, or monthly). For previous quarters, you can enter quarterly totals.
- If you tell QuickBooks that your live date is any date in the first quarter, you will have to enter historical data for each pay period before the live date.
- If you tell QuickBooks that your live date is in the second quarter, QuickBooks will ask you to enter a quarterly total for the first quarter, and then ask you for individual pay period totals for the second quarter up to the live date.
- If you tell QuickBooks that your live date is in the third quarter, QuickBooks will ask you to enter quarterly totals for the first two quarters, and then ask you for pay period totals up to the live date.

To avoid a lot of data entry, go live with payroll at the beginning of a calendar quarter.

Enter Employee History

In the next window, the wizard displays the list of your employees. Now it's time to enter the year-to-date information. You perform this task one employee at a time.

Select the first employee and click Enter Summary (or double-click the employee listing). QuickBooks presents a screen with the pay period for this employee so you can fill out the amounts, as seen in Figure 8-4.

Click Next Period to move to the next pay period for this employee. If you indicated a live date that's later than March 31, QuickBooks offers quarterly pay periods to fill in the YTD amounts, except for the current quarter (as explained in the previous section).

Click OK when you finish with this employee. You're returned to the list of employees, where you select the next employee and repeat the process.

When all the employee records are entered, click Next to move to the wizard window that accepts information about the payments you've made to remit withholding, pay employer taxes, and so on.

- If you haven't made those payments (perhaps you're setting up payroll in January, or any time in the first calendar quarter), click Finish.
- If you made those payments and recorded them in QuickBooks, click Finish.
- If you made the payments and didn't record them in QuickBooks, click Create Payment to open the Prior Payments dialog box, and enter the data.

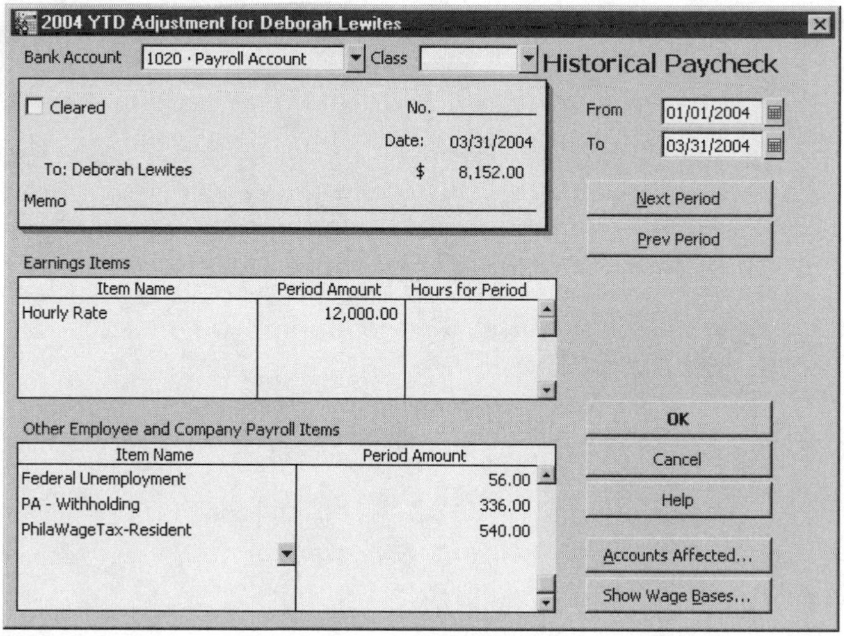

FIGURE 8-4   Enter all payroll items linked to this employee for the period.

Running a Payroll Checkup

QuickBooks has a feature that checks your payroll configuration to make sure there aren't any discrepancies. This Payroll Checkup feature should be run whenever you add or modify payroll items or deductions. It's also a good idea to run the checkup after you've entered historical data so that QuickBooks can check your payroll system before you run your first payroll. If QuickBooks finds discrepancies or problems, you're told about them and given the opportunity to make changes. Use one of the following methods to open the Payroll Checkup program:

- Choose Employees | Run Payroll Checkup.
- Choose Employees | Payroll Services | Set Up Payroll, and select Step 6.

Click Continue twice to begin the process. It takes a few seconds to check your system, and then a window opens to display the results:

```
┌─────────────────────────────────────────────────────────────────┐
│ ⚑ Payroll Setup                                       _ □ ✕       │
├─────────────────────────────────────────────────────────────────┤
│  ⬛ Payroll Setup – Checkup                                        │
│                                                                   │
│   1 ──────── 2 ──────── 3 ──────── 4 ──────── 5 ──────── ⬤       │
│                                                                   │
│  Incomplete or Invalid Tax Setup            ┌─────────────────┐   │
│                                             │   Questions?    │   │
│  QuickBooks found some potential problems   ├─────────────────┤   │
│  in your federal and/or state payroll       │ ▫ General       │   │
│  taxes.                                     │   questions about│  │
│                                             │   payroll setup. │  │
│  The taxes you need to correct are listed   └─────────────────┘   │
│  in the following table. Click Edit next to                       │
│  each item to display the payroll tax page, and then              │
│  correct the problem(s).                                          │
│            ┌──────────┬──────────────────────┐                    │
│            │      Please Review              │                    │
│            ├──────────┼──────────────────────┤                    │
│            │   Edit   │ Pennsylvania Payroll Taxes │                │
│            └──────────┴──────────────────────┘                    │
│                                                                   │
│   ┌──────────┐              ┌──────────┐  ┌──────────┐            │
│   │  Cancel  │              │   Back   │  │ Continue │            │
│   └──────────┘              └──────────┘  └──────────┘            │
│                                                                   │
└─────────────────────────────────────────────────────────────────┘
```

If QuickBooks indicates a problem with missing or incorrect data, click the Edit button to open the appropriate windows so you can fix the problems. Click Continue and follow the prompts to complete the Payroll Checkup (your tasks depend on the problems the checkup program found). When you've made all the changes, run the checkup again, just to be sure.

Getting the Tax Tables

Before you can process payroll checks, you must install the current tax tables. You must do this periodically, to make sure any changes in tax rules or government forms are installed in your payroll files.

If you selected the option to receive a CD from Intuit, follow the instructions that came with the CD to install the tax table.

If you choose to download the tax tables from the QuickBooks Payroll Services website, make sure you're connected to the Internet before you start. Choose Employees | Get Updates | Get Payroll Updates to open the QuickBooks Payroll Information dialog box. Your current tax table version displays, along with other information about your payroll subscription status.

NOTE: The dialog offers a choice between downloading only those files that have changed since you last installed a payroll update, or downloading all the payroll-related program files. You only need to download the full set of files if you've had a problem downloading the tax table update, or you've seen an error message about a missing file when you're running payroll functions.

Click Update. A progress bar displays to show you how things are going as you download the tax table to your computer. QuickBooks automatically installs the software, so you don't have to do anything else to begin working with the tax tables.

Running Payroll

It's payday. All the historical data is entered. It's time to run the payroll. If you're using direct deposit services, you need a two-day lead before the actual payday. If only some of your employees use direct deposit, you have two choices:

- Do all your payroll data entry two days before payday and hold the printed checks until payday (date the checks appropriately).
- Run the payroll procedure twice using the appropriate employees for each run.

Selecting Employees to Pay

To begin, choose Employees | Pay Employees, to open the Select Employees To Pay dialog box shown in Figure 8-5.

 NOTE: QuickBooks may display a message telling you it's been quite some time since you last checked for payroll updates and offering to perform that task. Always accept the invitation so you know you have the most current tax information.

The first time you run payroll, there's no information about the last payroll check for each employee. After you've completed this payroll run, that information will be available.

- For salaried employees, the information usually remains the same so you can create the checks without previewing information about hours.
- For hourly wage employees, if the number of hours is the same as the last check, you can repeat checks as if the employee were on salary.

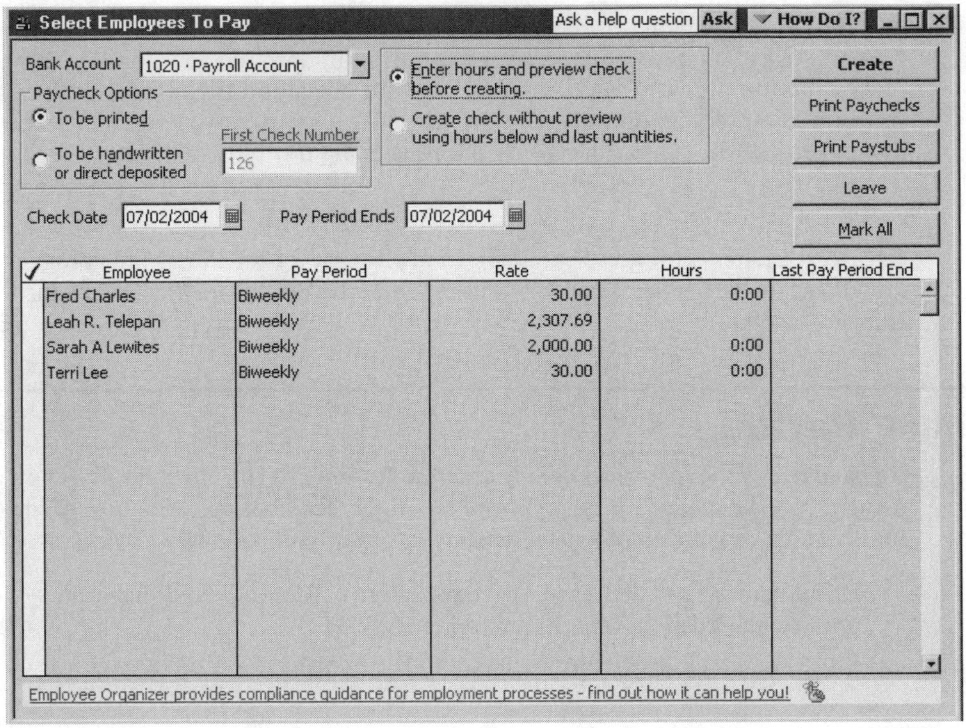

Select Employees To Pay   Ask a help question | Ask | ▽ How Do I? | _ □ ✕

Bank Account	1020 · Payroll Account ▼	● Enter hours and preview check before creating.		Create
Paycheck Options		○ Create check without preview using hours below and last quantities.		Print Paychecks
● To be printed	First Check Number			Print Paystubs
○ To be handwritten or direct deposited	126			Leave
Check Date 07/02/2004	Pay Period Ends 07/02/2004			Mark All

✓	Employee	Pay Period	Rate	Hours	Last Pay Period End
	Fred Charles	Biweekly	30.00	0:00	
	Leah R. Telepan	Biweekly	2,307.69		
	Sarah A Lewites	Biweekly	2,000.00	0:00	
	Terri Lee	Biweekly	30.00	0:00	

Employee Organizer provides compliance guidance for employment processes - find out how it can help you! 🖑

FIGURE 8-5   Select the employees who get a paycheck in this payroll run.

For this first payroll, however, you must check the details before printing payroll checks:

1. Make sure the correct bank account is selected.

> **TIP:** If you have a separate payroll account, be sure to go to Edit | Preferences and click the Checking icon. On the Company Preferences tab, select the default bank account for creating paychecks and the default bank account for paying payroll liabilities. This way, you won't accidentally use the wrong bank account when you're working in payroll.

2. Select the option Enter Hours And Preview Check Before Creating.
3. Select the employees to be paid by clicking next to their names in the check mark column. If all employees are included in this payroll run (they're all direct deposit, or all printed checks) click the Mark All button.

4. Specify the check date and the end date for this payroll period.

5. Click Create to begin entering paycheck information.

Filling Out the Paycheck Information

The first employee's Preview Paycheck window opens (see Figure 8-6). If the employee is on an hourly wage, everything is blank until you fill in the Hours column. If the employee is salaried, the amounts are displayed.

Complete the following steps:

1. Enter hours, if the employee is an hourly employee.

2. Make any corrections necessary. Perhaps you need to add an additional pay item such as a bonus or enter a one-time deduction.

3. When everything is correct, click Create.

4. The next employee's record appears so you can repeat the process.

5. Continue to move through each employee.

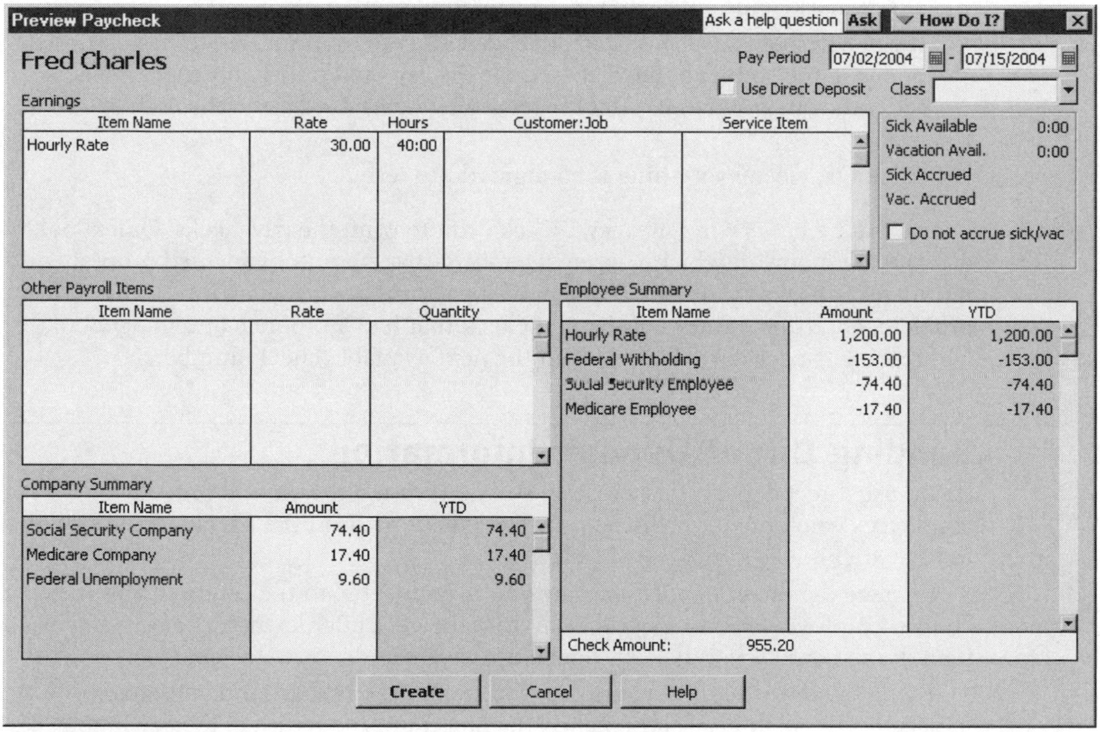

FIGURE 8-6 Enter any necessary data for each paycheck.

6. When the last employee check is created, you're returned to the original Select Employees To Pay window.

7. Click Print Paychecks if you're ready to do that; otherwise, click Leave and print the paychecks later.

Printing the Paychecks

When all the checks have been created, you must print the paychecks. Load the right checks in your printer (don't use your standard bank account checks if you have a separate payroll account).

1. Either click the Print Paychecks button in the Select Employees To Pay window, or choose File | Print Forms | Paychecks to open the Select Paychecks To Print window.

2. Select the bank account for this paycheck print run.

3. Make sure the First Check Number field contains the correct number for the first check loaded in the printer.

4. Deselect any paycheck you don't want to print at this time by clicking in the check mark column to remove the existing check mark.

5. If you have both paychecks and direct deposit stubs to print, select the appropriate option at the bottom of the dialog box to display (and print) only those items. Then select the other option to print the remaining items. By default, the Both option is enabled.

6. Click OK when everything is configured properly.

The Print Checks window opens. Click Print to print the paychecks. QuickBooks displays a window in which you must confirm that everything printed properly or reprint any checks that had a problem. If everything is fine, click OK. If there's a problem, enter the number of the first check that had a problem and QuickBooks will reprint as necessary, starting with the next available check number.

Sending Direct Deposit Information

If you use direct deposit services, you still go through the payroll process for the employees who opted for this service. You just don't print the checks. Instead, you notify QuickBooks to deposit the checks.

To make the direct deposit, be sure you're connected to the Internet, and then choose Employees | Send Payroll Data from the QuickBooks menu bar (the menu item doesn't exist if you haven't signed up for direct deposit services).

A window opens to display the data you're about to upload, and you must confirm its accuracy. If anything is amiss, cancel the procedure and return to the Pay Employees procedure to correct the information.

When the data is correct, click Go Online to begin the data transfer and follow the onscreen instructions.

Sending Payroll Liability Information to Assisted Payroll Services

If you've signed up for Assisted Payroll Services, you must upload the information about the payroll run you just completed so that the service can remit your withholding to the appropriate government agencies.

Choose Employees | Send Payroll Data from the QuickBooks menu bar. A window opens to display the data you're about to upload, and you must confirm its accuracy. Click Go Online to begin the data transfer, and follow the onscreen instructions. When the information is received by QuickBooks, a confirmation window appears to show you the transactions that are being performed (for example, remittance of withholding taxes to the appropriate authorities) and the fees being charged. The transactions are automatically entered in your checking account register.

Government Payroll Reporting

In this chapter:

- Make tax deposits

- Remit withheld amounts and employer taxes

- Prepare quarterly and annual returns

- Print W-2 forms

Doing payroll in-house means having a lot of reports to print, forms to fill out, and checks to write. There's a logical order to these tasks, although the logic differs depending on the state and city (or town) you're in. In this chapter, I'll go over the procedures in the order in which most businesses have to perform the tasks.

If you've signed up for QuickBooks Assisted Payroll services, you don't have to worry about the sections in this chapter that are concerned with remitting federal and state withholdings. You do, however, have to remit your local payroll tax withholding yourself.

Making Federal Payroll Tax Deposits

The federal government requires you to deposit the withholding amounts, along with the matching employer contributions, at a specified time. That time period is dependent upon the size of the total withholding amount you've accumulated. You may be required to deposit monthly, semimonthly, weekly, or within three days of the payroll. Check the current limits with the IRS or your accountant.

There's a formula for determining the size of the deposit check—it is the sum of the following amounts for the period:

- Federal withholding
- FICA withholding
- Medicare withholding
- FICA matching contribution from employer
- Medicare matching contribution from employer

You don't have to do the math—QuickBooks does it for you. But it's a good idea to know what the formula is so you can check the numbers yourself.

Select the Liabilities for the Federal Deposit Check

To prepare the check, choose Employees | Process Payroll Liabilities | Pay Payroll Liabilities from the QuickBooks menu bar. The Select Date Range For Liabilities dialog opens; select the date range the check covers by choosing an interval from the drop-down list, or by entering the start and end dates.

For a federal deposit, the date range must match your deposit frequency, which is determined by the amount of withholding. For most small businesses, monthly deposits are common. However, if your federal withholding amounts are large, you may have to make a federal deposit within several days of each payroll. (The IRS sends you a letter if your deposit frequency changes.)

When you click OK, the Pay Liabilities window appears, listing all the payroll liabilities currently due. Select the payroll bank account, if you use one. You could select all the liabilities and write all the checks (whether they're due at the moment or not) just to get them out of the way. I don't do that. I select only those liabilities that are due now. Besides, this section is about the federal deposit check.

Click in the check mark column to select the liabilities you want to pay. Notice that when you choose Medicare or Social Security, selecting the employee liability automatically selects the company liability (or vice versa). This is, of course, because you must pay the total of withholding and employer contributions at the same time.

Specify whether you want to create the check without reviewing it, or review the check before finalizing it (you don't usually need to review the check, unless you're adding penalties or changing the amount for some other reason).

Click Create when you've selected the liability payments you want to pay for your deposit payment. If you opted to review the check, it's displayed, and if you need to make changes, do so. Then click Save & Close to record the data.

Print the Check

The check is created and needs only to be printed. (If you don't use printed checks, just use the check register to enter your manual check, instead of following these steps for printing).

1. Choose File | Print Forms | Checks from the menu bar.
2. When the Select Checks To Print window opens, select the bank account you use for payroll.
3. Be sure all the payroll liability checks you created are selected.
4. Click OK to bring up the Print Checks window so you can print the checks.

 N O T E : Chapter 7 explains how to set up your printer for printing checks.

The federal government sent you a book of coupons (Form 8109) you must use when you deposit the funds you owe. Fill out a coupon and take it, along with your check, to the bank in which you have your payroll account. Make the check payable to the bank, unless you've been given different instructions by the bank or your accountant.

N O T E : Don't forget to fill in the little bullets on the coupon: one to indicate this is a 941 deposit, the other to indicate the quarter for which this payment is remitted.

Paying Federal Unemployment Taxes

The Federal Unemployment Tax Act (FUTA) provides unemployment compensation to workers who have lost their jobs, usually after the workers' state benefits have been exhausted. The FUTA tax is paid by employers; no deductions are taken from employee wages. Companies must make FUTA payments if either of the following scenarios exist:

- During this year or last year you paid wages of at least $1,500 in any calendar quarter.
- During this year or last year you had one or more employees for at least part of a day for a period of 20 weeks (the weeks do not have to be contiguous).

Use Form 8109 (the same coupon you use to deposit federal withholding and employer matching contributions) and mark the coupon for 940 Tax, and the quarter in which you are making your deposit. You don't have to make the deposit until you owe $100.00, but you can make deposits until you reach that amount if you wish.

Technically, FUTA tax is 6.2 percent of gross wages up to $7,000.00 per employee, but the federal government gives employers a 5.4 percent credit for paying their state unemployment taxes. Therefore, unless you deliberately ignore your state unemployment payments, you can calculate FUTA at the rate of .8 percent of gross wages ($.008 \times \$7,000.00$), which is $56.00 per employee who reaches the $7,000.00 goal. QuickBooks assumes you're paying your state unemployment taxes, and calculates your FUTA liability accordingly.

Remitting State and Local Liabilities

Your state and local payroll liabilities vary depending upon where your business is located and where your employees live (and pay taxes). Besides income taxes, you are probably liable for unemployment insurance, as well. And many states have withholding for disability.

State and Local Income Taxes

Most states have some form of an income tax, which might be calculated in any one of a variety of ways:

- A flat percentage of gross income
- A sliding percentage of gross income
- A percentage based on the federal tax for the employee

Local taxes are also widely varied in their approach:

- Some cities have different rates for employees of companies that operate in the city. There may be one rate for employees who live in the same city and a different rate for nonresidents.
- Your business might operate in a city or town that has a *payroll head tax* (a once-a-year payment that is a flat amount per employee).
- You may have a head tax for the town in which your business operates and still be required to withhold local taxes for employees who live in another city.

State and local taxing authorities usually provide coupons or forms to use for remitting income tax withholding. The frequency with which you must remit might depend on the size of your payroll, or it might be quarterly, semiannual, or annual regardless of the amount.

To remit the withheld income tax for your state and local taxing authorities, choose Employees | Process Payroll Liabilities | Pay Payroll Liabilities from the QuickBooks menu bar. Select the date range this payment covers and click OK to open the Pay Liabilities window. Locate the state and local income tax liabilities. Mark them by clicking in the check mark column, and then click Create. Follow the steps to print the checks as described earlier. Mail them, along with your coupon or form, to the appropriate addresses.

Other State Liabilities

If your state has SUI or SDI or both, you have to pay those liabilities when they're due. Commonly, these are quarterly payments.

> **TIP:** It's a good idea to create different vendor names for SUI, SDI, and income tax withholding to make sure you don't accidentally send checks for the wrong thing, and to prevent QuickBooks from issuing a single check for the grand total. The vendor record for each vendor name may have the same payee (Department of Revenue), but the records are kept separately.

Not all states have SUI or SDI, and some have one but not the other. Some states collect SUI from the employee and the company; some collect only from the company. Check the rules for your state.

Use the same process described earlier for selecting the amounts due from the Pay Liabilities window when it's time to pay your state liabilities.

Remitting Other Payroll Liabilities

The rules for remitting the paycheck deductions and employer contributions for other reasons—such as health benefits, pension, and so on—are specific to your arrangements with those vendors.

There are a great many ways to handle the way these payments are posted, and you have to decide what makes sense to you (or to your accountant). For example, if you pay a monthly amount to a medical insurer, you may want to post the employee deductions back to the same expense account you use to pay the bill. That way, only the net amount is reported as an expense on your taxes. Or you can track the deductions in a separate account and calculate the net amount at tax time.

You have to perform these tasks in a way that guarantees the vendors get the right amount. For example, before you write the check to the medical insurance company, you must enter a regular vendor bill for the difference between the deducted amounts and the actual bill. That difference is your company contribution, of course. Then, when you write the check, both bills will be in the hopper, and the check will be in the correct amount.

Preparing Your 941 Form

Every quarter you must file a 941 form that reports the total amount you owe the federal government for withheld taxes and employer expenses. If you have been paying the deposits regularly, no check is remitted with the 941. Instead, it's a report of amounts due and amounts paid, and they should match. The 941 is concerned with the following data:

- Gross wages paid
- Federal income tax withholding
- FICA (social security) withholding and matching employer contributions
- Medicare withholding and matching employer contributions

Many people fill out the 941 form they receive in the mail. You can gather the information you need from a QuickBooks report to do that, or you can have QuickBooks print the 941 form for you.

NOTE: The federal government is encouraging telephone filing, and instructions for that feature arrive with your 941 form every quarter. This is certainly an easy way to file. The government is also beginning to set up online filing via the Internet. For more information about setting up Internet filing of 941 forms, go to www.irs.gov/efile/.

QuickBooks will prepare your 941 report using the information in your QuickBooks registers. To prepare the report, follow these steps:

1. Choose Employees | Process Payroll Forms from the QuickBooks menu bar.
2. Select the option to Create Form 941 (which may include Schedule B).
3. Follow the onscreen instructions to complete the form and print it.

> **NOTE:** Schedule B is the Employer's Record of Federal Tax Liability. If you are a semiweekly depositor, or your payroll tax liability on any day in the quarter exceeds the standard amount for a monthly depositor, you must file Schedule B with Form 941.

The printed form can be sent to the IRS if you use these printing criteria:

- The form must be printed with black ink on white or cream paper.
- The paper must be 8"×11" or 8.5"×11".
- The paper must be 18 lb. weight or heavier.

The printed report doesn't look exactly like the blank form you received, but it's close. More importantly, it's perfectly acceptable to the government.

You could also use the information in the printed report to fill in the blank 941 form you receive or to transmit the information via telephone and save your QuickBooks printout as your copy.

Preparing Annual Returns

All the taxing authorities want annual returns. The feds, state, and local folks need reports and forms. Some of them need checks. You can get all the information you need from QuickBooks. In fact, all the usual QuickBooks reports work just fine, as long as you remember to set the Dates field to the entire year.

Preparing State and Local Annual Returns

The state and local taxing authorities usually send you a form that asks for a reconciliation for the year. You may have to present quarterly totals as you fill out the form, which you can accomplish by changing the date range in the QuickBooks payroll reports.

Finish your State Unemployment annual report as soon as possible, because the payments you make to the state are relevant to the Federal Unemployment report (Form 940). Incidentally, for many states, the year-end State Unemployment report doesn't require a check because there's a limit to the wages that are eligible for applying the unemployment contribution rate.

Preparing the 940 Report

For small businesses with only a couple of employees, the 940 report (FUTA) is frequently filed annually. To create your Form 940, choose Employees | Process Payroll Forms from the QuickBooks menu bar. Select the option to create the 940 form and follow the instructions that appear on the screen. Many small businesses qualify for Form 940EZ (which is shorter and easier).

Printing W-2 Forms

You must print W-2 forms for your employees, the government agencies, and your own files. Everybody needs them.

Choose Employees | Process Payroll Forms from the QuickBooks menu bar and select Form W-2 to open the Process W-2s window. Click Mark All to select all the employees, and then choose Review W-2. Each employee's W-2 form is presented on the screen. If there is nonfinancial data missing (such as an address or ZIP code), you must fill it in.

Click Next to move through each employee's form. When everything is correct, load your W-2 forms in the printer and choose Print W-2s. The Print W-2s window opens so you can choose a printer and print the forms. Click OK, and click Print.

You must also print the W-3 form, which is a summary of your W-2 forms. It must be in the package you send to the IRS when you transmit the W-2 forms. Unfortunately, you can't preview the W-3 form.

All these payroll reports are a bit time consuming, but you have no choice: these tasks are legally necessary. At least it's easier because QuickBooks keeps the records and does the math.

QuickBooks Electronic Filing Services

You can file all your federal forms, coupons, and tax payments electronically if you sign up for QuickBooks E-File & Pay. In addition, this service can handle state forms and remittances for many states.

E-File & Pay is only available if you signed up for Do It Yourself Payroll and you download your payroll files (users who receive their payroll files on a CD cannot use the QuickBooks electronic filing services). To learn more about this service, or to sign up, follow these steps:

1. Choose Employees | Payroll Services | Add/Change Payroll Service.

2. To learn about the service, click the link Learn More to the right of the option Service Add-Ons For Do-It-Yourself Payroll.

3. To sign up, select Service Add-Ons For Do-It-Yourself Payroll and click Continue.

4. Follow the onscreen instructions for signing up for E-File & Pay.

There are circumstances under which you cannot file your federal forms electronically, and there are states for which QuickBooks has no capability for e-filing. Specific information about E-File & Pay limitations is available when you choose the Learn More link.

Configuring and Tracking Inventory

In this chapter:

- Create inventory items
- Deal with physical inventory counts
- Adjust the count
- Create pre-builds
- Use backorders

For many businesses, the warehouse is a source of frustration, bewilderment, rage, and erroneous information. I'm using the term "warehouse" generically to indicate the place where you store inventory (which may not be a discrete building that looks like a warehouse).

Creating Inventory Items

Inventory items are part of the Item List in your QuickBooks system. That list contains all the elements that might ever appear on a customer invoice, a purchase order, or a vendor bill. If you track inventory, many of the items in your Item List are the things you sell to customers from stock.

Creating New Items

Instructions for adding items to the Item List are in Chapter 2, but it's worth taking a moment here to go over the steps for inventory items.

Click the Item icon on the QuickBooks Icon Bar (or choose Lists | Item List from the menu bar) to open the Item List window, where all your inventory items are listed, along with all the other types of items. The inventory items can be distinguished easily because they have their own type: Inventory Part. To display all the inventory items together, click the Type column heading to sort the list by type.

If you want to add a new item to your inventory items list, press CTRL-N while the Item List window is displayed. When the New Item window opens, select Inventory Part as the item type, and then fill in the information (Figure 10-1 is an example of an inventory item).

If you disabled automatic spell checks in the Preferences dialog box, click Spelling to make sure you have no spelling errors. This also lets the QuickBooks spelling checker add the words connected to this item to its dictionary (for example, the item code, the name of the vendor, and any technical jargon in the description). This obviates the need to check the spelling when you create an invoice or purchase order for the item. If you didn't disable automatic spell checks, the spelling tool will start when you click OK to save the item. (See Chapter 21 to learn all about configuring and using the spelling checker.)

If you created any custom fields for items (discussed in Chapter 2), click Custom Fields and enter data in any custom field that's appropriate for this item. (If you want to add additional custom fields, click Define Fields.)

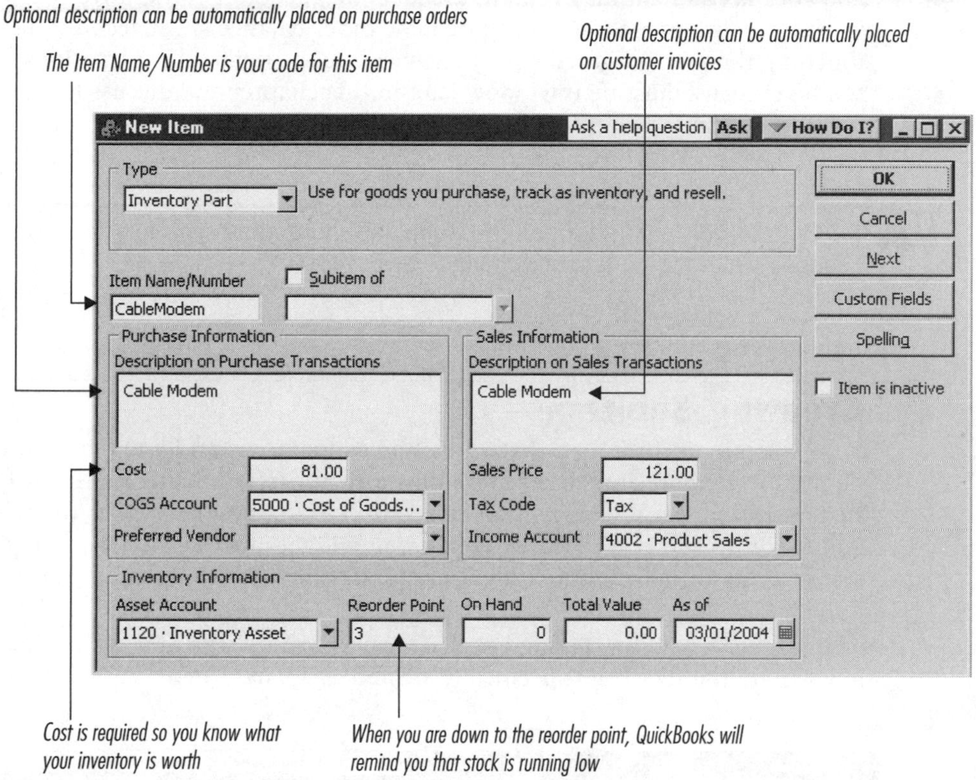

Optional description can be automatically placed on purchase orders

The Item Name/Number is your code for this item

Optional description can be automatically placed on customer invoices

Cost is required so you know what your inventory is worth

When you are down to the reorder point, QuickBooks will remind you that stock is running low

FIGURE 10-1 An item's record holds all the important information you need to use it in transactions and reports.

You can also enter the current quantity on hand in the New Item window. If you're creating inventory items as part of a QuickBooks setup, this is a suitable point for establishing the current quantity for the item. If you've already started QuickBooks with an opening balance sheet from your accountant, you should enter the quantity on hand through the inventory adjustment tool, discussed in the section "Making the Inventory Adjustments" later in this chapter. Ask your accountant for his or her advice on making the inventory adjustment before you start dealing with the quantity in stock. The reason to check with your accountant arises from the way inventory value is posted in QuickBooks. If you enter the quantity on hand through the New Item window, the value of that quantity is entered into your inventory asset account, and a balancing entry is made to your current equity account.

If you use the Inventory Adjustment window, the balancing entry is made to an account of your choice. When you're performing standard adjustments (after a physical count of the inventory), the account you use is the inventory adjustment account. However, you can invent and use any account for offsetting the inventory adjustment, and your accountant may want to use an equity account you've invented for prior years for your opening inventory, or some other balance sheet account instead of touching the preconfigured equity balance. See the detailed explanations for using the Inventory Adjustment window later in this chapter and discuss this issue with your accountant.

> **TIP:** To edit an item, open the Item List and double-click the item you want to change. Make the necessary changes and click OK.

Creating Subitems

Subitems are useful when there are choices for items and you want all the choices to be part of a larger hierarchy so you can track them efficiently. For instance, if you sell widgets in a variety of colors, you may want to create a subitem for each color: red widget, green widget, and so on. Or perhaps you sell widgets from different widget manufacturers: Jones widgets, Smith widgets, and so on.

In order to have a subitem, you must have a parent item. Figure 10-2 shows a new item that has been specifically created as a parent item.

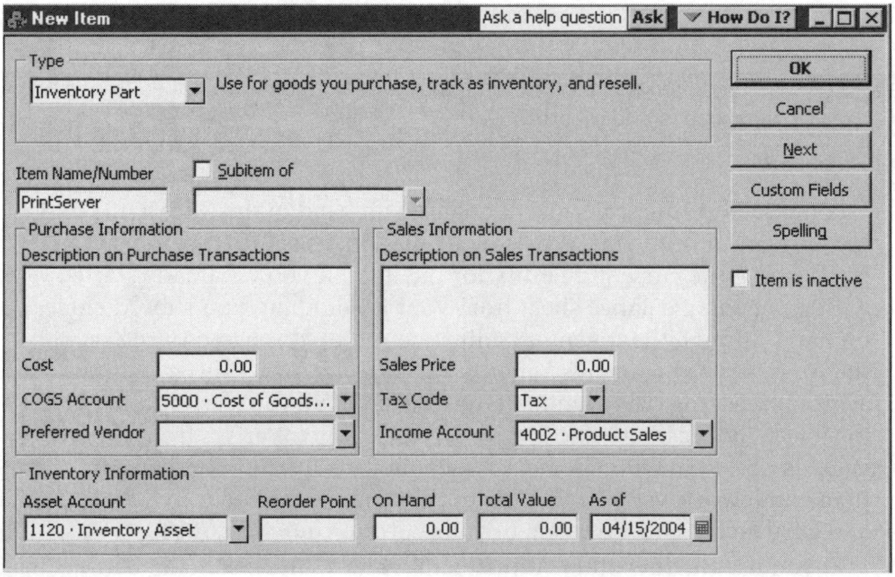

FIGURE 10-2 This item isn't sold to customers—it exists only as a parent item.

Here are the guidelines for creating an inventory item that's designed to be a parent:

1. Use a generic name for the item; the details are in the subitem names.
2. Don't enter a description, save that for the subitems.
3. Don't enter the cost.
4. Don't enter the price.
5. Don't enter a reorder point.
6. Don't enter the quantity on hand.
7. Enter the COGS account because it's a required field for all inventory items.
8. Enter the Income Account because it's a required field for all inventory items.

Having created the parent item, subitems are easy to create by opening a blank New Item window (press CTRL-N) and following these steps:

1. In the Item Name/Number field, enter the code for this item. It can be an item, a color, a size, a manufacturer name, or any other code that specifies this subitem as compared to other subitems under the same parent item. For instance, the first subitem I created under the parent item shown in Figure 10-2 was LinksysEPSX3, seen in Figure 10-3.
2. Check the box named Subitem Of, and then select the parent item from the drop-down list that appears when you click the arrow to the right of the field.
3. Enter the descriptions you want to appear on purchase orders and invoices.
4. Enter the cost and price.

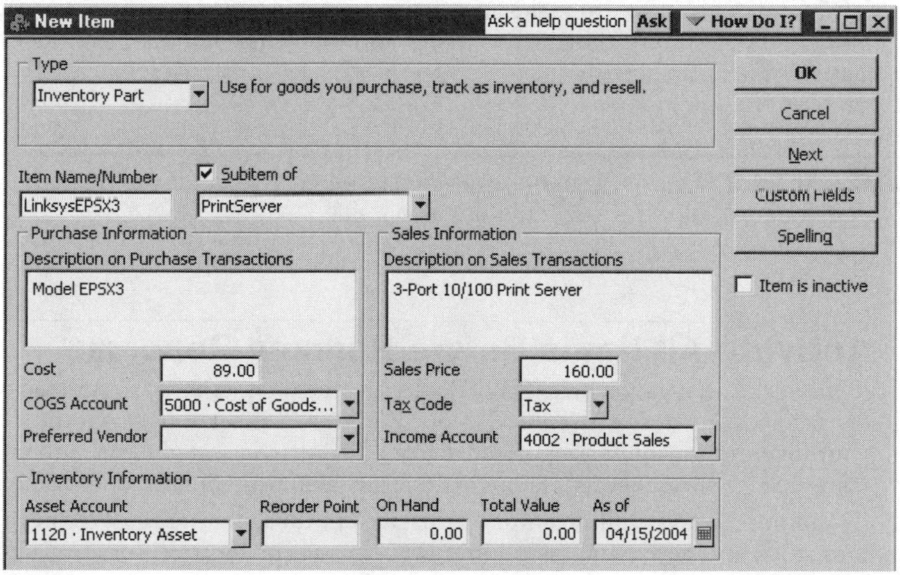

FIGURE 10-3 The subitem contains the descriptions the customer and vendor should see.

5. Enter the general ledger account information.

6. Enter the reorder point if you're using that feature.

7. Continue to add subitems to each parent item in your system.

Making Items Inactive

Sometimes you have inventory items that you aren't buying or selling at the moment. Perhaps they're seasonal, or the cost is too high and you want to delay purchasing and reselling the item until you can get a better price.

As long as you're not using the item, you can make it inactive. It doesn't appear on the Item List, which means that the list is shorter and easier to scroll through when you're creating an invoice. And QuickBooks won't nag you with reorder reminders.

To declare an item inactive, open the Item List window and right-click the item. Then choose Make Inactive from the shortcut menu.

When an item is inactive, it's not just invisible on the list of items for sale that appears during invoice data entry; it doesn't even appear on the Item List window. However, you can change the appearance of the Item List window to display inactive items.

When you make any item inactive, the Show All check box becomes activated in the Item List window. If no items are marked inactive, the Show All option is grayed out and inaccessible. Click the Show All check box to display the inactive items along with the active items. Any inactive item is displayed with an X to the left of the item listing. To make an inactive item active again, choose the Show All option so you can see the inactive items, and then click X to deselect the inactive status.

 C A U T I O N : You can make any subitem inactive, but if you make a parent item inactive, all of its subitems are also made inactive.

Activate All Items Before Running Reports

If you make an item inactive, QuickBooks pretends it doesn't exist. An inactive item doesn't show up in any inventory report. Worse, all calculations about the worth of your inventory, including reports that aren't directly connected to inventory (such as your balance sheet reports), fail to include any amounts connected to inactive items.

You must activate all inventory items, except those that have never been received into stock and never sold, before running any reports on inventory. You should also activate all inventory items before running financial statements.

Running Inventory Reports

You'll probably find that you run reports on your inventory status quite often. For most businesses, tracking the state of the inventory is the second most important and frequently run set of reports (right behind reports about the current accounts receivable balances).

QuickBooks provides several useful, significant inventory reports, which you can access by choosing Reports | Inventory. The available reports are discussed in this section.

> **NOTE:** Very few customization options are available for inventory reports—you can change the date range and the headers/footers, and some reports let you filter some of the items. You can't add or remove columns.

Inventory Valuation Summary Report

This report gives you a quick assessment of the value of your inventory. By default, the date range is the current month to date. Each item is listed with the following information displayed in columns:

Item Description   The description of the item, if you entered a description for purchase transactions.

On Hand   The current quantity on hand, which is the net number of received items and sold items. Because QuickBooks permits you to sell items you don't have in stock (let's hope you really do have them but you haven't used a QuickBooks transaction to bring them into stock), it's possible to have a negative number in this column.

Avg Cost   Each transaction for receipt of inventory is used to calculate this figure.

Asset Value   The value posted to your Inventory account in the general ledger. The value is calculated by multiplying the number on hand by the average cost.

% of Tot Asset   The percentage of your total inventory assets that this item represents.

Sales Price   The price you've set for this item. This figure is obtained by looking at the item's configuration window. If you entered a price when you set up the item, that price is displayed. If you didn't enter a price (because you chose to determine the price at the time of sale), $0.00 displays. QuickBooks does not check the sales records for this item to determine this number, so if you routinely change the price when you're filling out a customer invoice, those changes aren't reflected in this report.

Retail Value   The current retail value of the item, which is calculated by multiplying the number on hand by the retail price.

% of Retail Value   The percentage of the total retail value of your inventory that this item represents.

Inventory Valuation Detail Report

This report lists each transaction that involved each inventory item. The report shows no financial information about the price charged to customers, because your inventory value is based on cost. You can double-click any sales transaction line to see the details (and the amount you charged for the item).

Inventory Stock Status

There are two Stock Status reports: By Item and By Vendor. The information is the same in both reports, but the order in which information is arranged and subtotaled is different. You can use these Stock Status reports to get quick numbers about inventory items, including the following information:

- The preferred vendor
- The reorder point
- The number currently on hand
- A reminder (a check mark) for ordering items that are below the reorder point
- The number currently on order (purchase order exists but stock has not yet been received)
- The next delivery date
- The average number of units sold per week

Pending Builds

This report details the current state of items you assemble from existing inventory items (called *builds*, or *pre-builds*). Only QuickBooks Premier Editions offer built-in features for creating builds. This report is listed in case you've opened a company file in your copy of QuickBooks Pro that was created in QuickBooks Premier. You could use the report to view the details on pre-builds, but you can't access the QuickBooks pre-build features.

To learn about a workaround for pre-builds so you can create them in QuickBooks Pro/Basic, see the section "Creating Pre-Builds," later in this chapter. To learn how to create pre-builds in QuickBooks Premier Edition, read *Running*

QuickBooks 2004 Premier Editions from CPA911 Publishing. You can purchase the book at www.cpa911.com.

Getting Quick Inventory Reports

QuickBooks provides a reporting feature called QuickReports that provides valuable information about an individual inventory item or all inventory items. QuickReports are available from the Item List window.

In the Item List window, select an item and press CTRL-Q (or click the Reports button and choose QuickReport) to open the QuickReport shown in Figure 10-4. You can change the date range for the report, and you can double-click any transaction line to drill down to the transaction details.

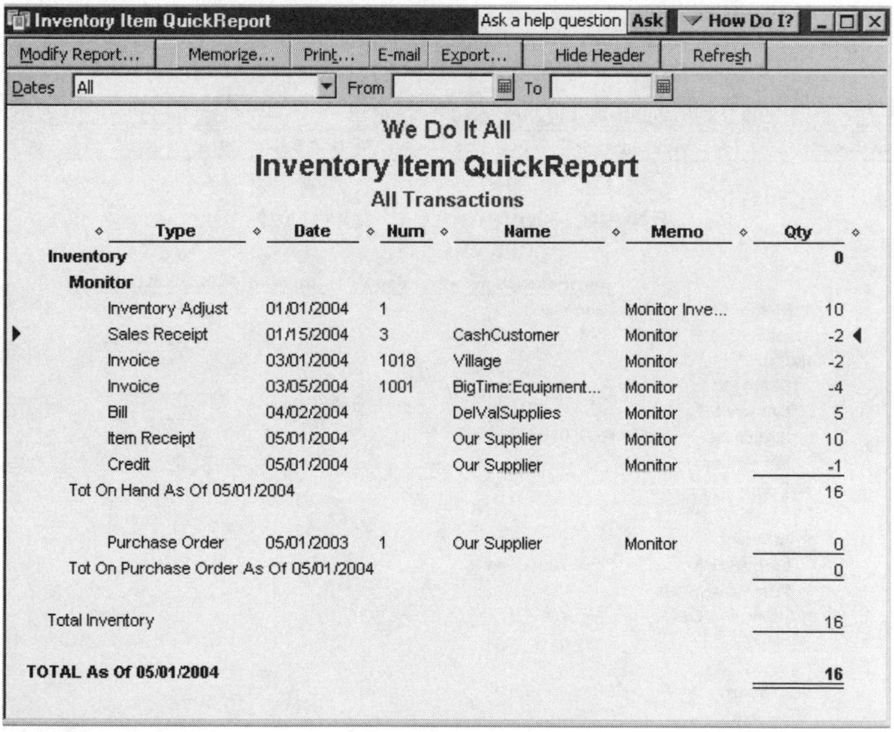

FIGURE 10-4   A QuickReport is an activity report for an item.

Counting Inventory

I can hear the groans. I know—there's nothing worse than doing a physical inventory. However, no matter how careful you are with QuickBooks transactions, no matter how pristine your protocols are for making sure everything that comes and goes is accounted for, you probably aren't going to match your physical inventory to your QuickBooks figures. Sorry about that.

Printing the Physical Inventory Worksheet

The first thing you must do is print a Physical Inventory Worksheet (see Figure 10-5), which is one of the choices on the Inventory Reports submenu. This report lists your inventory items in alphabetical order, along with the current quantity on hand, which is calculated from your QuickBooks transactions. In addition, there's a column that's set up to record the actual count as you walk around your warehouse with this printout in hand.

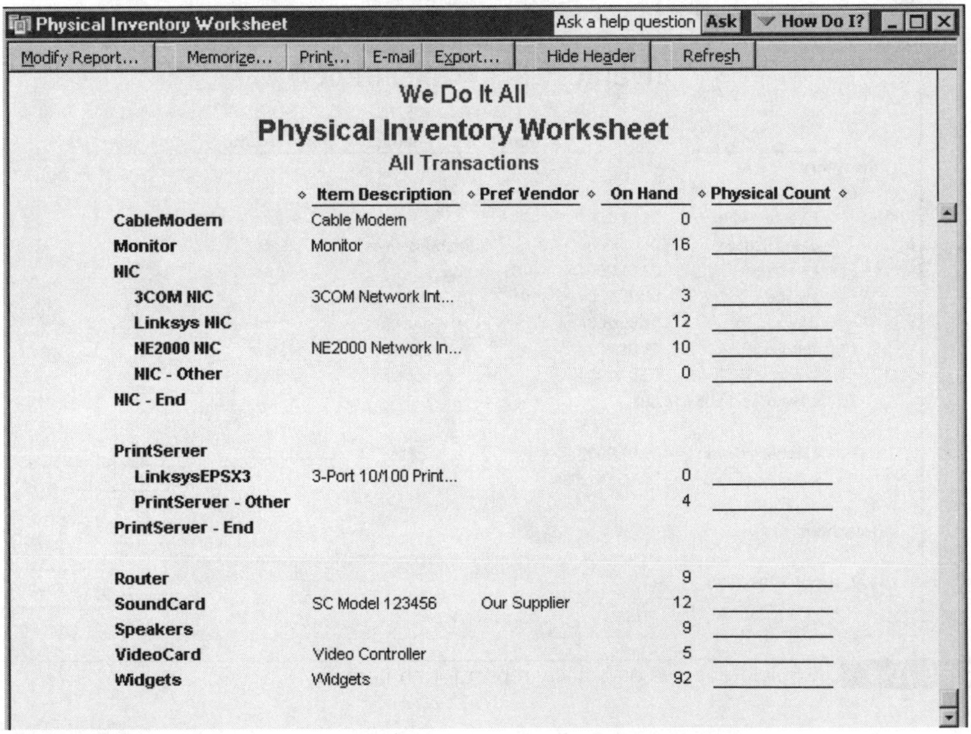

FIGURE 10-5 The worksheet's most important column is the one with blank lines, which is where you enter the physical count.

If you have a large number of inventory items, you may have some problems with this worksheet:

- You cannot change the way the worksheet is sorted, so you cannot arrange the items to match the way you've laid out your warehouse.
- If you use bins, rows, or some other physical entity in your warehouse, QuickBooks has no feature to support it, so you cannot enter the location on this worksheet (nor can you sort by location, which is an extremely useful method).

I have no idea why the Pref Vendor column exists, because I've never experienced a physical inventory in which that information was used. If you stock by manufacturer, the manufacturer's name is usually referred to in the code or description. You can't get rid of this column, but you can hide it by dragging its right border to the left.

Click the Print button in the worksheet window to bring up the Print Reports window. In the Number Of Copies box, enter as many copies as you need (one for each person helping with the count).

TIP: Don't hand every person a full report—cut the report to give each person the pages he or she needs, and keep one full copy to use as a master.

Planning the Physical Count

QuickBooks lacks a "freeze" feature like the one found in most inventory-enabled accounting software. Freezing the inventory means that after you've printed the worksheet and begun counting, any transactions involving inventory are saved to a holding file in order to avoid changing the totals. When you've finished your physical count, you unfreeze the inventory count and print a report on the holding file. You make your adjustments to the count using the information in that file, and then make the final adjustments to the count.

You can perform these actions manually, however. After you print the worksheet (which you don't do until you're ready to start counting), be sure that all sales invoices will be handled differently until after the inventory count is adjusted. There are a number of ways to do this:

- Print an extra copy of each invoice and save the copies in a folder. Don't pick and pack the inventory for the invoices until after the count.
- Prepare a form for sales people to fill out the name and quantity of inventory items sold during the freeze, and delay picking and packing the inventory until after the count.

- Delay entering invoices until after the count is over. (This is not a good idea if counting takes a couple of days.)
- Don't receive inventory in QuickBooks (don't fill out a Receive Items or Receive Bill form) until after the count.
- If inventory arrives in the warehouse, don't unpack the boxes until after the count.

When you start counting the inventory, be sure there's a good system in place. The most important element of the system is *having somebody in charge*. One person, with a master inventory worksheet in hand, must know who is counting what. When each counter is finished, his or her sheet should be handed to the person in charge and the numbers should be duplicated onto the master inventory worksheet. (This is why you print multiple copies of the worksheet.) Note the date and time the count was reported.

After the count, bring in any inventory that's arrived during the count. Then start picking and packing your orders so you can generate income again.

Making the Inventory Adjustments

After you've finished counting the inventory, you may find that the numbers on the worksheet don't match the physical count. In fact, it's almost a sure bet that the numbers won't match.

Most of the time the physical count is lower than the QuickBooks figures. This is called *shrinkage*. Shrinkage is jargon for "stuff went missing for an unexplained reason," but most of the time the reason is employee theft. Sorry, but that's a well-documented fact. Another reason for shrinkage is breakage, but most of the time that's reported by employees, and you can adjust your inventory because you know about it. When you don't know about it, suspect the worst, because statistics prove that suspicion to be the most accurate.

Adjusting the Count

You have to tell QuickBooks about the results of the physical count, and you accomplish that by choosing Vendors | Inventory Activities | Adjust Quantity/Value On Hand. The Adjust Quantity/Value On Hand window opens, which is shown in Figure 10-6.

 N O T E : Inactive items appear on the Adjust Quantity/Value On Hand window.

Here are the guidelines for filling out this window:

- Enter the date (usually inventory adjustments are made at the end of the month, quarter, or year, but there's no rule about that).

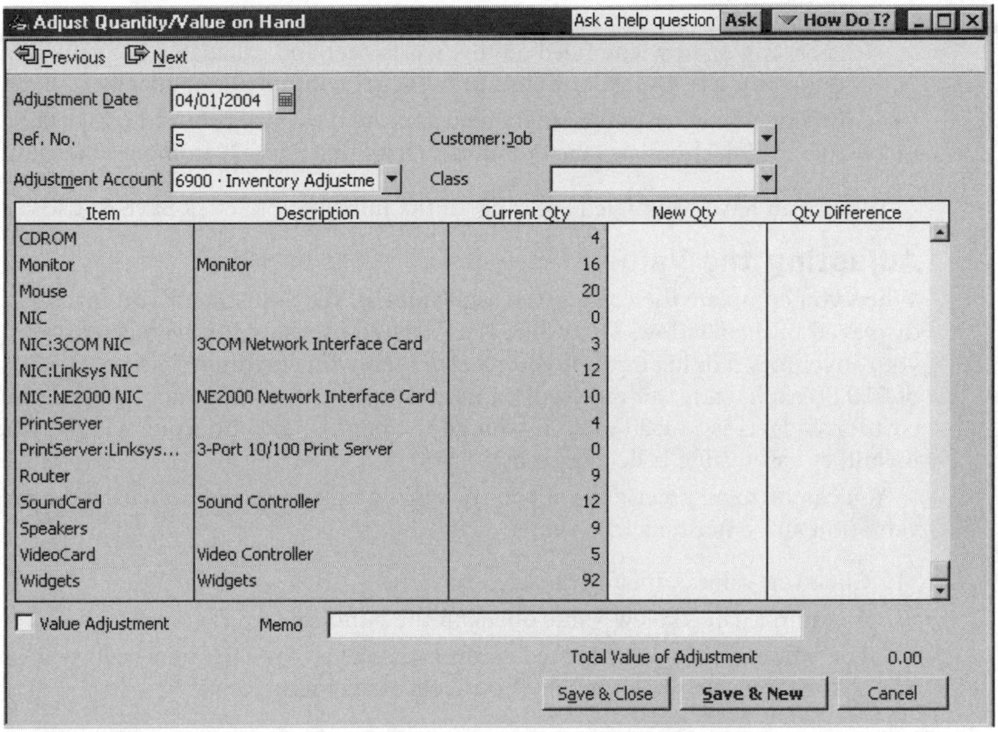

Item	Description	Current Qty	New Qty	Qty Difference
CDROM		4		
Monitor	Monitor	16		
Mouse		20		
NIC		0		
NIC:3COM NIC	3COM Network Interface Card	3		
NIC:Linksys NIC		12		
NIC:NE2000 NIC	NE2000 Network Interface Card	10		
PrintServer		4		
PrintServer:Linksys...	3-Port 10/100 Print Server	0		
Router		9		
SoundCard	Sound Controller	12		
Speakers		9		
VideoCard	Video Controller	5		
Widgets	Widgets	92		

Adjust Quantity/Value on Hand   Ask a help question Ask   ▼ How Do I?

◄】Previous   ▐⇨ Next

Adjustment Date 04/01/2004

Ref. No. 5   Customer:Job

Adjustment Account 6900 · Inventory Adjustme ▼   Class

☐ Value Adjustment   Memo

Total Value of Adjustment   0.00

Save & Close   Save & New   Cancel

FIGURE 10-6   Correct the value of your inventory by adjusting quantities to match the physical count.

- Use an optional reference number to track the adjustment. The next time you enter an adjustment, QuickBooks will increment the reference number by one.
- Enter the inventory adjustment account in your chart of accounts. Click the arrow to see a display of all your accounts. If you don't have an inventory adjustment account, choose Add New and create one.

 CAUTION: An inventory adjustment account must exist in order to adjust your inventory. It's an expense account.

- The Customer:Job field is there in case you're sending stuff to a customer (or for a job) but not including the items on any invoices for that customer or job. QuickBooks provides this feature to help you when you do that (which is usually as a result of a job-costing scheme you're using). The inventory count is changed and the cost is posted to the job.
- If you've enabled the Classes feature, a Class field appears.

- Use either the New Qty column or the Qty Difference column to enter the count (depending on how you filled out the worksheet and calculated it). Whichever column you use, QuickBooks fills in the other column automatically.
- Anything you enter in the Memo field appears on your Profit & Loss Detail report, which eliminates the question "what's this figure?" from your accountant.

When you have completed entering all the information, click Save & Close.

Adjusting the Value

When you complete the entries, the total value of the adjustment you made is displayed in the window. That value is calculated by using the average cost of your inventory. For example, if you received ten widgets into inventory at a cost of $10.00 each, and later received ten more at a cost of $12.00 each, your average cost for widgets is $11.00 each. If your adjustment is for minus one widget, your inventory asset value is decreased by $11.00.

You can be more precise about your inventory valuation by eliminating the average valuation and entering a true value:

1. Click the Value Adjustment check box.
2. A column named New Value opens in the window (see Figure 10-7).
3. The value of the total adjusted count is displayed for each item, and you can change the value to eliminate the effects of averaging costs.

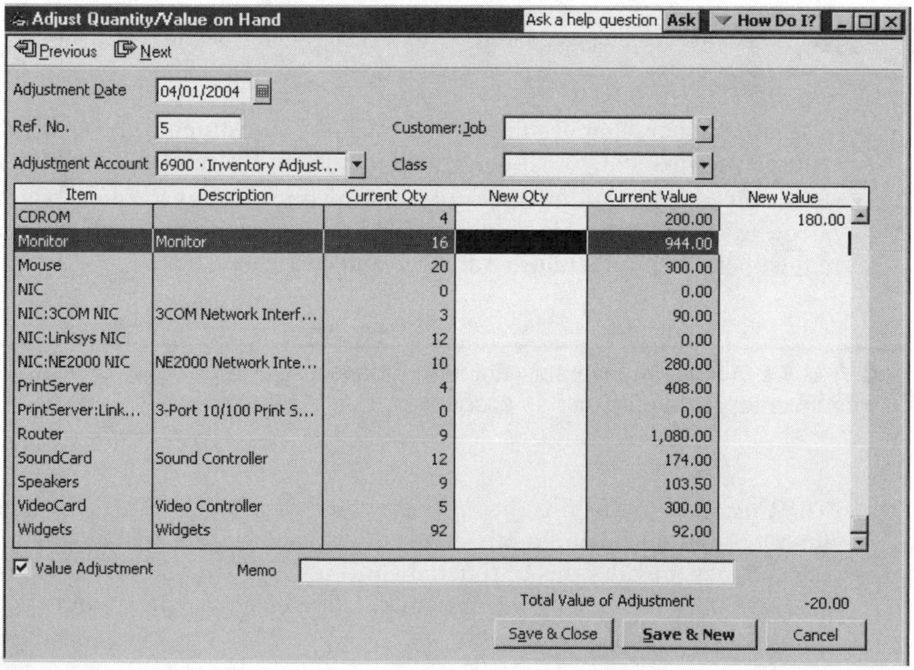

FIGURE 10-7   You can manually change the current value of any item.

Of course, in order to enter the correct total value, you must have the information you need and then make the appropriate calculations. To obtain the information, follow these steps:

1. Click the Item icon on the Icon Bar to open the Item List window.
2. Click the Reports button at the bottom of the window.
3. Choose Reports On All Items | Purchases | Purchases By Vendor Detail.

This report presents a history of your purchases so you can make the necessary calculations.

TIP: In case your accountant asks, QuickBooks does not support FIFO or LIFO costing for inventory. Essentially, you create your own FIFO/LIFO calculations by using the information in the vendor reports.

Return to the Adjust Quantity window and enter the data. When you've finished making your changes, click Save & Close to save your new inventory numbers.

Understanding the Postings

When you adjust the inventory count, you're also changing the value of your inventory asset. After you save the adjustment, the inventory asset account register reflects the differences for each item (see Figure 10-8).

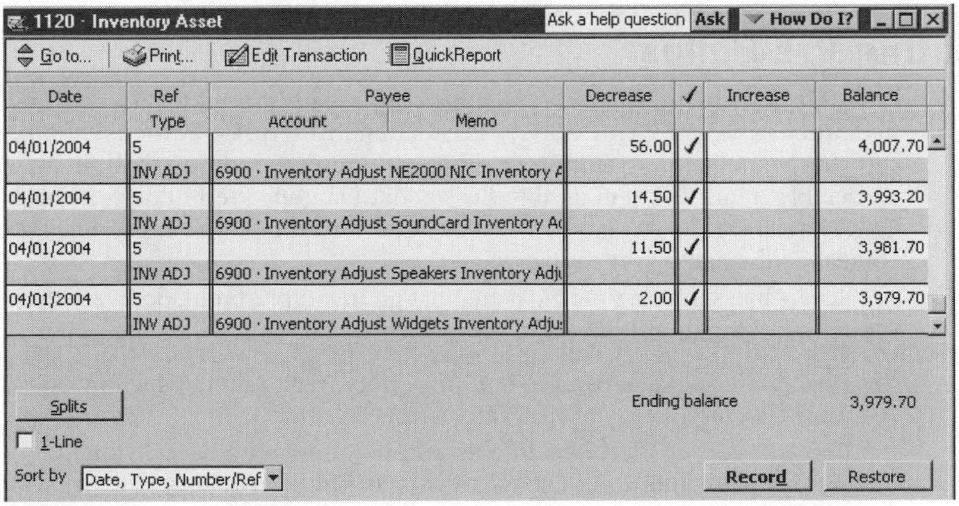

FIGURE 10-8 Inventory adjustments are posted with the transaction type INV ADJ.

But this is double-entry bookkeeping, which means there has to be an equal and opposite entry somewhere else. For example, when you sell items via customer invoices, the balancing entry to the decrement of your inventory account is made to cost of sales. When you're adjusting inventory, however, there is no sale involved (nor is there a purchase involved). In this case, the balancing entry is made to the inventory adjustment account, which must exist in order to adjust your inventory.

If your inventory adjustment lowers the value of your inventory, the inventory asset account is credited and the adjustment account receives a debit in the same amount. If your adjustment raises the value of your inventory, the postings are opposite.

Making Other Adjustments to Inventory

You can use the Adjust Quantity/Value On Hand window to make adjustments to inventory at any time and for a variety of reasons:

- Breakage or other damage
- Customer demo units
- Gifts or bonuses for customers or employees
- Removal of inventory parts in order to create pre-built or pre-assembled inventory items (see the upcoming section on pre-builds).

The important thing to remember is that tracking inventory isn't just to make sure that you have sufficient items on hand to sell to customers (although that's certainly an important point). Equally important is the fact that inventory is a significant asset, just like your cash, equipment, and other assets. It affects your company's worth in a substantial way.

Creating Pre-Builds

Pre-builds are products that are assembled or partially assembled using existing inventory parts. Only QuickBooks Premier and Enterprise Editions offer the software features for assembling pre-builds (and those editions call the items "Assembly Items," but I'm used to the standard jargon "Pre-Builds"). Even though QuickBooks Pro doesn't have any capacity for tracking pre-builds automatically, you can still create a system that works.

I'll start by examining the elements that go into a pre-build. Software that supports pre-builds automates all the processes, using the following steps:

- Permits the creation of a pre-built inventory item, asking which inventory parts (and how many of each) are used.
- Receives the pre-built item into inventory (after you physically build it), automatically removing the individual parts from inventory.

- Automatically creates a cost for the new pre-built item based on the cost of the individual parts.

TIP: Most software that supports pre-builds also permits a labor charge to be added as part of the cost.

Each of these steps can be performed manually in QuickBooks and, although it's more time consuming, it means you can create pre-builds if you need them.

TIP: If pre-builds are a large part of your business, you need to buy QuickBooks Premier, or QuickBooks Enterprise Edition. You can learn how to use this feature in *Running QuickBooks 2004 Premier Editions*, from CPA911 Publishing (www .cpa911.com).

Creating the Pre-Built Item

Start by putting the item into your items list, as shown in Figure 10-9.

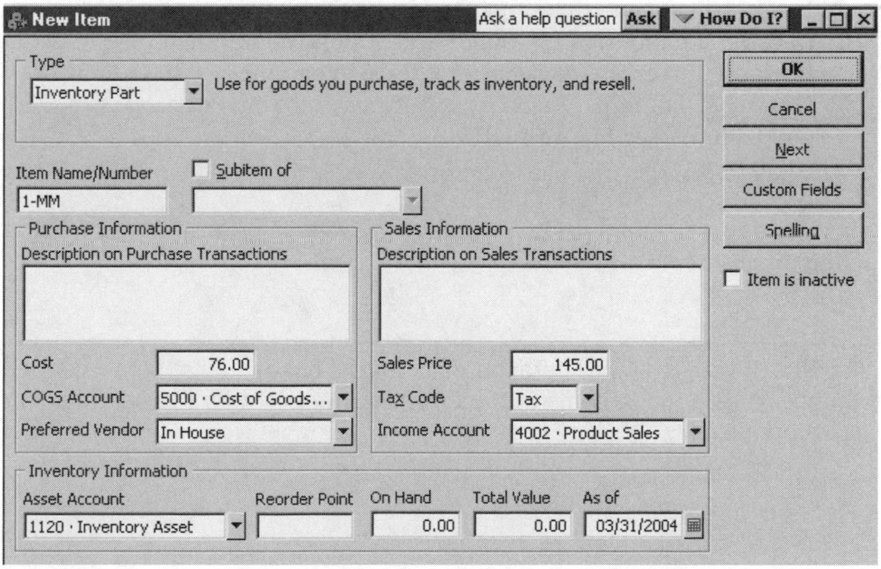

FIGURE 10-9 Create a pre-built item the same way you create a purchased item.

The protocols I used for entering the item shown in Figure 10-9 are specially designed for pre-builds, and you may find these guidelines helpful as you make your own entries:

- The Item Name/Number is unique in its starting character to make it clear that this is a special line of products. If you normally use numbers for items, use a letter for the first character of your pre-builds (X or Z usually works well).
- The cost is the aggregate current cost of the original inventory parts (which means you have to look them up before you perform this action).
- A vendor named InHouse was invented for this item.
- Notice that there is no startup quantity on hand (it's brought into inventory when built).

Putting Pre-Builds into Inventory

When you bring your pre-built items into inventory, you don't receive them the way you receive the inventory items you purchase (there's no vendor and you don't write a check to purchase the parts).

Instead, you must take the items you used to build the new product out of inventory and put the new pre-built product into inventory:

1. Choose Vendors | Inventory Activities | Adjust Quantity/Value On Hand.
2. In the Adjust Quantity/Value On Hand window, use the Qty Difference column to add the number of pre-builds and remove the number of original items that were used to create these pre-builds. As you enter each amount in the Qty Difference column, QuickBooks automatically makes entries in the New Qty column (see Figure 10-10).
3. Click OK to save the new quantities.

Notice that the total value of adjustment is zero, because you're replacing components with a pre-build.

TIP: If you use other paraphernalia for pre-builds (nails, screws, labels, whatever), add those items to the inventory items list so you can make the cost more exact.

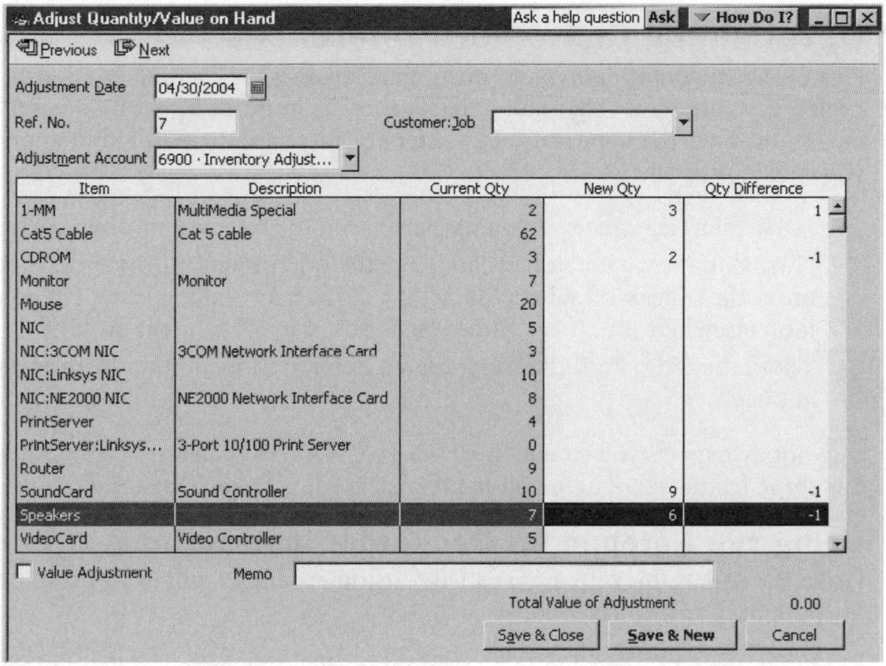

FIGURE 10-10 Add the pre-built item and remove its parts.

Handling Backorders

Backorders are nerve-wracking on both ends, whether you're waiting for items that your supplier didn't have (your supplier's backorder problem), or you need to ship items to customers and you're out of them (your backorder problem). Although QuickBooks Pro and Basic don't offer a backorder feature, you can use existing features to create your own backorder protocols.

NOTE: QuickBooks Premier and Enterprise Editions have backorder features built in. If you need a more convenient backorder function, consider upgrading. You can learn how to create and track backorders in *Running QuickBooks 2004 Premier Editions* from CPA911 Publishing (www.cpa911.com).

Determining Customer Preferences

Part of the trick of keeping your customers' business is keeping your customers' preferences straight. The issue of backorders is important, because not all customers have the same attitude. Generally, there are three different approaches your customers take:

- "Okay, ship me whatever you have and send the backorders when you get them."
- "Just ship me what you have and take the other items off the order, and I'll order the other stuff when you get it." (This may really mean, "I'm going to look elsewhere, but if everyone else is out of it, I'll call you back.")
- "Hold the order until the backordered items are in, and then ship everything at once."

Nobody expects you to remember each customer's preference, but QuickBooks has some features that help you handle backorders to each customer's satisfaction.

Using the Notepad for Backorder Instructions

QuickBooks has this nifty item called "customer notes," which you can use for keeping backorder instructions:

1. Open the Customer:Job List and double-click the customer listing to which you want to add a note.
2. When the Edit Customer window opens, click the Notes button.
3. In the Notepad window, enter a notation about the customer's attitude regarding backorders (see Figure 10-11).
4. Click OK twice to save the note and close the customer record.

When you're filling out an invoice for this customer, you can view the customer Notepad. With the customer's invoice on the screen, choose Edit | Notepad from the QuickBooks menu bar, and the notepad for that customer appears.

Using a Backorder Handling Field

You can formalize your backorder handling by creating a Backorders field on the customer cards. Then you can put the field on the invoice form so it's right in front of you when you're filling out an order. Actually, there are three tasks involved if you want to use this protocol (all of which are covered in this section):

1. Create the field for backorder preferences in the customer form.
2. Add data to the field for each customer.
3. Add the field to your invoice form.

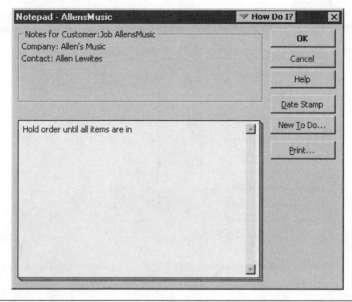

FIGURE 10-11 Use the Notepad so you can refer to its contents when a customer's order can't be filled.

Add the Field to the Customer Form

You can add a custom field to all the customer cards in your system by creating the new field in any existing customer record:

1. Click the Cust icon on the icon bar or press CTRL-J to open the Customer:Job List.
2. Double-click the listing for any existing customer.
3. Click the Additional Info tab, and then click Define Fields.
4. When the Define Fields window opens (see Figure 10-12), enter a label for the backorder field.
5. Select Customers:Jobs to use this field on your customer cards, and then click OK. QuickBooks displays a message telling you that you can use this custom field in templates (which is exactly what you're going to do). Click OK to make the message go away. Notice that you can tell it never to come back.
6. When you return to the customer window, click OK.

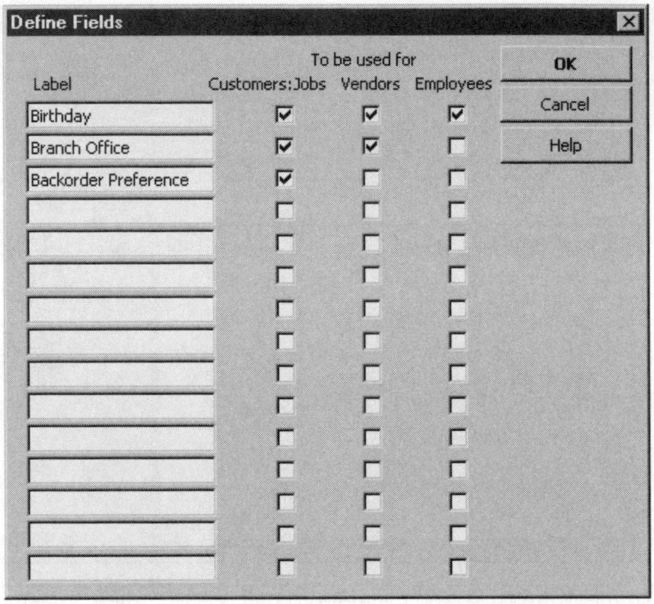

FIGURE 10-12 Create a label for the new field and place it in the entries of the Customer list.

Enter Data in the Customer Records

The customer list is still on your QuickBooks screen, which is handy because now you must enter information in the new field for each customer that orders inventory items from you:

1. Double-click a customer listing to open an Edit Customer window.
2. Move to the Additional Info tab.
3. Enter this customer's backorder preference in the Backorder Preference field you created (see Figure 10-13).
4. Click OK to save the information.
5. Repeat the process for each customer.

Unlike most of the fields that are built into the customer record, custom fields don't have their own list files; therefore, you don't have a drop-down list available when you want to enter data—data entry is manual. You should create some rules about the way you use this field so everyone in the office uses the same phrases. Don't let people create abbreviations or "cute" entries; make sure the data makes the customer's backorder status absolutely clear. For example, for a backorder preference, consider creating easy-to-understand data entries such as: Ship Separate, Hold Order, and No BOs.

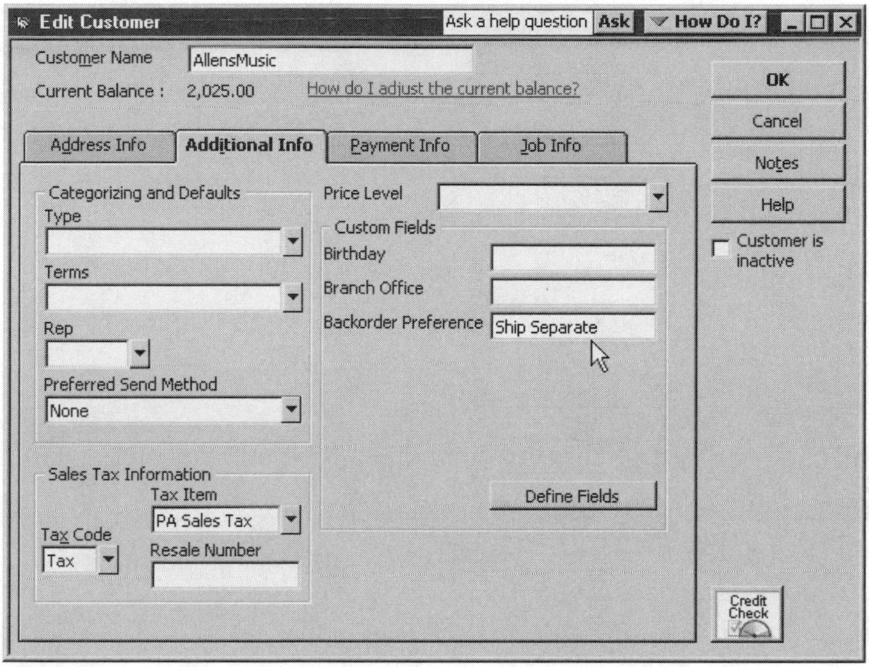

FIGURE 10-13 Enter data specific to each customer in your new field.

Put the Field on Your Invoice Forms

The information about a customer's backorder preferences is important when you're filling an order and you're out of something the customer wants. So you might as well have the information in front of you, which means putting it right on the invoice form. Complete instructions for customizing invoices appear in Chapter 3, but I'll go over the way you customize an invoice by adding a new field:

1. Click the Invoice icon on the icon bar to open the Create Invoices window.
2. Click the Customize button above the Template box.
3. In the Customize Template window, select the Intuit Product Invoice from the Template list and click New to open the Customize Invoice window.
4. Enter a name for this new invoice template.
5. Move to the Fields tab, where you'll find that the field you added to the customer form is listed.
6. Enter the text you want to use for this field on the invoice (see Figure 10-14).
7. Select Screen to make sure this field and its data are on the screen when you're filling out an invoice. If you want to print the field and its data when you print the invoice (so the customer is reminded of the preference), also select Print.
8. Click OK to save the new template.

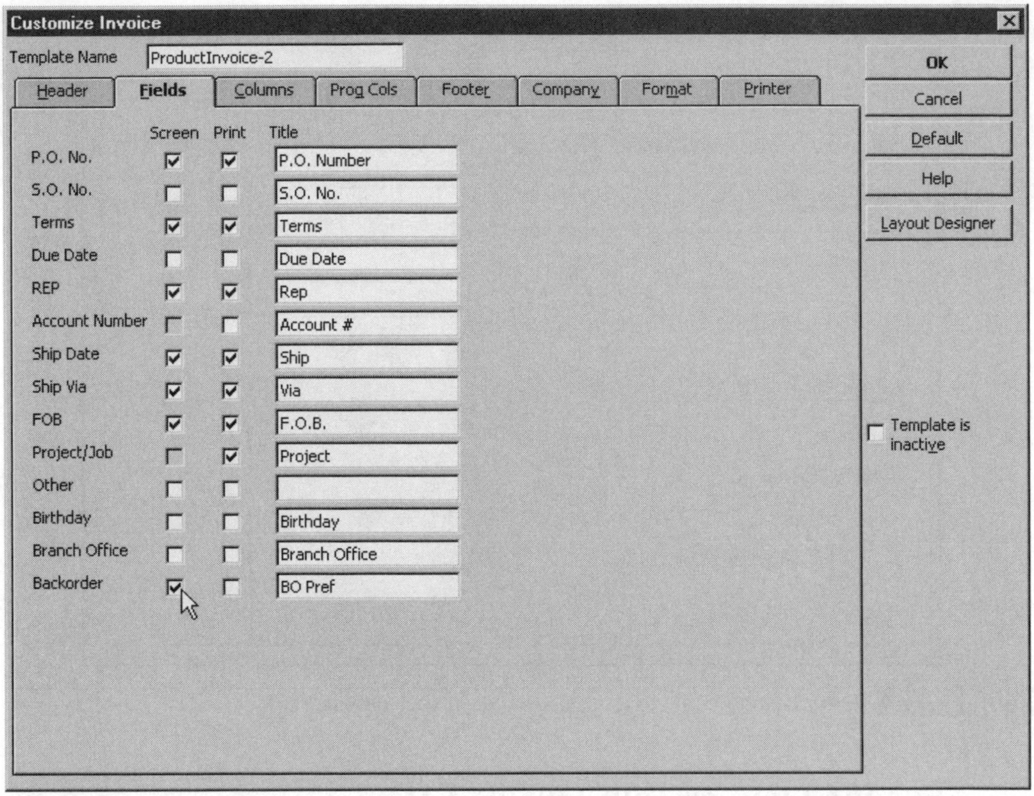

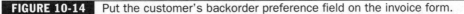

FIGURE 10-14 Put the customer's backorder preference field on the invoice form.

You may get a message from QuickBooks about the position of fields (adding a field may cause fields on the template to overlap), and usually it's best to opt to lay out the fields again. Check Chapter 3 for more information about field positions on templates, including moving your new field to a different position on the invoice.

Now when you need to enter a product invoice, use this new template. As soon as you enter the customer name in the Create Invoices window, the backorder preference for that customer is displayed (see Figure 10-15).

Recording a Backorder Invoice

Now that you're all set and can fill backorders the way your customers want them filled, here's how to create a backorder invoice in QuickBooks:

1. Fill out the invoice form, putting backordered items on the line items (see Chapter 3 for information about creating invoices). QuickBooks will flash

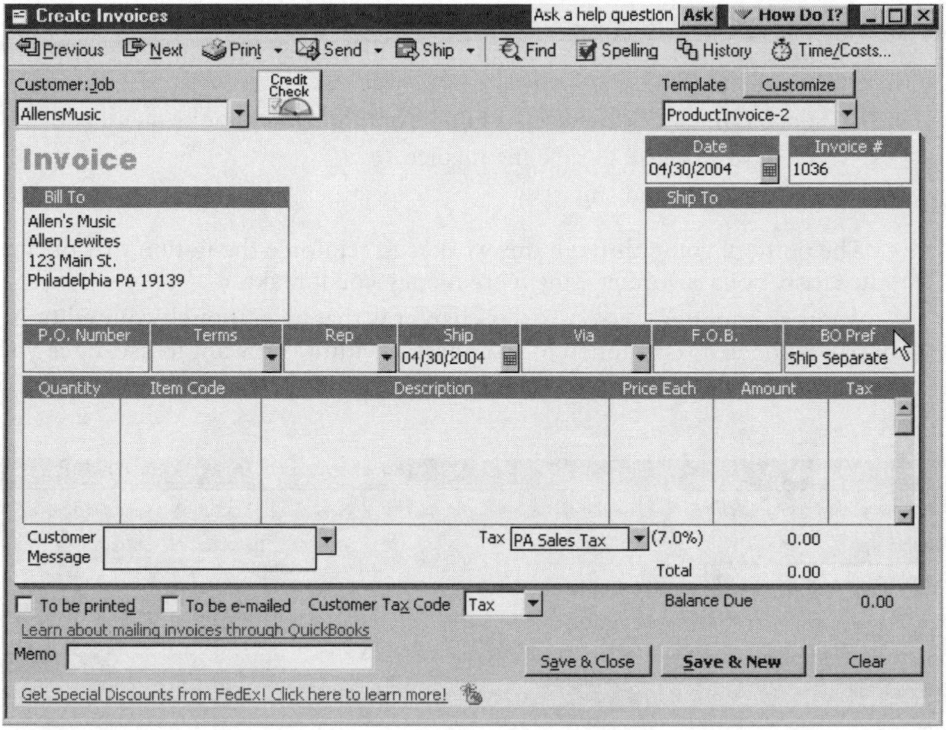

FIGURE 10-15 You won't make a mistake when the customer's backorder preference is in your face.

a message telling you there's insufficient quantity to fill the order (which is not a problem now, so click OK).

2. When the invoice form is completely filled out, right-click anywhere on the form and choose Mark Invoice As Pending from the shortcut menu. The word "Pending" appears on the invoice form (see Figure 10-16).

3. Save the invoice by clicking Save & Close (or click Save & New if you have more invoices to complete).

NOTE: A pending invoice does not post any amounts to the general ledger.

Later, when the backordered products arrive and have been entered into inventory, you can release the pending status:

1. Choose Reports | Sales | Pending Sales.

2. When the list of pending sales appears, double-click the listing for the sale you want to finalize. The original invoice (still marked "Pending") is displayed on your screen.

3. Choose Edit | Mark Invoice As Final from the QuickBooks menu bar.

4. Click Save & Close to save the invoice.

5. Pick it, pack it, and ship it.

The point of going through this work is to reinforce the notion that the better you satisfy your customers, the more money you'll make.

Another important lesson in this chapter is that even though your edition of QuickBooks doesn't inherently support a feature you want to use, once you understand the software you can frequently manipulate it to do what you need.

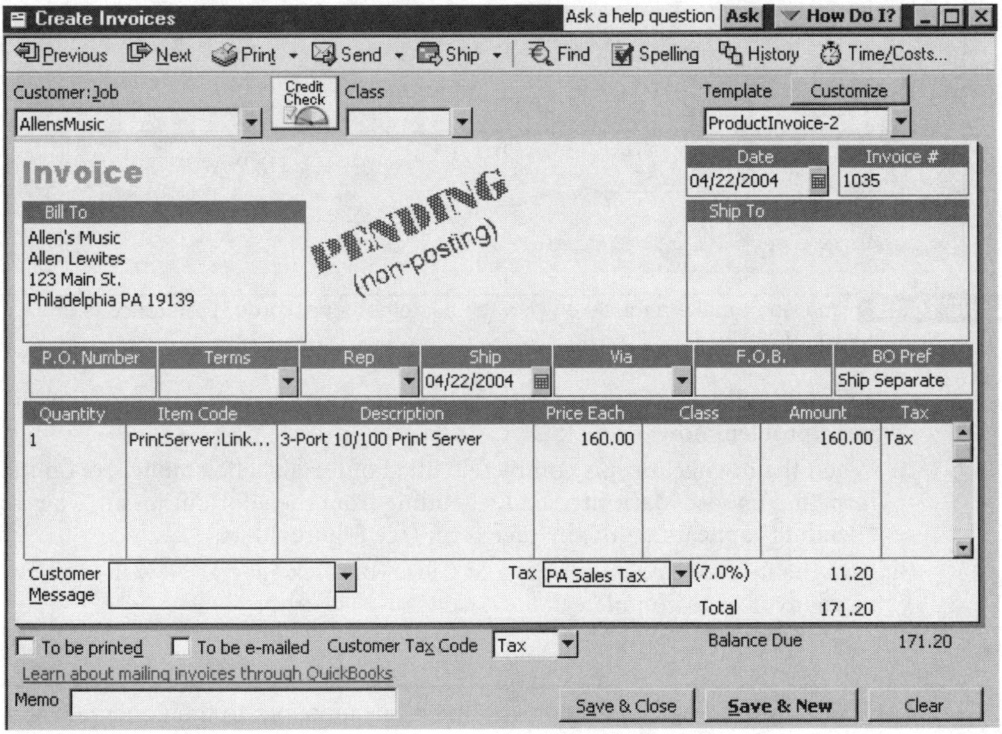

FIGURE 10-16   This order can't be filled until you receive the product, so it's not really a sale yet.

Managing Bank and Credit Card Accounts

In *this chapter:*

- Make deposits

- Transfer funds between accounts

- Deal with bounced checks

- Void disbursements

- Manage petty cash

- Balance credit card statements

Before you started using accounting software, did your checkbook register have entries crossed out? Pencil notes next to inked-in entries? Inked notes next to penciled-in entries? Transactions that were made in April entered in the middle of a string of June transactions ("The statement came—I forgot about that transaction")? Lots of corrections for math errors? If so, relax; QuickBooks can take care of all of those problems.

Making a Deposit

Even though QuickBooks takes care of depositing money into your bank account when you receive money from customers (covered in Chapter 4), there are times when you receive money that's unconnected to a customer payment.

Entering a deposit (one that's not a customer payment) into your QuickBooks check register isn't much different from entering a deposit into a manual checkbook register. Actually, it's easier because you don't have to make any calculations— QuickBooks takes care of that.

Press CTRL-A to open the chart of accounts and double-click the bank account you want to work with. Fill in the date, delete the check number if one automatically appears, and then click in the deposit column to enter the amount. Assign the deposit to an account. You should use the memo field for an explanation because your accountant will probably ask you about the deposit later (and, if necessary, create a journal entry to re-assign the amount to a different account). Click the Record button. That's it!

You can, if it's necessary, enter a payee name in the Payee column, but QuickBooks doesn't require that. Most of the time, you use this method of direct entry to record deposits that are unconnected to revenue you want to track (such as sales). For example, you may receive direct deposits as fees or commissions from other businesses, or a rebate on a purchase you made. If you enter a payee that doesn't exist in any of your name lists, QuickBooks displays a Name Not Found message offering you the following selections:

- Quick Add, which lets you enter a name without any additional information
- Set Up, which lets you create a new name using the regular New Name window
- Cancel, which returns you to the account register so you can either choose another name or delete the nonexistent Payee entry

If you select Quick Add or Set Up, you're asked which type of Name you're adding: Vendor, Customer, Employee, or Other. Unless this payee will become a Vendor or Customer (I think we can eliminate Employee from this procedure), choose Other.

If you're depositing your own money into the business, that's capital; you should post the deposit to a capital account (it's an equity account). If you're depositing the proceeds of a loan (from yourself, or from a bank), post the deposit to the liability account for the loan (or create a liability account). If you're making a deposit that's a refund from a vendor, you can post the amount to the expense account that was used for the original expense.

When in doubt, post the amount to the most logical place and call your accountant. You can always edit the transaction later or make a journal entry to post the amount to the right account.

> **TIP:** It's a good idea to set up accounts for transactions that you're unsure how to post. I have two such accounts. For income about which I want to ask my accountant, I use account #9998, titled MysteryIncome (it's an Other Income type). Account #9999 is titled MysteryExpense (it's an Other Expense type). If either account has a balance, it means I should call my accountant and find out where to post the income or expense I temporarily "parked" in that account. I can use a journal entry or edit the transaction to put the money into the right account.

Transferring Funds Between Accounts

Moving money between bank accounts is a common procedure in business. If you have a bank account for payroll, you have to move money out of your operating account into your payroll account every payday. Some people deposit all the customer payments into a money market account (which pays interest) and then transfer the necessary funds to an operating account when it's time to pay bills. Others do it the other way around, moving money not immediately needed from the business operating account to a money market account. Lawyers, agents, real estate brokers, and other professionals have to maintain escrow accounts and move money between them and the operating account.

The difference between a regular deposit and a transfer isn't clear if you think about the end result as being nothing more than "money was disbursed from one account and deposited into another account." However, that's not the way to think about it. When you work with accounting issues, every action has an effect on your general ledger, which means there's an effect on your financial reporting (and your taxes). A transfer isn't a disbursement (which is an expense that's assigned to a specific account), and it isn't a regular deposit (income received). A transfer has no effect on your profit and loss. If you don't use the transfer protocol, you run the risk of posting a deductible expense or taxable income to your profit and loss reports.

To make a transfer, follow these steps:

1. Choose Banking | Transfer Funds from the menu bar.
2. Fill out the fields (see Figure 11-1).
3. Click Save & Close (or Save & New if you have another transfer to make).

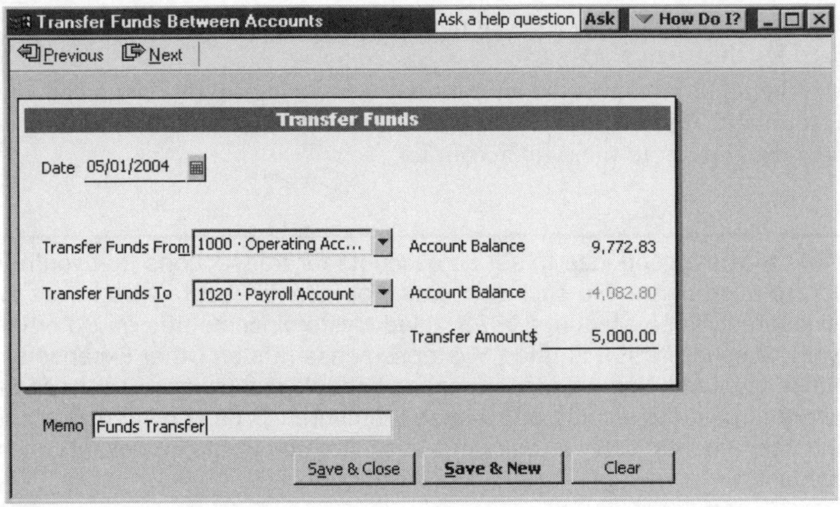

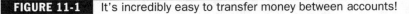

FIGURE 11-1 It's incredibly easy to transfer money between accounts!

QuickBooks posts the transaction (you'll see it marked as TRANSFR in both bank accounts if you open their registers) without affecting any totals in your financial reports. All the work is done on the balance sheet, but the bottom line of your balance sheet doesn't change as the following postings are made to the general ledger:

ACCOUNT	DEBIT	CREDIT
Sending Bank Account		Amount of Transfer
Receiving Bank Account	Amount of Transfer	

TIP: In order to facilitate a transfer of funds, you really should have both of the accounts set up in your QuickBooks system. Although you can create accounts during the transfer procedure, it's always quicker and easier to have everything set up in advance.

Handling Bounced Checks

Customer checks sometimes bounce. When that happens, you have several tasks in front of you:

- Deduct the amount of the bounced check from your checking account.
- Record any bank charges you incurred as a result of the bounced check.

- Remove the payment applied to the customer invoice (if it wasn't a cash sale).
- Recover the money from the customer.

In addition, you might want to collect a service charge from the customer (at least for the amount of any charges your own bank assessed).

Adjusting the Account Balances

You must remove the amount of the bounced check from your bank account and also adjust the Accounts Receivable account if the bounced check was an invoice payment. If the check was a payment for a cash sale, nothing was posted to Accounts Receivable; however, you must adjust the income account to which you posted the cash sale.

Using the Bank Account Register

If you deposited the check directly into the bank instead of using the Undeposited Funds account, and the deposit was an invoice payment, its listing in the bank register has a type of PMT. You must delete the payment (there's no Void option for payments) by pressing CTRL-D or by choosing Edit | Delete Payment from the QuickBooks menu bar.

QuickBooks displays a message telling you that the payment was used to pay an invoice and that deleting it will result in unpaid balances (which is exactly what should happen). Click OK, and the invoice that was paid returns to its balance due before the payment. The Accounts Receivable account is also adjusted. The invoice will show up as unpaid the next time you send a statement to the customer, and you should also invoice the customer for any bounced check charges you incurred, and for any service charge you want to charge the customer for the aggravation. (See "Invoicing Customers for Bounced Checks" later in this section.)

If you used the Undeposited Funds account, it's easiest to create a journal entry to remove the amount paid from the customer's balance. Then you must re-invoice the customer (see "Invoicing Customers for Bounced Checks" later in this section).

Using a Journal Entry

You can create a journal entry to adjust the amounts. Choose Banking | Make Journal Entry to open the General Journal Entry window. Then take these steps:

1. Click the Account column, then click the arrow and select the bank into which you deposited the payment.
2. Move to the Credit column, and enter the amount of the bounced check.
3. Move to the Memo column to write yourself a note (e.g., Smith Ck #2345 bounced).
4. Click in the Account column and choose the Accounts Receivable account. QuickBooks automatically fills in the amount in the Debit column.

5. Click in the Name column and select the customer whose check bounced.

6. Click Save & Close.

Recording Bank Charges for Bounced Checks

If your bank charged you for a returned check, you have to enter the bank charge. To do so, start by opening the register for your bank account with either of the following actions:

- Open the Chart of Accounts and double-click the bank account listing.
- Click the Reg icon on the toolbar and select the bank account from the drop-down list in the Use Register dialog box.

Then fill out the fields as follows:

1. Click the Date field in the blank line at the bottom of the register and enter the date that the bank charge was assessed.

2. In the Number field, QuickBooks automatically fills in the next available check number. Delete that number and press TAB. QuickBooks fills in the word "Number."

3. Leave the Payee field blank.

4. In the Payment field, enter the amount of the service charge for the returned check.

5. In the Account field, assign this transaction to the expense account you use for bank charges.

6. Optionally, enter text in the Memo field (such as the name of the customer whose check bounced).

7. Click the Record button in the register window to save the transaction.

Your bank account balance is reduced by the amount of the service charge. You should charge the customer for this, and in the following sections I'll cover the steps needed to accomplish that.

Invoicing Customers for Bounced Checks

In order to re-invoice your customers after a check bounces, you must create items for bounced checks and for any service charges. Then you can use those items in the invoice.

Creating an Item for a Bounced Check

You have to re-invoice the customer for the bounced check. To do that, you need an item for bounced checks:

1. Click the Item icon on the Icon Bar to open the Item List window.

2. Press CTRL-N to enter a new item.

3. Select Other Charge as the item type.

4. Name the item appropriately (for instance, "Returned Check").

5. Enter an optional description.

6. Leave the amount blank (you fill it in when you create the invoice).

7. Select Non as the tax code.

8. Link the item to the sales income account.

The reason you link the item to the sales income account is to replace the income that was removed when you voided the deposited check. After all, the customer still has the product or service you sold.

Creating an Item for Customer Service Charges

To create an item for invoicing customers for service charges, follow these steps:

1. Click the Item icon on the Icon Bar to open the Item List window.

2. Press CTRL-N to enter a new item.

3. Select Other Charge as the item type.

4. Name the item appropriately (for instance, "RetChkChg").

5. Enter a description (for example, "Service charge for returned check").

6. Leave the amount blank (you fill it in when you create the invoice).

7. Select Non as the tax code.

8. Link the item to an income account, such as to Other Income or to an account you create for situations like this (perhaps "Customer Service Charges").

9. Click OK.

Creating the Invoice

Now you need to send an invoice to the customer for the bounced check.

 TIP: You might want to use the Intuit Service Invoice template for this charge; it's easier and "cleaner" for this type of invoice.

1. Click the Invoice icon on the Icon Bar.

2. When the Create Invoices window opens, enter the name of the customer who gave you the bad check.

3. Enter the date on which the check bounced.

4. Click in the Item column and select the item you created for returned checks.

5. Enter the amount of the returned check.

6. Add another line item for the service charge you incurred for the bounced check, using the item you created for service charges.

Voiding Disbursements

Sometimes you have to void a check that you've written. Perhaps you decided not to send it for some reason, or perhaps it was lost in the mail. Whatever the reason, if a check isn't going to clear your bank, you should void it.

The process of voiding a check is quite easy, and the only trouble you can cause yourself is *deleting* the check instead of *voiding* it. Deleting a check removes all history of the transaction, and the check number disappears into la-la land. This is not a good way to keep financial records. Voiding a check keeps the check number, but sets the amount to zero.

To void a check, open the bank account register and click anywhere on the check's transaction line. Right-click to see the shortcut menu and choose Void Check. The corresponding entry in the expense account (or multiple expense accounts) to which the check was written is also adjusted. Click Record to save the transaction.

Tracking Petty Cash

Aren't those ATM gadgets wonderful? They're everywhere, even at the supermarket checkout! It's so easy to take cash out of your bank account. And it's so easy to forget to enter the transaction in your account register!

Another wonderful device is the petty cash box, which many businesses maintain to dispense cash to employees (or owners) who need cash to recover money they've spent for the company, or as an advance against future expenditures.

When you use cash, whether it's cash from the petty cash box, or a withdrawal via an ATM machine, you have to account for it. That means you have to account for the portion of it you spend and the portion that's still in your pocket. The cash belongs to the business. In this section, I'll cover the accounting procedures involved with petty cash transactions. Creating a system that ensures your ATM and petty cash withdrawals are accounted for is *your* problem—QuickBooks cannot help you remember to enter transactions. (Well, you could set up a QuickBooks reminder that appears frequently with the message "Did you ATM today????")

Creating a Petty Cash Account

If you spend cash for business expenses, your chart of accounts should have a petty cash account. This account functions like a cash till: you put money in it, then you account for the money that's spent, leaving the rest in the till until it, too, is spent. Then you put more money into the till. The petty cash account doesn't represent a real bank account; it just represents that portion of the money in the real bank account that moved into the till. If you don't have a petty cash account in your chart of accounts, create one as follows:

1. Click the Accnt icon on the Icon Bar to open the Chart Of Accounts window.
2. When the Chart Of Accounts window appears, press CTRL-N to open a blank New Account window.
3. Fill in the account information using the following guidelines:
   - The Account Type is Bank.
   - If you number your accounts, use a number that places your new petty cash account near the other (real) bank accounts in your chart of accounts.
   - Leave the opening balance at zero.

Putting Money into Petty Cash

You have to put money into your petty cash till, both literally (get cash) and figuratively (record a withdrawal from your bank account to your petty cash account). Most of the time you'll write a check for petty cash using the following guidelines:

- Create a name in the Other Names list for the payee (usually the name is "cash").
- Post the check to the petty cash account.
- If you're tracking classes, assign the transaction to the Other class, or omit the class.

You can use the Write Checks window to accomplish the task, or enter the transaction directly in the bank account register.

TIP: You don't post a petty cash check to an expense nor a class; those postings are recorded when you account for the spent funds (see "Recording Petty Cash Disbursements").

Recording ATM Withdrawals

When you withdraw money from your bank account with your ATM card, it's not an expense, it's just cash. You've put cash into a till (literally, the till is your pocket, but to QuickBooks it's a petty cash container). It becomes an expense when you spend it (remember to get a receipt so you can enter the expense into your system).

Bring the ATM receipt (and receipts for any stuff you purchased with the ATM cash) back to the office. Now you're ready to perform the procedures necessary to track the cash you took and the cash you spent.

The first thing you have to do is take the cash out of your QuickBooks bank account because you stood in front of an ATM dispenser and took cash out of your actual bank account. However, this is double-entry bookkeeping, and there has to be an equal and opposite posting to another account. That's what the petty cash account is for. You have a choice of methods for performing this task: transfer the funds between accounts, or enter a transaction in your bank account.

To transfer funds between the bank account and the petty cash account, use the following steps:

1. Choose Banking | Transfer Funds.
2. In the Transfer Funds Between Accounts window, fill out the information needed, which is just the two accounts and the amount you withdrew. Then click Save & Close.

To enter the withdrawal as a transaction, open the bank account register and follow these steps:

1. Enter the transaction date.
2. Delete the check number QuickBooks automatically enters in the Number field.
3. Skip the Payee field.
4. Enter the amount of transaction in the Payment column.
5. In the Account field, post the transaction to the petty cash account. QuickBooks automatically assigns the type TRANSFR to the transaction.

Some bookkeepers are uneasy about skipping the Payee field. If you fall in that category, create a payee named PettyCash in the Other Name list, and use that name for petty cash transactions.

Recording Petty Cash Disbursements

As you spend the money you withdraw via an ATM transaction or by taking cash out of the petty cash box in the office, you must record those expenditures in the petty cash register.

> **TIP:** Don't let anyone take money out of the petty cash till without a receipt. If the money is an advance against a purchase instead of payment for a receipt, use an IOU. Later, replace the IOU with the purchase receipt.

Open the petty cash account register and use the receipts you've collected to assign expense accounts to the transaction. You can enter one transaction, splitting the postings among all the affected expense accounts, or enter individual transactions. Use the following guidelines for entering the transaction:

- You can delete the check number QuickBooks automatically inserts in the Number field, or you can leave the number there (you'll never reconcile the petty cash account, so it doesn't matter).
- You can either skip the Payee field or use a payee named PettyCash, as explained in the previous section.

I constantly encounter bookkeepers who enter a real payee for each petty cash transaction ("Joe's Hardware Store," "Mary's Office Supplies," and so on). As a result, their QuickBooks files grow larger than they need to because the system is carrying the weight of all these vendors. The vendors they enter appear in all their vendor reports, crowding those reports with extraneous names that nobody has any interest in tracking.

Reserve vendors for those payees from whom you receive bills, or to whom you disburse checks, and for whom you want to track activity. If it's so important to know that you spent a buck eighty for a screwdriver at Joe's Hardware Store, enter that information in the memo field.

If you spent less than the amount of cash you withdrew from the till, the balance stays in the petty cash account. You'll probably spend it later, and at that point you'll repeat this task to account for that spending.

Managing Your Credit Cards

When you use a business credit card, you have a number of choices for tracking and paying the credit card bill. First, you can either pay the entire bill every month, or pay part of the bill and keep a running credit card balance. Second, you can choose between two methods of handling credit card purchases in QuickBooks:

- Treat the credit card bill as an ordinary vendor and enter the bill when it arrives.
- Treat the credit card bill as a liability and enter each transaction as it's made.

Treating Credit Cards as Vendors

You can set up the credit card as an ordinary vendor and enter the bill into QuickBooks when it arrives. Most of the time, the expenses are posted to multiple accounts, so the credit card bill transaction is a split transaction (see Figure 11-2).

If you don't pay off the card balance (you make a partial payment when you use the Pay Bills window, or you write a direct disbursement check for less than the amount due), each month you'll have a new bill to enter that has interest charges in addition to your purchases. Post the interest charges to the appropriate account.

When you pay the credit card bill, you can enter the amount you want to pay against each bill in the system. Always start with the oldest bill, making a partial payment or paying it in full. Then move to the next oldest bill, making a partial payment or paying it in full.

Treating Credit Cards as Liability Accounts

You can also treat credit cards as liability accounts, tracking each transaction against the account as it occurs. Then when the bill arrives, you match the transactions against the bill and decide how much to pay. Your running balance is tracked specifically against the credit card, instead of being part of your Accounts Payable balance.

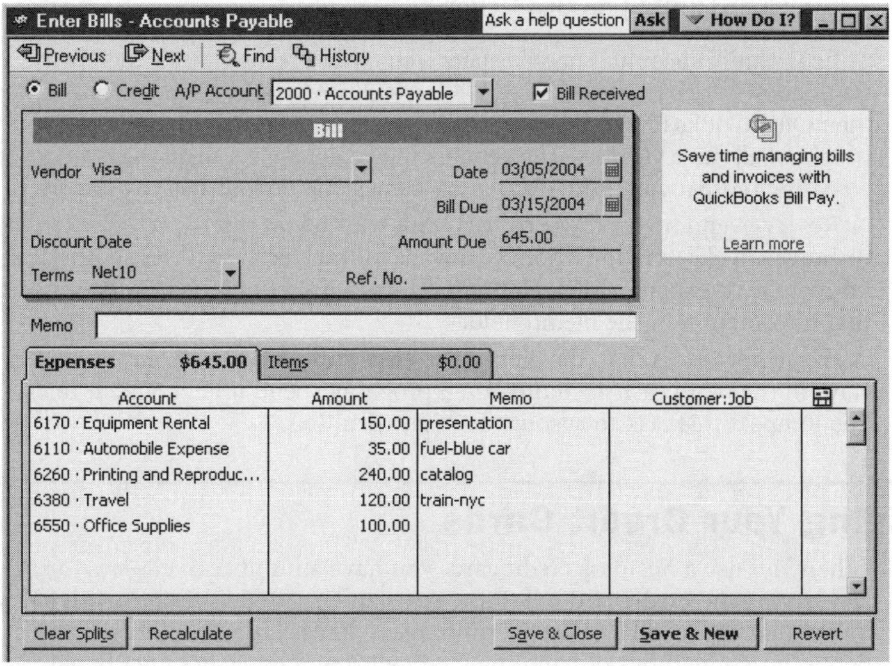

FIGURE 11-2 Credit card bills are usually split transactions.

Creating a Credit Card Account

To use credit cards in this manner, you must have an account for each credit card in your chart of accounts. If you don't have such an account as a result of the EasyStep Interview, you can create one now, using an account type of Credit Card. Check out Chapter 2 for information about adding items to your chart of accounts.

> **CAUTION:** QuickBooks arranges the chart of accounts by account types. If you're using numbers for your accounts, the numbering is ignored in favor of account types. To make sure your credit card accounts are displayed in the right order, use account numbers that fit into the right section of the chart of accounts—credit card accounts come right after accounts payable accounts.

Entering Credit Card Charges

If you want to track your credit card charges as they're assumed, instead of waiting for the bill, you have to treat your credit card transactions like ATM transactions— enter them as you go. QuickBooks offers two methods to accomplish this:

- Set up your credit card account for online banking, and download the transactions (covered in Chapter 16).
- Enter transactions manually.

If your credit card account is enabled for online banking, these are not mutually exclusive methods. You can enter the transactions manually and download data from your credit card server to match those transaction. Or, you can download the transactions and then add each transaction to the credit card register (instructions are in Chapter 16).

To enter credit card charges manually, choose Banking | Record Credit Card Charges | Enter Credit Card Charges, which opens the Enter Credit Card Charges window seen in Figure 11-3.

Select the appropriate credit card account and then use the store receipt as a reference document to fill in the transaction. Here are some guidelines for making this transaction easy and quick to complete:

- In the Purchased From field, enter a generic vendor. Create a vendor named Credit Card Purchase or something similar. Then use the Memo field for each transaction to note the name of the real vendor, if that information is important to you. If you use a real, individual vendor name in the Purchased from field, each time you use your credit card at a new vendor, QuickBooks will force you to add the vendor to your vendor list. You'll end up with a gazillion vendors with whom you don't have a real vendor relationship (they don't send you bills), and you won't be able to delete them from your QuickBooks file because they have transactions.

- If the transaction is a return, be sure to select the Credit option at the top of the window.
- Enter the receipt number in the Ref No. field.
- Enter the date of the purchase.
- Use the Expenses tab for general expenses; use the Items tab if you used the credit card to buy inventory items (items you sell to customers).
- If you use the credit card for an expense or an item for a customer, enter the customer information so you can bill the customer for reimbursement (see Chapter 6 for details about entering reimbursable expenses).

Click Save & New to save the record and move to another blank credit card entry window to enter another credit card transaction, or click Save & Close if you're finished entering credit card charges.

TIP: You can also enter these charges directly in the register of your credit card account. (Some people find it faster to work in the register.)

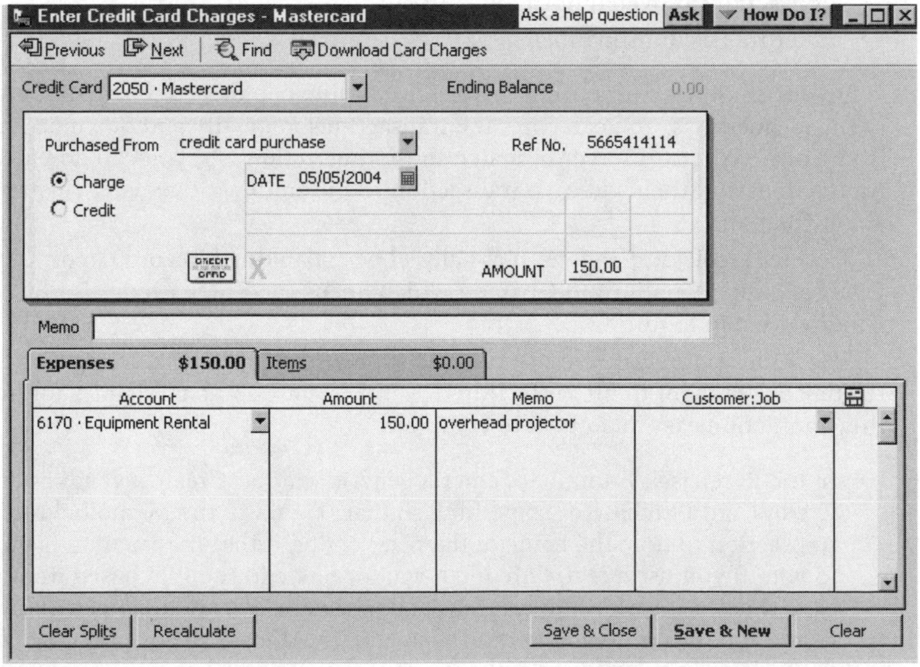

FIGURE 11-3 To track credit cards as liabilities, enter each credit card transaction as it occurs.

Reconciling the Credit Card Bill

Eventually, the credit card bill arrives, and you have to perform the following chores:

- Reconcile the bill against the entries you recorded.
- Decide whether to pay the entire bill or just a portion of it.
- Write a check.

Choose Banking | Reconcile from the QuickBooks menu bar to open the Reconcile window. In the Account field, select the credit card from the drop-down list. In the Begin Reconciliation dialog box enter the following data:

- The ending balance from the credit card bill.
- Any finance charges on the bill in the Finance Charge box, along with the date on which the charges were assessed.
- The account you use to post finance charges (create one if you don't have one—it's an expense).

NOTE: The first time you do this, there won't be a beginning balance for this credit card.

Click Continue to open the Reconcile Credit Card window, which displays the purchases you entered. Click the check mark column for each transaction on your window that has a matching transaction on the credit card bill (make sure the amounts match, too). That includes payments, credits, and charges.

Add any transactions you forgot to enter by opening the credit card register and entering the transactions. (To find the receipts, search your pockets, desk, pocketbook, the floor of your car, and the kitchen junk drawer.) When you return to the Reconcile Credit Card window, the new transactions are added and you can check them off.

TIP: Finance charges for businesses are tax deductible; the finance charges you incur for your personal credit cards, or for personal expenses, aren't.

Now look at the box at the bottom of the window where the totals are displayed. If the difference is $0.00, congratulations! Everything's fine. Click Reconcile Now (QuickBooks offers a congratulatory message).

If the difference is not $0.00, you have to figure out the problem and make corrections (read Chapter 12, which is dedicated to the subject of reconciling bank accounts, to learn how to troubleshoot reconciliations).

Paying the Credit Card Bill

When you finish working in the reconciliation window, QuickBooks moves on to pay the bill by asking you whether you want to write a check now, or create a vendor bill that you'll pay the next time you pay your bills.

Select the appropriate response and click OK. QuickBooks offers congratulations, and also offers to print a reconciliation report (see Chapter 12 to learn about printing reconciliation reports). Select the report type you want, or click Cancel to skip the report.

Next, a transaction window that matches your response to paying the bill opens, so you can either enter a vendor bill or write a check. Fill in all the fields and save the transaction.

TIP: All the detailed information you need to create vendor bills is covered in Chapter 6, and information about paying bills and printing checks is in Chapter 7.

Reconciling Bank Accounts

In *this chapter:*

- Get ready to reconcile

- The Begin Reconciliation window

- The first QuickBooks reconciliation

- Troubleshoot opening balance discrepancies

- Clear transactions

- Reconcile the differences

- Make adjustments

- Undo a reconciliation that didn't work properly

- Troubleshoot reconciliation problems

- Print reconciliation reports

Reconciling bank accounts is fancy terminology for "I have to balance my checkbook," which is one of the most annoying tasks connected with financial record keeping. In this chapter I'll go over all the steps required to reconcile your bank accounts.

 NOTE: If you also have to reconcile credit card statements, read Chapter 11 to learn how.

Getting Ready to Reconcile

After your bank statement arrives, you must find some uninterrupted moments to compare it to the information in the QuickBooks account register.

If your bank sends your canceled checks in the envelope along with the statement (some banks don't include the physical checks), you can arrange the checks in numerical order before you start this task. However, instead of sorting and collating the physical checks, it's much easier to use the list of check numbers, which appear in numerical order, on your statement. An asterisk or some other mark usually appears to indicate a missing number (usually a check that hasn't cleared yet, a check that cleared previously, or perhaps a voided check).

Open the register for the bank account you're about to reconcile by clicking the Reg icon and selecting the appropriate account, or by double-clicking the account's listing in the Chart Of Accounts window. If the bank statement shows deposits or checks (or both) that are absent from your bank register, add them to the register. If you miss any, don't worry, you can add transactions to the register while you're working in the Reconcile window, but it's usually quicker to get this task out of the way before you start the reconciliation process.

Interest payments and bank charges don't count as missing transactions, because the bank reconciliation process treats those transactions separately. You'll have a chance to enter those amounts during bank reconciliation.

Adding Missing Disbursements to the Register

The way you add missing checks to the register depends on whether the checks were payments of vendor bills you entered into your QuickBooks file, or direct disbursements.

- To enter a payment, use the Pay Bills command on the Vendors menu.
- To enter a direct disbursement, use the Write Checks window (press CTRL-W) or enter the check directly into the register.

Adding Missing Deposits to the Register

Check the Undeposited Funds account to see if you entered the deposits when they arrived but neglected to run the Make Deposits procedure. If so, choose Banking | Make Deposits, and select the deposits that appear on your statement. If you have multiple deposits listed, you can either deposit the funds to match the transaction list on the statement, or group deposits and don't worry about matching the transaction list on the statement.

For example, your bank statement may show a deposit of $145.78 on one date, and another deposit for $3,233.99 on another date. Both deposits appear in the Make Deposits window. Select one of the deposits, process it, and then repeat the procedure for the other deposit. When you reconcile the account, your transactions reflect the transactions in your bank statement.

On the other hand, you could select both deposits and process them in one transaction. When you reconcile the account, the joint deposit adds up correctly, so the reconciliation succeeds.

If a missing deposit isn't in the Undeposited Funds account, you have to create the deposit, which may have been a customer payment of an invoice, a cash sale, a transfer of funds between banks, a payment of a loan, or a deposit of capital.

For customer invoice payments, or cash sales, fill out the appropriate transaction window. If you deposit the proceeds to the Undeposited Funds account, don't forget to take the additional step to deposit the funds in the bank so the transaction appears in the reconciliation window. If you deposit the proceeds directly to the bank, the transaction appears in the reconciliation window automatically.

If you made deposits unconnected to customers and earned income, such as putting additional capital into your business, or depositing the proceeds of a loan, the fastest way to enter the transaction is to work directly in the bank account's register. Enter the deposit amount and post the transaction to the appropriate account. If you're not sure which account to use for the offset posting, ask your accountant.

Using the Begin Reconciliation Window

Reconciling your bank account starts with the Begin Reconciliation window, which you open by choosing Banking | Reconcile. If you have more than one bank account, or you have credit card accounts you reconcile in addition to bank accounts, select the bank account you want to reconcile from the drop-down list in the Account field.

Check the Beginning Balance field in the window against the beginning balance on the bank statement. (Your bank may call it the *starting balance*.)

If your beginning balances match, enter the ending balance from your statement in the Ending Balance field, and enter the statement date. Skip the next sections in this chapter on solving the problem of non-matching beginning balances. Head for the section "Enter Interest Income and Service Charges" and keep reading from there.

If the beginning balances don't match, and this is the first time you've reconciled this account in QuickBooks, that's normal. If the beginning balances don't match, and you've previously reconciled this account, that's *not* normal.

You cannot edit the beginning balance in the Begin Reconciliation window, but you can change it by making adjustments in your bank account register, and I'll go over those tasks in this section.

Adjusting the Beginning Balance for the First Reconciliation

The beginning balance in the Begin Reconciliation window probably doesn't match the opening balance on your bank statement the first time you reconcile the account. Your QuickBooks beginning balance is the initial entry you made for this bank account during setup. The number may have been posted to the bank account from the account balance you entered in the EasyStep Interview, or the account balance you entered when you set up the account from the Chart Of Accounts window.

The bank, of course, is using the last ending balance as the current beginning balance. The last ending balance represents a running total that began way back when, starting when you first opened that bank account. The only QuickBooks users who have it easy are those who opened their bank accounts the same day they started to use QuickBooks. (A minuscule number of people, if any, fit that description.)

You can change the beginning balance in your account register to match the bank's beginning balance, and the changed balance will appear as the Beginning Balance in the Begin Reconciliation window. Use the following steps to match beginning balances:

1. Click Cancel on the Begin Reconciliation window to close it.
2. Open the bank account register and find that opening balance entry. It's probably the earliest entry in the register and the Account field shows Opening Bal Equity as the posting account.
3. Change the amount to match the beginning balance on your bank statement.
4. Make sure there's a check mark in the Cleared column (the column heading is a check mark).
5. Click Record to save the transaction.

6. QuickBooks issues a warning message about changing this transaction and asks if you really want to record your changes. Click Yes.
7. Choose Banking | Reconcile to open the Begin Reconciliation window, which displays the same opening balance as the bank statement.

Now you can move on in this chapter to the section "Enter Interest Income and Service Charges" and keep reading from there. Also, write yourself a note so you can give your accountant a coherent explanation, because your Opening Bal Equity account changed and may have to be adjusted at the end of the year.

> **TIP:** If you don't want to change the beginning balance, QuickBooks can make an automatic adjusting entry to account for the difference when you finishing reconciling the account. In fact, QuickBooks posts the adjusting entry to the Opening Bal Equity account, so the bottom line is the same. See the section "Permitting an Adjusting Entry" later in this chapter for more information.

Resolving Unexpected Differences in the Beginning Balance

If this isn't the first time you've reconciled the bank, the beginning balance that's displayed on the Begin Reconciliation window should match the beginning balance on the bank statement. That beginning balance is the ending balance from the last reconciliation, and nothing should change its amount.

If the beginning balance doesn't match the statement, you have to find out why. Search your memory, because you probably performed one of the following actions (and you need to undo the damage):

• You changed the amount on a transaction that had previously cleared. Never do that.
• You voided a transaction that had previously cleared. Never do that.
• You deleted a transaction that had previously cleared. Never do that.
• You removed the cleared check mark from a transaction that had previously cleared. Never do that.

Now that you know all the things you should never do, you have to figure out which one of those actions you took after you last reconciled the account. QuickBooks has a tool to help you. Click the Locate Discrepancies button on the Begin Reconciliation window to open the Locate Discrepancies dialog box seen in Figure 12-1.

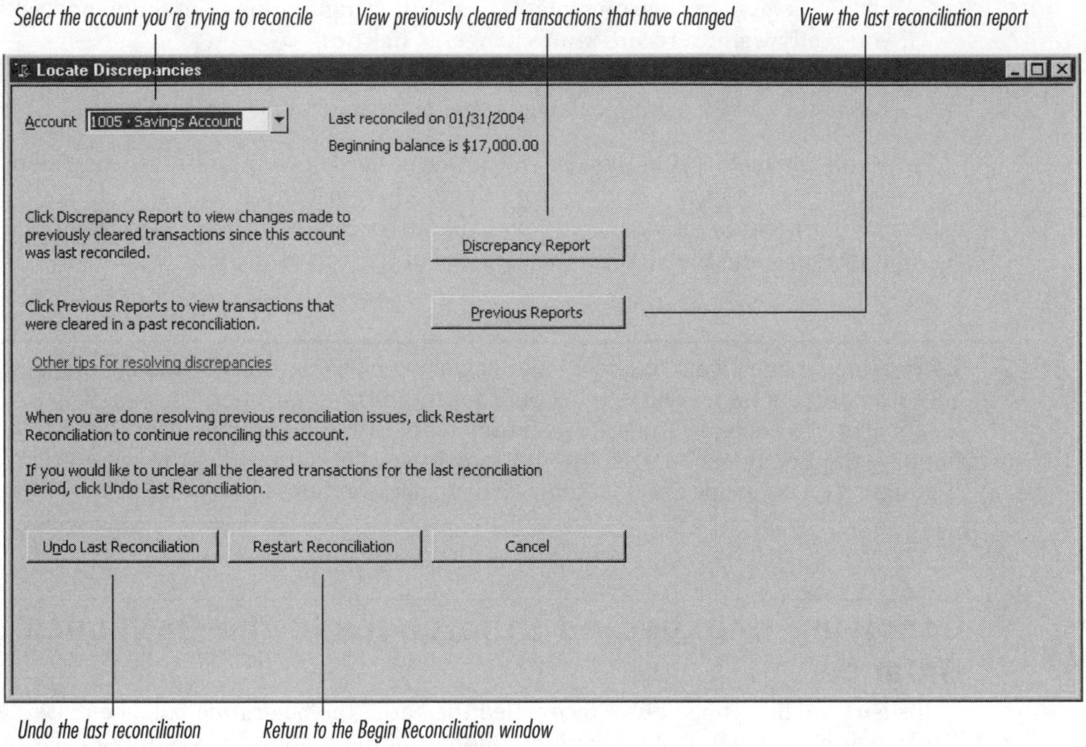

Select the account you're trying to reconcile   View previously cleared transactions that have changed   View the last reconciliation report

Undo the last reconciliation   Return to the Begin Reconciliation window

---

FIGURE 12-1 You have to track down the reason for an incorrect starting balance.

Viewing the Discrepancy Report

Click Discrepancy Report to see any transactions that were cleared during a past reconciliation, and then were changed or deleted.

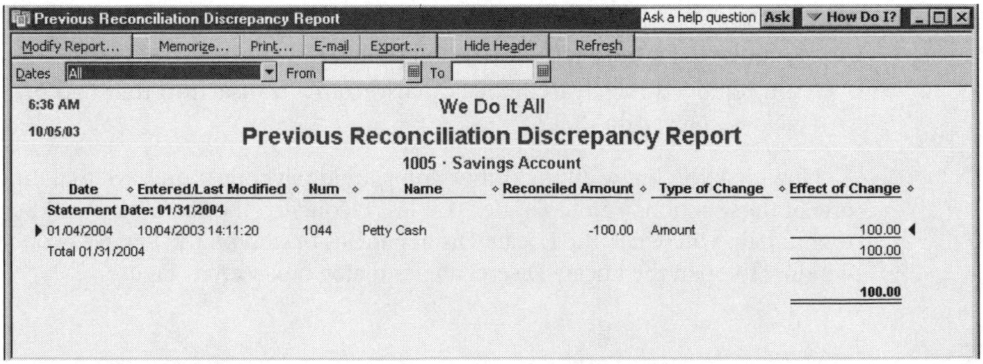

This report shows you the details of the transaction when it was cleared during a previous reconciliation and the change in the transaction since that reconciliation. If the reconciled amount is a positive number, the transaction was a deposit; a negative number indicates a disbursement (usually a check).

The Type Of Change column provides a clue about the action you must take to correct the unmatched beginning balances.

- Uncleared means you removed the check mark in the Cleared column of the register (and you persisted in this action even though QuickBooks issued a stern warning about the dangers).
- Deleted means you deleted the transaction.
- Amount is the original amount, which means you changed the amount of the transaction. Check the Reconciled amount and the amount in the Effect Of Change amount, and do the math; the difference is the amount of the change.

Unfortunately, QuickBooks doesn't offer a Type Of Change named "Void," so a voided transaction is merely marked as changed. A transaction with a changed amount equal and opposite of the original amount was probably voided.

Open the register and restore the affected transactions to their original state. This is safe because you can't justify changing a cleared transaction—*a transaction that cleared can't be changed, voided, deleted, or uncleared, it is what it is, forever*.

TIP: You don't have to be in the Begin Reconciliation window to see a Discrepancy Report. You can view the contents at any time by choosing Reports | Banking | Reconciliation Discrepancy.

Viewing the Last Reconciliation Report

Even if you don't display or print a reconciliation report after you reconcile an account, QuickBooks saves the report. If you're trying to track down a discrepancy in the beginning balance, viewing the last reconciliation report may be helpful. QuickBooks Pro/Basic Editions can save only the last reconciliation report, and each time you reconcile an account the report is overwritten.

TIP: QuickBooks Premier Editions save multiple reconciliation reports. Instructions for viewing and using older reconciliation reports are available in *Running QuickBooks 2004 Premier Editions*, from CPA911 Publishing (www.cpa911.com).

Click Previous Reports to open the Select Previous Reconciliation Report dialog box, and select the options for the type and format of the report you want to see.

TIP: You can view the Previous Reconciliation report at any time by choosing Reports | Banking | Previous Reconciliation.

Choose the Reconciliation Report Type

Select Summary to see the totals for transactions that were cleared and uncleared at the time of the reconciliation. The report also lists the totals for new transactions (transactions entered after the reconciliation). Totals are by type, so there is one total for inflow (deposits and credits), and another total for outflow (checks and payments).

Select Detail to see each transaction that was cleared or not cleared in a previous reconciliation, and also see each new transaction.

Select Both to open both reports (not one report with both sets of listings).

Choose the File Type for the Reconciliation Report

QuickBooks offers this report in two file types: PDF and the regular QuickBooks report window.

PDF, which you choose by selecting the option Transactions Cleared At The Time Of Reconciliation. (Report Is Displayed As A PDF File), is a Portable Document Format file. In order to view a PDF file, you must have Adobe Acrobat Reader (or another PDF reader program) installed on your computer. If you don't, when you select this report QuickBooks opens a dialog box with a link to the Adobe website, where you can download Acrobat Reader (it's free!).

PDF files are graphical and let you view and print information. You cannot drill down to see details, because this report is not directly linked to your QuickBooks data.

However, the report gives you an accurate report of the last reconciliation. (If you printed a reconciliation report the last time you reconciled the account, the PDF file matches your printout.)

The standard QuickBooks report window, which you choose by selecting the option Transactions Cleared Plus Any Changes Made To Those Transactions Since The Reconciliation, is neither useful nor accurate. It is not, as its name implies, a reconciliation report. It's merely a report on the current state of the account register, sorted in a way to display the account's transactions according to cleared/uncleared/new categories. If you, or someone else, changed a cleared transaction, the new information appears in this report, not the information that was extant at the time you reconciled the account. If you're viewing the previous reconciliation to try to determine whether any changes were made to cleared transactions, this report fools you—it's dangerous to rely on its contents.

Here's the bottom line: If you need to see an accurate, trustworthy, previous reconciliation report in order to track down discrepancies, either use the PDF file or make sure you print and file a detailed reconciliation report every time you reconcile a bank account.

Finding and Resolving Differences

If you view the Discrepancy Report, changed transactions are displayed. If you haven't found the problem that's causing the discrepancy in the beginning balances, and want to search for it manually, you can compare the reconciliation report and the account register. Any transaction that is listed in the reconciliation report should also be in the register.

- If a transaction is there, but marked VOID, re-enter it, using the data in the reconciliation report. That transaction wasn't void when you performed the last reconciliation, it had cleared. Therefore, it doesn't meet any of the reasons to void a transaction.

- If a transaction appears in the reconciliation report, but is not in the register, it was deleted. Re-enter it, using the data in the reconciliation report.

Check the amounts on the printed check reconciliation report against the data in the register to see if any amount was changed after the account was reconciled. If so, restore the original amount.

Undoing the Last Reconciliation

QuickBooks now lets you undo the last reconciliation, which means that all transactions cleared during the reconciliation are uncleared. This is a good way to start over if you're mired in difficulties and confusion during the current reconciliation, and the problems seem to stem from the previous reconciliation (especially if you'd forced reconciliation by having QuickBooks make an adjusting entry).

Just in case this process doesn't work, back up your company file so you can restore the data in its reconciled state. Then follow these steps to undo the last reconciliation:

1. Click the Locate Discrepancies button in the Begin Reconciliation dialog box.
2. In the Locate Discrepancies dialog box, select the appropriate account.
3. Click Undo Last Reconciliation.
4. Click Continue.

QuickBooks performs the following actions:

- Removes the cleared status of all transactions you cleared during the last reconciliation.
- Leaves the amounts you entered for interest and bank charges.

When the process completes, QuickBooks displays a message to inform you of that fact. Click OK to clear the message and return to the Locate Discrepancies dialog box.

If you'd let QuickBooks make an adjustment entry during the last reconciliation (which almost certainly is the case; otherwise you wouldn't have to undo and redo the reconciliation), click Cancel to close the dialog box. Open the account's register and delete the adjustment entry—it's the entry posted to the Opening Bal Equity account. Hopefully, this time the reconciliation will work and you won't need another adjusting entry.

Start the reconciliation process again. When the Begin Reconciliation window opens, the data that appears is the same data that appeared when you started the last reconciliation—the last reconciliation date, the statement date, and the beginning balance are back.

Enter the ending balance from the bank statement. Do *not* enter the interest and bank charges again, they weren't removed when QuickBooks undid the last reconciliation.

Good luck!

Giving Up the Search for a Reason

You may not be able to find a reason for the difference in the beginning balances. If a changed transaction cleared in a previous reconciliation, you can't compare the reconciliation report against the register if you didn't print and save those reports (unless you're running QuickBooks Premier Edition, which stores them).

There's a point at which it isn't worth your time to keep looking, so just give up. QuickBooks will make an adjusting transaction at the end of the reconciliation process, and if you ever learn the reason, you can remove that transaction.

In the Begin Reconciliation dialog box, enter the ending balance from the bank statement, and follow the instructions in the rest of this chapter.

Enter Interest Income and Service Charges

Your statement shows any interest and bank service charges if either or both are applicable to your account. Enter those numbers in the Begin Reconciliation window and choose the appropriate account for posting.

If you have online banking, and the interest payments and bank charges have already been entered into your register as a result of downloading transactions, don't enter them again in the Begin Reconciliation window.

By "bank charges," I mean the standard charges banks assess, such as monthly charges that may be assessed for failure to maintain a minimum balance. Bank charges do not include special charges for bounced checks (yours or your customers'), nor any purchases you made that are charged to your account (such as the purchase of checks or deposit slips). Those should be entered as discrete transactions (using the Memo field to explain the transaction), which makes them easier to find in case you have to talk to the bank about your account.

Reconcile the Transactions

After you've filled out the information in the Begin Reconciliation dialog box, click Continue to open the Reconcile window, shown in Figure 12-2.

Configuring the Reconcile Window

You can configure the way transactions are displayed to make it easier to work in the window.

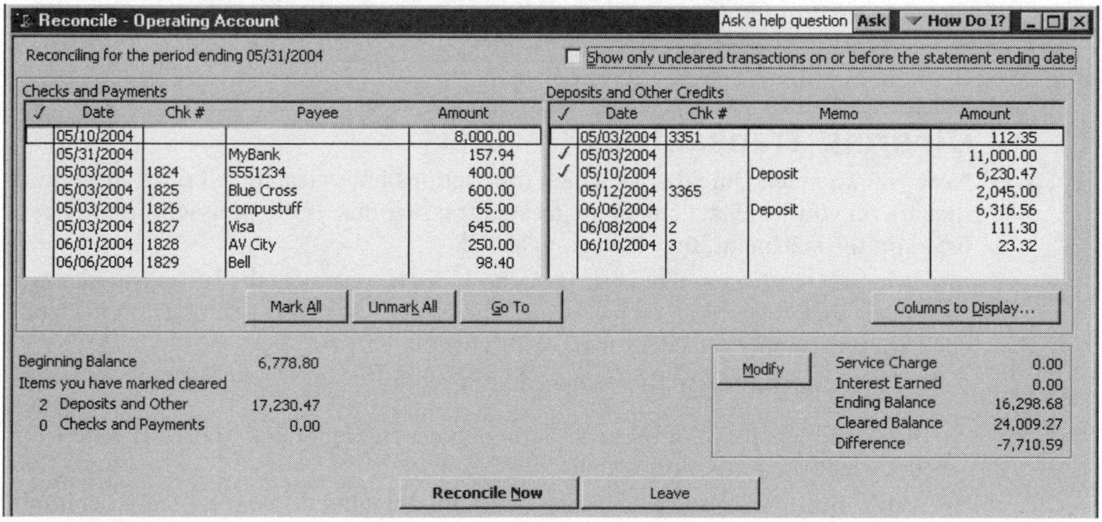

FIGURE 12-2   All uncleared transactions are displayed in the Reconcile window.

Eliminate Future Transactions

If the list is long, you can shorten the list by selecting the option Show Only Uncleared Transactions On Or Before The Statement Ending Date. Theoretically, transactions that weren't created before the ending date couldn't have cleared the bank. Removing them from the window leaves only those transactions likely to have cleared. If you select this option and your reconciliation doesn't balance, deselect the option so you can clear the transactions in case one of the following scenarios applies:

- You issued a post-dated check and the recipient cashed it early. Since it's rare for a bank to enforce the date, this is a real possibility.
- You made a mistake when you entered the date of the original transaction. You may have entered a wrong month, or even a wrong year, which resulted in moving the transaction date into the future.

Customize the Column Display

You can change the columns that display on each pane of the Reconcile window by clicking Columns To Display. Add or remove columns, depending on their usefulness to you as you clear transactions.

Clearing Transactions

Now you must tell QuickBooks which transactions have cleared. All the transactions that are on your bank statement are cleared transactions. If the transactions are not listed on the statement, they have not cleared.

Click each transaction that cleared. A check mark appears in the left-most column to indicate that the transaction has cleared the bank. If you clear a transaction in error, click again to remove the check mark—it's a toggle.

Use the following shortcuts to speed your work:

- If all, or almost all, of the transactions have cleared, click Mark All. Then de-select the transactions that didn't clear.
- Mark multiple, contiguous transactions by dragging down the Cleared column.

- If the account you're reconciling is enabled for online access, click Matched to automatically clear all transactions that were matched in the QuickStatements you've downloaded over the month. QuickBooks asks for the ending date on the statement, and clears each matched transaction up to that date.

As you check each cleared transaction, the Difference amount in the lower-right corner of the Reconcile window changes. The goal is to get that figure to 0.00.

Viewing Transactions During Reconciliation

If you need to look at the original transaction window for any transaction in the reconcile window, double-click its listing (or select the listing and click the button labeled Go To).

Adding Transactions During Reconciliation

While you're working in the Reconcile window, if you find a transaction on the statement that you haven't entered into your QuickBooks software (probably one of those ATM transactions you forgot to enter), you don't have to shut down the reconciliation process to remedy the situation. You can just enter the transaction into your register.

To open the bank account register, right-click anywhere in the Reconcile window and choose Use Register from the shortcut menu (or click the Reg icon on the toolbar). When the bank register opens, record the transaction. Return to the Reconcile window, where that transaction is now listed. Pretty nifty! Check it off as cleared, of course, because it was on the statement.

C A U T I O N : Right-clicking on a transaction toggles the clear/unclear check mark in addition to displaying the shortcut menu.

You can switch between the Reconcile window and the register for the account you're reconciling all through this process. Use the Open Windows list on the Navigators list, or the Windows menu item, to move between them.

T I P : I automatically open the register of the account I'm reconciling as soon as I start the reconciliation process, just in case.

Deleting Transactions During Reconciliation

Sometimes you find that a transaction that was transferred from your account register to this Reconcile window shouldn't be there. This commonly occurs if you entered an ATM withdrawal twice. Or perhaps you forgot that you'd entered a deposit, and a couple of days later you entered it again. Whatever the reason, occasionally there are transactions that should be deleted.

To delete a transaction, move to the account register and select that transaction. Press CTRL-D to delete it (QuickBooks asks you to confirm the deletion). When you return to the Reconcile window, the transaction is gone.

Editing Transactions During Reconciliation

Sometimes you'll want to change some of the information in a transaction. For example, when you see the real check, you realize the amount you entered in QuickBooks is wrong. You might even have the wrong date on a check. (These things only happen, of course, if you write checks manually; they don't happen to QuickBooks users who let QuickBooks take care of creating checks.)

Whatever the problem, you can correct it by editing the transaction. Double-click the transaction's listing in the Reconcile window to open the original transaction window. Enter the necessary changes, and close the window. Answer Yes when QuickBooks asks if you want to record the changes, and you're returned to the Reconcile window where the changes are displayed.

Resolving Missing Check Numbers

Most bank statements list your checks in order and indicate a missing number with an asterisk. For instance, you may see check number 1234, followed by check number *1236, or 1236*. When a check number is missing, it means one of three things:

- The check cleared in a previous reconciliation.
- The check is still outstanding.
- The check number is unused and is probably literally missing.

If a missing check number on your bank statement is puzzling, you can check its status. To see if the check cleared in the last reconciliation, open the Previous Reconciliation report (discussed earlier in this chapter) by choosing Reports | Banking | Previous Reconciliation.

To investigate further, right-click anywhere in the Reconcile window and choose Missing Checks Report from the shortcut menu. When the QuickBooks Missing Checks Report opens, select the appropriate account. You'll see asterisks indicating missing check numbers, as seen in Figure 12-3.

Type	Date	Num	Name	Memo	Account	Split	Amount
Bill Pmt -Check	04/21/2004	1818	AV City		1000 · Operating A...	2000 · Accou...	-200.00
Bill Pmt -Check	04/21/2004	1819	DHL		1000 · Operating A...	2000 · Accou...	-40.00
Bill Pmt -Check	04/21/2004	1820	Landlord		1000 · Operating A...	2000 · Accou...	-650.00
Bill Pmt -Check	04/21/2004	1821	Our Supplier		1000 · Operating A...	-SPLIT-	-234.90
Bill Pmt -Check	04/21/2004	1822	PhoneCompany		1000 · Operating A...	2000 · Accou...	-402.15
*** Missing numbers here ***							
Bill Pmt -Check	05/03/2004	1824	5551234	215-555-123...	1000 · Operating A...	2000 · Accou...	-400.00
Bill Pmt -Check	05/03/2004	1825	Blue Cross	123-456-789	1000 · Operating A...	2000 · Accou...	-600.00
Bill Pmt -Check	05/03/2004	1826	compustuff		1000 · Operating A...	2000 · Accou...	-65.00
Bill Pmt -Check	05/03/2004	1827	Visa	VOID:	1000 · Operating A...	2000 · Accou...	0.00
Check	06/01/2004	1828	AV City		1000 · Operating A...	6170 · Equipm...	-250.00
Check	06/06/2004	1829	Bell		1000 · Operating A...	6340 · Teleph...	-98.40

FIGURE 12-3 Check 1823 is missing because it's missing, not because it didn't clear.

If the check number is listed in your Missing Checks Report, it's just uncleared, and will show up in a future bank statement (unless someone is framing your checks instead of cashing them). If a check number is truly missing, you probably deleted the check.

Finishing the Reconciliation

If this isn't the first reconciliation you're performing, there's a good chance that that Difference figure at the bottom of the Reconcile window displays 0.00. If this is the first reconciliation, and you changed the opening balance in the account register (as explained earlier in this chapter), you probably also see 0.00 as the difference.

If that's true, you've finished this part of the reconciliation. Click Reconcile Now and read the section "Printing the Reconciliation Report" later in this chapter. If Difference shows an amount other than 0.00, read the following sections.

Pausing the Reconciliation Process

If the account doesn't reconcile (the Difference figure isn't 0.00), and you don't have the time, energy, or emotional fortitude to track down the problem at the moment, you can stop the reconciliation process without losing all the transactions you cleared.

Click the Leave button in the Reconcile window and do something else for a while. Have dinner, play with the cat, help the kids with homework, whatever. When you restart the reconciliation process, everything will be exactly the way you left it.

Finding and Correcting Problems

When you're ready to investigate the cause of a difference between the ending balance and the cleared balance, follow the guidelines I present here to find the problem.

Count the number of transactions on the bank statement. Then look in the lower-left corner of the Reconcile window, where the number of items you have marked cleared is displayed. Mentally add another item to that number for each of the following:

- A service charge you entered in the Begin Reconciliation box
- An interest amount you entered in the Begin Reconciliation box

If the numbers now differ, the problem is in your QuickBooks records; there's a transaction you should have cleared but didn't, or a transaction you cleared that you shouldn't have.

If that's not the problem, do the following:

- Check the amount of each transaction against the amount in the bank statement.
- Check your transactions and make sure a deposit wasn't inadvertently entered as a payment (or vice versa). A clue for this is a transaction that's half the difference. If the difference is $220.00, find a transaction that has an amount of $110.00 and make sure it's a deduction if it's supposed to be a deduction (or the other way around).
- Check for transposed figures. Perhaps you entered a figure incorrectly in the register, such as $549.00 when the bank clears the transaction as $594.00. A clue that a transposed number is the problem is that the reconciliation difference can be divided by nine.

If you find the problem, correct it. When the Difference figure is 0.00, click Reconcile Now.

TIP: You might want to let somebody else check over the statement and the register, because sometimes you can't see your own mistakes.

Permitting an Adjusting Entry

If you cannot find the problem, you can tell QuickBooks to make an adjusting entry to force the reconciliation to balance. The adjusting entry is placed in the bank account register, and is offset in the Beginning Bal Equity account. If you ever figure out what the problem is, you can make the proper adjustment transaction and delete the adjusting entry.

To force a reconciliation, click Reconcile Now, even though there's a difference. A message appears to offer the opportunity to make an adjusting entry. Click Enter Adjustment.

Printing the Reconciliation Report

When you have a balanced reconciliation (even if it results from an adjusting entry), QuickBooks offers congratulations and also offers to print a reconciliation report. (The dialog box has a Cancel button to skip the report, but it's not a good idea to do so). QuickBooks saves the report whether you print it, view it, or cancel it, and you can view it in the future by choosing Reports | Banking | Previous Reconciliation.

Deciding on the Type of Report

QuickBooks offers two reconciliation report types: Detail and Summary. Here are the differences between them:

- The Detail Report shows all the transactions that are cleared, and all the transactions that haven't cleared (called *in transit* transactions) as of the statement closing date. Any transactions dated after the statement closing date are listed as *new transactions*.
- The Summary Report breaks down your transactions in the same way, but it doesn't list the individual transactions; it shows only the totals for each category (Cleared, In Transit, and New).

Selecting the Detail Report makes it easier to resolve problems in the future. You have a list of every check and deposit, and when it cleared.

Print vs. Display

You also have to decide whether to Print or to Display the report. Make your decision according to how you think you might use the report.

Printing a Reconciliation Report

If you opt to print the report, the Print Reports dialog offers two options:

- Print the report to the selected Printer. You can file the printout in case you ever need to refer to it.
- Print the report to a file. The file option offers several formats in a drop-down list, so you can load the resulting file into the software of your choice. This gives you the opportunity to store multiple reports in one application (or even one file) and sort the data as you wish. The following file options are available:
  - **ASCII text**   Is straight, unformatted text
  - **Comma delimited**   Automatically puts a comma between each field (column). Select this option if you want to use the file in a spreadsheet or database program capable of importing comma-delimited files. Most spreadsheet software can handle comma-delimited files.
  - **Tab delimited**   Is the same as comma delimited, but the field delimiter is a tab marker instead of a comma. All spreadsheet and database software can handle tab-delimited files.

When you print a report to a disk file, QuickBooks opens a Create Disk File window with the folder that holds your QuickBooks software as the target folder. The file extension matches the file type you selected.

You can change the container to any other folder in the system—you might want to create a subfolder in your My Documents folder to hold these files. Hereafter, that folder becomes the default container for your reconciliation reports. Be sure to save each month's reconciliation report file with a unique name—the date and the account name (if you reconcile more than one bank account) are good selections for filenames.

Displaying a Reconciliation Report

If you choose to display the report, you see the usual QuickBooks report format. You can modify the report to change the font, the columns, etc. In addition, you can click the Export icon at the top of the report window and send the report to a spreadsheet or database program.

Using Budgets and Planning Tools

In this chapter:

- Configure a budget

- Report on budgets versus actual figures

- Export budgets

- Use QuickBooks Decision Tools

A budget is a tool for tracking your progress against your plans. A well-prepared budget can also help you draw money out of your business wisely, because knowing what you plan to spend on staff, overhead, or other expenses in the future prevents you from carelessly withdrawing profits and living high on the hog whenever you have a good month.

How QuickBooks Handles Budgets

Before you begin creating a budget, you need to know how QuickBooks manages budgets and the processes connect to budgets. If you've upgraded to QuickBooks 2004 from any previous version except QuickBooks 2003, you'll notice that the budget feature has changed dramatically.

In this section I'll present an overview of the QuickBooks budget features, so you can bear them in mind when you plan your budgets.

Types of Budgets

QuickBooks offers several types of budgets:

- Budgets based on your Balance Sheet accounts
- P&L budgets based on your income and expense accounts
- P&L budgets based on income and expense accounts and a customer or job
- P&L budgets based on income and expense accounts and a class (if you've enabled class tracking)

P&L budgets can be created from scratch or by using the actual figures from the previous year. The latter option, of course, only works if you've upgraded to QuickBooks 2004 from an earlier version.

> **NOTE:** QuickBooks Basic doesn't support creating budgets from the previous year's figures.

Budgets Aren't Really Documents

In QuickBooks, a budget is the data you enter in a budget window. Once you begin creating a budget, the data you record is more or less permanently ensconced in the budget window and reappears whenever you open that budget window.

You can only create one of each type of budget

For example, if you create a P&L budget, enter and record some figures, and then decide to start all over by launching the Create New Budget Wizard, you can't create a new P&L budget. Instead of creating a new budget, the wizard displays the data you already configured. You have no way of telling QuickBooks, "Okay, save that one, I'm going to do another one with different figures." You can change the figures, but the changes replace the original figures. You're editing a budget, you're not creating a new budget.

Creating Multiple Budgets

Once you've created your first budget, regardless of type, the next time you select Company | Planning & Budgeting | Set Up Budgets, the budget window opens with the last budget you created.

If the budget is a P&L or Balance Sheet budget, you cannot create a second budget of the same type. However, you can create a budget of a different type (P&L Customer:Job, or P&L Class). To do so, click the Create New Budget button in the budget window and go through the wizard to select different criteria (Customer:Job or Class).

After you've created a Customer:Job budget or a Class budget, you can create another budget using a different customer or job (or different accounts for the same customer or job). See the sections "Customer:Job Budgets" and "Class Budgets" for instructions on creating multiple budgets of those types.

Deleting a Budget

QuickBooks lets you delete a budget. This means if you want to create multiple budgets of the same type (perhaps you feel better if you have a "Plan B"), you have a workaround to the "no two budgets of the same type" rule. Export the original budget to a spreadsheet application, and then delete the original budget and start the process again. See the section "Exporting Budgets," later in this chapter.

To delete a budget, choose Edit | Delete Budget from the QuickBooks menu bar while the budget window is open.

Understanding the Budget Window

Before you start entering figures, you need to learn how to manage your work, using the buttons on the budget window.

- **Clear**   Deletes all figures in the budget window—you cannot use this button to clear a row or column.
- **Save**   Records the current figures and leaves the window open so you can continue to work.
- **OK**   Records the current figures and closes the window.
- **Cancel**   Closes the window without any offer to record the figures.

- **Create New Budget** Starts the budget process anew, opening the Create New Budget Wizard. If you've entered any data, QuickBooks asks if you want to record your budget before closing the window. If you record your data (or have previously recorded your data with the Save button), when you start anew, the budget window opens with the same recorded data.
- **Show Next 6 Months** Exists only if the display resolution of your computer is set lower than 1024×768; otherwise, you can see all twelve months in the budget window. With lower resolution, only six months of the budget can be seen in the window. In that case, QuickBooks adds buttons to the window to move the display to the next six-month display, and the button changes its name to Show Previous 6 Months.

The other buttons in the budget window are used when you're entering data, and I go over them later in this chapter. See the section "Enter Budget Amounts."

Tasks to Perform Before You Start Your Budget

Before you create a budget, you need to check the following details:

- The accounts you need must be available; you cannot add accounts while you're working in a budget.
- The first month of the budget must be the same as the first month of your fiscal year.

Activate All Necessary Accounts

Make sure all the accounts you want to include on the budget are included in the accounts list in the budget window. Any account you marked "inactive" is not available. If you want to create a budget that includes an account that's currently inactive, follow these steps:

1. Click the Accnt icon on the toolbar to open the Chart Of Accounts window.
2. Make sure a check mark appears in the Show All check box at the bottom of the window. Your inactive accounts have an X in the leftmost column.
3. Right-click any inactive account you want to use in the budget, and choose Make Active from the shortcut menu.
4. Close the Chart Of Accounts window.

Check the Starting Month

The first month that's displayed in the budget window must be the first month of your fiscal year, or your budget won't work properly. If you don't run your company on a calendar year (or if you want to create a budget that's not based on your fiscal year), you must make sure your company configuration has the correct starting month.

1. Choose Company | Company Information from the menu bar.

2. Enter the correct starting month for your fiscal year and click OK. (The tax year doesn't matter for budgeting, but if it's wrong, you should correct it.)

A Word About Balance Sheet Budgets

It's highly unusual to have a need to create a Balance Sheet budget, because you can't predict the amounts for most Balance Sheet accounts. Even if you want to keep an eye on the few accounts over which you have control (fixed assets and loans), there's little reason to use a budget to do so. The transactions for fixed assets and loans are usually planned, and therefore don't need budget-to-reality comparisons to allow you to keep an eye on them.

As a result, I'm not going to spend time discussing Balance Sheet budgets. If you feel you need to create one, choose Company | Planning & Budgeting | Set Up Budgets. If this is your first budget, the Create New Budget Wizard opens. Otherwise, when an existing budget appears, click the Create New Budget button. When the Create New Budget Wizard opens, select the year for which you want to create the budget and select the Balance Sheet option. Then click Next, and because the next window has no options, there's nothing for you to do except click Finish. The budget window opens, listing all your Balance Sheet accounts (see Figure 13-1),

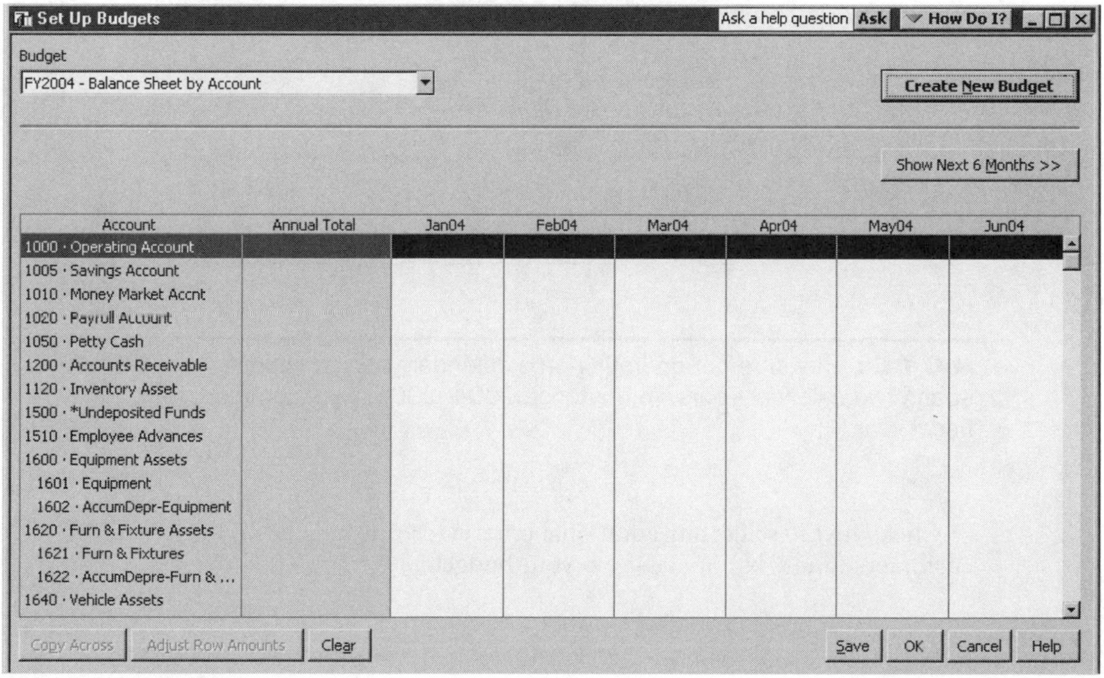

FIGURE 13-1   All your Balance Sheet accounts are listed, so you can begin entering budget figures.

and you can enter the budget figures. See the following sections on creating P&L budgets to learn the procedures for entering budget figures.

P&L Budgets

The most common (and useful) budget is based on your income and expenses. After you've set up a good chart of accounts, creating a budget is quite easy.

Create the Budget and Its Criteria

To create a P&L budget, choose Company | Planning & Budgeting | Set Up Budgets. If this is the first budget you're creating, the Create New Budget Wizard opens to walk you through the process. If you've already created a budget, the Set Up Budgets window appears with your existing budget loaded. Click Create A New Budget to open the Create New Budget Wizard. Enter the year for which you're creating the budget, and select the P&L budget option.

Create New Budget

Create a New Budget

Begin by specifying the year and type for the new budget.

2004

Choose the budget type

○ Profit and Loss (reflects all activity for the year)
○ Balance Sheet (reflects ending balance)

Prev | Next | Finish | Cancel

NOTE: If you're not operating on a calendar year, the budget year field spans two calendar years, for instance 2004–2005, to accommodate your fiscal year.

Click Next to select any additional criteria for this budget. You can include customers (and jobs) or classes in your budget.

Create New Budget

Additional Profit and Loss Budget Criteria

      ○ No additional critiera
      ○ Customer:Job
      ○ Class

    Prev   Next   Finish   Cancel

For this discussion, I'll go over regular P&L budgets (unconnected to customers or classes), and I'll explain later in this chapter how to budget for customers and jobs and for classes. Click Next to choose between creating a budget from scratch, or from the figures from last year's activities. I'll start by creating a budget from scratch. Click Finish to open the budget window, where all your income and expense accounts are displayed (see Figure 13-2).

Set Up Budgets   Ask a help question | Ask | ▽ How Do I?

Budget
FY2004 - Profit & Loss by Account ▾   Create New Budget

                                          Show Next 6 Months >>

Account	Annual Total	Jan04	Feb04	Mar04	Apr04	May04	Jun04
4000 · Revenue							
4001 · Consulting							
4002 · Product Sales							
4003 · Markups & Misc Income							
4020 · Other Regular Income							
4025 · Finance Charges Colle...							
4040 · Reimbursed Expenses							
4041 · Equip Rental Reimbu...							
4042 · Telephone Reimburs...							
4043 · Travel Reimburseme...							
4044 · Subcontractor Reim...							
4050 · Discounts Taken							
4060 · Markups to Customers							
4500 · Cost of Sales							
4510 · Vendor Discounts							
5000 · Cost of Goods Sold							

Copy Across   Adjust Row Amounts   Clear   Save   OK   Cancel   Help

FIGURE 13-2   All active income and expense accounts are available for your budget.

Enter Budget Amounts

To create budget figures for an account, select the account and then click in the column of the first month you want to budget. Enter the budget figure, press TAB to move to the next month, and enter the appropriate amount. Repeat until all the months for this account have your budget figures. As you enter each monthly amount and press TAB, QuickBooks automatically calculates and displays the annual total for the account (see Figure 13-3).

If you see the Show Next 6 Months button, when you enter the amount for the sixth month, you must click it to continue through the rest of the months. Pressing TAB in the sixth month column moves your cursor to the first month of the next account, not to the seventh month column of the current account (isn't that annoying?). When you finish entering the figures in the twelfth month, click Show Prev 6 Months to return to the first half of the year and the next row.

Using Budget Entry Shortcuts

To save yourself from contracting a case of terminal ennui, QuickBooks provides some shortcuts for entering budget figures.

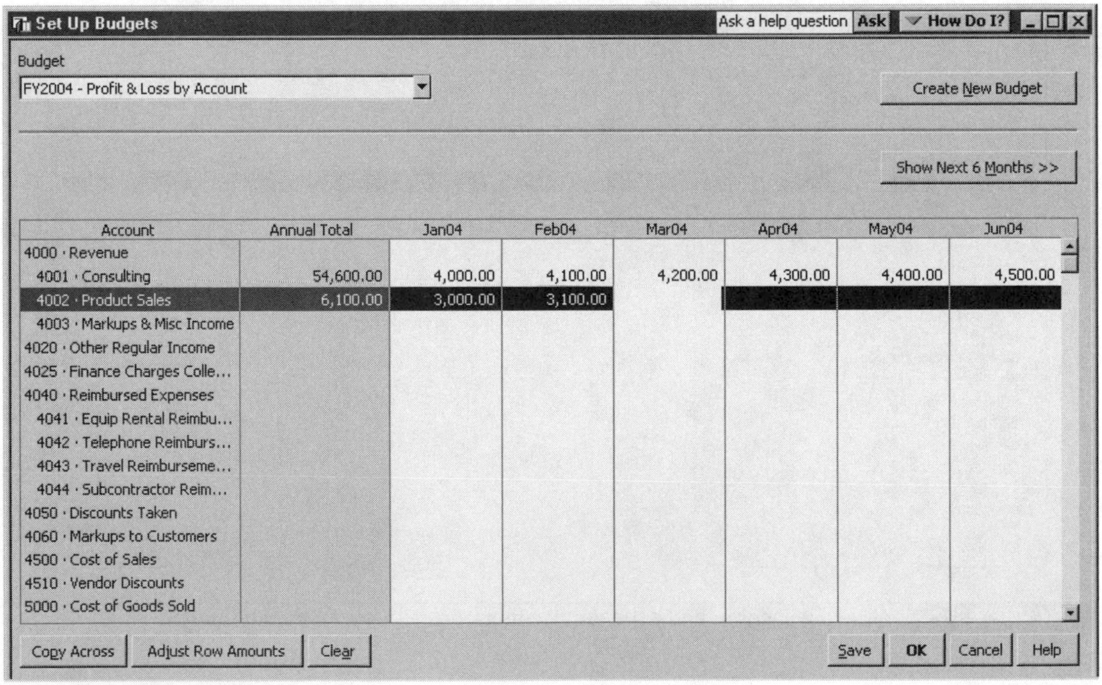

FIGURE 13-3 QuickBooks takes care of tracking the running totals.

Copy Numbers Across the Months

To copy a monthly figure from the current month (the month where your cursor is) to all the following months, enter the figure and click Copy Across. The numbers are copied to all months to the right, including the seventh through twelfth months if you're starting in one of the first six months.

You can perform this shortcut as soon as you enter an amount (but before you press TAB), or you can return to the month you want to designate the first month by clicking its column (useful if you've entered figures for several months and then remember this shortcut).

This is handier than it seems at first glance. It's obvious that if you enter your rent in the first month and choose Copy Across, you've saved a lot of manual data entry. However, suppose your landlord sends you a notice that your rent is increasing beginning in July? To adjust the July–December budget figures, just move your cursor to July, enter the new rate, and click Copy Across.

The Copy Across button is also the only way to clear a row. Delete the figure in the first month and click Copy Across. The entire row is now blank.

Automatically Increase or Decrease Monthly Figures

After you've entered figures into all the months on an account's row (manually, by using the Copy Across button, or by bringing in last year's figures), you can raise or lower monthly figures automatically. For example, you may want to raise an income account by an amount or a percentage starting in a certain month because you expect to sign a new customer or a new contract.

Select the first month that needs the adjustment and click Adjust Row Amounts to open the Adjust Row Amounts dialog.

Choose 1st Month or Currently Selected Month as the starting point for the calculations.

- You can choose 1st Month no matter where your cursor is on the account's row.

- You must click in the column for the appropriate month if you want to choose Currently Selected Month (you can click the first month to make that the currently selected month).
- To increase or decrease the selected month and all the months following by a specific amount, enter the amount.
- To increase or decrease the selected month and all columns to the right by a percentage, enter the percentage rate and the percentage sign.

Compound the Changes

If you select Currently Selected Month, the Adjust Row Amounts dialog adds an additional option named Enable Compounding.

Adjust Row Amounts

Start at   Currently selected month ▼

◉ Increase each remaining monthly amount in this row by   0.0%
   this dollar amount or percentage

○ Decrease each remaining monthly amount in this row by   0.0%
   this dollar amount or percentage

☐ Enable compounding

OK   Cancel   Help

TIP: Although the Enable Compounding option appears only when you select Currently Selected Month, if your cursor is in the first month and you select the Currently Selected Month option, you can use compounding for the entire year.

When you enable compounding, the calculations for each month are increased or decreased based on a formula starting with the currently selected month and taking into consideration the resulting change in the previous month.

For example, if you entered $1,000.00 in the current month and indicated a $100.00 increase, the results differ from amounts that are not being compounded, as seen here:

COMPOUNDING ENABLED?	CURRENT MONTH ORIGINAL FIGURE	CURRENT MONTH NEW FIGURE	NEXT MONTH	NEXT MONTH	NEXT MONTH	NEXT MONTH
Yes	1,000.00	1,000.00	1,100.00	1,200.00	1,300.00	1,400.00
No	1,000.00	1,100.00	1,100.00	1,100.00	1,100.00	1,100.00

Create a Budget from Last Year's Data

If you used QuickBooks last year, you can create a budget based on last year's figures. To use last year's real data as the basis of your budget, open the Create New Budget Wizard by choosing Company | Planning & Budgeting | Set Up Budgets. When the Create New Budget Wizard opens, enter the year for which you're creating the budget, and select the P&L budget option. In the next window, select any additional criteria. (I'm skipping additional criteria for this example.) In the next window, select the option to create the budget from the previous year's actual figures, and click Finish.

The budget window opens with last year's actual data displayed (see Figure 13-4). For each account that had activity, the ending monthly balances are entered in the appropriate month.

You can change any figures you wish, using the procedures and shortcuts described earlier in this chapter.

Customer:Job Budgets

If you have a customer or a job that warrants it, you can create a P&L budget to track the financials for that customer or job against a budget. Usually, you'd only do this for a project that involves a substantial amount of money and/or covers a long period of time.

Creating the First Customer:Job Budget

To create your first budget for a customer or a job, choose Company | Planning & Budgeting | Set Up Budgets. I'm assuming you're creating the budget from scratch, not from last year's P&L figures.

- If you already created another budget of a different type (P&L or Class), the budget window opens with the last budget you created. Click the Create New Budget button in the budget window to launch the Create New Budget Wizard.

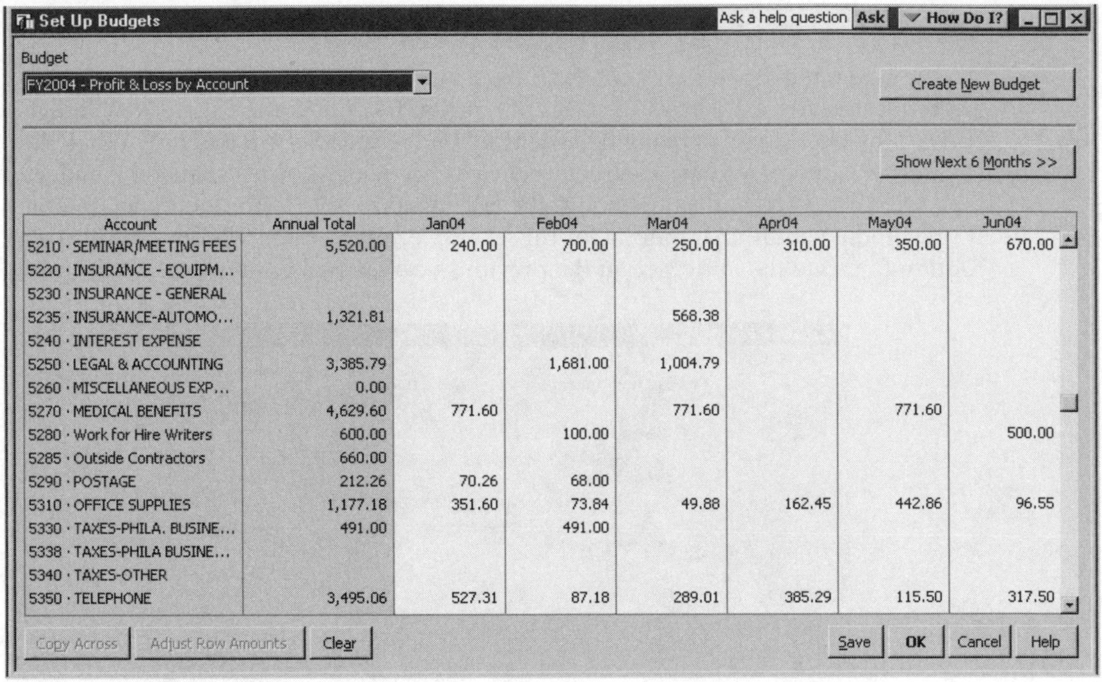

Account	Annual Total	Jan04	Feb04	Mar04	Apr04	May04	Jun04
5210 · SEMINAR/MEETING FEES	5,520.00	240.00	700.00	250.00	310.00	350.00	670.00
5220 · INSURANCE - EQUIPM...							
5230 · INSURANCE - GENERAL							
5235 · INSURANCE-AUTOMO...	1,321.81			568.38			
5240 · INTEREST EXPENSE							
5250 · LEGAL & ACCOUNTING	3,385.79		1,681.00	1,004.79			
5260 · MISCELLANEOUS EXP...	0.00						
5270 · MEDICAL BENEFITS	4,629.60	771.60		771.60		771.60	
5280 · Work for Hire Writers	600.00		100.00				500.00
5285 · Outside Contractors	660.00						
5290 · POSTAGE	212.26	70.26	68.00				
5310 · OFFICE SUPPLIES	1,177.18	351.60	73.84	49.88	162.45	442.86	96.55
5330 · TAXES-PHILA. BUSINE...	491.00		491.00				
5338 · TAXES-PHILA BUSINE...							
5340 · TAXES-OTHER							
5350 · TELEPHONE	3,495.06	527.31	87.18	289.01	385.29	115.50	317.50

FIGURE 13-4 Start your budget by looking at what last year's figures were.

- If this is your first-ever budget, the Create New Budget Wizard appears automatically.

Select the year for your budget and choose P&L as the type. In the next wizard window, select the option Customer:Job and click Finish.

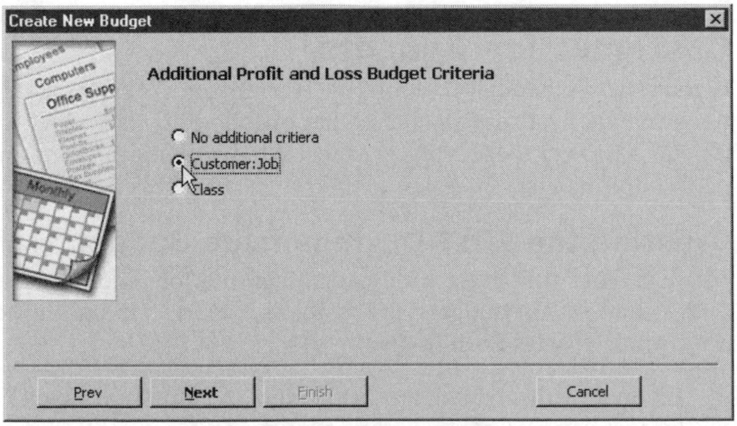

When the budget window opens, an additional field labeled Current Customer:Job appears so you can select the Customer:Job for this budget from the drop-down list (see Figure 13-5).

Select the account, or multiple accounts, for which you want to budget this job—these will probably be only expense accounts (your invoicing activity takes care of tracking anticipated income). The expenses you track depend on the scope of the job. For example, you may only want to budget the cost of outside contractors, or budget supplies so if prices rise you can have a conversation with the customer about overruns.

You can enter a monthly budget figure for each account or for each month the project exists, or enter a total budget figure in the first month. The latter option lets you compare accumulated data for expenses against the total budgeted figure by creating modified reports. Change the report date to reflect the elapsed time for the project, and filter the report for this job.

If the project is lengthy, you may budget some accounts for some months and other accounts for other months. For example, if you have a project that involves purchases of goods, followed by installation of those goods, or training for the customer's employees, you might choose to budget the purchases for the first few months and then the cost of the installation or training (either by tracking payroll or outside contractors) for the months in which those activities occur.

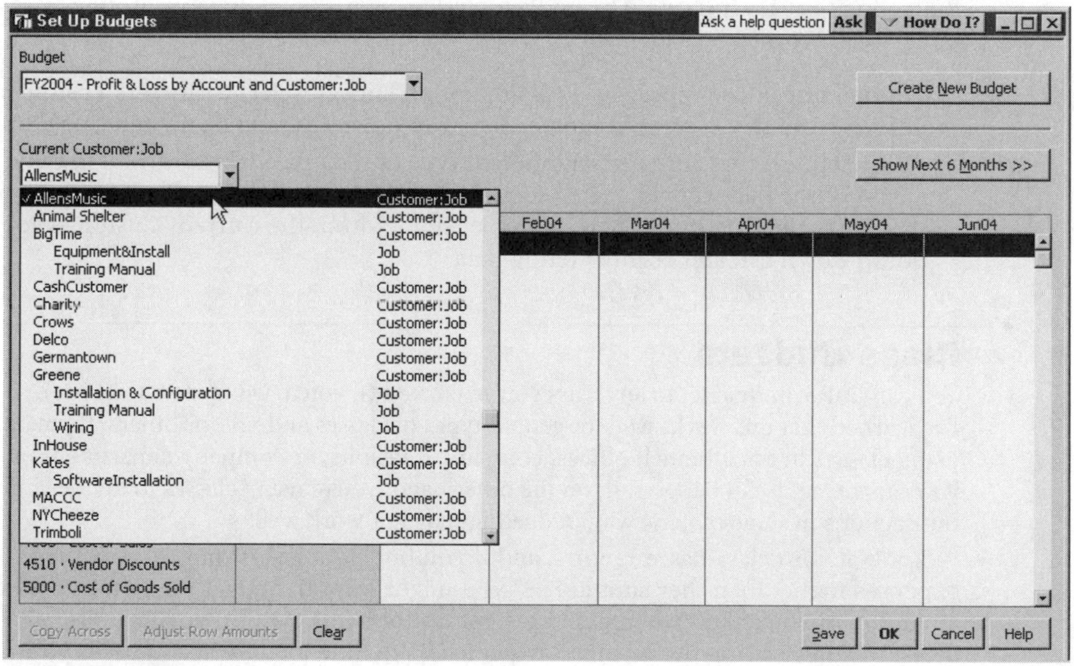

FIGURE 13-5 Link a customer or job to budget a project.

If you want to track payroll costs against a job, use the QuickBooks Time and Billing features that are discussed in Chapter 18. If you do your own payroll, also read Chapter 19 to learn how to move the Time and Billing features to your payroll computations. It's nerve-wracking to attempt payroll job-costing manually.

 C A U T I O N : Customer:Job budgets don't work unless you're faithful about assigning transactions to the customer or job. If you've only been filling in the Customer:Job fields when the customer is billable, you won't have accurate budget-to-reality reports.

Creating Additional Customer:Job Budgets

After you've created one budget based on a customer or job, creating a budget for a different customer or job requires different steps.

To create a budget for another customer immediately, while the Customer:Job budget you just created is still in the budget window, select another customer from the drop-down list. Begin entering data and click Yes when QuickBooks asks if you want to record the budget you just finished.

To create a budget for another customer later, choose Company | Planning & Budgeting | Set Up Budgets. The budget window opens immediately with the last budget you worked on.

- If the budget that appears is a Customer:Job budget, select a different customer or job from the Current Customer:Job drop-down list, and begin entering data.
- If the budget that appears is a different type of budget, click the arrow to the right of the Budget field and select Profit And Loss By Account And Customer: Job as the budget type. Then select a customer from the Current Customer:Job drop-down list, and begin entering data.

Class Budgets

You can link your budget to any class you've created (if you're using class tracking). I've learned that this works well for certain types of classes and not for others. If you're using classes to track branch offices, company divisions, or company departments, you can create useful budgets. If, on the other hand, you're using classes to divide your transactions in some esoteric way, budgeting may not work well.

Look at your class-based reports, and if you find yourself asking, "Aren't those expenses higher than they should be?" you might want to budget each month to get a handle on where and when expenses got out of hand. Also, if you ask, "Is this division contributing the income I expected?" include income accounts in your budget. You can use income accounts in class budgets to provide incentives to your employees—perhaps a bonus to a manager if the reality is better than the budget.

To create a class-based budget, use the steps described earlier to create a budget and choose Class in the Additional Profit and Loss Budget Criteria Wizard window. When the budget window opens, a Current Class field appears. Select the class for which you're creating a budget from the drop-down list. Then begin entering data.

To create additional class budgets (for other classes, of course), use the same approach discussed in the previous section on creating additional customer or job budgets.

Budget Reports

QuickBooks provides a number of budget reports you can use to see how you're doing. I'll discuss each of them in this section. To get to the reports, choose Reports | Budgets from the menu bar, and then select one of the following reports:

- Budget Overview
- Budget vs. Actual
- Profit & Loss Budget Performance
- Budget vs. Actual Graph

If you've only created one budget, as soon as you select the report you want to view, the report opens. However, if you've created multiple types of budgets, a Budget Report window opens first, so you can select the type of budget you want to view.

The window has a Next button, and the contents of the following window depend on the report you've selected from the menu and the type of budget you selected from the previous window. I'll go over the options as I discuss each report.

Budget Overview

This report shows the accounts you budgeted and the amounts you budgeted for each month. Accounts that you didn't include in the budget aren't displayed. The following choices are available in the Budget Report window that opens when you select Budget Overview from the submenu.

Profit & Loss Budget Overview

If you created a P&L budget, select Profit & Loss By Account in the first Budget Report window, and click Next. In the next window, you're asked to select a report layout, but the only option available in the drop-down list is Account By Month. Click Next, and then click Finish. The report opens and looks like the P&L budget report in Figure 13-6.

If you use subaccounts in your budget, you can click the Collapse button at the top of the budget window to see only the parent account totals. The button name changes to Expand, and clicking it puts the subaccount lines back into the display.

To condense the numbers, change the interval in the Columns list box by selecting a different interval. The default is Month, but you can choose another interval, and QuickBooks will calculate the figures to fit. For example, you might want to select Quarter to see four columns of three-month subtotals.

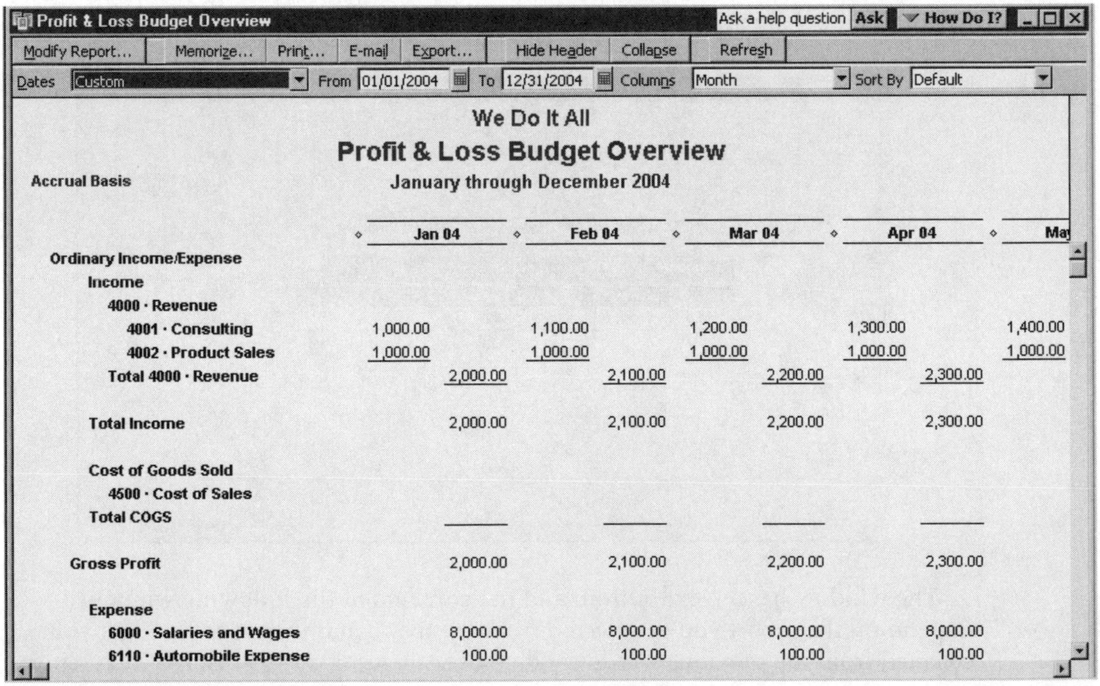

FIGURE 13-6 The Budget Overview report is a simple display of your budget.

If you want to tweak the budget, or play "what if" games by experimenting with different numbers, click the Export button to send the report to Microsoft Excel. See Appendix B for more information about integrating QuickBooks reports with Excel.

Balance Sheet Budget Overview

If you created a Balance Sheet budget, select Balance Sheet By Account in the first window, and then click Next. QuickBooks displays a graphical representation of the report's layout (it's a monthly layout similar to the layout for the P&L budget). Click Finish to see the report.

Customer:Job Budget Overview

If you created one or more budgets for a customer or a job, select Profit & Loss By Account And Customer:Job in the first window, and click Next. Select a report layout from the drop-down list (as you select each option from the list, QuickBooks displays a diagram of the layout). The following choices are available:

- **Account By Month**   Lists each account you used in the budget and displays the total budget amounts (for all customer budgets you created) for each month that has data. No budget information for individual customers appears.
- **Account By Customer:Job**   Lists each account you used in the budget and displays the yearly total for that account for each customer (each customer has its own column).
- **Customer:Job By Month**   Displays a row for each customer that has a budget and a column for each month. The budget totals (for all accounts—individual accounts are not displayed) appear under each month. Under each customer's row is a row for each job that has a budget.

 T I P : The name of each layout choice is a hint about the way it displays in the report. The first word represents the rows, and the word after the word "by" represents the columns.

Class Budget Overview

If you created a Class budget, select Profit & Loss By Account And Class in the first window, and click Next. Select a report layout from the drop-down list. You have the following choices:

- **Account By Month**   Lists each account you used in the budget and displays the total budget amounts (for all Class budgets you created) for each month that has data. No budget information for individual classes appears.
- **Account By Class**   Lists each account you used in the budget and displays the yearly total for that account for each class (each class has its own column).

- **Class By Month** Displays a row for each class that has a budget and a column for each month. The total budget (not broken down by account) appears for each month.

Budget vs. Actual

This report's name says it all—you can see how your real numbers compare to your budget figures. For a straight P&L budget (see Figure 13-7 for a sample), the report displays the following columns for each month, for each account:

- Amount posted
- Amount budgeted
- Difference in dollars
- Difference in percentage

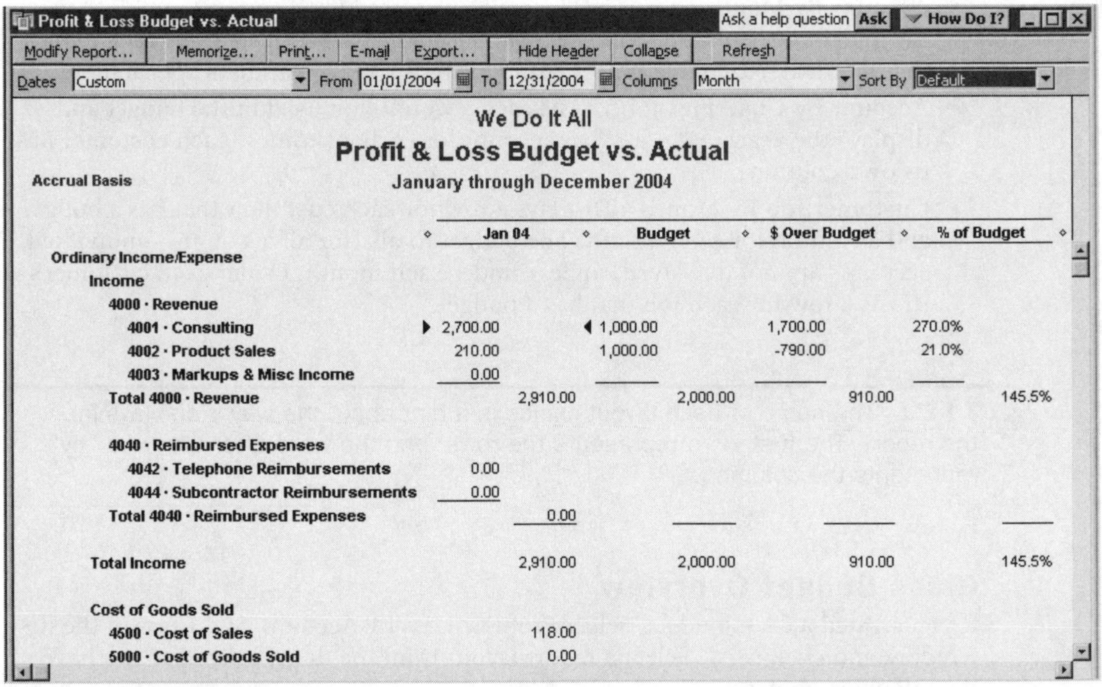

FIGURE 13-7 Check what you took in and spent against the budget you designed.

The choices for the budget type are the same as the Budget Overview, so you can see account totals, customer totals, or class totals to match the budgets you've created.

The first thing you'll notice in the report is that all the accounts in your general ledger are listed, regardless of whether or not you included them in your budget. However, only the accounts you used in your budget show budget figures. You can change that by customizing the report to include only your budgeted accounts.

Click the Modify Report button at the top of the budget report window. In the Modify Report window, click the Advanced button to open the Advanced Options window. Click the option labeled Show Only Rows And Columns With Budgets.

Click OK to return to the Modify Report window, and then click OK again to return to the Budget vs. Actual report window. The data that's displayed is only that data connected to your budgeted accounts.

You can also use the options in the Modify Report window to make other changes:

- Change the report dates.
- Change the calculations from Accrual to Cash (which means that unpaid invoices and bills are removed from the calculations, and only actual income and expenses are reported).

You should memorize the report so you don't have to make these modifications the next time you want to view a comparison report. Click the Memorize button at the top of the report window, and then give the report a meaningful name. Only the formatting changes you make are memorized, not the data. Every time you open the report, it displays current data. To view the report after you memorize it, choose Reports | Memorized Reports from the QuickBooks menu bar.

Profit & Loss Budget Performance

This report is similar to the Budget vs. Actual report, but it's based on the current month and the year to date. For that time period, the report displays your actual income and expenses compared to what you budgeted (see Figure 13-8).

By default, the date range is the current month, but you can change that to see last month's figures, or the figures for any previous month.

This report is also available for all types, as described in "Budget Overview," earlier in this section, and can also be modified to customize the display.

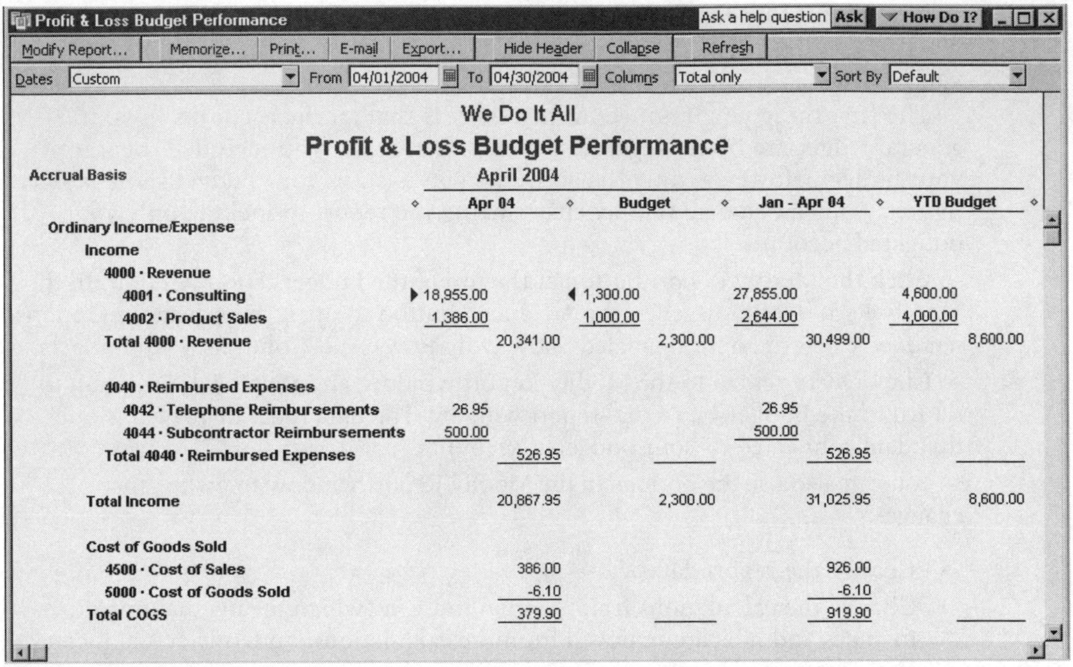

We Do It All
Profit & Loss Budget Performance
Accrual Basis — April 2004

	Apr 04		Budget		Jan - Apr 04		YTD Budget	
Ordinary Income/Expense								
Income								
4000 · Revenue								
4001 · Consulting	18,955.00		1,300.00		27,855.00		4,600.00	
4002 · Product Sales	1,386.00		1,000.00		2,644.00		4,000.00	
Total 4000 · Revenue		20,341.00		2,300.00		30,499.00		8,600.00
4040 · Reimbursed Expenses								
4042 · Telephone Reimbursements	26.95				26.95			
4044 · Subcontractor Reimbursements	500.00				500.00			
Total 4040 · Reimbursed Expenses		526.95				526.95		
Total Income		20,867.95		2,300.00		31,025.95		8,600.00
Cost of Goods Sold								
4500 · Cost of Sales		386.00				926.00		
5000 · Cost of Goods Sold		-6.10				-6.10		
Total COGS		379.90				919.90		

FIGURE 13-8 See how your budget stacks up against your actuals at this point in time.

Budget vs. Actual Graph

This report just opens; you have no choices to select first. All the choices are in the graph that displays, in the form of buttons across the top of the report window (see Figure 13-9). Merely click the type of report you want to see.

Exporting Budgets

If you need to manipulate your budgets, export them to other software applications. However, you can't select specific budgets to export—it's all or nothing.

You can export the budgets to any software program that supports documents that contain delimited fields (this usually means spreadsheet or database programs), using the following steps:

1. Choose File | Export | Lists to IIF Files from the QuickBooks menu bar.

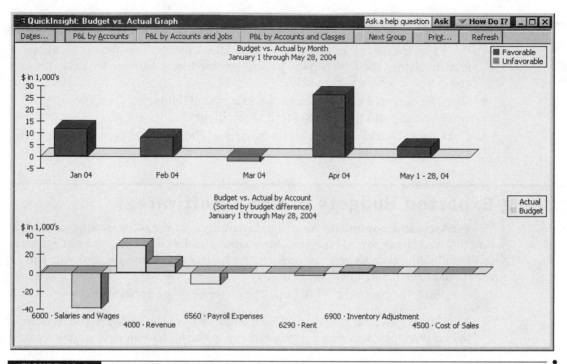

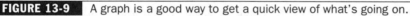

FIGURE 13-9   A graph is a good way to get a quick view of what's going on.

2. When the Export dialog box opens, it displays all the QuickBooks lists. Select the item named Budgets and click OK.

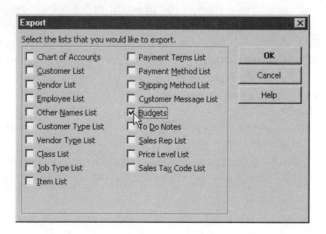

3. Another Export dialog box opens (this one looks like the Save dialog box you're used to seeing in Windows software). Select a folder in which to save this exported file, or leave it in your QuickBooks folder (the default location). I usually change the folder to the location where I keep files for the program I'm going to use for the exported file.

4. Give the exported list a filename (for example, 04Budgets). QuickBooks will automatically add the extension .iif to the filename.

5. Click Save. QuickBooks displays a message telling you that your data has been exported successfully. Click OK.

Using Exported Budgets in Other Software

You can view and manipulate your exported budgets in the software application that received the exported budgets. One common task is to change the budget dates to the following year, so you can import your budgets back into QuickBooks and use them as the basis of next year's budgets.

Here's how to import the .iif file into the target software application:

1. Click the Open icon (or use the Open command) in the software you're using. When the Open dialog box appears, move to the folder where you stored your .iif file.

2. In the Files Of Type field of the Open dialog box, change the specification to All Files (otherwise, you won't see your .iif file in the listings).

3. Double-click your exported .iif file to open it.

Your software application should recognize that this file doesn't match its own file type and therefore begin the procedures for importing a file. In case your software doesn't figure it out, your .iif file is a tab-delimited file.

When the import procedures are completed, your budget is displayed in the window of your software program.

You can use the features in this software to manipulate the budget by changing the way the items are sorted, or by applying formulas to budget data. If you want to change the budget dates so you can use the budgets next year in QuickBooks, move to the column labeled STARTDATE and update the dates so they apply to the following year.

If you're planning to import the budgets back into QuickBooks (covered next), be sure to save the file as a tab-delimited document and give the file the extension .iif.

Importing Budgets Back into QuickBooks

The only circumstances under which you'd import budgets back into QuickBooks is to copy a budget to another year. If you wanted to edit figures you'd work in the QuickBooks budget window. To play "what if" games, or to sort the budget differently, you'd work in the appropriate software (such as Excel) because QuickBooks doesn't provide those features.

If you changed the dates to next year, import the file so you can use the data in budget reports, or edit data right in the QuickBooks budget window. Import the budgets back into QuickBooks, using the following steps:

1. Choose File | Import | IIF Files from the menu bar.
2. When the Import dialog box opens, locate and double-click the file you saved.
3. QuickBooks displays a message to tell you the import was successful. Click OK.

You can view the imported budgets in any budget report or in the budget window. QuickBooks checks the dates and changes the budget's name to reflect the dates. Budget names start with FY*xxxx*, where *xxxx* is the fiscal year.

When you select a budget report, or choose a budget to edit in the budget window, the available budgets include both the budgets you created in QuickBooks (FY2004) and the budgets you imported after changing the date (FY2005). Next year, you can delete the FY2004 budgets.

Decision Tools

QuickBooks includes a number of tools you can use to analyze your fiscal condition and make decisions about the way you manage your business. You can see the list of tools on the submenu displayed when you choose Company | Planning & Budgeting | Decision Tools. In this section I'll provide an overview of some of these features.

Measure Profitability

The Measure Profitability tool looks at your profit margin and offers advice based on that data. Move through the tabs (see Figure 13-10) to gain specific information about improving your profits.

You can select the tab that piques your interest, or use the Next button to move through the tabs in order. You'll find advice, sample scenarios of successful businesses, and links to additional information.

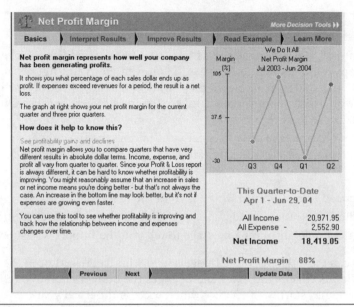

FIGURE 13-10 Check your profit margin and learn how to improve it.

Analyze Financial Strength

This tool concerns itself with your liquidity, which means the amount of cash and assets your business has available. A business that is financially strong has enough liquidity to manage emergencies and can continue to operate in spite of slow accounts receivable collections.

Your current working capital amount is displayed, which is the difference between your current assets and your current liabilities, and the difference is also displayed as a ratio. While a ratio of 2 or higher is considered healthy, sometimes working capital amounts and ratio figures can be deceiving. That's because your current assets include your inventory and accounts receivable, in addition to cash. If you've over-bought inventory and sales aren't vigorous enough to recoup the investment quickly, that's no good. If your current assets are enhanced by a large accounts receivable, don't assume that means you're experiencing a healthy number of sales of products and services. It could mean you have a lot of uncollected sales. Run an aging report (covered in Chapter 5) before you celebrate what seems to be a healthy financial condition.

Compare Debt and Ownership

This tool examines your data and calculates what's commonly called the debt-to-equity ratio, which is simply an analysis of the amount of assets in your business that's controlled by debt. The tool displays a graph that shows how much of your total assets came from ownership (equity), and how much came from creditors. The more equity-owned assets, the easier it is to use your company's assets as collateral. Inventory and accounts receivable are often used as collateral.

It's difficult to pinpoint a ratio that's "good" or "healthy," because the type of business has a great deal to do with that determination. Service-based businesses frequently don't have as high an asset total as product-based businesses, because of the lack of inventory assets. Retail businesses have inventory assets but lack the accounts receivable assets that wholesale businesses experience.

You can use the information you gain in this report to decide whether to seek credit in order to expand (or survive). Many banks want a debt-to-equity figure as part of your loan application.

Debt isn't necessarily a bad thing in business. If you can use borrowed funds to increase revenue to a point where your profit is larger than the cost of debt, borrowing money might be a good idea. Use the data you gain from this tool to discuss your borrowing options with your accountant.

Using Journal Entries

n this chapter:

- Work in the General Journal Entry window
- Enter the opening trial balance
- Make adjustments to the general ledger
- Depreciate fixed assets
- Journalize outside payroll services

Chapter 14

As you work in QuickBooks, the amounts involved in the financial transactions you complete are transferred to your general ledger. In addition to transaction totals, numbers can be placed into the general ledger directly. This is called making a *journal entry.*

Journal entries shouldn't be used without a specific purpose, and usually that purpose is to enter figures that cannot be added to an account via a standard transaction (e.g., an invoice or a check).

N O T E : The standard jargon for this transaction type is "journal entry," usually abbreviated "JE." However, QuickBooks refers to the transaction as "general journal entry" and uses "GJE" as the abbreviation.

Using the General Journal Entry Window

The Make General Journal Entries window, seen in Figure 14-1, represents the standard approach to viewing the general ledger: columns for account numbers,

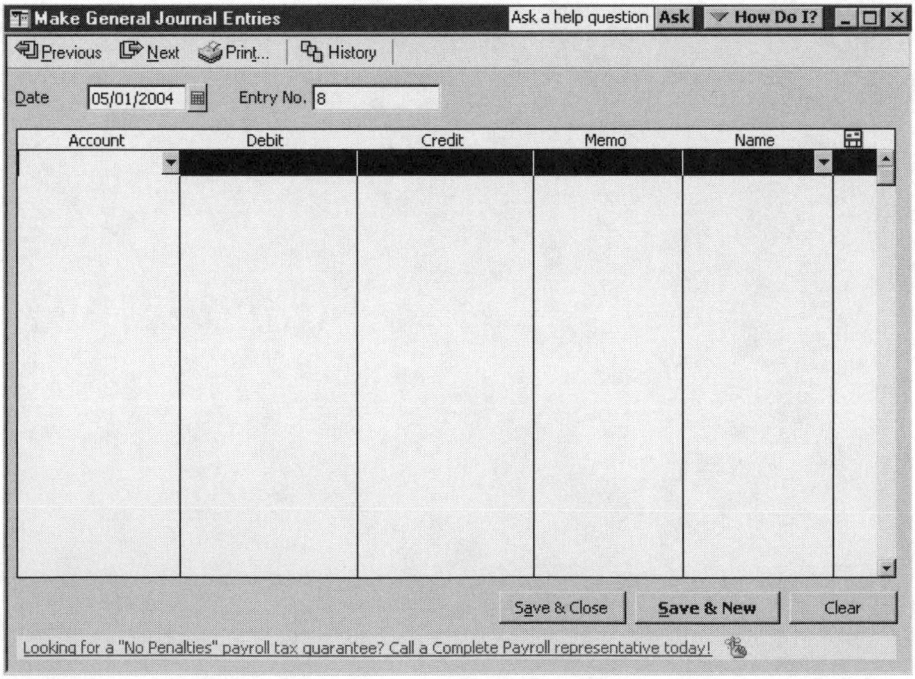

Make General Journal Entries	Ask a help question	Ask	How Do I?

Previous Next Print... History

Date 05/01/2004 Entry No. 8

Account	Debit	Credit	Memo	Name	

Save & Close   Save & New   Clear

Looking for a "No Penalties" payroll tax guarantee? Call a Complete Payroll representative today!

FIGURE 14-1 The QuickBooks GJE window has more columns than the standard T-Account format because you can link customer and class information to an entry.

debit amounts, and credit amounts. In addition, QuickBooks provides some additional columns that hold data related to the journal entry.

To create a journal entry, follow these steps:

1. Choose Banking | Make General Journal Entries. QuickBooks displays a message telling you that automatic numbers are now assigned to journal entries (a feature introduced several years ago). Unless you want to see this message every time you make a journal entry, select Do Not Display This Message In The Future, and then click OK to see the Make General Journal Entries window.

2. Click in the Account column, and then click the arrow to see a drop-down list of your chart of accounts. Choose the account you need.

3. Move to the Debit or Credit column (depending on the data you're entering), and enter the amount for that account.

4. Repeat for all the accounts in the journal entry.

As you enter each amount, QuickBooks presents the offsetting total in the next line. For example, if the line items you've entered so far have a higher total for the credit side than the debit side, the next entry presents the balancing offset (see Figure 14-2).

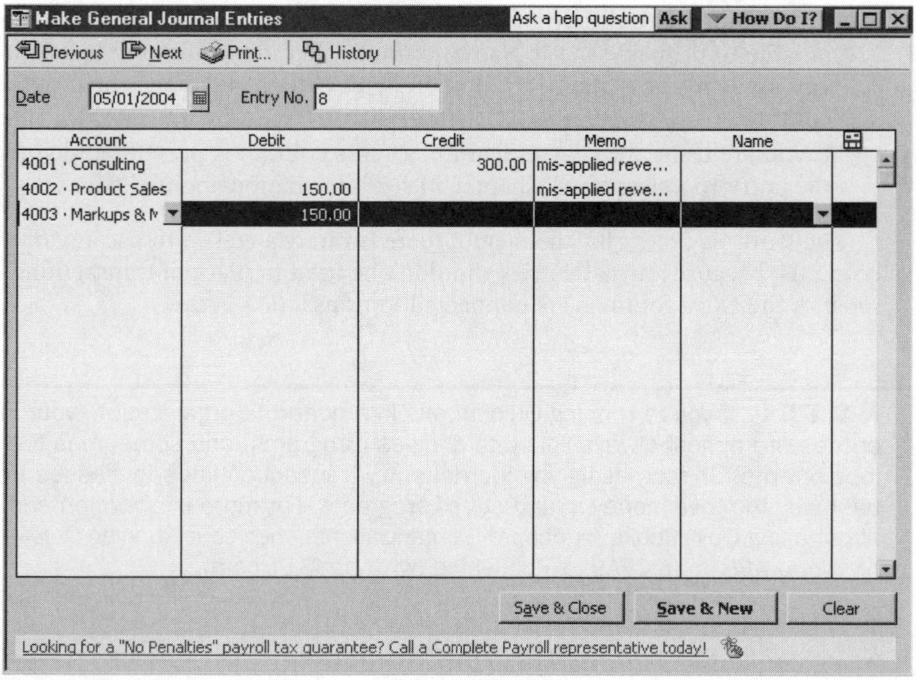

FIGURE 14-2 QuickBooks keeps the running offset figure available so you don't have to enter an amount for the last entry.

Here are the guidelines for using the columns QuickBooks adds to a traditional journal entry window:

- Use the Memo column to write a comment about the reason for the journal entry. The memo text appears in the entry of the account's register and on reports, so you should enter the text on every line of the entry in order to see the explanation no matter which account register you're viewing.

NOTE: If you're using QuickBooks Premier, you can select the Autofill Memo option to have the memo you enter on the first line appear automatically on all lines. This is frequently a very handy feature. To learn how to use this and other Premier Edition features, you can buy *Running QuickBooks Premier Editions* from CPA911 Publishing (www.cpa911.com).

- Use the Name column to assign a customer, vendor, employee, or other name to the amount on this line of the entry, if you're linking the entry to a name. If the account you're posting to is an A/R or A/P account, an entry in the Name column is required.
- The column with the icon is a "billable" flag, which means that the amount is billable to the name in the Name column. Click the column to insert the icon if you are using an expense account and you enter a customer name in the Name column.
- If you are using the Classes feature, a Class column is present, and you can link the entry to a class. (See Chapter 21 for information about classes.)

The truth is, except for the memo, there is rarely a reason to use any of those columns, because journal entries shouldn't be used in place of transactions, and most of the extra columns are connected to transaction issues.

NOTE: If you're running QuickBooks in a nonprofit organization, your journal entries are almost always linked to classes (programs) and sometimes linked to jobs (grants). In fact, assigning journal entry transaction lines to classes is the best way to move money in and out of programs. For more information and tips about using QuickBooks for nonprofit organizations, check out *Running QuickBooks for Nonprofits* from CPA911 Publishing (www.cpa911.com).

Opening Trial Balance

If you opted to skip entering opening balances during your EasyStep Interview or when you created accounts manually, eventually you'll need to enter the opening balances for your accounts. All that's necessary is the opening balances for the balance sheet accounts. Then you can add all the transactions that took place since the beginning of the year to create a thorough history of transactions while you're posting the current year's activity to the general ledger.

Entering the Opening Balances

QuickBooks does not have an item or feature called the "opening balance," per se. However, every account register is sorted by date, so using the first day of your fiscal year creates an opening balance automatically.

 TIP: Create a separate equity account for your previous equity; it makes it easier to maneuver numbers at the end of the year when you're closing books. QuickBooks will post profit (or loss) to the retained earnings equity account, but you'll have historical numbers in the other account. At the end of each year, you can make a journal entry to move the current year's equity change into the previous equity account.

Confer with your accountant to develop the opening balance, and then enter it as a journal entry by using the steps described in the previous section.

Workarounds for QuickBooks Limitations

There are a couple of QuickBooks idiosyncrasies you may run into when working with journal entries.

In QuickBooks, a journal entry can contain only the A/P account or the A/R account; you cannot use both of those accounts in the same journal entry (and the odds are good that both accounts have balances in your opening balance). You'll get an error message that says, "You cannot use more than one A/R or A/P account in the same transaction" (which is not a clear explanation). Unfortunately, QuickBooks doesn't issue the error message until after you enter all the data and try to save the journal entry. This restriction does not have its roots in accounting standards. It's an arbitrary rule built into the QuickBooks software.

Another problem is that QuickBooks insists you attach a single customer or vendor name to the entry if you're making a journal entry that involves either the A/R or the A/P account. You can't just enter an A/R or A/P balance against your previous equity (or against income or expenses, for that matter). If you're keeping customer info outside of QuickBooks (perhaps you have a retail business and keep customer charges elsewhere), you're out of luck.

If you decide that's OK, and you're willing to enter customer opening balances in your JE, you have another problem: You can't enter A/R for more than one customer. QuickBooks won't permit more than one A/R line in the journal entry (the same restrictions apply to A/P).

QuickBooks' approach is to enter the opening balance when you create a customer or vendor. Both the New Customer and New Vendor windows have a field for this purpose. Those totals are posted to A/R and A/P as of the date you enter, which should be the first day of the fiscal year if you're trying to create an opening trial balance.

Neither of these data entry methods—A/R lines or opening balances during customer setup—is a good idea anyway. The entry is only a total, and you cannot enter discrete invoices or bills, saddling you with several annoying drawbacks, such as:

- You can't easily deal with disputes over specific invoices or bills (you'll have to find the original paperwork).
- Customer payments have to be applied as partial payments against the total you entered. This makes it more difficult to have conversations with customers about their accounts.
- You don't have the opportunity to enter memos on invoices or bills.
- It makes it difficult to track those amounts that are for reimbursed expenses.

The solution is to enter your opening trial balance without the A/R and A/P entries. Adjust the equity account if your accountant preconfigured the opening trial balance for you. (Also, avoid using an opening balance when you set up customers and vendors). Then, enter the open invoices for customers and the open bills from vendors, using your opening balance date for the transactions, and let QuickBooks post the totals to the general ledger.

You can create one comprehensive invoice per customer/vendor and pay it off if you don't want to bother with the individual invoices that created the opening balance. The equity account will automatically adjust itself back to your accountant's original totals as you enter the transactions.

Making Adjusting Entries

There are some circumstances, such as changing accounts and tracking depreciation, that require adjusting entries to your general ledger. Read on to find out how to handle these situations.

Making Journal Entries for Changed Accounts

I've had many clients who decided, after they'd been using QuickBooks for a while, that they wanted to track income differently. Instead of one income account, they opted for separate income accounts that are more specific. For example, an income account for fees and another income account for products sold makes business analysis easier.

This transaction is quite simple. Create the new account and then take the appropriate amount of funds out of the original account and put it into the new account. Revenue is a credit-side item, so that means:

- Debit the original account for the amount that belongs in the new account.
- Credit the new account for that same amount.

Then, of course, you'll have to go to the items list and change the necessary items to reflect the new income account so you don't have to keep making journal entries. (If QuickBooks didn't force you to link items to accounts, this wouldn't be necessary—sigh!)

The same decision is frequently made about expenses, as business owners decide to split heretofore comprehensive accounts. Perhaps you feel Insurance accounts should be car insurance, equipment insurance, building insurance, malpractice insurance, and so on.

For expense accounts, the journal entry goes to the opposite side of the ledger because expenses are a debit-side item, so do the following:

- Credit the original expense account for the amount you're taking out of it and putting into the new account(s).
- Debit the new account(s) for the appropriate amount(s).

The same logic applies to a fixed-asset account named Vehicles that you want to divide into more specific accounts (to track the truck separately from the car, for instance, especially if they were purchased in different years). This means you can also separate out any accumulated depreciation so it's assigned to the correct asset. (You can get that information from your tax returns, or ask your accountant.)

Making Depreciation Entries

Depreciation is a way to track the current value of a fixed asset that loses value as it ages. The basis of an asset's depreciation from an accounting point of view is determined by a complicated set of rules. The IRS makes these rules, and the rules change frequently.

Depreciation is a journal entry activity. Most small businesses enter the depreciation of their assets at the end of the year, but some companies perform depreciation tasks monthly or quarterly.

Depreciation is a special journal entry because the accounts involved are very restricted—this is not a free choice where you can use whichever account strikes your fancy. The account that is being depreciated must be a fixed asset. The offset entry is to an account named Depreciation Expense (or Depreciation), and it is in the expense section of your chart of accounts.

Creating Accounts for Tracking Depreciation

I'm assuming that you've created your fixed-asset account and that the assets you've purchased have been posted there. You might have multiple fixed-asset accounts if you want to track different types of fixed assets separately. (For instance, my chart of accounts has three fixed-asset account sections: Equipment, Furn & Fixture, and Automobile.)

When it comes to accounting procedures that have a direct bearing on my taxes and for which I might need information at a glance (especially if I'm called on to explain it), I like to be very explicit in the way I work. Therefore, for every fixed-asset account in my chart of accounts I have families of accounts for depreciation. I create a parent (account) and children (subaccounts) for each type of fixed asset. For example, the fixed-asset section of a chart of accounts I create would look like this:

PARENT ACCOUNTS	SUBACCOUNTS
Equipment Assets	
	Equipment
	AccumDepr- Equipment
Furn & Fixtures Assets	
	Furn & Fixtures
	AccumDepr-Furn & Fixtures
Vehicle Assets	
	Vehicles
	AccumDepr-Vehicles

If you use numbers for your chart of accounts, create a numbering system that makes sense for this setup. For example, if Equipment is 1600, the subaccounts start with 1601; Furn & Fixture starts with 1620, and the subaccounts start with 1621; Vehicle starts with 1640, and so on.

I post asset purchases to a subaccount I create for the specific purchase, and I make my journal entry for depreciation in the AccumDepr subaccount. I never use the parent account. There are several reasons for this:

Both the asset subaccount and the depreciation asset subaccount are "pure." I can look at either one to see a running total instead of a calculated net total.

- Tracing the year-to-year depreciation is easy. I just open the depreciation asset subaccount register—each line represents a year.
- It's easier and quicker to open the depreciation asset subaccount if I'm asked about the depreciation total (handy if you sell the asset and have to add back the depreciation).

The net value of my fixed assets is correct. A Balance Sheet report shows me the details (see Figure 14-3).

Balance Sheet	Ask a help question	Ask	▼ How Do I?	_ □ X
Modify Report...	Memorize...	Print...	E-mail	Export...	Hide Header	Collapse	Refresh
Dates	Custom ▼	As of	04/30/2004	Columns	Total only ▼	Sort By	Default

We Do It All
Balance Sheet

Accrual Basis

	Apr 30, 04
Fixed Assets	
1600 · Equipment Assets	
1601 · Equipment	21,560.00
1602 · AccumDepr-Equipment	-18,450.00
Total 1600 · Equipment Assets	3,110.00
1620 · Furn & Fixture Assets	
1621 · Furn & Fixtures	10,200.00
1622 · AccumDepre-Furn & Fixtures	-10,200.00
Total 1620 · Furn & Fixture Assets	0.00
1640 · Vehicle Assets	
1641 · Vehicles	18,000.00
1642 · AccumDepr-Vehicles	-15,000.00
Total 1640 · Vehicle Assets	3,000.00
Total Fixed Assets	6,110.00

FIGURE 14-3   Use subaccounts for fixed assets to get a detailed view of depreciation activity.

You can further refine this paradigm by creating subaccounts for specific fixed assets. For instance, you may want to create a subaccount for each vehicle asset (or one for all cars and one for all trucks) and its accompanying accumulated depreciation. If your equipment falls under a variety of depreciation rules (e.g., manufacturing equipment vs. computer equipment), you may want to have a set of subaccounts for each type.

If you're really obsessive, you can create a different subaccount for each year of depreciation; for instance, under your AccumDepr-Vehicle subaccount, you could have Vehicle-Depr 2000, Vehicle-Depr 2001, Vehicle-Depr 2002, and so on. Then your balance sheet shows a complete year-by-year depreciation schedule instead of accumulated depreciation—and the math still works properly. Of course, after a number of years, you'll have destroyed an entire forest with all the paper it takes to print your balance sheet.

Creating a Depreciation Entry

To depreciate fixed assets, you must have a depreciation offset account in the Expense section of your chart of accounts. Once that account exists, here's how to make your depreciation entry:

1. Choose Banking | Make General Journal Entries from the menu bar.

2. Choose the first asset depreciation subaccount.

3. Enter the depreciation amount in the Credit column.

4. Choose the next asset depreciation subaccount and enter its depreciation amount in the Credit column. (QuickBooks automatically puts the offsetting amount in the Debit column, but you can ignore that as you work.)

5. Continue until all your depreciation figures are entered in the Credit column.

6. Choose the Depreciation Expense account. The total amount of the credits is automatically placed in the Debit column.

7. Click Save & Close.

For example, here's a typical journal entry for depreciation.

ACCOUNT	DEBIT	CREDIT
Equipment Assets:AccumDepr-Equip		5,000.00
Furn & Fix Assets:AccumDepr-Furn & Fix		700.00
Depreciation Expense	5,700.00	

Notice the colon in the account names for the two asset accounts—that's QuickBooks indication of a subaccount.

Using the QuickBooks Fixed Asset Tools

Starting with version 2004, QuickBooks has added some features to help you manage fixed assets: a new Fixed Asset Item list and a planning tool named Depreciate Your Assets.

The Fixed Asset Item list is designed to store detailed information about fixed assets. Information about the list and the kind of data you can store in each asset's record is in Chapter 2.

The Depreciate Your Assets tool can be used to determine depreciation rates, but it doesn't pay any attention to the Fixed Asset Item list—instead you have to enter your asset information to use the tool. This is a planning tool, and it doesn't perform depreciation journal entries.

NOTE: QuickBooks 2004 Premier: Accountant Edition has a terrific tool for managing assets on your Fixed Asset Item list. If your accountant has installed this product, depreciation calculations and entries can be written to your file when you send an Accountant's Copy. Chapter 15 explains how to create an Accountant's Copy of your file, and what it's for.

Reversing Entries

Your accountant may enter, or tell you to enter, *reversing entries*. These are general journal entries that are applied on one date and then reversed on another (later) date. For example, on 12/31/04, you may have a journal entry that adjusts your A/R and A/P accounts in order to prepare for tax filing on a cash basis (some accountants prefer this method to asking QuickBooks to print cash-basis reports). On 1/1/05, the entry has to be reversed. You enter both journal entries, and the totals you see are dictated by the dates selected in report windows.

 N O T E : QuickBooks Premier Editions have an automated reversing journal entry. Merely indicate the reversal date when you create the journal entry.

Journalizing Outside Payroll Services

If you have an outside payroll service, you have to tell QuickBooks about the payroll transactions that took place. You get a report from the service, so all the numbers are available. It's just a matter of entering them.

It's common for businesses to perform this task via a journal entry (businesses that don't use computers have to haul out the big ledger books). Like all other journal entries, this one is just a matter of entering debits and credits.

There are three parts to recording payroll:

- Transferring money to the payroll account
- Entering the payroll figures
- Entering the employer expense figures

Transferring Money to the Payroll Account

You should have a separate bank account for payroll if you have an outside payroll service—in fact, a separate payroll account is a good idea even if you do your own payroll with QuickBooks. Outside payroll services reach into your checking account; in fact, they have checks, and you certainly don't want to give away checks for your regular operating account.

Another reason for a separate payroll account, even if you do your own payroll, is the discipline involved in holding on to your employee withholdings until you pass them along to insurance companies, other vendors, and the government—*especially* the government. The money you withhold and leave in your bank account until you're ready to transmit it to the government is not your money. You cannot spend it. It doesn't matter if you need the money to save your business from total bankruptcy—you cannot spend the money. People have done that and gotten into serious trouble, including going to jail. Keeping all the money associated with payroll in a separate bank account removes it from the amounts you have available to run your business.

To transfer the money you need for this payroll, choose Banking | Transfer Funds. Then, transfer the money from your regular operating account to your payroll account. Be sure to transfer enough money for the gross payroll plus the employer payroll expenses, which include the following:

- Employer-matching contributions to FICA and Medicare
- Employer-matching contributions to pension plans
- Employer-matching contributions to benefits
- Employer state unemployment assessments
- Employer FUTA
- Any other government or benefit payments due

Even though some of these aren't transmitted every payday, you should transfer the amounts at that time anyway. Then, when it's time to pay them, the correct amount of money will have been amassed in the payroll account.

Recording the Payroll

The *payroll run* (jargon for "printing the paychecks") produces a fairly complicated set of debits and credits. Many businesses record a journal entry for the run, then a separate journal entry for the employer expenses when they're transmitted.

If your payroll service takes care of remitting employer expenses, you can journalize the payments. If you do the employer reports yourself and send the checks directly, your check-writing activity will record the payments.

It's possible that you don't have all the expenses shown in this list (for instance, not all states have employee unemployment assessments). And you may have additional withholding such as union dues, garnishments against wages, and so on. Be sure you've created a liability account in your chart of accounts for each withholding category you need, and a vendor for each transmittal check. Table 14-1 shows a typical template for recording the payroll run as a journal entry.

Recording Employer Payments

You need to journalize the employer remittances if your payroll service is taking care of them for you (if you do it yourself, just write the checks from the payroll account and each item will post to the general ledger correctly). Table 14-2 is a sample journal entry for recording payroll remittances.

ACCOUNT	DEBIT	CREDIT
Salaries and Wages (Expense)	Total Gross Payroll	
FWT (liability)		Total Federal Withheld
FICA (liability)		Total FICA Withheld
Medicare (liability)		Total Medicare Withheld
State Income Tax (liability)		Total State Tax Withheld
Local Income Tax (liability)		Total Local Tax Withheld
State SDI (liability)		Total State SDI Withheld
State SUI (liability)		Total State SUI Withheld
Benefits Contrib. (liability)		Total Benefits Withheld
401(k) Contrib. (liability)		Total 401(k) Withheld
Other Deductions (liability)		Total Other Deductions Withheld
Payroll Bank Account (asset)		Total of Net Payroll

TABLE 14-1   Typical Outside Payroll Service Journal Entry

ACCOUNT	DEBIT	CREDIT
Federal Payroll Expenses (expense)	FICA and Medicare Employer Total	
Federal Withholdings (liability)	All individual withholding totals (FIT, FICA, etc.)	
State and Local Withholdings (liability)	All withholding totals (taxes, SDI, SUI, etc.)	
SUTA (expense)	Employer SUTA	
FUTA (expense)	Employer FUTA	
Employer Contributions (expense)	All benefit, pension, other remittances	
Payroll Bank Account (asset)		Total of checks written

TABLE 14-2   Journal Entry for the Employer-Side Transactions

The entry involving the transmittal of withholdings is posted to the same account you used when you withheld the amounts. In effect, you "wash" the liability accounts; you're not really spending money, you're remitting money you've withheld.

You can have as many individual employer expense accounts as you think you need, or you can post all the employer expenses to one account named "payroll expenses."

CAUTION: Don't have your payroll service take their fee from the payroll account. Instead, write them a check from your operating account. The service is not a payroll expense; it's an operating expense.

Create Your Own Template

You can save a lot of time and effort by creating a template for the payroll journal entries. Open a Make General Journal Entries window and fill out the Account column only. Enter the first account, then press the DOWN ARROW and enter the next account, and keep going until all accounts are listed. QuickBooks automatically inserts 0.00 as you skip the Debit and Credit columns.

Account	Debit	Credit	Memo	Name	
6000 · Salaries and...					
2110 · FWT	0.00				
2120 · FICA Withheld	0.00				
2130 · Medicare Wi...	0.00				
2140 · PA Income ...	0.00				
2150 · Phila Wage ...	0.00				
1020 · Payroll Acco...	0.00				
	0.00				

When all the accounts are listed, press CTRL-M to open the Memorize Transaction dialog. Name the memorized transaction Payroll (or something similar), and select the option Don't Remind Me (the reports from the payroll company are your reminder).

Close the Make General Journal Entries window. QuickBooks displays a message asking if you want to save the transaction you just created. Click No (you don't have to save a GJE to memorize it, isn't that nifty?). Do the same thing for the journal entry you create to record employer remittances.

When you're ready to record payroll, click the MemTx icon on the toolbar and select the appropriate memorized transaction. When it opens, fill in the figures and save it.

Reconciling the Payroll Account

The problem with journal entries for payroll is that when the bank statement comes for the payroll account, reconciling it is a bit different. You don't have a record of the check numbers and payees. When you open the payroll account in the Reconcile window, you see the journal entry totals instead of the individual checks.

Reconciling Outside QuickBooks

You have the report from the payroll service, and it lists each check number. You can therefore reconcile the account outside of the Reconcile window (using a manual system or using your spreadsheet software).

TIP: See if your payroll service can send you a file containing check#/ payee/ amount information that can be opened in spreadsheet or database software. A tab-delimited file is the best file type.

Entering Fake Payroll Checks in QuickBooks

If you want to perform the reconciliation in QuickBooks, you can enter the checks and post them back to the payroll account. (The journal entry took care of all the real postings.) You have a little bit of setup to do, then you can perform this task every payday.

Create a name, "Payroll," with a type Other Name. (Choose Lists | Other Names List from the menu bar.) You can use this name for every check (and put the employee's name in the memo field).

Alternatively, you can create a name for each employee in the Other Name list, using initials, last name only, or some other name that isn't the same as the original employee name. The reason you have to create these fake names is that QuickBooks will not let you write a check directly to an employee. Employee checks can be written only via the real Payroll feature.

Now you have a payee name for the payroll checks. Grab the report from the payroll service and enter the individual checks:

1. Press CTRL-A to open the chart of accounts, and double-click the payroll account to open the register.
2. On the next available transaction line, enter the payroll check date.
3. Tab to the Number field and enter the first check number on the payroll service report.
4. Enter the payee Payroll (unless you've entered all your employee names as Other Name types, in which case enter the appropriate name).
5. Enter the amount of the net paycheck.
6. In the Account field, choose the Payroll account (the account you're currently working in). QuickBooks will flash a message warning you that you're posting the payment to the source account.
7. Click OK and click the check box that tells QuickBooks to omit this warning in the future.
8. Click the Record button to save this check, and then enter the next check.

Continue the process until all the checks are entered. Each entry is automatically duplicated (although the amounts are in different columns). The duplication occurs because QuickBooks is automatically writing the balancing entry (which is what double-entry accounting software does); in this case, the balancing entry is posted to the same account.

You can also enter the checks the payroll service wrote to transmit your withholdings or pay your taxes. As long as each entry you make was entered into the journal entry, you can post everything back to the payroll account. You're "washing" every transaction, not changing the balance of the account. Then, when you want to reconcile the payroll account, the individual checks are in the Reconcile window. The fact is, this procedure is quite easy and fast, and you have to do it only on payday (or once a month if you want to wait until the bank statement comes in).

Running Reports

In *this chapter:*

- Trial balance

- Balance Sheet

- Profit & Loss statement

- Accountant's Review Copy

- Cash flow

If QuickBooks is your first accounting software program, and you've been using manual bookkeeping procedures, you've already discovered how much easier it is to accomplish bookkeeping tasks. However, even with the ease and power you've gained with QuickBooks, bookkeeping probably isn't fun. I can't give you any QuickBooks tips to make it fun (it isn't—it's precise, repetitive work), but I can tell you how to feel better about all the work you do in QuickBooks.

It's the reports you get out of the software that make the work worthwhile. These are reports you'd have to spend hours on using a manual bookkeeping system. And you can change, customize, and manipulate these reports to get all sorts of information about your business. Most of the results you obtain from QuickBooks reports couldn't be gained from a manual system. (Well, maybe they could, if you made a lifetime career out of it and spent weeks on each report.)

Reporting the Trial Balance

A *trial balance* is a list of all your general ledger accounts and their current balances. It's a quick way to see what's what on an account-by-account basis. In fact, you can use the individual totals and subtotal them to create a Balance Sheet and a Profit & Loss (P&L) statement. However, you don't have to do that because both of those important reports are also available in QuickBooks. Most accountants ask to see a trial balance when they're preparing your taxes or analyzing the health of your business.

To see a trial balance, choose Reports | Accountant and Taxes | Trial Balance. Your company's trial balance is displayed on your screen and looks similar (in form, not content) to Figure 15-1. You can scroll through it to see all the account balances. The bottom of the report has a total for debits and a total for credits, and they're equal. Click the Print button on the report's button bar to print the report.

Configuring the Trial Balance Report

You can change the way the trial balance report displays information, using the configuration options available for this report. Click the Modify Report button on the report's button bar to bring up the Modify Report window shown in Figure 15-2. If you make changes that don't work as you thought they would, click the Revert button that appears on each tab of the Modify Report window to reset all options to their default state.

Accrual vs. Cash Trial Balance

One important control in the Display tab of the Modify Report window is the Report Basis selection. QuickBooks can show you your balances on an accrual basis or on a cash basis:

- Accrual numbers are based on your transaction activity. When you invoice a customer, that amount is considered to be revenue. When you enter a vendor bill, you've entered an expense.
- Cash numbers are based on the flow of cash. Revenue isn't real until the customer pays the bill, and your vendor bills aren't expenses until you write the check.

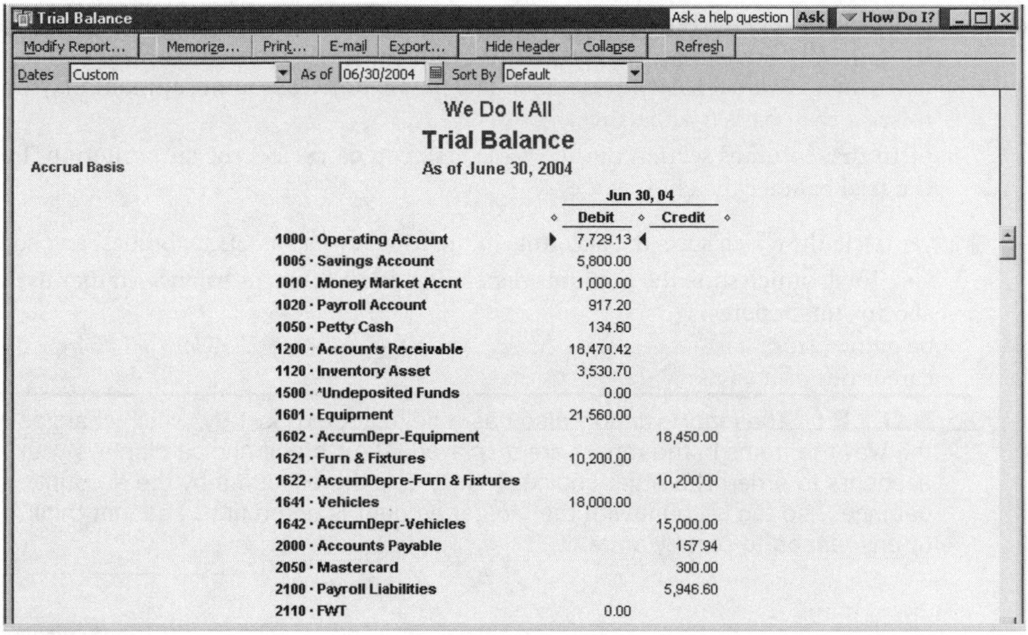

FIGURE 15-1   A trial balance reports the current balance for each account.

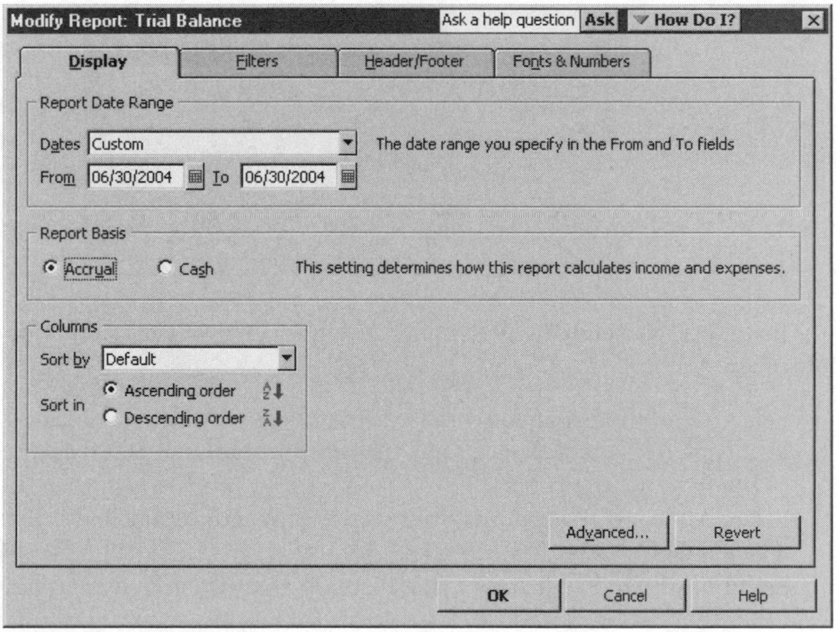

FIGURE 15-2   Modify the trial balance report by changing configuration options.

By default, QuickBooks, like most accounting software, displays accrual reports. It's generally more useful as you analyze your business. However, unless you pay taxes on an accrual basis (most small businesses don't), your accountant may want to see a cash basis trial balance.

In the Columns section of the Display tab you can select the sort criterion. For the trial balance the choices are

- Default, which sorts the accounts in the usual order (assets, liabilities, and so on)
- Total, which sorts the accounts depending on the current balance (rather useless for this report)

N O T E : The report window also has a field labeled Sort By, which changes the way the items in the report are displayed. The Default choice displays your accounts in order. The other choice, Total, sorts the accounts by the account balances, so the account with the largest amount is listed first. I cannot think of any reason to sort by amount.

Setting Advanced Options

Click the Advanced button on the Display tab to see the Advanced Options window, where you have two choices for changing the criteria for displaying information, and a choice for determining the calendar basis of the report.

The two display choices (Rows and Columns) change the criteria for displaying information.

- Select Active to display only those accounts in which financial activity occurred. This includes accounts that have amounts of $0.00 as a result of financial activity.
- Select All to see all accounts, irrespective of whether they had activity or have a balance of $0.00.
- Select Non-zero to see only those accounts that had activity and have a balance other than $0.00.

TIP: Most accountants want to see zero-balance accounts, because it's a way to see all the accounts in your system and because sometimes the fact that an account has a zero balance is significant.

The Reporting Calendar option determines the calendar basis of the report. You can change the option if your company preferences are not set for a fiscal and tax year that coincide with the calendar year:

- Fiscal Year sets the reporting calendar to start at the first month of your company's fiscal year.
- Calendar Year sets the reporting calendar to start at January 1.
- Income Tax Year sets the reporting calendar to start on the first day of the first month of your company's tax year.

Click OK to return to the Modify Report window.

Filtering the Data

Click the Filters tab in the Modify Report window to filter the contents of the report (see Figure 15-3). Select a filter from the list in the Choose Filter box and decide how it should be displayed. Different categories have different filtering criteria. For instance, you can filter amounts that are less or greater than a certain amount.

CAUTION: Once you start filtering accounts and amounts, you probably will have a trial balance that no longer balances. At that point, you can't call it a trial balance; you're merely creating a list of account balances.

Changing the Header and Footer

You can customize what appears on the header and footer of your report by changing the options on the Header/Footer tab, shown in Figure 15-4.

The options you configure here have no bearing on the figures in the report; this is just the informational stuff. Most of the fields are self-explanatory, but the Date Prepared field may confuse you. That's not a date that has anything to do with you, your QuickBooks files, or your system; it's a sample format. Click the arrow to the right of the field to see other formats for displaying the date.

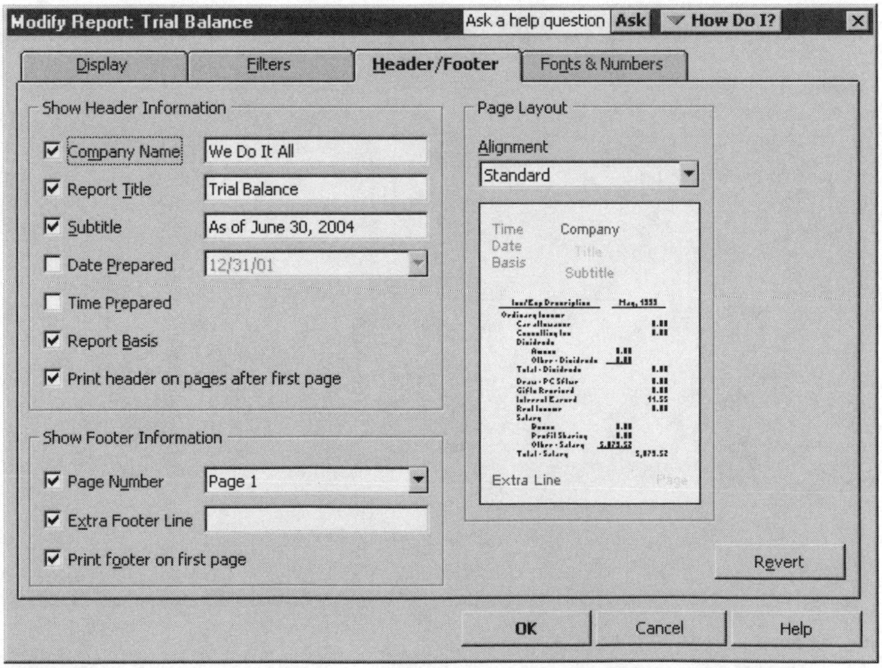

FIGURE 15-4 Change the information that isn't connected to the data you're reporting.

Changing the Fonts and Number Display

The Fonts & Numbers tab, shown in Figure 15-5, lets you change the font you use for the various elements in the report. Select any part of the report from the list on the left side of the dialog box and click Change Font. Then select a font, a style (bold, italic, etc.), a size, and special effects such as underline.

On the right side of the dialog box, you can configure the way numbers display and print on your report. Select a method for showing negative numbers. If you wish, you can also select a method for displaying all the numbers on the report:

- Divided By 1000 reduces the size of the numbers by showing them as multiples of 1000. This is useful for companies that report seven- and eight-digit numbers.
- Except Zero Amounts removes all instances of $0.00 and leaves the entry blank.
- Without Cents eliminates the decimal point and the two digits to the right of the decimal point from every amount. Only the dollars show, not the cents. QuickBooks rounds the cents to the nearest dollar.

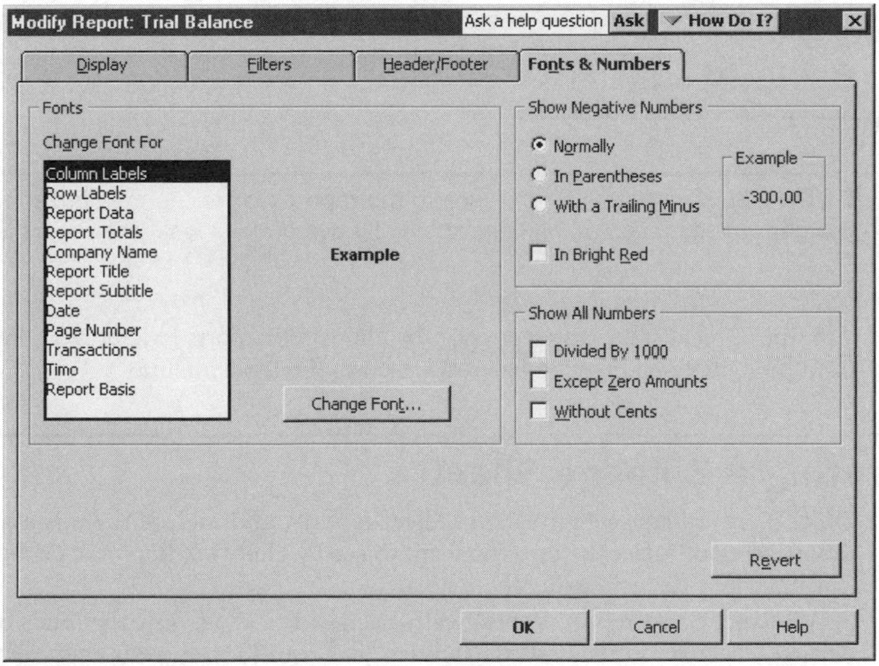

FIGURE 15-5 Change the appearance of the text and numbers.

Memorizing a Customized Trial Balance

I find that I like to glance at the trial balance report occasionally, just to see what certain totals are. Calling up the trial balance to view five or six account balances is faster than opening five or six account registers to examine the current balance. I only need to see the accounts that have a balance; I have no interest in zero-balance accounts. My accountant, on the other hand, likes to see all the accounts. He finds significance in some accounts being at zero.

TIP: Balance Sheet accounts display their current balances in the Chart of Accounts list window, so you don't have to print a report to see those numbers.

The solution to providing both of us with what we want is in memorizing each modified version of the report. After you've configured the report to display the information you want, in the manner in which you want it, click the Memorize button on the report's button bar. The Memorize Report window appears so you can give this customized format a name.

TIP: Be sure to use a reference to the report type in the memorized name. If you use a name such as My Report, you'll have no idea what the report is about.

You can recall a memorized report by choosing Reports | Memorized Reports from the QuickBooks menu bar and selecting the report name.

Generating a Balance Sheet

QuickBooks offers several Balance Sheet reports, and each of them is explained in this section. Select the one you want to see by choosing Reports | Company & Financial and then choosing the report.

A Balance Sheet report is specifically designed to show only the totals of the Balance Sheet accounts (assets, liabilities, and equity) from your chart of accounts. It's really a report on your financial health. The reason a Balance Sheet balances is that it's based on a formula:

$$\text{Assets} = \text{Liabilities} + \text{Equity}$$

Before you glance at the trial balance you just printed and prepare to write me a note saying, "Excuse me, you don't know what you're talking about; I just added those accounts up, and it doesn't balance," let me redefine one of the terms: equity.

When you generate a Balance Sheet report, the equity number is a calculated number and is arrived at with these steps:

1. All the income accounts are added up.
2. All the expense accounts are added up.
3. The expense total is subtracted from the income total.
4. The result of the calculation in Step 3 is added to the totals in existing equity accounts (which could be Opening Balance Equity, Prior Retained Earnings, Retained Earnings, and so on).
5. The total that's calculated in Step 4 becomes the figure for equity in a Balance Sheet.

If you have more expenses than you have income, you're operating at a loss; consequently, it's a negative number that is combined with the existing equity accounts. This means that the equity number that appears on your Balance Sheet could be lower than the equity number that shows on your trial balance.

Balance Sheet Standard Report

The Balance Sheet Standard reports the balance in every Balance Sheet account (unless the account has a zero balance) and subtotals each account type: asset, liability, and equity. The report is automatically configured for year-to-date figures, using your fiscal year and the current date. The fiscal year is the same as the calendar year for most small businesses.

Balance Sheet Detail

This report is similar to a detailed general ledger transaction report, showing every transaction in every Balance Sheet account. By default, the report covers a date range of the current month to date. Even if it's early in the month, this report is lengthy. If you change the date range to encompass a longer period (the quarter or year), the report goes on forever.

If you want to see a Balance Sheet only to get an idea of your company's financial health, this is probably more than you wanted to know.

Balance Sheet Summary

This report is a quick way to see totals, and it's also the easiest way to answer the question, "How am I doing?" All the account types are listed and subtotaled, as shown in Figure 15-6.

We Do It All
Summary Balance Sheet
As of June 30, 2004

Accrual Basis

	◇ Jun 30, 04 ◇
ASSETS	
Current Assets	
Checking/Savings	▶ 15,580.93 ◀
Accounts Receivable	18,470.42
Other Current Assets	3,530.70
Total Current Assets	37,582.05
Fixed Assets	6,110.00
TOTAL ASSETS	**43,692.05**
LIABILITIES & EQUITY	
Liabilities	
Current Liabilities	
Accounts Payable	157.94
Credit Cards	300.00
Other Current Liabilities	9,875.73
Total Current Liabilities	10,333.67
Total Liabilities	10,333.67

FIGURE 15-6 Do a quick checkup of your financial health with the Summary Balance Sheet report.

Balance Sheet Previous Year Comparison

The comparison Balance Sheet is designed to show you what your financial situation is compared to a year ago. There are four columns in this report:

- The year-to-date balance for each Balance Sheet account
- The year-to-date balance for each Balance Sheet account for last year
- The amount of change between last year and this year
- The percentage of change between last year and this year

If you've just started using QuickBooks this year, there's little reason to run this report. Next year, however, it'll be interesting to see how you're doing compared to this year.

Customizing and Memorizing a Balance Sheet

When your Balance Sheet is on the screen, you can use all of the customization features mentioned for the trial balance report. Then when you have the configuration you need, memorize the report by clicking the Memorize button in the report window.

Generating a Profit & Loss Statement

Your P&L report is probably the one you'll run most often. It's natural to want to know if you're making any money. A P&L report is sometimes called an *income report*. It shows all your income accounts (and displays the total), all your expense accounts (displaying the total), and then puts the difference between the two totals on the last line. If you have more income than expenses, the last line is a profit.

All of the P&L reports are available by choosing Reports | Company & Financial. The report types are explained in this section.

Profit & Loss Standard Report

The standard P&L report is a straightforward document, following the normal format for an income statement:

- The income is listed and totaled.
- The Cost of Goods Sold accounts are listed, and the total is deducted from the income total in order to show the gross profit.
- The expenses are listed and totaled.
- The difference between the gross profit and the total expenses is displayed as your Net Income (or Net Loss).

N O T E : If you don't sell inventory items, you probably don't have a Cost of Goods Sold section in your P&L.

While the format is that of a normal income statement, the end result isn't. The default date range for the QuickBooks standard P&L is the current month to date. This is not a year-to-date figure; it uses only the transactions from the current month. Click the arrow to the right of the Dates field and change the date range to This Fiscal Year-To-Date. The resulting display is what you want to see—a normal income statement for your business for this year.

Profit & Loss Detail Report

The Profit & Loss detail report is for terminally curious people. It lists every transaction for every account in the P&L format. It goes on forever.

This report is almost like an audit trail, and it's good to have if you notice some numbers that seem "not quite right" in the standard P&L. I don't recommend it as the report to run when you just need to know if you're making money.

Profit & Loss YTD Comparison Report

The YTD (year-to-date) comparison report compares the current month's income and expense totals with the year-to-date totals. Each income and expense account is listed.

Profit & Loss Previous Year Comparison Report

If you've been using QuickBooks for more than a year, this is a great report! If you recently started with QuickBooks, this will be a great report next year!

This is an income statement for the current year to date, with a column that shows last year's figure for the same period. This gives you an instant appraisal of your business growth (or ebb). So that you don't have to tax your brain doing the math, there are two additional columns: the difference between the years in dollars and the difference in percentage.

Profit & Loss by Job Report

This report presents a year-to-date summary of income and expenses posted to customers and jobs. In effect, it's a customer P&L. Each customer gets its own column, and the bottom row of each column is the net income (or loss) for this customer.

Profit & Loss by Class Report

If you've enabled class tracking, this report appears on the Reports menu. Each class is subtotaled for its own P&L. If you use classes for branch offices, or company divisions, this is the way to get a separate P&L for each.

You should also run the Profit & Loss Unclassified report, which displays a P&L generated from transactions that had no class assignment. Even if you think you don't care about assigning classes to these transactions, you should examine the report and drill down (double-click the listing) to view the individual transactions. If any transaction should have been assigned a class, you can add the class and click Yes when QuickBooks asks if you want to save the changes you made to the transaction.

Customizing and Memorizing P&L Reports

Use the QuickBooks Customize features discussed earlier in this chapter to tailor P&L reports so they print exactly the way you want to see the information. You might want to customize several formats: for you, for your accountant, and perhaps for your bank (if you have a loan or line of credit, or are applying for either, your bank also wants to see a Balance Sheet). Then memorize the perfect custom reports you design.

Creating an Accountant's Review

Many accountants support QuickBooks directly, which means they understand the software and know how to use it. In fact, they have a copy of QuickBooks on their own computer system.

At various times during the year, your accountant might want to look at your books. There might be quarterly reports and adjustments, a physical inventory that resulted in serious changes in your Balance Sheet, expenses that should be posted to different accounts, or any of a hundred other reasons. Almost definitely this will occur at the end-of-year process you have to go through in order to close your books for the year.

This could result in your accountant showing up and sitting in front of your computer, making the necessary changes (almost always journal entries), moving this, reversing that, and generally making sense out of your daily transaction postings. By "making sense," I mean putting transaction postings into categories that fit your tax reporting needs.

While your accountant is using the software, you can't get much accomplished. You could say, "Excuse me, could you move? I have to enter an invoice." But remember, you're paying for the accountant's time.

If your accountant doesn't want to visit, he or she may request printouts of various reports, then write notes on those printouts: "Move this, split that, credit this number here, debit that number there." Or you can receive a spreadsheet-like printout with an enormously long and complicated journal entry, which means you have to stop entering your day-to-day transactions to make all those changes.

QuickBooks has a better idea. Give your accountant a disk with a copy of your QuickBooks records. Let your accountant do the work back at his or her office. When the disk comes back to you, the necessary changes have been placed on the disk. QuickBooks merges the changes into your copy of the software. It's magic!

> **NOTE:** To work with your QuickBooks 2004 files, your accountant must have QuickBooks 2004 installed.

Creating an Accountant's Review Copy

You can create the accountant's review copy on a floppy disk, or save it to a file and send it to your accountant via e-mail:

1. Choose File | Accountant's Review | Create Accountant's Copy from the QuickBooks menu bar. You may see a message indicating you must be in single-user mode to do this, and you may see a message that all open QuickBooks windows will be closed, depending on your QuickBooks environment. Then the Save Accountant's Copy To dialog box appears so you can save the information for your accountant.

2. The location to which QuickBooks saves the file is the same location to which you last saved a backup. If necessary, change the location to match the media

you want to use for this file. For example, use your floppy drive if you plan to send a floppy disk to your accountant, or save it to your hard drive if you're going to transmit the file via e-mail.

3. The filename must have an extension of .qbx. You can change the name of the file if you want to, but generally it's a good idea to keep the filename QuickBooks suggests (which is based on your company name).

4. Click Save to create the accountant's copy.

QuickBooks notifies you when the process is complete. If the file won't fit on a floppy disk, you'll be asked to insert a second floppy disk to complete the process. If you've password-protected your QuickBooks data file, you must tell your accountant what the admin password is. Otherwise, your accountant won't be able to open the file.

Working During the Accountant's Review

Because parts of your QuickBooks data have been locked, it's important to know what you can and cannot accomplish until you receive data back from your accountant. Your accountant also has restrictions. Table 15-1 describes what you (the client) can and can't do while your files are locked, and Table 15-2 describes what an accountant can and cannot do with the accountant's copy file.

To remind you that an accountant's copy was created, the title bar of your QuickBooks software changes to include that fact.

CLIENTS CAN	CLIENTS CANNOT
Create transactions	Delete an entry in a list
Edit transactions	Rename an item in a list
Delete transactions	Change an account to a subaccount
Add new items to lists	Change a subaccount to an account
Edit items in lists	

TABLE 15-1   What You Can and Cannot Do During Review

ACCOUNTANTS CAN	ACCOUNTANTS CANNOT
Create journal entries	Delete list entries
Edit account names	Make list entries inactive
Change account numbers (if you use numbers for your chart of accounts)	Create transactions (except journal entries)
Edit tax information for accounts	
Adjust inventory quantities and values	
Print 1099 forms	
Print 941 forms	
Print 940 forms	
Print W-2 forms	

TABLE 15-2   What Your Accountant Can and Cannot Do With A ReviewCopy

Unlocking Your Files Without Receiving a Review

If you make an accountant's review copy in error, or if your accountant tells you there are no changes to be made, you can unlock your files. This puts everything back as if you'd never created an accountant's review copy. To accomplish this, choose File | Accountant's Review | Cancel Accountant's Changes. QuickBooks asks you to confirm your decision.

Merging the Accountant's Changes

When your accountant returns your files to you, the changes have to be imported into your QuickBooks files, as follows:

1. Place the floppy disk you received from your accountant into the floppy drive. If you received the file via e-mail, note the folder and filename you used to store it on your hard drive.
2. Choose File | Accountant's Review | Import Accountant's Changes.
3. QuickBooks closes all open QuickBooks window and insists on a backup of your current file before importing. Click OK and proceed with the backup.
4. When the backup is complete, QuickBooks automatically opens the Import Changes From Accountant's Copy window. Make sure the Look In field at the top of the window matches the location of the accountant's review file.
5. Choose the import file, which has an extension of .aif, and click Open (or double-click the .aif file).

Your QuickBooks data now contains the changes your accountant made, and you can work with your files normally.

> **TIP:** Make sure your accountant sends you a note or calls to tell you about the changes. QuickBooks does not indicate what has changed after the import, and you should know what specific alterations were made to your financial records.

Cash Flow Reports

QuickBooks offers two cash flow reports in the Company & Financial Reports menu: Statement of Cash Flows, and Cash Flow Forecast. Essentially, the difference between them is that the Statement of Cash Flows looks back, and the Cash Flow Forecast looks ahead. Both of these reports can be useful for analyzing the current state (health) of your business.

Cash flow reports are complicated documents and are accurate to the degree that the accounts included in the reports contain transaction figures that should actually be included. Your accountant can look at the activity in any account to determine whether it's appropriate to include or exclude that account's activities in the calculation of cash flow reports.

> **NOTE:** It's beyond the scope of this book to provide detailed instructions about verifying and modifying cash flow reports, because that's a complicated accounting subject.

Statement of Cash Flows

The Statement of Cash Flows report displays information about your cash position over a period of time (by default, year-to-date). You can see where your cash came from and where it went, categorized as follows:

- **Operating Activities** The transactions involved with maintaining the business
- **Investing Activities** The transactions involved with the acquisition of fixed assets
- **Financing Activities** The transactions involved with long-term liabilities and owners' activities (such as investments and draws)

Accounts Used for the Statement of Cash Flows

QuickBooks predetermines the accounts used in the Statement of Cash Flows report, and you can view the account list by choosing Edit | Preferences and selecting the Reports & Graphs icon in the left pane. On the Company Preferences tab, click Classify Cash to open the Classify Cash dialog box seen in Figure 15-7.

You can add and remove accountants and move selected accounts to a different category, but that's dangerous unless your accountant recommends such a step. By and large, the default settings that QuickBooks established work quite well. If your accountant knows you're using an account that's not selected for transactions that should be included in the report, or vice-versa, it's okay to make changes.

 CAUTION: Make sure your accountant knows that Balance Sheet accounts cannot be removed from the list, although they can be moved to a different category.

Creating a Statement of Cash Flows

To create the Statement of Cash Flows report, choose Reports | Company & Financial | Statement of Cash Flows. The report opens, showing your cash flow from the first day of your fiscal year to the current date, as seen in Figure 15-8.

| Classify Cash | Ask a help question | Ask | How Do I? | ✕ |

Assign accounts to a section of the Statement of Cash Flows:
* You can move a balance sheet account but you cannot remove it.
* You can add or remove an income or expense account but make sure that the account only tracks non-cash transactions.

Account Name	Operating	Investing	Financing
1200 · Accounts Receivable	✓		
1120 · Inventory Asset	✓		
1510 · Employee Advances	✓		
1600 · Equipment Assets		✓	
1601 · Equipment		✓	
1602 · AccumDepr-Equipment		✓	
1620 · Furn & Fixture Assets		✓	
1621 · Furn & Fixtures		✓	
1622 · AccumDepre-Furn & Fixtures		✓	
1640 · Vehicle Assets		✓	
1641 · Vehicles		✓	
1642 · AccumDepr-Vehicles		✓	

| OK | Cancel | Help | Default |

FIGURE 15-7 Look, but don't touch—unless your accountant instructs you to make changes.

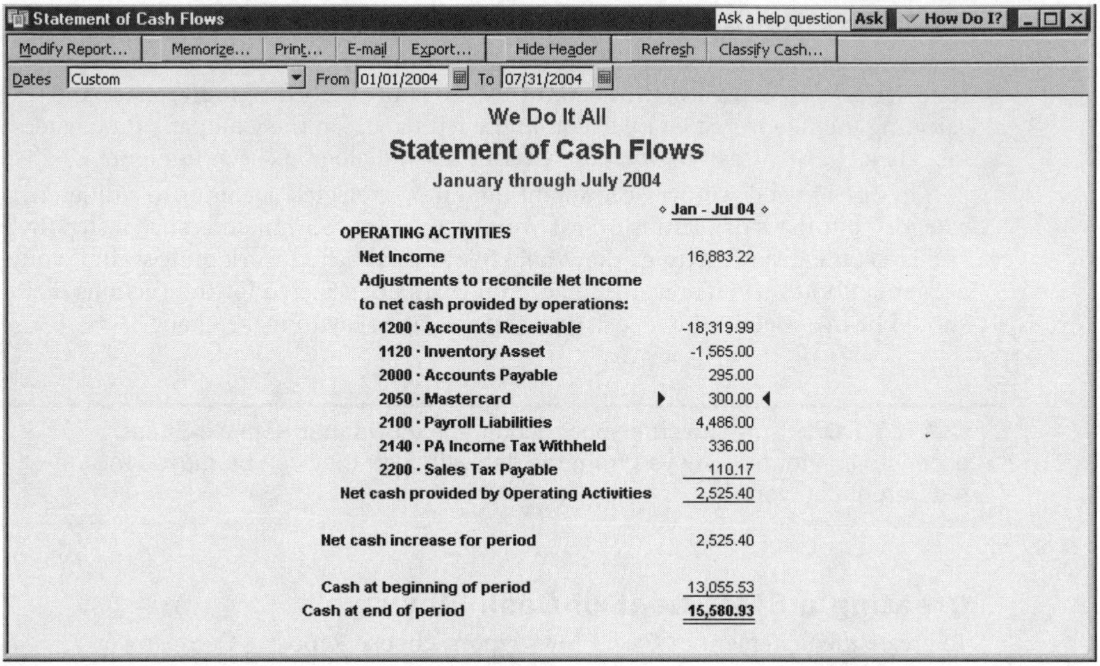

FIGURE 15-8 This report shows how your cash position changed during the interval specified in the Dates fields.

If you want to see how your cash flow changed during another interval (perhaps this month, this quarter, or during a previous month or quarter), change the date range.

This report is generated on an accrual basis, and unlike most QuickBooks reports, you can't specify accrual or cash-based calculations. Because cash flow is a cash-based figure, QuickBooks adjusts amounts to turn this accrual-based report into a cash-based report. The bottom line is cash-based, but instead of just displaying cash-based figures, QuickBooks takes an accrual-based report and shows you the adjustments that had to be made. Of course, if you have no accrual-based totals (you don't owe money, nobody owes you money), you won't see any adjustments.

Cash Flow Forecast

The Cash Flow Forecast reports does what its name implies—forecasts your cash flow as of a given future date (by default, four weeks hence). The forecast includes cash in, cash out, and the consequent cash (bank) balances.

To create the report, choose Reports | Company & Financial | Cash Flow Forecast. The report window opens with estimated cash flow figures for the next four weeks, as seen in Figure 15-9.

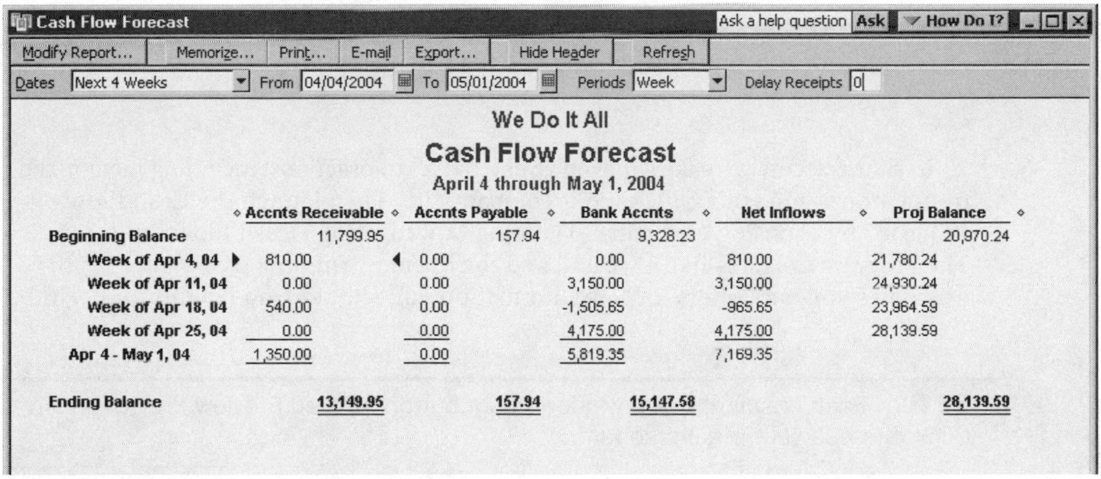

We Do It All

Cash Flow Forecast

April 4 through May 1, 2004

	Accnts Receivable	Accnts Payable	Bank Accnts	Net Inflows	Proj Balance
Beginning Balance	11,799.95	157.94	9,328.23		20,970.24
Week of Apr 4, 04	810.00	0.00	0.00	810.00	21,780.24
Week of Apr 11, 04	0.00	0.00	3,150.00	3,150.00	24,930.24
Week of Apr 18, 04	540.00	0.00	-1,505.65	-965.65	23,964.59
Week of Apr 25, 04	0.00	0.00	4,175.00	4,175.00	28,139.59
Apr 4 - May 1, 04	1,350.00	0.00	5,819.35	7,169.35	
Ending Balance	13,149.95	157.94	15,147.58		28,139.59

FIGURE 15-9 This report predicts what's coming in and going out in the near future.

Remember that this forecast is made with the assumption that all A/R will arrive when due, and all A/P will be paid when due. That may or may not be a realistic assumption for your business. To enhance the reality of the report, you can use the Delay Receipts field to tell QuickBooks to assume that your customers will pay late by the amount of days you specify in that field. This is useful if you know that by and large there's a pattern indicating your customers are late by an average of *x* number of days.

To view a forecast for a different date range, select a different interval from the drop-down list in the Dates field, or enter specific From and To dates.

Cash Flow Projector

New in QuickBooks 2004, the Cash Flow Projector is a tool you can use to build a report that projects your cash flows using your own criteria. Like the cash flow reports available in QuickBooks, this tool uses data in your company file, but you can remove and add accounts and adjust figures, which lets you achieve the projection parameters and results you need.

The Cash Flow Projector is rather powerful if you understand the accounting terminology and principles of determining cash flows. You can design very specific cash flows scenarios, which might be useful in planning for expansion or other major business events.

It's beyond the scope of this book to provide a detailed explanation of the best ways to use this tool, but in this section I'll give you an overview.

NOTE: Unless you have quite a bit of expertise in accounting, it's best to work with your accountant when you use the Cash Flow Projector.

To assure accuracy, make sure you've entered all transactions, including memorized transactions, into your QuickBooks company file. Then launch the Cash Flow Projector by choosing Company | Planning & Budgeting | Cash Flow Projector. The program operates like a wizard, and the opening window (see Figure 15-10) welcomes you, and offers links to information you should read before you begin.

TIP: Each ensuing wizard window has a button labeled Preview Projection. Click it to see your results so far.

Click Next to display the Beginning Balance window (see Figure 15-11), and select the cash accounts you want to include in your projection.

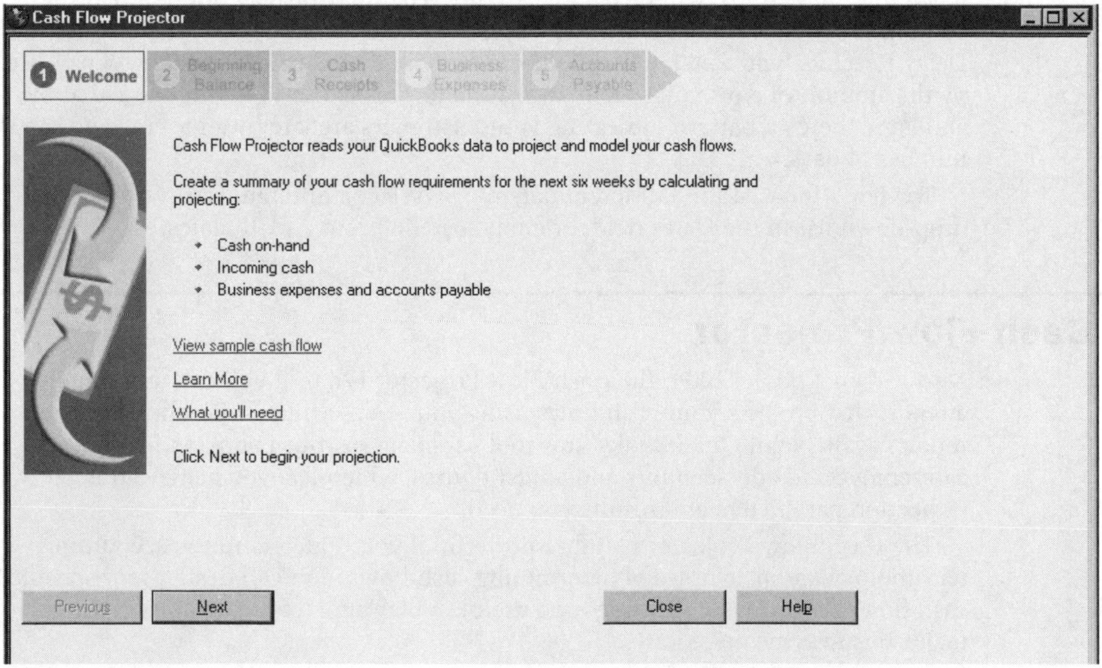

Cash Flow Projector

1 Welcome 2 Beginning Balance 3 Cash Receipts 4 Business Expenses 5 Accounts Payable

Cash Flow Projector reads your QuickBooks data to project and model your cash flows.

Create a summary of your cash flow requirements for the next six weeks by calculating and projecting:

* Cash on-hand
* Incoming cash
* Business expenses and accounts payable

View sample cash flow

Learn More

What you'll need

Click Next to begin your projection.

Previous   Next   Close   Help

FIGURE 15-10   Start by familiarizing yourself with the information the wizard will need.

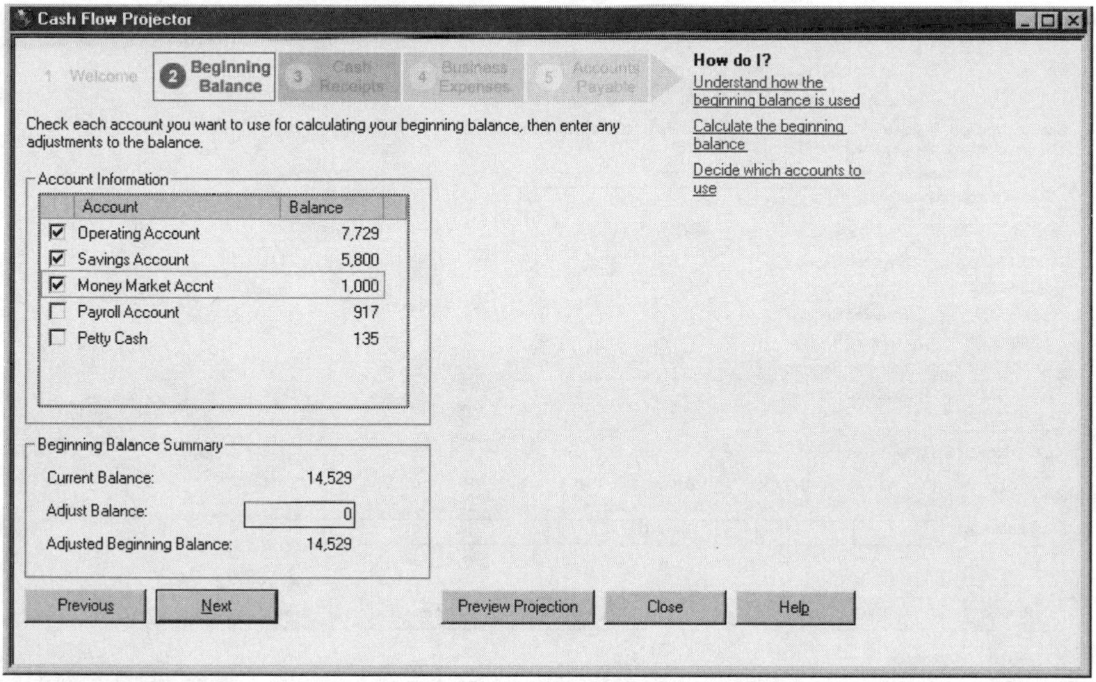

FIGURE 15-11 Select the accounts you want to use for your cash flow projection.

The software calculates a beginning balance by adding together the balances of all the accounts you select. You can make an adjustment to that calculated balance to change the beginning balance of the cash flows projection. This is useful if you know the current balance of any account contains an amount that you don't want included in the projection, such as an income item that is earmarked for spending tomorrow.

Click Next to move to the Cash Receipts window (see Figure 15-12). You must select a projection method from the drop-down list. If you don't understand the terminology in the list, discuss it with your accountant. One of the choices is manual entry, which is useful if your accountant has some particular paradigm in mind, or if you don't have A/R totals to guide you because you run a retail business.

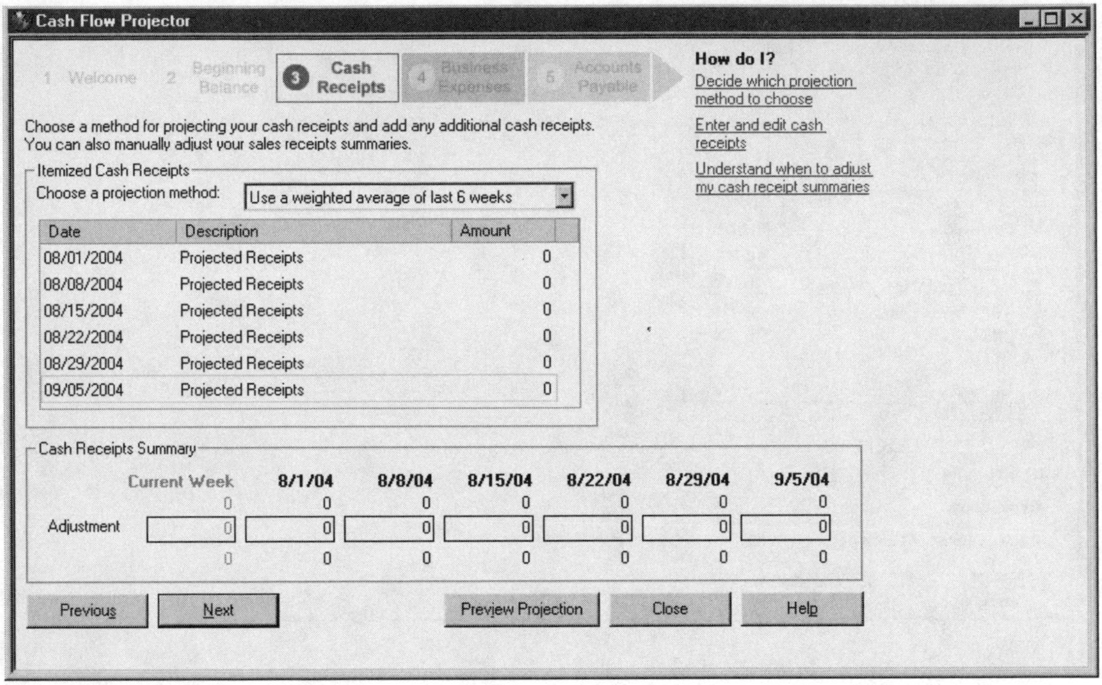

FIGURE 15-12   Summarize your projected cash receipts on a week-by-week basis.

The next two wizard windows look similar to Figure 15-12, but they deal with expenses, starting with expenses that are not accounts-payable expenses (such as unique expenses that qualify as "one-time-only"), and moving on to accounts payable expenses (including recurring bills you've entered into your system). In both windows you can enter specific expenses or enter adjusted total expenses.

This brief discussion should help you understand the possibilities in this tool. If you have a need for a variety of cash flows scenarios, you should go over this tool and its application to your business needs with your accountant.

Using Online
Banking Services

In this chapter:

- Understand online banking

- Set up a connection to QuickBooks on the Web

- Set up online bank accounts

- Perform online transactions

- Receive online payments from your customers

If you have an Internet connection, you can use the wide range of online services offered by QuickBooks. Internet-based banking chores are the subjects covered in this chapter. You'll discover that QuickBooks and its parent company, Intuit, have taken advantage of the Internet to make banking a snap.

You can sign up for online banking, which means you can view the status of your bank accounts, see which transactions have cleared, and generally maintain your accounts via your Internet connection.

You can also sign up for online payments, which means you send money to vendors via the Internet instead of writing checks. The money is deposited directly into your vendor's bank account, or a check for the vendor is automatically generated and mailed (depending on whether the vendor accepts electronic deposits).

Online banking also includes credit card accounts, so you can see credit card transactions and enter them in your credit card account register. To take advantage of online credit card tracking, you must set up your credit cards as liability accounts, which is discussed in Chapter 11.

Understanding Online Banking

Online banking is nothing more than using the Internet to access information about your accounts from your bank's computer. The bank's computer is a server, configured for secure exchange of data, that provides information about your accounts. QuickBooks provides two methods for using the online banking services your bank offers:

- **WebConnect** This is the method you use when your bank doesn't provide a way to connect your QuickBooks data directly to the data on the bank's server. Actually, this means your bank chose not to install the software required to work interactively with QuickBooks. Instead, the bank maintains a web page on its website that lets you view and download your bank statement.

- **Direct Connection** In which your bank exchanges data interactively with QuickBooks. This allows you to take advantage of all types of online banking services (transaction data downloads, transfers between bank accounts, e-mail messages between you and the bank, and online bill payments). Of course, those features are limited to the online services provided by your bank.

Instructions for using the WebConnect and Direct Connection features appear later in this chapter, in the section "Exchanging Data Online."

Setting Up a Connection

Before you can use the QuickBooks online services, you have to let the software know how you get online. After this simple, initial step, QuickBooks does its online work on autopilot.

The first step is to let QuickBooks know how you reach the Internet. Choose Help | Internet Connection Setup from the menu bar. This launches the Internet Connection Setup Wizard (see Figure 16-1).

The choices on the first wizard window cover all the possibilities. One of them fits your situation, and in this section I'll explain how QuickBooks handles the setup for each type of connection.

NOTE: No matter which selection you choose, when you click Next, the last window wizard appears (it's a small, efficient wizard). Click Done when you've read the information in the second window.

Dial-up Connections

The option Use The Following Connection refers to a dial-up connection, using a modem. This connection could be through an ISP (Internet service provider), which you reach using the dial-up capabilities built into your operating system (Dial-Up Networking). Or you may have a connection through a proprietary

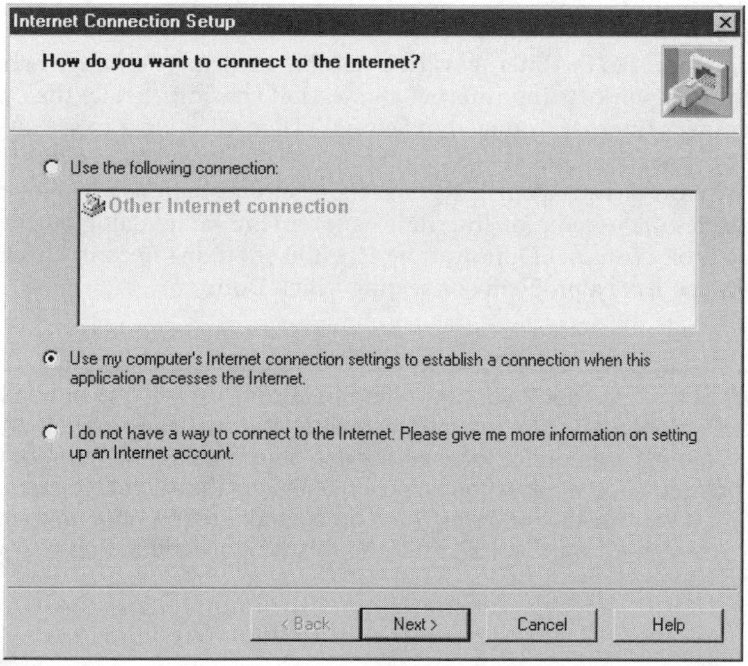

Internet Connection Setup

How do you want to connect to the Internet?

○ Use the following connection:

　　Other Internet connection

◉ Use my computer's Internet connection settings to establish a connection when this application accesses the Internet.

○ I do not have a way to connect to the Internet. Please give me more information on setting up an Internet account.

| < Back | Next > | Cancel | Help |

FIGURE 16-1 You have to tell QuickBooks how to get to the Internet on this computer.

software program that connects you to a particular host such as America Online. These proprietary programs first connect you to their host computer, where there are preconfigured sections of information. Then the systems permit you to wander off on your own on the Internet.

Any dial-up connections you've configured appear in the Internet Connection Setup window. If no connection appears and you know you've configured a dial-up connection to your ISP, QuickBooks had a problem finding it or identifying it. Close the window (but don't shut down QuickBooks), open your dial-up connection, and connect to the Internet. Then open this window again, and QuickBooks should find it.

Select (highlight) the connection. Then click Next, and click Done on the next window. You're all set. Any time you need to travel to the Internet while you're working in QuickBooks, QuickBooks will open the connection (unless you're already connected to the Internet) and take you to the right site.

 CAUTION: If QuickBooks doesn't detect your connection, and you had to connect to the Internet before configuring this wizard, you'll probably have to connect manually every time you want to use Internet services in QuickBooks.

Network or Always-on Connections

If you connect to the Internet via a DSL/cable modem, or through another computer on your network (using Internet connection sharing), select the option Use My Computer's Internet Connection Settings. Then click Next to see an explanation of the connection QuickBooks found, which is referred to as a direct connection. The window has an Advanced Connection Settings button, which opens the Internet Properties dialog box for Internet Explorer (the same dialog box you see if you select Tools | Internet Options from IE). You shouldn't need to check these settings unless you have a problem connecting. Click Done.

 NOTE: If you don't yet have Internet access, select the option I Do Not Have A Way To Connect To The Internet, and click Next, where you'll see an explanation that you must sign up for Internet service before using the Internet Connection Setup Wizard. The window has an option to launch the Microsoft Internet Connection Wizard, which walks you through the process of setting up a new connection. After you sign up with an ISP, return to this window and set up your QuickBooks online connection.

Setting Up Online Accounts

You have to establish online access for your accounts, both with your bank and with QuickBooks. Your bank must support QuickBooks online access procedures. There are three online banking services available:

- Online account access
- Online bill paying
- Online credit card services

You can sign up for any or all of these services. If your bank only supports online account access and doesn't support online bill paying or online credit card services, you can work directly with QuickBooks online banking sites. See "Using the QuickBooks Online Payment Service," and "Using a QuickBooks Credit Card," later in this chapter.

The process of enabling online banking has three steps:

1. Apply for online services with your bank.
2. Receive a personal identification number (PIN) from your bank to make sure your online account is secure.
3. Enable a QuickBooks account (or multiple accounts) for online services.

Finding Your Bank Online

You may already have learned about your bank's online services—many banks enclose information about this feature in the monthly statements or have brochures available when you visit the bank.

 N O T E : If you've already applied for online services, you can skip this part and move to the section "Enabling Your Online Bank Accounts."

Before you run to the neighborhood bank branch to sign up, you can go online to find out what tasks your bank wants you to complete. In fact, you may be able to sign up online. Choose Banking | Set Up Online Financial Services from the menu bar. The submenu has two commands:

- Setup Account For Online Access
- Online List Of Available Financial Institutions

The Setup Account For Online Access command is a wizard that walks you through either of the following functions (depending on your selections in the wizard windows):

- It searches for your bank on the Internet so you can apply online (if your bank supports online setup) or get information about applying by telephone or in person. These functions duplicate the functions you perform by choosing Online Financial Institutions List.
- It walks you through the process of enabling your bank account after you've completed the paperwork at your bank and received a PIN. These functions are discussed in the section "Enabling Your Online Bank Accounts."

If you haven't signed up for (or discussed) online services with your bank, choose Online List Of Available Financial Institutions to see if your bank participates. QuickBooks opens the Financial Institutions Directory website (see Figure 16-2).

The four choices at the top of the left pane determine the contents of the Financial Institutions Directory list. The window opens with the choice Any Services preselected, and all the banks listed provide some type of online service.

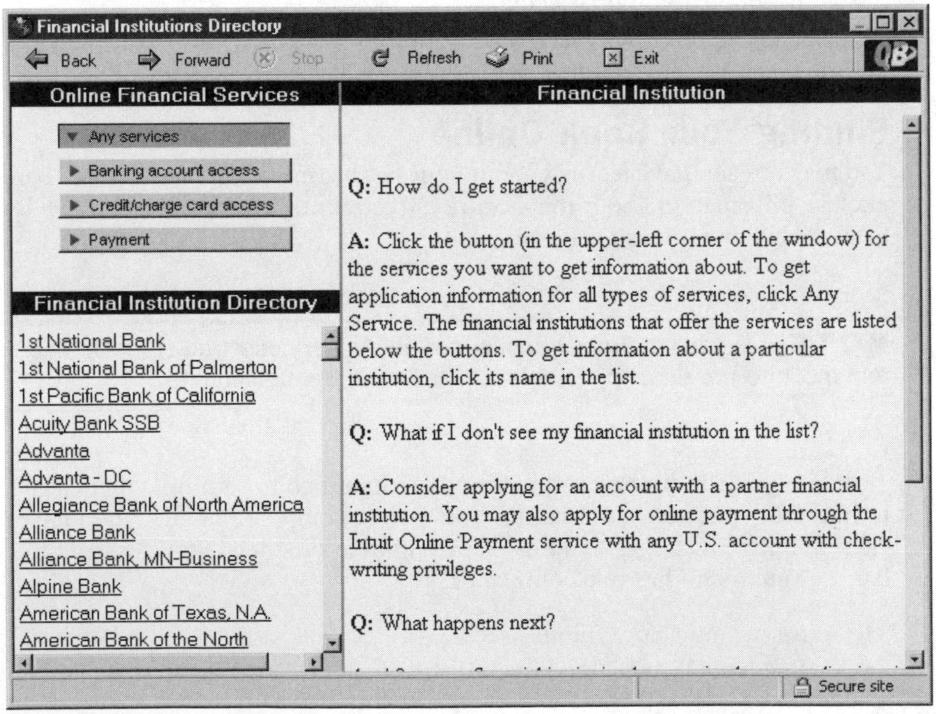

FIGURE 16-2 Select the type of online service you want, and then scroll through the list to see if your bank participates.

If you're interested in a particular online service (for example, you only care about online access), select that option, and the list of banks changes to those banks that offer the selected service.

Scroll through the list to find your bank and click its listing. The right pane of the Financial Institutions Directory window displays information about the bank's online services (see Figure 16-3) and a telephone number for more information or to apply for online services. You may also see an Apply Now button (or one similarly named).

Click the Apply Now button if you want to start the application process here and now. If no Apply Now button exists, follow the instructions for setting up online services at the bank—usually the bank displays a phone number. If online applications are available, fill out the form and submit the information. Your bank will send you information about using its online service, along with a PIN that's been assigned. All banks provide a method of changing the PIN to one of your own choosing. In fact, many banks insist that you change the PIN the first time you access online services.

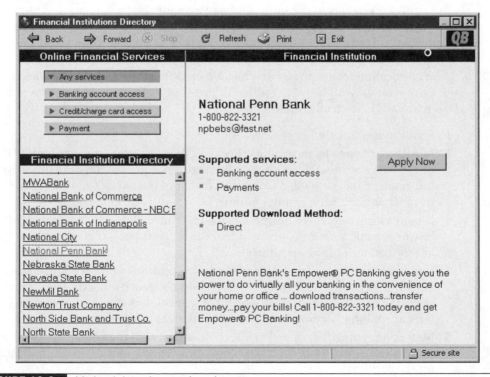

FIGURE 16-3   My bank has the services I want.

CAUTION: You may see a warning that you are about to send information to an Internet zone in which it might be possible for other people to see the data you send. Select Yes to continue (you might want to select the option not to be warned in the future). If this makes you nervous, forget online banking, because there's no guaranteed security on the Internet—even though Intuit and your bank both make every possible effort to keep data secure.

Using the QuickBooks Online Payment Service

If your bank doesn't participate in online services, and if your prime motivation for banking online is paying your bills via the Internet, you can sign up for online payments directly with QuickBooks.

When the Financial Institutions list is displayed in your browser window, scroll through the list to find and look for QuickBooks BillPay Service in the left pane. You'll see two listings—QuickBooks BilllPay—New!, and QuickBooks BillPay(TM). Choose QuickBooks BillPay—New! (the other listing is for existing customers of the service, which didn't provide online signup).

QuickBooks travels to the Intuit Online Payment Service site on the Internet. Read the information, and if you're interested, click Apply Now. Answer a couple of questions about your business (see Figure 16-4), and then click the Continue button at the bottom of the window.

An application form appears on your screen. Fill out the information and click the Print icon on your browser toolbar to print it (or print the blank form and fill it in manually). Then take these steps:

1. Sign the application.
2. Mark one of your bank account checks VOID (just write the word "VOID" in the payee section of the check). Be careful not to obliterate the important information that's encoded along the bottom of the check (your account number and the bank routing number).
3. If your check only has a business name imprinted (which is true for most business bank accounts), obtain a letter from your bank that says you're an authorized user of the account(s).
4. If you are signing up for online payment for multiple bank accounts, send a voided check for each account. QuickBooks collects its fees directly from your checking account, so indicate which bank account is the billing account by writing "Billing Account" on the back of the appropriate check.
5. Mail your completed, signed application, along with the voided check(s) and the authorization letter from your bank (if needed), to the address indicated on the application.

In a couple of weeks, you'll receive all the information you need to begin paying your bills online.

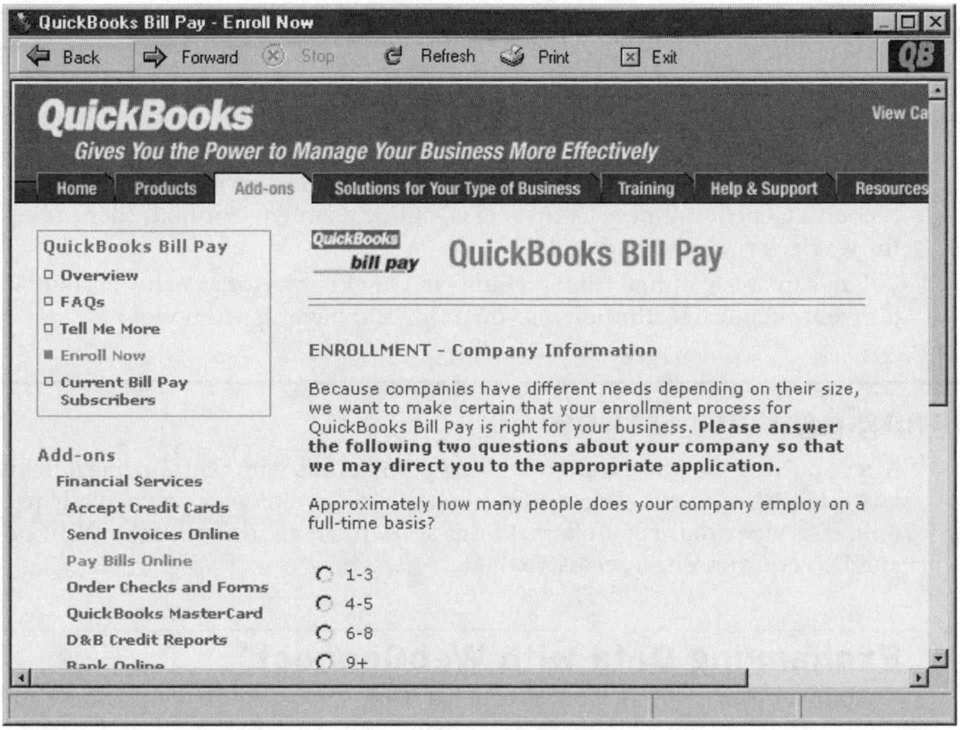

FIGURE 16-4 If your bank doesn't let you pay bills online via QuickBooks, QuickBooks will provide the service.

Using a QuickBooks Credit Card

If your credit card issuer doesn't support online access and that feature is important to you, you can sign up for a QuickBooks credit card. QuickBooks issues MasterCards (serviced by Citibank). In the Financial Institutions list, select QuickBooks Credit Card. Follow the instructions for signing up.

Enabling Your Online Bank Accounts

After you've signed up with your bank and have your secret PIN, you must configure your QuickBooks bank account(s) for online services.

NOTE: Some banks use passwords instead of PINs.

Choose Banking | Set Up Online Financial Services | Setup Account for Online Access. The Online Banking Setup Interview Wizard appears, and this time you should click the Enable Accounts tab. Follow the instructions and answer the questions as you proceed through the wizard. (Click Next to keep moving along.)

As you go through the steps in the wizard, you're configuring a bank account as an online account. You'll be asked to select the online services you'll use with this account. Choose online account access, online payments, or both (depending on the services you've signed up for).

You can create online bank accounts in QuickBooks for as many accounts and different financial institutions as you need (and have signed up for).

Exchanging Data Online

After you've set up your online banking permissions with your financial institutions and established your online bank account(s) in QuickBooks, you're ready use the online services your bank offers. In this section, I'll go over both the WebConnect and Direct Connection access methods.

Exchanging Data with WebConnect

To connect to your WebConnect-enabled bank, choose Banking | Online Banking Center. In the Online Banking Center dialog box, seen in Figure 16-5, select your bank from the Financial Institution drop-down list at the top of the dialog box. (The drop-down list only offers multiple entries if you've configured more than one bank for online access or credit card transaction access). Click Go Online.

When QuickBooks opens the bank's web page, log in and view your bank statements. You can either print the statement from your browser and then enter transactions manually, or download a file that you can import into QuickBooks. When you click the Download File button on the website, the standard Windows Download dialog box appears. Choose Save and select a location for the file (most people use the folder that holds their QuickBooks files).

Make sure you download the right file type; the download button should say QuickBooks. Many banks that provide download files offer selection buttons representing file types for Quicken, QuickBooks, and CSV (or other delimited formats). While it's possible to modify a CSV file so it will import transactions into QuickBooks, it's far from a cakewalk, and although I almost never recommend "key the data in manually." this is one scenario that elicits that response from me.

To import a downloaded QuickBooks transaction file, follow these steps:

1. Choose File | Import | Web Connect Files from the QuickBooks menu bar.
2. In the Open Online Data File dialog box, select the file you downloaded (the file extension is .qbo), and click Open.

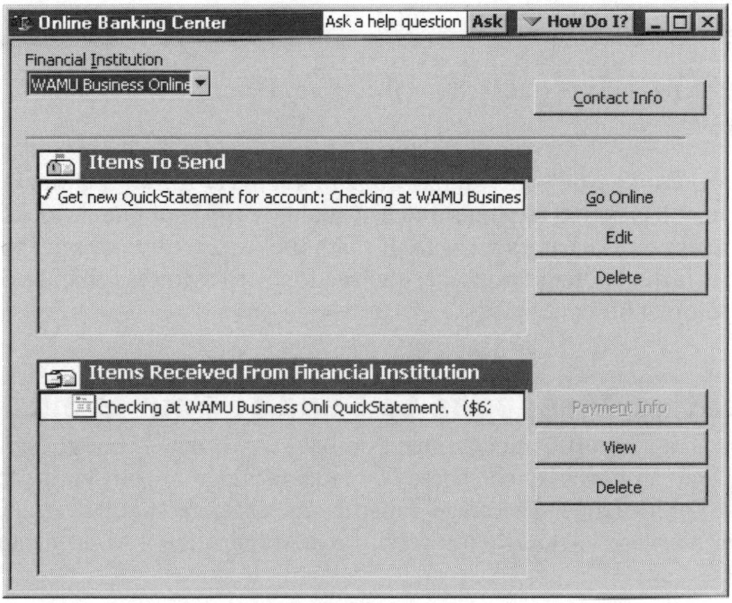

FIGURE 16-5   Online access starts in the Online Banking Center.

3. The Select Bank Account dialog box opens, offering you two options: use an existing online account or create a new one.

NOTE: The list of existing accounts includes only those accounts you configured for online access

4. Click Continue to begin the import process.

When the file is imported, QuickBooks issues a message to inform you of that fact. Click OK.

Exchanging Data with Direct Connection

If your bank supports the Direct Connection method of online banking, you can perform the following tasks online, although you're limited to functions your bank offers:

- Send a message (essentially an e-mail message) to your bank.
- Receive messages from your bank.

- Send data to the bank regarding the transfer of funds between accounts at that bank.
- Receive a list of transactions that have cleared your account.
- Pay bills.

Some banks won't let you pay bills interactively through QuickBooks, although they may have a bill paying service available outside of QuickBooks, which you can access on the bank's website. If that's the case, and you prefer to pay your bills online through QuickBooks, see the section earlier in this chapter on using the QuickBooks BillPay Service.

Creating Messages to Send to Your Bank

Banks that support Direct Connection have a two-way message feature; you can both send and receive messages. To send a message to your bank, choose Banking | Create Online Banking Message. Enter the message text in the Online Banking Message dialog box, and click OK. You send the message when you connect to your bank (covered next).

Connecting to Your Bank

To connect to your bank, choose Banking | Online Banking Center to open the Online Banking Center dialog box.

If you have online banking at more than one bank, select the appropriate bank from the drop-down list in the Financial Institution field at the top of the dialog box. For example, you may have online bank account access at one bank and online credit card access at another bank. The dialog box has two sections:

- Items To Send, which always includes a request for a QuickStatement and may include a message to your bank if you created one.
- Items Received From Financial Institution, which includes the latest QuickStatement from your bank, along with any messages from your bank. If the listing for the QuickStatement has a check mark, you haven't yet viewed it.

Details about these functions are covered in the following sections.

Sending Data to Your Bank

The Items To Send section of the Online Banking Center dialog box contains the data you send to your bank. A request for a QuickStatement is always on the list, and if you created any message to send to the bank, they're listed too. (A QuickStatement is a list of transactions that have cleared the account since the last time you received a QuickStatement.)

By default, all items have a check mark, which means they'll be sent to the bank when you click the Send button.

- If you don't want to send an item, click its check mark to remove it (it's a toggle). You can click again to put the check mark back when you're ready to send the item.
- You can edit any item except a request for a QuickStatement. Select the item, click the Edit button, make the necessary changes, and click OK.
- You can remove any item except the request for a QuickStatement. Select the item and click the Delete button.

Click the Send button to contact your bank over the Internet. A dialog box opens to accept your PIN or password (depending on the way your bank manages security).

> **NOTE:** If you want to change your PIN during this interactive session, click Change PIN and enter your new PIN.

Click OK to begin communications. You'll see progress messages as QuickBooks contacts the bank's server, sends any messages you created, and delivers the request for a QuickStatement.

If your bank account has not cleared any new transactions since the last time you received a QuickStatement, a dialog box reports that fact and encourages you to try again tomorrow. If new transactions have cleared, the Online Transmission Summary dialog box displays a report.

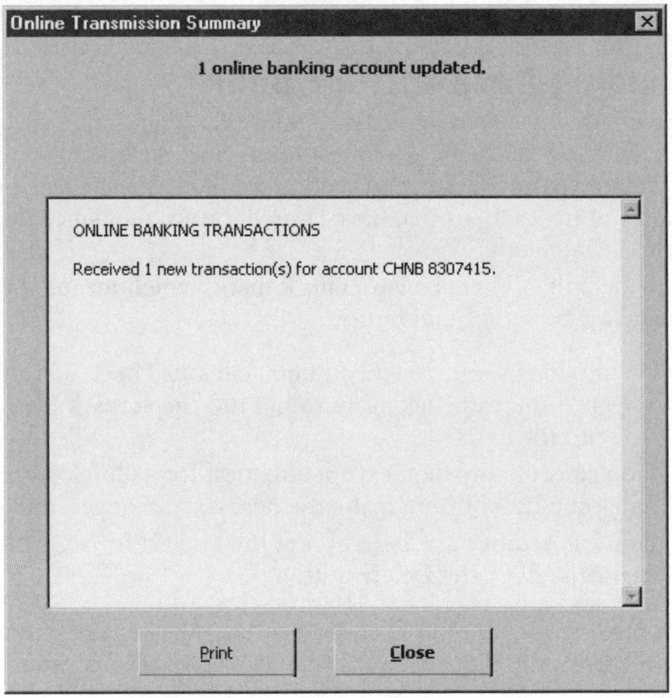

Click Print if you want to print the new transactions (I can't think of any reason to do so), and click Close to return to the Online Banking Center dialog box.

Viewing the Received Data

The Online Banking Center dialog box displays all the items received from your bank during the online session in the Items Received section. The list includes a QuickReport for each online account at that bank (the current online balance is displayed next to the bank's listing), and any e-mail messages from the bank. Select an item and click View to see it. Read any e-mail messages and delete those you don't care to save (although it would be unusual to want to save any, since most of the time the messages contain information about upcoming bank holiday closings or announcements about new mortgage or CD rates).

To see the new transactions in your account, select the QuickReport and click View. QuickBooks opens the Matched Transactions dialog box, which displays the account register at the top and the list of new transactions at the bottom. (If the account register isn't in the dialog box, select the Show Register option.)

Matching Transactions

QuickBooks automatically tries to match the transactions in the QuickStatement to the transactions in your register and marks each QuickStatement transaction with one of the following conditions:

- **Matched**   Means the downloaded transaction matches a transaction in the register.
- **Unmatched**   Means no match was found for the downloaded transaction.

If all the downloaded transactions are matched, you have nothing else to do. QuickBooks inserts a lightning bolt in the Cleared column of your register (the column with a check mark heading) for every matched transaction, indicating the fact that the transaction has cleared the bank. Whenever you open the register, you know which transactions have cleared:

- A check mark indicates a transaction has cleared and also been through reconciliation.
- A lightning bolt indicates a transaction has cleared but has not been through a bank reconciliation.

(Chapter 12 covers the topic of bank reconciliations.)

Matching Unmatched Transactions

If any transactions are marked unmatched, you have to correct the register. Any of several conditions will cause a failure when QuickBooks is trying to match transactions in the QuickStatement to the transactions in the register.

Differing Check Numbers and Amounts

If a transaction's check number and amount differs, QuickBooks won't match the transaction. For example, you may have entered check 2034 in the amount of $100.00 in your register, but the only $100 check in the QuickStatement is listed as check 2035. Or, you may have entered check 2034 for $100.00 in your register, but the QuickStatement shows check 2034 with an amount of 1000.00.

Correct the transaction in the register. If the problem is a check number, change the check number in the register, because it's unlikely the QuickStatement check number is wrong. Banks read check numbers electronically, using the metallic ink at the bottom of your check.

If the problem is a difference in the amount for a specific check number, it could be either your error or the bank's error. However, for the time being, change the registry to give the victory to the QuickStatement, because the QuickStatement always wins (by virtue of the fact that you can't change the items in the QuickStatement). Then contact your bank to find out what happened. If the bank made a mistake in the amount, it will credit or debit your account for the appropriate amount and that transaction will show up in a future QuickStatement, matching the adjusting entry you make in the register when you finish talking to the person at the bank.

Often, the QuickStatement contains transactions that aren't in your register. I'll go over some of the common reasons for this scenario and provide the remedies.

Unmatched Bank Charges

Bank charges appear in the QuickStatement when they're assessed (people who don't have online banking have to wait for the statement to arrive to learn what the monthly bank charge is). Add the bank charges to the register by selecting the transaction in the QuickStatement and clicking the Add To Register button. In the Unmatched Transaction dialog box, select the method you want to use to add the transaction (the choices differ depending on whether you're working with a bank account or a credit card account). Follow the prompts and enter the information. You don't have to enter a payee for a bank charge, you just have to enter the account to which you post bank charges.

If you have a merchant account (you accept credit cards for customer payments), you're assessed a monthly charge that appears as an unmatched transaction just like a bank charge. Use the same remedy described for entering bank charges, posting the merchant card fee/charge to the appropriate account.

Unmatched Checks

A check that has no matching transaction means you sent a check but didn't enter it in the register. (If this occurs frequently, you should stop writing manual checks and have QuickBooks print your checks.) Enter the check in the register and click Match.

Of course, if you print checks, or you know you entered every manual check you wrote in your QuickBooks register, you may have a more serious problem—someone has stolen a check. Call your bank immediately.

Unmatched Deposits

If a deposit appears in the QuickStatement for which no matching transaction is found in the register, it's usually rather easy to remedy.

Check to see whether income you recorded in a Sales Receipt or Received Payment transaction is still in the Undeposited Funds account (because you forgot to move the funds to the bank with the Make Deposits window). If so, open the Make Deposits window, select the appropriate transaction(s), and walk through the steps to make the deposit. As soon as you finish, QuickBooks automatically matches the deposit to the QuickStatement.

If a deposit doesn't exist in your QuickBooks file, either because you never entered it, or because it was a direct deposit about which you lacked prior knowledge (either lacking information about the date or the amount of the deposit), you need to create the transaction. Use either a Sales Receipt for a direct sale, or a Received Payment for a customer's invoice payment. When you finish recording the transaction, QuickBooks automatically matches it to the QuickStatement.

Matching Merchant Card Deposits

Most of the time, your merchant card deposits are unmatched in the QuickStatement, because you keep the merchant card funds in the Undeposited Funds account until your merchant card provider deposits the money (which could take several days). Merchant card deposits work in one of the two following ways:

- The entire amount of the sale is deposited, and all fees incurred during the month are removed from your account once a month.
- The fee is deducted before the proceeds of the sale are deposited (and your Undeposited Funds account lists the total amount of the sale).

If your merchant card provider deposits the gross sale proceeds, match the transaction by selecting the transaction in the Make Deposits window and following the steps for depositing the funds.

If your merchant card provider deposits the net after deducting the fee (and you didn't deduct the fee when you entered the sales transaction), you need to match that action. Choose Banking | Make Deposits, and select the credit card transaction in the Payments to Deposit dialog box. Click OK, and in the Make Deposits dialog box, create an additional line for this transaction, as follows:

- In the From Account column, enter the account to which you post merchant card fees.

- In the Amount column, enter the fee as a minus figure (you have to calculate the amount—it's the difference between your sale amount and the amount in the QuickStatement).

The net deposit, displayed at the bottom of the dialog box, matches the QuickStatement. When you click Save & Close, QuickBooks automatically matches the transaction.

Transferring Money Between Accounts Online

If you have multiple accounts at your financial institution, you can transfer money between those accounts. For example, you may have a money market account for your business in addition to your checking account.

To transfer money online, you must have applied at your financial institution for online banking for both accounts. You'll probably have a unique PIN for each account. To make your life less complicated, you should make changes while you're online to ensure both accounts have the same PIN. In addition, you must have enabled both accounts for online access within QuickBooks.

There are two methods you can use to transfer funds between online accounts: use the transfer funds function or use the register for either account.

Using the Transfer Funds Function

The simplest way to move money between your online accounts is to use the QuickBooks Transfer Funds Between Accounts window, which you reach by choosing Banking | Transfer Funds from the menu bar.

Specify the sending and receiving accounts (remember, both must be enabled for online access), and enter the amount you want to transfer. Be sure to select the option for Online Funds Transfer. Click Save & Close. Then choose Banking | Online Banking Center, make sure the transaction has a check mark, and click Send.

Using the Bank Register to Transfer Funds

You can enter a transfer directly into the account register of the bank account from which you are sending the money. The significant data entry is the one in the check number column; instead of a check number, type the word **send**. Don't enter a payee; enter the amount, and enter the receiving account in the account field. Then choose Banking | Online Banking Center, make sure the transaction has a check mark, and click Send.

Paying Bills Online

You can pay your bills in QuickBooks, then go online to send the payments to the payees. You can either use your own bank (if it's capable of working with QuickBooks to pay bills online) or use the QuickBooks bill paying service. In this section, when I say "bank," you can mentally substitute the QuickBooks service if that's what you're using.

When you make an online payment, the following information is transmitted to your vendor in addition to money:

- The date and number of the invoice(s)
- Information about any discounts or credits you've applied to the invoice(s)
- Anything you inserted as a memo or note when you prepared the payment

If the vendor is set up to receive electronic payments, the money is transferred directly from your bank account to the vendor's bank account. Incidentally, being set up to receive electronic payments does not mean your vendor must be using QuickBooks; there are many and varied methods for receiving electronic payments, and many companies have these arrangements with their banks. If the vendor's account is not accessible for online payments, your bank writes a check and mails it, along with all the necessary payment information.

If your vendor can accept electronic funds, making an online payment is a breeze. What happens is that your bank's software transmits the payment electronically, and the vendor's bank uses its software to accept it—no paper, no mail, no delays. If your vendor cannot accept electronic funds, your bank actually prints a check and mails it.

There are three methods for creating the transaction in QuickBooks:

- Use the Write Checks window.
- Use the Pay Bills window.
- Use the register for the account you use for online payments.

I think the easiest way is using the Write Checks window. Here's how it works:

1. Press CTRL-W, or choose Banking | Write Checks from the menu bar, to open the Write Checks window.
2. Select the bank account.
3. Select the Online Payment option (the label on the date field changes to Delivery Date).
4. Select the vendor. If your information on the vendor doesn't include an address, telephone number, and bank account number, QuickBooks will ask you to provide whatever information is missing.
5. Enter the delivery date, which is the date on which you want the funds to be delivered. The first time you use online bill paying, the default delivery date is two days after the current date. Thereafter, the default delivery date will be one day after the current date.
6. Enter the amount of the online payment.
7. Enter an optional memo if you want to include a message to the vendor.

 CAUTION: A memo can only be delivered as a voucher or stub, which means that your payment will not be made electronically even if the vendor is able to accept electronic payments. Instead, a check is sent, which delays the payment.

8. Assign the expense account (or item sale) in the line item section of the window.
9. Repeat this process for each payment you're making.

Finally, go online to transmit the information to the Online Banking Center. Choose Banking | Online Banking Center. In the Online Banking Center window, click Send. Your payments are sent to the big bill-paying machine on the Net.

Creating Online Transaction Reports

You can track your online activities using the available QuickBooks reports. The quickest way to see your online transactions is to choose Reports | Accountant & Taxes | Transaction Detail By Account.

In the report window, click the Modify Report button, and click the Filters tab. In the Filter list box, select Online Status. Click the arrow to the right of the Online Status box and select the online status option you need (most of the following options are only available for bank accounts that are enabled for Direct Connection online access):

- **All**   Reports all transactions whether they were online transactions or not (don't choose this option if you're trying to get a report on your online transactions).
- **Online To Send**   Reports the online transactions you've created but not yet sent online.
- **Online Sent**   Reports only the online transactions you've sent.
- **Any Online**   Reports on all the online transactions you've created, both sent and waiting.
- **Not Online**   Excludes the online transactions from the report. (Don't choose this option either.)

After you've set the filter options, click OK to return to the report window.

Receiving Customer Payments Online

Besides the online activities that permit you to track your own bank account activity, transfer money, and pay your own bills, QuickBooks offers a way for your customers to pay you online. This service is provided by the QuickBooks online billing service.

The QuickBooks online billing service offers your customers a way to pay your bills on the QuickBooks online payment site. The customer can enter a credit card number to pay the bills, or use an online payment service.

You can notify the customer about this online service by e-mailing the invoice with the online service URL in the cover note, or by snail-mailing the invoice and sending an e-mail message with the online service URL. The customer clicks the link to the URL to travel to the QuickBooks website and arrange for payment.

QuickBooks notifies you that the payment is made, and you can download the payment information into your bank register using the standard online banking procedures.

To learn more about this service, or to sign up, choose Customers | Customer Services | Get Paid Faster With Online Billing. In the QuickBooks Billing Solutions window, click the appropriate link to learn more about the service or to sign up.

Year-End Procedures

In *this chapter:*

- Run reports on your financial condition

- Print 1099 forms

- Make year-end journal entries

- Get ready for tax time

- Close the books

The end of the year is a mad house for bookkeepers, and that's true for major corporations as well as for small businesses. There is so much to do, so many reports to examine, corrections to make, entries to create—whew!

You can relax a bit. You don't have to show up at the office on January 1 (or the first day of your new fiscal year if you're not on a calendar year). Everything doesn't have to be accomplished immediately. QuickBooks is date-sensitive so you can continue to work in the new year. As long as the dates of new transactions are after the last day of your fiscal year, the transactions won't work their way into your year-end calculations.

Meanwhile, even after the first day of the next fiscal year, you can continue to work on transactions for the current fiscal year, making sure you change the transaction dates any time a transaction window opens with the current (next year) date.

Running Year-End Financial Reports

The standard financial reports you run for the year provide a couple of services for you:

- You can see the economic health of your business.
- You can examine the report to make sure everything is posted correctly.

To run financial reports, click the Reports menu listing. For year-end reports, you'll need to access several types of reports (see Chapter 15 for information about modifying and customizing reports).

Don't forget that reports have date ranges like "current year" and "last fiscal year." If you perform these tasks before the end of your fiscal year, you're still in the current year. However, if you're working after the last date of your fiscal year (which is the norm), the current year isn't the year of interest.

Year-End P&L Report

Start with a Profit & Loss Standard report (also called an *income statement*), which is one of the reports in the Company & Financial listing.

The report displays the year-end balances for all the income and expense accounts in your general ledger that had any activity this year. Examine the report, and if anything seems out of line, double-click the total to see the postings for that account. If the data you see doesn't reassure you, double-click any of the posting lines to see the original transaction.

If there's a transaction that seems to be in error, you can take corrective action. You cannot delete or void a bill you paid or a customer invoice for which you received payment, of course. However, you might be able to talk to a customer or vendor for whom you've found a problem and work out a satisfactory arrangement for credits. Or you may find that you posted an expense or income transaction to the wrong general ledger account. If so, make a journal entry to correct it (see Chapter 14 for information on journal entries). Then run the year-end P&L report again and print it.

Year-End Balance Sheet

Your real financial health is demonstrated in your Balance Sheet. To run a year-end balance sheet, choose Reports | Company & Financial | Balance Sheet Standard. The Balance Sheet figures are more than a list of numbers; they're a list of chores. Check with your accountant first, but most of the time you'll find that the following advice is offered:

- Pay any payroll withholding liabilities with a check dated in the current year in order to clear them from the Balance Sheet and gain the expense deduction for the employer taxes.
- If you have an A/P balance, pay some bills ahead of time. For example, pay your rent or mortgage payment that's due the first day of the next fiscal year during the last month of this fiscal year. Enter and pay vendor bills earlier than their due dates (if those dates fall in the next year) in order to pay them this year and gain the expense deduction for this year.

Issuing 1099 Forms

If any vendors are eligible for 1099 forms, you need to print and mail the forms to them. First, make sure your 1099 setup is correct by choosing Edit | Preferences and selecting the Tax: 1099 icon. Click Company Preferences to see your settings (see Figure 17-1).

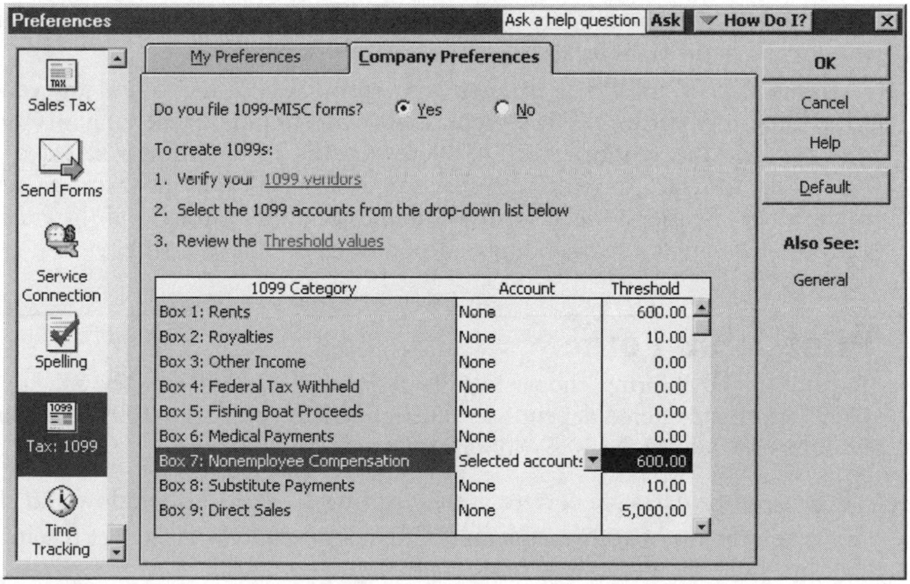

FIGURE 17-1   Make sure your 1099 configuration is correct.

Check the latest IRS rules and make any changes to the threshold amounts for the categories you need. Also assign an account to each category for which you'll be issuing Form 1099 to vendors. You can assign multiple accounts to a 1099 category, but you cannot assign any accounts to more than one 1099 category.

For example, if you have an expense account "subcontractors" and an expense account "outside consultants," both of the accounts can be linked to the 1099 category Nonemployee Compensation. However, once you link those accounts to that category, you cannot use those same accounts in any other category.

To assign an account to a category, click the category to select it. Click the text in the account column (it probably says "none") and then click the arrow to select an account for this category.

To assign multiple accounts to a category, instead of selecting an account after you click the arrow, choose the Selected Accounts option (at the top of the list). In the Select Account dialog box, click each account to put a check mark next to its listing. Click OK to assign the accounts. Then click OK to close the Preferences dialog.

Run a 1099 Report

Before you print the forms, you should print a report on your 1099 vendors. To do this, choose Reports | Vendors & Payables and select one of the following 1099 reports:

- 1099 Summary lists each vendor eligible for a 1099 with the total amount paid to the vendor.
- 1099 Detail lists each transaction for each vendor eligible for a 1099.

You can make adjustments to transactions, if necessary, to make sure your 1099 vendors have the right totals.

It's also a good idea to go through your entire Vendor list to find any vendors who did not appear on the 1099 report but who should be receiving a 1099. If you find any, edit the Vendor record to make sure the 1099 option is selected on the Additional Info tab. You must also have an identification number for the vendor in the form of either a social security number or an EIN number if the vendor is a proprietorship or a partnership—corporations do not receive 1099s.

Print 1099 Forms

To print the 1099 forms, choose File | Print Forms | 1099s/1096. The specific type of 1099 form that's offered depends on the preferences you set for 1099s and vendors. Most businesses use the 1099-MISC form.

- Be sure the dates are correct in the Printing 1099 Forms window and click OK.
- When the list of 1099 recipients appears, any vendor who is over the appropriate threshold should have a check mark.

- Click Preview 1099 to see what the form will look like when it prints. Zoom in to make sure your company name, address, and EIN number are correct. Click Close on the Preview window to return to the 1099 window. Then load the 1099 forms into your printer and click Print.
- If you're using a laser or ink-jet printer, set the number of copies so you have enough—you'll need three. Dot-matrix printers use multipart forms.

When the forms are printed, send one to the vendor, one to the government, and put the third copy in your files. You must deliver the forms to vendors by January 31.

Repeat these procedures for each type of 1099 form you are required to print (most businesses need to worry only about the 1099-MISC form).

Making Year-End Journal Entries

There are probably a couple of journal entries your accountant wants you to make before you close your books for the year:

> **NOTE:** See Chapter 14 for detailed information about creating journal entries.

- Depreciation entries
- Prior retained earnings moved to a different account, or retained earnings moved to owner or partner equity accounts
- Any adjustments needed for cash versus accrual reporting (these are usually reversed on the first day of the next fiscal year)
- Adjustment of prepaid expenses from asset accounts to expense accounts

You can send the P&L and Balance Sheet reports to your accountant, and ask for journal entry instructions. Or you can send your accountant an accountant's review copy of your company data, and let your accountant make the journal entries. You import the changes when the review copy is returned. See Chapter 15 to learn how to use the Accountant's Review Copy feature.

Running Tax Reports

Some small-business owners prepare their own taxes manually or by using a tax software program like TurboTax. Many small businesses turn over the tax preparation chores to their accountants. No matter which method you choose for tax preparation, you should run the reports that tell you whether your QuickBooks data files are ready for tax preparation. Is all the necessary data entered? Do the bottom line numbers call for some special tax planning or special tax considerations? Even if your taxes are prepared by your accountant, the more organized your records are, the less time the accountant spends on your return (which makes your bill from the accountant smaller).

Check Tax Line Information

If you're going to do your own taxes, every account in your chart of accounts that is tax-related must have the right tax form in the account's tax line assignment. To see if any tax line assignments are missing, choose Reports | Accountant & Taxes | Income Tax Preparation. When the report appears, all your accounts are listed, along with the tax form assigned to each account. If you created your own chart of accounts, the number of accounts that you neglected to assign to a tax form is likely to be quite large, as shown in Figure 17-2.

Before you can prepare your own taxes, you must edit each account to add the tax information. To do so, open the chart of accounts and select an account. Press CTRL-E to edit the account and select a tax form from the Tax Line entry drop-down list.

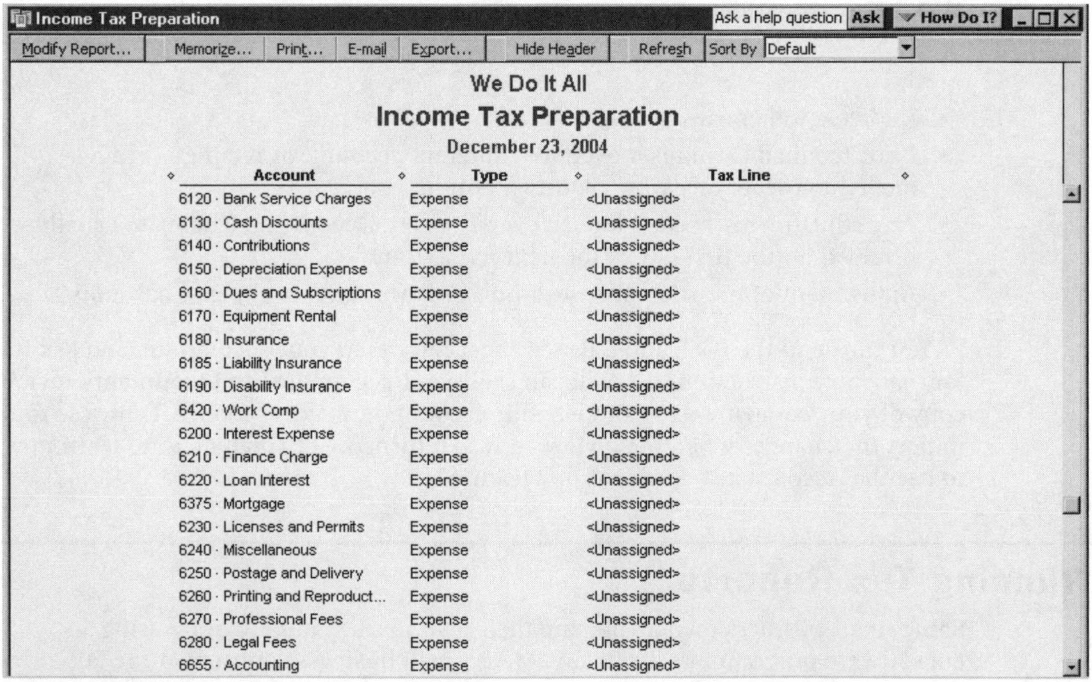

Account	Type	Tax Line
6120 · Bank Service Charges	Expense	<Unassigned>
6130 · Cash Discounts	Expense	<Unassigned>
6140 · Contributions	Expense	<Unassigned>
6150 · Depreciation Expense	Expense	<Unassigned>
6160 · Dues and Subscriptions	Expense	<Unassigned>
6170 · Equipment Rental	Expense	<Unassigned>
6180 · Insurance	Expense	<Unassigned>
6185 · Liability Insurance	Expense	<Unassigned>
6190 · Disability Insurance	Expense	<Unassigned>
6420 · Work Comp	Expense	<Unassigned>
6200 · Interest Expense	Expense	<Unassigned>
6210 · Finance Charge	Expense	<Unassigned>
6220 · Loan Interest	Expense	<Unassigned>
6375 · Mortgage	Expense	<Unassigned>
6230 · Licenses and Permits	Expense	<Unassigned>
6240 · Miscellaneous	Expense	<Unassigned>
6250 · Postage and Delivery	Expense	<Unassigned>
6260 · Printing and Reproduct...	Expense	<Unassigned>
6270 · Professional Fees	Expense	<Unassigned>
6280 · Legal Fees	Expense	<Unassigned>
6655 · Accounting	Expense	<Unassigned>

FIGURE 17-2 This is what happens if you don't take the time to assign tax lines when you create accounts.

Your selections vary depending upon the organizational type of your company (proprietorship, partnership, S corp, C corp, etc.).

> **NOTE:** Be sure the Income Tax Form Used field is filled out properly on your Company Information dialog box. If it's blank, you won't see the tax information fields on your accounts.

If you don't know which form and category to assign to an account, here's an easy trick for getting that information:

1. Choose File | New Company to create a new company in QuickBooks.
2. Begin answering the wizard questions, using a fake company name. You can skip the general information such as the company address, phone number, tax identification number, and so on.
3. Select the income tax form you use for tax returns.
4. Choose a company type that's the same as (or close to) your type of business.
5. When prompted, save the new company file.
6. Tell the EasyStep Interview wizard to create a chart of accounts.
7. After the chart of accounts is created, click Leave to stop the interview.
8. Open the chart of accounts list and press CTRL-P to print the list.

The printed list has the tax form information you need. Open your real company, open the chart of accounts, and use the information on the printed document to enter tax form information.

Calculate Other Important Tax Information

There are some taxable numbers that aren't available through the normal QuickBooks reports. One of the most common is the report on company officer compensation if your business is incorporated.

If your business is a C corporation, you file tax form 1120, while a Subchapter S corporation files tax form 1120S. Both of these forms require you to separate compensation for corporate officers from the other employee compensation. You will have to add those totals from payroll reports (either QuickBooks payroll or an outside payroll service).

You can avoid the need to calculate this by creating a separate Payroll item called Officer Compensation and assigning it to its own account (which you'll also have to create). Then open the Employee card for each officer and change the Earnings item to the new item. Do this for next year; it's probably too late for this year's end-of-year process.

Using TurboTax

If you purchase TurboTax to do your taxes, you don't have to do anything special in QuickBooks to transfer the information. Open TurboTax and tell it to import your QuickBooks company file.

Almost everything you need is transferred to TurboTax. There are some details you'll have to enter directly into TurboTax (for example, home-office expenses for a Schedule C form).

Closing Your Books

After all the year-end reports have been run, any necessary journal entries have been entered, and your taxes have been filed (and paid), it's traditional to go through the exercise of closing the books.

Typically, closing the books occurs some time after the end of the fiscal year, usually within the first couple of months of the next fiscal year (right after the tax forms have been sent to the government).

The exercise of closing the books is performed to lock the books; no user can change anything. After taxes have been filed based on the information in the system, nothing can be changed. It's too late. This is it. The information is etched in cement.

Understanding Closing in QuickBooks

QuickBooks doesn't use the traditional accounting software closing procedures. In most other business accounting software, closing the year means you cannot post transactions to any date in that year, nor can you manipulate any transactions in the closed year. Closing the books in QuickBooks does not etch the information in cement; it can be changed and/or deleted by users with the appropriate permissions.

QuickBooks does not require you to close the books in order to keep working in the software. You can work forever, year after year, without performing a closing process. However, many QuickBooks users prefer to lock the transactions for a year as a way to prevent any changes to the data except by users with the appropriate permissions.

Closing the Year

In QuickBooks, you close the year by entering a closing date. This inherently does nothing more than lock users out of the previous year's transactions. At the same time, you can reconfigure user rights to enable or prevent entry into closed transactions with the following steps:

1. Choose Edit | Preferences to open the Preferences dialog box.
2. Click the Accounting icon.
3. Select the Company Preferences tab.
4. Enter the closing date, which is the last date of your fiscal year (see Figure 17-3).

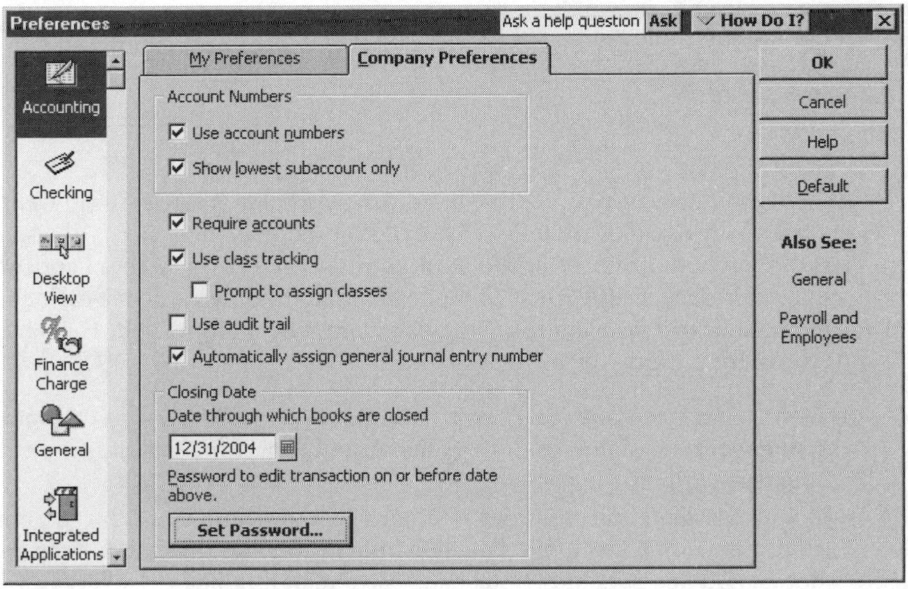

FIGURE 17-3 Entering the closing date is the first step in locking down the year's data.

If your fiscal year is different from a calendar year, don't worry about payroll. The payroll files and features (including 1099s) are locked into a calendar year configuration and closing your books doesn't have any effect on your ability to work with payroll transactions.

Preventing Access to Closed Books

To prevent users from changing transactions in the closed year (or to permit certain users to), assign a password for manipulating closed data. Click Set Password, and enter the password in the Set Closing Date Password dialog box. Press TAB and enter it again in the Confirm Password field.

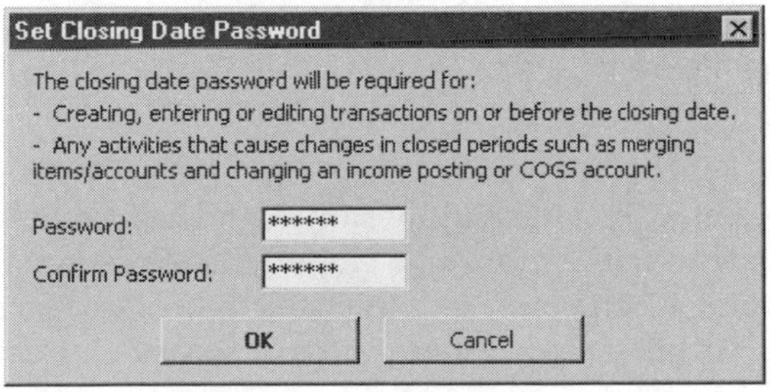

> **CAUTION:** If you've set up users and passwords for access to your QuickBooks data file, only the QuickBooks Administrator can set the closing date and password.

The characters you type are displayed on the screen as asterisks (in case somebody is peeking over your shoulder). If you don't enter exactly the same characters in both fields, QuickBooks asks you to start over. If that happens, you may have chosen a password so complicated that it invites typos, which could mean you'll have a problem using the password when you need it. Here are some guidelines for creating effective passwords:

- Don't use a password that is easy to figure out. Your birthday, your spouse's name, your nickname, your dog's name, and other similar phrases are easy to guess.

- If you distribute the password to other users to whom you want to grant the right to manipulate closed data, don't post a note on their desk lamps or office doors, and don't yell down the hall. Use e-mail if nobody else has access to their inbox. (Users who habitually leave their inbox window loaded on the screen can't say that.)

- Write yourself a note with the password and put it in a secure place (your wallet, a locked desk drawer, etc.). Even if you're sure you'll remember the password when you need it, don't fail to take this step. History has already proven you wrong (and you can confirm this by querying any QuickBooks consultant or any Intuit support technician, who had to pass along the bad news that the file had to be sent to Intuit for unlocking—for a fee).

If you're using password-protected usernames on your QuickBooks system (not necessary for using this closing date protection), you must know the admin password to enter the closing date and assign a password.

> **TIP:** If you think the password is compromised (security-tech-talk for "somebody who shouldn't know the password has learned what it is"), you can change it by repeating the same steps.

QuickBooks Premier Editions offer a feature that tracks and logs every change that's made to transactions in a closed year. Even when you (or other users to whom you gave the password to enable access to a closed year) make necessary changes, it's often a good idea to keep a record of those changes. After all, a figure on your tax return may differ from the total figure in your QuickBooks file after you change any individual transaction, and you may need to explain it to your accountant or (gasp!) the IRS.

 TIP: To learn how to set up and use the tracking feature (if you're using a Premier Edition or planning to upgrade), read *Running QuickBooks 2004 Premier Editions*, from CPA911 Publishing (www.cpa911.com).

Creating a Year-End Backup

After all the numbers are checked, all the journal entries are made, and the books have been closed by entering a closing date as described in the previous section, do a separate backup in addition to your normal daily backup. Don't put this backup on one of the disks you're using for your normal backups—use a fresh disk, label it "Year-End Backup 2004," and put it in a safe place.

Part Three

Tracking Time and Mileage

Most service businesses sell time; it's the most important commodity they have. Actually, most service businesses are really selling knowledge and expertise, but nobody's ever figured out how to put a value on those talents. The solution, therefore, is to charge for the time it takes to pass along and use all that expertise (that explanation was originally voiced by Abraham Lincoln as he explained why and how attorneys charge for time). Even businesses that are product-based might need to track time for employees or outside consultants.

Tracking mileage is a universal need for any business in which vehicles are used to deliver services or products. Vehicle expense deductions on your tax return need to be able to pass an audit, and many companies insist that every employee keep a travel log. In addition, many service businesses bill clients for mileage when employees work at the client site, or travel at the client's behest.

Beyond the need to track time and mileage, you may need to track time and activities by outside contractors, or off-site employees.

Part Three of this book covers all the steps you need to take to set your system up for tracking time and mileage with maximum efficiency and accuracy.

Using Time Tracking

In *this chapter:*

- Configure time tracking
- Fill out timesheets
- Edit timesheets
- Bill for time

All editions of QuickBooks 2004 except QuickBooks Basic offer time tracking, which lets you see how much time is spent completing a project, working for a customer, or working for your company (administrative tasks). You can use that information to invoice customers for time.

In addition to tracking billable time, you can also use this information for a variety of reasons. For example, if you charge retainer fees for your services, time tracking is a terrific way to figure out which customers may need to have the retainer amount raised.

Configuring Time Tracking

When you create a company in QuickBooks, one of the EasyStep Interview windows queries you about your desire to track time. If you respond affirmatively, QuickBooks turns on the time-tracking features. If you opt to skip time tracking, you can turn it on later if you change your mind. In fact, if you turn it on, you can turn it off if you find you're not using it.

If you're not sure whether you turned on time tracking when you installed your company, choose Edit | Preferences from the QuickBooks menu bar. Select the Time Tracking icon and click the Company Preferences tab. Make sure the Yes option is selected.

Configuring Your Work Week

By default, QuickBooks assumes your work week starts on Monday. However, if your business is open every day of the week, you might want to use a standard Sunday-to-Saturday pattern for tracking time.

If you're tracking time for employees and you plan to use the timesheets for payroll, it's a good idea to base the work week on the last day of the week that your pay period covers. Of course, this only works if your pay periods are based on weeks—not if your payroll is semimonthly or monthly.

Configuring Workers

If you're tracking time for your employees, outside contractors, or yourself, everybody who must keep track of his or her time must exist in the system. Each person must also fill out a timesheet.

Tracking Employee Time

If you are running the QuickBooks payroll feature, you already have employees in your QuickBooks system. You can track the time of any employee who fills out a timesheet (timesheets are covered later in this chapter).

You can also use the timesheet data to pay the employee, using the number of hours reported in the time-tracking system to determine the number of hours for which the employee is paid. For this to work, however, the employee must be linked to his or her timesheet. As a result, you must modify the employee record as follows:

1. Choose Lists | Employee List from the menu bar to open the Employee List.
2. Double-click the listing of the employee you want to link to time tracking.
3. In the Change Tabs field, select Payroll And Compensation Info from the drop-down list (see Figure 18-1).
4. Select the Use Time Data To Create Paychecks check box.
5. Click OK.

You don't have to link employees to time tracking in order for them to use the timesheets and record time—the time-tracking configuration is required only if you want to create the paychecks with the timesheets.

If you *do* link an employee to time tracking, while that employee is filling out timesheets, a QuickBooks message may appear saying that the activity the employee is reporting is not linked to an hourly rate. QuickBooks will report the rate at $0.00/hour, which is fine (especially if your employees are on salary).

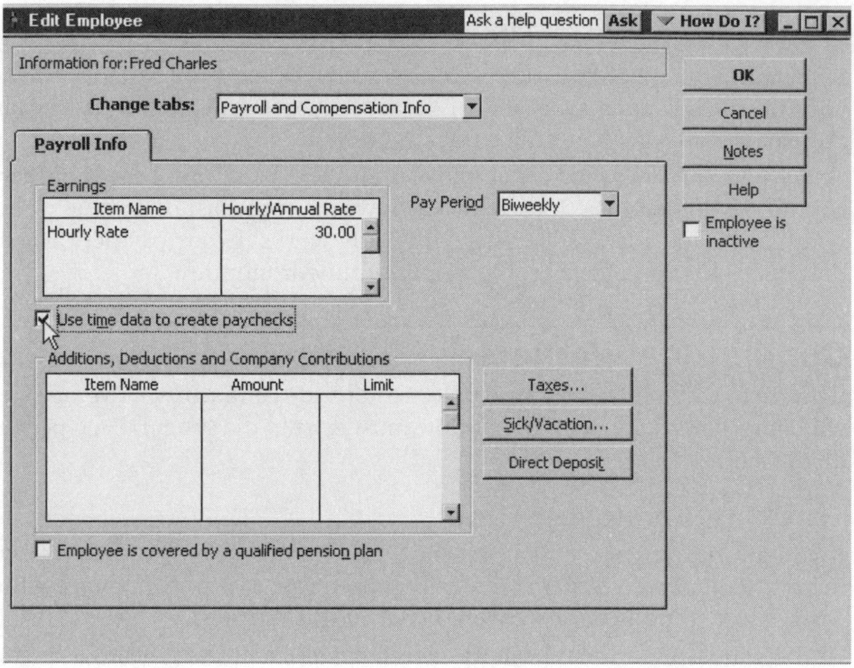

FIGURE 18-1   Link employees to the time tracking feature if you want to use timesheets to prepare paychecks.

Tracking Vendor Time

Any vendor in your system who is paid for his or her time can have that time tracked for the purpose of billing customers. Most of the time these vendors are referred to as outside contractors or subcontractors. You don't have to do anything to the vendor record to effect time tracking; you merely need to record the time used as the vendor sends bills.

Tracking Other Worker Time

You may need to track the time of people who are neither employees nor vendors. The word "employees" means you have established QuickBooks payroll services. If you have employees, but you don't use QuickBooks payroll, they're not employees to your QuickBooks software.

QuickBooks provides a system list called Other Names. You use this list to amass names that don't fit in the other QuickBooks lists. You can track time for people by entering their names into the Other Names List. Here are some situations in which you'll need to use the Other Names feature:

- You have employees and use QuickBooks payroll, but you are not an employee because you take a draw instead of a paycheck. In this case, you must add your name to the Other Names List if you want to track your own time.

- You have employees and are not using QuickBooks payroll, so there is no Employees list in your system. You must add each employee name to the Other Names List to track employee time.
- You have no employees and your business is a proprietorship or a partnership. Owner or partner names must be entered into the Other Names List in order to track time.

Configuring the Tasks

Most of the tasks you track already exist in your system as service items. These are the items you use when you bill customers for services. However, because you can use time tracking to analyze the way people in your organization spend their time, you may want to add service items that are relevant to noncustomer tasks.

For example, if you want to track the time people spend performing administrative tasks for the business, you can add a service item called Administrative to your items list. If you want to be more specific, you can name the particular administrative tasks you want to track (for example, bookkeeping, equipment repair, new sales calls, public relations, and so on).

To enter new items, click the Item button on the icon bar. When the Item List window opens, press CTRL-N to open a new item form. Select Service as the item type (only service items are tracked in timesheets) and name the new item. Here are some guidelines for administrative items:

- If you're specifying administrative tasks, create a service named Administration, and then make each specific administrative task a subitem of Administration.
- Don't put an amount in the Rate box. You're not charging a customer for this service, and you can calculate the amount you're paying the recipient when you make the payment (via payroll or vendor checks).
- Because QuickBooks insists that you assign an account to a service, choose or create an innocuous revenue account (such as Other Revenue, or Timetracking Revenue). Don't worry, no money is posted to the account because you don't ever sell these services to customers.

The option to configure the item for subcontractors, owners, or partners isn't important if you're creating a service for the purpose of tracking time, because you're entering time on the timesheets, not amounts. If you actually pay a subcontractor, owner, or partner for work, you must create specific accounts for those payments. For subcontractors, you post payments to an expense account that is linked to your 1099 configuration (covered in Chapter 17). For owners and partners, payments must be posted to a draw account (which is an equity account).

Because time tracking is connected to customers, in order to track administrative work, you must also create a customer for the occasions when no real customer is being tracked (those administrative tasks). The easiest way to do that is to create a new customer to represent your company. For example, you may want to create a customer named House, or InHouse.

Configuring User Permissions

If you're using multiple user and password features in QuickBooks, you must edit each user to make sure people can use the time-tracking forms. See Chapter 21 for detailed information about setting up users and permissions.

Using Timesheets

QuickBooks offers two methods for recording the time you spent on tasks: Single Activity and Weekly Timesheet.

- Single Activity is a form you use to enter what you did when you performed a single task at a specific time on a specific date. For example, a Single Activity form may record the fact that you made a telephone call on behalf of a customer, you repaired some piece of equipment for a customer, or you performed some administrative task for the company that is unrelated to a customer.
- Weekly Timesheet is a form in which you indicate how much time and on which date you performed work. Each Weekly Timesheet entry can also include the name of the customer for whom the work was performed.

Your decision about which method to use depends on the type of work you do and on the efficiency of your workers' memories. People tend to put off filling in Weekly Timesheets and then attempt to reconstruct their activities in order to complete the timesheets. This frequently ends up being a less-than-accurate approach. The method works properly only if everyone remembers to open the timesheets and fill them in as soon as they complete each task. Uh huh, sure.

 TIP: If you fill out a Single Activity form, every time you open a Weekly Timesheet form, any single activity within that week is automatically inserted into the Weekly Timesheet.

Using the Single Activity Form

Bring up the Single Activity form when you need to track one event or task. Use these steps to open and fill out the form:

1. Choose Employees | Time Tracking | Time/Enter Single Activity from the menu bar to open the Time/Enter Single Activity window (see Figure 18-2).

 NOTE: The time tracking menu items are also on the Customer menu.

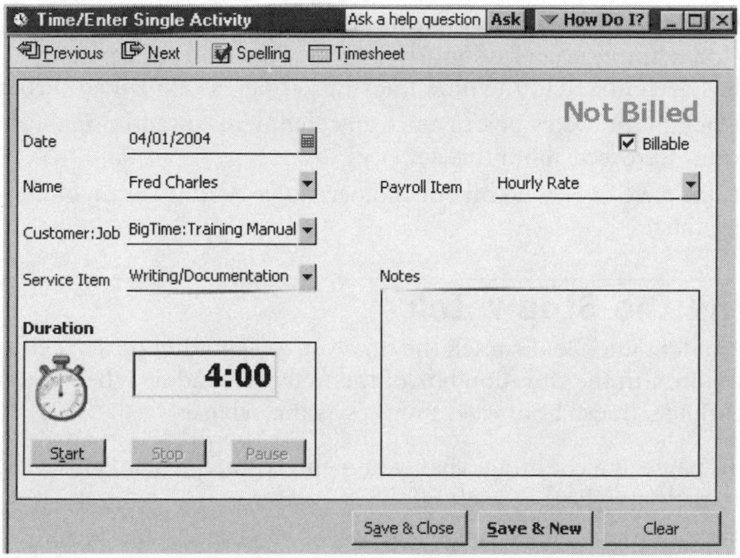

FIGURE 18-2 Fill out the details to indicate how you spent your time.

2. The Date field is automatically filled in with the current date. If this activity took place previously, change the date.

3. Click the arrow to the right of the Name field and select the name of the person who performed the work from the list that appears (usually the person who is filling out the timesheet). The list contains vendors, employees, and names from the Other Names List. (You can use <Add New> to add a new name.)

NOTE: If an employee is not configured for using time data to create paychecks, QuickBooks asks if you'd like to change that configuration. If the employee is just tracking time for job costing purposes, and is not paid from these timesheets, click No.

4. If this time was spent working on a task for a customer rather than performing an administrative task, select the customer or job in the Customer:Job field. Do this whether or not the customer is going to be billed for the time.

5. In the Service Item field, select the task.

6. In the Duration box, enter the amount of time you're reporting in the format hh:mm.

7. If this time *is* billable to the customer, the Billable check box should be marked (it is by default). If the time is not going to be billed to the customer, click the box to remove the check mark.

8. If the Payroll Item field appears, select the payroll item that applies to this time (for example, salary or hourly wages). This field appears only if an employee has been linked to the time-tracking system, as explained earlier in this chapter.

9. Click in the Notes box to enter any comments or additional information you want to record about this activity.

10. Click Save & New to fill out another Single Activity form, or click Save & Close to finish.

Using the Stopwatch

You can let QuickBooks track the time you're spending on a specific task. Click the Start button in the Duration box of the Activity window when you begin the task. QuickBooks tracks hours and minutes as they elapse.

- To pause the counting when you're interrupted, click Pause. Then click Start to pick up where you left off.
- To stop timing, click Stop. The time is recorded in the Weekly Timesheet.

Click Save & New to fill out the next activity; click Save & Close if you're finished recording your time.

You can set the format for reporting time, both on the activity sheet and in the stopwatch window. Some companies prefer the hh:mm format; others prefer a decimal format (such as 1.5 hours). To establish your preference, choose Edit | Preferences and click the General icon. Then select the Company Preferences tab, and use the options in the Time Format section of the dialog box to select the appropriate format.

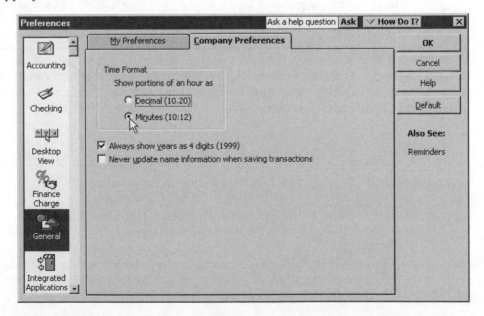

Using Weekly Timesheets

A Weekly Timesheet records the same information as the Single Activity form, except that the information is recorded in week-at-a-time blocks. To use this form, choose Employees | Time Tracking | Use Weekly Timesheet to open the Weekly Timesheet window (see Figure 18-3).

Use the following steps to fill out the timesheet:

1. Select your name from the list that appears when you click the arrow to the right of the Name field. (If you're filling out a timesheet for a subcontractor who reported time to you, select the subcontractor's name.)

2. If you want to enter time for a different week, click the Set Date button and enter the first day of any week for which you want to enter activities. (The first day of your company work week is set in Edit | Preferences | Time Tracking, as explained earlier in this chapter.)

3. Click in the Customer:Job column to display an arrow that you click to see the Customer List. Select the customer connected to the activity (or select the in-house listing if you're performing administrative work unconnected to a customer).

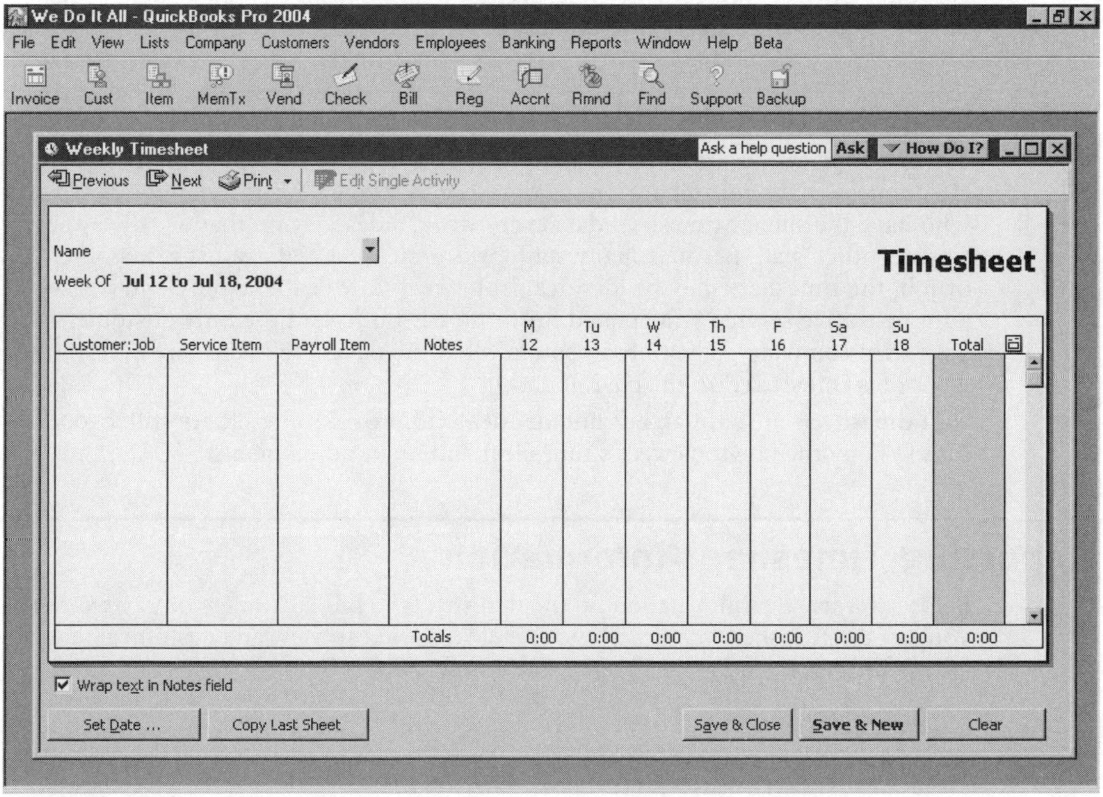

FIGURE 18-3 You may find it easier and faster to enter information on a weekly basis.

4. Enter the service item that describes your activity.

5. If you're an employee whose paycheck is linked to your timesheets, select the Payroll Item that fits the activity. If your name is attached to the Other Name or Vendor list, or you're an employee who is not paid from the timesheets, you won't see a Payroll Item column.

6. In the Notes column, enter any comments you feel are necessary.

7. Click the column that represents the day for which you are entering this activity and enter the number of hours worked on this task. Repeat for each day that you performed this activity. If you're linking the activity to a customer, all the days you indicate must be for this activity for this customer.

8. Move to the beginning of the next row to enter the next timesheet entry (a different activity, or the same activity for a different customer), repeating until you've accounted for your time for the week.

9. For each row, indicate whether the time is billable in the right-most column. By default, all time entries linked to a customer are billable. (The icon in the right-most column is supposed to look like an invoice.) Click the icon to put an X atop it if the time on this row is not billable.

10. Click Save & New to use a timesheet for a different week. Click Save & Close when you are finished entering time.

Copying Weekly Timesheets

You can copy the previous week's timesheet by clicking the Copy Last Sheet button after you enter the current date in the timesheet window. This is useful for employees who have the similar timesheet data every week, a description that usually applies to your office staff. Because many staff tasks aren't charged against a customer or job, the timesheet may be identical from week to week (the only entry is the administrative service you created for in-house work, and the only customer is your own company). The only reason to fill in the data is to make sure every hour worked is transferred to the payroll data.

If timesheets are similar, but not identical, from week to week, it's still a good idea to copy the previous week's timesheet and make adjustments.

Reporting Timesheet Information

Before you use the information on the timesheets to bill customers or pay workers, you can use timesheet reports to check the data. You can view and customize reports, edit information, and print the original timesheets.

Running Timesheet Reports

To run reports on timesheets, choose Reports | Jobs, Time & Mileage. You'll see a long list of available reports, but the following reports provide information on time tracking:

- **Time By Job Summary** Reports the amount of time spent for each service on your customers and their jobs.
- **Time By Job Detail** Reports the details of the time spent for each customer and job, including dates and whether or not the time was marked as billable (see Figure 18-4). A billing status of Unbilled indicates the time is billable but hasn't yet been transferred to a customer invoice.
- **Time By Name** Reports the amount of time each user tracked.
- **Time By Item** Provides a quick analysis of the amount of time spent performing services your company is providing and to whom.

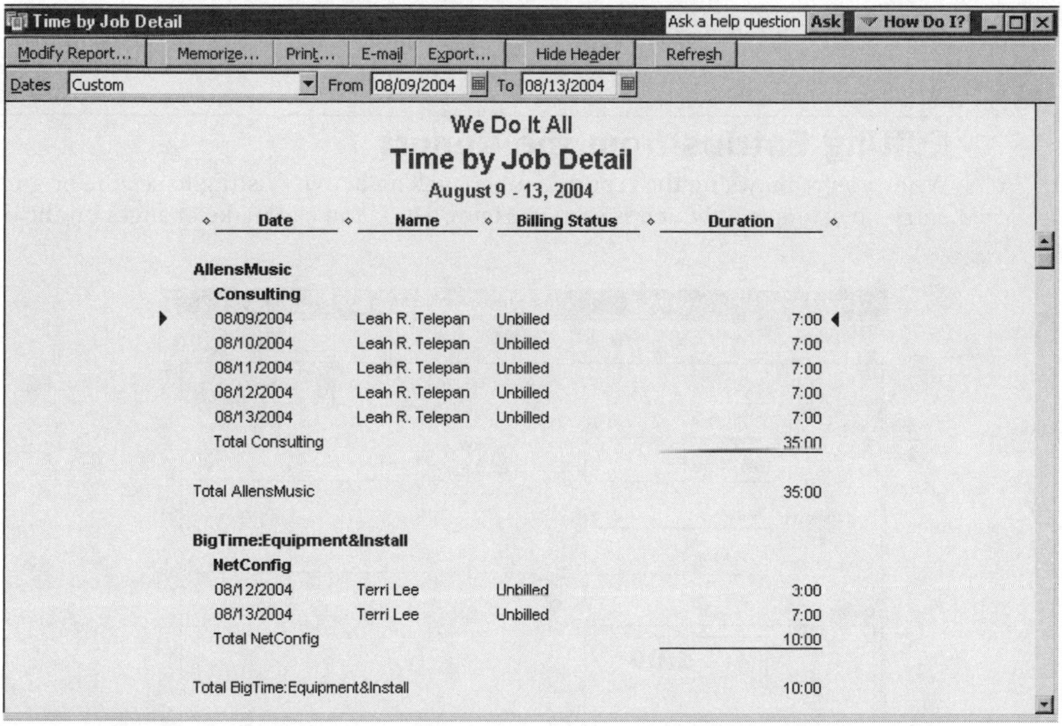

FIGURE 18-4 This report displays details from the timesheets entered during the period you select.

If you've made it a practice to encourage people to enter comments in the Notes section of the timesheet, you should change the report format so it includes those comments. You can do this only in the Time By Job Detail report:

1. Open the Time By Job Detail report and click the Modify Report button on the button bar.
2. In the Modify Report window, select Notes from the Columns list.
3. Click OK.

To make sure you always see the notes, you should memorize this report. Click the Memorize button on the report button bar and name the report. Hereafter, it will be available in the Memorized Reports list.

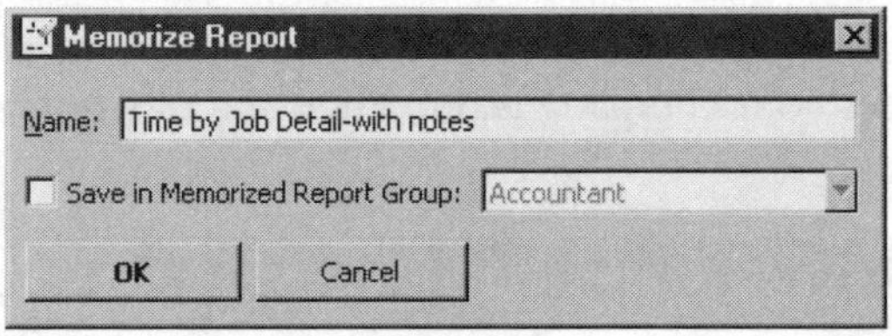

Editing Entries from the Report

While you're browsing the report, double-click an activity listing to see the original entry, an example of which is seen in Figure 18-5. You can make changes on the

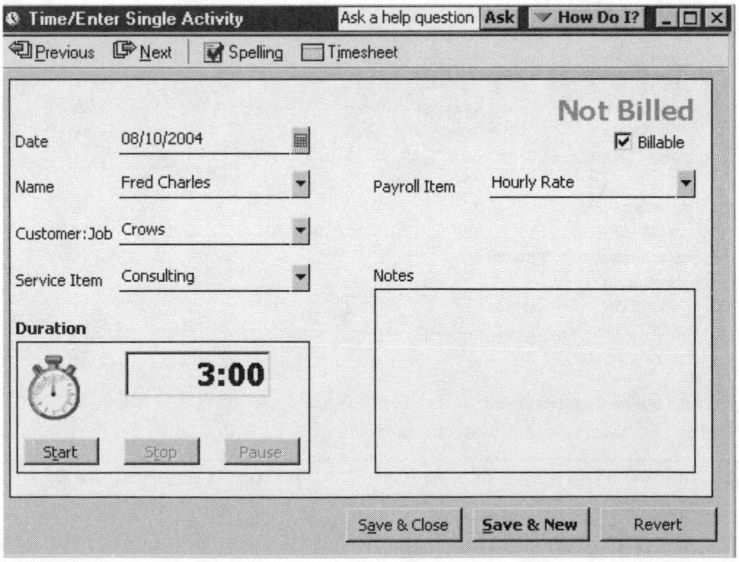

FIGURE 18-5 You can drill down to the original timesheet for any item in a Time report.

original entry, such as selecting or deselecting the billable option, or changing the note field by adding a note or editing the content of the existing note.

> **NOTE:** For all reports except Time By Job Detail, when you double-click an activity listing you see a Detail report, where you can locate the listing for the original entry and double-click that to drill down to original data.

If you make changes, when you click Save & Close to return to the report window, QuickBooks displays a message to ask whether you want to refresh the report to accommodate the changes. Click Yes to see the new, accurate information in the report. In fact, it's a good idea to select the option to stop asking you the question, because any time you make changes in transactions from a report window, you want to see the effect on the report.

Editing the Original Timesheets

Before you use the timesheets for customer billing or payroll, make sure you examine them and make any needed corrections. In fact, you may want to take this step before you view any of the Jobs & Time reports.

The common revision is the billable status. If you have outside contractors or employees filling out timesheets, it's not unusual to have some confusion about which customers receive direct time billings. In fact, you may have customers to whom you send direct time bills only for certain activities and provide the remaining activities as part of your basic services.

To check timesheets, just open a new timesheet (choose Employees | Time Tracking | Use Weekly Timesheet). Enter the name of the person connected to the timesheet you want to inspect. Use the Previous or Next arrows at the top of the timesheet window, or click the Set Date button at the bottom of the window, to move to the timesheet you want to inspect. Then edit the information as necessary:

- You can change the number of hours for any activity item.
- Click the icon in the Billable column (the last column) to reverse the current status (it's a toggle). Line entries that are not billable have an X over the icon.
- To view (and edit if necessary) any notes, first click in any of the weekday columns to activate the Edit Single Activity icon at the top of the timesheet window. Click that icon to see the entry as a single activity, with the entire note available for viewing or editing.

> **CAUTION:** If you've already used the timesheet data to bill the customer or pay the employee, the changes you make are useless. It's too late. Customer invoices and payroll records are not updated with your edits.

Printing the Weekly Timesheets

It's a common practice to have employees print their Weekly Timesheets and distribute them to the appropriate management people. Usually that means your payroll person (or the person who phones in the payroll if you use an outside payroll service) or a personnel manager. However, instead of having each user be responsible for handing in the timesheet, it's a good idea to designate someone (such as your payroll manager) to perform this task. That way, all the timesheets are printed and available in a timely manner.

To print timesheets, choose File | Print Forms | Timesheets from the QuickBooks menu bar to open the Select Timesheets To Print window shown in Figure 18-6.

- Change the date range to match the timesheets you want to print.
- By default, all timesheets are selected. To remove a timesheet, click the column with the check mark to deselect that listing. You can click Select None to deselect all listings, then select one or more specific users.
- To see any notes in their entirety, select the Print Full Activity Notes option. Otherwise, the default selection to print only the first line of any notes is empowered.

Click OK to open the Print Timesheets window, where you can change the printer or printing options. You should change the number of copies to print to match the number of people to whom you're distributing the timesheets.

The Select Timesheets To Print dialog box has a Preview button, and clicking it displays a print preview of the selected timesheets. If you click the Print button in the Preview window, the timesheets are sent to the printer immediately, giving you no opportunity to change the printer or any printing options. Clicking the Close

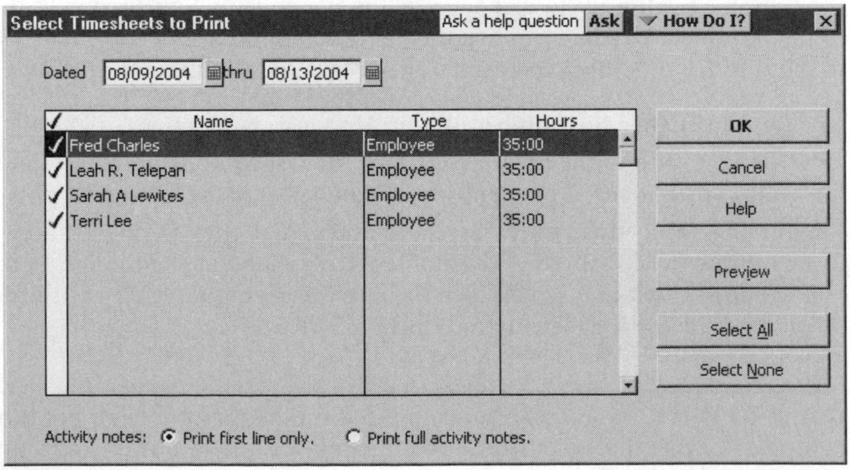

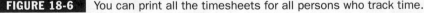

FIGURE 18-6 You can print all the timesheets for all persons who track time.

button in the Preview window returns you to the Select Timesheets To Print dialog box, where clicking OK brings up the Print Timesheets dialog box.

One thing you should notice about printed (or previewed) timesheets is the last column, which indicates the billing status. The entries are codes, as follows:

- **B** Billable but not yet billed to the customer
- **N** Not billable
- **D** Billable and already billed to the customer

Creating Invoices with Timesheets Data

After you've configured QuickBooks to track time, you can use the data you amass to help you create customer invoices quickly. For a full and detailed discussion about invoicing customers, please turn to Chapter 3.

Plugging In Time Charges

When you're ready to bill customers for time, click the Invoice button on the icon bar and follow these steps:

1. In the Create Invoices window, select the customer or job. If the customer or job as billable time charges, QuickBooks notifies you of that fact.

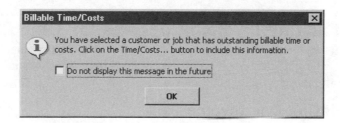

2. Enter the date of this invoice.
3. Click the Time/Costs button on the top of the invoice form to open the Choose Billable Time And Costs window. Click the Time tab to see the entries from timesheets, as shown in Figure 18-7.

4. Select the entries you want to include on this invoice (click Select All to use all the entries, otherwise click in the Use column to put a check mark on the entries you want to include).

5. If you don't want to change any options (see the following section if you want to make changes), click OK to transfer the items to the invoice.

6. Click Save & New to continue to the next invoice, or Save & Close if you are finished creating invoices.

Choose Billable Time and Costs					Ask a help question	Ask	▼ How Do I?	☒

Time and Costs For: **AllensMusic**

Items	$0.00	Expenses	$0.00	**Time**	**$0.00**	Mileage	$0.00

Select All   Click on Options... to customize how information from timesheets is brought into QuickBooks invoices   Options...

Use	Date	Employee	Service Item	Hours	Rate	Amount	Notes	Hide
	08/09/2004	Leah R. Telepan	Consulting	7:00	135.00	945.00		
	08/10/2004	Leah R. Telepan	Consulting	7:00	135.00	945.00		
	08/11/2004	Leah R. Telepan	Consulting	7:00	135.00	945.00		
	08/12/2004	Leah R. Telepan	Consulting	7:00	135.00	945.00		
	08/13/2004	Leah R. Telepan	Consulting	7:00	135.00	945.00		

☐ Print selected time and costs as one invoice item   Total billable time and costs   0.00

OK   Cancel   Help

FIGURE 18-7   Choose the timesheet entries you want to include on this invoice.

Changing Invoicing Options for Time Charges

You can change the way you transfer data from the timesheets to the invoice. You're not changing data or amounts, you're just altering the way in which data is presented on the invoice the client receives.

Printing One Invoice Item

If you just want to invoice the total amount for time charges instead of showing each activity, click the check box next to the selection Print Selected Time And Costs As One Invoice Item. Then click OK to return to the invoice.

Now you're going to go crazy unless you realize you have to take the word "print" literally. After you make the selection and return to the invoice form, you see every individual item listed on the invoice, with individual totals for each item. However, two things have changed on the invoice: the first line item is now an item named Reimb Group, and it has no amount. A new description appears below the individual time items, and it has an amount that is the total of the individual time charges. This entry is the description attached to the Reimb Group item.

Don't worry, the only thing that prints is this new Reimb Group, that last item. It prints as one item; the onscreen invoice is not the same as the printed invoice.

If you're a skeptic, click the arrow to the right of the Print button at the top of the invoice and select Preview to see what the printed invoice will look like (told ya so!).

If you don't want to combine all the time charges into one line, you can still be selective about the way information is transferred to the invoice. Click the Options button at the top of the Choose Billable Time And Costs dialog box to see your choices.

```
┌─────────────────────────────────────────────────────────┐
│ Options for Transferring Billable Time              [×]   │
├─────────────────────────────────────────────────────────┤
│  When transferring billable time to an invoice:          │
│       ⦿ Enter a separate line on the invoice for each activity │
│            ⦿ Transfer activity notes                     │
│            ○ Transfer item descriptions                  │
│            ○ Transfer both notes and descriptions        │
│       ○ Combine activities with the same service items   │
│                                                          │
│      [    OK    ]    [   Cancel   ]    [   Help   ]       │
└─────────────────────────────────────────────────────────┘
```

Transferring Notes and Item Descriptions to the Invoice

If you're entering each transaction as a discrete line item on the invoice, you can choose to print the notes on each timesheet, the service item description, or both. The text for both the notes and description appear in the Description column of the invoice.

Don't transfer notes unless you check every timesheet to make sure an employee hasn't entered a note you'd prefer the customer didn't see. Delete any such notes from the activity window when you edit the timesheets.

Subtotaling Line Items by Services

You can select the option Combine Activities With The Same Service Item to enter a single line item for each activity type. For example, if you have Consulting and Training as separate services, and there are several activities for each of those services, the invoice will have a line item for Consulting and another line item for Training. Each line will have the total for that service.

Using Timesheets for Payroll Job Costing

In this chapter:

- Configure payroll from timesheets
- Configure services and reports for job costing

When you turn on time tracking (covered in Chapter 18), you can connect it to your QuickBooks payroll functions. You just move the information about each employee's time into the employee's paycheck. In addition to speeding up the process of creating paychecks, this means you can improve job costing by tracking your payroll expenses against jobs.

Setting Up Payroll Data

If you want to link employee time to payroll or job costing, you must configure your QuickBooks system for those features.

Configuring the Employee Record

To link an employee to time tracking, you must select the time-tracking option on the Payroll Info tab of the employee record. To accomplish this, follow these steps:

1. Open the Employee List by choosing Lists | Employee List, or Employees | Employee List.
2. Double-click the list for an employee you want to link to time tracking.
3. In the Change Tabs drop-down list, choose Payroll And Compensation Info.
4. Select the option Use Time Data To Create Paychecks.

Opting to link paychecks to time tracking data doesn't mean that the employee's paycheck is absolutely and irrevocably linked to the employee's timesheets. It means only that when you prepare paychecks, QuickBooks checks timesheets before presenting the employee's paycheck form. You have total control over the number of hours and pay rate for the paycheck.

For hourly workers, if the employee's payroll information includes the hourly rate (and, optionally, the overtime hourly rate), that information is automatically inserted in that employee's timesheet.

If you haven't configured the employee's hourly rate, during the data entry process in the timesheet QuickBooks displays a message that no hourly rate exists, so the system will use a rate of $0.00. You can enter a rate when you're creating paychecks, or you can go through the employee information and set a rate for each hourly worker.

For salaried workers, the QuickBooks message about the lack of an hourly rate isn't "fixable." In fact, while the link to time tracking is advantageous for creating paychecks for hourly workers, the only reason to link salaried employees to time tracking is to track job costing.

Configuring Payroll Preferences for Job Costing

If your time tracking is just as important for job-costing analysis as it is for making payroll easier, you can configure your payroll reporting for that purpose:

1. Choose Edit | Preferences from the menu bar.
2. Click the Payroll & Employees icon, and then click the Company Preferences tab.
3. At the bottom of the window (see Figure 19-1), be sure the option Report All Payroll Taxes By Customer:Job, Service Item, And Class (if you're using classes) is selected. (QuickBooks preselects the option as the default setting.)
4. If you're using classes, specify the way to assign a class (see the next section, "Using Classes for Payroll Job Costing").
5. Click OK to save your preferences.

Using Classes for Payroll Job Costing

If you've established classes, you may be able to use those classes for the payroll expenses you're tracking as part of your job costing. The class feature won't work for payroll unless your classes match the available options in the Payroll & Employees Preferences dialog box. QuickBooks makes the following choices available:

• **Entire Paycheck** Means you assign a class to all payroll expenses on a check (including company-paid taxes), instead of assigning a class to individual payroll items.

• **Earnings Item** Means you can assign a class to each payroll item (in the Earnings section of the paycheck) that's used in the paycheck.

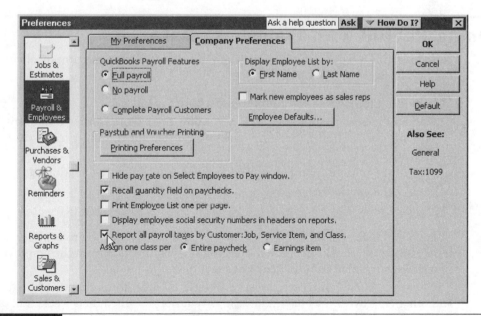

FIGURE 19-1 Use your payroll costs in job costing.

If your classes provide a tidy way to fit each employee into a class, the entire paycheck option will work. For example, if you have branch offices, each of which is a class, you can assign the paychecks according to the location of the employee. If your classes divide your company by the products or services you provide, then tracking classes by payroll item will produce useful reports. If your classes don't match the tracking options, you can just ignore the Class column when you're entering data or creating reports.

Using Timesheets Efficiently

If your employees only keep timesheets to indicate the billable work they do, that's not going to do much to automate the payroll process. Few employees fill every hour of their work day with billable activity, and you'll have to fill in the remaining information manually when you create the paycheck.

- Create at least one payroll item to cover nonbillable work. You can call it Administration, In-Office, or any other designation. The customer attached to this work is your own company (create a customer named In-House).
- Make sure employees account for every hour of the day and every day of the week.
- Have employees fill in days for sick pay or vacation pay on their timesheets. Those items are probably already part of your payroll items.

Running Payroll with Timesheet Data

When it's time to run the payroll, you can use the data from the timesheets to create the paychecks:

1. Choose Employees | Pay Employees from the menu bar.
2. When the Select Employees To Pay window opens, the Hours column displays the number of hours that employees accounted for in their timesheets (see Figure 19-2).
3. Select the option Enter Hours And Preview Check Before Creating.
4. Select the employees to pay.
5. Click Create.

Each employee's paycheck is previewed. For employees who are configured to have their paychecks generated from timesheets, the data from the employee's timesheet is transferred to the Earnings section.

Of course, some hourly employees will have billable hours that filled their week, and other employees may have administrative tasks that filled their week. Still others will have entered only the billable hours, and you'll have to fill in the hours devoted

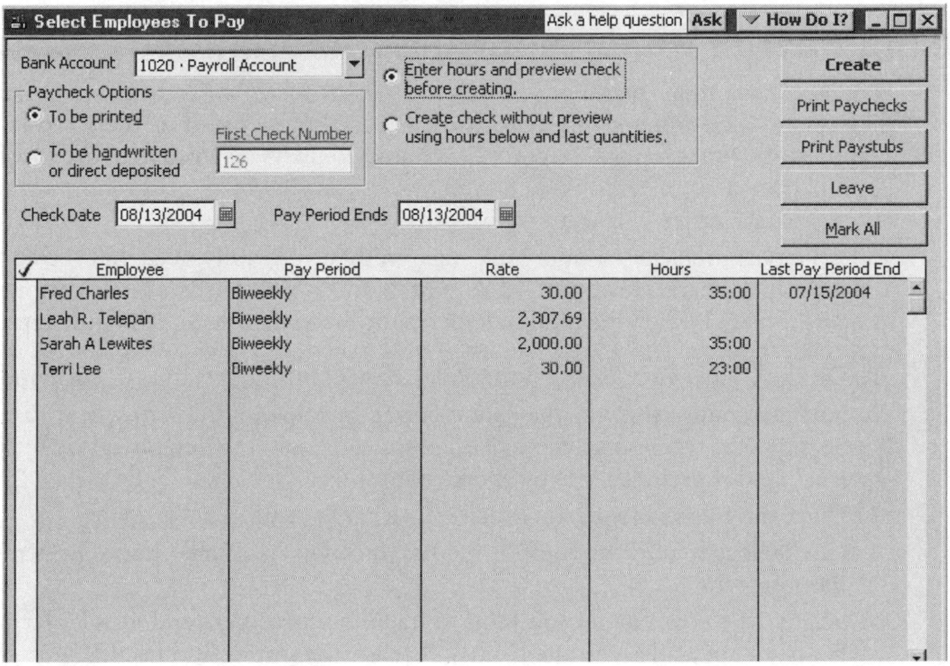

| Select Employees To Pay | | | | Ask a help question | Ask | How Do I? | _ □ × |

Bank Account 1020 · Payroll Account ▼

Paycheck Options
● To be printed
○ To be handwritten
   or direct deposited

First Check Number
126

○ Enter hours and preview check before creating.
○ Create check without preview using hours below and last quantities.

Create
Print Paychecks
Print Paystubs
Leave
Mark All

Check Date 08/13/2004   Pay Period Ends 08/13/2004

✓	Employee	Pay Period	Rate	Hours	Last Pay Period End
	Fred Charles	Biweekly	30.00	35:00	07/15/2004
	Leah R. Telepan	Biweekly	2,307.69		
	Sarah A Lewites	Biweekly	2,000.00	35:00	
	Terri Lee	Biweekly	30.00	23:00	

FIGURE 19-2 Not all the employees followed directions about filling out timesheets for every hour of work.

to administrative work yourself. If the timesheet data that is transferred to the paycheck doesn't account for all the time the employee is entitled to, you'll have to fill in the hours by adding administrative items:

1. Click the Item Name column in the Earnings section, and enter a nonbillable (administrative) payroll item.

2. In the Rate column, enter this employee's pay rate.

3. In the Hours column, enter the number of hours needed to complete this employee's work week.

4. Click Create.

 C A U T I O N : Changes you make to the payroll window are not updated on the timesheet.

See Chapter 8 for detailed information about creating payroll checks.

Running Payroll Reports for Cost Information

When you use time tracking, you can see reports on your payroll expenses as they relate to customers and jobs. The one I find most useful is the Payroll Transaction Detail report. To get to it, choose Reports | Employees & Payroll | Payroll Transaction Detail. When the Payroll Transaction Detail report appears, enter the date range you want to examine.

This report probably has more information than you really need, but the customer and job data is there. However, I've found that this report needs a bit of customization to make it useful. Click the Modify Report button to start customizing the report.

1. On the Display tab, deselect the Wage Base column, because it's not important.
2. You can change the way the data is sorted by clicking the arrow next to the Sort By text box and selecting a different category (the default sort is by date, but I find it useful to sort by source name).
3. Click the Filters tab; in the Filter list, select Payroll Item.
4. Click the arrow to the right of the Payroll Item field and choose Selected Payroll Items.
5. Select the payroll items you want to track for customers and jobs (Salary, Hourly Rate, and Overtime Hourly Rate are the ones I find useful).
6. Click OK twice to return to the report window with its new configuration.
7. Click the Memorize button to make this configuration permanent, giving it a name that reminds you of why you need the report (for example, payroll job costing).

Now you're all set! If you want to see the net profit for any customer or job, choose Reports | Jobs, Time & Mileage, and select one of the Job Profitability reports. The total costs, total revenue, and net gain appear for each customer and job. Double-click the costs and drill down to the individual costs that were posted to the job, and you'll find your payroll costs.

Using QuickBooks Timer

In this chapter:

- Install Timer

- Make copies for others

- Use Timer

- Export activities

- Export information to Timer users

- Import files from Timer

If you have QuickBooks Pro or QuickBooks Premier, you have QuickBooks Timer, a program that permits you and people who perform work for you to track time automatically. It works by providing an onscreen clock that ticks away as you perform tasks. Each time you start a task, you tell Timer what you're doing, and the program keeps track of the amount of time it takes to complete each task.

Installing Timer

The Timer software must be installed separately; it's not part of the standard QuickBooks Pro or Premier installation procedure. After you install it, you can give copies of the program to employees, subcontractors, or anyone else whose time you must track in order to send invoices to customers or perform cost analysis. Those folks do not have to have QuickBooks installed on their computers because Timer is a discrete software application.

The Timer program works on its own; you cannot launch it from within QuickBooks. It has its own menu choice on your computer's Program menu. Timer and QuickBooks interact by importing and exporting files between QuickBooks and the Timer software.

Installing the Program Files

To use Timer, you must install it on your computer from the original QuickBooks install disc. Before you begin the installation, close any programs that are open (including QuickBooks).

Put your QuickBooks software CD in the CD-ROM drive. If AutoRun launches the CD and asks if you want to install QuickBooks, click No. Choose Start | Programs | QuickBooks | Install QuickBooks Pro Timer (or Install QuickBooks Premier Timer).

 TIP: You can prevent the launch of the AutoRun program by holding down the SHIFT key after you insert the CD. Release the SHIFT key when the access light on the CD drive stops flashing.

The installation program launches, and you need only follow the prompts. The Installation Wizard displays the directory into which Timer will be installed (by default, C:\QBTIMER). If you have some reason to move the software to a different directory, choose Browse and select another location. You also have to approve the location of the Timer program listing on your Programs menu (by default, in a program listing named QuickBooks Pro/Premier).

The files are transferred to your hard drive, which takes only a short time. Then the installation program notifies you that the files have been installed and you must restart your computer to use the software. Choose Yes to restart your computer, and when you're up and running again the QuickBooks Pro Timer program listing appears on the submenu under QuickBooks Pro/Premier.

Distributing the Timer Software to Others

Everybody who performs work for you needs a copy of the Timer program. (This is perfectly legal, and your QuickBooks Pro Timer software license permits it.) As they track their activities, the data is saved in files that you can import into QuickBooks in order to fill out timesheets. The information in the files includes the customer for whom the work is being performed, the amount of time expended on tasks, and all the other information a timesheet should track. Using Timer is far more efficient and accurate than relying on everyone's memory as they attempt to fill out timesheets.

You can give recipients a copy of the Timer program in any of the following ways:

- On floppy disks that you create
- On a CD that you burn
- Via e-mail (for high-speed Internet connections only)

I'll go over the tasks involved for each of these methods in the following sections.

Creating Timer Software Floppy Disks

If you want to send the program on floppy disks to the people who will use the Timer program when working for you, use the following steps to create those disks:

1. Label three blank formatted floppy disks with a disk number (1, 2, and 3).

TIP: Be sure you indicate the word "Timer" on the floppy disk labels; It's confusing to your recipients to have a disk labeled #1 without a software name.

2. Put the QuickBooks CD in the CD-ROM drive. If it starts the installation program automatically, click Close.
3. Put the disk labeled Timer Disk #1 into your floppy disk drive.
4. On your Programs menu, point to the QuickBooks program item to display the submenu. Click the submenu program item named Create Timer Install Disks.

A wizard opens, presenting a series of instructions, all of which are easy to follow, except perhaps the Select Components window, which may be confusing.

Ignore the question about whether you want to install QuickBooks or QuickBooks Pro—it's there by mistake. The two options, A and B, refer to the floppy disk drive you're using to create the disks. (I haven't seen a computer with two floppy disk drives in many years, so I'm reasonably confident that I can tell you to select A.)

Just keep going until the three disks are created. It takes a while because you're copying files from a CD-ROM, which isn't as fast as a hard drive, and you're writing to a floppy disk drive, which is slower than a snail. After you create the first set of floppy disks, repeat the process for any other users to whom you need to send the program.

Creating a CD for the Timer Program

If your computer has a CD-R/CD-RW drive, you can burn a CD for the recipients. You might find this easier than creating floppy disks because you don't have to remain in front of the computer, switching disks, to complete the task. Also, I find more and more offices (and homes) where floppy disks just aren't available—people just don't keep them around the way they used to. Here's how to set up the Timer software for burning:

1. Put the QuickBooks 2004 software CD into the CD-ROM. If the installation program starts, click Close.
2. In Windows Explorer or My Computer, expand the hierarchy of the QuickBooks software CD to display its folders.
3. Right-click the folder QBTimer and choose Copy from the shortcut menu.
4. Right-click the icon for Drive C (or another hard drive, if you prefer), and choose Paste from the shortcut menu. This creates a folder named QBTimer on the hard drive, containing all the files from the QBTimer folder on the QuickBooks software CD.
5. Use your CD recording software to burn a CD of the files in the QBTimer folder. If you're running Windows XP, the recording feature is built in.
6. Label the CD and send it to the appropriate recipients.

 TIP: When you burn the CD, select only the files in the QBTimer folder, don't select the folder. If you select the folder, recipients will have to drill down into the folder to find the installation file.

E-mailing the Timer Software

If you and your recipients have high-speed Internet connections, and you both have a file compression program (such as WinZip or the built-in compression feature in Windows XP) you can e-mail the Timer software files (which measure about 3MB). Select all the files in QBTimer folder on the QuickBooks 2004 software CD, or in the QBTimer folder you created on your hard drive (see the previous section).

Right-click any file and choose the compression software command to create a single, compressed file. Then e-mail the file.

 NOTE: Compressing the file doesn't reduce the size of the files very much, because they're software files (only data files are filled with so much "air" that compressing them makes a substantial difference in size). The advantage of compressing the file is that you send only one file.

CAUTION: Don't e-mail the program to a recipient with an ISP that limits e-mail attachment sizes to 1MB.

Installing the Timer Program

On the receiving end, the installation of Timer is straightforward and easy (although you should provide specific directions to your recipients along with the files). Close all software, including any antivirus programs (always close software when installing software).

Installing from Floppy Disks

If you're installing from floppy disks, put floppy disk #1 into the floppy disk drive and start the installation in either of the following ways:

- Choose Start | Run, and in the Open text box enter **a:\install**. Then click OK.
- From Windows Explorer or My Computer, open Drive A and double-click Install.exe.

The Installation Wizard asks for each floppy disk as required, and when the Timer software is installed, a Programs menu listing for QuickBooks Pro appears on the Programs menu, and the Timer program is in the submenu. You must restart the computer after the installation is complete in order to use the Timer program.

Installing from CD

If you burned a CD for the recipient, the installation program doesn't launch automatically when the CD is inserted in the drive. In Windows Explorer or My Computer, access the CD and double-click Install.exe. Then follow the prompts to complete installation.

Installing from an E-mail File

If you e-mailed the file to the recipient, he or she should create a folder to hold the software files (name it TimerSoftware or something similar). Copy the compressed file into that folder and extract the files (the steps vary depending on whether the recipient uses WinZip, another compression application, or the Windows XP built-in file compression feature). When the files are extracted, double-click Install.exe and follow the prompts to install the software.

Installing from the QuickBooks Software CD

If you're giving the program to someone who works in your office but doesn't have QuickBooks installed on his or her computer, you don't have to spend all that time creating disks. Instead, follow these steps for a quick installation:

1. Insert the QuickBooks CD into the computer. If the QuickBooks installation program starts automatically, click Close to cancel it.
2. Open My Computer or Windows Explorer, right-click the icon for the CD drive, and choose Explore from the shortcut menu.
3. Select the folder named QBTimer to display its contents in the right pane.
4. In the right pane, double-click the file Install.exe.

Exporting Data Lists to Timer Users

You must export information from your company files to the Timer program so the program has data to use. The information is the data in your lists: employees and customers and jobs, vendors, and service items. If you're using classes in QuickBooks, the class list is also exported.

From the QuickBooks menu bar, choose File | Timer | Export Lists For Timer to open the Export Lists For Timer window. Click OK to begin the export process. You can also select the option to skip this opening screen in the future.

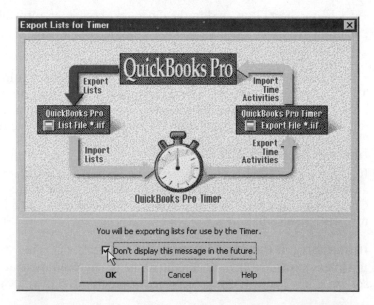

When the Export window opens (see Figure 20-1), choose a location for the file and give the file a name, using the following guidelines:

- Do not use more than eight characters in the filename (the .iif extension doesn't count, it's just the filename that's limited to eight characters). The Timer program doesn't recognize long filenames, so the recipient might have a difficult time finding the file if you give it one because the name will be truncated and contain the tilde (~) character.
- If you are creating the export file for your own use, save it in a folder on your hard drive. The default folder is your QuickBooks folder, which is as good a choice as any.
- If you are creating an export file that you're going to send on a floppy disk, click the arrow to the right of the Save In field and choose your floppy drive. Make sure you have a blank, formatted floppy disk in the drive.
- If you are creating the export file that you're going to send via e-mail, you can save it to any folder on your hard drive. However, it's faster if you save it to the default folder selected by your e-mail software when you choose to upload a file (usually My Documents).
- Give the file a name that will remind you of the company to which the data is attached. For instance, if the company name is A. J. Backstroke, Inc., you might want to name the export file AJB.iif. I also suggest you add a number to the filename (see the filename I used in Figure 20-1), because you may be sending replacement lists as you add customers, services, or other items to your QuickBooks company file. As the number in the filename increases, it's always clear which is the latest file.

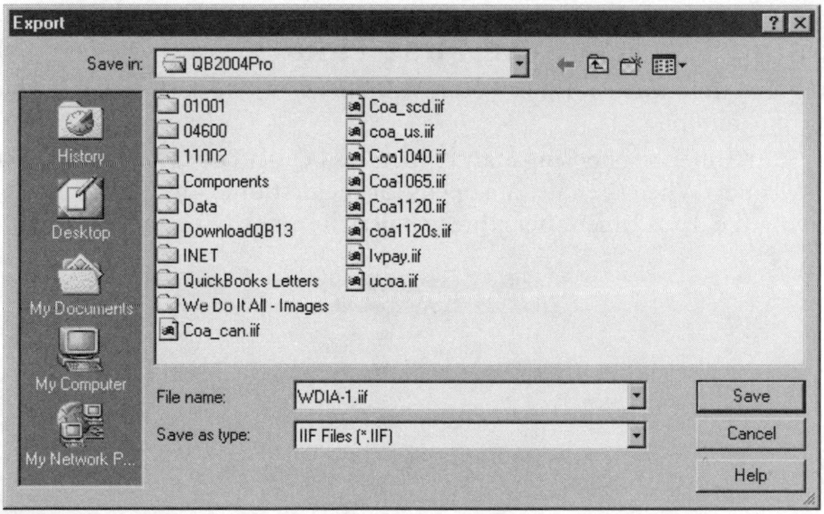

FIGURE 20-1   Name the export file and save it to a folder or a floppy disk.

NOTE: Don't forget to delete the asterisk (*) that QuickBooks places in the filename box.

QuickBooks adds an .iif file extension automatically, if you don't. Click Save to save the export file. QuickBooks displays a message announcing that the data has been exported successfully. Now you and other Timer users can use the file.

Incidentally, you only have to save this file once, even if you're shipping it to multiple Timer users. Save the file on your hard drive, then copy it to a floppy disk as many times as you need to, or send it via e-mail. However, if you add items, names, or other important data to your system file, you must create a new export file to include those items.

Using Timer

You use Timer to track your work and report the time you spend on each task. In order to report your time, the Timer software keeps a data file. That file can be brought into QuickBooks and imported into a timesheet, so you can get paid for the time.

You don't have to have QuickBooks installed on your computer to use Timer. You do, however, have to have information about the company for which you're doing the work. That information is contained in files that you import to your Timer software (the same exported files I discussed in the previous section). Then, when you use Timer, you can configure your tasks so the software knows who you are, what services you're performing, and which customer is being serviced.

Using Timer for the First Time

The first time you use Timer, you have a little setup work to do, after which you can go onto autopilot.

Start Timer by choosing Start | Programs | QuickBooks Pro/Premier | QuickBooks Pro Timer. When the software opens for the first time, there's no file established for saving the data. Timer offers three choices for remedying this problem.

No Timer File Is Open

- ● Create New Timer File
- ○ Open Sample Timer File
- ○ Open Existing Timer File

OK
Cancel
Help

Select Create New Timer File, and click OK.

TIP: QuickBooks provides a sample data file you can use to explore the software, but this program is easy enough to use that you can jump right in and use your own file.

When the New Timer File window opens, enter a location and a filename for your personal Timer data. By default, Timer offers to save the file in the same folder in which the software exists.

NOTE: If you're working on a network and saving your files to another computer on the network, click the Network button and map a drive to the folder you want to use.

Click OK to save the file. Timer displays a message telling you that you must import company information before you can use your new file, and it also offers to open a Help file that explains how to perform this task. You can click No, because the instructions are available right here.

The Timer window is on your screen, and the name of your file is on the Title Bar. However, because no data file is attached to it (yet), the important menu items aren't accessible.

The file with the needed data has already been created and exported (following the instructions in the previous section), so you can import it using the following steps:

1. Choose File | Import QuickBooks Lists from the menu bar of the Timer window to open the Import QuickBooks Lists introductory window (and click the option to stop displaying this window in the future).
2. Click Continue to display the Open File For Import window.
3. Select the folder (or floppy drive) that holds the lists file you received, and select the file.
4. Click OK.

> **N O T E :** If the person who prepared the file used a filename longer than eight characters, the filename appears with seven characters followed by a tilde (~).

Timer imports the file and then displays a message telling you that the file was imported successfully. Click OK to clear the message from the screen. Now it's time to go to work—and track your time as you work.

Using the Timer Window

All the menu items in the Timer software window are now accessible.

However, you have to set up an activity before the software can do its job. An *activity* is the work performed by a Timer user for one customer, during one day. Work performed for multiple customers requires multiple activities. An activity links three elements:

- The person using Timer
- The type of work that person is performing
- The customer for which that work is performed

Setting Up an Activity

Click the New Activity button to open the New Activity window and complete the form to establish this activity (see Figure 20-2).

The date is automatically filled in with the current date, and all the other fields are very easy to fill in. You just have to click the arrow to the right of each field to see the list that's been imported from the company you're working with. (Of course, there's no preconfigured list for the Notes field, which you can use to make comments.) If the activity is billable to the customer, be sure that option is selected.

 NOTE: Your name must be in the list that appears in the Your Name field, which means you've either been established as an employee, a vendor, or an "other name" in the original company's files.

 CAUTION: There is no option to add a new item to any list; you can only work with the items provided by the company's imported file.

After you've configured this activity, click Next to set up another activity, or click OK to return to the Timer window. Now the Timer window is ready to let you work. Select an activity from the drop-down list and get started (see Figure 20-3).

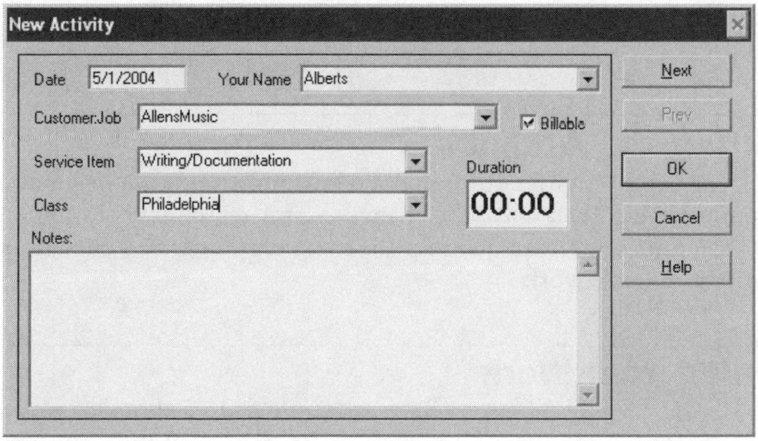

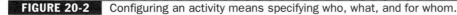

FIGURE 20-2 Configuring an activity means specifying who, what, and for whom.

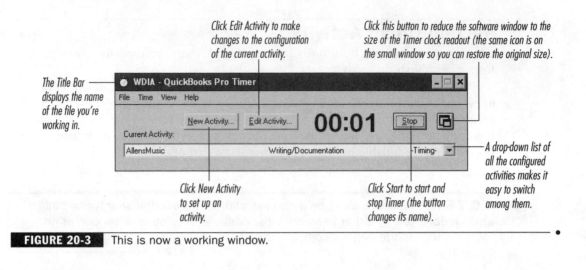

FIGURE 20-3 This is now a working window.

> **TIP:** Whether you leave the Timer window at its opening size or reduce it to a little square digital readout of time (like a digital clock), you can move it to a corner of your screen by dragging the Title Bar.

The activity you configured is a template containing the customer, the service, and your name (the user). All that's missing is the amount of time you spent working. The template is available all the time, and when you use it to time your activities, a copy of the template is loaded, and that copy is used for today's work (Timer works by the day). The original template, sans the elapsed time, remains in the system for later use.

Editing the Activity

Click the Edit Activity button to open a window with the original fields for the current activity. Then make the changes you need to make. Commonly, the changes involve a different service item for the same customer, or a change as to whether or not this is billable work.

Timing Your Work

Go to work. That might mean you're doing research, making telephone calls, building an ark, writing a white paper, or anything else for which the company pays you (and probably bills its customers).

1. Choose an activity from the Current Activity drop-down list.
2. Click the Start button. The Activity Bar displays "-Timing-" to indicate that timing is activated, and the elapsed minutes appear on the Timer window. The Start button changes to a Stop button.
3. If you need to stop working for a while, click the Stop button. The button changes its name to Resume.
4. If you stop working because you've finished the task, you can create another activity, choose a different activity from the Activity Bar, or close the software.

TIP: You can keep multiple activities running and switch among them. Each activity is automatically paused when you switch to another, and the new activity automatically starts the clock.

Each day, as you work with Timer, you can choose an activity from the Activity Bar. As you switch from activity to activity in the same day, you're resuming the activity, not starting a new one.

Setting Timer Preferences

After you've used Timer for a while, you may want to set preferences so the software works the way you prefer. To accomplish this, choose File | Preferences from the Timer menu bar to display the submenu, and use the following submenu items to configure Timer.

Default Name   You can select a name that is automatically entered in the Your Name field when you launch an activity.

Number Of Days To Remember Activities   You can specify the number of days that the Timer keeps an activity template (the default is 30). When the time expires, the template is removed.

Turn On All One Time Messages   You can bring back the message dialog boxes for which you selected the option Don't Show This Message Again.

Show Time When Minimized   Specify whether you want to see the elapsed time counter in the taskbar button when you minimize the Timer window. Minimize means minimized to a taskbar button, which is not the same as reducing the Timer window to a smaller size (which you accomplish by clicking the Reduce icon on the Timer window).

The most useful preference is the one that enters a default name every time you create a new activity. That name, of course, should be your own name. When you select this option, the Choose A Default Name window opens so you can select your name from the list. You can also set a default option for whether or not your work is billable to customers.

TIP: If more than one person uses Timer on your computer, it's probably better not to enter a default name. However, if you do enter a default name, the other user just has to choose an activity and click the Edit Activity button to change the name.

Exporting Timer Files

When you've completed your tasks or stopped for the day, you can send the company the information about your working hours. Some companies may want daily or weekly reports; others may want you to wait until you've completed a project.

Viewing the Log

Before you send your files back to QuickBooks, you should take a look at the information. Choose View | Time Activity Log from the Timer menu bar. When the Time Activity Log window opens, it shows today's activities (see Figure 20-4).

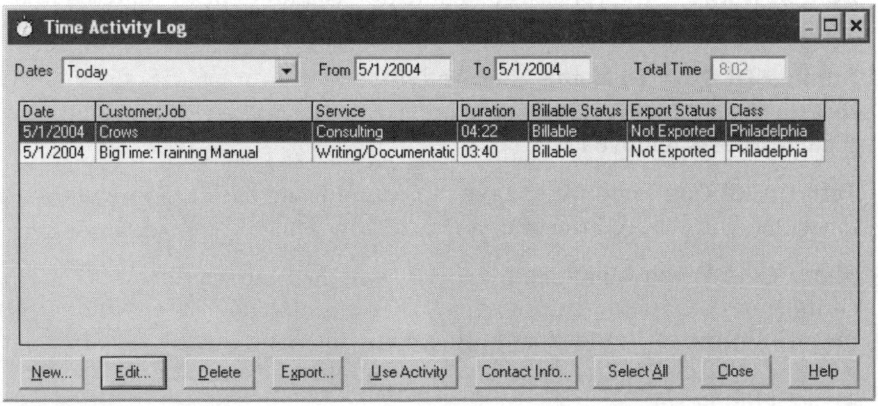

FIGURE 20-4 What did you do today?

If you wish, you can view a larger range of activities by changing the dates covered by this log. Click the arrow to the right of the Dates field and choose a different interval, or enter dates directly in the From and To fields.

Editing an Entry

You can change the information in any entry by double-clicking it (see Figure 20-5). The most common reasons to do this are to change the time (especially if you worked on this activity away from your computer, so no timer was running) or to add a note. If you want to change the time, enter the new time in the Duration field.

Creating an Export File

If you want to get paid, you must export your information to QuickBooks so your timesheet can be used to calculate payment. You can either choose specific entries for export, or export all the information in your Timer system.

1. Stop all Timer activities.
2. Choose View | Time Activity Log.
3. Choose the entries to export, as follows:
   - To export all entries click the Select All button.
   - To export multiple entries, click the first entry you want to export and hold down the CTRL key as you click any additional entries.
   - To export a single entry, select it.

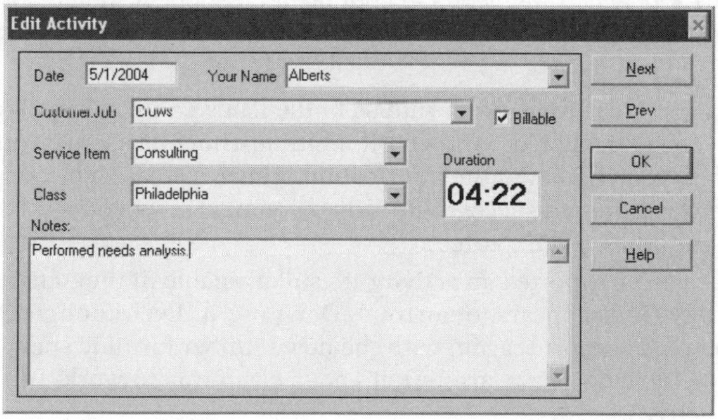

![Edit Activity dialog box showing fields: Date 5/1/2004, Your Name Alberts, Customer:Job Ciows, Billable checkbox checked, Service Item Consulting, Class Philadelphia, Duration 04:22, Notes: Performed needs analysis. Buttons: Next, Prev, OK, Cancel, Help.]

FIGURE 20-5 Make adjustments to the data, add a note, or do both.

4. Click the Export button to launch the Export Time Activities process.

5. Click Continue if the opening explanation window is displayed. (Remember, you can select the option to stop showing this window.)

6. In the Export Time Activities dialog box, select All Unexported Time Activities and enter the date you want to use as the cut-off date for selecting activities; or select Selected Activities, depending on your choice in Step 2.

Export Time Activities

Export
- All unexported time activities through 5/2/2004
- Selected activities

OK
Cancel
Help

7. Click OK.

8. When the Create Export File window opens, select a location for the file and give it an appropriate name.

 TIP: If you know you're ready to export all your files, you don't have to open the Time Activity Log. Instead, from the QuickBooks Pro Timer window, choose File | Export Time Activities. Timer exports all your unexported time activities.

CAUTION: Timer won't accept filenames longer than eight characters.

It's a good idea to use your initials in the name so there won't be any problems back at the QuickBooks computer if multiple Timer users are sending files. Click OK when you've entered the information. Timer displays a message telling you that the file was exported successfully. When you next view your activity log, the Export Status column says "Exported."

After you've exported an activity, it's still available in the Activity Bar for the rest of the day (it disappears tomorrow). Don't use it. Even though QuickBooks will permit you to export it again with the new number for time spent on the activity (although you do get a warning), it's not a clean way to work. Instead, start a new Timer activity.

Send the file back to the person who's responsible for entering this data into QuickBooks. You can send a disk or use e-mail.

Importing Timer Files Back into QuickBooks

When you receive Timer files from employees and subcontractors, you must import them into QuickBooks. This is a simple process, and QuickBooks takes care of putting the information you've received into the appropriate files.

Importing the File

On the QuickBooks menu bar, choose File | Timer | Import Activities From Timer. The first time you perform this task, you see another one of those Timer explanatory windows; this one is welcoming you to the file importing process. Select the option to skip this window in the future so you can get right to work. Then click OK. The Import window opens so you can locate and select the file. QuickBooks notifies you when the file has been imported and displays a summary of the contents.

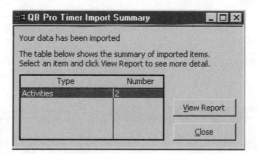

If you want to see details, click View Report to see a Timer Import Detail report, as shown in Figure 20-6.

Double-click a line item in the report to see even more details in the form of the timesheet that's created. You can edit the timesheet if you wish; it's common to make the final decision at this point about whether the activity is going to be billed to the client. You can also edit or remove any notes added by the user, as shown in Figure 20-7.

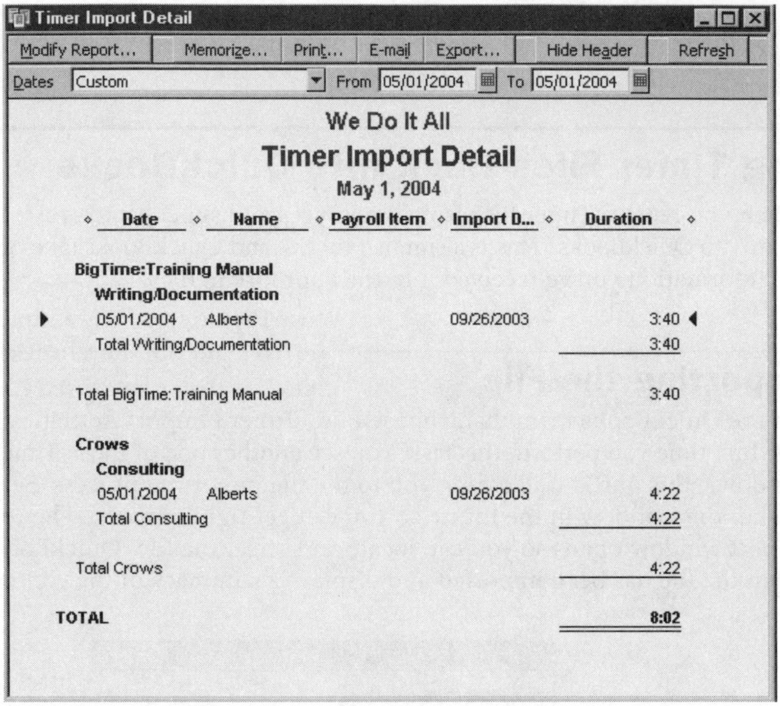

FIGURE 20-6 You can view the information that's in the Timer file.

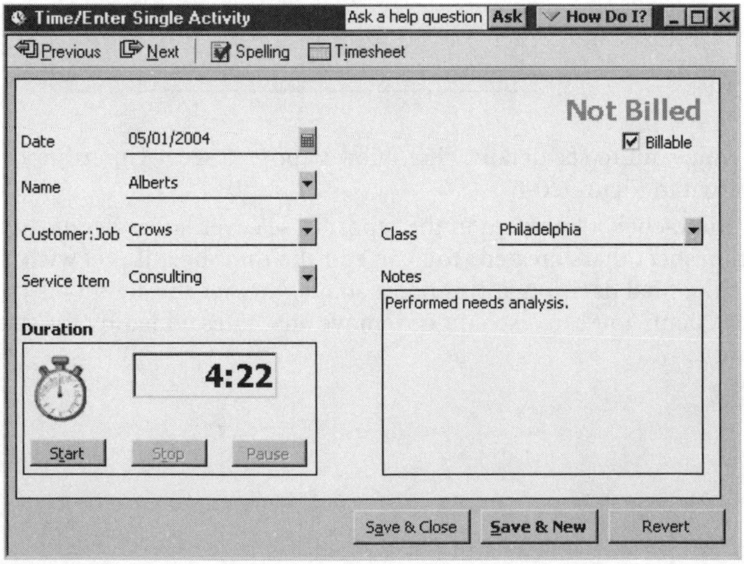

FIGURE 20-7 You can edit the timesheet to make sure it's accurate.

Using Timer Data with Timesheets

What makes all of this seem almost miraculous is the way you can use this data without doing anything. It's just there, waiting for you. Timer data is sent to the user's timesheet, and from there on, everything is on autopilot.

Open the Weekly Timesheets (choose Employees | Time Tracking | Use Weekly Timesheet), and select the name of the person who sent you the Timer file. Voilà! Everything's there.

For employees who are paid using their timesheets, wait until payday and head right for the Create Paychecks window (choose Employees | Pay Employees). Once again, everything's there (having been transferred from the timesheets).

See Chapter 18 for more information about using timesheets; see Chapter 19 for information about integrating timesheets with payroll.

Managing QuickBooks

All software needs TLC, and accounting software needs regular maintenance to ensure its accuracy and usefulness.

In Part Four of this book, you'll learn how to customize QuickBooks so it works more efficiently. The chapters in Part Four cover the features and tools you can use to make QuickBooks even more powerful. In addition, you'll learn how to maintain the file system, create additional company files, and use QuickBooks in network mode (so more than one person can be working in QuickBooks at the same time).

Of course, I'm going to cover backing up your data, which is the most important maintenance task in the world. Once you put your accounting data into QuickBooks, your business life depends on it. Hard drives die, motherboards freak out, power supplies go to la-la land, and all sorts of other calamities are just waiting to happen. Backing up saves your life (at least your business life).

Customizing QuickBooks

In this chapter:

- Change general preferences

- Customize the QuickBooks window

- Create users and passwords

- Use QuickBooks on a network

- Create classes

QuickBooks "out of the box" is set to run efficiently, providing powerful bookkeeping tools that are easy to use. However, you may have specific requirements because of the way you run your company, the way your accountant likes things done, or the way you use your computer. No matter what your special requirements are, it's likely that QuickBooks can accommodate you.

Changing Preferences

The preferences you establish in QuickBooks have a great impact on the way data is kept and reported. It's not uncommon for QuickBooks users to change or tweak these preferences periodically. In fact, the more you use QuickBooks and understand the way it works, the more comfortable you'll be about changing preferences.

You can reach the Preferences window by choosing Edit | Preferences from the QuickBooks menu bar. When the Preferences window opens for the first time, the General section of the window is selected (see Figure 21-1). If you've used the Preferences window previously, it opens to the section you were using when you closed the window.

Each section of the Preferences window is accessed by clicking the appropriate icon in the left pane. No matter which section you view, you see two tabs: My Preferences and Company Preferences.

- The My Preferences tab is where you configure your preferences as a QuickBooks user, and each user you create in QuickBooks can set his or her own preferences. QuickBooks will apply the correct preferences as each user logs in to the software. (Many sections lack options in this tab.)
- The Company Preferences tab is the place to configure the way QuickBooks accounting features work for the current company, regardless of which user logs in.

As you select options and move from one section of the Preferences window to another, you'll be asked whether you want to save the changes in the section you just left.

General Preferences

Since the Preferences window starts us in the General section, let's begin there.

Setting My Preferences for the General Section

The My Preferences tab of the General section offers a number of options you can select. They're all designed to let you control the way QuickBooks behaves while you're working in transaction windows.

Pressing Enter Moves Between Fields   This option exists for people who constantly forget that the default (normal) key for moving from field to field in Windows software is the TAB key. Of course, when they press ENTER instead of TAB, the record they're working on is saved even though they haven't finished filling out

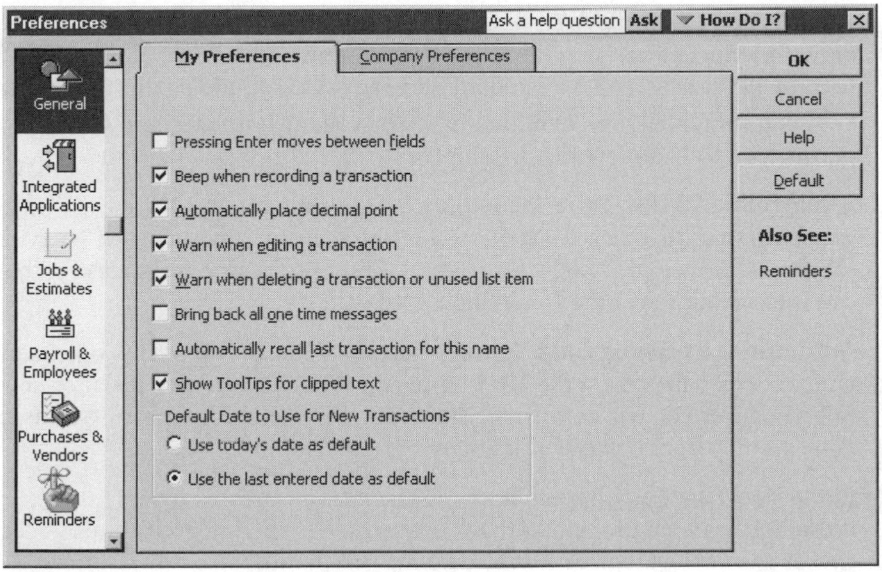

FIGURE 21-1   Configure QuickBooks to behave the way you prefer.

all the fields. Rather than force you to get used to the way Windows works, QuickBooks lets you change the procedure.

Beep When Recording A Transaction   If you don't want to hear sound effects as you work in QuickBooks, you can deselect the option. On the other hand, you can configure the sounds so that some actions produce sound effects and other actions don't. You can even specify which sound you want for the actions that you've configured to play sounds. To learn how to change the sound schemes, see the section "Desktop View Preferences," later in this chapter.

Automatically Place Decimal Point   This is a handy feature once you get used to it (I couldn't live without it—and my desk calculator is configured for the same behavior). When you enter monetary characters in a field, a decimal point is placed to the left of the last two digits. Therefore, if you type 5421, when you move to the next field the number changes to 54.21. If you want to type in even dollar amounts, type a period after you enter 54, and QuickBooks will automatically add two zeros to the right of the period (or you can enter the zeros, as in 5400, which automatically becomes 54.00).

Warn When Editing A Transaction   This option, which is selected by default, tells QuickBooks to flash a warning message when you change any transaction and try to close the transaction window without explicitly saving the changed transaction. This means you have a chance to abandon the edits. If you deselect the option, the edited transaction is saved, unless it is linked to other transactions (in which case, the warning message appears).

Warn When Deleting A Transaction Or Unused List Item   When selected, this option produces a warning when you delete a transaction or an item that has not been used in a transaction—it's a standard message asking you to confirm your action.

If you try to delete an item that has been used in a transaction, QuickBooks won't permit you to complete the deletion.

Bring Back All One-Time Messages   One-time messages are those introductory windows that include a Don't Show This Message Again option. If you've selected the Don't Show option, select this check box to see those messages again (and you can once again select the Don't Show option).

Automatically Recall Last Transaction For This Name   This option means that QuickBooks will present the last transaction for any name (for instance, a vendor) in full whenever you use that name. This feature is useful for repeating transactions, but you can turn it off if you find it annoying.

Show ToolTips For Clipped Text   This option (enabled by default) means that if there is more text in a field than you can see, hovering your mouse over the field causes the entire block of text to display. Very handy!

Default Date To Use For New Transactions   Tell QuickBooks whether you want the Date field to show the current date or the date of the last transaction you entered when you open a transaction window. If you frequently enter transactions for the same date over a period of several days (for example, you start preparing invoices on the 27th of the month, but the invoice date is the last day of the month), select the option to use the last entered date so you can just keep going.

Setting Company Preferences for the General Section

The Company Preferences tab in the General section has three choices, explained here.

Time Format   Select a format for entering time and choose between decimal (for example, 11.5 hours) or minutes (11:30).

Always Show Years As 4 Digits   If you prefer to display the year with four digits (01/01/2004 instead of 01/01/04), select this option.

Never Update Name Information When Saving Transactions   By default, QuickBooks asks if you want to update the original information for a name when you change it during a transaction entry. For example, if you're entering a vendor bill and you change the address, QuickBooks offers to make that change back on the vendor record. If you don't want to be offered this opportunity, select this option.

Accounting Preferences

Click the Accounting icon on the left pane of the Preferences window to move to the Accounting preferences. There are only Company Preferences available for this section (see Figure 21-2); the My Preferences tab has no options available.

Choose the options you require for efficiency and ease of use.

Use Account Numbers   Choose this option if you want to use numbers for your chart of accounts in addition to names.

Show Lowest Subaccount Only   This option, which is available only if you use account numbers, is useful because it means that when you see an account number in a drop-down list (in a transaction window), you only see the subaccount. If the option is not selected, you see the parent account followed by the subaccount, and since the field display doesn't show the entire text unless you scroll through it, it's hard to determine which account has been selected.

Require Accounts   When enabled, this option means that every item and transaction you create in QuickBooks has to be assigned to an account. If you disable this option, transaction amounts that aren't manually assigned to an account are posted to Uncategorized Income or Uncategorized Expense.

Use Class Tracking   This option turns on the Class feature for your QuickBooks system (which is discussed later in this chapter in the section "Configuring Classes"). The Use Class Tracking suboption for this setting is to have QuickBooks prompt you to fill in the Class field whenever you close a transaction window without doing so.

Use Audit Trail   Select this option to keep a log of changed transactions. What's important about this option is that deleted transactions are listed in the audit trail, and you should always have a way to see if a transaction has been deleted (for one thing, deletions make embezzling easier). To see the audit log, click the Reports listing on the Navigation bar. Choose the Accountant & Taxes report type, then choose Audit Trail.

Automatically Assign General Journal Entry Number This option means that every time you create a general journal entry, QuickBooks automatically assigns the next available number to it.

Closing Date Enabling this option lets you set a password-protected closing date for your QuickBooks data file. Once you set the date and create a password, nobody can manipulate any transactions that are dated on or before the closing date unless they know the password.

Checking Preferences

This section has options in both the My Preferences and Company Preferences tabs. On the My Preferences tab (see Figure 21-3), you can select default bank accounts for different types of transactions. You can skip these options if you only have one bank account.

The Company Preferences tab (see Figure 21-4) offers several options concerned with check printing, which are described here.

Print Account Names On Voucher This option is useful only if you print your checks and the check forms you purchase have vouchers (stubs). If so, selecting this option means that the stub will show the Payee, the posting account, and the

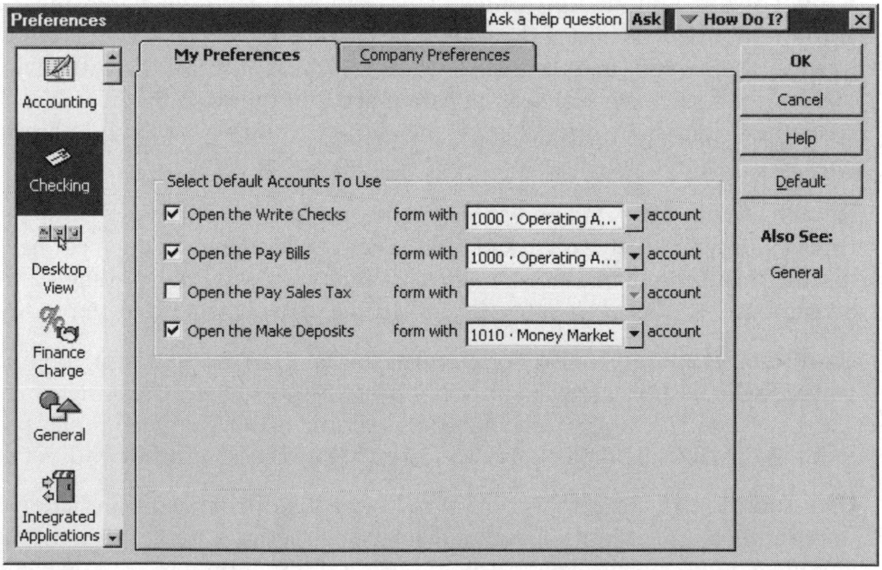

FIGURE 21-3 Save time and avoid mistakes by automatically selecting the right bank account when you create transactions.

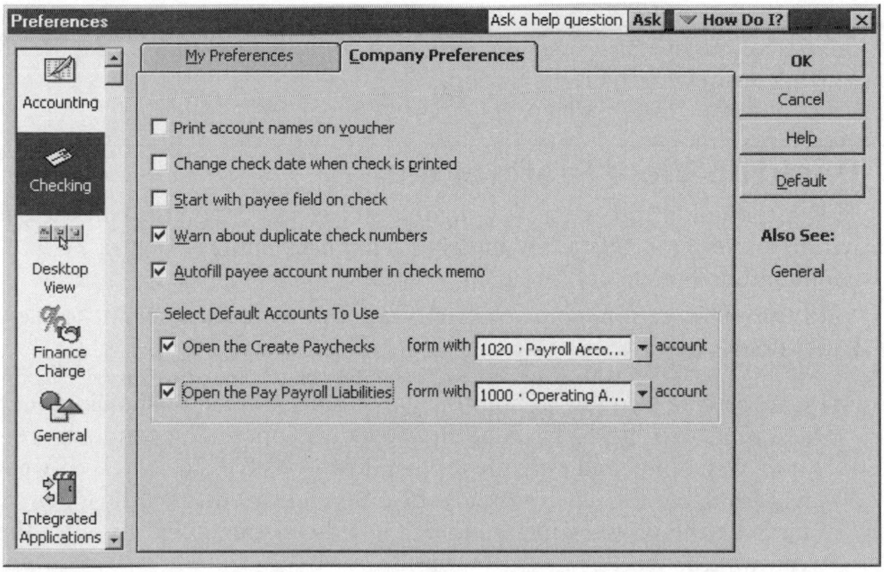

FIGURE 21-4   Select the options you need to make check writing more efficient.

first 16 lines of any memo you entered on the bill you're paying. If the check is for inventory items, the item name appears instead of the posting account. If the check is a payroll check, the payroll items and amounts are printed on the voucher.

Change Check Date When Check Is Printed   Selecting this option means that at the time you print checks, the current date becomes the check date. If you don't select this option, the check date you specified when you filled out the check window is used (even if that date has already passed).

Start With Payee Field On Check   This option forces your cursor to the Payee field when you first bring up the Write Checks window. If the option is off, the bank account field is the first active field. If you always write checks from one specific bank account, enable the option to save yourself the inconvenience of pressing TAB.

Warn About Duplicate Check Numbers   This option means that QuickBooks will warn you if a check number you're filling in already exists.

Autofill Payee Account Number In Check Memo   Most vendors maintain an account number for their customers, and your account number can be automatically printed when you print checks. In order for this to occur, you must fill in your account number in the Vendor card (on the Additional Information tab). The printout appears on the lower-left section of the check.

Select Default Accounts To Use   You can set the default bank accounts for payroll checks and payroll liability payments. Then, when you print these checks, you don't have to select the bank account from the transaction window (which usually displays the main bank account). This avoids the common error of printing the payroll on operating account checks, screaming "Eek!", voiding the checks, and starting again with the right account.

Desktop View Preferences

This section of the preferences configuration lets you design the way the QuickBooks window looks and acts. Only the My Preferences tab (see Figure 21-5) contains configuration options.

In the View section, you can specify whether you always want to see one QuickBooks window at a time, or view multiple windows.

- Choose One Window to limit the QuickBooks screen to showing one window at a time, even if you have multiple windows open. The windows are stacked atop each other, and only the top window is visible. To switch between multiple windows, use the Open Window List. If you don't display the Open Window List, use the Window menu on the QuickBooks menu bar to select the window you want to work in.
- Choose Multiple Windows to make it possible to view multiple windows on your screen. Selecting this option activates the arrangement commands on the Windows menu item, which allows you to stack or arrange windows so that more than one window is visible at a time.

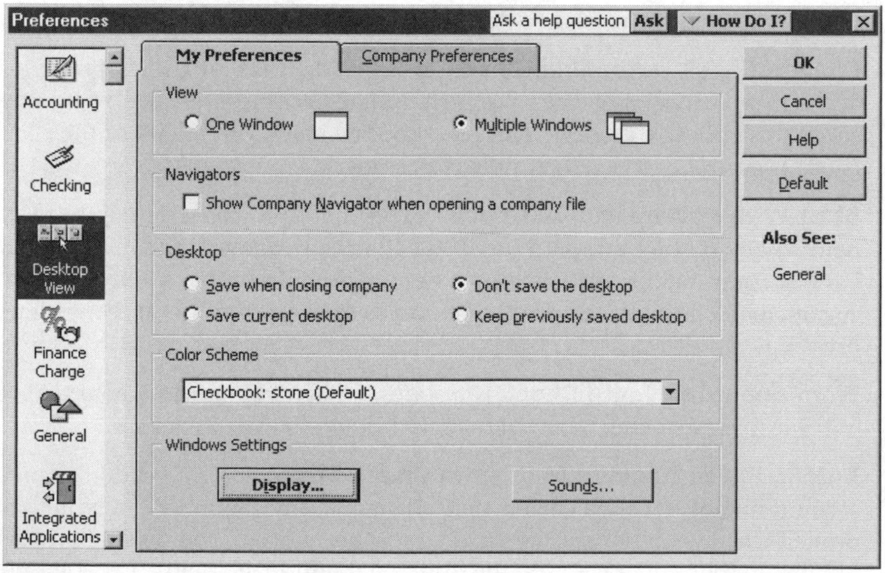

FIGURE 21-5   Configure the look and behavior of QuickBooks.

In the Navigators section, if you want to display the Company Navigator window whenever you open a company, select Show Company Navigator When Opening A Company File. This means the Navigator window appears when you start QuickBooks (which loads the last-used company during startup), or when you change companies while working in QuickBooks.

In the Desktop section, you can specify what QuickBooks should do when you exit the software, choosing among the following options:

- **Save When Closing Company**   Means that the state of the desktop is remembered when you close the company (or exit QuickBooks). Whatever QuickBooks windows were open when you left will reappear when you return. You can pick up where you left off.
- **Save Current Desktop**   Displays the desktop as it is at this moment every time you open QuickBooks. Select this option after you've opened or closed the QuickBooks windows you want to see when you start the software. If you choose this option, an additional choice named Keep Previously Saved Desktop appears on the window the next time you open Preferences.
- **Don't Save The Desktop**   Tells QuickBooks to display an empty QuickBooks desktop when you open this company or when you start QuickBooks again after using this company. The desktop isn't really empty—the menu bar, Icon Bar, and any other navigation bars are on the desktop, but no transaction or list windows are open.
- **Keep Previously Saved Desktop** (available only if you select Save Current Desktop)   Tells QuickBooks to display the desktop as it was the last time you used the Save Current Desktop option.

In the Color Scheme section, you can select a scheme from the drop-down list. In addition to a group of color schemes built into QuickBooks, you have the option of selecting the standards you set for Windows.

TIP: QuickBooks takes quite a bit of time to open after you select it from your Programs menu or a desktop icon. In addition, when you exit QuickBooks, it takes a long time for the program window to close. If you hate to wait, you can speed QuickBooks up by selecting the option Don't Save The Desktop and by deselecting the option to display the Company Navigator.

In addition to the options on this preferences tab, buttons are available to configure general settings for Display and Sounds. Clicking either button opens the associated applet in your Windows Control Panel. The configuration options you change in the Display applet affect your computer and all your software, not just QuickBooks.

Configuring sounds, however, only affects QuickBooks tasks (as long as you only manipulate the sounds attached to QuickBooks actions).

Select each QuickBooks action, and click the right arrow between the Name field and the Browse button to hear the sound. If you want to change the sound association, take one of the following steps:

- To remove the sound, click the small down arrow at the end of the Name text box and select None.
- To change the sound, click the small down arrow at the end of the Name text box and select another sound file. (If you've installed additional sound files, click Browse to locate them and select the one you want.)

Finance Charge Preferences

Click the Finance Charge icon (which has only Company Preferences available) to turn on, turn off, and configure finance charges. Finance charges can get complicated, so read the complete discussion about this topic in Chapter 5.

Integrated Applications Preferences

For all QuickBooks versions except QuickBooks Basic, you can let third-party software have access to the data in your QuickBooks files. Click the Integrated Applications icon and move to the Company Preferences tab to specify the way QuickBooks works with other software programs. You can give permission to access all data, no data, or some data. (See Appendix B for a discussion about finding and using applications that are designed to work with QuickBooks data.)

Jobs & Estimates Preferences

For QuickBooks Pro and QuickBooks Premier, you can configure the way your estimates and invoices work, as shown in Figure 21-6. The options are self-explanatory. Read Chapter 3 to learn everything about creating estimates and invoices.

Payroll & Employees Preferences

Use the Company Preferences tab of this section of the Preferences window to set all the configuration options for payroll. Read Chapter 8 to understand the selections in this window.

Purchases & Vendors Preferences

The Company Preferences tab (see Figure 21-7) has several configuration options for using purchase orders and paying vendor bills:

Inventory And Purchase Orders Are Active   Select this option to tell QuickBooks that you want to enable the inventory features; the purchase orders are automatically enabled with that action.

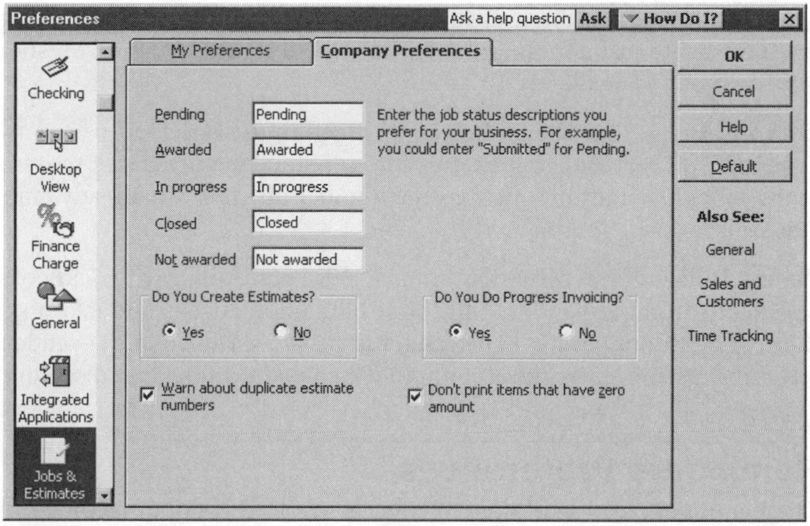

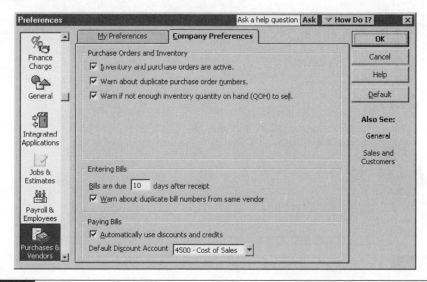

FIGURE 21-6 Turn estimating on or off and specify the jargon you want to use for tracking jobs.

Warn About Duplicate Purchase Order Numbers When this option is enabled, any attempt to issue a purchase order with a PO number that already exists will generate a warning.

Warn If Not Enough Inventory Quantity On Hand (QOH) To Sell This option turns on the warning feature that is useful during customer invoicing. If you sell ten widgets, but your stock of widgets is fewer than ten, QuickBooks displays

FIGURE 21-7 Configure QuickBooks to make it easier for you to manage inventory items.

a message telling you there's insufficient stock to fill the order. You can still complete the invoice; it's just a message, not a functional limitation, but you should order more widgets immediately.

Entering Bills   Use the options in this section to set default payment terms for vendors (you can change the terms for individual vendors) and to issue a warning if you enter a vendor bill that has the number of a bill you already entered from this vendor.

Paying Bills   If you select the automatic discounts option, QuickBooks will apply any credits from the vendor to the open bills automatically and take any discount that the vendor's terms permit. (The vendor terms are specified in the vendor's file.) If you select this option, enter the account to which you want to post discounts taken.

Reminders Preferences

The Reminders section of the Preferences window has options on both tabs. The My Preferences tab has one option, which turns on the Reminders feature. When the Reminders feature is enabled, QuickBooks displays a Reminders list when you open a company file.

The Company Preferences tab enumerates the available reminders, and you can select the ones you want to use (see Figure 21-8). Of course, these selections are meaningless unless you enabled Reminders in the My Preferences tab.

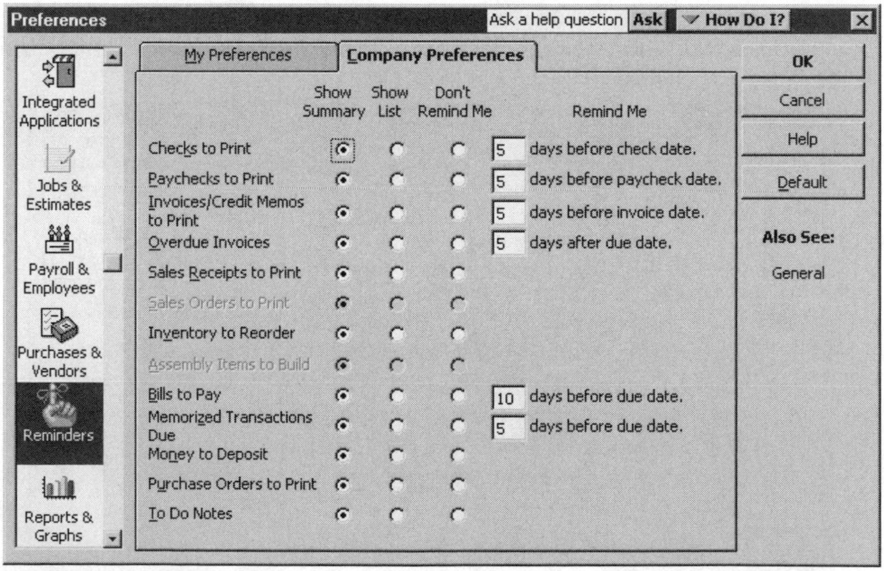

FIGURE 21-8   Decide which tasks you want to be reminded about.

For each item, decide whether you want to see a summary (just a listing and the total amount of money involved), a complete detailed list, or nothing at all. You can also determine the amount of lead time you want for your reminders.

NOTE: If you choose Show Summary, the Reminder List window has a button you can click to see the details.

Reports & Graphs Preferences

This is another section of the Preferences window that has choices on both tabs, so you can set your own user preferences and then set those options that affect the current company.

My Preferences Tab

The My Preferences tab (see Figure 21-9) configures performance issues for reports and graphs.

Reports and Graphs

While you're viewing a report or a graph, you can make changes to the format, the filters, or to the data behind it (by opening the appropriate transaction window and changing data). Most of the time, QuickBooks automatically changes the report/graph

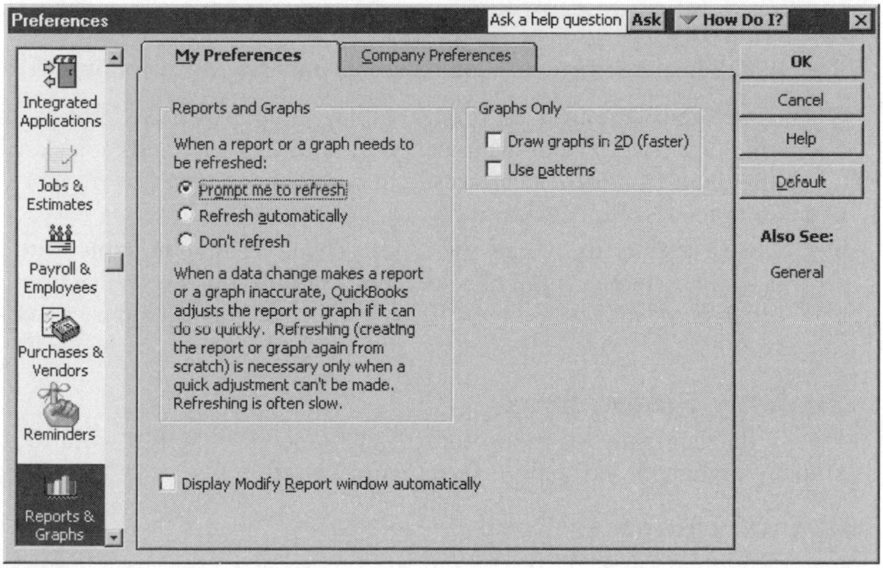

FIGURE 21-9 Set the parameters you want to use when you create reports and graphs.

to match the changes. However, if there is anything else going on (perhaps you're also online, or you're in a network environment and other users are manipulating data that's in your report or graph), QuickBooks may not make changes automatically. The reason for the shutdown of automatic refreshing is to keep your computer running as quickly and efficiently as possible. At that point, QuickBooks has to make a decision about when and how to refresh the report or graph. You must give QuickBooks the parameters for making the decision to refresh.

- Choose Prompt Me To Refresh to see a message asking you whether you want to be reminded to refresh the report or the graph after you've made changes to the data behind it. When the reminder appears, you can click Yes to refresh the data in the report.
- Choose Refresh Automatically if you're positively compulsive about having up-to-the-second data and don't want to bother to click the Refresh button. If you work with QuickBooks across a network, this could slow down your work a bit because whenever any user makes a change to data that's used in the report/graph, it will refresh itself.
- Choose Don't Refresh if you want to decide for yourself, without any reminder from QuickBooks, when to click the Refresh button on the report window.

Display Modify Report Window Automatically

If you find that almost every time you select a report you have to customize it, you can tell QuickBooks to open the Modify Report window whenever a report is brought to the screen. If you find this feature useful, click the check box next to Display Modify Report Window Automatically.

Graphs Only

Give QuickBooks instructions about creating your graphs, as follows:

- Choose Draw Graphs In 2D (Faster) to have graphs displayed in two dimensions instead of three. This doesn't impair your ability to see trends at a glance; it's just not as "high-tech." The main reason to consider this option is that the 2-D graph takes much less time to draw on your screen.
- Choose Use Patterns to draw the various elements in your graphs with black-and-white patterns instead of colors. For example, one pie wedge may be striped, another speckled. This is handy if you print your graphs to a black-and-white printer.

Company Preferences

Move to the Company Preferences tab of the Reports & Graphs window to set company preferences for reports (see Figure 21-10).

Summary Reports Basis

Specify whether you want to see summary reports as accrual-based or cash-based. You're only setting the default specification here, and you can always change the basis in the Modify Report dialog when you actually display the report.

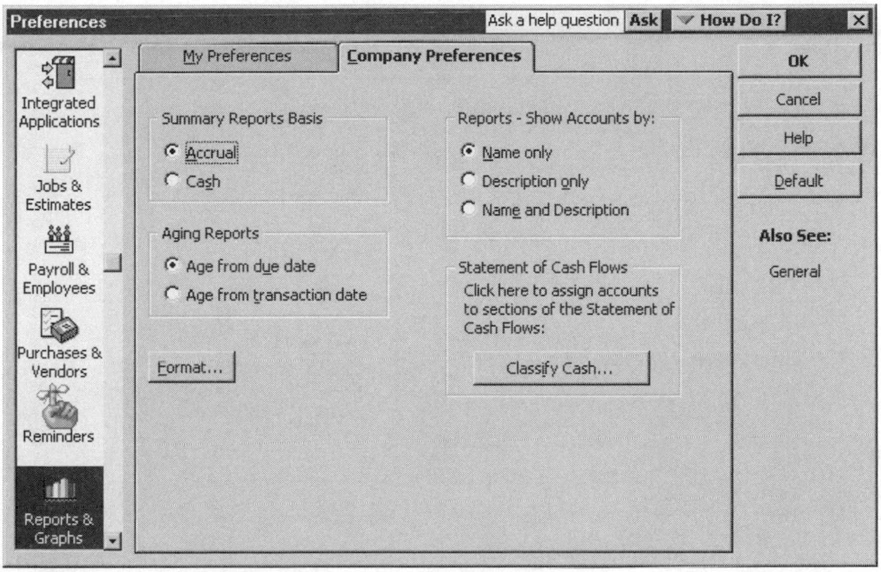

FIGURE 21-10   Set the default options for reports.

Aging Reports

Specify whether you want to generate A/R and A/P aging reports using the due date or the transaction date.

Reports—Show Accounts By

Specify whether you want accounts to display their account names, their descriptions, or both.

Setting Report Format Defaults

You can set the default formatting for reports by clicking the Format button and making changes to the default configuration options for parts of reports that aren't data-related, but instead control the look of the reports (see Figure 21-11). Use this feature if you find yourself making the same modifications to the formats over and over. See Chapter 15 for detailed information on creating and customizing reports.

Configuring the Cash Flow Report

A cash flow report is really a complicated document, and before the days of accounting software, accountants spent many hours creating such a report (and charged a lot of money for doing so). QuickBooks has configured a cash flow report format that is used to produce the cash flow reports available in the list of Company & Financial reports.

You can view the format by clicking the Classify Cash button, but you shouldn't mess around with the selections in the window that appears until you check with your accountant. You can learn about cash flow reports in Chapter 15.

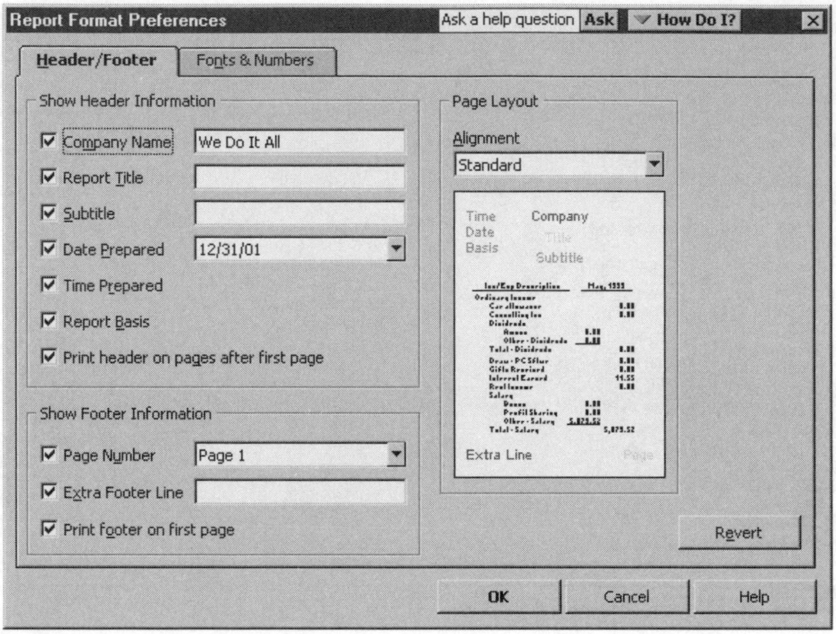

FIGURE 21-11 Set the default selections for report layout and fonts.

Sales & Customers Preferences

You can set a few options as defaults in the Sales & Customer section of the Company Preferences window:

Usual Shipping Method   Use this to set the default shipping method, if you use the same shipping method most of the time. This saves you the trouble of making a selection from the drop-down list unless you're changing the shipper for a particular invoice.

Default Markup Percentage   You can preset a markup for items that have both a cost and price (inventory items). Enter the number; QuickBooks automatically adds the percent sign.

QuickBooks uses the percentage you enter here to automate the pricing of inventory items. When you're creating an inventory item, as soon as you enter the cost, QuickBooks automatically adds this percentage and displays the result as the price. If your pricing paradigm isn't consistent, you'll find this automatic process more annoying than helpful, because you'll constantly find yourself re-entering the item's price.

Usual FOB   Set the FOB language for invoices. FOB (Free On Board) is the location from which shipping is determined to be the customer's responsibility. This means more than just paying for freight; it's a statement that says, "At this point you have become the owner of this product." The side effects include assigning responsibility if goods are lost, damaged, or stolen. FOB settings have no impact on your financial records. For instance, if your business is in East Overcoat, Iowa, EastOvercoat might be your FOB entry. Don't let the size of the text box fool you, you're limited to 13 characters. The FOB has absolutely nothing to do with your finances.

Track Reimbursed Expenses As Income This option changes the way your general ledger handles payments for reimbursements. When the option is enabled, the reimbursement can be assigned to an income account (which you should name "reimbursed expenses"). When the option is not enabled, the reimbursement is posted to the original expense account, washing away the expense. See Chapter 6 to learn how to enter and invoice reimbursable expenses.

Warn About Duplicate Invoice Numbers This option tells QuickBooks to warn you if you're creating an invoice with an invoice number that's already in use.

Use Price Levels This option turns on the Price Level feature, which is explained in Chapter 2.

Round All Sales Prices Up To The Next Whole Dollar If, after you apply a price level, the amount contains any cents over a penny, the price is rounded up to the next whole dollar.

Choose Template For Packing Slip Starting with QuickBooks 2004, a packing slip template is included with the list of invoice templates, and a Print Packing Slip command appears on the menu for the Print button on the invoice template. Select a default packing slip to use when you invoke that command. Detailed information on using invoice templates is in Chapter 3.

Automatically Apply Payments This option tells QuickBooks to apply payments automatically to open invoices. If the payment amount is an exact match for an open invoice, it is applied to that invoice. If the payment amount is smaller than any open invoice, QuickBooks applies the payment to the oldest invoice. If the payment amount is larger than any open invoice, QuickBooks applies payments, starting with the oldest invoice, until the payment amount is used up.

Without this option, you must manually apply each payment to an invoice. That's not as onerous as it may sound, and in fact, this is the way I prefer to work, because the customer's check almost always indicates the invoice the customer wants to pay (even if the check doesn't cover the entire amount of that invoice). Sometimes customers don't mark the invoice number on the check and instead enclose a copy of the invoice in the envelope. Read Chapter 4 to learn about receiving and applying customer payments.

Sales Tax Preferences

If you collect sales tax, you must set your sales tax options. These options are easy to configure, because most of the selections are predefined by state tax laws and state tax report rules. Check with your accountant and read the information that came with your state sales tax license. For more information about managing sales taxes, see Chapter 7.

Send Forms Preferences

If you send invoices to customers via e-mail, use this window to design the message that accompanies the invoice. See Chapter 3 for more information.

Service Connection Preferences

If you use QuickBooks services on the Internet, use this window to specify the way you want to connect to the Internet for those services.

My Preferences Tab

The My Preferences tab contains options related to online banking if your bank uses the WebConnect method of online access. (Chapter 16 has detailed information about online banking services.)

- **Give Me The Option Of Saving A File Whenever I Download Web Connect Data**   Select this option if you want QuickBooks to provide an option to save WebConnect data for later processing, instead of automatically processing the transactions.
- **If QuickBooks Is Run By My Browser, Don't Close It After Web Connect Is Done**   Selecting this option means that when QuickBooks is launched automatically when you download WebConnect data from your Financial Institution, QuickBooks remains open after you process the data. If you deselect this option, QuickBooks closes automatically as soon as your data is processed.

Company Preferences Tab

The following connection options are available on the Company Preferences tab:

- **Automatically Connect Without Asking For A Password**   Lets all users log in to the QuickBooks Business Services network automatically.
- **Always Ask For A Password Before Connecting**   Forces users to enter a login name and password in order to access QuickBooks Business Services.
- **Allow Background Downloading Of Service Messages**   Lets QuickBooks check the Intuit website for updates and information periodically when you're connected to the Internet.

Spelling Preferences

The Spelling section only presents options on the My Preferences tab. This is where you control the way the QuickBooks spell checker works. You can instruct QuickBooks to check spelling automatically before saving or printing any form. In addition, you can specify those words you want the spelling checker to skip, such as Internet addresses, numbers, and solid capital letters that probably indicate an abbreviation.

Tax:1099 Preferences

Use this window to establish the 1099 form options you need. For each type of 1099 payment, you must assign an account from your chart of accounts. See Chapter 17 for more information about issuing 1099 forms.

Time-Tracking Preferences

Use this section to turn on Time Tracking and to tell QuickBooks the first day of your work week (which becomes the first day listed on your timesheets). Read all about tracking time in Chapter 18.

Working with Multiple Users

Multiple users are users who access QuickBooks on the same computer; you're all taking turns using QuickBooks. This is not the same as running QuickBooks on a network.

Creating, Removing, and Changing User Information

When you want to create or modify users, choose Company | Set Up Users from the QuickBooks menu bar. If you are setting up multiple users for the first time, QuickBooks displays the Set Up QuickBooks Administrator window. You must have an administrator (I'm assuming it's you) to manage all the other user tasks.

The administrator can determine who can use the various features in QuickBooks, adding, deleting, and configuring permissions for users. It's a good idea to leave the administrator's name as Admin. If you want to password-protect the administrator's login, move to the Administrator's Password box and enter a password. Enter the same password in the Confirm Password box to confirm it. You won't see the text you're typing; instead, the system shows asterisks as a security measure (in case someone is watching over your shoulder). You don't have to use a password, but omitting this step could put your QuickBooks files at risk because an intruder could examine or manipulate your files.

CAUTION: If you forget the administrator's password, you can call QuickBooks support and arrange to have them recover the password—for a fee.

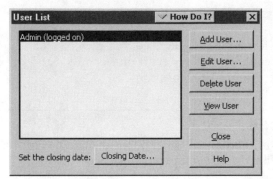

Creating a New User

When you click OK in the Set Up QuickBooks Administrator dialog (or if you set up the configuration option to have multiple users during the EasyStep Interview) you see the User List window.

To add a new user to the list, click Add User. This launches a wizard that assists you in setting up the new user. In the first wizard window, fill in the necessary information, as follows:

1. Enter the username, which is the name this user must type to log in to QuickBooks.
2. If you want to establish a password for this user (it's optional), enter and confirm the user's password.
3. Click Next to set up the user's access to QuickBooks features. See the section "Setting User Permissions" later in this section.

> **TIP:** Make a note of all user passwords and keep that list in a secure (hidden) place. Inevitably, a user will come to you because he or she cannot remember a password.

Deleting a User

If you want to remove a user from the User List, select the name and then click the Delete User button. QuickBooks asks you to confirm your decision. You can't delete the administrator.

Editing User Information

You can change the configuration options for any user. Select the user name in the User List window and click Edit User. This launches a wizard similar to the Add User Wizard, and you can change the user name, password, and access permissions.

Setting User Permissions

When you're adding a new user or editing an existing user, the wizard walks you through the steps for configuring the user's permissions. Click Next on each wizard window after you've supplied the necessary information.

The first permissions window asks if you want this user to have access to selected areas of QuickBooks or all areas. If you want to give the user full permission to do everything, you're asked to confirm your decision, and there's no further work to do in the wizard. Click Finish to return to the User List window.

Configuring Rights to Individual Areas of QuickBooks

If you want to limit the user's access to selected areas of QuickBooks, select that option and click Next. The ensuing wizard windows take you through all the QuickBooks features (Accounts Receivable, Check Writing, Payroll, and so on) so you can establish permissions on a feature-by-feature basis for this user. You should configure permissions for every component of QuickBooks. Any component not configured is set as No Access for this user. For each QuickBooks component, you can select from these permission options:

No Access   The user is denied permission to open any windows in that section of QuickBooks.

Full Access   The user can open all windows and perform all tasks in that section of QuickBooks.

Selective Access   The user will be permitted to perform tasks as you see fit.

If you choose to give selective access permissions, you'll be asked to specify the rights this user should have. Those rights vary slightly from component to component, but generally you're asked to choose one of these permission levels:

- Create transactions
- Create and print transactions
- Create transactions and create reports

TIP: You can select only one of the three levels, so if you need to give the user rights to more than one of these choices, you must select Full Access instead of configuring Selective Access.

Configuring Special Areas of QuickBooks

There are two wizard windows for setting permissions that are not directly related to any specific area of the software: sensitive accounting activities and sensitive accounting reports.

Sensitive accounting activities are those tasks that aren't directly related to specific QuickBooks features, such as

- Making changes to the chart of accounts
- Manipulating the register for any balance sheet account
- Using online banking
- Transferring funds between banks
- Reconciling bank accounts
- Creating journal entries
- Preparing an accountant's review
- Working with budgets

Sensitive financial reports are those reports that reveal important financial information about your company, such as

- Profit & Loss reports
- Balance Sheet reports
- Budget reports
- Cash flow reports
- Income tax reports
- Trial balance reports
- Audit trail reports

Configuring Rights for Existing Transactions

If a user has permissions for certain areas of QuickBooks, you can limit his or her ability to manipulate existing transactions within those areas. This means the user can't change or delete a transaction, even if he or she created it in the first place.

When you have finished configuring user permissions, the last wizard page presents a list of the permissions you've granted and refused. If everything is correct, click Finish. If there's something you want to change, use the Prev button to back up to the appropriate page.

Configuring Classes

QuickBooks provides a feature called Class Tracking that permits you to group items and transactions in a way that matches the kind of reporting you want to perform. Think of this feature as a way to "classify" your business activities. To use classes, you must enable the feature, which is listed in the Accounting section of the Preferences window.

Some of the common reasons to configure classes include

- Reporting by location if you have more than one office
- Reporting by division or department
- Reporting by business type (perhaps you have both retail and wholesale businesses under your company umbrella)

You should use classes for a single purpose; otherwise, the feature won't work properly. For example, you can use classes to separate your business into locations or by type of business, but don't try to do both. If you need to further define a class or narrow its definition, you can use subclasses.

When you enable classes, QuickBooks adds a Class field to your transaction windows. For each transaction, you can assign one of the classes you created.

Creating a Class

To create a class, choose Lists | Class List from the QuickBooks menu bar to display the Class List window. Remember that you must enable the feature in the Accounting Preferences dialog box to have access to the Class List menu item. Press CTRL-N to add a new class. Fill in the name of the class in the New Class window.

Click Next to add another class, or click OK if you are finished. It's a good idea to create a class called "Other." This gives you a way to sort reports in a logical fashion when a transaction has no link to one of your real classes.

Creating a Subclass

Subclasses let you post transactions to specific subcategories of classes, and they work similarly to subaccounts in your chart of accounts. If you set up a subclass, you must post transactions only to the subclass, never to the parent class. However, unlike the chart of accounts, classes have no option to force the display of only the subclass when you're working in a transaction window. As a result, if you're using subclasses you must keep the name of the parent class short, to lessen the need to scroll through the field to see the entire class name.

You create a subclass using the same steps required to create a class. Choose Lists | Class List from the QuickBooks menu bar, and follow these steps:

1. Enter the subclass name.
2. Click the check box next to the option Subclass Of to insert a check mark.
3. Click the arrow next to the field at the bottom of the dialog box, and choose the appropriate parent class from the drop-down list.

Editing Deleting and Merging Classes

You can change, remove, and merge classes right from the Class List window, which you open by choosing Lists | Class List.

To edit a class, double-click the class listing you want to modify. You can enter a new name, turn a parent class into a subclass, turn a subclass into a parent class, or mark the class Inactive.

To delete a class, select its listing in the Class List window and press CTRL-D. If the class has been used in transactions or has subclasses, QuickBooks won't let you delete it. (If the problem is subclasses, delete the subclasses and then you can delete the class.)

To merge two classes, start by editing the class you want to get rid of, which you do by double-clicking its listing. Change the name to match the name of the class you want to keep. QuickBooks displays a message telling you that the name is in use and asking if you want to merge the classes. Clicking Yes tells QuickBooks to go through all transactions that contain the now-removed class and replace the Class field with the remaining class.

Using a Class in Transactions

When you're entering transactions, each transaction window provides a field for entering the class. For example, the invoice form adds a Class field at the top (next to the Customer:Job field) so you can assign the entire invoice to a class. However, you can instead link a class to each line item of the invoice (if the line items require links to separate classes).

Reporting by Class

There are two types of reports you can run for classes:

- Individual class reports
- Reports on all classes

Reporting on a Single Class

To report on a single class, open the Class list and select the class you want to report on. Then press CTRL-Q to open a QuickReport on the class. When the Class QuickReport appears, you can change the date range or customize the report as needed.

Reporting on All Classes

If you want to see one report in which all classes are used, open the Class list and click the Reports button at the bottom of the list window. Choose Reports On All Classes and then select either Profit & Loss By Class, or Graphs. The Graphs menu item offers a choice of an Income & Expenses Graph or a Budget vs. Actual Graph.

Profit & Loss by Class Report   The Profit & Loss By Class report is the same as a standard Profit & Loss report, except that each class uses a separate column. The Totals column provides the usual P&L information for your company.

Totals for items not assigned to a class appear in a column called Unclassified. This is likely to be a rather crowded column if you chose to enable class tracking after you'd already begun using QuickBooks.

You can find detailed information about running and customizing Profit & Loss reports in Chapter 15.

Graphs That Use Class Data   You can also display a graph for Income & Expenses sorted by class, or one that compares budget versus actual figures sorted by class.

Customizing Other Reports for Class Reporting

Many of the reports you run regularly can also be customized to report class information (for example, aging reports). Use the Filters tab to add all, some, or one class to the report.

Using QuickBooks on a Network

If you're using a multi-user version of QuickBooks, you and other users can use the software on a network. Multiple users can work in QuickBooks at the same time.

Setting Up the Network Installation

The first thing you must do is install QuickBooks Pro on every computer that will be involved in this network setup. Designate one of those computers as the QuickBooks server—the computer that holds the main copy of your company data. All of the other computers are called *clients*.

 N O T E : The QuickBooks server doesn't have to be running a version of Windows Server; you can designate any computer running any version of Windows 95 or later to act as a QuickBooks server.

Set Up Shared Access on the Server

On the server that's holding company data, make the file accessible to all QuickBooks users on the network by creating a network share. The steps required for sharing a folder differs depending on your version of Windows, so if you don't know how to perform this task, check your Windows help files.

Don't restrict permissions on the shared folder; all users on the network must have full access to all files and folders in the shared folder.

Set Up Mapped Drives on the Client Computers

It's a good idea to map the shared folder as a drive on the other users' computers. It's not usually an absolute necessity, but my experience is that QuickBooks doesn't work well with UNC paths, and besides, mapping often speeds up access.

If you aren't familiar with network jargon, UNC means Universal Naming Convention, which is the established protocol for entering a path to a resource on another computer. The format of a UNC is *ServerName**ShareName*. On your network, *ServerName* is the name of the computer that has been designated "keeper of the QuickBooks data files," and *ShareName* is the name you assigned to the share when you shared the QuickBooks folder.

To map a drive to the QuickBooks folder on the server, perform the following tasks on each client computer:

1. Open the Network icon (Network Neighborhood or My Network Places) and open the remote computer that's acting as the server for QuickBooks Pro.
2. Right-click the listing for the shared QuickBooks folder.
3. Choose Map Network Drive from the shortcut menu.

4. In the Map Network Drive dialog box, select a drive letter for this resource (or accept the default drive letter).

5. Select the Reconnect At Logon option.

6. Click OK or Finish, depending on your version of Windows.

Windows automatically opens a window that displays the contents of the folder you just mapped. This is one of Windows' really annoying habits—just close the window. You can prevent this by holding down the SHIFT key while you click OK/Finish.

Switching Between Multi-User Mode and Single-User Mode

On the computer that's acting as the server, you must enable multi-user mode before other users can access the data files. To accomplish this, make sure the company you want users to work in is the current company. Then choose File | Switch To Multi-user Mode from the QuickBooks menu bar.

All the QuickBooks windows are closed while the switch is made. Then a message appears to tell you that the company file is working in multi-user mode. The title bar of the QuickBooks window also announces that the software is in multi-user mode and displays the name of the user. If you haven't set up any users, QuickBooks offers to begin that process now.

If you need to return to Single-user Mode, use the File menu, where the command has changed to Switch To Single-user Mode. You'll need to return to Single-user Mode when you perform certain administrative tasks:

- Backing up
- Restoring
- Compressing files
- Deleting items from lists
- Exporting or importing accountant's review copies
- Certain other setup and preferences tasks (QuickBooks displays a message telling you to switch to single-user mode when you access those setup tasks)

Accessing QuickBooks Pro from Client Computers

Users at client computers use the following steps to reach the network data:

1. Launch QuickBooks (from the Programs menu or a desktop shortcut).

2. Choose File | Open Company/Login from the QuickBooks menu bar to see the Open A Company dialog.

3. Click the arrow to the right of the Look In field to display a hierarchy of drives and shared resources.

4. Select the drive letter of the QuickBooks share you mapped. If the resource is not mapped, select Network Neighborhood or My Network Places. Then select the host computer and continue to make selections until you find the shared QuickBooks folder (see, I told you mapping made everything easier).

5. In the Open A Company window, choose the company you want to use and click Open, or double-click the company name.

 N O T E : If you attempt to open a company that someone else on the network is currently using, you see a message that QuickBooks has opened in multi-user mode because someone else is using the file. Click OK.

6. When the QuickBooks Login window appears, enter your login name and password. Then click OK.

C A U T I O N : Your login name exists in the User List, and if anyone is already accessing QuickBooks with that name, you are told to use a different name or try later. If nobody else is supposed to be using your name, hunt down the culprit and make sure this doesn't happen again. Change your password to provide a roadblock to poachers.

The first time each user logs on, it's a good idea to choose Edit | Preferences and establish personal preferences in all the My Preferences tabs that contain configuration options. (Only the administrator can make configuration changes to the Company Preferences tabs.)

Customizing the Icon Bar

QuickBooks put icons on the Icon Bar, but the icons QuickBooks chose may not match the features you use most frequently. Putting your own icons on the Icon Bar makes using QuickBooks easier and faster. You can also change the way the Icon Bar and the icons it holds look.

C A U T I O N : The Icon Bar must be visible in order to customize it. If it's not on your QuickBooks screen, choose View | Icon Bar from the QuickBooks menu bar.

To customize the Icon Bar, choose View | Customize Icon Bar to open the Customize Icon Bar dialog box, which displays a list of the icons currently occupying your Icon Bar.

If you log in to QuickBooks, either because a single computer is set up for multiple users, or because you're using QuickBooks on a network, the settings you establish are linked to your user name. You are not changing the Icon Bar for other users.

Changing the Order of Icons

You can change the order in which icons appear on the Icon Bar. The list of icons in the Customize Icon Bar dialog reads top-to-bottom, representing the left-to-right display on the Icon Bar. Therefore, moving an icon's listing up moves it to the left on the Icon Bar (and vice versa).

To move an icon, click the small diamond to the left of the icon's listing, hold down the left mouse button, and drag the listing to a new position.

Changing the Icon Bar Display

You can change the way the icons display in several ways, which I'll explain in this section.

Display Icons Without Title Text

By default, icons and text display on the Icon Bar. You can select Show Icons Only to remove the title text under the icons. As a result, the icons are much smaller (and you can fit more icons on the Icon Bar). Positioning your mouse pointer over a small icon displays the icon's description as a Tool Tip.

Change the Icon's Graphic, Text, or Description

To change an individual icon's appearance, select the icon's listing and click Edit. Then choose a different graphic (the currently selected graphic is enclosed in a box), change the Label (the title), or change the Description (the Tool Tip text).

Separate Icons

You can insert a separator between two icons, which is an effective way to create groups of icons (after you move icons into logical groups). The separator is a gray vertical line. In the Customize Icon Bar dialog, select the icon that should appear to the left of the separator bar and click Add Separator. QuickBooks inserts "(space)" to the listing to indicate the location of the separator.

Removing an Icon

If there are any icons you never use, or use so infrequently that you'd rather use the space they take up for icons representing features you use a lot, remove them. Select the icon in the Customize Icon Bar dialog box and click Delete. QuickBooks does not ask you to confirm the deletion; the icon is just zapped from the Icon Bar.

Adding an Icon

You can add an icon to the Icon Bar in either of two ways:

- Choose Add in the Customize Icon Bar dialog box.
- Automatically add an icon for a window (transaction or report) you're currently using.

Using the Customize Icon Bar Dialog Box to Add an Icon

To add an icon from the Customize Icon Bar dialog box, click Add. If you want to position your new icon at a specific place within the existing row of icons (instead of at the right end of the Icon Bar), first select the existing icon that you want to sit to the left of your new icon. Then click Add. The Add Icon Bar Item dialog box opens.

Scroll through the list to select the task you want to add to the Icon Bar. Then choose a graphic to represent the new icon (QuickBooks selects a default graphic, which appears within a box). If you wish, you can change the name (the title that appears below the icon) or the description (the text that appears in the Tool Tip when you hold your mouse pointer over the icon).

NOTE: New to QuickBooks 2004 is the ability to add icons for printing forms such as checks and bill payment stubs.

Adding an Icon for the Current Window

If you're currently working in a QuickBooks window, and it strikes you that it would be handy to have an icon for fast access to this window, you can accomplish the deed quickly. While the window is active, choose View | Add *Name of Window* To Icon Bar. A dialog box appears so you can choose a graphic, name, and description for the new icon.

Using the Navigators List

The Navigators List is a vertical toolbar that has two functions:

- It provides a list of navigators. Click an item to open its Navigator window.
- It provides a list of the currently open windows (in the Open Windows List box). Click an item to switch to that window.

The real name of this vertical toolbar is Open Window List, but because it has the title "Navigators" at the top, it's common to refer to it as the Navigators List. However, if you remove it from your QuickBooks window (by clicking the X at the top of the toolbar), you won't be able to put it back unless you realize that the View menu lists it as Open Window List.

Navigator windows are an assortment of related functions and features. For example, the Customer Navigator has links to QuickBooks customer functions and reports, as well as to Web-based information and features (see Figure 21-12).

TIP: When any navigator is open, you can also quickly switch to any other navigator window by clicking the arrow next to the word "Navigators" in the upper-right corner of the window to see a drop-down list of navigators.

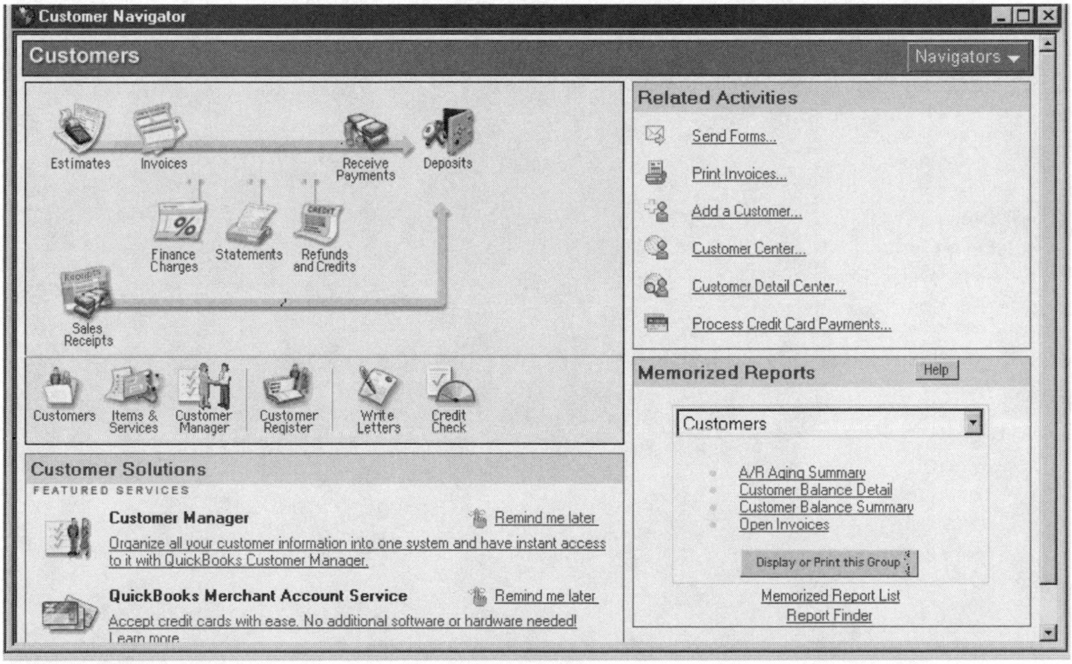

FIGURE 21-12 Tasks, activities, and information related to managing customers are all available in the Customer Navigator.

The Open Windows list is like your Windows task bar, providing quick access to any currently opened window.

To display or hide the Navigators/Open Window list, choose View | Open Window List. The command is a toggle, and if the list is on the screen, a check mark appears on the command. When the list is displayed, you can quickly close it by clicking the X in its upper-right corner.

If you log in to QuickBooks, either because a single computer is set up for multiple users, or because you're using QuickBooks on a network, the settings you establish are linked to your username. You are not changing the off/on setting for the Navigators/Open Windows list for other users.

Using and Customizing the Shortcut List

The Shortcut List is a vertical toolbar that combines the features of the Icon Bar, the menu bar, and the Navigators List (see Figure 21-13). You can add it to your QuickBooks screen by choosing View | Shortcut List.

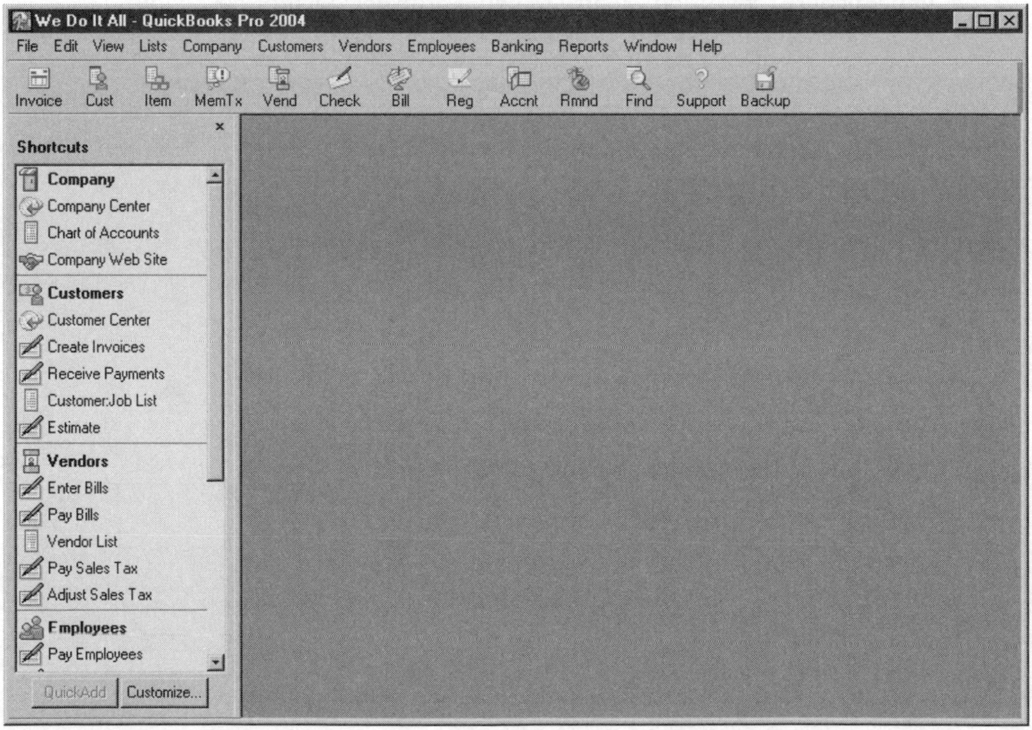

FIGURE 21-13 The Shortcut List groups tasks by category.

> **TIP:** If you opt to use the Shortcut List, you should turn off the Navigators List, because having both vertical bars on your screen leaves little room for your QuickBooks windows.

> **TIP:** When you customize the Shortcut List so it has all the shortcuts you use frequently, you can turn off the Icon Bar.

Changing the Appearance of the Shortcut List

By default, the Shortcut List has the following characteristics:

- It's positioned on the left side of your QuickBooks window.
- It displays both icons and text for each listing.

To change those settings, click the Customize button at the bottom of the Shortcut List to open the Customize Shortcut List window shown in Figure 21-14.

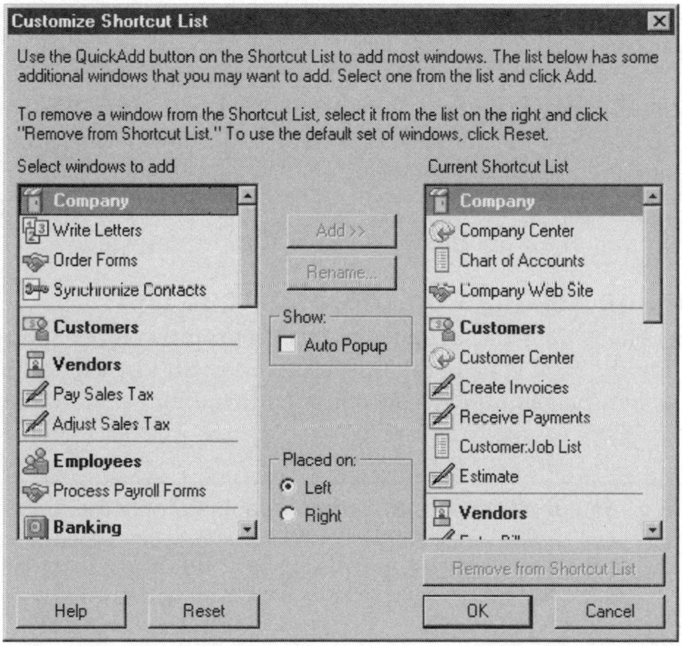

FIGURE 21-14 You can change the location and contents of the Shortcut List.

- Select Show: Auto Popup to hide the list by shrinking it until you place your mouse pointer over it. At that point, the bar gracefully slides open. This is a way to use all your screen space for QuickBooks windows and open the Shortcut List only when you need it.
- Select Placed On: Right to move the Shortcut List to the right side of your QuickBooks window. The auto popup feature continues to work the same way.

> **TIP:** You can also change the width of the Shortcut List by positioning your mouse pointer over its outside edge. When the mouse pointer turns into a double-arrow, hold down the left mouse button while you drag to enlarge or reduce the width of the bar.

Customizing the Shortcut List Contents

You can add or remove listings to make the Shortcut List a totally customized tool. You'll probably change your mind a lot, adding and removing listings as you continue to use QuickBooks.

Adding Listings to the Shortcut List

You can add a QuickBooks feature listing to the Shortcut List in two ways:

- Add the listing from the Customize Shortcut List window
- Add the listing when you're using the window for the task you want to add

To add listings while you're working in the Customize Shortcut List window, select the listing in the left pane and click Add to move the listing to the right pane. The right pane holds the contents of the Shortcut List.

To add a listing for a task you're currently performing, click the QuickAdd button on the bottom of the Shortcut List to add the current window to the listings.

Renaming Listings on the Shortcut List

You can change the name of any item that is currently on the Shortcut List. Select the item in the right pane of the Customize Shortcut List window and click Rename. Enter the new name in the Rename Shortcut List Item window and click OK.

> **NOTE:** You can't rename the group headings, only the items.

Removing Listings from the Shortcut List

If you decide you don't use an item often enough to let it take up space on your Shortcut List, open the Customize Shortcut List window and select that item in the right pane. Click the Remove From Shortcut List button at the bottom of the right pane. You can restore the item in the future by selecting it from the left pane.

 TIP: If you decide you really didn't mean to add items to or delete items from the Shortcut List, click Reset to put everything back the way it was the day you first started using QuickBooks.

 CAUTION: Watch out! If you remove one of the default items from the right pane, you won't find it later in the left pane. Instead you have to use the Reset option to start over. This doesn't happen to items you added yourself.

If you log in to QuickBooks, either because a single computer is set up for multiple users or because you're using QuickBooks on a network, the settings you establish are linked to your username. You are not changing the on/off state or customized appearance of the Shortcut List for other users.

Managing Your QuickBooks Files

In this chapter:

- Back up and restore company files
- Archive and condense data
- Update QuickBooks software

In addition to performing bookkeeping chores in QuickBooks, you need to take care of some computer file housekeeping tasks. It's important to keep your software up-to-date and to make sure your data is accurate and available. QuickBooks provides some features to help you accomplish these responsibilities.

Creating Companies in QuickBooks

You can create as many companies in QuickBooks as you wish. You can have your business in one company and your personal finances in another company. If you have enough time and energy, you can also volunteer to run the local community association, open a second business, keep your mother-in-law's books, or create companies for any of a zillion reasons.

> **TIP:** If you volunteer to use your QuickBooks software for a nonprofit organization, check out *Running QuickBooks for Nonprofits* (CPA911 Publishing), which shows you how to adapt QuickBooks for nonprofit needs. The book is available on the company's website, www.cpa911.com, and there's a link on the site to purchase the book at amazon.com if you prefer to use your Amazon account.

To create a new company, choose File | New Company from the QuickBooks menu bar. This opens the EasyStep Interview Wizard (you saw this wizard the first time you used QuickBooks). You don't have to go through the entire EasyStep Interview, but you should fill out the General sections, which are represented by tabs across the top of the window. The questions are easy to answer, and you just need to keep clicking Next to move through all the sections of the interview.

If you don't want to go through the interview process, the third Welcome screen has an escape hatch in the form of a button named Skip Interview. Click it to use the shortcut method of creating a company, which begins with the Creating New Company window, shown in Figure 22-1.

Click Next to see a list of company types, and select the one that comes closest to this company's mission. QuickBooks uses this information to create a chart of accounts for the company.

Click Next to save the information in a company file. QuickBooks suggests a filename based on your company name, but you can invent your own filename if you wish. Click Save to make this company a file in your QuickBooks system.

QuickBooks loads the new company as the current company, and you can start setting preferences, entering data, and doing all the other tasks involved in creating a company. Read Chapters 1 and 2 for information about company setup and configuration.

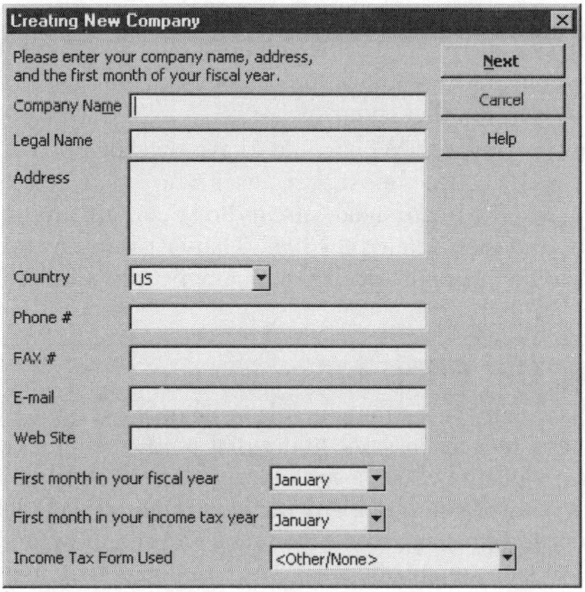

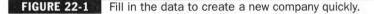

Creating New Company

Please enter your company name, address, and the first month of your fiscal year.

Company Name

Legal Name

Address

Country   US

Phone #

FAX #

E-mail

Web Site

First month in your fiscal year   January

First month in your income tax year   January

Income Tax Form Used   <Other/None>

Next

Cancel

Help

FIGURE 22-1   Fill in the data to create a new company quickly.

Deleting Company Files

Sometimes you have a valid reason to get rid of a company file. Perhaps you created a company to experiment with and you no longer use it, or you sent a copy of the local community association's file to another QuickBooks user who is taking over your job as treasurer.

So, how do you delete a company file? In an amazing display of convoluted logic, QuickBooks, the only accounting software I've ever worked with that lets users delete transactions (a dangerous thing to do), has no provision for deleting unwanted company files.

There's a workaround, of course (I wouldn't mention this topic if I didn't have a workaround to offer), but you must use it carefully, and pay attention to the order in which you perform tasks.

You've probably guessed the basic workaround: delete the file from Windows Explorer or My Computer. However, before you click the file's listing and press the DELETE key, read on so you don't encounter a problem when you next open QuickBooks.

How QuickBooks Loads Company Files

QuickBooks automatically opens the company file that was loaded when you last exited the software. If it can't find that file it gets confused, and when software gets confused it sometimes stops working properly (or at all). Even if QuickBooks accepts the fact that the file it's trying to open is missing and displays the No Company Open dialog box, it's cleaner to make sure you don't have the about-to-be-deleted company file loaded when you close QuickBooks. Use File | Open or File | Open Previous Company to select another company file.

I can hear you saying, "Why would I have that file open if I no longer use it?" The answer is, "Because almost every user who has called me for help in this situation opened the file to make sure it didn't contain anything important, closed QuickBooks, and then deleted the file." That last-minute check to make sure it's okay to delete the file is the quicksand many people wander into.

Deleting the Files

To delete a company, just delete the file *companyname*.qbw. By default, QuickBooks stores company files in the same folder that holds the QuickBooks software, but you may have opted to create a subfolder to store your files. If you've created an accountant's copy of your company file, you might as well delete that also; it has the filename *companyname*.qbx. If you saved a backup to your hard drive (not a good idea, but some people do this), you can delete that also—look for the file *companyname*.qbb.

TIP: I always create a subfolder for my QuickBooks company files, because in addition to using the QuickBooks backup feature, I back up documents and datafiles across my network with batch files and scripts. I also store any exported QuickBooks files I create in that subfolder and move files I want to import into QuickBooks into that subfolder. Having a discrete folder for my data is safer and more efficient.

Eliminating Deleted Files from the Previous Company List

QuickBooks tracks the company files you've opened and lists the most recently opened files on the File menu to make it easier to open those files. You don't have to open a dialog box to select one of those files, you just point to the appropriate listing on the submenu under the File | Open Previous Company command. The submenu lists the company files you've opened starting with the most recent.

After you delete a company file, if its listing appears on the submenu, a user (including you), could inadvertently select it, which produces a delay followed by an error message. To eliminate this possibility, use the following steps to remove the file from the list:

1. Choose File | Open Previous Company |
   Set Number of Previous Companies.
2. Change the number of companies to list
   from 4 (the default) to 1, and click OK.

Set Number of Previous Companies

QuickBooks can list companies that you've
previously opened, starting with the most
recent.

How many companies do you
want to list (1 to 20)? `1`

OK   Cancel

The next time you open QuickBooks, repeat
these steps and change the number back to 4, or
to any other number that's efficient (depending
on the number of companies you work with). QuickBooks begins tracking your
work to rebuild the list.

 T I P : If you have advanced computing skills, and you know how to work with
.ini files, you can accomplish all of these tasks in qbw.ini. If you're not an expert
in working with .ini files, don't try—QuickBooks may never work properly (or at
all) again.

Backing Up and Restoring Files

Backing up your QuickBooks data is an incredibly important task and should be
done on a daily basis. When QuickBooks performs a backup, it doesn't make an
exact copy of your company file; instead the data in the file is compressed, making
the resulting file much smaller than your original company file.

Backing Up

To create a backup of the current company, choose File | Back Up from the menu
bar to open the Back Up Company File tab of the QuickBooks Backup dialog box
seen in Figure 22 2.

Choose a Location

Choose a location for the backup file. QuickBooks names the backup file for you,
which you can change if you wish (but there's rarely a good reason to do so). The
default filename is the same as your company filename, with the extension .qbb.

If you're on a network, you can back up to a remote folder by clicking Browse,
selecting Network Neighborhood or My Network Places, and choosing the shared
folder that's been set up for your backups. It's better, and faster, however, to map a drive
to the remote backup location and enter the mapped drive letter Location field of the
Backup dialog. (See Chapter 21 to learn about mapping drives to network folders.)

Never back up onto your local hard drive. Use removable media, such as a floppy
drive, a Zip drive, or use a network drive (if you're on a network), because the point of
backing up is to be able to get back to work in case of a hard drive or computer failure.

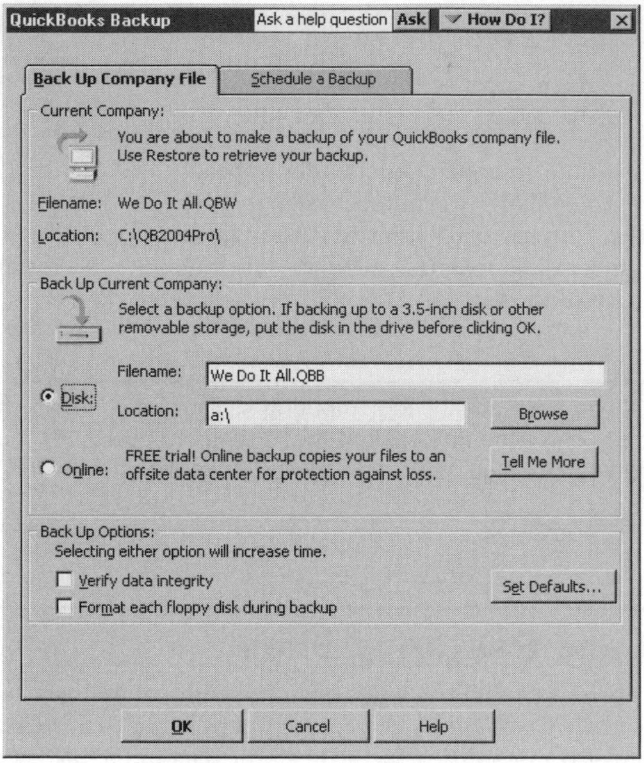

FIGURE 22-2 Back up your company file daily.

QuickBooks compresses the data in your files to create the backup file, but if you have a great many transactions, and you're backing up to a floppy disk, you may be asked to put a second floppy disk in your drive to complete the backup. If so, be sure to label the floppy disks so you know which is the first disk. (You must start with the first disk if you need to restore the backup.)

Don't back up on top of the last backup, because if something happens during the backup procedure, you won't have a good backup file to restore. The best procedure is a backup disk (or set of disks) for each day of the week.

If you're using expensive media, such as a Zip drive, and you don't want to purchase that many disks, have one disk for odd days and another for even days.

If you're backing up across a network, create two network shares on the remote computer, and map them to different drive letters. Name one share "Odd" and the other share "Even" so you rotate the backups on odd and even days.

When you use a disk that's already received a backup file, QuickBooks will ask if you want to replace the existing file with the new one. Click Yes, because the current backup file is newer and has up-to-the-minute data. The old file is at least two days old, and perhaps a week old, depending on the way you're rotating media.

Periodically (once a week is best, but once a month is essential), make a second backup copy on a different disk and store it off-site. Then, if there's a catastrophe (fire or flood), you can buy, rent, or borrow a computer, install QuickBooks, and restore the data (which escaped the catastrophe by being stored elsewhere).

 NOTE: The Online location is available if you buy the QuickBooks online backup service. Click Tell Me More if you're interested in learning about using QuickBooks servers to store your backed up data.

Choose Options

The Backup dialog offers two options for the backup process:

- Verify Data Integrity
- Format Each Floppy Disk During Backup

Verifying data is a process that QuickBooks runs against the current data file (your company file) to make sure its structure is valid. Data verification features can detect corrupt files or corrupt portions of files. If you choose the option to verify the data during the backup procedure, the time it takes to back up your file is substantially longer. The Verify Data command is available on the QuickBooks menu system (choose File | Utilities | Verify Data), and it's not necessary to run it on a regular basis.

The option to format the floppy disk(s) you're using for the backup is a way to make sure the disk is "clean." When you buy floppy disks, they're preformatted, but if they've been used and files have been written and deleted, it's probably a good idea to format them once in a while. Formatting destroys all data on a disk, so make sure the disk doesn't contain any important information before taking this step.

Set Defaults

Click Set Defaults to open a dialog box in which you can establish default settings for your backups.

- If you want to be reminded to perform a manual backup, select the option for reminders, and enter the frequency specification for the reminder. The frequency is linked to the number of times you close your QuickBooks company file; it's not a specification for elapsed days. If you open and close your QuickBooks files numerous times during the day, and you specify a small number, you'll see the reminder at least once every day (not a bad thing).

Set Defaults	×
☑ Re<u>m</u>ind me to back up when closing the data file every `4` times.	
<u>D</u>efault Backup Location: `a:\`	B<u>r</u>owse...
☑ <u>A</u>ppend date and timestamp to the name of this backup file	
<u>O</u>K Cancel Help	

- Select a default location, which can be an external drive, such as a floppy drive or a Zip drive, or a mapped drive to a shared folder on another computer on your network.
- If you select the option to append a date/time stamp to the filename, the backup filename contains the date and time information for the backup. This means you can tell at a glance when the latest backup was performed, instead of changing your view settings to display the date/time in Windows Explorer or My Computer.

Automatic Backups

QuickBooks lets you schedule automatic backups. To configure the feature, click the Schedule A Backup tab on the Backup dialog (see Figure 22-3).

This dialog offers two types of automatic backups:

- Automated backup when closing a company file
- Scheduled backup at a time you specify

You can configure either or both, using the guidelines presented here.

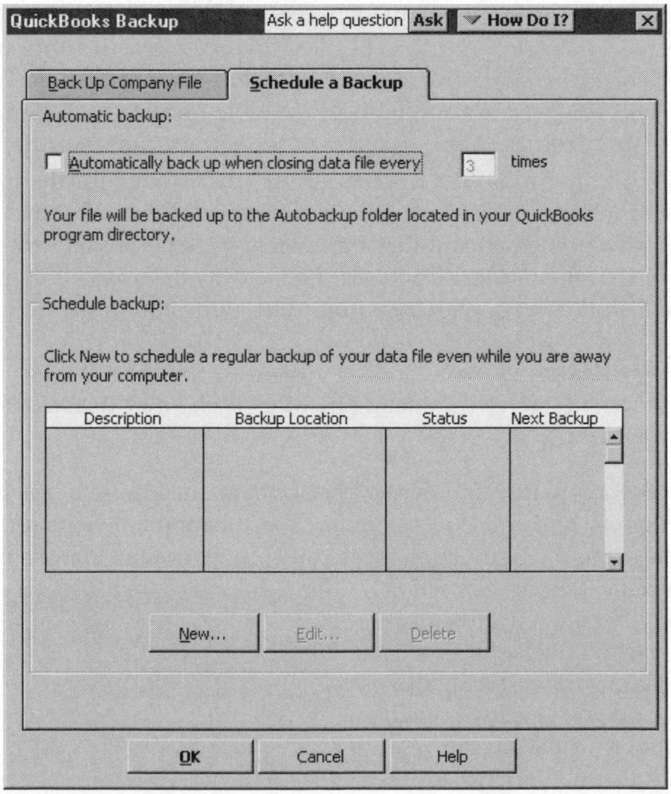

FIGURE 22-3 Automatic scheduling is the way to make sure backups occur regularly.

Automated Backup When Closing Files

The Automatic Backup section of the Backup dialog presents an option to back up your company data file whenever you close that file. The word "close" is literal, so an automated backup takes place under either of the following conditions:

- While working in QuickBooks, you open a different company file or choose File | Close
- You exit QuickBooks

The backup takes place, and the backup file is located in the subfolder named Autobackup under the folder in which you installed QuickBooks. QuickBooks maintains three discrete automated backup files:

- The first time the automated backup runs, the filename is ABU_0_<*Company Filename*><*TimeStamp*>.QBB.
- The second time the automated backup runs, the file that starts with ABU_0 is copied to a file named ABU_1_<*CompanyFilename*><*TimeStamp*>.QBB, and the latest backup becomes ABU_0.
- The third time the automated backup runs, the pattern continues, as previous files are copied to the next highest number and the most recent backup file starts with ABU_0.

NOTE: As an example of the filename structure, my company backup filename is ABU_0_We Do It All Jan 09,2004 06 34 PM.QBB.

If you have some reason to think your current file is corrupt, you can go back to a previous backup instead of restoring the latest backup (which may be a backup of corrupted data). However, you'll have to reenter all the transactions that aren't in the last-saved backup (which is a good reason to back up every day—you don't want to have to reconstruct several days worth of transactions).

Automatic Unattended Backups

You can also configure QuickBooks to perform a backup of your company files at any time, even if you're not working at your computer. This is a cool feature, but it doesn't work unless you remember to leave your computer running when you leave the office. Before you leave, make sure QuickBooks is closed so all the files are available for backing up (open files are skipped during a backup).

To create the configuration for an unattended backup, click New to open the Schedule A Backup dialog seen in Figure 22-4.

You can give the backup a descriptive name (it's optional), but if you're going to create multiple unattended backup configurations, it's a good idea to identify each by name.

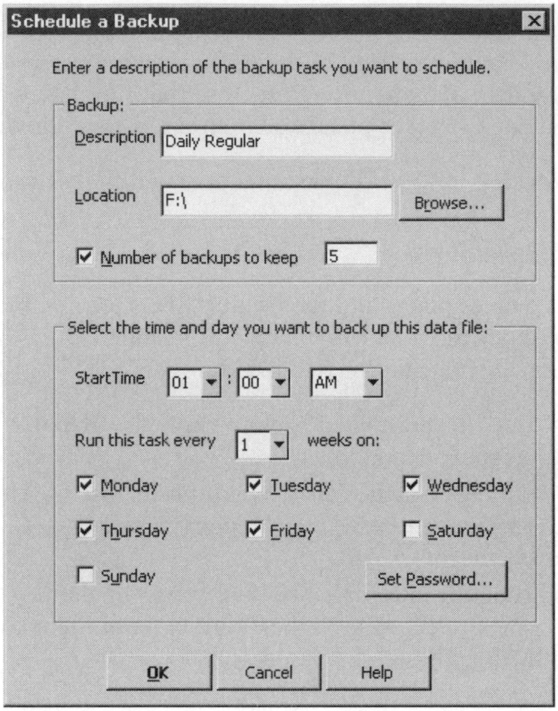

Schedule a Backup

Enter a description of the backup task you want to schedule.

Backup:

Description Daily Regular

Location F:\ Browse...

☑ Number of backups to keep 5

Select the time and day you want to back up this data file:

Start Time 01 ▾ : 00 ▾ AM ▾

Run this task every 1 ▾ weeks on:

☑ Monday ☑ Tuesday ☑ Wednesday

☑ Thursday ☑ Friday ☐ Saturday

☐ Sunday Set Password...

OK Cancel Help

FIGURE 22-4 Configure the specifications for a backup that runs automatically.

Enter a location for the backup file. In Figure 22-4, the location is a mapped network drive. You can use a Zip drive or another hard drive on your computer if you have two drives. It's not a good idea to back up to the same hard drive that holds your QuickBooks files. It's also not a good idea to use the floppy drive, because this backup is unattended, and when your company file grows too large to fit on a floppy disk, you won't be there to see the message "please insert the next disk." If you don't have a network, or a large removable drive, you should skip the unattended backup feature and manually back up frequently to floppy drives.

 CAUTION: Be sure the target drive is available—insert the Zip or other removable drive before leaving the computer; be sure the remote network computer isn't shut down.

If you don't want to overwrite the last backup file every time a new backup file is created, select the option Number Of Backups To Keep, and specify the number. QuickBooks saves as many discrete backup files as you specify, each time replacing the first file with the most recent backup, and copying older files to the next highest number in the filename, which always begins with SBU_0.

> **NOTE:** Unattended backup files are saved with the filename pattern SBU_0_<*CompanyFileName*><*Date/Time Stamp*>. If you specify two backup files in the Number Of Backups To Keep field, the second filename starts with SBU_1_. This pattern continues for the number of backups you specified.

Create a schedule for this unattended backup by selecting a time and a frequency. For this example, I created a daily schedule (weekdays) that runs every week.

The Set Password button is not related to your QuickBooks user and password configuration; it's for your operating system, and it's quite possible you don't have to use this function. The username and password you enter into the dialog are for a Windows logon name and password, and it's needed only if you're running Windows with permissions and rights configured under NTFS (the secure file system available in Windows NT/2000/XP/2003 Server).

> **TIP:** If you're using Windows 2000/XP/2003 Server, and you're familiar with the RunAs feature, this Set Password dialog works similarly.

You can create multiple unattended backups and configure them for special circumstances. For instance, in addition to a nightly backup, you may want to configure a backup every four weeks on a Saturday or Sunday (or during your lunch hour on a weekday) to create a backup on a Zip or other removable drive that is earmarked for off-site storage. Be sure to bring the office backup media to the office on that day and take it back to the off-site location when the backup is finished.

I'm a backup freak (my entire professional life is on my computers), so in addition to the nightly backup that runs at 11:00 P.M., I have a second unattended backup running at 1:00 A.M. to a different mapped drive (on a different network computer). A third backup is configured for Fridays at 3:00 A.M., and its target is a Zip drive (that's my off-site backup). On Fridays, before I leave the computer, I insert the cartridge into the drive, confident that all three backups will run while I'm gone. On Monday, I take the removable media off-site. In fact, I alternate between two removable media disks, so I'm never backing up over the only existing backup.

Backing Up to a CD-ROM

If you're running Windows XP or Windows Server 2003, you can back up to a CD from within QuickBooks. If you're running an earlier version of Windows, you can back up to a CD outside of QuickBooks. A CD is a good media choice for a weekly or monthly backup that is taken off-site. Of course, I'm assuming you have a CD-R or CD-RW drive.

If you're not using Windows XP/Windows Server 2003, periodically use your CD-burning software to copy your QuickBooks company files (all of them, if you're running multiple companies). You can copy the company file directly to the CD; you don't have to make a backup first. If you have to restore from this file, you can copy the file back to your QuickBooks folder; you don't have to use the Restore command.

In Windows XP, which has built-in CD writing features, QuickBooks supports backups to CD-ROM. Use the following steps to back up to CD:

1. Choose File | Back Up.
2. In the Location field of the QuickBooks Backup dialog box, enter *x*: (substitute the drive letter of your CD-R/CD-RW drive for x).
3. When QuickBooks displays a message warning you that backing up to your hard drive isn't a good idea and asking if you're sure if you want to back up to your hard drive, click Yes. (The message appears because the way Windows XP writes to your CD is to write the file to the hard drive before burning the CD.)
4. When the backup file has been written to the hard drive, QuickBooks displays a message telling you your data has been backed up successfully. A balloon appears over the notification area of your taskbar, telling you that files are waiting to be written to the CD. Click the balloon.
5. The folder window for the CD drive opens, displaying a listing for your backup file. Select the file.

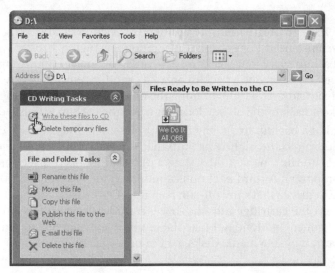

6. In the left pane, click Write These Files To CD.
7. Follow the prompts in the Windows XP CD Burning Wizard to transfer the file to the CD.

The next time you select the backup command, the location for the backup file is automatically set to the folder that Windows XP uses to store files that are going to be transferred to a CD, to wit:

C:\Documents and Settings*YourUserName*\Local Settings\Application Data\ Microsoft\CD Burning\

You could have entered that location in the Backup dialog box the first time, but why type all those characters? Windows XP understood what you were doing and adapted the data appropriately, which is pretty nifty. In addition, the next time you perform this task, you won't see the warning about backing up to your hard drive, because by then, both QuickBooks and Windows XP will have figured out what you're doing.

Restoring a Backup

You just turned on your computer and it sounds different—noisier. In fact, there's a grinding noise. You wait and wait, but the usual startup of the operating system fails to appear. Eventually, an error message about a missing boot sector appears (or some other equally chilling message). Your hard drive has gone to hard-drive heaven. You have invoices to send out, checks to write, and tons of things to do, and if you can't accomplish those tasks, your income suffers.

Don't panic; get another hard drive or another computer (the new one will probably cost less than the one that died because computer prices keep dropping). If you buy a new hard drive, it will take some time to install your operating system. If you buy a new computer, it probably comes with an operating system installed.

If you're running on a network (and you were backing up your QuickBooks files to a network drive), create the mapped drive to the shared folder that holds your backup. Then install your QuickBooks software.

▶ FYI

Bypassing the Windows XP CD Writing Wizard

QuickBooks 2004 introduces a way to back up to CD without using the wizard and the built-in CD burning features of Windows XP. Instead, you can write your backup file to the CD immediately, omitting the step of manually moving the file from your hard drive to the CD. This means you can write your backup file to a CD during an automated, unattended QuickBooks backup.

In order to accomplish this you must have packet writing software, such as Roxio's DirectCD, or Nero's InCD (not Nero's Burning ROM) installed on your Windows XP computer, and the software must be configured to launch during startup so it's always available (which is the default configuration).

In QuickBooks, configure the backup feature to bypass the Windows XP wizard by clicking the Set Defaults button on the QuickBooks Backup dialog box. In the Set Defaults dialog box, clear the check mark in the check box for the option Use Windows CD Writing Wizard. (This option is only on the Set Defaults dialog box if QuickBooks is installed on a computer running Windows XP.) QuickBooks will use your packet writing software to write the backup file to the CD.

Sometimes it's only your QuickBooks file, or your QuickBooks software, that experiences a disaster, and your computer is fine. QuickBooks won't open, or QuickBooks opens but reports a corruption error when it tries to open your file. In this case, you don't have all the work of rebuilding hardware. If QuickBooks won't open, or opens with error messages about a software problem, reinstall QuickBooks, and then restore your backup. If QuickBooks opens, but your company file won't open, restore your backup.

Here's how to restore a backup file:

1. Start QuickBooks. If the opening window tells you there's no company open and suggests you create one, ignore that message.
2. If you backed up to removable media, put the disk that contains your last backup into its drive. If you backed up to a network share, be sure the remote computer is running. If you purchased the QuickBooks Online backup service, be sure you've configured your Internet connection.
3. Choose File | Restore from the QuickBooks menu bar. When the Restore Company Backup window appears (see Figure 22-5), change any settings that are incorrect.
4. Click Restore. If your backup occupies multiple floppy disks, you'll be prompted to insert disks.
5. If you're restoring to an existing company (because the problem was a corrupt data file), you receive a warning that you're about to overwrite the existing file. That's fine, it's what you want to do.

QuickBooks displays a message that your data files have been restored successfully. You did it! Aren't you glad you back up regularly? Click OK and go to work!

> **TIP:** If this backup wasn't saved yesterday, you must re-create every transaction you made between the time of this backup and the last time you used QuickBooks.

Archiving and Condensing Data

QuickBooks provides a feature that enables you to condense certain data in your company file in order to make your file smaller. You can use it to make backing up faster (using fewer disks) or to save room on your hard drive. While this seems to be a handy feature, it carries some significant side effects in the loss of details about transactions. Before using this feature, consider other ways to survive with a very large file.

Alternatives to Condensing Data

Condensing data is a last-resort solution to a problem that might be resolved by other means. If your intent is to make the backup faster by eliminating the need to

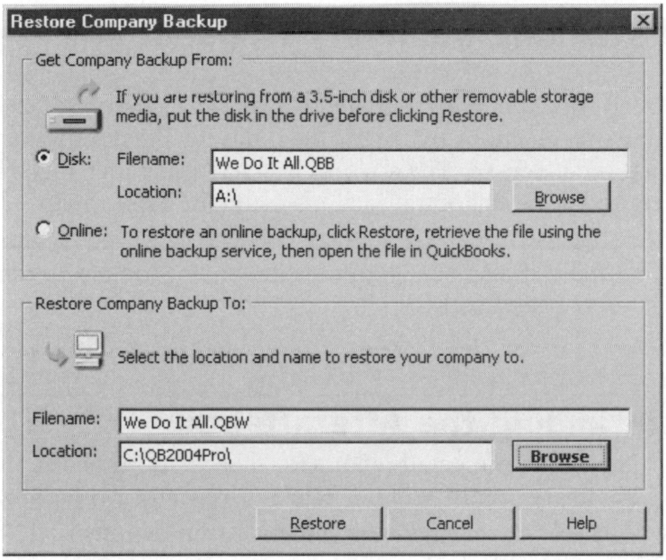

FIGURE 22-5 Specify the location of your backup file.

insert additional floppy disks, consider getting removable media that is larger in capacity, such as a Zip drive or a CD.

If your problem is a lack of sufficient hard-drive space, do some housekeeping on your hard drive. Get rid of temporary files, especially those stored by your browser when you visit the Internet. All browsers provide a menu command to empty the temporary files directory (sometimes called the *cache*).

Understanding the Condensing Procedure

If none of these suggestions is workable, and you feel your file size has gotten out of hand, you should condense your data. Consider this solution only after you've been using QuickBooks for more than a year or so, because you don't want to lose the details for the current year's transactions.

When your files are condensed, the details about closed transactions are deleted and replaced by a journal entry that shows totals posted to accounts. (If you subscribe to any QuickBooks payroll services, no current year transactions are condensed.) Open transactions (such as unpaid invoices and bills) are not condensed.

Choosing a Condensing Date

When you condense your data, QuickBooks asks you for the date you want to use as the cutoff date. Everything you no longer need before that date is condensed. No open transactions are condensed; only those data items that are completed, finished, and safe to condense are targeted. Also, any transactions before the condensing date that affect current transactions are skipped, and the details are maintained in the file.

Understanding Summary Transactions

The transactions that fall within the parameters of the condensing date are deleted and replaced with summary transactions. Summary transactions are nothing but journal entry transactions that show the totals for the transactions, one for each month that is condensed. The account balances are not changed by condensing data, because the summary transactions maintain those totals.

 NOTE: You can also configure the condensing feature to remove list items that have never been used.

Understanding the Aftereffects

You won't be able to run detail reports for those periods before the condensing date. However, summary reports will be perfectly accurate in their financial totals.

You will be able to recognize the summary transactions in the account registers because they will be marked with a transaction type GENJRNL.

Condensing Your File

Condensing your QuickBooks file is very simple, because a wizard walks you through the process. To start, choose File | Archive & Condense Data to open the Archive & Condense Data Wizard window seen in Figure 22-6.

NOTE: You may see a warning about losing your budget data when your file is condensed (because some budgets are based on detailed postings). Read Chapter 13 to learn how to export your budgets and import them back into QuickBooks.

The wizard offers two choices for proceeding: Condense Transactions As Of A Specific Date (which you choose), or Remove All Transactions. QuickBooks automatically displays the last day of the previous year as the condensing date for the first option. You can use this date or choose an earlier date (a date long past, so you won't care if you lose the transaction details). Be sure to choose the last day of a month, quarter, or year.

The option to remove all transactions is really an option to wipe all your data in order to create a new (empty) company file with the same name. It's unusual to do this, but be sure you have a full backup of the original company file in case you change your mind.

Click Next to see a list of the transaction types that are not removed (see Figure 22-7). You can select any of them to include them in the "to be removed" list, if you know you don't need to keep details about those transaction types.

Click Next and select the lists (accounts, customers, vendors, etc.) you want QuickBooks to empty of unused items.

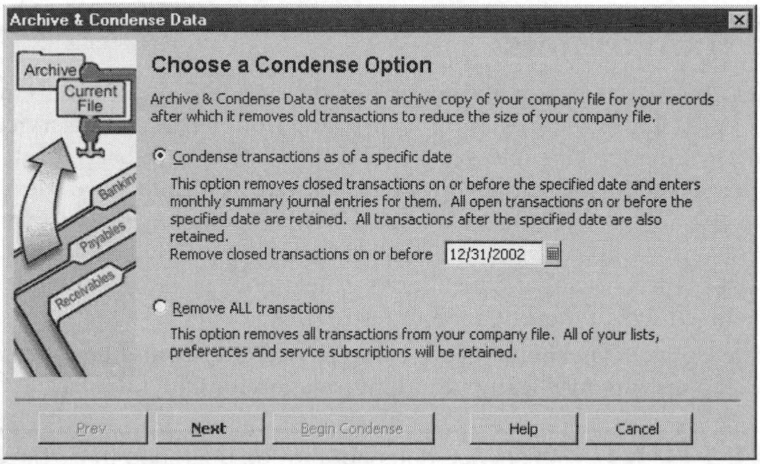

Archive & Condense Data

Choose a Condense Option

Archive & Condense Data creates an archive copy of your company file for your records after which it removes old transactions to reduce the size of your company file.

⊙ Condense transactions as of a specific date

This option removes closed transactions on or before the specified date and enters monthly summary journal entries for them. All open transactions on or before the specified date are retained. All transactions after the specified date are also retained.

Remove closed transactions on or before 12/31/2002

○ Remove ALL transactions

This option removes all transactions from your company file. All of your lists, preferences and service subscriptions will be retained.

Prev | **Next** | Begin Condense | Help | Cancel

FIGURE 22-6 Select the option you want to use for the condensing feature.

Click Next to see an informational window in which the condense process is explained. Click Begin Condense to start the process. QuickBooks displays a message telling you that first your data file needs to be backed up. This is not an everyday backup, it's the last backup of a full data file before information is removed—before the condensing takes place. Therefore, use new disks for this backup (if you use floppy disks). Click OK to begin the backup.

As soon as QuickBooks finishes backing up, it starts condensing data. You'll see progress bars on your screen as each step completes. When the job is complete, you're given the name of the archive copy of your data file (which is intact, so you can open it if you need to see transaction details).

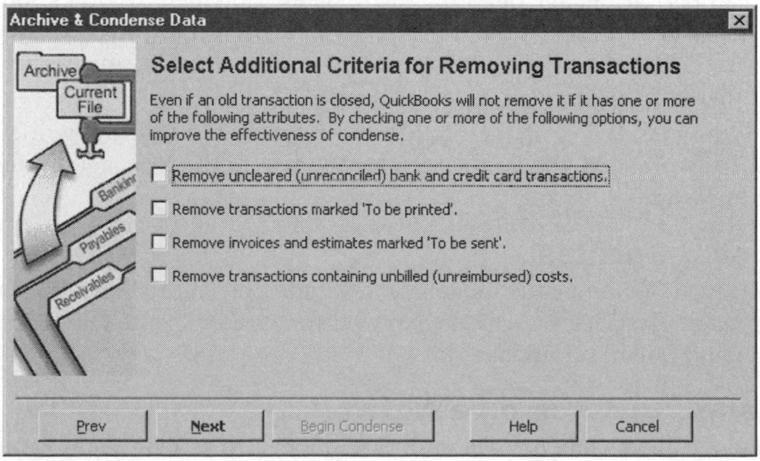

Archive & Condense Data

Select Additional Criteria for Removing Transactions

Even if an old transaction is closed, QuickBooks will not remove it if it has one or more of the following attributes. By checking one or more of the following options, you can improve the effectiveness of condense.

☐ Remove uncleared (unreconciled) bank and credit card transactions.

☐ Remove transactions marked 'To be printed'.

☐ Remove invoices and estimates marked 'To be sent'.

☐ Remove transactions containing unbilled (unreimbursed) costs.

Prev | **Next** | Begin Condense | Help | Cancel

FIGURE 22-7 You can remove transactions that QuickBooks would normally keep.

Updating QuickBooks

QuickBooks provides an automatic update service you can use to make sure your QuickBooks software is up-to-date and trouble-free. This service provides you with any maintenance releases of QuickBooks that have been created since you purchased and installed your copy of the software. A maintenance release is distributed when a problem is discovered and fixed. This is sometimes necessary, because it's almost impossible to distribute a program that is totally bug-free (although my experience has been that QuickBooks generally releases without any major bugs, since Intuit does a thorough job of testing).

The Update QuickBooks service also provides notes and news from Intuit so you can keep up with new features and information for QuickBooks.

 C A U T I O N : This service does not provide upgrades to a new version; it just provides updates to your current version.

The Update QuickBooks service is an online service, so you must have configured QuickBooks for online access (see Chapter 16). When you want to check for updated information, choose File | Update QuickBooks from the menu bar to open the Update QuickBooks window shown in Figure 22-8.

Configuring QuickBooks Update Service

Click the Options tab to configure the Update feature. You have several choices for updating your software components. You can always change these options in the future.

Automatic Updates

You can take advantage of automatic updates, which allow QuickBooks to check the Intuit update site on the Internet periodically while you're connected to the Internet. QuickBooks doesn't have to be running for this function to occur.

If new information is found, it's downloaded to your hard drive without notifying you. If you happen to disconnect from the Internet while updates are being downloaded, the next time you connect to the Internet, QuickBooks will pick up where it left off.

Manual Updates

If you turn off automatic updates, you should periodically check for new software files manually. Click the Update Now button in the Update QuickBooks window to select and download updated files.

Sharing Updates on a Network

If you're using QuickBooks in multi-user mode across a network, you must configure the Update QuickBooks service to share downloaded files with other users. When this

Update QuickBooks   _ □ ✕

v.13.0.3.1

| Overview | Options | Update Now |

Occasionally, Intuit provides updates to QuickBooks that you can download over the Internet.
An update might be a maintenance release, a new feature, a new service, and/or timely
information that is relevant to your business.

Automatic Update is OFF

Select the Options tab to turn on Automatic Updates

Select the Update Now tab to get the updates that you want to download
immediately from the Intuit server. The update feature transmits technical
information to Intuit about the computer's connection and the QuickBooks
software being updated. A secure connection protects customer-sensitive
information during an update. Under no circumstances do Intuit servers
access or read any other information on your computer. During an update,
QuickBooks downloads only the necessary files to your PC.

[Update Now]

[Close] [Help]

FIGURE 22-8 Use the Update QuickBooks window to change update options or to download
an update.

option is enabled, QuickBooks creates a subfolder on the computer that holds the
shared QuickBooks data files, and the other computers use that subfolder as the
source of updated files. For this to work, every user on the network must open his
or her copy of QuickBooks and configure the Update options for Shared Download
to reflect the folder location. The folder location is displayed on the Options tab
when you select the Shared Download option.

Selecting Update Types

Select the types of files you want QuickBooks to download when you update. The most
important selection is Maintenance Releases, which fixes problems and adds features.

Determining Update Status

The Update Now tab displays information about the current status of the service,
including the last date that QuickBooks checked for updates and the names of any
files that were downloaded.

Click the check boxes next to each specific type of update to select/deselect
those file types. Then click Get Updates to tell QuickBooks to check the Internet
immediately and bring back any files. After files are downloaded, click the listing to
see more information about that download. Most of the time, the files are automatically
integrated into your system. Sometimes an information box appears to tell you that
the files will be integrated when you exit QuickBooks.

Part Five

Appendixes

Technical and instructional books always have at least one appendix. Those of us who write computer books include them so we can organize the books in a way that lets you jump right into the software starting with Chapter 1. However, for most computer software, there's a configuration routine to manage before you dive into using the software, and we use the appendixes to instruct you on the appropriate methods for accomplishing these chores.

For accounting software, the setup and configuration procedures are far more important than for any other type of software. If the structure isn't right, the numbers won't be right.

You must read Appendix A before you do anything. In fact, you should read it and use the suggestions in it before you even install QuickBooks. That's why I named it "Do This First!"

Appendix B gives you guidance and instructions for using other software in conjunction with QuickBooks, including add-on services available from Intuit and other companies that might make your bookkeeping life easier.

Do This First!

Before you do anything with your QuickBooks software, you have to do three things:

- Decide on the starting date for your QuickBooks records.

- Find all the detailed records, notes, memos, and other items that you've been using to track your financial numbers.

- Create an opening trial balance to enter into QuickBooks.

If you don't prepare your records properly, all the advantages of a computer bookkeeping system will be lost to you. The information you enter when you first start using QuickBooks will follow you forever. If it's accurate, that's great! It means you have the right foundation for all the calculations that QuickBooks will perform for you, and all the reports you generate to keep an eye on your business and file your tax returns.

If it's not accurate, that fact will haunt you. It's not that you can't change things in QuickBooks; it's that if you start with bad numbers you frequently can't figure out which numbers were bad. Your inability to trace the origin of a problem will be what makes the problem permanent.

So get out that shoebox, manila envelope, or whatever container you've used to keep numbers. We're going to organize your records in a way that makes it easy to get QuickBooks up and running—accurately.

Deciding on the Start Date

The *start date* is the date on which you begin entering your bookkeeping records into QuickBooks. Think of it as a conversion date. In the computer consulting field, we call this "the date we go live." Things went on before this date (these are historical records and some of them must be entered into QuickBooks), but from this date on, your transactions go through QuickBooks.

This is not a trivial decision. The date you select has an enormous impact on how much work it's going to be to set QuickBooks up. For example, if you choose a starting date in September, every transaction that occurred in your business prior to that date has to be entered into your QuickBooks system before you start entering September transactions. Okay, that's an exaggeration, because you can enter some numbers in bulk instead of entering each individual transaction, but the principle is the same. If it's March, this decision is a lot easier, because the work attached to your QuickBooks setup is less onerous.

Here's what to think about as you make this decision:

- The best way to start a new computer accounting software system is to have every individual transaction in the system—every invoice you sent to customers, every check you wrote to vendors, every payroll check you gave an employee.
- The second best way to start a new computer accounting software system is to have running totals, plus any open transactions, in the system up to a certain date (your starting date), and then after that every single transaction is in the system. Open transactions are unpaid bills (either customer or vendor).

There is no third best way, because any fudging on either of those choices makes your figures suspect.

If it's the first half of the year when you read this, make your start date the first day of the year and enter everything you've done so far this year. It sounds like a lot of work, but it really isn't. When you start entering transactions in QuickBooks, such as customer invoices, you just pick the customer, enter a little information, and move on to the next invoice. Of course, you have to enter all your customers, but you'd have to do that even if you weren't entering every transaction for the current year. (Chapter 2 is all about entering lists: customers, vendors, and so on.)

If it's the middle of the year, toss a coin. Seriously, if you have goo gobs of transactions every month, you might want to enter large opening balances and then enter real transactions as they occur beginning with the start date.

If it's late in the year as you read this, perhaps September or October or later, and you usually send a lot of invoices to customers, write a lot of checks, and do your own payroll, think about waiting until next year to start using QuickBooks.

Gathering the Information You Need

You have to have quite a bit of information available when you first start to use QuickBooks, and it's ridiculous to hunt it down as each particle of information is needed. It's much better to gather it all together now, before you start working in QuickBooks.

Cash Balances

You have to tell QuickBooks what the balance is for each bank account you use in your business. Don't glance at the checkbook stubs—that's not the balance I'm talking about. The balance is the reconciled balance. And it has to be a reconciled balance as of the starting date you're using in QuickBooks.

If you haven't balanced your checkbooks against the bank statements for a while, do it now. In addition to the reconciled balance, you need to know the dates and amounts of the transactions that haven't yet cleared.

Customer Balances

If any customer owes you money as of your starting date, you have to tell QuickBooks about it. You have a couple of ways to do this:

- Skip the customer balance information during the QuickBooks setup procedure. Then enter each unpaid customer invoice yourself, giving the real dates for each invoice. Those dates must be earlier than your QuickBooks start date. This is the preferred method, because you have accurate, detailed information on your customers' activities.
- During the QuickBooks setup procedure (the EasyStep Interview), tell QuickBooks the total amount owed to you by each customer. The amount for each customer is treated as one single invoice, and payments are applied to this invoice.

This means you have to assemble all the information about unpaid customer invoices, including such details as how much of each invoice was for services, for items sold, for shipping, and for sales tax.

Vendor Balances

This is like the customer balances. You have the same chores (and the same decisions) facing you regarding any unpaid bills you owe to vendors. If you have the financial wherewithal, it might be easiest to pay them, just to avoid the work of entering all that data.

Asset Balances

Besides your bank accounts, an asset I've already covered, you have to know the state, as of the starting date, of all your assets. You'll need to know the current value, and also what the accumulated depreciation is for fixed assets. The open customer balances you enter determine the A/R asset automatically.

Liability Balances

Get all the information about your liabilities together. The open vendor bills you enter determine your A/P balance automatically. You'll need to know the current balance of any loans or mortgages. If there are unpaid withholding amounts from payroll, they must be entered (but this is definitely something that's easier to pay instead of entering.)

Payroll Information

If you do the payroll instead of using a payroll service, you'll need to know everything about each employee: social security number, all the information that goes into determining tax status (federal, state, and local), and which deductions are taken for health or pension. You have all this information, of course; you just have to get it together. If your employees are on salary, you've probably been repeating the check information every payday, with no need to look up these items. Dig up the W-4 forms and all your notes about who's on what deduction plan.

You also need to know which payroll items you have to track: salary, wages, federal deductions, state deductions (tax, SUI, SDI), local income tax deductions, benefits, pension, and any other deductions (garnishments, for example). And that's not all—you also have to know the name of the vendor to whom these withholding amounts are remitted (government tax agencies, insurance companies, and so on). See Chapter 8 to learn how to enter payroll data that occurred before your start date.

Inventory Information

You need to know the name of every inventory item you carry, how much you paid for each item, and how many of each item you have in stock as of the starting date.

Other Useful Bits of Paper

Find last year's tax return. QuickBooks is going to want to know which tax forms you use. Also, there's usually other information on the tax forms you might need (depreciation schedules, for example).

If you have a loan or mortgage, have the amortization schedule handy. You can figure out the year-to-date (the "date" is the QuickBooks starting date) principal and interest amounts.

Opening Trial Balance

Your opening trial balance, which probably should be prepared with the help of your accountant, almost creates itself during the setup process. If your QuickBooks start date is the beginning of the year, it's a snap. The opening trial balance for the first day of the year has no income or expenses. It should look something like this:

ACCOUNT TYPE	ACCOUNT	DEBIT	CREDIT
Assets	Bank	$10,000	
	Fixed Assets	$50,000	
	Accumulated Depreciation/Fixed Assets		$5,000
Liabilities	Loan from Corner Bank		$15,000
Equity	Equity		$40,000

Notice that there is no inventory figure in this opening balance. The reason is that you want to receive the inventory into your system, using QuickBooks transaction windows for receiving inventory, so there's a quantity available for each inventory item. Otherwise, no matter what you want to sell, QuickBooks will think you don't have it in stock. As you bring the inventory in and assign it a value, your inventory asset will build itself.

If your QuickBooks starting date is any other date except for the beginning of the year, your trial balance will also contain information about sales and expenses.

You're now ready to set up and configure QuickBooks!

Integrating with Other Programs and Services

f you're using QuickBooks Pro/Premier, you can integrate your QuickBooks system with other software and QuickBooks services. This brings more power to your QuickBooks installation. In addition, QuickBooks offers a number of add-on services you can purchase to enhance the range and power of the software.

Exporting Reports to Other Software

Every QuickBooks report can be exported so you can load the information in another software application. This is handy if the target application can do things that QuickBooks can't, or if you want to include data from a QuickBooks report in a document prepared in other software. To export a report, click the Export button on the report window to open the Export Report dialog box, and choose an export target.

Exporting to a CSV File

CSV stands for comma-separated values, and most spreadsheet and database software applications can handle this file type. A CSV file contains a series of text lines with the following characteristics:

- Each column is indicated by a comma
- Each row is a new record
- Text is surrounded by quotation marks
- Amounts are not surrounded by quotation marks

The presence or absence of quotation marks is code for the receiving application, so it knows whether to apply formatting for text (usually justified left), or for an amount (usually justified right). You don't see the quotation marks when you open the report in the receiving application.

Choose Export and select a location (folder) and name for the file. Then open the file in the appropriate software.

Exporting to Excel

QuickBooks makes it very easy to export reports directly to Excel. You merely have to choose whether you want to start a new Excel worksheet or integrate this report with an existing Excel worksheet.

 C A U T I O N : QuickBooks doesn't check to see if Excel is installed on your computer. If it's not, after you make your choices in the dialog box, QuickBooks will eventually figure it out and display an error message.

If you select the option to add the contents of this report to an existing workbook, the Browse button activates so you can locate and select the Excel file.

When you select either Excel option, QuickBooks makes an additional option available: Include A New Worksheet In The Workbook That Explains Excel Worksheet Linking. This means a worksheet labeled QuickBooks Export Tips is added to the workbook, and it provides general directions on managing exported reports, including an overview of setting up links among multiple Excel worksheets.

Click the Advanced tab to configure the options and features you want to use for this worksheet.

| Export Report | Ask a help question | Ask | ▽ How Do I? | ✕ |

Basic   **Advanced**

Preserve the following QuickBooks report formatting options:

☑ Fonts   ☑ Space between columns

☑ Colors   ☑ Row height

Turn on the following Excel features for this report:

☑ AutoFit (set column width to display all data)

☑ Freeze panes (keep headers and labels visible)

☑ Show Gridlines

☐ Auto Outline (allows collapsing / expanding)

☐ Auto Filtering (allows custom data filtering)

Printing options

◉ Send header to Page Setup in Excel

○ Send header to screen in Excel

☑ Repeat row labels on each page

Export   Cancel   Help

Click OK to return to the Export Report To Excel dialog box. Click OK again, and Excel opens automatically with the report in the worksheet window. This is a great way to play "what if" games: to see the effect of rising costs, higher salaries, more benefits, or any other change in your finances. Exporting to Excel also provides the opportunity to sort data in any manner you wish.

Mail Merge with Word

Need to send letters to some or all of your customers? Now it's easy, because QuickBooks Pro/Premier and Microsoft Word work together to provide this feature. QuickBooks supplies a number of prewritten letters for you to use, or you can design your own letter. In fact, you can use an existing Word document for your mail merge activities. To get started, choose Company | Write Letters from the QuickBooks menu bar.

Sending a Collection Letter

When you open the Write Letters window, you see three choices for letter types (see Figure B-1). This is a wizard, so you fill out each window and click the Next button to move along.

If you're sending a collection letter, click Next to define the criteria for adding a customer to the mail merge list (see Figure B-2).

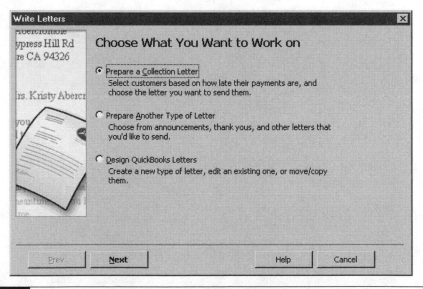

FIGURE B-1   Send collection letters to late-paying customers.

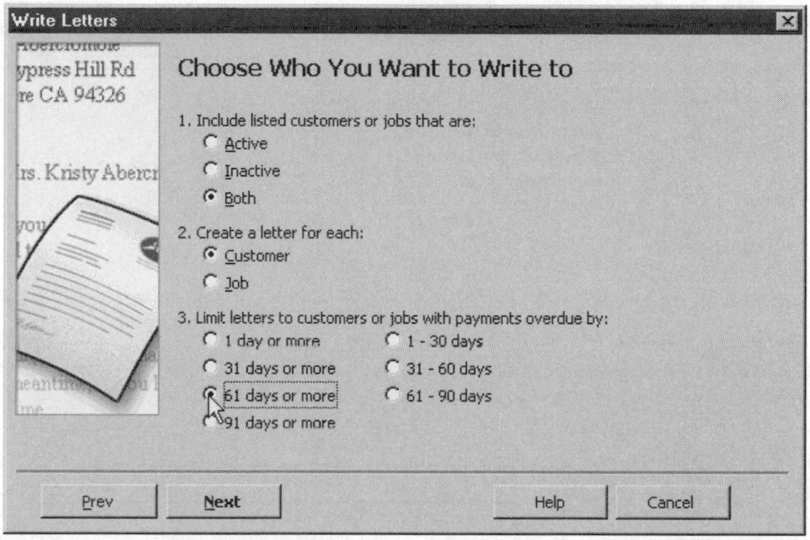

Write Letters

Choose Who You Want to Write to

1. Include listed customers or jobs that are:
   - ○ Active
   - ○ Inactive
   - ● Both

2. Create a letter for each:
   - ● Customer
   - ○ Job

3. Limit letters to customers or jobs with payments overdue by:
   - ○ 1 day or more   ○ 1 - 30 days
   - ○ 31 days or more   ○ 31 - 60 days
   - ● 61 days or more   ○ 61 - 90 days
   - ○ 91 days or more

Prev   Next   Help   Cancel

FIGURE B-2 Any customer who is more than two months late needs to hear from you.

> **NOTE:** If any customers who fall within the criteria have unapplied credits, QuickBooks reminds you of that fact. Cancel the wizard and apply the credits so the customers who don't deserve this letter are omitted from the mailing list.

The list of customers who match your criteria appears, along with the customers' balances. You can deselect any customer you don't want to send your letter to.

Click Next to choose the collection letter you want to send. QuickBooks has created a number of different collection letters, as you can see in Figure B-3.

You should look at each of the letters before you make your selection, and you can accomplish that with these steps:

1. Open Microsoft Word (you don't have to close QuickBooks).
2. Click the Open icon on the Word toolbar (or choose File | Open).
3. In the Open dialog box, use the Look In text box to move to the folder that holds the QuickBooks letters. You'll find it in a folder named QuickBooks Letters, under the folder in which you installed the QuickBooks software. There's a folder for each type of QuickBooks letter.

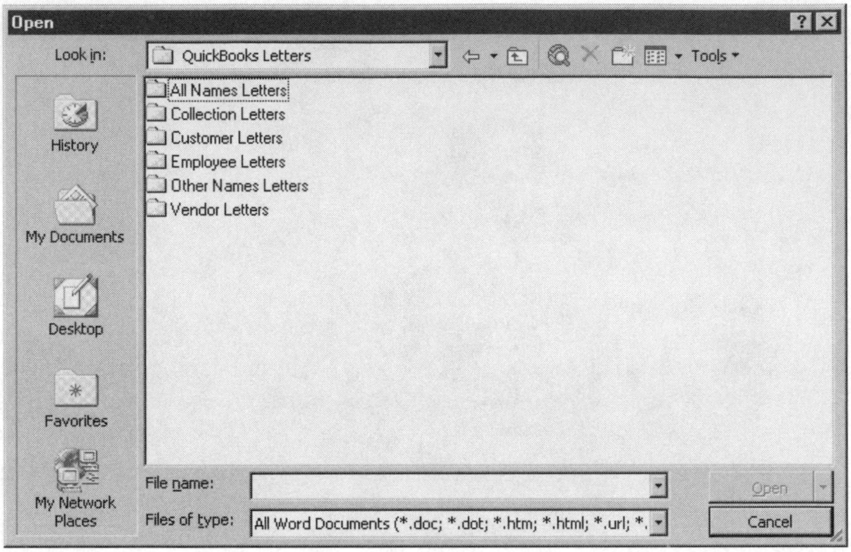

4. Open the Collection Letters folder, and then open each letter to see which one you prefer to use. When you've examined the letters and determined the ones you think suitable, close Word and return to the QuickBooks window.

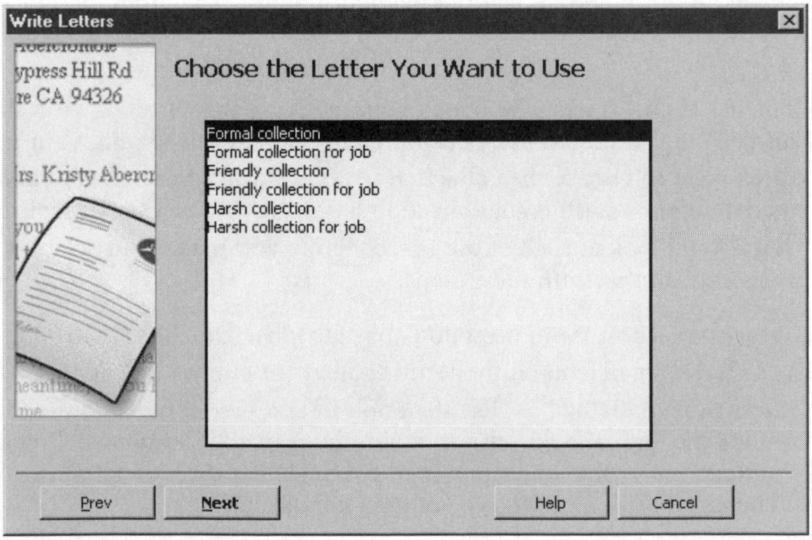

FIGURE B-3   Do you want to be gentle, firm, or nasty?

CAUTION: The letters contain codes for mail merges; don't make any changes to them, or your mail merge may not work properly.

The next wizard window asks you to fill in your name and title, the way you want it to appear in the letter. After you complete that information, click Create Letters to open Word. If your customer records don't contain data for all the fields QuickBooks requires (addresses, ZIP codes, and so on), a dialog box appears, informing you of that fact. (You can deselect that option, but that may be risky.)

QuickBooks provides a toolbar that's specifically designed for the type of letter you selected, and sometimes the toolbar automatically appears in the document window when Microsoft Word opens. If you don't see it, right-click the Word menu bar or toolbar, and choose the appropriate QuickBooks toolbar (Collection Letter Fields, Vendor Letter Fields, and so on).

All of your letters are displayed in a single document in the Word software window. Here are some guidelines for using this mail merge document:

- There's a page break at the end of each individual letter.
- If you want to make a change in the text, you must change each individual letter.
- Changes you make to the text are not saved back to the original QuickBooks letter.
- You don't have to save the mail merge document unless you think you're going to resend the same letter to the same people (which would be unusual).

When it's all perfect, print the letters.

Sending Other Types of Letters

You're not restricted to customers for mail merge; you can send mail to lots of different names in your QuickBooks files (vendors, employees, and others). Just select Prepare Another Type Of Letter in the first wizard window and choose Next. Then select a Name List, choose a type of letter, and specify the names you want to use from the list. The rest of the steps are the same as those for creating a collection letter.

 TIP: You can use the options in the wizard to create your own letters or change a pre-existing QuickBooks letter.

Synchronizing Contacts

If you use Microsoft Outlook or Symantec ACT! to manage information about business (or personal) contacts, you can synchronize the data in your contact program with QuickBooks. This means you don't have to enter information about customers, vendors, or other contacts in both programs. Synchronization makes even minor changes easier to handle. If a vendor's telephone number changes, you can enter the new information in either program, and then update both programs.

 N O T E : Although the wizard indicates you can only synchronize with Outlook 97/98/2000, I was able to synchronize with Outlook 2002. ACT!, on the other hand, is restricted to those versions listed (ACT! 3.0.8, 4.0.2, or 2000). If you have a later version of ACT! (such as version 6), synchronization fails with a message indicating you're not using a supported version of ACT!.

Understanding Synchronization

You can synchronize the following data:

- **Customer contact information**   Use the QuickBooks Customer:Job List
- **Vendor contact information**   Use the QuickBooks Vendor List
- **Other contact information**   Use the QuickBooks Other Names List

C A U T I O N : QuickBooks names that are marked Inactive are never involved in the synchronization process (in either direction).

You can establish synchronization as a one-way process, which is useful when you first begin to use this feature because most of your contact data likely is in one software application. The one-way direction will depend on whether you installed your contact management program before or after you installed QuickBooks.

Synchronizing the Data

Before you begin, back up your QuickBooks files and your contact software files. Close your contact program when you're finished with the backup. Then choose Company | Synchronize Contacts from the QuickBooks menu bar. QuickBooks displays a message urging you to perform a backup before you synchronize.

If you've just backed up, click Continue. Otherwise, click Cancel, perform the backup, and then return to the synchronization feature.

> $ **CAUTION:** You cannot synchronize contacts if you're working in multi-user mode. Wait until nobody else on the network is working in QuickBooks and switch to single-user mode.

Synchronization is performed with the help of a wizard, which means you click Next to move through all the windows:

1. The first wizard window suggests you backup your data before continuing. In addition, it lists your current synchronization settings (which are blank the first time you synchronize).

2. The second window asks you to select your contact management program. Choose Outlook or ACT!, depending on the software you use.

3. In the next window, select a type of synchronization: Two Way or One Way (if you choose One Way, indicate the direction).

4. If you're synchronizing with ACT!, the next window asks for the path and name of the database. Unless you have an excellent memory, click the Browse button to navigate through your computer to find and select the database. For Outlook, you must specify the Outlook folder (Contacts). If you're performing a two-way sync, or a one-way sync into QuickBooks, also select a folder to receive names.

5. If you're performing a two-way synchronization, select the QuickBooks lists you want to synchronize with your database. Your choices include Customer, Vendor, and Other Names. You may also be asked if you want to exclude any types of names from your contact program.

6. Tell QuickBooks what to do to resolve conflicts between contacts that exist in both QuickBooks and your PIM (perhaps the addresses don't match exactly). Select the solution you prefer from the options displayed in the wizard window, and click Next.

7. Click Sync Now to perform the synchronization, or click Sync Later to exit the Synchronization Setup Wizard and run the file transfers at a later time.

If you opt to synchronize later, the window that opens when you select Company | Synchronize Contacts offers you a chance to enter the Setup program again (in case you want to change something), or go ahead and perform the synchronization.

After running the synchronization, QuickBooks displays information about the process. Any data QuickBooks wasn't sure how to handle is presented so you can make a decision (perhaps it isn't clear which type of name the contact is—vendor, other, etc.). When you clear up any confusion, QuickBooks opens a confirmation window showing you all the contacts that will be synchronized. Accept the data if it's correct, and QuickBooks will complete the synchronization. If the data is incorrect, cancel the synchronization, clean up your databases, and start the process again.

Now you can use your contact program to track conversations and correspondence with your QuickBooks names.

Integrating QuickBooks with Third-Party Add-on Software

A number of software companies offer programs that work directly with QuickBooks to deliver additional features and power to your QuickBooks software. QuickBooks has an information window (the Solutions Marketplace window) you can see by choosing Company | Company Services | Find Integrated Applications. However, to get hard information, you'll have to click through a series of links to travel to the Intuit Marketplace website and find the right page.

It's faster to go directly to the information by opening your browser and traveling 3to http://marketplace.intuit.com/. When you get there, you can read about the way third-party software works with QuickBooks, see lists of software, read reviews, look at software titles by category, or search for software using keywords you think will produce the right results.

Using QuickBooks Business Services

QuickBooks isn't limited to the repetitive functions involved with filling out transaction windows and creating reports. You have a wide choice of extra goodies you can use to enhance the way you run your business. To see what's available, and to sign up for the business services you need, choose Company | Business Services Navigator. As you can see in Figure B-4, a wide range of extra services is available.

 CAUTION: Some services are only available for QuickBooks Premier Editions.

All of the services are fee-based and require Internet access. Many of the services offer a free trial period. After your free period ends, you'll be asked to give QuickBooks a credit card number to continue using the service.

To complete your signup process for any of the services, QuickBooks performs the following actions:

1. Opens Internet Explorer to travel to the QuickBooks marketplace website.

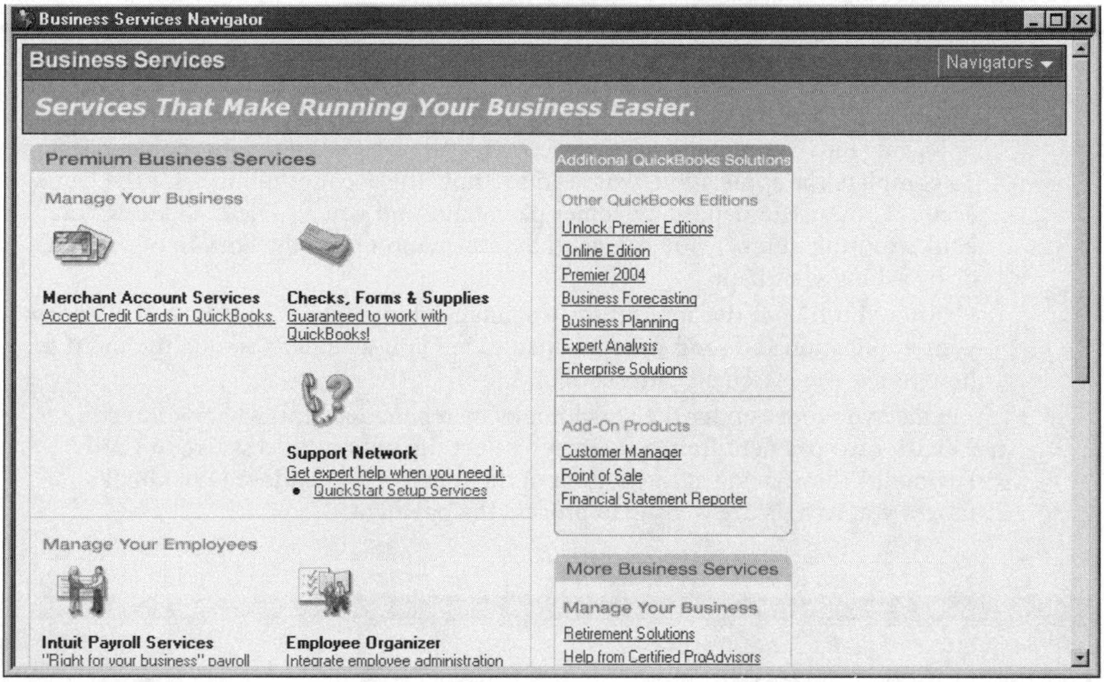

FIGURE B-4   QuickBooks offers plenty of useful services you can buy.

2. Authenticates your copy of the software (checks to see that you registered it).

3. Asks you for your e-mail address in order to create a QuickBooks services account for you. This is a one-time procedure, and when you want to apply for another QuickBooks business service, you'll only need to log in to your services account.

In this appendix, I'll discuss only some of the services (going over all of them would require a whole 'nother book).

QuickBooks Merchant Card Account Services

If you want to accept credit card payments from customers and process the credit card payments right in the Receive Payments window, get a QuickBooks merchant account.

To set up credit card services, in the Business Services Navigator, click the link under Merchant Account Services. The QuickBooks Merchant Account Service page opens so you can read about the service. Select the Tell Me More tab, or choose Quick Tour to travel to the QuickBooks website and learn more about the way a QuickBooks merchant account works.

From the Tell Me More window, or the QuickBooks Quick Tour website, click Sign Up Now! to open the window seen in Figure B-5.

Select the bank you want to work with and click Continue. Follow the prompts to move through the process (either signing up for a QuickBooks services account or logging into your existing services account). You'll be asked to fill out an application. To complete the application, you need to know the account number for the bank account you use to deposit customer payments, and you also need to know your bank's routing number. You can get that information from the bottom of a check, or by asking your bank.

After you fill out the application, the financial institution you chose will review your application and send you an e-mail to tell you whether you qualify, and if so, how to use the merchant card services.

Once you're set up for the QuickBooks merchant account, when you receive a credit card payment from a customer, select the option Process Credit Card Payment When Saving at the bottom of the transaction window. QuickBooks moves you to a secure website to process the payment.

Merchant Account Service Application

⇐ Back ⇒ Forward ⊗ Stop ⟳ Refresh 🖨 Print **QB**

You're on your way to processing credit cards from your QuickBooks financial software!

Follow these steps:

❶ Select a financial institution
❷ Complete the merchant account application

Common Questions

What do I need to complete the application?

Can I use my existing merchant account?

I have an account elsewhere. How do these prices compare?

Select a Financial Institution
Credit card processing is provided by Wells Fargo and Chase Merchant Services LLC. Please select one of these financial institutions:

	Wells Fargo Merchant Services		Chase Merchant Services
Discount rate for MasterCard and Visa	1.89% *† (card-swiped)	2.39% * (key-entered)	2.39% (key-entered)
Monthly fee	$17.95/month (includes paper statement)		$13.95/month
Statement fee	None		$ 4.00/month
Per authorization fee	$0.25		$0.25
Setup fee	$39.95		$39.95
No cancellation fees, no leasing fees and no extra phone lines!			

Select a financial institution 📄 ○ Wells Fargo Merchant ○ Chase Merchant Services

Done 🔒 Secure site

FIGURE B-5   Signing up for a merchant account is amazingly easy.

> **NOTE:** A secure website uses encryption to protect data as it travels to and from the Internet.

Bill Customers Online and Accept Online Payments

You can conduct business electronically if you sign up for QuickBooks online services. To learn about this QuickBooks service, in the Business Services Navigator, click the link for QuickBooks Billing Solutions.

Read the information in the QuickBooks Billing Solutions window (see Figure B-6), and if you're interested in this service, sign up. You can use the Internet to send invoices, statements, and other customer documents, and let your customers click a link to arrange for online payments. You can even give your customers access to a secure website where they can view their own account information.

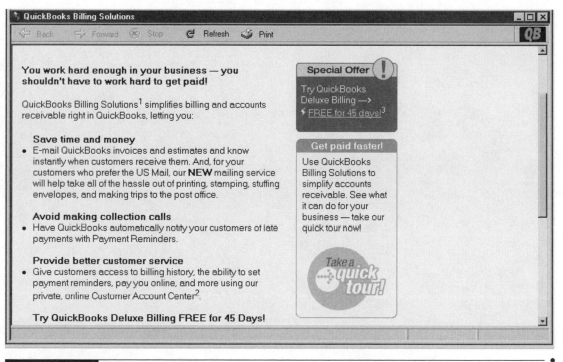

FIGURE B-6 Move to electronic invoices and collections with QuickBooks Billing Solutions.

Use FedEx Within QuickBooks

Click the FedEx Shipping Solutions link under More Business Services to sign up for discounted shipping rates and make shipping processes available right from your QuickBooks transaction windows. You can create the shipping label while you're working in an invoice, and you can track shipments while you're working in QuickBooks.

I've noted only a small number of the variety of QuickBooks services available to you, and many of them have a free trial period, so you can try before you buy. Go through the offerings to see which services would make the work of running your business easier.

Index

Sound Off!

Visit us at **www.osborne.com/bookregistration** and let us know what you thought of this book. While you're online you'll have the opportunity to register for newsletters and special offers from McGraw-Hill/Osborne.

We want to hear from you!

Sneak Peek

Visit us today at **www.betabooks.com** and see what's coming from McGraw-Hill/Osborne tomorrow!

Based on the successful software paradigm, Bet@Books™ allows computing professionals to view partial and sometimes complete text versions of selected titles online. Bet@Books™ viewing is free, invites comments and feedback, and allows you to "test drive" books in progress on the subjects that interest you the most.

Brilliance

Enlightened answers for your electronics, computers, and applications